NALA Manual
for Paralegals and Legal Assistants
A General Skills & Litigation Guide for Today's Professionals
FIFTH EDITION

DELMAR CENGAGE Learning

Options.

Over 300 products in every area of the law: textbooks, online courses, CD-ROMs, reference books, companion websites, and more – helping you succeed in the classroom and on the job.

Support.

We offer unparalleled, practical support: robust instructor and student supplements to ensure the best learning experience, custom publishing to meet your unique needs, and other benefits such as Delmar Cengage Learning's Student Achievement Award. And our sales representatives are always ready to provide you with dependable service.

Feedback.

As always, we want to hear from you! Your feedback is our best resource for improving the quality of our products. Contact your sales representative or write us at the address below if you have any comments about our materials or if you have a product proposal.

Accounting and Financials for the Law Office • Administrative Law • Alternative Dispute Resolution • Bankruptcy Business Organizations/Corporations • Careers and Employment • Civil Litigation and Procedure • CLA Exam Preparation • Computer Applications in the Law Office • Constitutional Law • Contract Law • Court Reporting Criminal Law and Procedure • Document Preparation • Elder Law • Employment Law • Environmental Law • Ethics Evidence Law • Family Law • Health Care Law • Immigration Law • Intellectual Property • Internships Interviewing and Investigation • Introduction to Law • Introduction to Paralegalism • Juvenile Law • Law Office Management • Law Office Procedures • Legal Nurse Consulting • Legal Research, Writing, and Analysis • Legal Terminology • Legal Transcription • Media and Entertainment Law • Medical Malpractice Law Product Liability • Real Estate Law • Reference Materials • Social Security • Sports Law • Torts and Personal Injury Law • Wills, Trusts, and Estate Administration • Workers' Compensation Law

DELMAR CENGAGE Learning
5 Maxwell Drive
Clifton Park, New York 12065-2919

For additional information, find us online at:
www.delmar.cengage.com

NALA Manual
for Paralegals and Legal Assistants

FIFTH EDITION

Prepared by

NALA

DELMAR
CENGAGE Learning™

Australia • Brazil • Japan • Korea • Mexico • Singapore • Spain • United Kingdom • United States

NALA Manual for Paralegals and Legal Assistants, Fifth Edition
NALA

Vice President, Career and Professional
    Editorial: Dave Garza

Director of Learning Solutions: Sandy Clark

Acquisitions Editor: Shelley Esposito

Managing Editor: Larry Main

Senior Product Manager: Melissa Riveglia

Editorial Assistant: Lyss Zaza

Vice President, Career and Professional
    Marketing: Jennifer McAvey

Marketing Director: Deborah Yarnell

Marketing Manager: Erin Brennan

Marketing Coordinator:
    Jonathan Sheehan

Production Director: Wendy Troeger

Production Manager: Mark Bernard

Senior Content Project Manager:
    Betty Dickson

Senior Art Director: Joy Kocsis

Senior Director of Product Management for
    Career, Professional, and Languages:
    Tom Smith

Production Technology Analyst:
    Thomas Stover

For product information and technology assistance, contact us at
Cengage Learning Customer & Sales Support, 1-800-354-9706

For permission to use material from this text or product,
submit all requests online at **www.cengage.com/permissions.**
Further permissions questions can be e-mailed to
permissionrequest@cengage.com

Library of Congress Control Number: 2009920620

ISBN-13: 978-1-4354-0025-2
ISBN-10: 1-4354-0025-9

Delmar
5 Maxwell Drive
Clifton Park, NY 12065-2919
USA

Cengage Learning is a leading provider of customized learning solutions with office locations around the globe, including Singapore, the United Kingdom, Australia, Mexico, Brazil, and Japan. Locate your local office at:
international.cengage.com/region

Cengage Learning products are represented in Canada by
Nelson Education, Ltd.

To learn more about Delmar, visit **www.cengage.com/delmar**
Purchase any of our products at your local college store or at our preferred online store **www.ichapters.com**

NOTICE TO THE READER

Publisher does not warrant or guarantee any of the products described herein or perform any independent analysis in connection with any of the product information contained herein. Publisher does not assume, and expressly disclaims, any obligation to obtain and include information other than that provided to it by the manufacturer. The reader is expressly warned to consider and adopt all safety precautions that might be indicated by the activities described herein and to avoid all potential hazards. By following the instructions contained herein, the reader willingly assumes all risks in connection with such instructions. The reader is notified that this text is an educational tool, not a practice book. Since the law in constant change, no rule or statement of law in this book should be relied upon for any service to any client. The reader should always refer to standard legal sources for the current rule or law. If legal advice or other expert assistance is required, the services of the appropriate professional should be sought. The publisher makes no representations or warranties of any kind, including but not limited to, the warranties of fitness for particular purpose or merchantability, nor are any such representations implied with respect to the material set forth herein, and the publisher takes no responsibility with respect to such material. The publisher shall not be liable for any special, consequential, or exemplary damages resulting, in whole or part, from the readers' use of, or reliance upon, this material.

Printed in the United States of America
2 3 4 5 6 7 12 11 10

DEDICATION

More than 100 leading authorities in a wide range of experience in legal disciplines and management have contributed to this comprehensive manual since it was introduced in 1976. The expertise and commendable dedication of these individuals has consistently produced an authoritative and reliable reference for paralegals with each updated edition.

We are indebted to these selfless professionals and wish to express our earnest gratitude to each person who contributed original material or carefully revised and updated material. Their careful and expert work has ensured that this manual represents the best and most current information available at the time of publication.

Contents

3   ETHICS | 81

4   JUDGMENT AND ANALYTICAL ABILITY | 109

5   COMMUNICATIONS | 132

7   INVESTIGATION | 178

Acknowledgments

This Fifth Edition of the NALA Manual for Legal Assistants has been a project of the NALA Continuing Education Council, Dawnne L. Linenbrink, ACP, Chairperson. The committee chairs for this revision project were Dorothe J. Howell, ACP, of Baltimore, Maryland, and Debra D. Taylor, of Lincoln, Illinois. The Council would also like to express its appreciation to Patricia Gustin, CFEI, CP, of Harrisburg, Pennsylvania, for her extensive work on Chapter 7, Investigation.

The National Association of Legal Assistants, Inc., gratefully acknowledges the contributions of the following members to the successful completion of this Fifth Edition:

Vanessa Beam, ACP
Parkersburg, WV

Jonathan Kafka
Campbell, CA

Jimmie Murvin, ACP, LCP
Baton Rouge, LA

Tita A. Brewster, ACP
Las Cruces, NM

Kay Kasic, CP
Napa, CA

Candy Pederson Reilly, ACP
Bismarck, ND

Annette R. Brown, ACP
Missoula, MT

Connie Kretchmer, ACP
Omaha, NE

Joey Phelps, ACP
Charlevoix, MI

Lynn Dean, CLA
Tampa, FL

Kelly LaGrave, ACP
Lansing, MI

Karen Sanders-West, ACP
Wichita, KS

Karen Dunn, ACP
Vail, CO

Cynthia McClelland, ACP
Hilton Head Island, SC

Jane Terhune, ACP
Georgetown, SC

Amy J. Hill, ACP
Raleigh, NC

Karen Greer McGee, ACP
Shreveport, LA

Vicki Voisin, ACP
Charlevoix, MI

Kimberly Houser, ACP
Enola, PA

Kathy Miller, ACP, CAS
Irvine, CA

Linda J. Wolf, ACP
Dallas, TX

Marcy L. Jankovich, ACP
Jackson, MI

Deb Monke, ACP
Bloomington, IL

We would also like to thank the following reviewers for their contributions to the manuscript:

Orsolya Furi-Perry, J.D.
Bridgewater State College
Bridgewater, MA

Lisa Santos, J.D.
Keiser University
Pembroke Pines, FL

Bernadette Young, J.D.
Florida Technical College
Auburndale, FL

Foreword

The National Association of Legal Assistants, Inc. (NALA) presents this manual as an educational contribution to the paralegal profession. It was originally developed:

To serve as a quick reference guide for working paralegals

For use by schools as a teaching aid to expose students to the practical skills and techniques required for entry into the profession

To support paralegals preparing to take the voluntary NALA Certified Legal Assistant/Certified Paralegal Examination

This revised manual was completed by many dedicated members who unselfishly gave their time and energy for this very worthwhile project. None of that dedication has gone unnoticed, and it is here that NALA gratefully acknowledges the exemplary and concentrated efforts of those professionals.

This manual is a collection of techniques and procedures which can be used by paralegals nationwide. It is compatible with the Federal Rules of Civil Procedure. However, the purpose of the manual is not to teach federal law or procedures since there are many excellent treatises available on that subject. Further, this book is not intended to offer specific guidance on any state law or procedure since the fifty jurisdictions differ too widely to capsulize all the laws adequately within one volume.

The techniques described are examples of past successful solutions to actual assignments accomplished by working paralegals. These should be considered as starting points from which changes, adaptations, and modifications can be made by other paralegals in similar situations.

This manual will serve its purpose if it:

Helps paralegals achieve a comfortable perspective of themselves

Inspires them to dedicate themselves to high standards of professional performance and strong ethical and moral commitment to the client and attorney

Generates enthusiasm and a willing sense of loyalty between paralegals and their employers

Introduction

What is a paralegal? What does one do? What does a job as a paralegal entail? How much responsibility can or should one assume?

If you are a paralegal and have not encountered these questions, you are unusual! You may only need this manual for reference or guidance in a particular area of the law. For those who have questions, for students, and for those entering the profession, the National Association of Legal Assistants, Inc. (NALA) offers this practical aid.

As the number of paralegals increases, there is a corresponding need for a workable reference on "what to do" and "how to do it." Realizing that those best qualified to present this information are paralegals themselves, the NALA called upon its members to share their knowledge and expertise. This manual is a culmination of that effort. It is designed to further the understanding of this profession, as well as its duties, responsibilities, and limitations.

What Is NALA?

NALA is a professional association for paralegals which was incorporated in 1975 (nonprofit). By the 2000's, NALA had grown to represent over 18,000 paralegals through its individual members, affiliated state and local associations, and certified legal assistants.

Headquartered in Tulsa, Oklahoma, NALA is managed by a professional staff under the direction of a board of directors consisting of members from across the nation.

NALA's goals and programs have been defined to:

- Increase the professional standing of paralegals throughout the nation
- Provide uniformity in the identification of paralegals
- Establish national standards of professional competence for paralegals
- Provide uniformity among the states in the utilization of paralegals

NALA is associated most often with the administration of the Certified Legal Assistant (CLA)/Certified Paralegal (CP) and Advanced Certified Paralegal (ACP) certifying programs, the profession's national credentialing mechanism designed to support the paralegal profession. Other services and programs for member and nonmember paralegals include:

- **Publications.**   Since the late 1970s, NALA has published educational materials for paralegals such as this Fifth Edition of the NALA *Manual for Legal Assistants.* In addition, the association also publishes, through Cengage, the NALA *CLA Study Guide and Mock Examination.*
- **Periodicals.**   *Facts & Findings,* the NALA quarterly magazine, is the professional journal for paralegals, offering in-depth educational articles and treatises to keep readers informed of current developments in specialized practice areas.
- **Workshops and Seminars.**   The association's annual convention, held in July, offers specialized workshops for both beginning and advanced paralegals. The association also sponsors courses for preparation for the CLA/CP examinations, a number of online self study and live continuing education courses, and advanced certification courses (APC). NALA's Web-based CLE programs are found online at **www.NALACampus.com** and **www.NALA-APC.org.**

- **Occupational Research.** In 1986, NALA initiated its biannual survey of paralegals to begin extensive research of the profession. The questionnaires used for this survey are very detailed in their request for information on the respondents' educational backgrounds and experiences, descriptions of employers, definitions of duties and responsibilities, billing rates, compensation, and benefits. Through this biannual survey, NALA developed a significant study of the profession. In addition to providing a description of this career field about every two years, NALA is storing and summarizing a tremendous amount of data showing the growth and development of this field. Much of the information in this introductory chapter is based on these research efforts and the work and contributions of NALA members and committees. The findings of NALA's latest survey are available free of charge to the legal community either in published form or electronically by visiting the NALA Web site at **www.nala.org.**

- **Online Services.** In addition to on-line interactive continuing education courses offered through NALA Campus LIVE!, NALA also offers its members and other legal professionals to network online through NALANet. NALANet is a communications link to other paralegals, and it is a source of relevant information concerning such issues as ethics, bar guidelines, case law updates, legislative activities, bar activities and significant research articles about the utilization of paralegals. NALANet Campus gives paralegals a forum to discuss trends in the profession and issues effecting the profession, request assistance from other professionals, exchange information and views and provide encouragement and advice to colleagues.

What Is a Paralegal?

It has become evident through the years that every law-related organization has its own definition of a paralegal. This myriad of definitions caused such confusion in the industry that at times even paralegals wondered who they really were and what, exactly, they were supposed to be doing. Members of NALA decided to do something about this, and at the NALA 2001 annual meeting, the membership adopted the following definition of a legal assistant:

> A legal assistant or paralegal is a person, qualified by education, training, or work experience who is employed or retained by a lawyer, law office, corporation, governmental agency, or other entity, who performs specifically delegated substantive legal work for which a lawyer is responsible.

This definition is the same as that approved by the American Bar Association (ABA) House of Delegates in 1997.

The issues surrounding the adoption of this definition are interesting. Members of the profession should be aware of them because they are historically significant to the evolution of the paralegal profession.

In 1984, NALA adopted the following definition of a legal assistant:

> Legal assistants, also known as paralegals, are a distinguishable group of persons who assist attorneys in the delivery of legal services. Through formal education, training, and experience, legal assistants have knowledge and expertise regarding the legal system and substantive and procedural law which qualify them to perform work of a legal nature under the supervision of an attorney.

Two years later, the American Bar Association (ABA) defined legal assistants as:

> Persons who, although not members of the legal profession, are qualified through education, training or work experience, who are employed or retained by a lawyer, law office, governmental agency, or other entity in a capacity or function which involves the performance, under the direction and supervision of an attorney, of specifically delegated substantive legal work, which work, for the most part, requires a sufficient knowledge of legal concepts such that, absent the legal assistant, the attorney would perform the task.

These definitions shared many similarities. Both stated that paralegals work under the supervision of a lawyer, that paralegals are qualified through education, training, or work experience, and that paralegals do substantive legal work. The ABA further stated that the work of paralegals is of such a nature that "absent the legal assistant, the attorney would perform the task."

In 1997, the ABA House of Delegates approved a streamlined definition of a paralegal which is the same as that adopted by the NALA membership in 2001. This definition maintains the similarities of those discussed previously by keeping the requirement that paralegals work under the supervision of a lawyer, that delegated work be substantive in nature, and that paralegals are qualified through education, training, or work experience. These similarities are the ingredients that separate this profession from other occupations and other professions in the legal field. They are the concepts that make the legal assistant/paralegal profession unique. There are numerous positions and responsibilities for nonlawyers within the legal profession. However, the membership and services of the NALA, including this publication, are designed for those persons whose positions and duties meet the NALA and ABA definitions of a legal assistant.

Paralegals who freelance are included in this same definition. Rather than being full-time employees of a law firm, freelance paralegals work for law firms on a contract basis, either through their own businesses or through other contractors. These individuals work on the same professional basis and under the same supervisory provisions as paralegals who work for only one law firm. In recent years, the numbers of freelance paralegals and independent contractor businesses have increased. However, the only differences between these paralegals and those working on a full-time basis for a single employer are the terms of their employment and delivery of services. Freelance paralegals are subject to the same, if not more, ethical proscriptions and responsibilities as all paralegals. The chapter on ethics in this manual will explain the variety of considerations and concepts of law that apply to all paralegals. Additionally, the Appendix to this manual contains an article authored by NALA which tracks the progress of the paralegal profession through case law, statutes, and regulation.

For Whom Do Paralegals Work?

The vast majority of paralegals work in private law firms, although some are also employed in banks, insurance companies, corporations, government offices, or are self-employed (freelance). They may work under the direction of just one attorney or several, have a private office or no office, have secretarial assistance or no support, and travel frequently or never travel.

NALA surveys have established that paralegals generally work in private law firms (64 percent of those surveyed in 2008) on a full-time basis. Most paralegals (50 percent) receive direction from one or more specific attorneys or from specific departments. However, the number of those receiving direction from an office administrator is about 33 percent. The paralegal's work environment depends in large part on the employer, the geographic region, and how the paralegal's skills are used.

One of the questions facing the profession and management studies is that of identifying the relationship between the size of a law firm, as defined by the number of lawyers, and the number of paralegals. The findings of the 2008 survey show that in smaller firms (1–10 attorneys) there are about 1 to 2 attorneys per paralegal. In firms of 11 to 30 attorneys, there are usually 2 to 3 attorneys per paralegal. In comparing this with findings of previous surveys, we find that in larger firms, the number of attorneys per paralegal is falling. In 1995, the average number of attorneys to paralegals in firms of 31 to 60 attorneys was between 5 to 6 attorneys. This number has decreased steadily, and in 2008, the number of attorneys to paralegals in firms of this size dropped to 3 attorneys per paralegal. This indicates a greater utilization of paralegals.

Professional Standards: Education and Experience

With the recent overwhelming increase in educational programs designed for paralegal training, a growing number of paralegals have some sort of formal education beyond high school. The most common educational degree available is a two-year associate degree with paralegal training or a post baccalaureate certification program in paralegal studies. Some colleges and universities are offering a bachelor degree program in paralegal studies, and some are offering a masters degree program, although the associate's degree remains the largest category of education. The growth of educational programs for paralegals coincides with predictions for a phenomenal growth of the paralegal profession.

In addition to the training offered through formal education programs, many law firms and other employers provide in-house training for their paralegals. In-house training refers to education of the employee by the attorney with regard to paralegal duties. In addition to review and analysis of assignments, the paralegal should receive a reasonable amount of instruction directly related to his or her duties and obligations. This preparation of paralegals is important because most codes of ethical and professional responsibility adopted by bar associations require that attorneys must be assured of the professional competence of their employees.

As a hiring criterion for entry-level employees, many employers require prior legal experience, a minimum level of education, and/or successful completion of the Certified Legal Assistant/Certified Paralegal (CLA/CP) certifying examination. The NALA *Model Standards and Guidelines for the Utilization of Legal Assistants* suggests to the profession the following as the minimum qualifications for a legal assistant:

1. Successful completion of the Certified Legal Assistant (CLA)/Certified Paralegal (CP) certifying examination of the National Association of Legal Assistants, Inc.;

2. Graduation from an ABA approved program of study for legal assistants;

3. Graduation from a course of study for legal assistants which is institutionally accredited but not ABA approved, and which requires not less than the equivalent of 60 semester hours of classroom study;

4. Graduation from a course of study for legal assistants, other than those set forth in (2) and (3) above, plus not less than six months of in-house training as a legal assistant;

5. A baccalaureate degree in any field, plus not less than six months in-house training as a legal assistant;

6. A minimum of three years of law-related experience under the supervision of an attorney, including at least six months of in-house training as a legal assistant; or

7. Two years of in-house training as a legal assistant.

These minimum qualifications recognize law-related work and formal educational backgrounds, both of which should provide the paralegal with a broad exposure to and knowledge of the legal profession. This background is necessary to assure the public and the legal profession that the one being identified as a paralegal is qualified.

What Does a Paralegal Do?

A paralegal is allowed to perform a task that is properly delegated and supervised by an attorney, who is ultimately responsible to the client and assumes complete responsibility for the work product. The chapter on ethics in this manual will explain in greater detail what a paralegal cannot do, as well as the variety of considerations and concepts of law that are involved in working as a paralegal.

Generally, and except as otherwise provided by statute, court rule or decision, administrative rule or regulation, or the attorney's codes, a paralegal may perform any function delegated by an attorney including, but not limited to, the following:

1. Conduct client interviews and maintain general contact with the client.

2. Locate and interview witnesses.

3. Conduct investigations and statistical and documentary research.

4. Conduct legal research.

5. Draft correspondence, pleadings, and other legal documents.

6. Summarize depositions, interrogatories, and testimony.

7. Attend execution of wills, real estate closings, depositions, court or administrative hearings, or trials with the attorney.

8. Author and sign letters, provided the paralegal status is clearly indicated and the correspondence does not contain independent legal opinions or direct legal advice.

The tasks of paralegals vary but usually fall within those functions listed previously. Empirical studies show a definite trend toward a concentration of paralegal time in specialized areas of practice due to the tendency of lawyers to move toward specialized practice. However, NALA surveys continue to show very strong data which suggests the continuing trend that paralegals generally are assigned a wide range of tasks and responsibilities in varied areas of practice. For instance, 65 percent of the respondents to NALA's most recent survey worked in up to four specialty areas of practice. These are not competing ideas or contradictory statements. It is difficult, if not impossible, to segregate the areas of practice of law or to compartmentalize these specialties so neatly that there is no overlap.

How assignments are given to paralegals also vary. Some employers have defined levels of paralegals; others have no structure. Assignments most commonly come from individual attorneys or through specific departments. Some paralegals participate in meetings with clients, do legal research, and attend court hearings, while others do not.

Remember, there will be diversity in each and every position filled by a paralegal. This diversity will depend in large part on the particular requirements for the position, the needs of the attorney and the firm, as well as the background and experience of the paralegal.

Utilization and Billing

The standards, responsibilities, and utilization of paralegals received significant endorsement in June 1989, when the U.S. Supreme Court announced its decision in *Missouri v. Jenkins,* 491 U.S. 274, 109 S. Ct. 2463 (1989). The Eighth Circuit Court of Appeals placed several issues before the Supreme Court regarding the general subject of attorney fee awards under 42 U.S.C. Section 1988 (the Civil Rights Attorney's Fees Awards Act of 1976). The issue related to the utilization of paralegals was whether or not, in attorney fee awards, paralegal time may be reimbursed at market rates, rather than at actual cost. While the question before the Court already assumed that the time was reimbursable under the Code, the question of how the time may be reimbursed required the Court to examine the utilization of paralegals. NALA participated in this case as an *amicus* and filed a brief in the U.S. Supreme Court in support of the award of paralegal fees at market rates.

Ultimately, the Court agreed with the decision of the Eighth Circuit Court, which had allowed the compensation of paralegal time at market rates (*see* Appendix). There are matters of great significance to the profession in the Court's decision. First is the Court's acknowledgment of the general practice of billing paralegal time at market rates and that these rates are significantly lower than the hourly market rates for attorney time. Second, the Court allowed the time of paralegals to be considered in the same manner as all professional fees and separate from costs or expenses associated with a case. Finally, the Court encouraged the use of lower cost paralegals wherever possible as a practice that ensures the cost-effective delivery of legal services and reduces the spiraling cost of litigation.

The Court cautioned that "purely clerical or secretarial tasks should not be billed at a paralegal rate, regardless of who performs them." Herein lies the significance of the Court's decision on the utilization of paralegals. While strongly encouraging the use of paralegals through its comment and decision, the Court cautioned just as adamantly that when billing for paralegal time (or time for any other professional), firms should not bill for any tasks that are clerical or secretarial in nature. The assumption is that the costs for these tasks are already included as overhead expenses in the hourly rates of professionals such as attorneys and paralegals.

The Court's decision in *Missouri v. Jenkins* has been relied on by other courts in reviewing the propriety of attorney fees awards and compensation within those awards for paralegal time.[1]

In 2008, NALA was again before the U.S. Supreme Court, and the issue was, again, the award of paralegal fees at market rates. The difference this time was whether the award of paralegal fees is provided for under the Equal Access to Justice. Act. The case was *Richlin Security Service Co. v. Michael Chertoff, Secretary of Homeland Security.* The case involves a contract dispute between Richlin Security Service Co. and the Immigration and Naturalization Service (then). Richlin was engaged by INS to provide guard services for detainees at LAX. The parties contracts misclassified Richlin's employees and ultimately the Department of Labor ordered Richlin to pay its employees back wages. Richlin then filed a claim against the Government and sought reformation of the two contracts in order to force the government to make additional payments necessary to cover Richlin's liability. Richlin prevailed.

Richlin then filed an application for reimbursement of attorney fees, expenses, and costs under the Equal Access to Justice Act. The U.S. Court of Appeals for the Federal Circuit held the term "fees" embraced only the fees of attorneys, experts, and agents. The U.S. Supreme Court issued its opinion on June 2, 2008. In the opinion, the court relied heavily on the opinion in *Missouri v. Jenkins* and found that a prevailing party that satisfies EAJA's other requirements may recover its paralegal fees from the Government at prevailing market rates. The court also stated that it is "self evident that attorneys fee embraced the fees of paralegals as well as attorneys. . . . the EAJA must be interpreted as using the term attorney fees to reach fees for paralegal services . . . since these sections generally provide for recovery of attorney fees at prevailing market rates, it follows that paralegal fees must also be recoverable at those rates." The court also stated that separate billing of paralegal time has become increasingly widespread.

The impact of the decisions in both *Missouri v. Jenkins* and *Richlin v. Chertoff* cannot be underestimated in terms of the recognition of the value of paralegal work and its contribution to the effectively delivery of legal services. Now, not only in cases that are filed under the Civil Rights Act, but also in those filed against the government under the Equal Access to Justice Act, paralegal time may be awarded on the same basis as professional fees of attorneys. The *Richlin* decision, also may suggest that this practice is so accepted, it may likely not be before the Court again.

The Court's decision is also included in the appendix.

The following list of factors should be helpful in defining billing practices for paralegals:

1. The firm customarily bills clients at an hourly rate for paralegal time.
2. The paralegal has the necessary qualifications through education, training, professional certification, or work experience to function in that capacity under the direction and supervision of an attorney.
3. The paralegal time and the services performed are clearly identified and documented in the fee request.
4. The tasks performed by the paralegal are not clerical or ministerial in nature.
5. The tasks performed by the paralegal involve substantive legal work specifically delegated by and conducted under the direct supervision of an attorney.
6. The tasks performed by the paralegal are cost-effective in the delivery of legal services in that, absent the use of a paralegal in the litigation, the attorney would have performed the tasks at a higher hourly rate.
7. There is no duplication of efforts by the use of a paralegal, as the only necessary time for the attorney is in review and supervision of the paralegal's work to merge it into the attorney's final work product.
8. The training and expertise of the paralegal are such that they support the requested hourly services performed.
9. In specialized or complex litigation where a higher hourly rate may be sought, emphasis should be placed on the paralegal's experience, expertise, and type and quality of work.
10. Affidavits, other documentation, or evidence are presented on the prevailing hourly rate in the relevant market area for paralegal services.[2]

Compensation

A paralegal's compensation will likely depend on a number of factors: type of employer, such as a private law firm or corporation and its size; geographic region of employment; number of years of paralegal experience; level of education; and other professional achievements, such as the CLA/CP or the ACP (Advanced Certified Paralegal) credentials.

Depending on these variables, paralegal salaries typically range from almost $40,000 to over $80,000 annually. In its 2008 survey, NALA found an average salary of $48,211 and average annual compensation of $52,119. . . Increasingly, lawyers have come to recognize the high cost of replacing an experienced paralegal. Because educational institutions are generally better equipped than law firms to train paralegals, more positions than ever before are being filled by paralegals with some formal education. The number of Certified Legal Assistants/Certified Paralegals has increased dramatically within the past few years, and the NALA surveys reflect a slight increase in the compensation of those with the Certified Paralegal in comparison with the average compensation reported by those without the credential. Those with the Advanced Certified Paralegal designation report about 9 percent higher compensation.

The majority of paralegals are salaried and frequently work in excess of their employers' normal working hours. Fringe benefits can include vacation, medical or other insurance, parking, professional dues, and retirement plans.

Professional Certification and Activities

Paralegals work under the supervision of attorneys, and attorneys have the ultimate responsibility for the work product of paralegals. However, this does not relieve a paralegal of his or her individual obligation to exhibit ethical conduct and responsibility to the paralegal profession itself. For example, paralegals must remain current on such subjects as ethical guidelines, opinions, and case law that affect their professional status, continue their legal education, and demonstrate their competence and their commitment to professional standards. It is through their local, state, and national professional associations that they may address these goals and responsibilities.

NALA offers a national voluntary certification program for paralegals. This peer-established certification program provides a means for paralegals to demonstrate their knowledge and expertise in this profession and their commitment to professional development. The Certified Legal Assistant (CLA)/Certified Paralegal (CP) designation is generally recognized within the legal community as one means of identifying competent paralegals. This certification and the use of the CLA/CP designation are available to paralegals who meet certain eligibility requirements and successfully complete a two-day examination covering the range of skills and knowledge required of paralegals. All Certified Legal Assistants/Certified Paralegals must meet certain continuing education requirements in order to maintain the CLA/CP designation, which must be renewed every five years.

Paralegals who achieve the CLA/CP designation may continue their professional certification through the NALA Advanced Paralegal Certification program. At the present time, Advanced Certified Paralegal (ACP) designations are available in the areas of Alternative Dispute Resolution, Business Organizations: Incorporated Entities, Contract Management/Contracts Administration, Discovery, Social Security Disability, and Trial Practice, and APC Courses are being added at the rate of three or four a year. The ACP designation is earned through successful completion of a comprehensive online course in a specialty area of practice mentioned previously. Continuing education credit is also awarded for successful completion of an APC course.

Recognition of the Certified Legal Assistant program is nationwide. An example of the high regard in which it is held by attorneys in general is the discussion of the program which appears in the 1993 publication *Leveraging with Legal Assistants,* published by the ABA Section of Law Practice Management. On the subject of recruiting legal assistants:

> The legal assistant who can use the CLA designation has a number of advantages, not the least of which is that a hiring lawyer can assume from the CLA appellation that he or she is dealing with an experienced legal assistant who has performed to a high standard. It would be safe to assume that a CLA can immediately bring experience and capability to the practice.

The CLA program has been in existence over thirty years. As of June 2008, there were 14,752 Certified Legal Assistants/Certified Paralegals in the United States. Over 1,200 have achieved an Advanced Certified Paralegal credential. Three states (Florida, Louisiana, and California) have adopted the CLA/CP as the standard for paralegals within their own state specialty certification programs. The only other states to offer statewide certification are North Carolina, Ohio, and Texas, with the CLA being one of the means of qualifying for their program.

Numerous bar associations offer guidelines for paralegals, as well as associate membership for paralegals. Half of the bar associations and bar association sections offering this membership include the CLA/CP credential among the alternate eligibility requirements for membership. The South Dakota Supreme Court has recognized the CLA/CP as a means of identifying competent paralegals, and other courts have awarded higher fees to paralegals with the CLA/CP designation. In 1995, the Mississippi Bar Ethics Committee Opinion 223 (1/19/95) described the CLA as a reputable program and allowed the use of the CLA and CLAS credentials on law firm letterhead listings. The New York State Bar Association Committee on Professional Ethics, in Opinion 695, August 25, 1997, also addressed the issue of use of the designation "certified legal assistant" on firm letterhead and promotional materials and determined law firms may do so. The legal community has also been supportive of the credential economically. Paralegals with the CLA/CP may stand to receive higher salaries nationwide, and their work is billed at higher rates. The Certified Legal Assistant/Certified Paralegal and Advanced Certified Paralegal programs exist for the paralegal profession. They are valuable tools for use by paralegals in the development of their career path and growth.

Summary

The word *assist* is the basis for the title *legal assistant*. This one word is the key reason for the emergence of and the ever-growing need and demand for qualified legal assistants. Legal assistants *assist* attorneys in the delivery of legal services by performing whatever tasks the attorneys' delegate. This frees attorneys to do that which only they can do. This *assisting* can be in a direct one-to-one relationship with an attorney, as part of an attorney-legal assistant-legal secretary team, or with a number of attorneys. It is in this spirit of assisting that we must approach the legal assistant profession. This, above all others, is the criterion upon which we will build and expand this exciting, promising, and vital career.

A Final Word . . . Is it Paralegal or Legal Assistant?

NALA has long stated that the terms "legal assistant" and "paralegal" are synonymous terms. This is not a choice or opinion of NALA, but a fact—the terms are defined as such throughout the United States in state supreme court rules, statutes, ethical opinions, bar association guidelines, and other similar documents. These are the same documents which provide recognition of the legal assistant profession and encourage the use of legal assistants in the delivery of legal services.

However, the association has become increasingly aware that while the terms may be used in a similar fashion as "lawyer" and "attorney," preference in terms is emerging—different geographic areas use one term more than another. For this reason, NALA filed for a certification mark "CP" with the U.S. Patent and Trademark Office. The certification mark CP® was successfully registered on July 20, 2004. Our survey is also showing a preference for the term "paralegal." In the 2008 survey, 78 percent of the respondents reported a preference for the term "paralegal." This number is growing. In 2004, 62 percent of respondents preferred "paralegal"; in 2000, the respondents were almost split on the preferred term—49 percent preferred "legal assistant," and 42 percent preferred "paralegal."

Endnotes

1. For a discussion of the reliance of the courts on *Missouri v. Jenkins* see "The Ripple Effect of *Missouri v. Jenkins* Begins: Special Report of NALA President Karen B. Judd, *CLA, Facts & Findings* (January, 1990).

2. See Judd, Karen B., "Legal Assistant Time in Attorney Fee Awards: A Separate and Distinct Compensation," VIII *Facts & Findings* (June, 1988).

1

Introduction to the American Legal System

The American legal system reflects complexity and diversity in its structure and procedure. In the United States, two sovereigns exercise jurisdiction. The federal government exercises authority according to the powers granted by the U.S. Constitution, and each state exercises authority through its own constitution and through the federal constitution.

In each case, the power exercised is a grant from the people, an expression of the people's choice as to how they will be governed and the limitations upon that governance.

1.00 LAW IN AMERICAN SOCIETY

What is law? *The American College Dictionary* defines law as "the principles and regulations emanating from a government and applicable to a people, whether in the form of legislation or of custom and policies recognized and enforced by judicial decision." *Oran's Dictionary of the Law* also offers a general definition: "1. That which must be obeyed. 2. A statute; an act of the legislature. 3. The whole body of principles, standards, and rules put out by a government." Thus, "law" can best be described as rules of conduct made by a controlling body (usually a government) which are enforceable.

How has the government of the United States earned the right or power to make and enforce rules for its people? The answer can be found in the history and theory of legal principles.

1.001   History, Theory, and Philosophy

Legal traditions develop from history, theory, and philosophy. The American legal system is most often thought to be based upon previous English systems of law. In the development of Anglo-American law, four basic schools of thought are commonly identified.

1.0011 Natural Law.   In ancient times, the great philosophers from Athens and the great jurists from Rome believed humankind could discover, by reason, the perfect rules of human conduct that were separate from enacted laws. These "natural laws" are not peculiar to any one people; rather, they conform to the inherent nature of all people. In other words, they are unchanging rules of conduct discovered only by the rational intelligence of humankind.

Our Founding Fathers, particularly Thomas Jefferson and Alexander Hamilton, adopted a revised "natural law" school of thought. Jefferson and Hamilton were particularly influenced by the written works of John Locke (1632–1704), an English philosopher. Locke wrote about individual rights and government obligations. In keeping with Locke's philosophy, Thomas Jefferson wrote the following portion of the *Declaration of Independence*:

> When in the Course of human events, it becomes necessary for one people to dissolve the political bands which have connected them with another, and to assume among the powers of the earth, the separate and equal station to which the Laws of Nature and of Nature's God entitle them, a decent respect to the opinions of mankind requires that they should declare the causes which impel them to the separation. We hold these truths to be self-evident, that all men are created equal that they are endowed by their Creator with certain unalienable Rights, that among these are Life, Liberty and the pursuit of Happiness.

Consequently, one of the major forces behind the American colonists declaring revolution against the King of England was the belief that new rules must be established that are consistent with an individual's natural rights.

1.0012 Positive Law/Divine Law.   Early positivism developed in Europe, reflecting Judeo-Christian traditions and the canon law of the early Holy Roman Empire. Fundamentally, believers held that all law is of divine origin and handed down by the sovereign. The positivist focused on four basic principles: (1) law consists of rules, (2) law is different from morals, (3) the sovereign establishes the rules, and (4) legal rules carry sanctions.

1.0013 Sociological Jurisprudence.

This school of thought is concerned with the effects of law and its justifications. When a law is enacted, the proponents of sociological jurisprudence analyze the effects and reasons for the law by applying methods of the social sciences. The adequacy of a legal system is judged by weighing its effect on society against individual interest, special group interest, and the good of the general public.

1.0014 Legal Realism.

This school, which best describes American legal philosophy, has its roots in natural law and sociological jurisprudence. The great jurist Oliver Wendell Holmes (1841–1935) was a pioneer of the realist school. Fundamentally, realists examine what the law is and not what the law ought to be. Realists use social science to analyze how the law functions and to look for underlying policy.

1.01   SOURCES OF AMERICAN LAW

Federal and state laws come from many different sources. Most individuals think of the "law" as the statutes or ordinances enacted by a legislative body. To understand the American legal system and its sources of law, we must look further.

For the most part, American government systems are divided into three branches: executive, legislative, and judicial. Within each branch, there are several levels: federal, state, and local. The United States executive branch is headed by the president, the state executive branch by a governor, and the local executive branch by a mayor or similar officer. The same pattern can be found in the legislative branch of government. The United States legislative body is the Congress, the state legislative body is the legislature, and the local legislative body is generally called a city or town council. The judicial branch of government also has three basic levels: the United States (federal) courts, consisting of the U.S. Supreme Court and the lower federal courts of appeals and district courts; state courts reflect this system as well by also having a court of last resort usually referred to as the supreme court, and/or their appellate court; and a trial court. Administrative agencies are sometimes referred to as the "fourth" branch of government because the regulations that they promulgate have the effect of law. Administrative regulations are created at the federal, state, and local levels. (*See* Exhibit 1-1, Sources of American Law.)

EXHIBIT 1-1 Sources of American Law

FOUR SOURCES OF LAW			
Statutory (Legislatures)	Administrative Agencies	Common Law (Courts)	Constitutions
Federal Level — Congress (Statues)	Federal Agencies (Regulations)	Federal Courts (Cases or opinions)	U.S. Constitution
State Level — State Legislatures (Statues)	State Agencies (Regulations)	State Courts (Cases or opinions)	State Constitution
Local Level — City Council (Ordinances)	City Agencies (Regulations)	Local Courts (Cases or opinions)	Charter

1.011   Common Law

The individual states of the United States can trace the development of their legal principles, and to some degree their judicial systems, to medieval England. Common law principles have evolved through judicial decision-making. The judge applies principles of law through the analysis of prior court decisions. This process is known as *stare decisis,* in which the courts follow the reasoning and decisions of earlier courts when presented with a similar fact situation unless a clear, convincing reason exists to depart from the established precedent. Judicial adherence to the principle of *stare decisis* creates consistency in the law. When a similar fact situation arises, the parties and their attorneys can, with some degree of certainty, predict and explain what the law has been and how the courts are likely to decide the dispute. Clearly, there are exceptions because the law is ever changing. Fortunately, this system offers stability and consistency in how legal principles are applied.

1.012   Statutory Law

Laws that have been enacted by a legislative body are known as statutes or ordinances. Statutes are enacted by either the United States Congress or a state legislative body. The term *ordinance* is generally used when a city or town council passes a local law. The federal legal system is exclusively statutory in nature. There is no federal common law source. When a federal statute is challenged, it is interpreted by judges. The state legal system is a combination of statutory law and common law principles.

1.013   Administrative Law

Administrative law is similar to statutory law (legislation). It is now well established and judicially accepted that Congress and the state legislatures may delegate some of their constitutional lawmaking authority to administrative agencies. In fact, without these agencies, government could not effectively function. Agencies of the federal government, such as the Social Security Administration, promulgate rules and regulations that have the effect and force of law.

Administrative agencies have the power to exercise quasi-judicial, quasi-legislative, and quasi-executive authority. Their authority is limited by the power granted to them. Through legislation, Congress can grant to the Social Security Administration the power to hear and decide violations of Social Security regulations. This grant is not unlimited because under the United States Constitution, Congress is restricted as to what authority it can delegate. In this way, agencies carry out many functions that are simply not possible for Congress to do alone. Because the separation of powers through the three branches of government is fundamental, this "fourth branch" can only function through the authority granted by one of the original branches, specifically, the legislative branch or the executive branch.

1.014   Constitutional Law

The final major source of law is the constitution. The constitutions may be found at federal, state, and local levels. The United States Constitution is the supreme law of the land. Legislative, administrative, and common law are all subject to the principles of the U.S. Constitution. The Constitution embodies general principles regarding: (1) the powers granted to the federal government, (2) the powers reserved to the states, and (3) the rights held by citizens. The Bill of Rights, or the first ten amendments to the Constitution, specifically restates the rights held by citizens. Because the principles of the U.S. Constitution are general in nature, they frequently require interpretation by the judiciary.

In addition to the U.S. Constitution, state and local governments have constitutions. A state's constitution is the supreme law of that particular state; however, it is subordinate to the U.S. Constitution when their provisions overlap. Local governments also may adopt constitutions, generally referred to as charters, and these are subordinate to federal and state constitutions.

1.02 THE AMERICAN LEGAL SYSTEM

The American legal system is founded in common law principles the colonists brought with them from England.

Common law does not operate in isolation within our legal system. In addition to common law, each governmental unit (federal, state, and local) has adopted a document that defines and limits its powers in relation to its citizens. At the federal and state levels, this document is called a constitution. A local government, such as a city, may adopt a charter for this purpose.

The U.S. Constitution reflects the method of government adopted by the founders through the creation of three governmental branches: legislative, executive, and judicial. The legislative branch is authorized to make laws, the executive branch is authorized to enforce laws, and the judicial branch is authorized to interpret laws. The creation of the three branches of government is known as "separation of powers." In addition, the U.S. Constitution and most state constitutions include a Bill of Rights. Typically, a Bill of Rights defines the rights of an individual that a governmental branch can not remove, such as the right to a jury trial and the right to freedom of speech.

The U.S. Constitution gives Congress the authority to legislate in specific areas, such as interstate commerce and federal taxation. The U.S. Supreme Court is the only court specifically created by the Constitution, although Congress is given authority to add such other, inferior courts as it deems necessary. Since most state constitutions follow a format similar to that of the U.S. Constitution, many parallels can be drawn between the two systems of government. Yet, federal and state governments exist independently of each other. Their authority or jurisdiction is distinct. For further discussion, see Chapter 2, Legal Research.

1.021 Court Systems

At both the federal and state levels, court systems have been established for judicial resolution of legal disputes. Each court system is generally organized in four levels: specialty courts, trial courts, intermediate appellate courts, and supreme courts. Some decisions and appeals, heard and adjudged in state courts, may be appealed further to the U.S. Supreme Court if a federally protected right is involved and if the Court consents (grants *certiorari*) to hear the case. (*See* Exhibit 1-2, United States Judicial System.)

1.022 Federal Court System

The federal judiciary is established in Article III of the U.S. Constitution. However, only the Supreme Court is specifically mentioned: "The judicial Power of the United States, shall be vested in one supreme Court, and in such inferior Courts as the Congress may from time to time ordain and establish." Thus, the federal court system is in a large part determined by Congress. In addition, Congress may establish courts under Article I, Section 8 of the Constitution, which states that "Congress shall have power... To constitute Tribunals inferior to the supreme Court." For example, Congress has established the U.S. Tax Court under this section of the Constitution. The difference between the two articles is that under Article III, Section 1, judges hold office for life and compensation cannot be reduced during their term. Article I, Section 8 makes no statement regarding the length of office or the level of compensation; thus Congress may establish specialty courts, such as tax or bankruptcy, without appointing judges for life

EXHIBIT 1-2 United States Judicial System

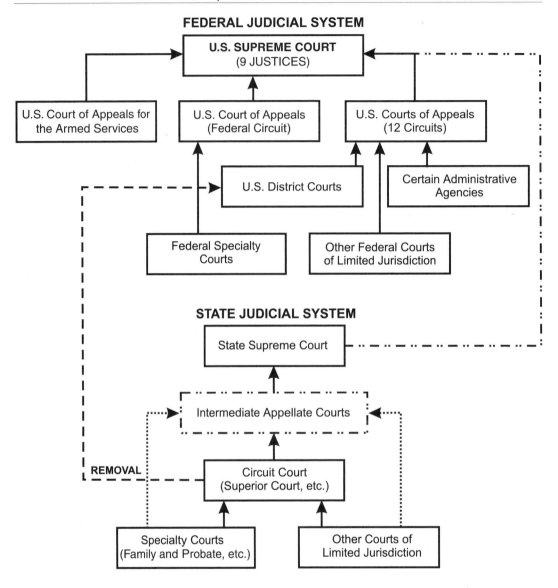

or guaranteeing a level of compensation. However, Congress cannot establish all courts under Article I because Article III, Section 2 describes certain judicial powers granted to the Supreme Court and inferior courts.

The federal court system is composed of four types of courts: (1) the district court, a trial court; (2) the court of appeals, an intermediate appellate court; (3) the Supreme Court, the final appellate court; and (4) specialized courts such as the U.S. Court of Federal Claims and the U.S. Tax Court. This basic four-tier federal system is generally repeated at the state level.

1.0221 District Courts.   The federal court system covers the United States, Puerto Rico, the Virgin Islands, Guam, and the Northern Mariana Islands. The U.S. District Courts are the federal trial courts. U.S. District Courts are geographically located to serve each state and the District of Columbia and Puerto Rico and have one or more courtrooms located in each state. These courts have federal jurisdiction over civil and criminal matters. The U.S. District Court of the District of Columbia has both federal and local jurisdiction.

The U.S. District Courts are organized by departments, with judges and courtrooms assigned to each department within the court. The number of courtrooms assigned to a district depends upon the population of the district and the amount of litigation filed within the district. Trials may be held before a judge, a jury, or a specially selected and qualified master(s) whose powers and limitations are defined by the district court making the appointment.

The district courts are established geographically, with a minimum of one established per state. District courts do not cross state lines. Currently, there are more than ninety district courts established in the United States. Larger states, such as Texas, California, and New York, have several district courts within their boundaries. District courts are trial-level courts of original jurisdiction. The district court evaluates testimony, hears witnesses, and makes findings of fact and law. Most types of trials brought within the federal court system originate in the district court. District courts are general jurisdiction courts; they hear most types of cases. Specialty courts, such as the U.S. Tax Court or U.S. Court of Federal Claims, hear only single-subject cases. Judges are appointed for life by the President, subject to confirmation by the U.S. Senate.

Certain circumstances allow the removal of some cases or issues from state courts into federal courts, such as diversity of citizenship (parties are domiciled in different states) or when the amount in controversy exceeds a minimum amount. When no federal question exists, but there is: (1) diversity of citizenship, (2) the amount in controversy exceeds the minimum proscribed in Title 28, U.S.C. 1332, and (3) the federal court accepts the right of removal as one properly exercised and procedurally correct, the U.S. District Court will apply the law of the appropriate state, whether it is common law, civil code, or the statutes of the state.

1.0222 Courts of Appeals.   The U.S. Courts of Appeals (also referred to as circuit courts) were established as intermediate appellate courts to help relieve the workload of the U.S. Supreme Court. The United States has thirteen circuits. Eleven represent geographic areas, the District of Columbia is the twelfth circuit, and the thirteenth is known as the Federal Circuit. The Federal or Thirteenth Circuit Court of Appeals handles appeals from the U.S. Court of Federal Claims, U.S. Court of International Trade, and other specialized federal courts. There may be more than one division within a single circuit. Three judges are designated from all the judges in the division to sit in each case in each division. Appeals are not heard before juries but before the judges of the division. At least two judges are always present, but the judges may sit *en banc* (all three judges present). When two of the three judges assigned to a particular case agree on an outcome, the decision is binding.

The courts of appeals hear cases where the appellant (the party appealing) argues that the evidence did not support the trial court's finding or that the trial court erred in the application of the law. The appellate court reviews the record only. No new evidence is admitted, and no witnesses are heard. This court will hear the arguments of the parties' attorneys, review the record of the trial proceedings, and read written briefs submitted by both parties. The court will make its decision based on this information. Most appeals end here. The next level of appeal would be to the U.S. Supreme Court, which exercises discretion in accepting cases. About 7,000 cases are appealed to the Supreme Court annually; the number actually heard averages less than 200.

1.0223 The Supreme Court.

The U.S. Supreme Court is the ultimate interpreter of the United States Constitution. This is the court of last resort; although in most cases, litigants do not have a right to have their appeal heard by the highest court. There are two ways that an appeal reaches the Supreme Court: (1) through a *writ of certiorari* (an order to the lower court to send the Supreme Court the record of the case for review), which may or may not be granted by the high court; or (2) through an appeal of right, (which exists in certain cases). An example of an appeal of right occurs when a state or federal court of appeals has held that a state statute violates the U.S. Constitution.

The Supreme Court consists of one chief justice and eight associate justices. Justices are nominated by the President and confirmed by the Senate. These are lifetime appointments. The Supreme Court has original jurisdiction in cases affecting ambassadors, other public ministers, and consuls, and in those cases where one of the fifty states is a party. Original jurisdiction is exercised in very few cases. The Supreme Court has appellate jurisdiction in all other cases. The Supreme Court itself is subject to some regulation by Congress. Article III, Section 2 of the U.S. Constitution establishes the powers and limitations of the federal judiciary. Sections 1251–1259, Title 28, Chapter 81 of the U.S. Code confer jurisdiction on the Supreme Court.

1.0224 Specialized Courts.

Federal specialized courts have jurisdiction limited to a specialized subject area and are considered *inferior courts.* Examples of such courts include the Court of International Trade, the U.S. Court of Federal Claims, and the U.S. Tax Court. These courts function as a trial court. Appeals from these first tier courts are made directly to the U.S. Court of Appeals for the Federal Circuit, which was established by Congress as part of the Federal Courts Improvement Act of 1982.

The U.S. Court of Federal Claims renders judgments on the validity of certain types of claims against the United States. Also separate from the U.S. District Court, the U.S. Tax Court renders judgments in federal taxation matters.

A separate U.S. Court of International Trade deals exclusively with matters of imported merchandise and the activities of customs collectors. The U.S. Court of Appeals for the Federal Circuit hears appeals and reviews decisions of the U.S. Court of International Trade, the U.S. Patent and Trademark Office, and the U.S. International Trade Commission.

1.0225 Administrative Agencies.

As a part of the executive branch, the administrative agencies of the federal government carry out the directions of the President. Each administrative agency is established and authorized by a specific legislative act (enabling act) passed by Congress. Within the boundaries of its particular enabling act, each administrative agency adopts rules and regulations to carry out its purpose. In addition, it is empowered to hold hearings and to render binding decisions in quasi-judicial proceedings that resemble trials. Hearing officers in contested matters may be administrative law judges, referees, hearing examiners, commissioners, or other persons authorized by the agency. Hearing officers are not generally required to be attorneys. Although the work of an administrative agency is not controlled or directed by the courts, all appeals from their decisions proceed directly to the U.S. Courts of Appeals. Examples of administrative agencies are the Federal Communications Commission, Federal Trade Commission, National Labor Relations Board, Federal Aviation Administration, Occupational Safety and Health Administration, and Equal Employment Opportunity Commission.

1.023 State Court Systems

Although state court systems are not uniform across the country, they share some typical elements. Most state court systems have trial and appellate level courts, specialized courts, and courts with general and limited jurisdiction. Examples of trial courts with limited jurisdiction would include magistrate's courts, small claims courts, and municipal courts that enforce local ordinances. Examples of specialized courts would include family or domestic relations courts and probate courts. States also have trial courts with general jurisdiction to hear civil and criminal cases.

Most states have an intermediate appellate court where the losing party has a right of appeal. The appeals court of last resort in most states is the state's supreme court. If the state has an intermediate appellate court, its supreme court may use discretion in accepting cases.

State courts handle an immense volume of litigation, both civil and criminal. Largely because of the defendant's constitutional right to a speedy trial, most courts give priority to criminal cases, which can cause problems in scheduling and rescheduling civil cases, both for procedural matters leading to trial as well as for the trials themselves. It is not unusual to have civil trial dates canceled or postponed on the court's calendar because of a sudden influx of criminal cases. Attorneys and paralegals recognize that the litigation process has inherent elements of uncertainty that require an attorney to be ready for trial on schedule, with the understanding that the trial may be postponed. This uncertainty is the basis for at least a portion of the pressures experienced by the litigation team as trial dates draw near. From state to state, trial court systems may differ (particularly in titles) but usually fit the general outline shown in Exhibit 1-2.

State supreme courts have minimal, if any, original jurisdiction. The bulk of their workload derives from their appellate jurisdiction over civil and criminal cases that are appealed from state superior courts and state administrative agencies. Depending on the state, five to nine judges provide appellate review based upon the record made at the respective trial court level or intermediate appellate court level, if any. No jury exists at this level and no new evidence is received. In some states, citizens have an absolute right of review by the state supreme court. In other states, supreme court review is discretionary with the court itself.

Superior courts (sometimes called district, circuit, common pleas, or sessions courts) are usually established in each county, parish, or similar region and have sufficient judges and courtrooms to handle the population or litigation within that particular county. Occasionally, judges are "borrowed" from other counties to handle heavy litigation loads. Superior courts generally handle the trial of all felonies, as well as civil litigation over a minimum dollar amount. In many states, this court is one of general jurisdiction in which there is no minimum or maximum dollar amount for the civil suits that it handles. These courts may also handle appeals from inferior courts as a separate and distinct responsibility.

The county court or municipal court is a lower-level court that hears criminal misdemeanor cases and civil cases having a maximum dollar value. Sometimes this court has a separate small claims court limited to very small dollar amounts (i.e., five hundred dollars or less), does not provide for trial by jury, and does not allow parties to be represented by attorneys.

1.024   Jurisdiction

The complexity of law and its administration, together with the multilevel regulation of modern life, often make it hard to identify the best *forum,* that is the location or type of court, in which to present the client's case. Even after all the relevant forums have been identified, difficult decisions often remain. A state may have laws that parallel those of the federal government in certain areas, such as antitrust statutes, securities regulation, equal employment opportunity, and utility regulation. If so, the lawyer must decide whether to file the client's claim in the appropriate state or federal court or at the administrative level (if applicable).

A decision as to whether to file a civil action in a state superior court or in a county court may depend on the dollar value of damages and the length of time necessary to bring the case to trial. While trials usually can be completed more quickly in a county court, a successful plaintiff may still need to register the judgment with the superior court before it will be given full faith and credit by other courts in different jurisdictions. This can be a critical factor when it appears likely that judicial enforcement will be required to collect the judgment.

Further decisions must be made if the potential defendant (or defendants) is domiciled outside the geographical jurisdiction of the forum court. In that case, facts must be established that will give the forum court personal jurisdiction over the defendant. Most states have long-arm statutes that authorize jurisdiction over persons who commit torts within the forum state (such as causing an automobile accident) or who do other things to establish minimum contacts with the forum state.

Even if all of the parties live in the same state, it may still be necessary to decide which court has proper venue to hear the case. Venue relates to the place where the case should be tried, assuming that there is more than one division or department of a court that has jurisdiction. When venue becomes an issue, it is usually resolved by balancing convenience to the plaintiff, convenience to the defendant, where the events occurred, and where the witnesses and other evidence are most readily available.

1.025 Legislative Systems

The power to make law originates with the federal and state legislative bodies. (*See* Exhibit 1-3, How a Bill Becomes a Law.) As stated before, the "supreme law of the land" is the U.S. Constitution and all other laws are subordinate. The Constitution states in Article I, Section 1, "All legislative Powers herein granted shall be vested in a Congress of the United States, which shall consist of a Senate and House of Representatives." The Constitution grants broad powers to Congress, but those powers not specifically granted to Congress are reserved to the states or to the people through the Tenth Amendment, which says "The powers not delegated to the United States by the Constitution, nor prohibited by it to the States, are reserved to the States respectively, or to the people." This is referred to as the Reserved Power Clause.

State constitutions similarly grant the power to legislate to a state body, often referred to as the legislature. This legislative body acts within the power granted by the state constitution or by the power reserved through the Tenth Amendment. Collectively, these powers are the police power of the state because they allow the state to enact laws to promote public health, safety, and welfare. Police power is very broad and permits states, for example, to set standards for licensing professionals, requirements for operating vehicles, minimum age for marriage, and generally to control any areas unique to the state.

State and federal legislative bodies have many potentially conflicting areas of power. When there is a legitimate conflict, the Supremacy Clause of the Constitution (Article VI) makes clear that the Constitution is the ultimate law: "This Constitution, and the Laws of the United States which shall be made in Pursuance thereof; and all Treaties made, or which shall be made, under the Authority of the United States, shall be the supreme Law of the Land; and the Judges in every State shall be bound thereby, any Thing in the Constitution or Laws of any State to the Contrary notwithstanding."

Article IV, Sections 1 and 2 of the Constitution clarifies the relationship between state and federal power. Section 1 states, "Full Faith and Credit shall be given in each State to the public Acts, Records, and judicial Proceedings of every other State. And the Congress may by general Laws prescribe the Manner in which such Acts, Records and Proceedings shall be proved, and the Effect thereof." This is called the Full Faith and Credit Clause, wherein a judgment or record shall have the same faith, credit, conclusive effect, and obligatory force in other states as it has by law or usage in the state from which it was originally decreed. Section 2, Clause 1 is referred to as the Privileges and Immunities Clause, and it states, "The Citizens of each State shall be entitled to all Privileges and Immunities of Citizens in the several States." Both of these sections of Article IV have been interpreted, through case law, by the U.S. Supreme Court. Laws enacted by Congress are enforced by the executive, judicial, and administrative systems.

EXHIBIT 1-3 How a Bill Becomes a Law

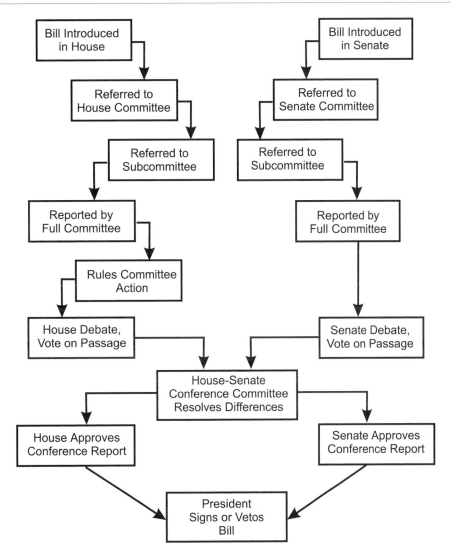

1.026 Administrative Systems

Administrative agencies are established by a specific act of the legislative branch but are usually considered an arm of the executive branch. The U.S. Constitution does not specifically provide for the agencies. Some examples of federal agencies are the Federal Deposit Insurance Corporation, Federal Reserve Board, U.S. Environmental Protection Agency, U.S. Securities and Exchange Commission, Federal Trade Commission, Farm Credit Administration, U.S. Consumer Product Safety Commission, and National Labor Relations Board. The administrative agencies, which may fall under the control of any one of the three branches of government or be classified as independent (*see* Exhibit 1-4, The United States Government), are often authorized by the act creating them to engage in quasi-legislative, quasi-executive, or quasi-judicial activities. In their quasi-executive status, they manage a particular area of

EXHIBIT 1-4 The United States Government

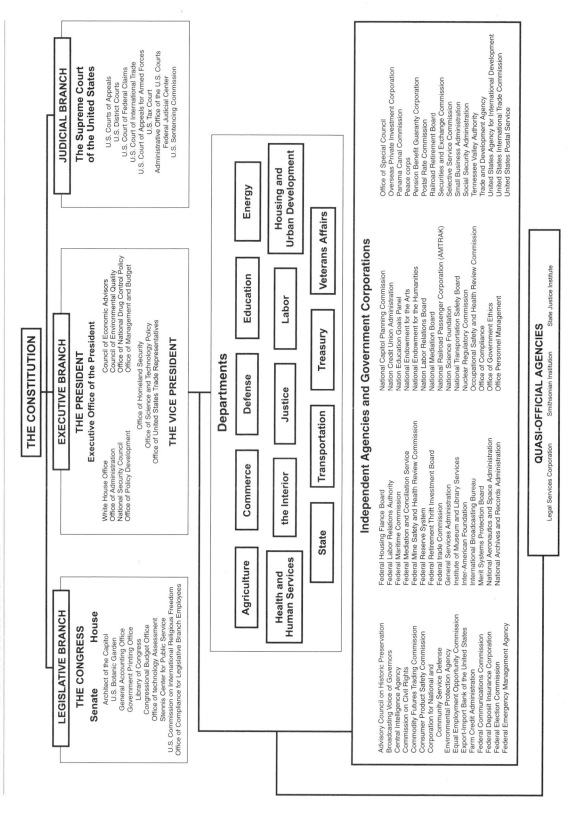

law assigned to them by their respective enabling acts; in their quasi-legislative role, they promulgate rules and regulations that have the force and effect of law; and in their quasi-judicial status, they conduct hearings and render and order the enforcement of decisions.

Under the theory of exhaustion of administrative remedies, a person must seek an administrative remedy to a problem, if a remedy is available, before seeking relief through a court system. The Administrative Procedures Act (APA), originally adopted in 1946, controls the majority of the administrative processes through the establishment of procedures which must be followed by an agency in its rulemaking and quasi-judicial functions. It is these procedures which generally control whether or not an individual is deemed to have exhausted administrative remedies. Many states have adopted similar administrative procedures acts which mirror the federal act and function at the state level in the same manner.

1.03   CLASSIFICATIONS OF LAW

It is not a simple task to break down our large accumulated body of laws into simple classifications to study. In general, we speak of our laws in terms of whether they are substantive or procedural, public or private, civil or criminal. As shown in Exhibit 1-5, a law often belongs to more than one classification.

1.031   Substantive and Procedural Law

Substantive law includes laws that regulate, define, and establish legal rights and obligations. Examples of the areas of substantive law are contracts, torts, criminal law, corporations, limited liability companies, real property, administrative, trusts and wills, and constitutional law.

Procedural law establishes the methods of enforcing the substantive laws. Examples of the areas of procedural law are federal and state rules of evidence, rules of civil procedure, and rules of criminal procedure.

Basically, the difference between substantive and procedural law is that the former describes our rights and obligations and the latter describes how we apply and enforce the substantive rights.

1.032   Public and Private Law

Public law is best described as the relationship between persons and their government. For example, constitutional law, administrative law, and criminal law all describe the relationship between the government and the people. Constitutional law provides the right to vote, a voice in the government; administrative law describes what entitlement might be available through an agency, such as Social Security benefits; and criminal law defines crime against society, even though the crime may be committed against an individual person.

Private law deals with relationships between people. A breach of contract, a tort, wills and trusts, and corporate law are all examples of private law since they affect person-to-person relationships.

EXHIBIT 1-5 Classifications of Law

CIVIL LAW				CRIMINAL LAW	
Public Law		Private Law		Public Law	
Substantive	Procedural	Substantive	Procedural	Substantive	Procedural

1.033   Civil and Criminal Law

Civil law embodies the whole area of law that exists between persons or between citizens and their government. Civil law can be considered either public or private. A suit by the government against a citizen is public even though it may involve a civil wrong.

In contrast, criminal law involves a wrong against the public as a whole. A person convicted of a crime has violated society's standard of conduct. Although a crime may involve a civil wrong, such as assault and battery, criminal law is considered public law.

1.04   REMEDIES

Oran's Dictionary of the Law defines remedy as "The means by which a right is enforced or satisfaction is gained for a harm done." In civil litigation, courts and/or juries determine the type of relief that a prevailing party shall receive. The type of relief awarded is dependant upon what the party requested and what is permissible under the applicable laws.

1.041   Law and Equity

Historically, remedies were divided into legal and equitable. Courts were also divided in this way, so that only a court of law could award a legal remedy and only an equity court could award an equitable remedy. Therefore, if a party desired a legal remedy such as land, money, or something of value, only a court of law could provide this type of remedy. If a party wanted an equitable remedy, such as an order for a person to perform an obligation under a contract, the party had to seek this remedy from a court of equity. As mentioned earlier in this chapter, the common law principle of *stare decisis* controls in courts of law, while courts of equity apply what are known as "equitable maxims." Some examples of equitable maxims are: "He who seeks equity must do equity;" "Equity must follow the law;" and "He who comes into equity must come with clean hands."

Today our courts are merged, and these distinctions are not as dramatic. Each state has at least one court of general jurisdiction that can issue a legal or equitable remedy. The adage "no remedy, no right" still applies. For example, in the area of contract law, if damages are inadequate, *rescission* (an equitable remedy modifying or canceling the parties' obligations) may be sought.

1.05   ALTERNATIVE DISPUTE RESOLUTION

No examination of the history of the American legal system would be complete without a glimpse into the future. In what direction is the legal system evolving? Discussions earlier in this chapter focused on the various sources of American law and its history, theory, and philosophy. The word "alternative" implies something new and different, apart from the mainstream. To the contrary, alternative dispute resolution (ADR) is far from new. Some historians view adjudication or litigation as the alternative method. The high rate of negotiated settlements prior to trial seems to support this theory.

1.051   Historical Perspective

Some form of negotiation and mediation has been employed for centuries. It is as ancient as human civilization itself and is not limited to Western tradition. In early China and Japan, religion and philosophy placed a strong emphasis on consensus, persuasion, and harmony. In Anglo-Saxon England, a wide array of dispute resolution processes were employed, predating English common law. Some of the dispute resolution methods were remarkably similar to our modern day arbitration, mediation, conciliation, and negotiation.

Valerie A. Sanchez, noted author and ADR expert, indicates that these processes were available to litigants on a "dispute processing continuum." Sanchez states that in Anglo-Saxon England, judges and arbitrators "often encouraged parties to reach settlement agreements... *after* the decision makers had reached a winner-take-all judgment on the merits of the claim *and* announced it to the parties, *but before* those judgments were procedurally 'finalized' in keeping with Anglo-Saxon legal procedure." Thus, the decisionmakers became third-party facilitators—commonly known today as mediators.

The major difference between adjudication and ADR is reflected in the Anglo-Saxon methods which gave disputants access to other options, rather than accepting the judgment of the third-party decisionmakers. Negotiation was adjunct to the adjudication process. Then, as now, ADR permits parties to forge their own resolutions. The control of the outcome of the process is shifted to the parties themselves. Along with control came power—the key to ADR.

1.052   The Multidoor Courthouse Experiment

Though widely credited with coining this metaphor, "multidoored courthouse," Frank E. A. Sander, Harvard professor and noted authority on ADR did not actually call for a "multidoored courthouse" but a "Dispute Resolution Center." In a paper delivered at the National Conference on the Causes of Popular Dissatisfaction with the Administration of Justice (1976), known as the "Pound Conference," Professor Sander envisioned a flexible system where a litigant could be channeled through a diverse array of processes—mediation, arbitration, fact-finding, and/or court processes.

As the practice of ADR has evolved, so have the various processes available to disputants. Arbitration (both binding and nonbinding) and mediation (in some jurisdictions known as case evaluation) are the most prevalent types of ADR used today. Also available in some jurisdictions are the minitrial, summary jury trial, and moderated settlement conference. A brief description of these processes is included.

1.053   Arbitration

Oran's Dictionary of the Law defines arbitration as "A method of dispute resolution involving one or more neutral third parties who are usually agreed to by the disputing parties and whose decision is binding." Arbitration may be binding or nonbinding depending on prior agreement of the parties. The arbitration hearing is similar to a trial proceeding but is less formal and does not follow strict rules of evidence. Arbitration is often employed in disputes involving labor relations, commercial contracts, and intellectual property matters. Parties may enter into arbitration by informal agreement, contractual agreement, or by order of a court. Statutory authority for the Federal Arbitration Act is found at 9 U.S.C. Section 1, et seq., and the Uniform Arbitration Act (UAA) is found at 7 U.L.A. Business & Financial Laws. A majority of states have adopted some form of the UAA. The UAA serves to validate arbitration agreements by allowing for the filing of motions to enforce, confirm, modify, or vacate arbitration agreements and awards.

The American Arbitration Association, a private, nonprofit organization, serves to assist parties by promulgating rules and regulations, providing lists of qualified arbitrators, and assisting with logistical matters. Qualification requirements for arbitrators vary by region. Some jurisdictions require a law degree; others do not. The primary requirement for an arbitrator is that the arbitrator be impartial.

Disputes in arbitration are best decided by skilled arbitrators who are knowledgeable in that particular field. Arbitrators have virtually total control over the proceedings, including subpoena power. One of the major advantages of arbitration, like most forms of ADR, is cost. One of the major disadvantages of arbitration is that it places the decision-making capability in the hands of a third party.

1.054 Mediation

Mediation is a process in which an impartial third party assists the parties in a direct negotiation of their dispute. Parties voluntarily work out their own agreement in an informal, private setting. Mediation may be employed outside the court system or as a result of a court order. Many jurisdictions are enacting court-ordered mediation in certain substantive areas, most notably domestic law. Other cases that lend themselves especially well to mediation are those where the parties have an ongoing relationship, such as business partners, neighbors, and students.

The mediator assists the parties in focusing on their interests, not their positions. Positional bargaining is dangerous because parties have the tendency to become entrenched. The mediator must guide the parties to identify, analyze, and separate the issues and then to rephrase the issues within the context of resolution. To accomplish these goals, the mediator strives to help parties develop their BATNA (best alternative to a negotiated agreement).[1] Mediators help parties to explore options that will satisfy some of the goals of each party, creating an end result that is usually a win-win situation for all, not the typical winner-take-all result of the court system.

What makes a good mediator? Credential requirements vary by jurisdiction, particularly for court-ordered mediation. First, as with arbitration, the mediator must be impartial. He or she must not only be a good listener, but also must be able to get the parties to listen to each other. The mediator must show all the parties involved that they should seek to understand the position of the other party before they themselves can be understood. In addition, a mediator must be able to maintain confidentiality and be unbiased, open, courteous, tolerant, reliable, attentive, observant, and encouraging.

The procedures involved in a mediation conference consist of educating the parties to the process (including attorneys who may be unfamiliar with mediation), negotiating dates and fee schedules (mediator fees are split among the parties), arranging for the facility where the mediation will occur, and arranging for the execution of any agreements to mediate.

As the plenary session of the mediation conference begins, the mediator makes opening remarks which acclimate those present to the process and the expected roles of all participants. These remarks establish the tone of the conference and stimulate interest in the process. The mediator must lay out ground rules so all know what steps the mediator will follow as he or she controls the process. Next the parties, and/or their attorneys, will be asked to make opening statements. Thereafter, the mediator summarizes the key points of each presentation, separating personalities from the problem. This summary is crucial, since it lets the parties know they have been heard, sorts out the issues, and reframes the problem as a search to satisfy interests.

The mediator may caucus with each party and their respective attorneys separately, in a private, confidential meeting. The caucus permits parties to share concerns, hidden agendas, and perceptions with the mediator in a confidential forum. The mediator also may employ a technique called settle-try analysis, asking questions designed to get parties thinking about probable results of delegating the problem-solving to a judge or strangers on a jury. Brainstorming and other option-generating techniques may also be employed, both in caucus and in plenary session.

When and if agreements are reached, the mediator continues to manage the process by having counsel prepare a settlement memorandum to be executed by all parties. The mediator must bring closure to the conflict by memorializing the agreement and, if necessary, reporting the results to the court.

1.055 Other ADR Forms: Minitrial, Summary Jury Trial, and Moderated Settlement Conference

A minitrial (MT) or summary jury trial (SJT) usually takes place after parties have completed substantial discovery. The SJT typically takes place on the eve of a trial. Paralegals are often as involved in

MT and SJT preparation as they would be for a traditional court trial. The juries of the MT and SJT differ. SJTs take place before juries of impartial strangers, and MTs take place before corporate representatives of the parties. Usually the MT is voluntary, generated by motions of the parties. The court may order a SJT if the matter has already proceeded to pretrial conference. The SJT often is the final alternative before an actual trial. Judge Thomas D. Lambros, of the U.S. District for the Northern District of Ohio, is generally credited for creating the SJT form of ADR in 1980.[2]

The moderated settlement conference (MSC) is a hybrid form of ADR, combining the minitrial, summary jury trial, and mediation. In MSC, a panel of three attorneys issues a nonbinding opinion.

1.056   ADR Fears and Misconceptions

Parties to lawsuits are often concerned that if they initially use the arbitration method and it fails, any information that is discussed during arbitration can be used against them at trial. Fortunately, Federal Rule of Evidence Rule 408 protects the parties, since any evidence of conduct or statements made in compromise negotiations are not admissible in court (unless the evidence is otherwise discoverable or provided for another purpose). Therefore, it usually is in the best interest of parties to try ADR for the following reasons: parties are not prejudiced by any efforts to settle, the process often opens lines of communication, and the process can typically shorten the time necessary to resolve a dispute, even if the matter is not fully settled.

1.057   Role of the Paralegal

What is the role of the paralegal in ADR? Roles may vary depending on jurisdiction and practice. Some jurisdictions permit nonlawyers to serve as arbitrators, mediators, and/or other third-party facilitators, particularly in the area of construction and business disputes. Experts in these fields, such as architects, real estate professionals, medical and dental technologists, accountants, engineers, and so forth, are found serving as such facilitators. In some jurisdictions, paralegals are serving as mediators and service providers; in others, paralegals act as ADR Coordinators assisting service providers. The key for the paralegal interested in ADR, as with any other legal specialty, is knowledge and continuing education. Potential for using ADR in informal settings, such as community groups, abounds and is not limited to licensed attorneys.

There are many questions about who should train and regulate ADR providers. Some state bar associations are drafting rules and guidelines that exclude nonlawyers from court-approved rosters of mediators and ADR service providers. Education of the general public, legal practitioners, and legislators is an ongoing requirement if ADR is to expand into the mainstream of the legal profession and society. One thing is clear—the "dispute resolution center" idea envisioned by Professor Sander has become a reality.

PRACTICE TIP

For an excellent review of the ADR options, see the NALA Campus Course on Alternative Dispute Resolution, written by attorney and law school professor Martin A. Frey. This course was published in 2004 and updated frequently. It is a condensed version of a text written by Martin A. Frey entitled Alternative Methods of Dispute Resolution and published by Delmar Learning, 2003. Details may be found on the NALA website, www.nala.org and the NALA Campus website, www.nalacampus.com.

BIBLIOGRAPHY

Dillon, Fonda M., *From Litigation to ADR,* in *Facts & Findings, The Journal for Legal Assistants.* Vol. XXIII, Issue 2, August, 1996.

Duvall, Suzanne Mann and Scheske, Jack J., *No Mediator is an Island. Relationship Based Management of Legal Assistants and Other Staff in Mediation and Alternative Dispute Resolution Practices. Dispute Resolution Across the Continents,* 22nd Annual International Conference [Society of Professionals in Dispute Resolution], Dallas, TX, October 27–29, 1994.

Federal Civil Judicial Procedure and Rules, as amended to May 19, 2006. St. Paul, MN: Thompson West, 2006.

Fisher, Roger and Ury, William, *Getting to Yes; Negotiating Agreement Without Giving In,* edited by Bruce Patton, 2nd ed. New York: Penguin Books USA, 1991.

Goodheart, Harry G., III and Harness, Cotton C., III, *Circuit Court Civil Mediator Training Program.* Hilton Head Island, SC, December 1–5, 1994.

Koerselman, Virginia, American Legal System, 2000, A NALA Campus Course, On-line Self Study Program for Paralegals. www.NALACampus.com.

Koerselman, Virginia, *CLA Review Manual,* 2nd ed. West Publishing, 1998.

Lambros, Thomas D., *The Summary Jury Trial and Other Alternative Methods of Dispute Resolution,* in *A Report to the Judicial Conference of the United States Committee on the Operation of the Jury System.* 103 F.R.D. 461, 463 (1984).

Oran's Dictionary of the Law, 4th ed. Albany, NY: Delmar Cengage Learning, 2008.

Sanchez, Valerie A., *Towards a History of ADR: The Dispute Processing Continuum in Anglo-Saxon England and Today,* 11 Ohio St. J. on Disp. Resol. 1 (1996).

Sander, Frank E. A., *Varieties of Dispute Processing,* 70 F.R.D. 111, 131 (1976).

Scaletta, Phillip J., Jr. and Cameron, George D., III, *Foundations of Business Law.* Business Publications, Inc., 1986.

Schantz, William T. and Jackson, Janice E., *The American Legal Environment,* 2nd ed. West Publishing Company, (1984).

The United States Government Manual, 2005–2006 ed. Government Printing Office.

ENDNOTES

1. Roger Fisher and William Ury, *Getting to Yes; Negotiating Agreement Without Giving In*, Bruce Patton, Editor, 2nd ed. New York: Penguin Books USA, 1991.

2. Judge Thomas D. Lambros, *The Summary Jury Trial and Other Alternative Methods of Dispute Resolution*, in *A Report to the Judicial Conference of the United States Committee on the Operating of the Jury System*, 103 F.R.D. 461, 463 (Jan. 1984).

3. Judy Quan, *Legal Assistant's Guide to Alternative Dispute Resolution*, Clark Boardman Callaghan/Estrin Paralegal Practice Series. Deerfield, IL, Clark Boardman Callaghan, 1994, 1995.

2

Legal Research

2.00 INTRODUCTION

This chapter is an introduction and is not intended to be a complete course in legal research. It will provide the inexperienced paralegal with a working background of the mechanics of research but will not satisfy the highly sophisticated needs of an attorney or a fully trained and experienced paralegal. Most inexperienced paralegals first may receive very limited and specific research assignments. The parameters of the research will be clearly defined, some research sources suggested, cases cited, and past research efforts of others often will be made available for guidance in form, style, and preferred format. These tools will help in determining starting points or checkpoints during the research and reporting tasks. Research assignments will increase in difficulty and complexity as the paralegal demonstrates skill and craftsmanship and gains the attorney's trust and confidence.

Paralegals should not be discouraged if first efforts do not result in immediate success. In all likelihood, the initial assignment will take more time than anticipated, with the odds against achieving perfect results. However, those efforts will not be wasted, since they contribute to a practical foundation in research, providing opportunities to try different methods and to identify those most effective. As familiarity with research material and resources increases, the time required to find applicable law and analyze case decisions will decrease. As individual research techniques become more refined, even less time will be needed to research a given fact situation. Experience, practice, and constructive criticism by others will help the paralegal develop expertise in stating facts and analyses in professional, concise legal writing.

The law library seems overwhelming and complex, but as the paralegal gains familiarity and confidence, it will become a friend. While most lawyers maintain a library sufficiently complete to meet the needs of their practice, other libraries are highly specialized and sophisticated with multiple copies of source material and several varieties of sources on the same topics. Looking at the different topic titles and sets of books to determine exactly what sources of information are available in the library, understanding how the library is arranged, and locating the specialized sections is time well spent. It will aid research planning and improve confidence. Where other law libraries are available to the public (such as law school, county, district, state, or federal libraries), write or visit them, meet the librarians, and take note of the procedures that allow access to use or borrowing of material. Competence in using the library is the key to success in legal research. Use of library resources via the Internet can exponentially increase your information sources with text libraries as well as through card catalogue searches. Library resources at universities as well as government agencies are regularly updated, maintained, and available for public access on a limited online basis as well. Additionally, many law schools have the full text of their law review articles online.

Compact Disk Read Only Memory (CD-ROM) technology reduces the size of many library sources to a compact disk with keyword searching ability. Although the updates are not as frequent as weekly supplements and certainly not as frequent as the hourly updates of available online subscription services such as Westlaw® or LexisNexis®, CD-ROM technology provides even the smallest firm with the ability to store rooms of books in a CD carrying case. Research from online Websites also may be downloaded and burned onto a CD with editing capability and the necessary hardware (CD-R/W drive), thus developing a local library resource for a given topic. [*See* Section 2.0812.]

If the paralegal is diligent, confidence will be acquired in the ability to research. Legal research is a very rewarding experience and an exciting challenge; it requires full understanding of the research objective accomplished only when the employing attorney identifies each of the legal principles and issues underlying each assignment.

2.01   PRINCIPLES OF LEGAL RESEARCH

Legal research is an integral part of the practice of law, and its impact on a case can be critical. It is essential that all research be accurate and includes the most current data available. The authority controlling the status of the law can change very quickly as decisions come down from higher courts; therefore, the importance of fully updated research cannot be overemphasized.

A working rapport must be established between the attorney and the paralegal. Mutual respect and trust are essential. The attorney must thoroughly discuss the issue or subject of the research with the paralegal, including the legal principles, legal issues involved, scope of the research, fact situation, and time deadline. These must be completely understood by the paralegal before proceeding. Always remember that the research must be thorough and precise with up-to-the-minute accuracy, or it will have to be redone completely by the attorney. Leave no stone unturned, no case or statute (and the updated pocket parts) unread, and no conflict unresolved without being clearly pointed out. If confusion sets in, seek help.

2.011   Case Law and Statutory Law

The paralegal must become comfortable with the dual origins of law and legal principles that may influence the client's case. There is case law and statutory law to consider in most situations. The courts, both federal and state, must apply statutory law where applicable, even in the face of contradictory case law. The only exception to this hierarchy is when a court determines that the statute in question is inconsistent with the state's constitution or the U.S. Constitution. When applying case law, the courts are obligated to follow the appropriate precedents established by prior decisions unless the present circumstances can be distinguished in some way. This method of adhering to the same legal principles in similar cases is the doctrine of *stare decisis* ("let the decision stand"). The product of this doctrine is the ability of the public to examine existing legal standards and predict with some degree of accuracy the likely outcome in a current situation. With respect to goals in legal research, this translates to the following equation: (1) search for applicable statutory law and then (2) search for case law (especially if there is some basis upon which the statutory law is likely to be declared unconstitutional).

2.0111 Case Law.
Case law is based in part on legal principles developed from the written opinions by judges in past cases. Case law is part of the tradition of common law dating as far back as medieval England. The exception to this is case law developed in the state of Louisiana, which has its legal origins in France, resulting in case law based upon French legal principles of civil law. While the legal terminology may be different, there are many striking similarities in English and French legal principles.

In essence, the written opinions of judges in past cases have established legal principles which are to be followed in future similar cases. These principles, or rules of law, are known as precedents. Most judicial opinions that are reported (published) are those of appellate courts, which establish standards for entire jurisdictions, such as the federal court system or the courts of a particular state. As a result, these are the precedents that can be cited as authority in subsequent cases.

When researching case law, keep in mind that the law of a particular jurisdiction is usually controlling. The law of other jurisdictions may be used to influence and persuade the court, but the court has no obligation to follow it. For example, when performing research for a case that is pending in a particular state, the statutory law and appellate decisions of that state are controlling. However, the law of other states or federal courts may be cited as persuasive authority.

It is important to understand that appeals may be made on nearly any area of the law involved with the trial, such as the basic legal questions involved; the procedural rules, including but not limited to jurisdiction and discovery procedures; introduction of witnesses or evidence; instructions to the jury on the law to apply; and standards. Only the issues tried, appealed, and ruled upon at the appellate level may be properly cited as authority from the appellate decision. All the rest is *dictum:* interesting in showing how the appellate court reached its decision but not binding. *Dicta* may be helpful in determining how the court might rule on a given matter in the future, even persuasive in arguing that another court should so rule, but it is not law.

2.0112 Statutory Law.
Statutory law is different from case law in that statutes are the stated intention of a legislative body to create a standard of permitted or proscribed conduct. The U.S. Constitution, Bill of Rights, and subsequent amendments to the Constitution are controlling as the primary written expression of the rights of individuals, and state and federal laws must be consistent with them and encourage the observance of similar desirable objectives. Each state also has its own constitution

upon which its statutes are based, and these must be consistent with the U.S. Constitution as well. Counties, as subordinate governmental units of the state, are granted certain powers by the state to legislate rules of conduct within the county by ordinances and codes. Cities and towns are organized under the permission of the state and are granted certain powers to create rules necessary for the execution of their public responsibilities. Each of these entities follows the same basic process of creating a law, whether titled as such or called a "rule," "regulation," "ordinance," or "code."

2.0113 Codes.   Codes are collections of statutory or regulatory law by jurisdiction and sometimes by subjects of law within a jurisdiction. A similar term used by some states is *revised statutes*. These collections are updated frequently to include new statutory law and to reflect amendment or repeal of existing statutory law. These codes are organized to facilitate the research process. Typically, all of the laws on a particular area of legislation, such as motor vehicles, are placed under a single heading. This is sometimes known as a title or chapter. The titles are arranged in alphabetical order and then assigned consecutive numbers as well. For example, "agriculture" would be one of the first numbered titles since it begins with "A." The main headings are also arranged in alphabetical order. Within each heading, all of the laws on the particular subject are individually numbered. Thus, new laws can be added to the subject simply by adding new numbers. In addition, each code is accompanied by an extensive subject index that assists the reader in locating the needed information. For example, if one wanted to locate the law that indicated a driver's duty when road conditions are dangerous, one would look in the subject index for such topics as motor vehicles, automobiles, and traffic. Below each main topic are more specific references to the individual laws on the subject. When the correct heading and subheading are located in the index, a two-part number will be found. This generally corresponds to the number assigned to the main heading and the number assigned to the particular law.

Included with the actual text of the statute in the code may be a reference to the initial publication of the statute in the session laws. This enables the reader to locate historical information about the passage of the statute. Many codes are also *annotated*, which simply means that a brief description and reference to any judicial opinions that have interpreted the statute follow the text of the statute. These can be helpful in determining how the statute has been applied in specific past situations and consequently how it is likely to be applied in a present situation.

2.0114 Legislative Intent.   Each statute exists for the purpose intended by the entity that passed it. Where the language of a particular statute cannot be clearly understood or, as is more often the case, opponents claim different meanings for the same words, the researcher may have to look back into the recorded minutes of hearings, committee discussions, and legislative rhetoric to define the original purpose. Many times this is an onerous task, which involves tracking the statute back to its origins as a bill, through committee and public hearings, even to the personal files of the original author of the proposed legislation. In some cases, a federal statute is so important that the U.S. Government Printing Office will publish all the written materials pertaining to it in one or more volumes. The historical data, debates, and comments can be a great aid to the researcher. The legislative intent, more often described as "legislative history" on the federal level, also may be published in loose-leaf services available to its subscribers or on the Internet (e.g., the U.S. Environmental Protection Agency makes such information concerning environmental legislation available to the public over the Internet). Some states provide staff members to handle requests for legislative history, or intent. Administrative agencies also have archives of historical information concerning rules they establish from the date of their proposal until publication. It may be necessary when contending with administrative agency rules and regulations to research first the rule and then the agency's own enabling legislation to ensure the agency is not exceeding its own authority as shown by the legislative intent in the statutory law that created the agency.

2.02 FIVE STEPS OF RESEARCH

While efficiency and productivity in legal research can only be the product of extended practice, some basic steps can help the researcher locate valid authority more quickly and easily. After years of performing legal research, many practitioners still follow these basic steps as a normal course of action. The five basic steps are:

1. Analyzing the facts and identifying the problem and subject of research
2. Recognizing the issues or points of law involved
3. Finding the law and expanding the research to access all necessary information, including adverse authority
4. Updating the search
5. Reporting the research

2.021   Step One: Analyzing the Facts

Know the factual situation completely and know the client's objective. There may be occasions when the paralegal will be able to discover an alternative way of obtaining the client's purpose when direct methods, as the client may have proposed, cannot be used. For example, if a man wants an advertising sign erected on his building and city ordinances prohibit certain kinds of signs, there may be an alternative way to accomplish the desired advertising to his satisfaction.

Legal research will be easier if the facts and desired end result are clearly understood. Analyzing the facts and identifying the problem and/or subject are musts. Every legal problem arises from a factual situation; the facts determine whether there is a legitimate cause of action or a valid defense. The facts are the basis of the document to be prepared, such as a will, bill of sale, lease agreement, or complaint.

a. The first essential element in the factual analysis is to identify the parties involved. Determine whether they have any special standing under the law, such as a tenant, landowner, or particular class of people (such as all the purchasers of Product X) or whether they are immune from suit.

b. Next, determine the subject matter, such as real or personal property, bodily injury and damages, issues of governmental regulation, or contract execution.

c. Then determine the basis of the action or issue, such as negligence, breach of contract, or strict liability.

d. Now determine what types of relief are available, such as temporary restraining order, specific performance of the contract, or compensatory money damages.

e. Determine the defenses to the claim. Consider the facts and evaluate whether the claim has merit and whether any extenuating circumstances, facts, or law might legally exonerate the opponent, such as self-defense, comparative or contributory negligence of the plaintiff, or impossibility of performance of the contract.

2.022   Step Two: Identifying the Law

When defining the legal problems and areas, try to determine:

a. What court or agency has primary jurisdiction
b. If there are statutes, codes, or administrative agency rules or regulations involved
c. Whether it is a substantive or procedural law problem

2.023   Step Three: Finding the Law

Finding the law and expanding the search to include all necessary information is the next step and the point at which the true research begins. Again, there are many approaches open to the paralegal. One of the most useful actions at this point is identifying all related terms, synonyms (same or similar meaning), and antonyms (opposite meaning) for the subject of research. Legal research is aided tremendously by the existence of subject indexes for most authorities. However, one must know what terminology the author used when preparing the index. By first identifying a number of possibilities, the speed of research can be increased while at the same time decreasing the level of frustration at not being able to locate the proper authority.

If the research problem is in an area of law unfamiliar to the paralegal, the first step would usually be to read some secondary authority that contains a general commentary and explanation of the subject. (*See* Section 2.04, Sources of the Law in Research.) This allows the paralegal to become familiar with the general nature and past history of and approaches to the problem and to decide which path the research must follow. The secondary authority generally cites cases and sometimes statutes. These can often provide a starting point for the research. Identifying the leading case on an issue provides a key to many other cases that follow, distinguish, or depart from the leading case holding. At the very least, these sources contain basic principles and relevant terminology and can provide a general familiarity with the subject matter. Because the majority of legal research resources can be accessed through various types of subject indexes, this basic knowledge can greatly assist the researcher when searching for commentary, case law, or statutory law.

Following examination of secondary sources, it is often necessary to go to the codes and reported judicial opinions of the jurisdiction whose law is being applied in the case under research. While more attention is given to this in the subsequent discussion, it is briefly noted here that codes are accompanied by extensive subject indexes that allow easy access to the particular statute sought. Similarly, all published judicial decisions are briefly described and arranged by subject in what is known as a *digest*. A digest also has a subject index (called a "descriptive word index") that allows the researcher to locate the specific subject area of research. A key element in both statutory and case law research is knowledge of the relevant terminology. What one might consider the appropriate subject heading for a topic might vary significantly from the actual heading used in the legal resources. Familiarity with the subject, as well as such aids as a legal thesaurus, can take much of the frustration out of this aspect of legal research.

2.024   Step Four: Updating the Search

Updating the search accomplishes two very important objectives. First, it confirms that the legal authority is still accepted as valid by the legislature and the judiciary. Second, it allows the researcher to learn of any subsequent statutes or judicial opinions on the subject that may not yet have been incorporated into the code or published. The most commonly accepted method of updating is through a process referred to as "Shepardizing." This describes the use of *Shepard's Citations* to locate all references to or approval, amendment, or repeal of published statutory or case law. (*See* Section 2.06, Use of *Shepard's Citations* or "Shepardizing.") In addition to examining the subsequent treatment of the case or statute in *Shepard's Citations*, one should also read the actual text of the case or statute to determine if there are any distinguishing characteristics that may affect its applicability to the case at hand. With respect to statutes, it is important to note the date upon which the statute became effective to ensure that it was in effect on the relevant dates in the case being researched.

The completeness of the updating is of paramount importance since the research must reflect the law as it is currently interpreted. The review of advance sheets, pocket parts, and supplements of codes or statutes is essential. The paralegal who cites a case as authority for a positive position and later is proved to be in error because a more recent decision reversed the cited authority may find overnight that the attorney's confidence has been lost, along with any further assignments in this interesting and highly important work area.

 Caveat: Most cases involve the law as it was on the date of the occurrence; for example, changes in the vehicle code or other law are seldom retroactive. Therefore, be certain to research the applicable law individually from the current date back to the origin of the cause of action. There can be some shocking exceptions. For example, in *Li v. Yellow Cab Co.*, 13 Cal.3d 804, 119 Cal. Rptr. 858, 532 P.2d 1226 (1975), a case establishing in California the system of comparative negligence to assign responsibility and liability for damage in direct proportion to the degree of negligence of each of the parties, the California Supreme Court concluded that the rule of contributory negligence (which had prevailed for years in California law) was overturned and that a rule of limited retroactivity should prevail. The court held that in view of the many pending cases involving matters similar in issue to that in *Li* at the trial and appellate levels, *Li* would apply to all cases in which the trial had not begun before the date the decision became final but would not apply to any case in which trial had begun before that date. It also provided that if any judgment were reversed on appeal for other reasons, the opinion would be applicable to any retrial. Another example is *California Code of Civil Procedure* Section 1048, which was completely reworded in 1971 to be operative July 1, 1972. The new act applied to actions commenced on or after July 1, 1972, but not to actions pending on July 1, 1972, and provided that any action to which the act did not apply would be governed by the law as it would exist had the act not been enacted.

 Admittedly, these are exceptions, but this type of limited retroactivity or limited applicability of operative dates must be considered in any research.

2.025 Step Five: Reporting the Research and Commenting on the Opposing Party's Position

Everything done must be reported concisely to the attorney, including the positive research and, if the work effort goal is to rebut the position of another, the research and review of every case cited in support of the opposing party's position. Do not accept at face value the opposing party's cited positions or authorities as either factually or legally correct statements of the positions taken by the courts in the cited cases. Citing cases out of context, from headnotes, or only from synopsis is a common, though dangerous, activity. Similarly, citing dictum from a case as though it were a tried and considered issue is a technique the paralegal can avoid only by reading the case in its entirety.

 Reviewing the opposing party's cited cases provides several benefits, one being an appreciation of the opposing party's legal reasoning and/or legal foundation. Many times the paralegal may find the opposing party cited a case that does not help the opposing party's position nearly so persuasively as it does the client's; also, other cases favorable to the client's position may be found by Shepardizing the cases developed in the opposing party's citations. These finds occur when the paralegal reads the full case text, not just the headnotes, to be certain the context of the citation is applicable, the interpretation is correctly reported, and it is current law and not a case that has been overturned by subsequent decisions. If the cases cited in the initial document are not valid authority or have been incorrectly interpreted, the report of research must point out these facts as well as the reasoning and cases supporting the paralegal's own conclusions.

 While a report on all the research is essential, carefully think about and consider each bit of information accumulated and decide whether to include or exclude it. This is critical to the clarity of the end result and conclusion. Research requires an intelligent and active mind and the ability to analyze information and to concentrate all efforts single-mindedly and fixedly on the goal. Practice in legal writing requires familiarity with legal writing styles. Go to the library and read some decisions at random. Learn to analyze the case content. The first few cases may not make any sense, but familiarity with the legal writing style and careful rereading will create skill in analysis, perception, and measuring the written cases against a given issue. It also will increase the paralegal's ability to detect relevance or analogy between the reported cases and the factual situation in the instant problem.

The office file of past legal research reports can offer pointers on style and form for the paralegal to follow. Briefs filed in appellate proceedings can clearly show the organized manner of expression that may be helpful or desired by the office (*see* Section 2.031, Retention of Legal Research). Adapting to the style preferred in the office simplifies the lawyer's review of the finished effort, since the form of the report is familiar and he or she can concentrate on the substance of the report or memorandum.

Finally, while most research will entail only a review of authority and will not be incorporated in any formal pleading, the purpose is to provide the lawyer with case law, statutory law, and statements sufficient to enable him or her to measure the law against the facts, thereby reaching a final determination and stating a positive position. Even drafting pleadings requires research, as do law and motion matters, particularly the points and authorities for such documents. In any event, the written product should be clear and to the point, and the writing quality should be above reproach. An evaluation of the factors should be presented in an appropriate, logical, and effective manner, and the paralegal must be confident of the position recommended. Strong decisions in opposition to the proposed point of view must be brought to the attention of the attorney, as well as any distinctions between those cases and the instant problem. If, at any time during the research procedures, the paralegal becomes unsure of a point, it must be discussed fully and freely with the attorney to resolve the doubt, redirect the effort, or get back on the right track. If the attorney will not help, the paralegal is working in the wrong office.

2.03 BASIC RESEARCH PROCEDURES AND PRACTICES

Certain basic beneficial procedures should be instituted at the start of a career in research to avoid duplication of effort; also, they will be invaluable later as starting points.

2.031   Retention of Legal Research

This sounds self-explanatory, but it is not necessarily a simple matter. Some offices maintain complete legal memoranda files, whether in hard copy or in their computer network, and all research in the office is categorized, indexed, and filed in a control file. If the office has such a research file system, the paralegal must become familiar with both the file and the indexing system. Clearly, it is important to take advantage of the past research contained within the file. In large firms, examining and/or updating past research is often one of the functions of the law librarian. Some firms with such files also have procedures to continuously update the material or selected categories of material, depending on the specialties of the office. If the employer does not maintain such a file, take the initiative and start one. In any event, the paralegal must adapt to or devise a suitable system and maintain his or her own research for use in the future, taking care to update the cites in any past memorandum or report before again citing that material as authority. Each update is posted to the research file as well. If the paralegal is working in a specialized field, such as malpractice, it is helpful to read the West advance sheets on that topic as they come into the office.

The paralegal can establish the protocol for the research file system through an attorney review process to maintain the integrity of the law stored. If a new associate prepares a draft brief, not yet reviewed, it should not be immediately downloaded or printed for storage into a research file system. The firm will need to support the law used and maintain whatever is placed in that file through updates and supervision. In a large firm, with a large number of practice areas, this can be a full-time job for a paralegal or librarian. A justification in maintenance time by the use of coded topics familiar to all firm members (such as the West Key System) can facilitate maintenance and also increase the use by attorneys and paralegals.

Through the use of Internet software and capabilities offered through some online services, West-law and LexisNexis, articles and news releases can be automatically downloaded to the paralegal's computer for review as they become available. This may be the first notice of a new decision to overrule or modify the existing standard relied upon in a firm's brief, released to the public by a news service that day. In addition, there are also electronic daily news summaries, often limited by practice area, that many firms and corporate law departments subscribe to which provide breaking news or case information. Nevertheless, some research is so current that it may not be available without a telephone call (e.g., a decision reached that day with no published case law at that time) and a copy request from the deciding court or agency. The paralegal appears efficient with this up-to-the-minute information for the attorneys.

2.032   Compilation of a Personal Case Book

As the paralegal researches problems and as new decisions are handed down, he or she should file or record the citations in a case book by topic. An alternative to the case book is to create and maintain an electronic document with the same general format. Also, when researching a problem which is common from both "for and against" sides, that is, filing a claim with a public entity, as opposed to relief from the requirement of filing a claim, or filing a late claim, note the case as applicable to both sides. This book, or electronic document as the case may be, normally is not a detailed description of the case, but rather it is a loose-leaf system with general categories, such as malpractice, fraud, or strict liability, which contains the cite or code sections along with the particular point of law to which it applies, along with a few lines setting forth the theory as shown in the following example.

PRODUCTS LIABILITY
** Lessor of Personal Property...
Doctrine of strict liability in tort applicable.
Fakhoury v Magner, 25 Cal. App. 3d 58, 101 Cal. Rptr. 473 (1972) lessor of furnished apartment liable
     for injuries when couch partially collapsed.
Price v.Shell Oil Co., 2 Cal. 3d 245, 85 Cal. Rptr. 178, 466 P.2d 722 (1970) lessor of truck and ladder to
     plaintiff's employer liable when ladder collapsed.

2.033   Devise a Workable System to Avoid Duplication in Research

When paralegals begin their initial efforts to research, many find themselves returning to the same case several times. This is wasted effort and should be avoided. This seems to happen most frequently in the updating process, where the paralegal is reading many cases and Shepardizing. (*See* Section 2.06, Use of *Shepard's Citations* or "Shepardizing.") Many methods can be utilized, such as keeping lists of citations or titles as cases are read. Find a method and use it faithfully.

2.034   Save Time and Steps

One essential tool for beginning research is a legal dictionary or combination dictionary/thesaurus (*see* Section 2.0511). Dictionaries provide meanings, origins, spellings, and pronunciations. A legal thesaurus can provide synonyms to aid the paralegal in locating information during research and in writing in a more concise and professional manner. "Words and Phrases" dictionaries are another useful tool for beginning a research project. These references provide case citations to the subtle meanings which have developed through case law where courts have defined and construed the particular meaning of certain words and phrases.

Up-to-date word processing software is available which includes legal terminology as part of the software package and which contains both a dictionary and a thesaurus. Legal dictionary and thesaurus materials as well as "words and phrases" publications are also available electronically on CD-ROM and through online services.

2.035   Be Familiar with the Hierarchy of the Courts and the Reporting Systems

Each of the fifty states has established its own court system and rules for those courts, including appellate procedures (*see* Chapter 1, Section 1.023, State Court Systems). A good place to start when researching the structure and procedures of a court system in another state is the *Martindale-Hubbell Law Digest*. These volumes contain summaries of statutory law from all states (as well as U.S. Territories) and are also available electronically through online services such as LexisNexis. For example, if you looked in the volume which contained a summary of California statutory law, you would be able to determine that California has four courts: small claims court, superior court (both of which comprise the trial-level courts), the courts of appeal, and the supreme court (the appellate-level courts). Each court has established procedural rules that must be followed. The appellate procedures provide for appeal to the next higher court, for example, from superior court to a court of appeal. The paralegal must be familiar with the state's court system, which decisions are published, the reporting systems of the courts' official reports, and the corresponding commercial (unofficial) reporters and the decisions they cover. The decisions of the trial-level courts are seldom published; the decisions of the appellate-level courts usually are. For instance, the official reports of the California Courts of Appeal are contained in the *California Appellate Reports* (in several series), while *California Reports* contains the official decisions of the California Supreme Court. The *Pacific Reporter* (part of the national reporter system, *see* Section 2.0543) contains the *unofficial* reports of the California Supreme Court, as well as reports of other Western states, but does not contain reports for the California Courts of Appeal. The separate West's *California Reporter* (still of the national reporter system) contains the *unofficial* reports of both appellate-level courts. Therefore, most California paralegals, in researching California law, rely on *California Reporter* rather than the *Pacific Reporter*.

In addition to the preceding more traditional sources, a search of the Internet will locate official Websites for states providing court decisions online to the public. For instance, Florida Supreme Court decisions are available to the public via the Internet as are decisions of the South Carolina Supreme Court. *Florida Administrative Weekly* publishes and maintains past issues and lists recent decisions, and the *Florida Law Weekly* is available on the Internet for a fee. Online resources are still evolving and do not constitute a comprehensive or complete resource, but neither does the library "down-the-hall" in most law offices. Supplement resources with other material and determine an effective and efficient method to utilize the strengths of both.

The federal court system has a hierarchy of trial and appellate courts (*see* Chapter 1, Section 1.021, State Court Systems) with separate and distinct reporter systems, official and unofficial, which are similar to those of the states discussed previously.

2.04   SOURCES OF THE LAW IN RESEARCH

Generally, the law is contained in two types of authority—primary and secondary. Law books and finding aids are categorized in the same manner—primary and secondary.

2.041   Primary Authority

Primary authority is that which is valid authority as to the exact status of the law on any given point, in any state or area, and at any given time. The most persuasive primary authority that can be cited is that of the official report of the highest court, state or federal, (above the trial court level) that has rendered a decision on the point of law being researched. This may be cited as the controlling law. Examples of this type of authority are the U.S. Supreme Court decisions or the supreme court decisions of the state in which the issue is located; then the Constitution (state or federal); codified laws; Statutes at Large or session laws; administrative rules, regulations, orders, and decisions; and court rules and court decisions in the state where the issue is located. Similar authority from other jurisdictions may be persuasive authority on matters not previously decided in the state, but it is not mandatory authority.

2.042   Secondary Authority

Secondary authority is any compilation of opinions and/or comments by various authors setting forth their interpretation of the law. This kind of authority is most helpful as an aid in research but does not have the force and effect of law. Examples of this type of authority are annotated case reports, annotated codes and statutes, "restatements" of various laws, encyclopedias, loose-leaf services, index books, dictionaries, digests, form books, treatises, and periodical literature.

Secondary authority is a basic tool. It provides insight into the disputed issue and, many times, quickly directs the researcher to the primary authority being sought. There are occasions when secondary authority can be cited and effectively used to sway or persuade the court to accept a given position as the correct one, but it should be clearly referenced to the attorney as a secondary authority—distinctly different from case law or statutory law or any administrative agency rule. In so-called test cases (a case where the particular legal issue has not been tried and appealed in the state before), where there is no substantive or case law, it may be the only authority available.

2.05   SEARCH METHODS—FINDING THE LAW

It is impossible to include in this chapter a detailed discussion of each and every search aid available to the serious researcher. This will review the types of materials available and give a brief discussion of the general categories. Entire books are devoted to this topic (see the Bibliography of this chapter).

Regardless of whether you are researching using printed books or electronic media, the same general search methods, techniques, and reasoning apply.

2.051   The Subject or Text Approach

The subject or text approach to the law requires the use of general information sources (secondary authority). In the absence of a specific case or a definite starting place, this is probably the logical starting point.

2.0511 Dictionaries.   There are various kinds of dictionaries, including single-volume and multivolume glossaries. The single-volume type is represented by *Oran's Dictionary of Law, Ballentine's Law Dictionary*, and, of course, *Merriam-Webster's Dictionary*. The definitions in the law dictionaries are usually derived from court opinions and are quoted verbatim with citations to the cases. The best known of the multivolume dictionaries is probably *Words and Phrases* by West Publishing Company. This set covers, as nearly as possible, every word and phrase defined by the federal and state courts in opinions rendered since 1658, and the words and phrases are listed in alphabetical order. A smaller version of

Words and Phrases is produced for some states, for example, *Florida Words and Phrases*. These sets are kept up-to-date with annual pocket parts and revisions. Other standard law dictionaries may be in the firm's library. Dictionaries are secondary authority and often are cited as persuasive authority. They are often good tools for finding references to primary authority. As previously noted, many of these resources, if not all, are available in electronic format via CD-ROM, Westlaw, Lexis, and the Internet.

2.0512 Textbooks, Treatises, and Law Reviews.

As the primary authorities became more voluminous, lawyers, students, and others began to follow the development of the law in certain fields. As attorneys became more knowledgeable, they began to write treatises and textbooks relating to certain areas of the law. The bibliography at the end of this chapter provides an idea of some of the texts and references available on legal research. Textbooks are available on nearly every area of the law, including discovery procedures, evidence, and punitive damages. Periodically, judges, attorneys, and law school professors jointly agree that the law in a particular area needs clarification, modernization, or adjustment to the demands of our changing, complex society. Study groups are formed, such as the American Law Institute, and produce definitive restatements of a law for the area under study, such as the *Restatement of the Law Second, Torts* or the *Restatement of the Law Second Contracts*. This type of authority is secondary and is not the law itself, but it is a strong and persuasive presentation of the way the law should be. Such studies have, in the past, become the law by a court agreeing and overturning the existing law or by being codified and the code being enacted by the various jurisdictions. The *Uniform Commercial Code* is the result of such a restatement and codification procedure. The restatements are widely respected as quotable authority, though secondary, because of the distinguished and highly respected authors who participate in their preparation and because of the sound logic and legal reasoning they represent. Such authority has value to the attorney particularly if directly on point in the instant case, whether in direct conflict with past case law or not.

Law schools publish law reviews, such as the *Cornell Law Review, Harvard Law Review*, and *Hastings Law Journal*. Law reviews contain articles written by professors, lawyers, and students usually including detailed analysis of a particular problem, area of law, or particular case, with copious commentary and voluminous footnote references to primary and secondary authorities on the topic. These materials are secondary authority in that they contain one person's discussion, opinion, viewpoint, and conclusions after examination of the footnoted sources; the theories expressed, therefore, are not universally accepted, so the cases cited in support of their opinions should be read.

2.0513 Newspapers.

Newspapers often contain articles concerning lawsuits of local or national interest, as well as reports on matters being considered by state and federal courts of appeal. Access to newspapers across the United States and even around the world has become increasingly inexpensive and available through such online sources as the Internet, Westlaw, and LexisNexis. There also are newspapers that deal only with legal matters. Examples of such publications on the national level are *Inside Counsel, National Law Journal*, and *The American Lawyer*. This kind of exclusive legal newspaper also exists on a local level in many metropolitan areas and is represented by such publications as *The Recorder, Los Angeles Daily Journal, Texas Lawyer*, and *KC Daily Record*. These are secondary, though valuable, sources of current information.

2.0514 Legal Encyclopedias.

Many researchers find legal encyclopedias are the best secondary source of information and an excellent place to start research. Encyclopedias give an overall view of the given legal topic and, when properly used, provide an enormous amount of background information, sometimes set out the necessary elements or meaning for any given term, and get the paralegal off on the right foot in finding the law. Because they contain numerous case citations, the paralegal who studies them will have a general feeling for the point being researched as well as a place to start the case research to determine the present state of the law. Normally, encyclopedias are multivolume publications, arranged alphabetically and indexed. They are updated continually with cumulative pocket parts or replacement volumes. Here again, do not cite cases from encyclopedias without reading the cases.

Two general legal encyclopedias are available: *Corpus Juris Secundum* and *American Jurisprudence 2d* (both of which are also available in electronic media). *Corpus Juris Secundum*, generally known as *C.J.S.*, purports to cite all American cases. Footnotes in these volumes are extensive. Since this is a West publication, it carries references to the West topic and key numbers, which allows easy transition from one to another of the West publications. As a bound volume created from past cases, extensively edited and proofed, the information is very informative but may be out of date. Every item of interest in the basic volumes must be checked by reference to the cumulative annual pocket parts and by seeking out updated case citators to find any cases on the same matter that may have been decided since the publication of the pocket part. An example of pages in a *C.J.S.* volume and its updating pocket part are shown in Exhibits 2-1 and 2-2. These exhibits clearly show the number of cases concerning issues of contributory negligence and avoidance of injury that occurred between the publication of the 1972 bound volume and the 1996 Annual Cumulative Supplement on the one topic of "What Constitutes Ordinary or Reasonable Care."

Three search methods can be applied to *C.J.S.* through the (1) descriptive word index, the fact method of search; (2) the topic analysis method, through its topical outlines; and (3) the words and phrases method or words sprinkled throughout. A separate "Words and Phrases Defined" listing in alphabetical order is located at the back of each volume. *American Jurisprudence 2d (Am.Jur.2d)* reports selected cases. It also contains a general index system. If the researcher is familiar with the area of law, he or she may proceed directly to the volume that contains that topic. If the researcher has difficulty using this method, the volume itself has a volume index (to be used in the same manner as the general index volumes). In the front of every volume of *Am.Jur.2d* are tables of statutes and parallel references. These tables indicate where the statutes cited in the volume are located and the references covered by articles formerly in the first edition of this work. Cross-references are cited to *American Law Reports (ALR); United States Supreme Court Reports, Lawyer's Edition; U.S. Code Service; Am. Jur. Legal Forms; Pleading and Practice Forms*; and *Proof of Facts* and *Trials*.

Out of the national legal encyclopedias have evolved state legal encyclopedias, examples of which are *California Jurisprudence, Texas Jurisprudence, Florida Jurisprudence*, and practice sets, such as *Illinois Law and Practice*.

The value of encyclopedias becomes obvious through examination and use, since they give extensive coverage of the law in broad treatment covered by known cases within specific jurisdictions and footnoted to those cases.

2.0515 Indexes, Words and Phrases.

Almost every publication contains an index. Some indexes also contain a section entitled "Words and Phrases" containing significant words and phrases used within that publication, in alphabetical order. These are useful in leading the reader quickly to the proper section of the publication.

There also are special indexes for legal periodical literature and periodicals, as well as law review citations. Among these are *Jones-Chipman's Index to Legal Periodical Literature* (covering the period from 1803 until it ceased publication in 1937); *Index to Legal Periodicals* (covering the period from 1926 to date), and *Shepard's Law Review Citations*. These sources can be found in larger libraries, such as law school, county, state, or federal law libraries, as well as in electronic versions, such as Heinonline.

Some states, in addition to the indexes in the volumes of the state codes and statutes, have other indexes that may prove more adaptable to the individual researcher's thinking. For example, the state

EXHIBIT 2-1 Sample C.J.S. Page

CJS NEGLIGENCE § 381
65A C.J.S. Negligence § 381

Corpus Juris Secundum
Database updated June 2003

Negligence

John Bourdeau, J.D.; Romualdo Eclavea, J.D.; Edward K. Esping, J.D.; Stephanie
Giggetts, J.D.; John R. Kennel, J.D.; Steve Lease, J.D.; Jane E. Lehman, J.D.;
Lucas Martin, J.D.; Thomas Muskus, J.D.; Carmela Pellegrino, J.D.; Eric
Surette, J.D.; Susan L. Thomas, J.D.; Mitchell Waldman, J.D.
VI. Premises Liability
A. Persons Liable
1. Overview

Topic Contents List of Topics

§ 381. OWNERSHIP, CUSTODY AND CONTROL, GENERALLY

**Liability for a dangerous condition on property is predicated upon the occupancy, ownership, control,
possession, or a special use of such premises.**

Research References

West's Key Number Digest, Negligence ☞1001, 1002, 1011, 1260

Liability for a dangerous condition on property is predicated upon the occupancy, ownership, control, possession,
or a special use of such premises; [FN1] the existence of one or more of these elements is sufficient to give rise to a
duty to exercise reasonable care, [FN2] and where none of these elements is present, a party cannot be held liable
for injuries caused by the dangerous or defective condition. [FN3] In other words, ordinarily, a person who does
not own, occupy, or otherwise control real property cannot be held liable for defective or dangerous conditions
thereon, [FN4] since it is possession and control that generally must be shown to establish premises liability. [FN5]

CUMULATIVE SUPPLEMENT:

Cases:

Liability for injuries caused by defective premises does not depend on who holds legal title, but rather on who has
possession and control of the property. LaFlamme v. Dallessio, 261 Conn. 247, 802 A.2d 63 (2002).

Copr. © West 2004 No Claim to Orig. U.S. Govt. Works

Source: Reprinted with permission of Thomson Reuters/West

EXHIBIT 2-2   Pocket Part

CORPUS JURIS
SECUNDUM™

2008
Cumulative
Annual Pocket Part

Issued June, 2008

Volume 65A

Insert this Pocket Part in back of volume
It replaces prior Pocket Part

This Cumulative Annual Pocket Part contains supplementary material
derived from principles and decisions including pertinent federal
legislation and selected federal and state cases added to
WESTLAW through March 31,2008.

THOMSON
WEST

Mat #40642328

IT-116

(continues)

NEGLIGENCE

KeyCite®: Cases and other legal materials listed in KeyCite Scope can be researched through the KeyCite service on Westlaw®. Use KeyCite to check citations for form, parallel references, prior and later history, and comprehensive citator information, including citations to other decisions and secondary materials.

VI. PREMISES LIABILITY

Research References

Westlaw Databases

Modern Tort Law: Liability and Litigation (2d ed.) (MTLLL)

A.L.R. Library

A.L.R. Index, Attractive Nuisance; Comparative Negligence; Contributory Negligence or Assumption of Risk; Degree and Standard of Care; Guests, Invitees, or Licensees; Negligence

A.L.R. Digest, Negligence §§ 38, 39, 63 to 71(6), 72 to 93, 114, 117, 119, 120, 145, 146, 175, 176

West's A.L.R. Digest, Negligence ☞1000 to 1320

Liability Of Owner, Operator, Or Other Parties, For Personal Injuries Allegedly Resulting From Snow Or Ice On Premises Of Parking Lot, 74 A.L.R. 5th 49

Liability Of Hotel, Motel, Resort, Or Private Membership Club Or Association Operating Swimming Pool, For Injury Or Death Of Guest Or Member, 55 A.L.R. 5th 463

Liability For Injury To Customer From Object Projecting Into Aisle Or Passageway In Store, 40 A.L.R. 5th 135

Liability Of Owner Or Operator Of Shopping Center, or Business Housed Therein, For Injury To Patron On Premises From Criminal Attack By Third Party, 31 A.L.R, 5th 550

Violation Of Governmental Regulations As To Conditions And Facilities Of Swimming Pools As Affecting Liability In Negligence, 79 A.L.R. 4th 461

Tort Liability Of Private Nursery School Or Day-Care Center, Or Employee Thereof, For Injury To Child While Attending Facility, 58 A.L.R. 4th 240

Liability To Adult Social Guest Injured Otherwise Than By Condition Of Premises, 38 A.L.R. 4th 200

Modern Status Of Rules Conditioning Landowner's Liability Upon Status Of Injured Party As Invitee, Licensee, Or Trespasser, 22 A.L.R. 4th 294

Liability Of Theater Owner Or Operator For Injury To Or Death Of Patron Resulting From Lighting Conditions On Premises, 19 A.L.R. 4th 1110

Treatises and Practice Aids

Modern Tort Law: Liability and Litigation §§ 8:1 to 8:5, 8:15, 30:1 to 30:12, 35:5. 39:1 to 39:23, 39:30 to 39:35, 39:37, 39:38

A PERSONS LIABLE

Research References

Westlaw Databases

Modern Tort Law: Liability and Litigation (2d ed.) (MTLLL)

A.L.R. Library

A.L.R. Index, Attractive Nuisance; Comparative Negligence; Degree and Standard of Care; Negligence

West's A.L.R. Digest, Negligence ☞ 1001, 1002, 1011, 1260 to 1269

Liability Of Owner Or Operator Of Shopping Center, Or Business Housed Therein, For Injury To Patron On Premises From Criminal Attack By Third Party, 31 A.L.R 5th 550

Treatises and Practice Aids

Modern Tort Law; Liability and Litigation §§ 8:1 to 8:5, 8:15, 35:5, 39:1 to 39:4, 39:37, 39:38

1. Overview

§ 381 Ownership, custody and control, generally

Cases

Liability for injuries caused by defective premises does not depend on who holds legal title, but rather on who has possession and control of the property LaFlamme v. Dallessio, 261 Conn. 247, 802 A. 2d 63 (2002).

A public or private entity which owns, operates, or controls a property, including a roadway, owes a duty to maintain that property, and a corresponding duty to warn of and correct dangerous conditions thereon. Pollock v. Florida Dept. of Highway Patrol, 882 So. 2d 928 (Fla. 2004).

2. Owners of Property

§ 382 Generally

Cases

Under New York law, defining the nature and scope of landowner's duty and to whom the duty is owed requires consideration of the likelihood of injury to another from a dangerous condition or instrumentality on the property; the severity of potential injuries; the burden on the landowner to avoid the risk; and the foreseeability of a potential plaintiff's presence on the property. In re September 11 Litigation, 280 F. Supp.

Source: Reprinted with permission of Thomson Reuters/West

library (usually in the capital city) may publish a special directory listing the types of legislative documents within the library and providing procedural guidance on searching the library for the volumes and on the types of information within them, their availability for loan, the methods of arranging to check out the books, and the names and telephone numbers of persons in the library who can assist the researcher. Additionally, there are commercial sources for more detailed indexes that can be helpful. For instance, the Recorder Printing and Publishing Company of San Francisco, California, published Larmac, *Consolidated Index to the Constitution and Laws of California*, a very comprehensive index with an effective subject cross-index. Other states have similar publications. Indexes sometimes are difficult to use for finding the specific area of interest. An alternative is to use the table of contents, which will lead to the general area of interest, and persistence and review of the general material will suggest or lead to the specific subject of interest, if it is contained in the legal publication. Municipal codes, including many city and county ordinances, are currently located at http://www.municode.com, including the ordinance index and the text of the code. Without such a site, the paralegal must travel to the locale or call, write, and send money for copies before identifying the necessary sections desired for research. This Website permits a preliminary review of the local code's index and format.

2.0516 Digests.   Legal digests are arranged much like legal encyclopedias, except that they do not contain a summary of the law or a particular point. Legal digests are really indexes to the law. The *American Digest System* constitutes the most comprehensive index to American decisions that is available. The system is based on a topic and key number classification scheme that divides the entire body of law into seven major headings, thirty-two subheadings, and over four-hundred digest topics. There are over 75,000 subtopics, each representing decisions accumulated under the topic-key number system.

The topic name and the key number, together, serve as a research reference for points of law abstracted from reported judicial decisions. The digest paragraphs are short summaries of the decisions arranged to help locate the decision and its holding(s). Digests also have indexes and tables of cases, as well as "Words and Phrases" compendia, which refer the reader to judicial definitions of words and phrases in court opinions.

An example of the indexes found in digests is Exhibit 2-3. This exhibit clearly reflects the helpful organization and explicit outline of the matters covered or excluded, suggests sources for near-synonymous topics and outlines, and provides topic and key number references to the material covered. Anyone interested in "proximate cause of injury" quickly finds the same topic and key number within the text as shown in Exhibit 2-3.

2.0517 Other Sources.   Some other methods that some researchers find expeditious will be mentioned because they can be effective for persons with particular research needs. Every method is only a tool to accomplish a task, and each should be designed to fit the individual and the special task when possible.

One such method takes advantage of a resource that many states have and some do not: an approved state book for forms, pleading and practice, and/or points and authorities. There are many form books commercially published for pleadings and for preparation of legal documents for the client. When one is asked to draft a motion for summary judgment, for example, the state form book of pleading and practice details the specific items that must be included for a meritorious motion to be acceptable based on the law of that state. It often cites the code section, rule of court, and so on that makes such a requirement. A state-approved points and authorities book can provide the form and language of any issue and cite the actual case giving rise to the acceptable authority. Naturally, the cases must be read to ensure that they are on point and do support the proposed motion.

EXHIBIT 2-3   Sample Pages from Federal Practice Digest Index

---

NEGLIGENCE

SUBJECTS INCLUDED

General civil negligence law and premises liability, including duty, standards of care, breach of duty, proximate cause, injury, defenses, and comparative fault, whether based on the common law or statute, as well as procedural aspects of such actions

General civil liabilities for gross negligence, recklessness, willful or wanton conduct, strict liability and ultrahazardous instrumentalities and activities

Negligence liabilities relating to the construction, demolition and repair of buildings and other structures, whether based on the common law or statute

General criminal negligence offenses and prosecutions

SUBJECTS EXCLUDED AND COVERED BY OTHER TOPICS

Accountants or auditors, negligence of, see ACCOUNTANTS ☞ 8, 9

Aircraft, accidents involving, see AVIATION ☞ 141–153

Asylums and assisted living facilities, see ASYLUMS AND ASSISTED LIVING FACILITIES

Attorneys' malpractice liability, see ATTORNEY AND CLIENT ☞ 105–129.5

For detailed references to other topics, see Descriptive-Word Index

---

Analysis

   I. IN GENERAL, ☞ 200–205.
   II. NECESSITY AND EXISTENCE OF DUTY, ☞ 210–222.
  III. STANDARD OF CARE, ☞ 230–239.
  IV. BREACH OF DUTY, ☞ 250–259.
   V. HEIGHTENED DEGREES OF NEGLIGENCE, ☞ 272–276.
  VI. VULNERABLE AND ENDANGERED PERSONS; RESCUES, ☞ 281–285.
 VII. SUDDEN EMERGENCY DOCTRINE, ☞ 291–295.
VIII. DANGEROUS SITUATIONS AND STRICT LIABILITY, ☞ 301–307.
  IX. TRADES, SPECIAL SKILLS AND PROFESSIONS, ☞ 321–323.
   X. SPORTS, GAMES AND RECREATION, ☞ 331–333.
  XI. FIRES, ☞ 341–344.
 XII. NEGLIGENT ENTRUSTMENT, ☞ 351–355.
(XIII.) PROXIMATE CAUSE, ☞ 370–454.
 XIV. NECESSITY AND EXISTENCE OF INJURY, ☞ 460–463.
  XV. PERSONS LIABLE, ☞ 480–484.
 XVI. DEFENSES AND MITIGATING CIRCUMSTANCES, ☞ 500–575.
 XIX. CRIMAL NEGLIGENCE, ☞ 1800–1809.

I. IN GENERAL.

   ☞ 200. Nature.
     201. Distinction between negligence and intentional conduct.

(continues)

☞387   NEGLIGENCE

For later cases, see same Topic and Key Number in Pocket Part

XIII. PROXIMATE CAUSE.——Cont'd

☞ 387.——**Foreseeablility.**

C.A.D.C. 1997.   Rieser v. District of Columbia, 563 F.2d 462, 183 U.S.App.D.C. 375, opinion reinstated in part on rehearing 580 F.2d 647, 188 U.S.App.D.C. 384.

C.A.8 (Ark.) 1997.   Plaintiff in negligence action in Arkansas must show, inter alia, that negligent act proximately caused damages sustained and that such damages were reasonable foreseeable.
Duston v. Daymark Foods, Inc., 122 F.3d 1146.

If act or omission is of itself negligent and likely to result in injury to others, then person guilty thereof is liable under Arkansas law for natural consequences which occurred, whether he might have foreseen it or not.
Duston v. Daymark Foods, Inc., 122 F.3d 1146.

C.A.9 (Cal.) 2003.   Under California law, proximate cause limits the defendant's liability to those foreseeable consequences that the defendant's negligence was a substantial factor in producing.
Ileto v. Glock Inc., 349 F.3d 1191, rehearing en banc denied 370 F.3d 860, certiorari denied China North Industries Corp. v. Ileto, 125 S.Ct. 865 543 U.S. 1050, 160 L.Ed.2d 770, on remand 421 F.Supp.2d 1274.

C.A.9 (Cal.) 1995.   Under California law, question of proximate cause is usually defined with reference to scope of foreseeable risks of actor's conduct.
Hines v. U.S., 60 F.3d 1442.

C.A.10 (Colo.) 2004.   Under Colorado negligence law, the test for establishing that an incident is foreseeable is whether the defendant reasonable should have anticipated any injury.
Elliot v. Turner Const. Co., 381 F.3d 995.

Under Colorado law, foreseeability includes whatever is likely enough in the setting in modern life that a reasonably thoughtful person would take account of it in guiding practical conduct; in other words, for an injury to be a foreseeable consequence of a negligent act, it is not necessary that the tortfeasor be able to foresee the exact nature and extent of the injuries or the precise manner in which the injuries occur, but only that some injury will likely result in some manner as a consequence of his negligent acts.
Elliot v. Turner Const. Co., 381 F.3d 995.

C.A.2 (Conn.) 1998.   Under Connecticut law, in order to determine whether a defendant's conduct is the proximate cause of an injury, it is necessary to determine whether the harm caused is within the foreseeable scope of the risk created by the defendant's conduct.
Chylinski v. Wal-Mart Stores, Inc., 150 F.3d 214.

C.A.11 (Ga.) 1988.   "Negligence" which is proximate cause of injury is act which person exercising ordinary caution and prudence could have foreseen producing an injury.
George v. Brandychase Ltd. Partnership, 418 F.2d 1094.

C.A.7 (Ill.) 2003.   Under Illinois law, "legal cause" is essentially question of foreseeability; relevant question is whether injury is of type that reasonable person would see as likely result of his or her conduct.
Palay v. U.S., 349 F.3d 418.

Under Illinois law, so long as defendant could have foreseen that **h**is negligence would result in some type of injury, precise nature or method of injury need not have been foreseeable.
Palay v. U.S., 349 F.3d 418.

C.A.7 (Ill.) 2002.   Legal cause, as element of proximate cause under Illinois law, exists where injury was of type that reasonable person would foresee as likely result of his or her conduct.
Cleveland v. Rotman, 297 F.3d 569.

C.A.7 (Ill.) 1996.   Defendant's conduct is proximate cause of plaintiffs injury if all events following that conduct, including any actions by plaintiff, are its reasonably foreseeable results.
Suzik v. Sea-Land Corp., 89 F.3d 345.

Negligence defendants are not required under Illinois law to foresee every injury-causing accident that can possibly arise from dangers they have created; law provides that it is reasonable for defendants to foresee some, but not all, accidents arising from their conduct, and if accident that injures plaintiff is not of the kind that defendant could have foreseen, court may decide proximate cause as a matter of law.
Suzik v. Sea-Land Corp., 89 F.3d 345.

C.A.7 (Ind.) 1996.   Under Indiana law, act of negligence is not proximate cause of injury unless consequence was one which, in light of attending circumstances, ought, could, or should reasonably have been foreseen or anticipated.
Lockwood v. Bowman Const. Co., 101 F.3d 1231.

C.A.7 (Ind.) 1995.   Proximate cause is established if injury caused by defendant is natural and probable consequence which was, or should have been, reasonably foreseen or anticipated in light of attendant circumstances; thus, intervening cause, e.g., act or omission of third party, will not operate to defeat recovery from

† This Case was not selected for publication in the National Reporter System
For cited U.S.C.A. sections and legislative history, see United States Code Annotated

— *(continues)* —

West's
FEDERAL PRACTICE
DIGEST 4th

Vol. 77D

Negligence 387 to 1649

2008
Cumulative Annual Pocket Part

THE WEST DIGEST TOPIC NUMBERS WHICH CAN
BE USED FOR WESTLAW® SEARCHES ARE LISTED ON
PAGE III OF THIS POCKET PART.

*All Federal Case Law of
The Modern Era*

**Up-Dated Weekly by West's Reporter Advance Sheets
or WESTLAW**

**For Prior Cases Consult Federal Digest,
Modern Federal Practice Digest,
Federal Practice Digest 2d and Federal
Practice Digest 3d**

99 F P D 4th-323   **NEGLIGENCE**

References are to Digest Topics and Key Numbers

NEGLIGENCE—Cont'd
PROFESSIONS—Cont'd
   Jury questions and directing verdict, **Neglig** ☞1700
   Medical malpractice
     See heading HOSPITALS,
       NEGLIGENCE; PHYSICIANS AND
       SURGEONS, NEGLIGENCE or
       malpractice.
   Physicians and surgeons. See heading
     PHYSICIANS AND SURGEONS,
     NEGLIGENCE or malpractice.
   Plaintiff's conduct or fault,
     Generally, **Neglig** ☞502(3)
     Last clear chance, **Neglig** ☞530(3)
   Pleading,
     Complaint, **Neglig** ☞1519
     Proof at variance with pleading, **Neglig** ☞1542
   Standard of care, **Neglig** ☞322
   Travel and tour, **Neglig** ☞323
PROOF at variance with pleading,
     Generally, **Neglig** ☞1537–1542
   Contributory and comparative negligence,
     Neglig ☞1541
   Defenses and mitigating circumstances in general,
     Neglig ☞1541
   Fires, **Neglig** ☞1542
   General issue, allegation or denial, **Neglig** ☞1538
   Heightened degrees of negligence, **Neglig** ☞1540
   Intentional conduct, **Neglig** ☞1540
   Multiple acts, **Neglig** ☞1539
   Professions, **Neglig** ☞1542
   Specific acts, **Neglig** ☞1539
   Violation of statutory requirements, **Neglig** ☞1542
PROSECUTING attorneys, **Dist & Pros Attys** ☞10
PROTECTION,
   Due process, **Const Law** ☞253(1)
   Duty to protect,
     Due process, **Const Law** ☞253(1)
   Failure to protect, Due process, **Const Law** ☞253(1)
   PROXIMATE cause. See heading
     PROXIMATE CAUSE, NEGLIGENCE.
PUBLIC buildings or other public property,
   Injuries,
     Condition or use, **Mun Corp** ☞847–857
PUBLIC employees and officials,
   Liability, **Office** ☞115–118

NEGLIGENCE—Cont'd
PUBLIC policy, duty of care, **Neglig** ☞211
RAILROADS. See heading RAILROADS, generally.
REASONABLE care standard, **Neglig** ☞233
RECKLESSNESS, **Neglig** ☞274
RECREATION,
   Generally, **Neglig** ☞331
   Assumption of risks, **Neglig** ☞565
   Complaint, **Neglig** ☞1520
   Evidence,
     Burden of proof, **Neglig** ☞1557
     Presumptions and inferences, **Neglig** ☞1588
     Sufficiency, **Neglig** ☞1663
   Instructions to jury, **Neglig** ☞1729
   Jury questions and directing verdict, **Neglig** ☞1701
   Sports. See subheading SPORTS under this heading.
REGISTERS of deeds, **Reg of Deeds** ☞6
REGULATORY requirements. See subheading
   STATUTORY requirements under
   this heading.
REPAIRS,
   Assumption of risks, **Neglig** ☞560
   Breach of duty, **Neglig** ☞252–253
   Complaint, **Neglig** ☞1515
   Instructions to jury, **Neglig** ☞1724
   Jury questions and directing verdict, **Neglig** ☞1696
   Res ipsa loquitur, **Neglig** ☞1625
   Standard of care, **Neglig** ☞235
   Sufficiency of evidence, **Neglig** ☞1658
RES ipsa loquitur,
   Generally, **Neglig** ☞1610–1625
   Application of doctrine in general, **Neglig** ☞1624
   Elements of application,
     Generally, **Neglig** ☞1612–1617
     Absence or unavailability of direct evidence,
       Neglig ☞1616
     Cause of accident or injury, **Neglig** ☞1617, 1625
     Contributory or comparative negligence,
       Neglig ☞1617
     Control or custody, **Neglig** ☞1614, 1625
     Defendant's superior knowledge or means to
       explain, **Neglig** ☞1615
     Occurrence of accident or injury as negligence,
       Neglig ☞1613
   Fires, **Neglig** ☞1625

(continues)

99A F P D 4th-139   # PROXIMATE

References are to Digest Topics and Key Numbers

| PROXIMATE CAUSE |

AUTOMOBILE accidents. See heading
   AUTOMOBILE ACCIDENTS,
   PROXIMATE cause.

AUTOMOBILES,
   Products liability, **Prod Liab** ☞38

AVIATION, injuries from operation of aircraft. See
   heading **AVIATION,** PROXIMATE cause, injuries
   from operation of aircraft.

BRIDGES, injuries from defects or obstructions,
   Bridges ☞43, 46(11)

CARGO, improper stowage as proximate cause of
   injury to or loss of, **Ship** ☞123(5)

CARRIERS,
   Goods, loss or injury,
      Generally, **Carr** ☞123
   Baggage of passenger, **Carr** ☞397
   Warehouseman, liability of carrier as, **Carr** ☞144
   Livestock, loss or injury, **Carr** ☞217(2)
   Passengers, injuries to,
      Generally, **Carr** ☞305
   Instructions, **Carr** ☞321(19)
   Jury questions, **Carr** ☞320(30)
   Pleading, **Carr** ☞314

CHILDREN. See heading **CHILDREN AND MINORS**,
   NEGLIGENCE, Proximate cause.

CIVIL rights violations. See heading CIVIL RIGHTS,
   CAUSATION.

COLLISION of vessels, **Collision** ☞18

COMMODITY futures trading regulation,
   Com Fut ☞28

CONSUMER protection,
   As element in general, **Cons Prot** ☞ 4
   Particular contexts, **Cons Port** ☞ 6–12

DAMAGE,
   Intervening cause, **Damag** ☞19
   Proximate or remote consequences, **Damag** ☞17–19

DEATH actions. See heading DEATH, PROXIMATE
   cause, actions for death.

ELECTRICITY, injuries from
   Generally, **Electricity** ☞16(7)
   Contributory and comparative negligence,
      Electricity ☞18(4)

Source: Reprinted with permission of Thomson Reuters/West

PROXIMATE CAUSE—Cont'd

EMPLOYERS' liability. See heading **EMPLOYERS'
   LIABILITY**, PROXIMATE cause of injury.

EXPERT witnesses. See heading EXPERT WITNESSES,
   PROXIMATE cause.

FRAUD, **Fraud** ☞25

INDEPENDENT business judgment rule, **Torts** ☞15

INJURIES to employee. See heading EMPLOYERS'
   LIABILITY, PROXIMATE cause of injury.

INSTRUCTIONS,
Contributory negligence, **R R** ☞351(13)
   Railroads,
      Accidents, **R R** ☞485(9)

INSURANCE, **Insurance** ☞2103 (1, 2)

INTOXICATING liquors, injury from sale, **Int
   Liq** ☞291

NEGLIGENCE,
   Generally, **Neglig** ☞370–454
Act of god, intervening cause, **Neglig** ☞440 (2–3)
Actions
   See also heading NEGLIGENCE, ACTIONS.

   Directing verdict. See Questions for jury and
      directing verdict, post.
   Evidence. See Evidence, post.
   Instructions to jury. See Instructions to jury, post.
   Pleading, complaint, **Neglig** ☞1526
   Questions for jury and directing verdict.
      See Questions for jury and directing verdict, post.
But–for causation, **Neglig** ☞379
Cause in fact or causation, Necessity,
   Neglig ☞371
   Relation to legal or proximate cause,
   Neglig ☞373
Common sense or experience, **Neglig** ☞377
Comparative negligence. See Contributory and
   comparative negligence, post.
Concurrent causes,
Generally, **Neglig** ☞421–424
   Fires, **Neglig** ☞424
   Joint and several liabilities, **Neglig** ☞421, 423
   Liability for, in general, **Neglig** ☞423–424
   Multiple causes, possibility of, **Neglig** ☞422
   Owners, **Neglig** ☞424

Another method that can be effective is best demonstrated by an example:

A paralegal has the assignment to review a complaint to determine whether an action for strict liability against the client has been properly stated and to draft interrogatories sufficient to reveal the existence of facts known by the adversary that support the cause of action.

Some researchers are very successful in immediately finding the essential elements to prove strict liability by consulting their state book of approved jury instructions. These books are collections of standardized jury instructions, also known as jury "charges," which are approved by the court as to form and language for presentation to a jury by the judge before the jury is sequestered to consider and decide a case. The theory of framing jury instructions has led to creating succinct expressions of each essential element that must be proved for a cause of action to be supported by a jury verdict. Since the pleadings are generally phrased in very broad terms, the jury instructions are a guide to framing interrogatories which develop the exact facts that support or attack the allegations in a set of pleadings, as well as the facts relied upon which hold the party in as a proper party-defendant or (as often is the case in strict liability) as a cross-defendant.

2.052   The West Topic and Key Number System

The West Publishing Company topic and key number system of classification was developed as a comprehensive indexing system to be used by researchers to locate points of law or legal principles. This system is a hallmark of the West Publishing Company encyclopedias, digests, unofficial reporters (such as the national reporter system volumes), and annotated codes and was made available for licensing to other publishing companies in 1996. Some of the major topic headings are shown in Exhibit 2-2, and Exhibit 2-4, showing the relationship between the topic and the key number subtopics. A quick perusal of the topic and key number chart reveals there are many topics within each division and each topic is further subdivided according to the legal principles or the points of law that fall within its scope. Finer breakdowns within the individual subtopics naturally result, and each subdivision topic is given a *key number*. Every case reported using the West system is first provided with *headnotes*. Each headnote summarizes a salient point of law decided in the case. Then, the headnotes of every published decision are further reviewed for specific case elements, and each headnote is provided with a topic and key number reference. For example, headnotes 1 and 2 might be on "Evidence," and headnote 3 might be on "Appeal and Error." Theoretically, this results in a system where all cases with the same elements are assigned the same topic and key number and will involve fact situations or points of law that have some similarity. The topic and key numbers from all the cases are consolidated into digests which West publishes. Digests are finding tools, and a researcher must check the appropriate digest for a given jurisdiction. As an example, for an action in Montana, the appropriate digest would be *West's Montana Digest*. These digests are kept up-to-date with cumulative annual *pocket parts* and supplemental pamphlets, in the same manner as the national reporter volumes are kept current using pamphlets and advance sheets with indexes. The most comprehensive digest published by West is the *American Digest System*, which indexes and classifies all American case law, state and federal, into digests called *Decennials*. Starting with the *Ninth Decennial Digest*, West began publishing the series in two parts, Part I covering the first five-year period and Part II covering the second five-year period to make up a full *Decennial Digest*. Prior to the *Ninth Decennial*, the digests were published once every ten years.

Other digests published individually cover the decisions of different courts, such as the *United States Supreme Court Digest* and *West's Federal Practice Digest, 4th*. The ultimate value of the West topic and key number system is that once a researcher locates a particular topic and key number, he or she has the "key" to reported American cases that have litigated a particular point or principle of

EXHIBIT 2-4   West Topics

DIGEST TOPICS

See, also, Outline of the Law by Seven Main Divisions of Law
preceding this section.

The topic numbers shown below may be used in WESTLAW searches for cases
within the topic and within specified key numbers.

1	Abandoned and Lost Property	44	Attachment	81	Colleges and Universities
2	Abatement and Revival	45	Attorney and Client	82	Collision
4	Abortion and Birth Control	46	Attorney General	83	Commerce
5	Absentees	47	Auctions and Auctioneers	83H	Commodity Futures Trading Regulation
6	Abstracts of Title	48	Audita Querela		
7	Accession	48A	Automobiles	84	Common Lands
8	Accord and Satisfaction	48B	Aviation	85	Common Law
9	Account	49	Bail	88	Compounding Offenses
10	Account, Action on	50	Bailment	89	Compromise and Settlement
11	Account Stated	51	Bankruptcy	89A	Condominium
11A	Accountants	52	Banks and Banking	90	Confusion of Goods
12	Acknowledgment	54	Beneficial Associations	91	Conspiracy
13	Action	55	Bigamy	92	Constitutional Law
14	Action on the Case	56	Bills and Notes	92B	Consumer Credit
15	Adjoining Landowners	58	Bonds	92H	Consumer Protection
15A	Administrative Law and Procedure	59	Boundaries	93	Contempt
		60	Bounties	95	Contracts
16	Admiralty	61	Breach of Marriage Promise	96	Contribution
17	Adoption	62	Breach of the Peace	96H	Controlled Substances
18	Adulteration	63	Bribery	97	Conversion
19	Adultery	64	Bridges	98	Convicts
20	Adverse Possession	65	Brokers	99	Copyrights and Intellectual Property
21	Affidavits	66	Building and Loan Associations		
23	Agriculture			100	Coroners
24	Aliens	67	Burglary	101	Corporations
25	Alteration of Instruments	68	Canals	102	Costs
26	Ambassadors and Consuls	69	Cancellation of Instruments	103	Counterfeiting
27	Amicus Curiae	70	Carriers	104	Counties
28	Animals	71	Cemeteries	105	Court Commissioners
29	Annuities	72	Census	106	Courts
30	Appeal and Error	73	Certiorari	107	Covenant, Action of
31	Appearance	74	Champerty and Maintenance	108	Covenants
33	Arbitration	75	Charities	108A	Credit Reporting Agencies
34	Armed Services	76	Chattel Mortgages	110	Criminal Law
35	Arrest	76A	Chemical Dependents	111	Crops
36	Arson	76D	Child Custody	113	Customs and Usages
37	Assault and Battery	76E	Child Support	114	Customs Duties
38	Assignments	76H	Children Out-of-Wedlock	115	Damages
40	Assistance, Writ of	77	Citizens	116	Dead Bodies
41	Associations	78	Civil Rights	117	Death
42	Assumpsit, Action of	79	Clerks of Courts	117G	Debt, Action of
43	Asylums	80	Clubs	117T	Debtor and Creditor

(continues)

DIGEST TOPICS

118A	Declaratory Judgment	171	Fences	225	Joint-Stock Companies and Business Trusts
119	Dedication	172	Ferries	226	Joint Tenancy
120	Deeds	174	Fines	227	Judges
122A	Deposits and Escrows	175	Fires	228	Judgment
123	Deposits in Court	176	Fish	229	Judicial Sales
124	Descent and Distribution	177	Fixtures	230	Jury
125	Detectives	178	Food	231	Justices of the Peace
126	Detinue	179	Forcible Entry and Detainer	232	Kidnapping
129	Disorderly Conduct	180	Forfeitures	232A	Labor Relations
130	Disorderly House	181	Forgery	233	Landlord and Tenant
131	District and Prosecuting Attorneys	183	Franchises	234	Larceny
132	District of Columbia	184	Fraud	235	Levees and Flood Control
133	Disturbance of Public Assemblage	185	Frauds, Statute of	236	Lewdness
		186	Fraudulent Conveyances	237	Libel and Slander
134	Divorce	187	Game	238	Licenses
135	Domicile	188	Gaming	239	Liens
135H	Double Jeopardy	189	Garnishment	240	Life Estates
136	Dower and Curtesy	190	Gas	241	Limitation of Actions
137	Drains	191	Gifts	242	Lis Pendens
141	Easements	192	Good Will	245	Logs and Logging
142	Ejectment	193	Grand Jury	246	Lost Instruments
143	Election of Remedies	195	Guaranty	247	Lotteries
144	Elections	196	Guardian and Ward	248	Malicious Mischief
145	Electricity	197	Habeas Corpus	249	Malicious Prosecution
146	Embezzlement	198	Hawkers and Peddlers	250	Mandamus
148	Eminent Domain	198H	Health	251	Manufactures
148A	Employers' Liability	200	Highways	252	Maritime Liens
149	Entry, Writ of	201	Holidays	253	Marriage
149E	Environmental Law	202	Homestead	255	Master and Servant
150	Equity	203	Homicide	256	Mayhem
151	Escape	205	Husband and Wife	257	Mechanics' Liens
152	Escheat	205H	Implied and Constructive Contracts	257A	Mental Health
154	Estates in Property			258A	Military Justice
156	Estoppel	206	Improvements	259	Militia
157	Evidence	207	Incest	260	Mines and Minerals
158	Exceptions, Bill of	208	Indemnity	265	Monopolies
159	Exchange of Property	209	Indians	266	Mortgages
160	Exchanges	210	Indictment and Information	267	Motions
161	Execution	211	Infants	268	Municipal Corporations
162	Executors and Administrators	212	Injunction	269	Names
163	Exemptions	213	Innkeepers	270	Navigable Waters
164	Explosives	216	Inspection	271	Ne Exeat
165	Extortion and Threats	217	Insurance	272	Negligence
166	Extradition and Detainers	218	Insurrection and Sedition	273	Neutrality Laws
167	Factors	219	Interest	274	Newspapers
168	False Imprisonment	220	Internal Revenue	275	New Trial
169	False Personation	221	International Law	276	Notaries
170	False Pretenses	222	Interpleader	277	Notice
170A	Federal Civil Procedure	223	Intoxicating Liquors	278	Novation
170B	Federal Courts	224	Joint Adventures	279	Nuisance

(continues)

DIGEST TOPICS

280	Oath	325	Recognizances	367	Subscriptions
281	Obscenity	326	Records	368	Suicide
282	Obstructing Justice	327	Reference	369	Sunday
283	Officers and Public Employees	328	Reformation of Instruments	370	Supersedeas
284	Pardon and Parole	330	Registers of Deeds	371	Taxation
285	Parent and Child	331	Release	372	Telecommunications
286	Parliamentary Law	332	Religious Societies	373	Tenancy in Common
287	Parties	333	Remainders	374	Tender
288	Partition	334	Removal of Cases	375	Territories
289	Partnership	335	Replevin	376	Theaters and Shows
290	Party Walls	336	Reports	378	Time
291	Patents	337	Rescue	379	Torts
294	Payment	338	Reversions	380	Towage
295	Penalties	339	Review	381	Towns
296	Pensions	340	Rewards	382	Trade Regulation
297	Perjury	341	Riot	384	Treason
298	Perpetuities	342	Robbery	385	Treaties
300	Pilots	343	Sales	386	Trespass
302	Pleading	344	Salvage	387	Trespass to Try Title
303	Pledges	345	Schools	388	Trial
305	Possessory Warrant	346	Scire Facias	389	Trover and Conversion
306	Postal Service	347	Seals	390	Trusts
307	Powers	348	Seamen	391	Turnpikes and Toll Roads
307A	Pretrial Procedure	349	Searches and Seizures	392	Undertakings
308	Principal and Agent	349A	Secured Transactions	393	United States
309	Principal and Surety	349B	Securities Regulation	394	United States Magistrates
310	Prisons	350	Seduction	395	United States Marshals
311	Private Roads	350H	Sentencing and Punishment	396	Unlawful Assembly
313	Process	351	Sequestration	396A	Urban Railroads
313A	Products Liability	352	Set-Off and Counterclaim	398	Usury
314	Prohibition	353	Sheriffs and Constables	399	Vagrancy
315	Property	354	Shipping	400	Vendor and Purchaser
316	Prostitution	355	Signatures	401	Venue
316A	Public Contracts	356	Slaves	402	War and National Emergency
317	Public Lands	356A	Social Security and Public	403	Warehousemen
317A	Public Utilities		Welfare	404	Waste
318	Quieting Title	357	Sodomy	405	Waters and Water Courses
319	Quo Warranto	358	Specific Performance	406	Weapons
319H	Racketeer Influenced and	359	Spendthrifts	407	Weights and Measures
	Corrupt Organizations	360	States	408	Wharves
320	Railroads	361	Statutes	409	Wills
321	Rape	362	Steam	410	Witnesses
322	Real Actions	363	Stipulations	411	Woods and Forests
323	Receivers	365	Submission of Controversy	413	Workers' Compensation
324	Receiving Stolen Goods	366	Subrogation	414	Zoning and Planning

Source: Reprinted with permission of Thomson Reuters/West

law. If a state digest is checked and there are no cases under the topic and key number assigned to a particular point, then the researcher knows there is a strong possibility that the particular point has not been decided or litigated in that state. The search is then extended to the cases of other states and courts. *Caveat:* Careful consideration must be made when selecting the topic word under which a search for the key number is made since our vocabulary is filled with near synonymous words. The absence of a topic and key number should not be accepted without exhausting the reasonable synonyms, which is another way of saying the human element of decision exercised by West employees in deciding how a subject should be indexed may not always match how the researcher would index a subject. Certain invaluable methods for finding the correct topic and key number are outlined in the following sections.

2.0521 Descriptive Word Method.

The descriptive word method becomes the most effective tool when the researcher does not have the name of a case on point or has not yet determined the topic that deals with the issue of interest. Every case decided is based on a fact situation, and the aim is to find other cases based on the same, or similar, fact situation that will provide the authority with which to argue the client's case.

In classifying and indexing cases, editors use words consistently when describing the facts of a case. These words are arranged alphabetically in volumes called "Descriptive Word Indexes" which will, in turn, direct the researcher to the topic and key number relating to cases with similar facts or legal issues. To use this search method, the researcher must analyze the fact situation and list the key words and phrases describing the essential elements. The researcher may have difficulty analyzing problems and choosing descriptive words at first, but the skill will develop with practice. Most descriptive words naturally group themselves around the five elements common to every case, namely:

a. Parties

b. Places and things

c. Acts or omissions that provide a basis for the action or issue

d. Defenses that might apply to an action or issue

e. The ultimate relief sought

The problem for most researchers at the start is to select words that are the same as a significant descriptive word to which a key number has been assigned. The pamphlet *West's Law Finder, a Legal Research Manual* contains an excellent example of the process. (*See* Exhibits 2-5 and 2-6.) *West's Federal Practice Digest, 4th* (Exhibit 2-3) uses a similar method of topic analysis. Additionally, at the beginning of each digest topic is a note specifying the scope of the topic and a complete breakdown of all subtopics, which are arranged numerically. Each subtopic bears what is called a key number. These numbers are often preceded by a drawing of a small key. This is simply a reminder that the number and title that follow are part of the organized group of topics and subtopics, as seen in Exhibits 2-5 and 2-6.

Beginning at page 21 of *West's Law Finder* (Exhibit 2-6), the researcher is shown how the descriptive word method works:

a. "Parties" equals spectator and a synonym patron, or arena owner, or wrestler, or referee, or promoter, all words that might have been the issue parties in past litigation. Other synonyms could be generated if a search for each proved negative. As it is, patron immediately leads to the topic "Theatre" and the key number 6.

b. "Places" equals wrestling match, amusement place, theatre, and show and could include auditorium, arena, or others. "Theatre," however, is the title of a topic on point.

c. "Basis of Action" produces "Personal Injury" (to a spectator).

d. "Defense" finds an easy entry under "Assumption of Risk."

e. "Relief Sought" produces references to several sources of information.

EXHIBIT 2-5   Copy of Page 19, West's Law Finder; a Legal Research Manual

mind that most descriptive words naturally group themselves around the five elements common to every case, namely:

1. PARTIES
   Aliens, Children Out-of-Wedlock, Landlords, Physicians, Sheriffs
2. PLACES AND THINGS
   Playground, Theater, Office Building, Roller Coaster, Puck, Automobile, Engagement Ring
3. BASIS OF ACTION OR ISSUE
   Negligence, Breach of Contract, Slander, Restraint of Trade, Title to Property, Admission of Evidence
4. DEFENSE
   Act of God, Assumption of Risk, Contributory Negligence, Usury
5. RELIEF SOUGHT
   Damages, Injunction, Eviction, Rescission, Divorce

At a professional wrestling match the referee was thrown from the ring in such a way that he struck and injured plaintiff who was a front row spectator. Does plaintiff have a cause of action? The following analysis shows how the descriptive words for this problem should be selected.

1. PARTIES—Spectator, Patron, Arena Owner, Wrestler, Referee, Promoter
2. PLACES AND THINGS—Wrestling Match, Amusement Place, Theater. Show
3. BASIS OF ACTION OR ISSUE—Negligence, Personal Injury to Spectator, Liability
4. DEFENSE—Assumption of Risk
5. RELIEF SOUGHT—Damages

The following are actual excerpts from the Descriptive-Word Index of the 6th Decennial Digest showing how several of the above words refer to Theaters 6 which is the Topic and Key Number that carries the wrestling injury cases in all Key Number Digests.

Descriptive-Word Index

ASSUMPTION OF RISKS—Cont'd

Automobiles—
   Burden of proof in action for injuries from operation or use of highways. **Autos 242(8)**
   Evidence of assumption of risk by occupant. **Autos 244(56)**
   Guest passenger, host's failure to look. **Autos 224(1)**
Hockey spectator. **Theaters 6**
Hunting party members. **Weap 18(1)**
Motorboat race, voluntary entry. **Collision 15**
Operation of doctrine. **Neglig 105**
Passengers. **Carr 323**
Patron of amusement device. **Theaters 6**

Swimming pool patron. **Theaters 6**
Tenant. **Land & Ten 168(1)**
Tenant's injuries, evidence. **Land & Ten 169(6)**
Tractor operator voluntarily assisting truck driver. **Autos 202**
Willful and wanton conduct of defendant. **Neglig 100**
Workmen's compensation—
   Abrogation or modification of defense. **Work Comp 772, 2110**
   Failure of employee to elect to come under act. **Work Comp 2114**
Wrestling match spectator injured by referee thrown from ring. **Theaters 6**

ASSUMPTION OF SKILL
Master as chargeable with knowledge

Source: Reprinted with permission of Thomson Reuters/West

EXHIBIT 2-6   Copy of Page 21, West's Law Finder, a Legal Research Manual

Nebraska Digest

⬗6(5)   THEATERS & SHOWS   10 Neb D—222

THEATERS AND SHOWS.

Library references

▸ C.J.S. Theaters and Shows § 1 et seq.

⬗2. Statutory and municipal regulations.

Neb. An act prohibiting "all public exhibitions of Hypnotism, Mesmerism, Animal Magnetism, or so-called Psychical Forces, for gain", does not prohibit spiritualistic seances, unless they are public and open and for gain, the words "psychical forces" applying to a seance conducted by a spiritualistic medium, but his act as such not violating statute unless it is public and open and for gain. Comp.St. 1929, § 28–1111.—Dill v. Hamilton, 291 N.W. 62, 137 Neb. 723.

The act prohibiting "all public exhibitions of Hypnotism, Mesmerism, Animal Magnetism, or so-called Psychical Forces, for gain", is a valid exercise of police power, since police power to prohibit public exhibitions for money-making purposes or for gain extends to harmful, immoral or indecent performances, though conducted in the name of religion, and violators of such prohibitions are subject to statutory penalties therefor. Comp.St.1929, § 28–1111.—Dill v. Hamilton, 291 N.W. 62, 137 Neb. 723.

A guaranty of $15 to remunerate a medium for conducting spiritualistic seance as religious ceremony in the worship of God and creation of the fund by voluntary contributions of communicants of Spiritualistic Church do not constitute "gain" within statute forbidding public seances for gain. Comp.St.1929, § 28–1111.—Dill v. Hamilton, 291 N.W. 62, 137 Neb. 723.

⬗6. Liabilities for injuries to persons attending.

    (1). In general.

    (2). Duty affected by charging for admission, insuring safety or assuming special legal status.

    (3). Licensees or invitees.

    (4). —— Particular invitees.

    (5). Persons liable or entitled to sue.

    (6). Limitation of liability.

    (7). Particular duties toward participants.

    (8). —— Amusement devices.

    (9). —— Swimming or bathing.

    (10). Particular duties toward spectators.

    (11). —— Athletic events.

    (12). —— Floor and ground.

    (13). —— Lighting, and ushering in darkness.

    (14). —— Protection against crowds, assaults and acts of others and ushering in general.

    (15). —— Seats and structural defects.

    (16). —— Stairs, steps and ramps.

    (17). Contributory negligence and assumption of risk.

    (18). —— Athletic events.

    (19). —— Participants.

    (20). Actions in general.

⬗6(5). Persons liable or entitled to sue.

Neb. In personal injury action by spectator at wrestling match, instruction that if jury found that while two wrestlers were on ground outside ring they continued to wrestle and when referee attempted to separate them, one of the wrestlers shoved the referee into the spectator and injured spectator, there was no liability against anyone except wrestler who did the pushing, because such pushing was outside that wrestler's scope of employment, was erroneous, since such wrestler was not, as a matter of law, outside the scope of his employment.—Klause v. Nebraska State Bd. of Agriculture, 35 N.W.2d 104, 150 Neb. 466.

Action for injuries sustained by spectator at wrestling match when referee was thrown or knocked from ring and came in contact with spectator was properly dismissed as to one who procured one of the wrestlers, where such wrestler was in nowise in such person's employ or under his control.—Id.

⬗6(10). Particular duties toward spectators.

Neb. One who operates a place of public amusement or entertainment is held to a stricter accountability for injuries to patrons than owners of private premises generally; and is not insurer of safety of patrons but owes to them only what under the particular circumstances, amounts to ordinary and reasonable care.—Fimple v. Archer Ballroom Co., 35 N.W. 2d 680, 150 Neb. 681.

⬗6(14). —— Protection against crowds, assaults and acts of others, and ushering in general.

Neb. Ordinance rendering it unlawful for operators of public dance halls to permit persons therein while under influence of liquor or engaging in boisterous conduct is for benefit of individual patrons of dances as well as public at large and could properly be made basis of civil action for damages where dance hall patron was injured by bottle thrown by second patron who was intoxicated.—Fimple v. Archer Ballroom Co., 35 N.W.2d 680, 150 Neb. 681.

⬗6(17). Contributory negligence and assumption of risk.

Neb. Patron who attended large dance at public dance hall did not assume risk of injury from bottle thrown by second patron who was intoxicated.—Fimple v. Archer Ballroom Co., 35 N.W.2d 680, 150 Neb. 681.

⬗6(18). —— Athletic events.

Neb. A spectator at hockey game assumes risk of, and owes duty to protect himself against, such dangers incident to playing of game as are known to him or should be obvious and apparent to reasonable and prudent person in exercise of due care under circumstances.—Tite v. Omaha Coliseum Corporation, 12 N. W.2d 90, 144 Neb. 22.

Neb. A spectator at a wrestling match is required to exercise due care in protecting himself against known dangers or such as should be known and appreciated by a reasonable person in exercise of due care.—Klause v. Nebraska State Bd. of Agriculture, 35 N.W.2d 104, 150 Neb. 466.

Spectator at wrestling match who was injured when referee was thrown or knocked from ring and came in contact with spectator was not contributorily negligent, so as to preclude recovery for his injuries, because he sat in front row.—Id.

Spectator at wrestling match who was injured when referee was thrown or knocked from ring and came in contact with spectator, did not assume risk of injury because he sat in front row.—Id.

A spectator at a wrestling event assumes risk only of such dangers as are incident to such events, of which he had knowledge or

21

Annotation labels (margin):

- Corpus Juris Secundum reference
- Internal Key Number breakdown
- Point of law in illustrative example

2.0522 Topic Method.   The topic method involves locating the topic under which the point of law has been previously classified. Before relying on this method, be very familiar with the key number classification system. Researchers, particularly those just beginning, very often arrive at the wrong topic. Study and analyze the key number system law chart (Exhibit 2-3); almost invariably it will lead the researcher to the correct topic. If problems still exist, refer to the alphabetic list of digest topics that appears in the front of each digest volume and the *C.J.S.* indexes. In using the descriptive word indexes, the researcher may have difficulty locating the precise key number needed, but they will always lead the researcher to the proper topic and, sometimes, to additional topics for consideration. Every digest has a topic analysis that begins with a "scope-note." Review of the scope-note will often quickly reveal whether the selected topic matches the case factual situation. Select an example based on page 1 of the current key chart to replace this example: For instance, presume a client is involved in an automobile accident where her car was pushed into another because a third vehicle rammed the side of the client's car. This will require a search to determine whether the client is liable for damage to the vehicle she hit. Review of the key number system law chart (Exhibit 2-3) suggests the transaction fits best in the category of "Collision."

2.0523 Table of Cases Method.   The table of cases search method is useless unless, or until, the researcher has the name of at least one case that deals with the particular point of law of concern. The name of a case allows the researcher to go immediately to the table of cases in the appropriate state key number digest, reporter key number digest, or the *Decennial Digest* and find from that case what topics and key numbers were used. Once the proper topic and key number are located, all other American cases dealing with the same general point become available for review, analysis, and report.

2.053 The Statutory Approach to Law

Once an initial review of the secondary source material has been completed on a particular issue, the paralegal has a general understanding of the problem and in all probability has discovered some case on point and found references to one or more statutes or codes. When researching a problem involving a statute, a good rule of thumb is to first read the statute (including all updates) and relevant annotations that may be listed after the statute. As mentioned previously, an annotation is a brief description of a judicial opinion.

Locating a statute is a relatively simple procedure. Statutory laws can be divided into three subdivisions:

  a. Federal—U.S. Constitution, congressional legislation, treaties, executive orders, administrative rules and orders, and court rules

  b. State—state constitutions, session laws, uniform laws, administrative rules and orders, and court rules

  c. Local—municipal charters, county and municipal ordinances, and court rules

When statutes are initially published, they are arranged in chronological order according to the date of passage. However, the statutes passed in a particular legislative session are ultimately incorporated into statutes that were in existence prior to that legislative session, thus creating an ever-growing and changing collection of laws. Because these change so frequently, they are arranged topically. Consequently, if one is familiar with the appropriate terminology relating to a particular subject of law, one can locate all current laws on a specific topic through the use of a subject index to the statutes. Various names for these collections of statutes are used by the different states and jurisdictions. Very often the terms code, annotated statutes, compiled laws, or revised statutes appear in the title of the publication. There are a large number of codes in this country, and each may be composed of one, five, or even several hundred volumes, as in the case of the *United States Code Annotated*. Additionally, some states subdivide their state codes into smaller codes, such as a code of civil procedure, a code of criminal procedure, an insurance code, and so on. A researcher who is encountering a code for the first time should try to become familiar with the organization of the state code, including any smaller codes, and become comfortable with the form and style of the text. At the beginning of the code will be noted the order in which the topics are arranged as titles, parts, or chapters, as well as the system of numbering of the sections and subsections.

The difference between chronologic (such as statutes at large and session laws) and the topical arrangements of codes is of primary importance to the researcher for speed of location, clarity of reading, and ease of updating.

2.0531 Federal Reports.　Federal question research is technical and advanced, and although it will not be discussed in detail, it is important for paralegals to be aware of common sources of federal statutory and case law.

The U.S. Constitution was signed in 1787 and took effect in 1789. It was the origin of federal law and, as amended, still stands as the supreme law of the land. Most Americans are affected continuously by its provisions, and the discussion of cases and terminology arising directly from the rights guaranteed to individuals by the Constitution (for example, freedom of speech, freedom of the press, and due process) regularly appears in the media. The Constitution is the highest authority available, and the U.S. Supreme Court is the final arbiter in disputes over its provisions. All other federal and state statutes must conform to the guarantees of this document or they will fail. West's *U.S. Code Annotated (U.S.C.A.)* has several volumes devoted exclusively to the Constitution and the cases that have arisen from disputes over its provisions. A key to statutory research is that statutes can be found in several places: in session laws, in an unannotated code, and in an annotated code. As bills are enacted by Congress, they enter the *U.S. Statutes at Large*, the session laws of the U.S. Congress, and may, if permanent, general, and public in nature, be included in the *U.S. Code*. Official copies of the *U.S. Code* can be obtained through the U.S. Government Printing Office. Each such provision as it becomes law can be found in the *Congressional Record* and may be located through the Congressional Information Service/Index. Unofficial reports include the *U.S.C.A.*, *U.S. Code Service (U.S.C.S.)*, and *U.S. Code Congressional and Administrative News (USCAAN)*. *USCAAN* publishes new federal laws as they are enacted and includes some legislative history. Remember when checking annotations to check both the *U.S.C.A.* and the *U.S.C.S.*, because different editors make different decisions about what materials to include in annotations. Additionally, there are numerous publishers of *loose-leaf services*. These services monitor and publish new laws along with updated material for subscribers in particular fields of law, such as trade regulation, taxation, antitrust, environmental law, labor, and occupational safety and health law in a loose-leaf format for insertion into binders. Firms that have a substantial specialty practice will generally subscribe to such a service at both the federal and state levels.

Each publisher supplies the legal community with a particular style and format they believe is helpful, easy to use, and clear to its readers. The *U.S.C.A.* supplies the researcher with a variety of routes to the significant material of the statutes and cases which refer to them. Each volume of the *U.S.C.A.* contains all or a portion of the U.S. Constitution or the *U.S. Code,* as well as a title page describing the extent of material covered in the volume, which is supplemented by detailed tables of contents and indexes.

The *U.S.C.A.* also contains a special index of the popular name of each law enacted by Congress, references to the date of its passage, any amendments, the chapter and statute reference to the statutes at large, its public law designation (if any), the titles and sections under the *U.S. Code*, and any alternative names under which it is listed. (*See* Exhibit 2-7.)

EXHIBIT 2-7   Sample Entry, U.S.C.A. Popular Name Table

POPULAR NAME TABLE
FOR
ACTS OF CONGRESS
Through Pub.L. 110–180

Generally, the initial entry under the name of an Act in this Table is the citation for the Act of Congress or Public Law which enacted the Act. The subsequent entries under each Act are the citations for Public Laws which amended the Act.

The convention of citing laws beginning with the Public Law number commenced in 1957. Prior to that time, laws were cited with the date of enactment first, followed by the chapter number. Since this Popular Name Table consists of laws from the first Congress in 1789 to today, it contains laws in both styles. As a matter of consistency, post-1957 amendments to laws which were originally enacted before 1957 follow the date-first style.

Parentheticals.   The references within the parentheses following Public Law citations indicate the classifications of that Public Law to the United States Code by Code title and section. In some instances, Code classifications may not be indicated for Acts of Congress that have been repealed, superseded, obsolete, or not classified to the Code.

Notes.   A reference in parentheses to a "note" indicates material set out below the text of a section in the Code. A reference in parentheses in the initial entry under an Act just to a note generally indicates an Act that was codified as a whole as a note under the referenced section of the Code.

Tables.   A reference in parentheses to the Tables following the citation of a Public Law means Table 1—Revised Statutes 1878 and Table 2—Statutes at Large. These tables contain a chronological listing of Public Laws that have been classified to the Code together with their Code classifications and current status.

"See".   The word "See" set out in parentheses preceding the Code title and section indicates that the Public Law has been repealed (in whole or in part) and that certain provisions thereof have been restated in the Code title and section specified, generally a Code title that was revised when enacted into positive law. The name of an Act preceded by the word "See" indicates an alternate name for the Act and the location within the Table for the list of Public Law citations for that Act.

"See, also,".   The name of an Act preceded by the words "See, also," indicates either an Act related to the named Act or another Popular Name Act contained entirely within the named Act.

"Prec."   The word "prec." set out in parentheses preceding the Code title and section indicates that the Public Law has been classified in whole or in part to a heading above that section.

AA
  See Agricultural Act of 1970

AAA
  See Agricultural Adjustment Act of 1938

(continues)

AAA Farm Relief and Inflation Act (Wagner-Lewis $500,000,000 Emergency Relief Act)
  May 12, 1933, ch. 25, 48 Stat. 31 (7 §§ 601 to 604, 607, 608, 608a to 608e, 608e-l, 609
        to 620, 623, 624; 12 §§ 347, 462b, 636, 723, 771, 781, 810, 823 note, 992, 993,
        1016 to 1019; See 31 §§ 5301, 5304)

AAIA
  See Airport and Airway Improvement Act of 1982

AAPA
  See Antarctic Protection Act of 1990

Abacá Production Act of 1950
  Aug. 10, 1950, ch. 673, 64 Stat. 435 (50 §§ 541 to 546)

Abandoned Barge Act of 1992
  Short title, see 46 USCA § 4701 note
  Pub.L. 102–587, Title V, Subtitle C, Nov. 4, 1992, 106 Stat. 5081 (46 §§ 4701 to 4705)

Abandoned Infants Assistance Act of 1988
  Short title, see 42 USCA § 670 note
  Pub.L. 100–505, Oct. 18, 1988, 102 Stat. 2523 (42 § 670 note)
  Pub.L. 102–236, §§ 2 to 8, Dec. 12, 1991, 105 Stat. 1812 to 1816 (42 § 670 note)
  Pub.L. 104–235, Title II, Subtitle C, §§ 221, 222, Oct. 3, 1996, 110 Stat. 3091, 3092
        (42 § 670 notes)
  Pub.L. 108–36, Title III, §§ 301 to 305, June 25, 2003, 117 Stat. 822 to 824 (42 § 670 note)

Abandoned Infants Assistance Act Amendments of 1991
  Short title, see 42 USCA § 670 note
  Pub.L. 102–236, Dec. 12, 1991, 105 Stat. 1812 (29 § 623 note; 42 § 670 note)

Abandoned Military Reservations Acts
  July 5, 1884, ch. 214, 23 Stat. 103 (43 § 1071 et seq.)
  Aug. 23, 1894, ch. 314, 28 Stat. 491
  July 3, 1916, ch. 217, 39 Stat. 342

Abandoned Mine Reclamation Act of 1990
  Short title, see 30 USCA § 1201 note
  Pub.L. 101–508, Title VI, Subtitle A, Nov. 5, 1990, 104 Stat. 1388–289 (30 §§
        1231, 1231 note, 1232 to 1237, 1239, 1240a, 1241 to 1243, 1257, 1302)

Abandoned Property Collection Act
  Mar. 12, 1863, ch. 120, 12 Stat. 820

Abandoned Shipwreck Act of 1987 (ASA)
  Short title, see 43 USCA § 2101 note
  Pub.L. 100–298, Apr. 28, 1988, 102 Stat. 432 (43 §§ 2101, 2101. note, 2102 to 2106)

————— *(continues)*—————

Abie Seamen Act

July 8, 1941, ch. 279, 55 Stat. 579 (46 § 672–2)

Abolition of Slavery Acts (District of Columbia)

Apr. 16, 1862, ch. 54, 12 Stat. 376

July 12, 1862, ch. 155, 12 Stat. 538

Abolition of Slavery Act (Territories)

June 19, 1862, ch. 112, 12 Stat. 432

Abraham Lincoln Bicentennial Commission Act

Pub.L. 106–173, Feb. 25, 2000, 114 Stat. 14 (36 prec. § 101 note)

Pub.L. 107–20, Title II, § 2804, July 24, 2001,115 Stat. 185 (36 prec. § 101 note)

Pub.L. 107–68, Tide II, § 209, Nov. 12; 2001, 115 Stat. 588 (36 § prec. 101 note)

Pub.L. 108–7, Div. H, Title I, § 1304, Feb. 20, 2003,117 Stat. 379 (36 prec. § 101)

Pub.L. 108–59, § 1, July 14, 2003, 117 Stat. 860 (36 prec. § 101 note)

Abraham Lincoln Bicentennial 1-Cent Coin Redesign Act

Pub.L. 109–145, Title III, Dec. 22, 2005,119 Stat. 2673 (31 § 5112 note)

Abraham Lincoln Birthplace National Historic Site Acts

July 17,1916, ch. 247, 39 Stat. 385 (16 §§ 211 to 214)

Feb. 11, 1929, ch. 176, 45 Stat. 1162 (16 §§ 215, 216)

Mar. 2, 1934, ch. 38, 48 Stat. 389 (16 § 214)

Aug. 11, 1939, ch. 686, 53 Stat. 1405 (16 §§ 217, 440a)

May 27, 1949, ch. 149, 63 Stat. 140 (16 § 218)

Sept. 8,1959, Pub.L. 86–231, 73 Stat. 466 (16 § 217a)

Abraham Lincoln Commemorative Coin Act

Pub.L. 109–285, Sept. 27, 2006, 120 Stat. 1215 (31 § 5112 note)

ACA

See Agricultural Credit Act of 1987

Source: Reprinted with permission of Thomson Reuters/West

Because not all statutes at large are codified and published in the *U.S. Code,* it is essential to be able to move between the *U.S. Code* and the *U.S. Statutes at Large.* The *U.S.C.A.* provides indexes which meet this need by providing: (1) the year and the session of Congress in which the law was passed; (2) the statute volume in which it is recorded; (3) the date of passage of the statute; and (4) its public law number, along with the sections and pages all cross-referenced to the *U.S.C.A.,* as shown in Exhibit 2-8.

Administrative agencies of the United States must publish their rules and regulations (these terms are used synonymously in administrative law vernacular) in the *Federal Register.* The codification of the

EXHIBIT 2-8   Sample Page, Index of U.S. Code Cross-Reference to Statutes at Large

1990   STATUTES AT LARGE

1990—101st Cong.—104 Stat.				USCA		
May P.L.	**Sec.**		**Page**	**Tit.**	**Sec.**	**Status**
4 ...... 101–280	5(d)		159	18	207	
	5(e)		159	18	208	
	5(f)		159	18	216	
	6(a)(1)		160	26	1043	
	6(a)(2), (3)		160	26	1043	nts
	6(b)		160	31	1344	nt
	6(c)		160	18	208	nt
	6(d)(1)		160	5	3393	
	6(d)(2)		160	5	7701	
	6(d)(3)		160	22	3945	
	6(d)(4)		161	10	1601	
	7(a)		161	5 App. 7	501	
	7(b)		161	5 App. 7	502	
	7(b)(1)		161	2	441i	
	7(b)(2)		161	2	31–1	
	7(c)		161	5 App. 7	503	
	8		162	2	31–2	
	9		162	5 App. 6	105	nt
	10(a)		162	31	3730	
	10(b)		162	10	2397a	
	10(c)		162	10	2397a	nt
	11		163	5 App. 6	101	nt
101–281	1(a)		164	49 App.	1475	
	1(b)		164	49 App.	1475	nt
	2		164	49 App.	2210	
9 ...... 101–286	1		171	16	551	nt
	101 to 106		174	16	551b	nt
	201		174	16	551b	nt
	202		174	16	551b	
	203		175	16	551c	
	204(a)		175	16	558c	
	204(b)		175	16	18i	
	204(c)		175	43	1737	
17 ...... 101–292	1		185	16	460aaa	
	2		185	16	460aaa–1	
	3		185	16	460aaa–2	
	4		187	16	460aaa–3	
	5		188	16	460aaa–4	
	6		188	16	460aaa–5	
	7		188	16	460aaa–6	
	8		189	16	460aaa–7	
	9		190	16	460aaa–8	
101–293	1, 2		192	13	23	nt
101–296	1 to 4		197 to 199	31	5111	nt
22 ...... 101–298	1		201	18	175	nt
	2		201	18	175	nt
	3(a)		201, 202	18	prec. 175, 175 to 178	
	3(b)		203	18	2516	
	3(c)		203	18	prec. 1	
24 ...... 101–301	1(a)(2)		206	25	450m–1	
	1(a)(3)		206	25	608	
	1(b)		206	25	608	
	2(a)(1) to (3)		206	25	450b	
	2(a)(4)		206	25	450c	
	2(a)(5)		206	25	450e–1	
	2(a)(6)		206	25	450i	
	2(a)(7)		207	25	450j	
	2(a)(8), (9)		207	25	450j–1	
	2(a)(10)		207	25	450m	
	2(b)		207	25	450m–1	
	2(c)		207	5	3371	
	3(a)		207	25	478–1	
	3(b)		207	25	473	
	3(c)		207	25	477	
	4		207	25	713f	nt
	5(a)		207	25	2019	
	5(b)		207	25	2508	

644

Source: Reprinted with permission of Thomson Reuters/West

various rules of these agencies is found in the *Code of Federal Regulations (C.F.R.)*, the official record for such law. The topics in the *C.F.R.* correspond to those found in the *U.S. Code*. Because of the volume of agency rules promulgated, one-quarter of the *C.F.R.* is updated every three months. Therefore, although the *C.F.R.* is well indexed and revised annually, at any given time some volumes will be three months old, some six months old, and some nine months old. The date on the cover of the particular *C.F.R.* volume will tell the researcher when that particular title was last updated and include a cumulative history of changes from 2001 forward. Anything older is found in a special volume set, list of *C.F.R. Sections Affected 1949–1963, 1964–1972, 1973–1985,* and *1986–2000*, published by the U.S. Government Printing Office in 1966. The *C.F.R.* contains indexes which aid the researcher in finding the *U.S. Code, U.S. Statutes at Large*, proclamation, executive order, or reorganization plans relied upon by a particular rule or regulation for authority. The *United States Code Service Index and Finding Aids to the Code of Federal Regulations* is another useful tool for moving between the *U.S. Code* and the *Code of Federal Regulations*.

To assist a researcher in delving into the governmental regulatory and administrative agency maze, the U.S. Government Printing Office annually publishes the *United States Government Manual*. This manual describes all executive branch and regulatory agencies and cites the statutes under which they function, their subordinate units, and other organizational data, as well as the types of information each agency can provide. It is an excellent general reference and informational tool.

Many of the loose-leaf services, mentioned previously, follow the publications of these agencies and supply their subscribers with the most recent changes in a timely fashion. Additionally, electronic versions of the government publications and official reports mentioned previously, as well as some of the loose-leaf services, such as *Bureau of National Affairs (BNA)*, are available on the Internet and in CD-ROM versions.

2.0532 Federal Court Rules.

Federal courts establish rules of procedure to guarantee a uniform system of presentation of cases. These rules are subject to controversy and interpretation, and the courts are sometimes requested to decide the meaning of a rule. Court resolutions of questions about the proper interpretation of rules from 1940 to the present will be found in a series of volumes called the *Federal Rules Decisions*. The *Federal Rules Service* is a similar publication which reports on decisions interpreting and construing federal rules. Both are excellent tools for researching questions concerning the federal rules of civil procedure. Of course, the U.S. Government Printing Office publishes *Rules of Civil Procedure* for U.S. District Courts and all other federal rules. This official publication, like all other official publications, provides only the text of the material without reference to cases. The unofficial publications by the commercial firms, such as the *Federal Civil Rules Handbook*, provide explanations of the meaning and intent of the rules in the form of footnoted cases.

2.0533 State Reports.

Each state has a similar range of statutory authority controlling or directing the lives of its citizens. The same basic procedures for proposing legislation, introducing bills, and enacting them into law are followed whether the state legislature meets annually or every other year. The executive branch of the state government (the governor and the regulatory and administrative agencies) generates executive orders and rules and regulations in a manner similar to the federal system. In many cases, there are areas of overlapping responsibilities between the state and federal jurisdictions that must be considered by the researcher. Some of these areas are education, health and welfare, housing, occupational health and safety, and utility regulation. Great care must be exercised to determine the exact problem and whether it is responsive to state statute, federal statute, or both. The basic sources of state statutory law are:

a. **State Constitution.** The constitution of each state is the ultimate source of the laws for that state. Here, again, check to be certain some article or section has not been amended or repealed.

The state's highest court, the supreme court in most states, is the final authority on the interpretation of the state's constitutional provisions, though some of those rulings may be appealed for decision by the U.S. Supreme Court where a conflict between rights under the state constitution and the U.S. Constitution is alleged.

b. **State Codes and Statutes.** These are the laws of the state, passed by the legislature and signed by the governor (or passed over his or her veto). Once the governor signs the legislation, the statute is published as a session law and consolidated chronologically with the current legislative session's accumulation. If the particular bill provided for the acceptance of a code is in its codified form, it will be found both in the chronologic and the code version of the law. The researcher will find parallels between the research aids for the federal system and the research aids for the state statutory law. Each state has a printing office that supplies official copies of the statutes and codes. Similarly, there are commercial publishers that produce the unofficial publications. In California, for example, there are two publications that cover the state's codes: *West's Annotated California Codes* and *Deering's California Codes, Annotated.* California's codes are divided topically much like the *U.S. Code* and the *U.S.C.A.* The arrangement of the content is similar to the *U.S.C.A.* in that it provides quick reference in the code to the statutes for each section, historical notes, library references, and derivation of any section, as well as the West Topic and Key Number references for research in other West sources. Clearly, care must be taken to ensure the latest amendments are included. Each volume is updated annually with pocket parts containing amendments to the sections in the volume, as well as additional annotations. (Annotations are compilations of cases and historical matter dealing with various aspects of a code or statute, with short summaries of decisions and case citations. They contain cases ruling both for and against.) Always check the volume to determine its date of publication and for a pocket part. If there is a pocket part, check to see if there have been any changes. If there is no pocket part, it may be the most recent replacement volume. If there are several years between the publication date in the front of the volume and the time of the research, take the extra step of checking for a missing pocket part. CD-ROM versions of the state statutes, with and without annotations, are also available. This provides better searching capabilities but is not updated as frequently (annually) unless the law firm is with a service which provides updates of the CD-ROM as laws are modified, repealed, and so forth, even in special sessions of the legislature. The librarian in the office or in the nearest major law library can be of assistance. The volumes also contain legislative history, cross-references, and collateral references. Each book of codes and statutes reflects the effective dates of the statutes and the date the statutes were passed in a given year.

State regulatory and administrative agencies are empowered by the legislature that created them to propose and publish (after public comment or hearing) rules and regulations necessary for the discharge of their responsibilities. Often they also are empowered to enforce their own regulations, subject to appeal. Many times these state agencies parallel federal ones and must work in concert with them on matters of mutual concern but within their specified areas of jurisdiction. *Caveat:* Research in statutes alone is ineffectual unless the cases (cited in the annotated code volumes) are studied to determine how the courts construed and interpreted the rules. It is obvious that finding cases analogous to the researcher's problem is helpful, whether the decisions support or refute the client's desired position. The attorney, armed with the past decisions, can adapt the theory, choice of jurisdictions, and strategy or at least advise the client of the most effective and economic course of action.

2.054 Case Approach to the Law

Case research is clearly the backbone of all legal endeavors in the United States. Even in cases of "first impression," where the court never before has heard or decided the disputed issue, the decision is influenced by the principles and reasoning of the courts in past similar cases and decisions. Sometimes, a dissent (the individual opinion of a judge disagreeing with the majority decision) becomes the choice of later judges who recognize that changes in social structure or mores call for a change in the law. These landmark cases do not come about without persuasion based on logic and the views presented in past decisions, by study groups (such as the American Law Institute), and in law review articles, among other sources. Reading and distinguishing the cases is essential. Reporting the results of the research in easily recognizable form contributes to the value of the research by aiding the reader's understanding and appreciation of the researcher/writer's views.

2.0541 Case Citation.   The uniform procedure for citing cases is:

a. Parties' surnames (full names of business entities should be included)

b. Volume number of the reporter containing the case

c. Abbreviated name of the reporter

d. Page number where the case begins

e. Parallel citation (if the case is published in two separate law reports)

f. Date

g. Court that rendered the decision (if necessary)

The latter is required if the reporters (official and parallel) in which the case is published contain decisions of more than one court. It is essential to know which of the courts rendered the decision because the authority of one court may be more persuasive than another or even mandatory. The Harvard Law Review Association publishes *The Bluebook, A Uniform System of Citation*, which illustrates the proper way to cite cases, statutes, and other legal authorities. The researcher is cautioned to follow these rules rather than to follow the form used in an authority. It is not uncommon for incomplete citations to appear within a published authority.

"Parallel citation," mentioned previously, refers to the fact that some cases are printed in more than one publication. When this occurs, one will be designated as the official reporter and the other as the unofficial reporter. As a general rule, the state-authorized publication is the official cite, and the commercially published copy of the decision is the unofficial cite or parallel cite. When the same decision is published in more than one location, the citations are referred to as parallel cites. *The Bluebook* includes a table of the federal and state governments and indicates the appropriate method of citing to the official (and unofficial, if any) publication. It should be noted that many states no longer publish their own cases and instead adopt the commercial publication as the official citation. In these states, the case is published in one location, so there is only one citation reference to a reporter. Parallel cites are not generally used in the statutory citation of laws that have been incorporated into a code.

Citations should omit the first names or initials of natural persons who are plaintiffs or defendants (except in administrative cases), but the entire name of fictitious entities, such as companies or corporations, should be used. For example, cite *Smythe v. Jones*, **not** *John Smythe v. Earl Jones*, but cite *J. M. Smythe Co. v. Smith and Sons Inc.*, **not** *Smythe v. Smith et al.*

With the advent of the availability of court decisions, statutes, and regulations on the Internet, published directly by the courts and other electronic services, a system of "neutral citation" not dependant on the national or official reporter volume and page number has also become acceptable. These citation forms are set forth in the latest edition of *The Bluebook*. An example of citing to other electronic publications which appear on the Internet appeared in the U.S. Supreme Court opinion *Denver Area Education Telecommunications Consortium, Inc. v. FCC*, 518 U.S. 727, 116 S. Ct. 2374, 135 L. Ed. 2d 288 (1996), at footnote 7. The form of the citation was Author (when known), Title, URL (which is the Internet address), and Date last modified (or visited) and looked like this: "[4]See, *e.g.*, Lynch, Speedier Access: Cable and Phone Companies Compete, at **http://www.usatoday.com/life/cyberl/bonus/cb006.htm*** (June 17, 1996) (describing cable modem technology); Gateway 2000 ships first Destination big screen TV-PCs, at **http://www.gw2k.com/corpinfo/press/1996/destin.htm*** (April 29, 1996) (describing computer with both cable TV and Internet reception capability)." The most widely referred to sources for citing to the Internet are Janice R. Walker and Todd Taylor's "The Columbia Guide to Online Style," **http://www.columbia.edu/cu/cup/cgos/idx_basic.html** (Columbia UP, 1998) and Andrew Harnack and Gene Kleppinger's "Beyond the MLA Handbook: Documenting Electronic Sources on the Internet," (June 10, 1996), **http://english.ttu.edu/kairos/1.2/inbox/mla_archive.html.**

2.0542 Federal Reports.

Certain federal cases are reported both officially and unofficially. U.S. Supreme Court cases are reported officially in *United States Reports. Caveat:* Volumes one through ninety must be cited with the name of the official court reporter who compiled the volume and the volume number, for example, *Marbury v. Madison*, 5 U.S. (1 Cranch) 137. There were a number of different reporters over the years who imposed their own numbers on the volumes they compiled. Citing their name and volume obviates any confusion. The unofficial reporters include the *Supreme Court Reporter* (a portion of the national reporter system), which began at Volume 106 of the *United States Reports*, and the *United States Supreme Court Reports, Lawyer's Edition*. Some researchers like the *Supreme Court Reporter* since it incorporates the topic and key number system in the annotation, while others prefer the *Lawyer's Edition* series because it includes a summary of the arguments of counsel on both sides of the question.

The U.S. Supreme Court publishes its decisions immediately upon ruling on an issue as a "slip" decision; slip opinions from the U.S. Supreme Court are available electronically on the day of the ruling or by mail subscriptions. Subscribers to the mail service receive their copy about two weeks after the decision is announced. There are unofficial loose-leaf services that fill the same function but even more quickly than the mail subscription to the official report. Subscribers to both the *Supreme Court Reporter* and the *Lawyer's Edition* also receive advance sheets containing the decisions as they will appear in the forthcoming bound volumes. Slip opinions are also available on Westlaw and on Lexis. The U.S. Supreme Court and many state supreme courts also publish the text of recent decisions on the Internet.

U.S. Courts of Appeals decisions are originally published in nominative reports (reports carrying the name and volume number of the reporter who compiled them) for each federal court, both district courts and circuit courts of appeals, creating a confusing and voluminous problem. West Publishing Company compiled the most important federal decisions, both of district and courts of appeal cases, and published them in a thirty-volume set called *Federal Cases*, dated up to 1880. United States District Courts and Courts of Appeals stopped publishing volumes of decisions and now publish some (but not all) of their decisions as slip opinions. West compiled the slip opinions and published them in bound volumes as the *Federal Reporter* until 1932. In that year, West began the *Federal Supplement*, which accumulated the selected district court and customs court decisions, leaving the *Federal Reporter* to cover only the decisions of the courts of appeals, court of patent appeals, and the court of claims.

In 1940, West began publishing the *Federal Rules Decisions* series, which covers decisions of all the federal courts on procedural law matters as well as articles or speeches on the topic.

---

* These links are simply examples. Please do not expect them to open.

Another source for federal case reporting is the *American Law Reports—Federal*, which includes specially selected and annotated federal court decisions. Citation to any of the preceding "unofficial" reporters is usually acceptable under local district or appellate court rules, a matter easily checked by examination of the court rules in the jurisdiction of the researcher's interest.

The *Supreme Court Reporter, Federal Reporter*, and *Federal Supplement* are part of the national reporter system and use the West topic and key number system.

2.0543 The State Court Reports.

Most states have official reports. In California, for example, there are two official reports: *California Reports*, containing reports of cases decided by the California Supreme Court since March 1850, and *California Appellate Reports*, containing reports of cases determined in the state's district courts of appeal since May 1905. Not all state decisions are published in the official reports because the supreme court can mark some decisions "Not to be Published in Official Reports."

California decisions too recent to be bound are reported in paperback volumes called "advance sheets," that contain both supreme court and appeal decisions, appropriately paginated as they will be in their respective future bound volumes.

Many states do not have a satisfactory method of reporting recent decisions, and the delay in publication of the decisions is a distinct disadvantage to the lawyer and the researcher. As a result, about one-fifth of the states have discontinued production of an official state reports system in favor of a commercial series, which is more efficient to use, current, and indexed. In such states, the series is designated as the official reporter of the state; for example, the *Southern Reporter* is the official reporter for Florida in lieu of the *Florida Reporter,* which ceased publication in 1948.

The *Southern Reporter* is a unit of the national reporter system developed by West Publishing Company, which includes the federal units described previously and the following state and regional reporters:

Atlantic Reporter: contains cases for Connecticut, Delaware, District of Columbia, Maine, Maryland, New Hampshire, New Jersey, Pennsylvania, Rhode Island, and Vermont.

North Eastern Reporter: contains cases for Illinois, Indiana, Massachusetts, New York (court of appeals only), and Ohio.

North Western Reporter: contains cases for Iowa, Michigan, Minnesota, Nebraska, North Dakota, South Dakota, and Wisconsin.

Pacific Reporter: contains cases for Alaska, Arizona, California (supreme court only), Colorado, Hawaii, Idaho, Kansas, Montana, Nevada, New Mexico, Oklahoma, Oregon, Utah, Washington, and Wyoming.

South Eastern Reporter: contains cases for Georgia, North Carolina, South Carolina, Virginia, and West Virginia.

South Western Reporter: contains cases for Arkansas, Kentucky, Missouri, Tennessee, and Texas.

Southern Reporter: contains cases for Alabama, Florida, Louisiana, and Mississippi.

West's California Reporter: contains all California cases from the supreme court, court of appeal, and appellate division of the California Superior Courts since 1960.

West's New York Supplement: contains cases for New York only from 1887 to the present.

West's Texas Cases contains opinions and decisions issued by the state courts of Texas.

Since the inception of the national reporter system in the late 1800s, the states (which had or have official reporters) had parallel reporters—one official and the other unofficial, the commercially published edition. Many decisions reported in the unofficial reporters were not reported in the official reporters. This, together with the headnote system, makes research in the unofficial publications a bit more thorough and informative than that allowed in the official reporters. Unofficial reporters published by West will contain the same topic name and key numbers that are used in all West digest series, making it possible to research the same issue in several jurisdictions very quickly.

All reporters, whether official or unofficial, include similar elements in their publication format, such as:

1. Docket number assigned by the court and the date of the decision
2. Full caption of the case
3. Summary of the case
4. Headnotes
5. Identity of counsel for the parties, including any counsel submitting briefs as *amicus curiae* (friend of the court)
6. Actual opinion

The actual opinion of the court on the subjects at issue is the only "authority" in the reports. Unless otherwise indicated, the summary is prepared by the editor of the reporter to assist the researcher in deciding whether to read the entire opinion or not. While this is helpful, it is not authority and, conceivably, may be in error. The headnotes (short paragraphs with numbers) list the legal issues and points of law covered in the opinion but are not authority. The headnotes are prepared by the editor and are a great aid in quickly determining (1) whether the opinion deals with or relates in any way to the researcher's current specific problem and (2) where in the opinion the particular point of law covered by the headnote is discussed. They are also very important when updating research by Shepardizing (*see* Section 2.06). The actual language in the opinion must be checked to verify that what the summary and the headnotes indicate is truly supported by the opinion text.

The opinion usually starts with the name of the judge writing it, though opinions may be written as *per curiam* decisions—those written expressing the court's view (even if all the judges were not there) or as *en banc* views—those written with all members of the court present and agreeing on the decision. The opinion is followed by a statement of the fact situation of the case, analysis of the points of law argued by the various parties, and the court's opinion and decision on each point raised. The court then states its decision(s) on the case as a whole. Because judges sometimes disagree, a decision also may carry one or more dissenting or minority opinions. The footnotes can also be helpful in finding supporting cases. Many lawyers start by reading the decision at the end of the report as an aid in understanding the language of the opinion that resulted in that decision.

As mentioned in other sections, many state court opinions are now available on the Internet, although most such state court sites do not contain cases any older than 1990.

2.06 USE OF SHEPARD'S CITATIONS OR "SHEPARDIZING"

Query: "Can the cases and laws be brought up to date? Have any of the cases been reversed on appeal or overruled by subsequent cases? Have the laws been amended or repealed? In essence, is our authority really valid authority?"

Shepard's Citations are published for the cases in the U.S. Supreme Court reports, federal reports, National Labor Relations Board (NLRB) reports, some other federal departments' reports, national reporter system, and state reports. This material is accumulated through searches of the various court decisions, agencies' decisions, opinions of attorneys general, articles in legal periodicals, and annotated reports and is available in electronic editions, via CD-ROM or via the Internet.

Shepard's publishes for statutory citations as well, including the *U.S. Constitution, U.S. Code, U.S. Statutes at Large*, treaties and other international agreements, United States court rules, state constitutions, codes, session laws, municipal charters, ordinances, and state court rules. These resources are also available in electronic media, such as CD-ROM and via online services such as LexisNexis and Westlaw (which has replaced Shepard's with its own similar system, Keycite). While *Shepard's* is available both in the hard-bound version and online, it should be pointed out that today's courts expect that cases will be validated online since the online version is much more up-to-date; some court decisions are entered into *Shepard's* within twenty-four hours of being decided.

Every reported case is collected and examined at Shepard's, and the cases and statutes mentioned in each reported case are recorded and printed under their own citations in the Shepard's publications. By this process, the history of the cited cases and laws is developed. Editors read the cases and, where required, note the history and treatment of the case. A table of abbreviations for consultation is provided at the front of each volume. If the same case is affirmed on appeal, a lowercase *a* appears in front of the citation; *cc* represents a connected case that is a different case but arising out of the same subject matter; capital *D* stands for dismissed, *m* for modified, *r* for reversed, *s* for same case, and *v* for vacated. Capital *S* for superseded case and parentheses indicate parallel citations. In the treatment of the case, *c* indicates criticized, *d* distinguished, *e* explained, *f* followed, *h* harmonized, *j* dissenting opinion, capital *L* limited, *o* overruled, *p* parallel, and *q* questioned. If any of these symbols appears at the front of a citation, for example, "s 167 FS 405," check the table of abbreviations at the front of the volume to confirm what the abbreviation means.

Frequently a case will cite another case for only one point of law in the cited case that may have had as many as twenty points of law analyzed in headnotes. In the book version, in order to indicate to the researcher that the citing case discussed only one point of law, a smaller number, called a superior figure, appears before the page number a little elevated from the line of type to show which headnote relates to the discussion in the citing case, e.g., "377 US[1] 555."

In the electronic version, the annotations are simplified. The report on the case is broken into three sections. The first section is the summary and contains the summary of how the case has been treated, along with colored bookmarks. Green indicates that the case has not been reversed and is still good case law; a yellow triangle replaces the "c" in the books for criticized; and a red stop sign indicates that the case has either been vacated or reversed. The summary breaks down how the case is treated; i.e., the number of cases which followed it, concurred with it, explained it, etc.

The second section provides the prior history for the case. The third section provides the citing decisions and breaks them down by courts. The U.S. Supreme Court cases are first, followed by the appellate and then the district courts. (*See* Exhibit 2.9.)

As stated before, the resources of the law library will control the scope of the research to a large extent. This chapter covers a variety of the Shepard's publications in the hope that the paralegal has access to some of the titles or at least similar titles so that these techniques may be applied to the resources at hand.

2.061   Case Research

The scope of case research in *Shepard's* can be limited to the state jurisdiction, expanded to neighboring states, federal cases, or all reported cases in accordance with the titles selected.

2.062   State Shepard's Citations

As discussed in Section 2.06, the courts recommend that the use of Shepard's should be done online for more current information. Both the online version and hard bound version of *Shepard's Citations* cover every state with volumes listing every case in that state that has been subsequently discussed in any

EXHIBIT 2-9   Sample Pages from Shepard's

UNITED STATES SUPREME COURT REPORTS						Vol. 364
Cir. 4	237FS¹566	456FS³673	j306F2d¹476	255So2d69	379US¹143	j568FS1461
537FS393	CtCl	506FS³2	313F2d¹38	Md	380US¹540	Cir. 1
— 297 —	198CCL624	541FS¹872	314F2d1228	226Md600	383US¹311	376F2d¹541
s278F2d446	461F2d1379	76FRD³600	355F2d¹362	174A2d783	j383US¹672	570F2d¹1075
Cir. D.C.	Mo	82FRD⁴609	362F2d¹120	NY	385US¹130	295FS¹206
292F2d756	352SW681	94FRD³241	410F2d81	33Msc2d521	387US¹108	385FS¹882
293F2d153	NY	Cir. 7	445F2d832	227S2d87	d391US¹384	405FS¹1394
294F2d221	13Ap2d209	346F2d³251	191FS¹683	Ore	393US¹391	j451FS¹154
j294F2d228	215S2d191	f525F2d¹764	d222FS¹986	229Or246	j393US589	70FRD¹655
547F2d699	Pa	408FS⁴1161	238FS¹757	230Or6	j396US453	Cir. 2
Cir. 2	497Pa63	68FRD⁴385	242FS¹298	235Or66	j398US¹193	j294F2d¹44
380F2d777	498Pa535	85FRD20	326FS530	366P2d886	400US¹126	j379F2d497
205FS836	439A2d103	98FRD721	Cir. 3	367P2d400	j400US¹283	j487F2d¹265
— 298 —	448A2d1048	13BRW860	486F2d¹1105	383P2d1004	400US¹389	c482F2d266
s371US807	Wis	18BRW⁴798	330FS¹496	Pa	402US141	510F2d814
s371US907	53Wis2d400	Cir. 8	361FS21	222PaS372	403US⁵	e510F2d¹522
s371US944	192NW897	476F2d²60	28FRD440	295A2d100	d403US¹149	j510F2d530
s374US203	47ABA458	Cir. 9	28FRD495	Wash	j403US¹177	512F2d49
s177FS398	— 310 —	316F2d⁴789	39FRD¹340	63W2d323	403US¹225	e191FS¹184
s184FS381	(5LE8)	337F2d¹750	Cir. 4	387P2d80	j403US¹264	196FS¹762
s195FS518	(81SC13)	f399F2d895	344F2d¹742	— 336 —	405US¹70	202FS¹744
s201FS815	s361US958	481F2d⁴1190	351F2d¹422	Case 1	j406US¹576	202FS¹754
Cir. 3	s364US938	487F2d¹675	202FS¹664	s76Nev157	407US¹194	202FS755
j465F2d863	s270F2d290	708F2d⁴1492	218FS¹597	Nev	j407US¹483	d211FS¹466
Cir. 9	s301F2d133	38FRD²197	237FS¹65	s350P2d724	j408US¹390	j211FS¹468
77FRD36	379US¹158	Cir. 10	Cir. 5		409US¹521	j211FS¹473
Cir. 10	401US⁴335	446FS⁴908	286F2d¹752	Case 2	412US¹751	d214FS¹901
689F2d914	406US¹17	76FRD346	290F2d¹398	s18Il2d506	413US¹368	j229FS¹779
Md	j449US926	Alk	290F2d¹431	Ill	j418US¹778	d238FS¹926
228Md247	52FCC1271	499P2d602	291F2d¹420	s165NE322	j418US¹808	260FS¹208
228Md259	Cir. D.C.	632P2d543	297F2d¹417	— 337 —	422US1378	d266FS¹325
179A2d702	424F2d⁴907	DC	319F2d¹366	Case 1	425US¹142	j271FS¹16
179A2d709	Cir. 2	305A2d530	325F2d¹159	s364US925	j425US¹148	271FS¹499
— 299 —	392F2d384	468A2d1342	335F2d¹197	s170OS393	426US¹254	290FS¹883
s279F2d289	522F2d158	Ind	346F2d¹874	Ohio	429US¹266	j311FS¹55
s290F2d858	f541F2d¹952	263Ind195	405F2d¹949	s165NE642	430US¹165	341FS¹148
Cir. 6	568F2d⁴906	325NE843	585F2d¹741		430US¹170	d377FS¹1166
311F2d47	668F2d108	Mich	249FS¹379	Case 2	430US¹179	386FS7
— 300 —	226FS²372	99McA858	331FS1289	s359Mch430	j430US¹181	429FS¹212
s271Ala22	349FS705	390Mch656	426FS¹375	Mich	j430US¹511	473FS¹495
Ala	359FS⁹14	213NW136	514FS¹1204	s102NW552	433US¹414	476FS323
s122So2d280	440FS1092	298NW870	Cir. 6		442US¹272	f535FS¹1017
— 301 —	445FS⁴722	Mo	340F2d¹730	— 338 —	j442US283	Cir. 3
(5LE1)	506FS⁴308	572SW867	662F2d¹434	Case 1	446US¹62	j535F2d¹812
s185Kan274	63FRD50	Ohio	305FS¹1185	Mo	e446US¹85	563F2d¹582
Kan	66FRD⁴228	330A228	Cir. 7	s335SW118	j446US102	564F2d¹141
s341P2d1002	82FRD4	293NE329	322FS519	Case 2	j446US127	d648F2d¹182
Cir. D.C.	23BRW283	Ore	Cir. 8	s171OS192	j446US214	233FS¹620
419F2d¹312	Cir. 3	271Or311	401FS17	Ohio	j458US652	262FS¹828
Cir. 1	312F2d³372	532P2d4	Cir. 9	s168NE409	51USLW [4858	j262FS¹857
f254FS¹255	407F2d673	Tenn	d343F2d¹221	— 339 —	51USLW [4861	419FS¹273
369FS¹1114	420F2d⁴1276	637SW884	369F2d¹300	(5LE110)	j51USLW [5116	468FS¹951
Cir. 2	534F2d569	Wash	371F2d¹783	(81SC125)	Cir. D.C.	536FS¹584
190FS¹625	663F2d⁴425	100W2d349	495F2d916	s362US916	395F2d587	567FS¹1515
Cir. 3	346FS⁴994	670P2d243	d203FS¹725	s270F2d594	452F2d¹306	Cir. 4
561FS⁴137	382FS474	MFP§6.16	213FS¹356	s167FS405	459F2d1247	397F2d¹41
356F2d¹654	484FS409	— 325 —	Cir. 11	j366US1573	465F2d¹638	442F2d¹572
347FS1254	519FS1562	(5LE20)	224FS¹249	369US1229	j481F2d530	459F2d¹1097
Cir. 5	58FRD447	(81SC6)	Calif	369US1244	j489F2d¹1174	j459F2d¹1100
333F2d¹640	81FRD³662	s362US909	228CA2d697	j369US¹284	520F2d¹70	j459F2d¹1109
523F2d1286	89FRD64	s271F2d194	44CA3d355	j369US1335	j559F2d694	462F2d1068
319FS522	96FRD⁴235	j375US212	39CaR763	d372US¹376	593F2d1111	j462F2d1078
Cir. 6	484FS312	379US¹672	118CaR518	j372US1386	661F2d1303	463F2d56
421F2d¹765	37FRD⁴435	51USLW [4103	Conn	376US156	255FS¹299	j473F2d¹1021
489FS¹43	Cir. 5	63MC935	153Ct78	376US¹58	j333FS¹590	573F2d¹190
Cir. 9	413F2d1281	66MC1561	171Ct276	376US¹59	349FS¹729	588F2d¹424
377FS¹152	616F2d¹747	67MC2155	214A2d366	376US¹68	d354FS¹1030	664F2d919
Cir. 10	639F2d⁴1284	Cir. 1	368A2d230	377US¹206	374FS¹377	710F2d¹135
513F2d137	661F2d¹52	434F2d¹122	Fla	376FS1352	198FS¹503	
620F2d779	Cir. 6	608F2d18	139So2d403	377US¹555	411FS¹654	245FS¹245
	429FS183	608F2d¹20	Ill	j377US¹615	568FS¹1460	d267FS267
		Cir. 2	79Il2594	j377US¹744		269FS848
		297F2d¹11	399NE175	378US¹287		d276FS¹668
			La			313FS386
			260La46			Continued

— (continues) —

Gomillion v. Lightfoot, 364 U.S. 339,81 S. Ct. 125, 5 L. Ed. 2d 110,1960 U.S. LEXIS 189 (1960)

SHEPARD'S Signal(TM): ▲ **Caution: Possible negative treatment**
Restrictions: *Unrestricted*
FOCUS(TM) Terms: *No FOCUS terms*
Print Format: *FULL*
Citing Ref. Signal: *Hidden*

SHEPARD'S SUMMARY

Unrestricted *Shepard's* Summary

No subsequent appellate history. Prior history available.
Citing References:

▲ Cautionary	**Criticized (1), Distinguished (40)**
Analyses:	
Positive Analyses:	Followed (18)
Neutral Analyses:	Concurring Opinion (16), Dissenting Op. (99), Explained (17), Harmonized (1)
Other Sources:	Law Reviews (747), Secondary Sources (3), Statutes (23), Treatises (13), Annotations (3), Court Documents (178)

LexisNexis Headnotes: **HN1 (69), HN2 (24), HN3 (35), HN4 (29), HN5 (3), HN6 (46), HN7 (38), HN8 (9), HN9 (46),HN10(22)**

PRIOR HISTORY (2 citing references)

1.   *Gomillion v. Lightfoot*, 167 F. Supp. 405, 1958 U.S. Dist. LEXIS 3431 (D. Ala. 1958)

2.   **Affirmed by:**
     Gomillion v. Lightfoot, 270 F.2d 594, 1959 U.S. App. LEXIS 3363 (5th Cir. Ala. 1959)

     Reversed by (CITATION YOU ENTERED):
     Gomillion v. Lightfoot, 364 U.S. 339, 81 S. Ct. 125, 5 L. Ed. 2d 110, 1960 U.S. LEXIS 189 (1960)

CITING DECISIONS (630 citing decisions)

U.S. SUPREME COURT

3.   **Cited in Dissenting Opinion at:**
     Parents Involved in Cmty. Sch. v. Seattle Sch. Dist. No. 1, 127 S. Ct. 2738, 168 L. Ed. 2d 508, 2007 U.S. LEXIS 8670, 75 U.S.L.W. 4577, 20 Fla. L. Weekly Fed. S 490 (U.S. 2007)
         127 S. Ct. 2738 *p.2817*
         168 L. Ed. 2d 508 *p.394*

4.   **Cited in Dissenting Opinion at:**
     League of United Latin Am. Citizens v. Perry, 548 U.S. 399, 126 S. Ct. 2594, 165 L. Ed. 2d 609, 2006 U.S. LEXIS 5178, 19 Fla. L. Weekly Fed. S 425 (2006)
         548 U.S. 399 *p.457*
         126 S. Ct. 2594 *p.2632*
         165 L. Ed. 2d 609 *p.656*

(continues)

5.   **Cited in Concurring Opinion at:**
      Cox v. Larios, 542 U.S. 947,124 S. Ct. 2806, 159 L. Ed. 2d 831,2004 U.S. LEXIS 4765 (2004)
         542 U.S. 947 *p. 950*
         124 S. Ct. 2806 *p.2808*
         159 L. Ed. 2d 831 *p.833*

6.   **Cited in Dissenting Opinion at:**
      Vieth v. Jubelirer, 541 U.S. 267, 124 S. Ct. 1769, 158 L. Ed. 2d 546, 2004 U.S. LEXIS 3233, 72 U.S.L.W. 4301,
      17 Fla. L. Weekly Fed. S 237 (2004)
         541 U.S. 267 *p.321*
         124 S.Ct. 1769 *p.1801*
         158 L. Ed. 2d 546 *p.585*

7.   **Cited by:**
      Grutter v. Bollinger, 539 U.S. 306, 123 S. Ct. 2325, 156 L. Ed. 2d 304, 2003 U.S. LEXIS 4800,71 U.S.L.W. 4498,
      16 Fla. L. Weekly Fed. S 367, 2003 Cal. Daily Op. Service 5378, 84 Empl. Prac. Dec. (CCH) P414I5, 91 Fair
      Empl. Prac. Cas. (BNA) 1761 (2003)
         539 U.S. 306 *p.327*
         123 S. Ct 2325 *p.2338*
         156 L. Ed. 2d 304 *p.331*

8.   **Followed by, Cited by:**
      Rice v. Cayetano, 528 U.S. 495, 120 S. Ct. 1044, 145 L. Ed. 2d 1007, 2000 U.S. LEXIS 1538, 68 U.S.L.W. 4138,13
      Fla. L. Weekly Fed. S 105, 2000 Cal. Daily Op. Service 1341, 2000 Colo. J. C.A.R. 898, 2000 D.A.R. 1881 (2000)
      LexisNexis Headnotes HN1
         Followed by:
         528 U.S. 495 *p.522*
         120 S. Ct. 1044 *p.l060*
         145 L.Ed. 2d 1007 *p.1029*

         Cited by:
         528 U.S. 495 *p.513*
         120 S.Ct. 1044 *p.1055*
         145 L. Ed. 2d 1007 *p. 1024*

9.   **Explained by, Cited in Dissenting Opinion at:**
      Reno v. Bossier Parish Sch. Bd., 528 U.S. 320,120 S. Ct. 866, 145 L. Ed. 2d 845,2000 U.S. LEXIS 993, 68 U.S.L.W.
      4086, 13 Fla. L. Weekly Fed. S 87, 2000 Colo. J. C.A.R. 444, 2000 D.A.R. 873 (2000) **LexisNexis Headnotes
      HN1, HN7**
         Explained by:
         528 U.S. 320 *p.334*
         120 S. Ct. 866 *p.875*
         145 L. Ed. 2d 845 *p.860*

         Cited in Dissenting Opinion at:
         528 U.S. 320 *p.360*
         120 S. Ct. 866 *p.888*
         145 L. Ed. 2d 845 *p.875*

later case in that state or federal system. The state *Shepard's* edition also incorporates any state case that is not reported in the national reporter system (primarily those decided prior to 1887). *ALR* and legal periodical citations are included in the *Citator*. The first time a case is mentioned in *Shepard's Citations*, the parallel citation to the national reporter system is given but not repeated in subsequent volumes.

Every unit of West's national reporter system has a companion *Shepard's Citator*. To use the contents, convert the state citation to the regional reporter citation. Under the reporter citation will be listed every case discussed in any later case in that regional reporter and all other reporters in the national reporter system as well as federal reporters. *ALR* and *American Bar Association Journal* citations are also included. The first time a case is mentioned in *Shepard's Citations*, the parallel citation to the state reports is given but not repeated in subsequent volumes.

2.063   Federal Shepard's Citations

Again, the online version of Shepard's is recommended to ensure the most up-to-date information. Both the online version and hard bound version of *Shepard's United States Citations* and *Shepard's Federal Citations* list every case citing the federal cases in alphabetical order by state, given the state or national reporter citation.

To research a federal case in Florida, for instance, consult the proper federal *Shepard's* and find a Florida case or a *Southern Reporter* citation. Then take that citation to the *Florida Shepard's Citations* or the *Southern Reporter Citations* and research that case through the state or regional system.

2.064   Statutory Research

Knowing the wording of a law may be insufficient to resolve a controversy between litigants, and resorting to court interpretation of the law is required. *Shepard's Citations* exist for state and federal statutory research, giving the citations to cases interpreting the laws as well as editorial notations as to changes in the law by legislative bodies.

Armed with the proper citation to state or federal constitutions, codified law, or session laws, it is possible to determine what courts have mentioned the laws in their opinions as well as subsequent changes in the law. Cases holding a law unconstitutional will have *U* prior to the citation alerting the researcher to this important fact. Tables of abbreviations at the front of the volume explain the meaning of the symbols used in the text. Again, law review articles, attorney general opinions, and *ALR* annotations specifically identifying the law will be cited in *Shepard's*.

Laws frequently are known by popular names but cannot be identified in indexes that way. *Shepard's* incorporates a "Table of Acts by Popular Names or Short Titles" in its statutory division as well as in a separate publication, *Shepard's Acts and Cases by Popular Names*. This is frequently the best source to consult for the proper statutory citation.

Municipal or county ordinances are included in the state *Shepard's Citations* when they have been interpreted and construed by the courts. These are usually arranged in alphabetical order by geographical unit and then alphabetically within the unit by catchword identification of the ordinance. Usually an index accompanies these for easy identification.

2.065   Court Rules

State and federal court rules can be Shepardized either in the state *Shepard's Citations* or *Shepard's Federal Citations*. The latest cases are cited under the number of the rule along with changes in the rules and periodical citations.

2.066   Administrative Decisions

Shepard's United States Administrative Citations includes other decisions by administrative agencies, such as the tax court, Interior Department, Federal Communications Commission, Federal Trade Commission, Treasury decisions, opinions of the Attorney General of the United States, and many others. Again, these decisions will be included if they have been mentioned specifically by name in later decisions. Notes will accompany the citations of subsequent changes in the points of law considered.

2.067   Shepard's Labor Law Citations

This very specialized system includes decisions and laws relating to labor. NLRB decisions and orders form the basis for the content. Extensive coverage of periodical literature is included. One of the distinct advantages of this title is the reporting of the parallel citations for the different commercial services publishing editions of labor materials. Patents and trademarks are also the subjects of specialized treatment in *Shepard's United States Citations*.

2.068   Law Review Articles

Shepard's Law Review Citations lists law review articles by citation and subsequent articles and court decisions that cite the original article. This permits one to locate a good article on a given subject and then trace it through later literature for other good articles on the same subject. New in 1974 was *Shepard's Federal Law Citations in Selected Law Reviews*. This compiles references from nineteen law reviews to federal court cases, federal rules decisions, and the *U.S. Constitution, U.S. Code*, and federal court rules. From these federal sources of primary authority, it is now possible to pinpoint law review articles that mention them specifically by name.

2.069   Supplements

Supplements to *Shepard's Citations* take the form of bound volumes and cumulative paper pamphlets in red or ivory color, with individual advance sheets in white. As information accumulates, the red pamphlet is revised and reissued with instructions to discard previous pamphlets. Be sure to check the notice on the front cover of the pamphlet as to the parts of the series that make up the whole unit of *Shepard's Citations*. The hard copy supplements to *Shepard's Citations* are published and delivered several weeks behind the available information. With online services such as Westlaw or Lexis, the time for *Shepard's Citations* updates moves to within twenty-four to forty-eight hours. Many judges (or their clerks) will check case law submitted via Westlaw or Lexis to confirm it is good law before a ruling. It is crucial that all memoranda are citing good law when submitted to the court to as close to the date of filing as possible.

     Total reliance on *Shepard's Citations* without substantiation from other sources could be harmful. *Shepard's* gives the history and treatment of a case by judges in later decisions. It does not cite all cases on a point of law. It should not be used as a substitute for a researcher bringing the search up-to-date through the reporter or statute being searched. *Shepard's* is designed as a complementary aid to research. Cases can cite other cases, not for the point of law involved, but for the amount of damages or some other phase of the case; therefore, cases cited in *Shepard's* must be checked for their pertinence to the question at hand. On the other hand, a case can completely change the areas of the law by a grand, sweeping statement that "all former decisions not in accord with this opinion are overruled." If such statements include no reference to cases affected (either by name or citation), they never will appear in *Shepard's Citations*.

The use of *Shepard's Citations* may yield more cases on the subject of inquiry and shed some light on the direction the law is taking in the area. In addition, it should turn up related sources that were not uncovered in prior research. Finding a case in *Shepard's Citations* may at first glance seem to be confusing, but it is easily resolved by consulting the back side of the title page to each volume. This page indicates the volumes of citing materials included in the *Shepard's* volume. Start with the first volume of *Shepard's Citations* (of any series) and examine the contents indicated on the spine. If the case or statute is of early vintage, in all likelihood it will be in this volume. Examine every subsequent volume for newer cases, law review articles, and other sources that cite the given case or statute. If the case is a relatively recent one, it may not be in the first volume. Advance forward through the volumes until you find the first mention of the case citation of interest. This procedure should become apparent when the volume itself is used.

2.07 REVIEW OF THE BASIC RESEARCH PROCESS

1. If unfamiliar with the particular area of law, locate a reference that discusses it, such as a legal encyclopedia or other commentary.

2. Identify a number of different terms that pertain to the topic of research. A legal thesaurus or dictionary may be helpful in doing this task.

3. If the research question involves or is likely to involve a statute, go to the subject index of the appropriate code and use the terms previously identified to locate the appropriate reference to a statutory chapter (title) and section number.

4. After locating the statute, read the text and examine any relevant annotations that might follow. If the allocation of billable hours permits, check the legislative history (analysis) available either in the firm's legal research file system or other official sources.

5. If the issue is not statutory or if there are no annotations, go to the digest. Again, use the identified terms with the descriptive word index (subject index) of the digest. These will help locate the topic and key number (section) for finding annotations or case summaries (also called headnotes) on the specific subject.

6. After reading the annotations, select those most applicable to the case at hand and locate the complete decision in the reporter system by using the citation given in the annotation. This citation will contain the case name, reporter volume and page, and year of the decision.

7. After reading the complete judicial opinions, note those that most closely resemble the research issue and general facts of the case at hand. Generally, those decisions that come from the same jurisdiction and most closely parallel the case being researched will be the most persuasive.

8. Prepare the correct citation for those authorities that are going to be used to respond to the research issue. Develop a handwritten outline, based on the priority of the cases and the issues each represents. This is the beginning of your memoranda, and because these notes may be discarded after preliminary research, it should be only a rough map, so you will not get lost along the way. Then go to the *Shepard's Citations* volume for the reporter where the case or statute is published, and, using the volume and page number, locate the *Shepard's Citations* volume for that particular case or statute. The volume and page appear in boldface, and any subsequent references appear immediately below.

9. In all stages of research, be aware that most publications, whether commentary, statutes, digests, or *Shepard's*, contain supplements or pocket parts with the most up-to-date information. These must be consulted to determine the most current law on a particular subject.

2.071 Let's Research

As you prepare to do your research, get ready to be alert, dig out facts needed to prove the client's side of the case, alert the lawyer to strong cases adverse to the client's position, and find or distinguish cases in rebuttal. Above all, be prepared to accept constructive criticism. Such criticism is an invaluable learning aid, and a lawyer who takes time to give thoughtful advice and constructive criticism is one who is interested in helping the paralegal advance and improve. One common criticism of a new paralegal's work is that it does not express the lawyer's own personal style. In both legal research and legal writing, a paralegal should try to style his or her work in a way that complements the attorney's. Do not be offended if the lawyer does not accept the offered writings in every instance or totally rewrites a proffered offering; try to think as the lawyer does and gear the style of the work product to his or her liking.

The research examples given here will be simple; they are illustrations of the sequence of researching and will pertain to one point of law only.

2.072 Facts—Example No. 1

In 1994, Sam Smith (plaintiff) sued General Hospital (defendant) and other medical practitioners at the hospital (codefendants) for malpractice. In 1995, that suit was settled, and an order of dismissal, with prejudice, was entered by the court.

In 1997, General Hospital (plaintiff), represented by the paralegal's firm, filed a collection suit against Sam Smith (now the defendant) in the amount of $1,800, representing the 1994 hospitalization expense. Smith filed an answer and counterclaim, alleging malicious prosecution among other things. In Smith's counterclaim, the amount sought for relief exceeded the jurisdictional dollar amount in Municipal Court and the action was transferred to Superior Court.

The paralegal for the firm representing General Hospital is asked to determine whether (1) the counterclaim of Smith states a valid cause of action for malicious prosecution and (2) can an action for malicious prosecution be raised by way of a counterclaim.

A review of defendant Smith's counterclaim by the paralegal reveals that Smith alleged the amount of the bill ($1,800) was included in the settlement of his medical malpractice claim in 1994 and that General Hospital waived payment of the bill as part of the settlement at that time. General Hospital's position is that the settlement only included the cause of action for malpractice against the hospital, the release signed by Smith released only General Hospital from such a claim, and the release neither contained a provision for waiving the amount of the bill nor was authority for waiving the bill given by the hospital in settlement of that case.

Beginning with a secondary source, such as *Corpus Juris Secundum* (*also see* 2.042, Secondary Authority and 2.0514, Legal Encyclopedias) or in California perhaps, Witkin, *Summary of California Law,* 10th edition, the paralegal determines that to establish a cause of action for "malicious prosecution of a civil proceeding" a plaintiff must plead and prove three points:

    a. that the prior action was commenced by or at the direction of the defendant and was pursued to a legal termination in his (the plaintiff's) favor;

    b. that the prior action was brought without probable cause, and

    c. that the prior action was initiated with malice.

In reading the secondary sources, the paralegal noted the cases cited or referred to and now begins reading them. The paralegal quickly learns that malicious prosecution is a cause of action not favored by law. Shepardizing (*see* 2.06, Use of Shepard's Citations or "Shepardizing") develops cases the paralegal reads and finds that malicious prosecution cannot be raised by way of cross-complaint. The paralegal's memorandum to the lawyer might take the form shown in Section 2.074.

2.073 Facts—Example No.2

John Law, a California highway patrolman, was injured while making an arrest and attempting to prevent Willy Henry from falling down. Law subsequently filed a civil suit against Henry and John Smith for personal injury. Law's employment records were subpoenaed, and the state of California claimed they were privileged. Determine whether the claimed privilege applies, and draft a letter in support of the contention that they are not privileged, if so indicated. The state claims privilege under California Government Code Section 6254 and California Evidence Code Section 1040. Begin the research by reading the code sections cited.

It appears clear that the code sections cited to not apply to a private citizen who files a civil suit for injury. Then read the California Code of Civil Procedure's applicable sections relating to discovery and confirm that the records are not privileged under those provisions.

2.074 Research Memorandum—Example No.1

MEMO

To: Ace, Attorney at Law
From: Deuce, Paralegal
Re: *General Hospital v. Smith*
Date: 1/26/2007

Issue 1:   Does Smith's counterclaim state a valid cause of action?
Issue 2:   Can malicious prosecution be raised by way of a counterclaim?

Issue 1: Elements of Proof

1. Prior action was commenced by or at the direction of the Defendant (General Hospital) and pursued to legal termination in favor of Plaintiff (Smith).
2. Prior action was brought without probable cause.
3. Prior action was initiated with malice.

Conclusion:

Smith's counterclaim fails to state a cause of action upon which relief can be granted, or facts sufficient to constitute proof of any of the above necessary elements. Smith's inability to plead favorable termination of the prior action will prove fatal through a motion to dismiss. *Bertero v. National General Corp.*, 13 Cal. 3d 43, 118 Cal. Rptr. 184, 529 P.2d 608 (1974); *Tool Research & Engineering Corp. v. Henigson*, 46 Cal. App. 3d 675, 120 Cal. Rptr. 291 (1975).

Issue 2: Discussion

The case of *Babb v. Superior Court*, 3 Cal. 3d 841, 92 Cal. Rptr. 179, 479 P.2d 379 (1971), involved the question of whether a defendant in a civil action might file a cross-complaint seeking declaratory judgment; that in the event the action terminated favorably to him the action be adjudged to have been instituted and prosecuted maliciously and without probable cause. The trial court overruled a demurrer contending that favorable termination of the prior proceeding is a necessary precondition to the maintenance of a malicious prosecution action, on the ground the cross-complaint was not premature since it sought only declaratory relief. The Supreme Court reversed the ruling and ordered the lower court to vacate its order and sustain the demurrer without leave to amend. This decision was based on the conclusion "that precedent, principle, practicality and policy forbid such a cross-complaint, which entails the risk of discouraging legitimate claimants." The Court stated, at page 846:

> First, there is a certain metaphysical difficulty in permitting a counterclaim for malicious prosecution since theoretically that cause of action does not yet exist.

The Court further stated, at pages 847 and 848:

> Third, the rule of favorable termination is supported by strong policy considerations. (5) Since malicious prosecution is a cause of action not favored by the law, (*Sebastian v. Crowley* (1040), 38 Cal. App. 2d 194, 202 [101 P.2d 120]; Note (1949) 58 Yale L.J. 490, 494), it would be anomalous to sanction a procedural change which not only would encourage more frequent resort to malicious prosecution actions, but would facilitate their use as dilatory and harassing devices. Abolition of the requirement that malicious prosecution suits be filed as separate actions after termination of the main litigation would surely increase the incidence of such suits, since filing a cross-action requires less time, expense, and preparation than does initiation of a separate action. Furthermore, the introduction of evidence on the issues of malice and probable cause may prejudice the trier of fact against the plaintiff's underlying complaint, or enhance the possibility of a compromise verdict. Even if, as here requested, consideration of those issues is deferred until the principal action has been completed, an outcome of that trial adverse to the plaintiff may unduly enhance the defendant's chances in his malicious prosecution action. Finally, as was the case here, the plaintiff and his attorney may be joined as cross-defendants in the malicious prosecution suit. This not only places the attorney in a potentially adverse relation to his client, but may well necessitate the hiring of separate counsel to pursue the original claim. (*See* Note, *supra,* 58 Yale Law Journal 490, 493, and fn. 13.) *The additional risk and expense thus potentially entailed may deter poor plaintiffs from asserting bona fide claims.* (Emphasis added.)

It is hornbook law that the plaintiff in a malicious prosecution action must plead and prove that the prior judicial proceeding of which he complains terminated in his favor.

> Because of this requirement it is obvious that a defendant cannot cross-complain or counterclaim for malicious prosecution in the first or main action, since a claim cannot state a cause of action at that stage of the proceedings. This appears to be the rule, not only in California, but generally. (*Baker v. Littman, supra,* 138 Cal. App. 2d 510, 514; 2 Witkin, Summary of Cal. Law (1960) Torts, 97, P. 1268).

Conclusion:

Malicious prosecution should not be allowed by way of cross-complaint in the main action. Failure to plead prior favorable termination is fatal; cross-complainants cannot allege a favorable determination of the underlying action.

2.075   Memorandum and Draft Letter—Example No.2

MEMO

To: Ace, Attorney at Law
From: Deuce, Paralegal
Date: 6/6/2007
Re: Privileged Records—Draft of Letter to State

Gentlemen:

We are in receipt of your records, forwarded to Naida Love, C.S.R., with your letter of May 11, 2007. We are also in receipt of the declaration attached thereto for the records withheld and deemed privileged, signed by Jack W. Lewis, state services analyst. You cite as authority for claiming privilege Government Code section 6254(b), (c), and (f) and Evidence Code section 1040. We submit that under the fact situation in this lawsuit, the privilege does not apply to "(3) Correspondence and reports pertaining to the December 10, 2004, injury which occurred on duty and from which Officer Law sustained a lower back injury. Injury Record card excluded." We are not concerned with the records listed in the balance of the declaration.

In support of our position, we call your attention to the following facts:

1. Enclosed is a copy of the amended complaint for personal injury filed by John Law. You will note that the charging allegations are that John Smith provided defendant Willy Henry with alcoholic beverage during the course and scope of his employment, that defendant Henry negligently and wrongfully assaulted, battered, and struck plaintiff about the face, head, back, body, and legs, causing severe bodily injuries, frightened plaintiff, and placed plaintiff in great fear for his life and physical well-being. In addition, the complaint alleges that these acts were done with malice and ill will and with the intent and design of injuring and oppressing plaintiff. The claim for punitive damages in the complaint has been dropped by stipulation of counsel. These injuries allegedly were the result of acts required of plaintiff in the course and scope of his employment. Further, in verified answers to interrogatories, plaintiff contends that defendant violated "ordinances, codes and statutes relating to reckless driving, speeding, improper lane change, failure to yield to a red light, resisting arrest, failure to obey lawful order of police officer, drunk driving and public drunkenness, and assault and battery."

2. Mr. Law is claiming back pain at the conclusion of putting the defendant in the car and that he later developed left leg problems. Further, he had surgery that he relates to this accident and may need further surgery. Asked why the facts surrounding the arrest as described by him in deposition were not included in his arrest report, he pointed out it is the Garden City's California Highway Patrol office policy not to charge intoxicated persons with resisting arrest or assault and battery on a peace officer unless the officer has actual signs of injury, such as lacerations, broken bones, etc., and, therefore, he felt the facts stated by him in deposition were not relevant to the charge of driving under the influence. He further testified that he reported the incident at the jail to his superior, Sgt. Lager, and later that evening the sergeant completed an injury report.

3. Your cited subdivisions to Government Code section 6254 (b), (c), and (f) are not applicable in this instance. Subsection (b) relates to "pending litigation to which the public agency is a party or to claims made pursuant to Division 3.6 (commencing with section 810)..." In this instance, the "public agency," or the California Highway Patrol, is not a party, nor is this suit filed against public entities or public employees (section 810). Rather, it is a private lawsuit by a California Highway Patrol officer for injuries resulting from an arrest made by him while on duty as an officer. Subsection (c) relates to personnel, medical, or similar files, the disclosure of which would constitute an unwarranted invasion of personal privacy. Here, again, we submit that by filing a civil action for personal injuries as a private citizen, plaintiff Law has subjected himself to the normal discovery available to defendant to prepare a defense to the suit and, thus, correspondence and reports pertaining to the injury are a proper subject of discovery to substantiate the injuries and

the circumstances surrounding same and that he has, in essence, waived the privilege regarding his reports and work records relating to the injury. This material is relevant and should be produced. Subsection (f) does not appear to state a privilege insofar as this lawsuit is concerned.

4. Your cited Evidence Code section 1040 refers to "official information," which is defined as "information acquired in confidence by a public employee in the course of his or her duty...." We submit that the correspondence and reports pertain to the December 10, 2004, injury of plaintiff Law. We suggest that they are, in view of his personal civil lawsuit, business records and should be produced as such under the provisions of California Evidence Code section 1560. Further, provision (b)(2) of Section 1040 provides for privilege if disclosure of the information is against public interest because there is a necessity for preserving the confidentiality of the information that outweighs the necessity for disclosure in the interest of justice. Our position is that the withholding of this information would be against public interest and prejudicial to the defendants in preparation of their defense.

Defendants cannot obtain this information through their own efforts, and under the facts, the necessity for disclosure in the interest of justice outweighs the necessity for preserving the confidentiality of the information.

We will appreciate your forwarding the material described under number (3) of your declaration relating to privileged and withheld records.

Sincerely,
Ace, Attorney at Law

2.08 MODERN TECHNOLOGY AND LEGAL RESEARCH

The reliance by courts and lawyers on precedent, the recorded accounts of the decisions in past litigation, as well as the gradual proliferation of statutes (whether amplifying old law or creating new) have made big business out of libraries and publishing houses. The increasing volume of decided cases and learned dissertations on facets of the law, the growth in regulatory agencies with their obligatory rules and regulations, increasing numbers of law schools and students, and the continuing legal education courses across the country all assure that the production of law source, reference, and citator books will greatly expand in the years ahead. It also ensures that an adequate law library is no mean investment to create or to maintain. Large firms find it necessary to equip their libraries with more than one volume of some law books, even of some sets of books. It is one of the observed, but untitled, laws that whenever a particular law book is desperately needed to check an authority, form, or reference for a last minute filing at court, that book will be checked out or misfiled within the library or another attorney is also engaged in a last-minute research project in the same volume.

Other types of library problems are the need for a dedication of labor time in posting and updating the reference books with pocket parts, rearranging shelves to make space for new acquisitions and replacement volumes, restoring books to the proper shelf, and performing emergency searches for wanted but checked out volumes. The space needed to create a law library is another consideration. At current commercial property rates in metropolitan areas, the financial impact of space alone is substantial.

The modern technologies of photography and computers can be applied to solve some of these nagging problems. Many public legal offices and private law firms are reducing the size of their library while at the same time increasing their library resources through the use of CD-ROM and Internet technology.

Perhaps the greatest strides in legal research have been made in the area of computer access to resource materials. The developments in the last few years alone are phenomenal and can only be expected to continue. It is entirely conceivable, if not probable, that most bound-volume libraries have been replaced by computer terminals with access to the resources located in databases (collections of information that can be retrieved through a computer) on-site or across the country. Certainly these terminals are an integral part of most comprehensive libraries.

One of the major computer research systems is Westlaw, created by West Publishing, which provides access to such sources as statutes, the West digest series, the national reporter system, *Shepard's Citations*, and *Oran's Dictionary of Law*. Another similar system is LexisNexis, a division of Reed Elsevier Inc. There is also a system similar to *Shepard's Citations* known as *Auto-Cite*, offered by the Lawyers Cooperative Publishing Company. One of the more recent developments is West Publishing's CD-ROM Libraries, which allow research for a specific jurisdiction rather than a nationwide scope, a much less expensive system. CD-ROM will be discussed in greater detail later. Additionally, certain governmental entities have similar computer research systems. In all of these systems, the user inputs a query into the system and receives an information response relevant to the query. This is seemingly a simple process. As with all legal research, a particular skill must be developed in formulating the appropriate question in order to gain the most valuable information and the least amount of irrelevant information.

2.081   Computer-Based Systems

2.0811 Online Sources.
Online sources generally refers to those resources available through use of a computer with a modem, although many use the term loosely to include any computer-based reference material.

2.08111 Database Service Providers.
The two major database service providers for legal research are Westlaw and LexisNexis. Both services require that accounts be established in advance and charge for use on a per-minute basis, although some "flat rate" plans are also available. Because charges for use are time-based, it is imperative that the attorney or paralegal have a query formulated prior to "signing on." It is also a wise practice to narrow the issues as much as possible before using these resources.

The benefits to both of these services is that they are updated on a daily basis and contain thousands of state and federal legal documents such as published and unpublished opinions, constitutions, statutes, regulations, court rules, presidential papers, law reviews, legal periodicals, and special databases on select topics of wide interest. Some of the special topical databases include civil rights, workers' compensation, family law, insurance, commercial litigation, asbestos litigation, and many others. Additionally, each has an online system for Shepardizing cases.

Search results from both these systems, including the full text of any document, are available by downloading the information to the computer's hard drive (allowing the ability to cut-and-paste quoted portions into legal memoranda and briefs), by fax transmission (useful when away from the office), and by printing to a printer attached to the computer. The ability to send the results via fax is especially helpful in situations where the attorney needing a printed copy of a case is elsewhere, such as in a judge's chambers or a courtroom.

2.08112 The Internet.
One of the fastest growing online legal research sources is the Internet. Many Websites providing such resources on the Internet are available free of charge—which is a great benefit—or require a nominal subscription fee. For access to the Internet, Internet Service Providers (ISPs) provide flat fee accounts at extremely low cost when compared to the online time-based access charges of some legal research services.

The organizations that sponsor sites of interest for legal research purposes tend to be major universities and law schools, state and federal governmental agencies, state and federal court systems, the U.S. Congress, and national legal professional organizations. The legal sources available are not as extensive as those available through Westlaw and Lexis, although the collections are growing by the hour, with the largest limitation being the time period covered (many collections do not have materials prior to 1990). The other major drawback to Internet research is that the search engines available are often not as discriminating as those provided by Westlaw and Lexis, making it more difficult to narrow a search quickly. In general, this is because Westlaw and Lexis are a series of structured, related, and linked databases, while the Internet is a collection of unrelated and often unlinked databases with no consistent structure.

The most effective use of the Internet for legal research is to consider it a secondary source for locating information. For example, the U.S. Supreme Court maintains a Website where its decisions are published instantly when announced. An independent student publication, *LLI Bulletin*, is a Cornell Law School electronic journal. *LLI Bulletin* prepares a synopsis of the opinions which it sends its subscribers within hours by e-mail. The e-mail, in addition to containing the opinion synopsis, contains a hypertext link to the U.S. Supreme Court's official full text opinion as well as to a related site at Cornell University which maintains a collection of prior decisions. Another excellent resource in the area of constitutional law is provided by the House of Representatives in the form of a full text version of the U.S. Constitution, Amendments, and the Bill of Rights which is annotated by citation and linked to interpreting decisions of the U.S. Supreme Court.

2.08113 Court System Services.   In addition to the Internet, the federal courts (and a growing number of state and local courts) are providing bulletin board systems (BBS) which allow certain kinds of access to court files. In general, these services are more useful for pretrial investigation purposes because they usually do not include access to case law or statutory law, although they do provide access to court rules (*see* Chapter 7, Section 7.0331, Court Records).

2.0812 CD-ROM Libraries.   Another component of computer-assisted research is CD-ROM libraries. The development of this system has made computer research affordable for virtually any size firm or organization. The concept is quite simple. Compact discs containing research materials for a particular subject of law or jurisdiction are loaded into a compact disc player attached to a personal computer and the information on them is retrieved by the computer. As with Westlaw, one can retrieve headnotes, cases, statutes, and so on. Because the user purchases only those discs his or her library needs, there is no cost for access through telephone lines to the Westlaw database or for access to all published statutes and cases nationally. Because approximately three hundred thousand pages of information can be contained on a single disc, space requirements are extremely low, compared with a standard library. Additionally, updated discs allow the researcher to retrieve the most current information. CD-ROM also has word processing capabilities that enable the researcher to copy information from the disc and incorporate it into a brief or other document.

2.082 Computer-Assisted Research Methods

2.0821 Formulating a Query.   The first step in computer-based research is to formulate a query. This is the discipline of writing down what it is you are really interested in finding. It is always a good practice to refine your search topic before you log on to an online service because this saves significant time—and online services charge for the time you spend using them.

2.0822 Boolean Logic and Wildcards—Tools to Refine a Search.

George Boole, a nineteenth-century mathematician, developed a system to describe language in mathematical/logical terms. Traditionally, the Boolean Search system is used by most online services, as well as by many Internet search engines, to retrieve documents. Although "natural language" tools also exist, they are based on the Boolean system. Boolean logic uses words and connectors to create phrases and concepts based on certain set rules. When using the basic framework of Boolean logic, the computer can search for documents containing specific words or combinations of words requested. Some common words such as "the," "and," or "when" cannot be used as search terms, because of the extremely large number of hits a search containing those terms would generate. (A "hit" is a document that matches search criteria.) Some letters in a word can be replaced in the search by an asterisk (*) or exclamation point (!) to denote variations of a root word or a different spelling (for example: wom*n will search for women and woman; child! will search for child, children, and childish in addition to any plural or possessive forms). By placing quotation marks around words, the entire word grouping will be searched (example: "clean air act"—without the quotes, it would list every document that contained either "clean," "air," or "act" or any combination of those three words).

"Natural" or freestyle language is also used by online services to enable simple queries, such as "Does Massachusetts law contain a common law marriage provision?" The search is broader in this form but will find documents or cases based on a computer-generated Boolean search.

2.0823 Example of a Westlaw Search Query

STEP 1:

Understand how the system works. The user logs on to a computer with Internet capabilities. The user then accesses the Westlaw site and, based on the user's queries, receives information back from the Westlaw databases. The user is able to review the information and, if desired, print a hard (paper) copy to his or her local printer, e-mail the results, or cut and paste selected/highlighted information to a word-processing document.

Though the query process will be discussed briefly here, since most Westlaw or other computerized legal research programs charge a fee for conducting the research, it is very important that the paralegal become proficient in how to efficiently and effectively conduct the research. The current training offered by Westlaw can be found at **http://west.thomson.com/westlaw/training** and consists of your choice of Web-based training, telephone (one-on-one) training, classroom training, on-site training for groups where a trainer comes to your office, and various user guides. Some of the training is directed specifically to paralegals. Westlaw also has telephone support lines where you can walk through your query before actually logging on.

The process of legal research is quite similar for most systems. For the purposes of demonstration here, reference will be made to the Westlaw system. As with any type of legal research, the first step is to identify the jurisdiction whose authority is being sought. For example, if research is being done for a case pending in Pennsylvania, the researcher would be primarily concerned with the legal standards issued by the courts and legislature of that state. In computer research, this step is known as identifying the "field." Once the correct field has been entered into the computer, all queries will be directed to the law of that field.

STEP 2:

Formulate the query. The cost of computer research is based on either (1) the time the system is in use (incremental hourly fee for online time) or (2) transactional use (the user is billed for each search and the price per search varies). In cases where the firms do not offer both types of passwords, the default for both Lexis and Westlaw is the transactional password, which means the user is also billed for each search in addition to incremental hourly fees for online time. Because of the cost factor, research should be performed efficiently. In all legal research, including that which is computer-assisted, it is necessary to determine the issue with as much specificity as possible. Once the issue has been defined, the researcher must select those terms relevant to the issue and identify any variations or synonyms of them. It is also important to make it broad so that you can use the "focus" feature of both Westlaw and Lexis to narrow down your search to the most relevant cases. Otherwise you would be charged for each search you conduct.

One law firm teaches their paralegals and associates to use the transactional ID when they are going to run one to two searches and to use the hourly ID when they want to run a lot of searches. If they are going to read the cases online, they need to be sure they are in transaction mode instead of hourly mode. Also, remember that not all files are created equal; some are three times as expensive as others. Obtaining a cost sheet of the cost of searching the various files would reflect which are more expensive tools in formulating searches accordingly when using the transactional ID.

To arrive at variations that might be used in place of the original term, the researcher needs only to identify the root of the term and follow it immediately with an exclamation point (!). This instructs the database to produce all authorities in the field that contain the root of the word and any variation. If the only relevant variations differ by only a few letters, an asterisk (*) can be used within the original term at any place where a different letter might appear in a variation. The system automatically searches for plural forms of terms, so these need not be identified as variations.

STEP 3:

After the terms and their variations are selected, it is important to connect the terms properly using Boolean logic. This will aid in limiting the information retrieved to relevant authorities. The system interprets a space between letters as the word or; for example, the system would interpret a query of "malicious prosecution" to mean locate any authority containing the word malicious or the word prosecution or both.

Connectors are symbols that tell the computer how closely terms in the query must appear to one another in order to be retrieved. For example, the symbol "/s" between two terms means that the terms must appear within the same sentence of an authority before the system will retrieve it. Similarly, the symbol "/p" means that the terms must appear within the same paragraph of an authority before the system will retrieve it. The "/s" symbol is so limiting that relevant cases or statutes may be missed, while the "/p" symbol may cause numerous irrelevant authorities to appear. Basically, knowledge of the subject and the likelihood of authority will guide the researcher in determining which connectors or combination of connectors to use between terms. When an authority is retrieved, the terms of the query will be highlighted where they appear in the authorities. It is possible to retrieve only the citations of the authorities or to examine the specific text of each authority.

The researcher who has a specific citation of a relevant authority may call up that citation without going through the query process by using the "find" command or by doing a field search. To do this, the researcher enters the name of the statute or case or volume, page, and report citation, or both, if available. The computer will then retrieve all cases in the field by that name; if the volume and page are available, the specific case is called up. Instacite can be used to provide the researcher with direct and indirect history in the particular case.

STEP 4:

Identify variations of the terms that might be used in authorities on this issue:

Elements—element

Malicious—maliciously, maliciousness, malice

Prosecution—prosecute

STEP 5:

Construct the query. Element requirement factor component and or /p malic! malevolent wanton and /p prosecut***

STEP 6:

Input the query, review the headnotes, and select the decisions that appear to address the issue most directly.

STEP 7:

If the results are not satisfactory, modify the query and input it.

STEP 8:

Call up the complete decisions of the selected headnotes and review.

STEP 9:

Shepardize those decisions that will be used as authority.

At virtually any point, the research process can be converted to standard book research. For example, if the printed materials are also available, it may be more cost effective to perform the research by computer through Step 7 and then read the decisions in the actual books. This compatibility with book research is an additional benefit of computer-assisted research.

Courts expect that cases will be Shepardized online. Court decisions are constantly being updated, and *Shepard's* online is much more up-to-date than the books. Some court decisions are even entered into *Shepard's* within twenty-four hours of being decided. *Shepard's* has two options: (1) to find cases and (2) to verify your citations. In verifying your citations, you can limit *Shepard's* to negative treatment which will only give information on cases that have negative impact on the case's validity.

2.083   Benefits of Computer-Based Media

As the power, efficiency, ease of use, and economics of computer research continues to improve, it is becoming more widespread and commonplace. Computer-based libraries have become more cost-effective than traditional bound-volume collections because of the cost savings available in terms of both shelf space and updates of hardbound volumes. Additionally, the portability of CD-ROM volumes along with the capability of using laptop computers with modems to access the growing number of online services are benefits of computer-based media that simply cannot be matched by traditional bound-volume libraries. One of the biggest advantages of computer research through Lexis or Westlaw is that you can use Boolean logic to refine and focus your searches to narrow the hits to useable information.

2.084 Photography, Microfilm, Microfiche, and Microform

Photography, microfilm, microfiche, and microform are older technologies for storage of data which the researcher may encounter in public libraries, government institutions, and private industry, although the trend has been and continues to be a move toward electronic and digital media such as CD-ROM. Because these various media may still be encountered, this section will briefly describe them.

Photography can reduce printed pages to the size of a typewriter's letter with resolution quality that allows a lighted viewing screen to restore the image to clear, readable size, even allowing the production of hard copy prints of the image. Whole volumes can be reduced onto one or several cards of microfiche or microform or rolls of microfilm.

Microfilm usually refers to the reduction of material into photographs on film rolls. Several thousand page-size images can be stored on one roll. The roll of film can be equipped with keyed film image counters that allow the indexing of its contents.

Microfiche began as transparent cards with sleeves into which microfilm strips were slipped, allowing the assembly to be handled as a four-by-six-inch card, easily filed and easily adapted to the assembly of one increment of information or topic. The reader equipment is less expensive than for microfilm, since no transport mechanism is needed and focusing problems are minimized. Copying requires slightly different equipment.

Microforms are microfiche further reduced to exceptionally small size, allowing hundreds or thousands of images on one card. One such form, "ultrafiche," has been used to provide units of the *National Reporter System* to subscribers. Each volume (approximately 1,450 pages) is on one ultrafiche card. The readers for the process have a nine-by-twelve-inch screen and can be mounted on a library table or office desk. Separate equipment is needed to make paper copies. Such devices as these eliminated the space requirements where mass storage of hard copy volumes was involved, producing a major space and economic benefit. They also reduced the problem of the "borrowed but not returned volume."

2.09 RESEARCH DELEGATION CONSIDERATIONS

The most commonly delegated research assignments to paralegals consist of Sheppardizing cited cases, reviewing cases for proper citation, and locating cited cases for review by the attorney. As the attorney becomes more confident in the paralegal's abilities, the types of research projects may be expanded to include finding relevant cases, statutes, or relevant sections of constitutions underlying a point of law, reviewing and summarizing cases, and preparing internal memoranda of law.

At first the paralegal's research projects will be basic and carefully detailed in scope, purpose, form, and time allowed for completion. Typically the problem may be one requiring little interpretation, such as "identifying each state code section or reference relating to riparian water rights." The project has easily defined parameters and can be checked easily by the attorney in order to verify the accuracy and thoroughness of the paralegal's work. A second assignment might be "locate each riparian water rights case decided since 1850 and distinguish each to our present case issue of beneficial water use, briefing chronologically those cases which mention this issue."

Legal research requires skill, perception, hard work, and a candid and forthright recognition by the paralegal of his or her own limitations. The lawyer has a wealth of knowledge obtained both at law school and in practice which allows him or her relatively quick recognition and appreciation of the sometimes complex and/or convoluted views expressed in some case opinions. The paralegal cannot, without equivalent training and experience, expect to, nor be expected to, perform with the same insight, legal writing skills, and appreciation of legal expressions as the employing attorney.

Both the attorney and the paralegal must adopt a mutually confident and comfortable posture which recognizes these differences in training and performance.

2.10   RESEARCH TASKS

Before allowing a paralegal to do legal research, the attorney must have confidence that the paralegal is trained, well-informed, and capable. A working rapport and understanding must be established between the attorney and the paralegal. Most of the tasks shown following can be performed either by the attorney or the paralegal; however, some require more knowledge and insight than a paralegal might have or more than his or her training will allow. Other tasks can and should be performed by a paralegal as a great time saver to the attorney.

RESEARCH TASKS	Attorney	Paralegal
Check cites and Shepardize a case or statute.	X	X
Prepare a table of authorities for a brief.	X	X
Given a West key number, a fact situation, and a point of law:		
Read summaries of cases listed under this number to find relevant cases.	X	X
Given a fact situation and a point of law:		
Go to appropriate sources to find relevant cases; update those cases to see if there have been any decision changes regarding that point of law.	X	X
Given a fact situation and a point of law:		
Find statutes or ordinances bearing on the issue and update statutes through supplements and session laws.	X	X
Given a particular question or point of consideration:		
Find relevant sections of constitution (federal and state).	X	X
Read cases and prepare a brief synopsis of each.	X	X
Organize research results into memo form.	X	X
Given a fact situation and a point of law:	X	
Determine whether there are constitutional considerations.		
Write a brief.	X	*

* *Primarily an attorney's job; however, a paralegal can assist in drafting and supplying technical information, such as legal descriptions, cites, and organizing exhibits.*

2.11   SUMMARY

The more experience and expertise the paralegal demonstrates, the more complex the research possibilities will become. Be absolutely certain to understand what is expected and avoid assignments totally beyond current skills and knowledge, since this will result in disaster both for the paralegal and the supervising attorney. As with all research topics, validate the information by review and corroboration of the issues and the facts.

One of the basic concepts of the role of the paralegal is to enable the lawyer to provide legal services at less cost to the client. The competent research of paralegals will enhance this aim, and the paralegal will become an even more valuable member of the staff in the law office.

BIBLIOGRAPHY

Cohen, Morris L., *Legal Research in a Nutshell,* 6th ed. St. Paul, MN: West, 1996.

Cohen, Morris L., Berring, Robert C., and Olson, Kent C., *How to Find the Law,* 9th ed. St. Paul, MN: West, 1989.

Harnack, Andrew and Kleppinger, Gene, "Beyond the MLA Handbook: Documenting Electronic Sources on the Internet," June 10, 1996, http://english.ttu.edu/kairos/1.2/inbox/mla_archive.html.

How to Use Shepard's Citations. Colorado Springs, CO: Shepard's Citations, n.d.

Jacobstein, J. Myron and Mersky, Roy M., *Fundamentals of Legal Research,* 8th ed. Westbury, NY: Foundation Press, 2002.

Jacobstein, J. Myron and Mersky, Roy M., *Legal Research Illustrated: An Abridgement of Fundamentals of Legal Research.* Westbury, NY: Foundation Press, 1987.

Koerselman, Virginia, Legal Research, 2000, A NALA Campus Course, On-line Self Study Program for Paralegals. www.NALACampus.com.

Price, Miles O., et al., *Effective Legal Research,* 4th ed. Boston: Little, Brown & Co., 1979.

Rombauer, Marjorie Dick, *Legal Problem Solving: Analysis, Research, and Writing,* 5th ed. St Paul, MN: West, 1991.

Statsky, William P., *Legal Research and Writing: Some Starting Points,* 3rd ed. St. Paul, MN: West, 1985.

Statsky, William P., *Legislative Analysis and Drafting,* 2nd ed. St Paul, MN: West, 1983.

Statsky, William P., *West's Legal Thesaurus-Dictionary.* St. Paul, MN: West, 1986.

The Bluebook, A Uniform System of Citation, 17th ed. Cambridge, MA: Harvard Law Review Association, Gannett House, 2000.

Walker, Janice R. and Taylor, Todd, "The Columbia Guide to Online Style," http://www.columbia.edu/cu/cup/cgos/idx_basic.html (Columbia UP, 1998).

West's Law Finder: A Legal Research Manual. St. Paul, MN: West, 1990.

3

Ethics

3.00 INTRODUCTION

Codes of ethics in the legal profession, whether promulgated by courts or professional associations, are not mere guidelines, which practitioners may follow or ignore—they are standards to which attorneys and paralegals must adhere or risk their professional careers. Paralegals must heed not only the ethics required by their profession, but must also be aware of and abide by those required of lawyers. Traditionally, the

legal profession has pursued and maintained a goal of assuring high standards of professional competence and ethical conduct. As part of the legal profession, the paralegal must maintain the same high
standards of professional conduct.

The past two decades have brought many changes and advances in the paralegal profession and the
recognition and increased utilization of paralegals by attorneys. This advancement and utilization have
also raised questions about what activities a paralegal may perform and still remain within accepted
professional boundaries and ethical limitations. One must ascertain what standards and principles exist
for a paralegal to follow to assure that the conduct and activities performed do not cross the boundary
into the realm of potential liability for the unauthorized practice of law. Questions on legal ethics are not
always easily answered. Conduct cannot always be simply categorized as right or wrong. A knowledge
of ethical considerations will assist in this decision process. The NALA *Code of Ethics and Professional
Responsibility*, NALA *Model Standards and Guidelines for Utilization of Legal Assistants* (Annotated),
provisions of the American Bar Association (ABA) *Model Rules of Professional Conduct*, provisions of
the American Bar Association *Model Guidelines for the Utilization of Legal Assistant Services*, and similar state codes of professional conduct for attorneys and paralegals and case law are necessary sources
for the paralegal to obtain this knowledge. The NALA *Code of Ethics and Professional Responsibility* with
its *Model Guidelines* has provided paralegals with meaningful guidelines to enable them to perform
their duties and remain within all ethical boundaries relating to standards of competence and ethical
requirements imposed on attorneys.

The American Bar Association has traditionally provided attorneys with meaningful guidelines
for competent and proper representation of their clients and the public interest as a whole. The most recent formal attorney conduct guidelines of the ABA are found in the Model Rules of Professional Conduct, adopted in 1983. The predecessor to the Model Rules was the ABA Model Code of Professional
Responsibility, which consisted of canons, ethical considerations, and disciplinary rules. Provisions of
the former Model Code have been incorporated into the present *Model Rules,* and the provisions of each
consider substantially similar subject matter or reflect similar concern. To the extent that the ethics and
disciplinary rules of the Model Code offer further explanation or clarification, they can and should be
relied on as a resource for professional standards and as a supplement to the current Model Rules. The
ABA Model Guidelines for the Utilization of Paralegal Services, adopted August 1991 and last revised in
2003, is another source of ethical guidelines. Guidelines 2 and 3 relate to the actual utilization of paralegals, while Guidelines 1 and 4–10 are specific to the ethical requirements imposed on the lawyer who
employs paralegals. All states have at least some equivalent code of professional conduct or responsibility statute governing the conduct of attorneys within their jurisdiction. The paralegal should be familiar
with the provisions of the attorneys' code applicable in his or her jurisdiction because the employing
attorney has a responsibility to see that the paralegal abides by the standards for ethical conduct set out
in the code. Rule 5.3 of the ABA Model Rules specifically requires that in employing a nonlawyer, the
attorney "shall make reasonable efforts to ensure that the person's conduct is compatible with the professional obligations of the lawyer." This requirement is imposed on the attorney because the "assistants,
whether employees or independent contractors, act for the lawyer in rendition of the lawyer's professional services" (Comment, Rule 5.3, ABA Model Rules of Professional Conduct).

Courts also continually render opinions interpreting the ABA Model Code and Model Rules, in
addition to disciplinary code provisions for a particular jurisdiction. The American Bar Association
President appoints a Standing Committee on Ethics and Professional Responsibility, which publishes
formal and informal opinions relating to code provisions. State and local bar associations also may offer
formal and informal opinions on questions relating to ethical conduct.

Self-regulatory efforts to pursue and maintain professional conduct and provide meaningful
guidelines for ethical behavior are also a tradition in the paralegal profession. In 1975, the National

Association of Legal Assistants (NALA) adopted its own Code of Ethics and Professional Responsibility. The NALA Code has been refined and amended over the years and is provided in its current form in Section 3.061 of this chapter. Each canon of the NALA Code considers the same types of subject matter and concerns that are addressed in the rules and codes governing attorney conduct, including attorney conduct involving the utilization of nonlawyers. NALA recognized that the paralegal's conduct must be compatible with the obligations of the attorney since the ultimate interests served are the same. Accordingly, Canon 10 of the NALA Code mandates that a paralegal is governed by bar associations' codes of professional responsibility and rules of professional conduct.

In 1984, NALA determined that the growing employment of paralegals by attorneys made it necessary to develop an educational document relating to utilization standards and guidelines as guidance to the legal profession on acceptable conduct for paralegals. The culmination of NALA's research and efforts in this area is the Model Standards and Guidelines for Utilization of Legal Assistants (Annotated), which is provided in Section 3.062 of this chapter. These guidelines were developed from existing case law, professional standards of conduct governing attorneys and their use of paralegals, and other authorities. In short, the guidelines served to answer three basic questions about paralegals: who are they, what are their qualifications, and what duties may they perform. Section IV of the Model provides an excellent outline of the ethical standards and principles for paralegals and guidance for the attorney in utilizing a paralegal.

3.01 DUTIES A PARALEGAL MAY PERFORM UNDER THE SUPERVISION OF AN ATTORNEY

As noted in the introduction to this book, the NALA definition of a paralegal includes the caveat that the legal work being performed by the individual is done under the supervision of an attorney. The rationale for inclusion of this aspect will become obvious in the discussion of guidelines, codes, and case law that follows.

Kentucky was the first state to actually adopt a separate paralegal code within its supreme court rules; this code recognizes the use of paralegals and sets forth certain exclusions to the unauthorized practice of law. But the code also expressly mandates that the attorney must supervise the paralegal and must remain responsible for the work:

> For purposes of this rule, the unauthorized practice of law shall not include any service rendered involving legal knowledge or advice, whether representation, counsel or advocacy, in or out of court, rendered in respect to the acts, duties, obligations, liabilities or business relations of the one requiring services where:
>
> a. The client understands that the paralegal is not a lawyer;
>
> b. The lawyer supervises the paralegal in the performance of his duties; and
>
> c. The lawyer remains fully responsible for such representation, including all actions taken or not taken in connection therewith by the paralegal to the same extent as if such representation had been furnished entirely by the lawyer and all such actions had been taken or not taken directly by the attorney.

Canon 2 of the NALA Code of Ethics and Professional Responsibility addresses this question as follows: "A paralegal may perform any task which is properly delegated and supervised by an attorney, as long as the attorney is ultimately responsible to the client, maintains a direct relationship with the client, and assumes

---

Paralegal Code, *Ky. S. Ct. R. 3.700, Sub-Rule 2.*

professional responsibility for the work product." This language is not only compatible with the Kentucky Code but also with EC 3-6 of the ABA Model Code of Professional Responsibility, which provides:

> A lawyer often delegates tasks to clerks, secretaries, and other lay persons. Such delegation is proper if the lawyer maintains a direct relationship with his clients, supervises the delegated work, and has complete professional responsibility for the work product.

Various states have included similar provisions in attorney professional responsibility codes. For example, EC 3-6 of the *Florida Rules of Professional Conduct* provides:

> A lawyer or law firm may employ nonlawyers such as secretaries, law clerks, investigators, researchers, paralegals, accountants, draftsmen, office administrators, and other lay personnel to assist the lawyer in the delivery of legal services. A lawyer often delegates tasks to such persons. Such delegation is proper if a lawyer retains a direct relationship with his client, supervises the delegated work, and has complete professional responsibility for the work product. The work that is delegated is such that it will assist the employing attorney in carrying the matter to a completed product either by the lawyer's personal examination and approval thereof or by additional effort on the lawyer's part. The delegated work must be such as loses its separate identity and becomes either the product or else merged in the product of the attorney himself.

In addition to the general professional responsibility codes regulating the use of nonlawyers by attorneys, many states have adopted specific guidelines for the use of paralegals.[1] These guidelines are generally not part of the attorney's professional responsibility code but have been developed to emphasize the requirement that attorneys must supervise the work that is delegated to the paralegal and must accept complete responsibility for the final work product. Case law is also useful in determining what constitutes the unauthorized practice of law. The paralegal should from time to time research recent decisions relating to the unauthorized practice of law. Thus, the paralegal should be familiar with not only the professional code for attorneys in his or her state or practice jurisdiction, but also with any additional guidelines or decisions regarding the use of paralegals.

PRACTICE TIPS

- Be familiar with the content and know where to find all rules, codes, and other regulations governing the attorneys in your firm and locale.
- Confirm answers to any ethical questions you may have by consulting the regulations and following up with your supervising attorney.
- Know that an attorney's livelihood demands that paralegals strictly adhere to the ethical rules.

3.02 ETHICAL CONSIDERATIONS IN THE WORK ENVIRONMENT

The ethical considerations for paralegals do not end with proper delegation and supervision by the attorney. The paralegal must be conscious of other ethical considerations when carrying out assigned tasks. The paralegal must examine and be aware of the relationship between specific concepts and principles contained in the codes of professional responsibility and the conduct and activities performed by the paralegal as part of the legal services team.

3.021 The Paralegal in the Client-Lawyer Relationship

3.0211 Accepting Clients and Setting Fees. Canon 3 of the NALA *Code* specifically prohibits a paralegal from engaging in the practice of law by accepting cases and setting fees. (*Also see* NALA Model Standards and Guidelines, Guideline 2 for a discussion of case law regarding such prohibited acts.)

The paralegal may not establish the attorney-client relationship. While the paralegal may be involved in obtaining initial information from a prospective client, the attorney must make the final decision to accept the case. The paralegal must also be extremely cautious in quoting fees for legal services. Making general statements about approximate fees that might be charged for a particular service is a very unwise practice, even when the employer may have an established schedule listing fees for various services. There may always be exceptions to the set fees, and until the attorney has discussed the specific legal problem with the client, neither the services required nor the reasonable fee is certain.

PRACTICE TIPS

- Make it clear to prospective clients or existing clients with new matters that only the attorney may agree to provide legal services.
- Be aware that in some kinds of cases, for example, class actions, paralegals in some jurisdictions may accept as new clients, members of the class who meet specific criteria which has been defined by the attorney.
- Tell individuals who are persistent in asking for an estimate of the fee that it is unethical for you to quote fees.

3.0212 Competence and Integrity. Canon 6 of the NALA Code stresses competence and integrity. Rules 1.1 and 8.4 are the counterpart rules in the ABA Model Rules of Professional Conduct. As with attorneys, paralegals must not only maintain present skills and knowledge, but they must also keep current and informed about changes in procedures and the law. Knowing how things used to be done and what the law was will not enable the paralegal to perform competently. The paralegal is a professional. To retain that status, a competent paralegal must pursue a continuous program of self-education and reeducation. Attendance at workshops and seminars in substantive areas of the law and in the paralegal's specialty is essential. Reading legal publications, case summaries, and professional association publications will keep the paralegal on the cutting edge. Integrity means strict personal honesty and independence and is generally understood to preclude any dishonest or unethical conduct. The paralegal must adhere to the highest standards of truth, honesty, and loyalty to assist the attorney in maintaining integrity, not only in the attorney-client relationship, but also in all activities conducted in the professional capacity.

PRACTICE TIPS

- Arrange to receive announcements of upcoming seminars given for attorneys or paralegals.
- Submit a request to attend relevant seminars.
- Supplement your request with the seminar brochure and comment on how such attendance would benefit your employer.
- Read promptly periodicals from attorneys' professional organizations as well as those from paralegal organizations.

3.0213 Diligence and Communication.

Canon 9 of NALA's Code of Ethics requires a paralegal to do "all other things incidental, necessary, or expedient for the attainment of the ethics and responsibilities as defined by statute or rule of court." In a profession fraught with deadlines, diligence and an absence of procrastination cannot be emphasized too strongly.

A paralegal is often responsible for docket control on matters involving time deadlines. A supervising lawyer must make reasonable efforts to ensure that a paralegal's conduct is compatible with the professional obligations of the lawyer, including the duty to act with "reasonable diligence and promptness in representing clients" as required by ABA Model Rule of Professional Conduct 1.3. The paralegal will also frequently keep clients updated on the status of cases or matters. Clients will often rely on the paralegal to get information because they may prefer to talk to the paralegal rather than the attorney. A paralegal may explain procedural matters to clients, but making a legal judgment on a client's behalf as to what procedure is best would be improper. If the paralegal is merely passing on information or a decision made by the attorney, the communication by the paralegal is not improper. A paralegal must be on guard in these situations to ensure that he or she does not give legal advice or perform any acts that involve professional legal judgment. Such activities are addressed in Canons 3, 4, and 5 of the NALA Code because the exercise of professional legal judgment is the practice of law.

PRACTICE TIPS

- Discipline yourself to timely performance of duties and responsibilities.
- Advise your supervisor if your workload is so excessive you are unable to perform tasks in a timely manner.
- Learn to prioritize your work.
- Other things being equal, tackle first the tasks you are unsure how to do.
- Remember many tasks are not difficult once you start.
- Be cautious in communications with clients and others to avoid giving legal advice.
- Make certain that all with whom you communicate are aware that you are not an attorney.
- Make certain that a system of docketing filing deadlines, statutes of limitations, and other important dates is used and that such information is regularly communicated to the attorneys.

3.0214 Confidential Information and Privileged Communications.

A paralegal is constantly exposed to confidential matters that concern the affairs of clients as well as information about client matters or cases in performing job functions. All of this information must be kept confidential and should not be revealed in casual or indiscreet conversations, particularly with individuals outside the workplace. Canon 7 of the NALA Code addresses this ethical responsibility for paralegals, and the ABA counterpart for attorneys is Rule 1.6.

A communication made to an attorney in professional confidence within the realm of the attorney-client relationship is considered a privileged communication. Under the Federal Rules of Evidence, these communications are generally not permitted to be disclosed, or allowed to be discovered, by third parties except where there may exist an exception to the general rule. Other similar privileged relationships exist, such as those between physician and patient or husband and wife, which are established by statute, constitutional mandate, or common law. Any communication made by a client to the paralegal in confidence while in the course and scope of professional employment is generally considered to be as if the communication were made to the attorney and therefore will be considered to come under the attorney-client privilege. Disclosures to third persons of any such communications should never be made by the paralegal unless directed to do so by the attorney, by court order, or expressly consented to by the client.

Work done by the attorney for a client as part of the attorney's work product is also subject to privilege considerations. When the work of the paralegal is directed, supervised, authorized, and required by the attorney as part of the service provided the client, it is generally considered to fall under this same attorney work product privilege. The paralegal must assume that each communication sent or received, each document generated, every note taken, and so on falls under this privilege and must protect the privilege until the attorney, the client, or the court authorizes or orders disclosure. It is critical to remember at all times that these privileges can be lost through unintentional and inadvertent disclosure to third persons.

Confidentiality takes on a whole new meaning with the advent of computerized information and electronic data transfer. The use of cellular phones carries with it responsibility for safeguarding information that can be accessed by outside parties. The paralegal should be aware that the confidentiality of sensitive information may be at risk when such information is transmitted by cellular phone. Courts in some jurisdictions have held that there is no reasonable expectation of privacy in the content of cellular or cordless phone conversations. Others have held that one has the same expectation of privacy with a cellular or cordless phone as one has with a "landline." Fax transmittals should always be accompanied by a cover sheet containing a disclaimer that the information is confidential and for the use of the intended recipient only. Care should be taken to ensure that faxes are sent to the correct location. By the same token, Internet e-mail should be used with caution, since it carries with it the same risk characteristics as fax transmittals and cellular or cordless phone transmission—all can be intercepted by or inadvertently disclosed to third persons. Always ascertain what ethical considerations apply in your jurisdiction and what procedures your supervising attorneys prefer. Another concern is that metadata (data about data) is embedded in nearly every form of digital information. When sending e-mail attachments, and especially those sent to opposing counsel or the court, attachments should be stripped of this metadata to avoid revealing competitive or confidential information.

Internet and digital technologies provide a broader level of communication, but that benefit is at the expense of privacy and confidentiality. Rule 34(a) of the *Federal Rules of Civil Procedure* allows a party to serve on any other party a request to permit the "inspection and copying of…data compilations…through detection devices." Courts have interpreted this language to include access to computer disks, hard drives, backup tapes, e-mail, and other electronic data. Every user should be aware that e-mail messages, file transfers, and Internet conduct are all potentially discoverable by a knowledgeable party. (*See* Wendi Webb, "The New Age of Electronic Discovery," *Legal Assistant Today,* May/June 1996 and James A. Powers, "O What A Tangled Web We Weave," *Facts & Findings,* May 1996.)

PRACTICE TIPS

- When speaking with a client, close doors and make sure that no third party is listening to the conversation.
- Protect your computer screen from being read by other persons by turning it away from office doors and windows or by obtaining a filter screen to place over the monitor.
- Do not talk about work-related matters when socializing with friends or in any public place.

3.0215 Conflict of Interest.   The avoidance of any conflict of interest or the appearance of impropriety is important to consider because loyalty is an essential element of the attorney-client relationship. Canon 3 of the NALA Code expands the general requirement for protection of the confidences of a client to include the avoidance of conflicts of interest or any activities that might present the appearance of impropriety. Rule 1.7 of the ABA Model Rules addresses the attorney's responsibility to avoid conflicts of interest.

The growth in the utilization of paralegals has increased the potential for conflicts of interest. Recognizing that conflicts may arise when a paralegal moves from one employer to another, the ABA Standing Committee on Ethics and Professional Responsibility issued an opinion on this topic:

> A law firm that hires a nonlawyer employee, such as a paralegal, away from an opposing law firm may save itself from disqualification by effectively screening the new employee from any participation in the case the two firms have in common.

This screening (sometimes referred to as the "Chinese wall," the "firewall," the "cone of silence," or the "ethical wall") seeks to protect the confidences of a client and any information that pertains to the attorney-client relationship. Several courts have been faced with requests for disqualification on the basis of nonlawyers' conflicts of interests, primarily resulting from a job change from one firm to another.[2] Just how far disqualification may extend is an issue still under scrutiny by the courts. It certainly extends to the new employer who utilizes the paralegal to perform work on cases it has in common with the old employer. While the New Jersey Supreme Court Advisory Committee on Professional Ethics issued Opinion 665 (1993) supporting its position for the "Chinese wall" theory, the Nebraska Supreme Court rejected the "Chinese wall" as a means of avoiding disqualification stating that it does little or nothing to ease the appearance of impropriety.[3]

EC4-2 and DR4-101(D) of the ABA Code of Professional Responsibility impose requirements on the attorney to exercise care in selecting and training employees to ensure that such client confidences are preserved. In addition, the new employer is prohibited from attempting to obtain information from a paralegal that was acquired as a result of a prior employment. The California Court of Appeal addressed the issue of whether there were any additional precautions a new employer might take to prevent disqualification when it discovers that a paralegal was previously employed by an adverse party in a common case. In its 1993 ruling on a case involving a change of employment by nonlawyer employees, the Court found that in addition to the cone of silence, a law firm has the option of obtaining a waiver from the former employer that it does not object to the switch in employment.[4] It is important that the paralegal be alert to any situations that might present a conflict of interest or the appearance of impropriety as a result of information gained during a past employment and should immediately disclose any questionable situation to the employer.[5]

Recent cases involving screening have been heard in state supreme courts. In Oklahoma, in an order issued July 12, 2001, in the matter of *Mark A. Hayes, M.D. v. Central States Orthopedic Specialists, Inc.*, a Tulsa County District Court Judge disqualified a law firm from representation of a client on the basis that an ethical screen was an impermissible device to protect from disclosure confidences gained by a nonlawyer employee while employed by another law firm. In applying the same rules that govern attorneys, the court found that the Rules of Professional Conduct pertaining to confidentiality apply to nonlawyers who leave firms with actual knowledge of material, confidential information and a screening device is not an appropriate alternative to the imputed disqualification of an incoming paralegal who has moved from one firm to another during ongoing litigation and has actual knowledge of material, confidential information. Because of the effect of this finding on the employment opportunities for paralegals and its potential nationwide effect, NALA, the Oklahoma Paralegal Association, the Central Oklahoma

---

ABA Opinion No. 88-1526 (6/22/88).

Association of Legal Assistants, and the Tulsa Association of Legal Assistants, filed an amicus brief with the Oklahoma Supreme Court on November 8, 2001. The brief, included in the appendix, offers a detailed discussion of the issue of screening and is a careful analysis of how it has been handled among the states through ethical opinions and case law. The Oklahoma Supreme Court disagreed with the trial court and determined that under certain circumstances, screening is an appropriate management tool.

In 2004, the Nevada Supreme Court also addressed this issue at the urging of the state's paralegals. The Nevada Supreme Court granted a petition to rescind the Court's 1997 ruling in *Ciaffone v. District Court*. In this case, the court clarified the original ruling, stating "mere opportunity to access confidential information does not merit disqualification." The opinion stated instances in which screening may be appropriate and minimum screening requirements. The opinion also set forth guidelines that a district court may use to determine if screening has been or may be effective. These considerations are:

1. substantiality of the relationship between the former and current matters;
2. the time elapsed between the matters;
3. size of the firm;
4. number of individuals presumed to have confidential information;
5. nature of their involvement in the former matter;
6. timing and features of any measures taken to reduce the danger of disclosure;
7. whether the old firm and the new firm represent adverse parties in the same proceeding rather than in different proceedings.

PRACTICE TIPS

- Keep track of former employment and former clients to prevent any potential conflicts.
- Do not enter into business transactions with clients or ever use any information you receive from a client to your own advantage.
- Do not accept gifts from clients.

3.0216 Safekeeping of Property.   A final area deserving of mention is the safekeeping of property. Rule 1.15 of the ABA Model Rules prohibits the commingling of funds. Law offices maintain separate trust accounts for holding monies related to client transactions, and strict accounting procedures must be followed in these accounts. The paralegal is often involved in setting up these accounts or in disbursements and should become familiar with, and strictly follow, all procedures required of the law firm in such transactions.

PRACTICE TIPS

- If you are given responsibility for handling client trust fund accounts, maintain a separate ledger that shows the date and amount of funds received; the date and amount deposited; and the date, amount, and purpose of any disbursements.
- Keep bank deposit slips for client trust fund accounts separate from other law office deposit slips.
- Beware of credit card transactions related to trust fund accounts because of issues related to comingling of funds.

3.022   Transactions with Persons Other than Clients

The paralegal's ethical obligations are not confined solely to activities within the employer's office or activities involving the clients represented by the employer.

3.0221 Truthfulness in Statements.

Rule 4.1 of the ABA Model Rules mandates that false statements cannot be made and facts cannot be misrepresented. Such a responsibility extends to the paralegal. The paralegal's nonlawyer status must be clearly stated and conveyed in any communications, oral or written, to anyone with whom the paralegal has contact during the course and scope of employment. This practice will ensure that there is no misrepresentation or misunderstanding about the paralegal's nonlawyer status and will avoid the problems that arise from the failure to disclose nonlawyer status.

3.0222 Improper Communications.

Just as attorneys are prohibited from any direct communications with persons and adverse parties known to be represented by counsel (*see* Rule 4.2 of ABA Model Rules), paralegals cannot make such a contact or be utilized in such a manner as to circumvent that prohibition.

PRACTICE TIPS

- Do not communicate with parties to litigation or employees of such parties where opposing counsel is not present.
- Do not initiate communications with a judge and avoid communications with members of a jury.

3.023   The Paralegal and the Law Firm

3.0231 Attorney Responsibility Regarding Nonlawyer Assistants.

As noted in the introduction to this chapter, Rule 5.3 of the ABA Model Rules specifically discusses the responsibilities of an attorney regarding the use of nonlawyer assistants and the need to take measures to ensure the nonlawyer's conduct is compatible with the professional obligations of the lawyer.

Some states have enhanced Rule 5.3 to provide that a partner in the law firm, in addition to the supervising attorney, has these responsibilities (e.g., Montana, Idaho, and South Carolina). EC 3-5 of the ABA Model Code of Professional Responsibility also relates to the attorney's use of nonlawyers.

3.0232 Sharing of Legal Fees and Partnership.

Rule 5.4 of the ABA Model Rules states that legal fees may not be shared with nonlawyer personnel. This rule is not intended to deny paralegals salary, bonuses, or benefits, even though they may be tied to the profitability of the law firm. Instead, the prohibition applies to any form of compensation that is based on the existence or amount of a particular fee. Bonuses paid to nonlawyers are to be distinguished from fee splitting. Fee splitting occurs when a payment to the nonlawyer is tied to a particular client; however, bonuses are not tied to receipt of a particular fee for a particular case. Thus, a paralegal's regular compensation may not include a percentage of the profits of a law firm, nor can the compensation be based on fees received in the general course of business, from any referrals of legal business, or from a particular client or case. Subparagraph (a)(3) of Rule 5.4 provides an exception to the extent that the law firm may include nonlawyers in a compensation or retirement plan, even though that plan is based in whole or in part on a profit-sharing arrangement. This is permitted since participation in these plans does not encourage or aid nonlawyers in the unauthorized practice of law and because such plans have been authorized by Congress (i.e., qualified plans under ERISA, 401K, etc.)

The same rule also prohibits the lawyer from establishing any business with a nonlawyer if any part of that relationship would involve the practice of law (DR 3-103). This rule is supplemented by DR 5-107(C), which forbids an attorney to practice law in any organization or professional corporation where a nonlawyer holds any interest or is a director or officer of such group.

PRACTICE TIPS

- Do not participate in, or agree to, any compensation arrangement which involves, or appears to involve, the sharing of legal fees with an attorney.
- You may refer clients to an attorney, as long as you are asked to do so by the client and you do not accept a fee for such referral.
- Do not go into business with an attorney when such business involves, or appears to involve, the practice of law.

3.0233 Listing on Letterhead, Use of Business Cards, and Signing of Letters.
Questions arise frequently as to whether a law firm may list paralegals and other nonlawyers on the firm letterhead, whether such individuals may have business cards also containing the law firm name, and whether paralegals can sign letters under the lawyer's letterhead.

ABA Model Rules 7.1 and 7.5 govern what information may be provided on lawyers' letterhead. While these rules do not specifically address the listing of nonlawyer personnel, the ABA has issued an informal opinion (89-1527, 2/22/89) stating that the listing of nonlawyer support personnel is not prohibited by the rule or any other rules, provided the listing is not false or misleading. To avoid being misleading, the title of the nonlawyer personnel should clearly appear on the letterhead so that the public is not misled into believing that the nonlawyer is an attorney. The same findings are made with regard to business cards for nonlawyers. The primary concern is to avoid confusion about the status of the nonlawyers that may arise from the use of any title or other designation. The use of letterhead and business cards by freelance or independent paralegals must also conform to these rules as well as the specific rulings of the jurisdiction in which the paralegal operates.

Rules regarding nonlawyer use of business cards and listing on letterheads vary from state to state. A paralegal should be familiar with and follow the appropriate rules of the jurisdiction involved. The form and language of any listing on letterhead or business cards should also be approved by a supervising attorney. Freelance or independent paralegals should seek the advice of an attorney and/or request an opinion from the appropriate state bar entity or supreme court commission prior to printing or disseminating letterhead or business cards.

It is generally accepted that a paralegal may sign letters on law firm letterhead as long as the nonlawyer status of the paralegal is clear. This is accomplished by stating an appropriate nonlawyer title immediately below the signature. The contents of a letter signed by a nonlawyer must also be considered. No direct legal advice or opinion should be contained in correspondence sent under the paralegal's name. If any doubt exists, a supervising attorney should be consulted.

3.024 The Paralegal and Public Service/Pro Bono Activities

Attorneys have a basic responsibility to provide public-interest legal services without a fee or at a reduced fee (ABA Model Rule 6.1). To meet public concern about the availability of legal services to the indigent, many bar associations have established programs to provide such low-cost or free services to these individuals. Some paralegal professional associations are even working with the organized bar associations in these programs. Paralegals may assist attorneys in these public service activities in the same manner and under the same delegation and supervisory obligations previously discussed. As with the attorney, the paralegal is bound by the same standards of professional conduct in offering pro bono services as with any other services.

3.03 THE PARALEGAL AND THE UNAUTHORIZED PRACTICE OF LAW

ABA Model Rule 5.5 specifically prohibits an attorney from assisting a nonlawyer in the performance of any activity that would constitute the unauthorized practice of law. Canon 3 of the NALA Code of Ethics and Professional Responsibility prohibits a paralegal from engaging in any activity that would constitute the unauthorized practice of law. Canon 1 of the NALA Code prohibits a paralegal from the performance of any duties that may only be performed by lawyers.

The proper starting point for any discussion of the unauthorized practice of law is to have a basic understanding of what constitutes the practice of law. The ABA has been reluctant to formulate a single specific definition of what constitutes the practice of law except to stress that it relates to the rendering of services to others which call for the exercise of professional legal judgment (*see* Model Code EC 3-5).

Various courts have addressed the definition of the practice of law. In *Davis v. Unauthorized Practice Commission*, 431 S.W.2d 590 (Tex. 1968), that Court stated:

> According to the generally understood definition of the practice of law, it embraces the preparation of pleadings and other papers incident to actions of special proceedings, and the management of such actions in proceedings on behalf of clients before judges in courts. However, the practice of law is not confined to cases conducted in court. In fact, the major portion of the practice of any capable lawyer consists of work done outside of the courts. The practice of law involves not only appearances in court in connection with litigation, but also services rendered out of court, and includes the giving of legal advice or the rendering of any service requiring the use of legal skill or knowledge, such as preparing a will, effect of which under the facts and conclusions involved must be carefully determined.

A cursory reading of this definition might lead one to the inaccurate conclusion that anyone who prepares legal documents could be engaged in the practice of law. The important distinguishing fact, not present in the *Davis* case but later articulated by other courts in other opinions, is that a paralegal performs these functions under the direct supervision of a licensed attorney. An example of the continuing development of this line of thought is represented by opinions from South Carolina:

> Paralegals are routinely employed by licensed attorneys to assist in the preparation of legal documents such as deeds and mortgages. The activities of a paralegal do not constitute the practice of law as long as they are limited to work of a preparatory nature, such as legal research, investigation, or the composition of legal documents, which enable the licensed attorney-employer to carry a given matter to a conclusion through his own examination, approval, or additional effort. *In re: Easler*, 272 S.E.2d 32 (1980).

[T]he preparation and filing of legal documents involving the giving of advice, consultation, explanation, or recommendations on matters of law [is the practice of law]. *State v. Despain*, 460 S.E. 2d 576 (S.C. 1995) and *State v. Buyers Service Co.*, 357 S.E.2d 15 (S.C. 1987).

[T]o legitimately provide services as a paralegal, one must work in conjunction with a licensed attorney. *State v. Robinson,* Opinion 24391, SC Supreme Court, March 1996.

In addition, as discussed previously, attorney standards of professional conduct recognize the use of nonlawyer personnel in performing many tasks that the lawyer would otherwise do.

PRACTICE TIPS

- When in doubt, do not proceed! Ask your supervising attorney for guidance.
- Join a local, state, or national paralegal association which may provide guidance.
- Know your state's professional responsibility codes for attorneys and paralegals.
- You may relay legal advice and opinions from the supervising attorney to the client but may not independently give legal advice or opinion.

The importance of being familiar with your jurisdiction's definition of the unauthorized practice of law cannot be overemphasized. Most states have adopted their own definition of the unauthorized practice of law, which have been interpreted according to specific areas of law. California Attorney General Opinion 93-416 found that a nonlawyer, acting on the basis of a power of attorney, may not engage in the practice of law on behalf of the client. Idaho has opined that lawyers may not enter into an arrangement with a corporation of nonlawyers to review living trust documents. It was found that the preparation of such documents is the practice of law (*see* Op. 135). Representation of individuals at real estate closings has been found to be the unauthorized practice of law in Pennsylvania (Op. No. 96-102).

Another aspect of the practice of law is the appearance in proceedings on behalf of clients in courts. Canon 3 of the NALA Code of Ethics prohibits the appearance of a paralegal in court in a representative capacity for a client, unless such appearances are authorized by court or agency rules. The basis for this guideline is the requirement that the paralegal's work must be under the direct supervision of an attorney. Unless there has been a waiver, either through statute or a court or agency rule specifically permitting a nonlawyer to perform such services independently and without the supervision of an attorney, the paralegal will be crossing the boundary and could be subject to charges of unauthorized practice of law. As an example, Kentucky is a state which has long held that an attorney may not send a nonlawyer to do anything in a courtroom with respect to the representation of a client. This would be the unauthorized practice of law. (Ethics Opinion E-266, Supreme Court of Kentucky, 93-C-159-KB, 4/20/83). Kentucky also extended this provision to include the taking of depositions by nonlawyers (*see* Op. 341, 11/90).

The appearance by nonlawyers in a representative capacity in administrative proceedings is authorized by a number of state and federal agencies. Before a paralegal engages in such activities, appropriate steps should be taken to ensure that such appearances are sanctioned by the agency rules, the supervising attorney has authorized and endorsed the appearance, court approval for the paralegal to appear has been obtained, and, if appropriate, the client has consented to the paralegal appearing on his or her behalf.[6]

What constitutes a court appearance is somewhat vague, depending on the activities involved in the appearance, and at least one court has held that preparation of a court order and transmission of information to the court was not the unauthorized practice of law because of the ministerial nature of the act.[7] As noted in the NALA Code (Canon 3), exceptions allowing court appearances by paralegals may exist, and local, state, and federal rules applicable for the jurisdiction where the paralegal works should be consulted. (As noted in Section 3.01 of this chapter, the *Kentucky Paralegal Code* specifically allows for some court appearances by paralegals but only if the client understands the paralegal is not an attorney, the lawyer supervises the paralegal in the performance of his or her duties, and the lawyer remains fully responsible for such representation, including all acts taken and not taken.)

In the early 1990s, a movement developed for nonlawyers to offer legal services directly to the public. These individuals are often referred to as legal technicians. In 1992, in response to the push to allow nonlawyers to serve the public, the ABA established a Commission on Nonlawyer Practice. The Commission consisted of lawyers and nonlawyers and received written statements, along with hearing testimony at sites across the United States. The Commission published a 173-page report entitled *Nonlawyer Activity in Law-Related Situations.* One of the items noted in the report is that the role of traditional paralegals should be expanded, while still under the supervision of lawyers. In 1996, Pennsylvania addressed their concerns on this issue by revising their UPL statute to include a reference to paralegals. It states:

> (a) General rule—Except as provided in subsection (b), any person, including, but not limited to, a paralegal or paralegal, who within this Commonwealth shall practice law, or who shall hold himself out to the public as being entitled to practice law, or use or advertise the title of lawyer, attorney at law, attorney and counselor at law, counselor, or the equivalent in any language, in such a manner as to convey the impression that he is a practitioner of the law of any jurisdiction, without being an attorney at law or a corporation complying with 15 Pa. C .S. Ch. 29 (relating to professional corporations), commits a misdemeanor of the third degree, upon a first violation. A second or subsequent violation of this subsection constitutes a misdemeanor of the first degree. Penn. Cons. Stats. Title 42 Sect. 2524(a).

Many states have adopted definitions of paralegals. In 1992, South Dakota adopted a definition for paralegals and included a list of seven minimum qualifications for paralegals. In Illinois, Senate Bill 995, effective January 1, 1996 states:

> Sec. 1.35 Paralegal. "Paralegal" means a person who is qualified through education, training, or work experience and is employed by a lawyer, law office, governmental agency, or other entity to work under the direction of an attorney in a capacity that involves the performance of substantive legal work that usually requires a sufficient knowledge of legal concepts and would be performed by the attorney in the absence of the paralegal. A reference in an Act to attorney fees includes paralegal fees, recoverable at market rates.

Many bar associations are also adopting definitions in an effort to clarify proper utilization of paralegals, all in an attempt to stay clear of the unauthorized practice of law.

3.04 ADEQUATE SUPERVISION BY THE ATTORNEY

The requirement that a paralegal work under the direct supervision of an attorney is embodied in ethical guidelines, case law involving the unauthorized practice of law, and rulings in disciplinary proceedings against attorneys. As a result of this clear ethical precept for the use of nonlawyers in the delivery of legal services, NALA has incorporated this principle into its definition of a paralegal, as discussed in the introduction of this book. The importance of adequate supervision by the employing attorney cannot be overemphasized. As is made clear in the guidelines and accepted standards of professional conduct for attorneys, the ultimate responsibility rests with the supervising attorney. The professional codes and case law establish that the attorney must be responsible for the assignment of the tasks to be performed, must supervise the manner in which the paralegal performs the duties and tasks, and must merge the work products of the paralegal into the attorney's final work product. The attorney must maintain a direct relationship with the client and a managerial role in the representation of the client.

The managerial role came into question in New Jersey with lawyers entering into contracts with independent or freelance paralegals. Opinion No. 24 was entered in November 1990, stating this practice was an unauthorized practice of law. This ruling was appealed. The Supreme Court opinion issued May 14, 1992, found:

> The evidence does not support a categorical ban on all independent paralegals practicing in New Jersey. Given the appropriate instructions and supervision, paralegals, whether as employees or independent contractors, are valuable and necessary members of an attorney's work force in the effective and efficient practice of law.

On March 1, 1997, the North Dakota Rules of Professional Conduct were amended to include:

Rule 5.3 Responsibilities Regarding Nonlawyer Assistants. This rule was amended August 1, 2006 and is as follows:

RULE 5.3 RESPONSIBILITIES REGARDING NONLAWYER ASSISTANTS

With respect to a nonlawyer employed or retained by or associated with a lawyer:

(a) a partner, and a lawyer who individually or together with other lawyers has comparable managerial authority in a law firm, shall make reasonable efforts to ensure that the firm has in effect measures giving reasonable assurance that the nonlawyer's conduct is compatible with the professional obligations of the lawyer;

(b) the lawyer having direct supervisory authority over the nonlawyer shall make reasonable efforts to ensure that the nonlawyer's conduct is compatible with the professional obligations of the lawyer; and

(c) a lawyer shall be responsible for conduct of a nonlawyer that would be a violation of these Rules if:

    (1) the lawyer orders or, with knowledge of the specific conduct, ratifies the conduct involved; or

    (2) the lawyer is a partner or has comparable managerial authority in the law firm in which the nonlawyer is employed, or has direct supervisory authority over the nonlawyer, and knows of the conduct at a time when its consequences can be avoided or mitigated, but fails to take reasonable action.

(d) In addition to paragraphs (a), (b) and (c), the following apply with respect to a legal assistant employed or retained by or associated with a lawyer:

    (1) A lawyer may delegate to a legal assistant any task normally performed by the lawyer except those tasks proscribed to one not licensed as a lawyer by statute, court rule, administrative rule or regulation, controlling authority, or these Rules.

    (2) A lawyer may not delegate to a legal assistant:

        (i) responsibility for establishing a lawyer-client relationship;

        (ii) responsibility for establishing the amount of a fee to be charged for a legal service;

        (iii) responsibility for a legal opinion rendered to a client; or

        (iv) responsibility for the work product.

    (3) The lawyer shall make reasonable efforts to ensure that clients, courts, and other lawyers are aware that a legal assistant is not licensed to practice law.

Failure by an attorney to adequately supervise nonlawyer staff can result in harsh disciplinary consequences, including disbarment. Guidelines 2 and 4 of the NALA Model Standards and Guidelines for Utilization of Legal Assistants provides detailed annotations to case law dealing with the duties of the attorney and instances where sanctions have been imposed for the attorney's failure to perform these duties.

PRACTICE TIPS

- Do not sign the attorney's name to any legal documents. The supervising attorney must review and sign any legal document that you have drafted.
- Make sure the work you are doing has been delegated by your attorney.
- If you are unsure of any aspect of any delegated work, ask for guidance from the supervising attorney.

3.05 SUMMARY

The placement of responsibility on the attorney does not relieve the paralegal from an independent obligation to follow the same professional conduct obligations required of attorneys and certainly to refrain from illegal conduct. (**As of this writing, the terms "paralegal" and "legal assistant" are defined by statute in the states of California, Florida, Indiana, Illinois and Maine. The definitions define paralegals and legal assistants as nonlawyers working under the supervision of a licensed attorney.**) While the provisions of standards and disciplinary rules for attorneys are not binding on nonlawyers, the very nature of a paralegal's employment imposes an obligation not to engage in conduct that would involve the supervising attorney in a violation of attorneys' codes. This obligation has been codified in Canon 10 of the NALA Code.

The paralegal must take additional individual steps to ensure protection from potential liability for the unauthorized practice of law. While statutory provisions concerning the unauthorized practice of law often do not describe such conduct with exactitude, precautionary steps can be taken by the paralegal to stay within proper and accepted boundaries. As an example, the Virginia Alliance of Legal Assistant Associations has adopted *Educational Standards and Professional Responsibility Guidelines* for paralegals.

From the compendium of material discussed in this chapter, the paralegal can analyze professional conduct by considering the presence or absence of the following factors:

1. Are the tasks the paralegal performs being delegated by an attorney?
2. Are the tasks and activities of the paralegal being performed under the supervision of an attorney?
3. Are the tasks being performed ministerial or information gathering for an attorney's use?
4. Are the tasks and activities performed being given final approval and/or personal examination by an attorney, and does the work performed by the paralegal merge into the attorney's final work product?
5. Has the attorney maintained a direct relationship with the client, or is the paralegal managing the attorney-client relationship?
6. Has the paralegal disclosed his or her nonlawyer status at the outset of any professional relationship with a client, other attorneys, a court or administrative agency (and personnel), or members of the general public?

7. Has the paralegal established attorney-client relationships by accepting cases?

8. Has the paralegal set the fees for the services to be performed?

9. Has the paralegal rendered professional legal opinions or advice?

10. Has the paralegal represented a client before a court when such activity is not authorized by the court or agency rules and when appropriate approval is obtained?

3.06 CODES AND GUIDELINES

3.061 National Association of Legal Assistants, Inc. Code of Ethics and Professional Responsibility (Copyright 2007; Adopted 1975; Revised 1979, 1988, 1995, 2007)

PREAMBLE

A paralegal must adhere strictly to the accepted standards of legal ethics and to the general principles of proper conduct. The performance of the duties of the paralegal shall be governed by specific canons as defined herein so that justice will be served and goals of the profession attained. (*See* NALA *Model Standards and Guidelines for Utilization of Legal Assistants,* Section V.)

The canons of ethics set forth hereafter are adopted by the National Association of Legal Assistants, Inc., as a general guide intended to aid paralegals and attorneys. The enumeration of these rules does not mean there are not others of equal importance although not specifically mentioned. Court rules, agency rules and statutes must be taken into consideration when interpreting the canons.

DEFINITION

Legal assistants, also known as paralegals, are a distinguishable group of persons who assist attorneys in the delivery of legal services. Through formal education, training and experience, legal assistants have knowledge and expertise regarding the legal system and substantive and procedural law which qualify them to do work of a legal nature under the supervision of an attorney.

In 2001, NALA members also adopted the ABA definition of a legal assistant/paralegal, as follows:

A paralegal is a person qualified by education, training or work experience who is employed or retained by a lawyer, law office, corporation, governmental agency or other entity who performs specifically delegated substantive legal work for which a lawyer is responsible. (Adopted by the ABA in 1997.)

Canon 1—A paralegal must not perform any of the duties that attorneys only may perform nor take any actions that attorneys may not take.

Canon 2—A paralegal may perform any task which is properly delegated and supervised by an attorney, as long as the attorney is ultimately responsible to the client, maintains a direct relationship with the client, and assumes professional responsibility for the work product.

Canon 3—A paralegal must not: (a) engage in, encourage, or contribute to any act which could constitute the unauthorized practice of law; and (b) establish attorney-client relationships, set fees, give legal opinions or advice or represent a client before a court or agency unless so authorized by that court or agency; and (c) engage in conduct or take any action which would assist or involve the attorney in a violation of professional ethics or give the appearance of professional impropriety.

Canon 4—A paralegal must use discretion and professional judgment commensurate with knowledge and experience but must not render independent legal judgment in place of an attorney. The services of an attorney are essential in the public interest whenever such legal judgment is required.

Canon 5—A paralegal must disclose his or her status as a legal assistant at the outset of any professional relationship, with a client, attorney, a court or administrative agency or personnel thereof, or a member of the general public. A legal assistant must act prudently in determining the extent to which a client may be assisted without the presence of an attorney.

Canon 6—A paralegal must strive to maintain integrity and a high degree of competency through education and training with respect to professional responsibility, local rules and practice, and through continuing education in substantive areas of law to better assist the legal profession in fulfilling its duty to provide legal service.

Canon 7—A paralegal must protect the confidences of a client and must not violate any rule or statute now in effect or hereafter enacted controlling the doctrine of privileged communications between a client and an attorney.

Canon 8—A paralegal must disclose to his or her employer or prospective employer any pre-existing client or personal relationship that may conflict with the interests of the employer or prospective employer and/or their clients.

Canon 9—A paralegal must do all other things incidental, necessary, or expedient for the attainment of the ethics and responsibilities as defined by statute or rule of court.

Canon 10—A paralegal's conduct is guided by bar associations' codes of professional responsibility and rules of professional conduct.

3.062 National Association of Legal Assistants, Inc. Model Standards and Guidelines for Utilization of Legal Assistants (Annotated) (Copyright 2007; Adopted 1984; Revised 1991, 1997, 2005, 2007)

INTRODUCTION

The purpose of this annotated version of the National Association of Legal Assistants, Inc. Model Standards and Guidelines for the Utilization of Legal Assistants (the "Model," "Standards" and/or the "Guidelines") is to provide references to the existing case law and other authorities where the underlying issues have been considered. The authorities cited will serve as a basis upon which conduct of a legal assistant may be analyzed as proper or improper.

The Guidelines represent a statement of how the legal assistant may function. The Guidelines are not intended to be a comprehensive or exhaustive list of the proper duties of a legal assistant. Rather, they are designed as guides to what may or may not be proper conduct for the legal assistant. In formulating the Guidelines, the reasoning and rules of law in many reported decisions of disciplinary cases and unauthorized practice of law cases have been analyzed and considered. In addition, the provisions of the American Bar Association Model Rules of Professional Conduct, as well as the ethical promulgations of various state courts and bar associations have been considered in the development of the Guidelines.

These Guidelines form a sound basis for the legal assistant and the supervising attorney to follow. This Model will serve as a comprehensive resource document and as a definitive, well-reasoned guide to those considering voluntary standards and guidelines for legal assistants.

I.
PREAMBLE

Proper utilization of the services of legal assistants contributes to the delivery of cost-effective, high-quality legal services. Legal assistants and the legal profession should be assured that measures exist for identifying legal assistants and their role in assisting attorneys in the delivery of legal services. Therefore, the National Association of Legal Assistants, Inc., hereby adopts these Standards and Guidelines as an educational document for the benefit of legal assistants and the legal profession.

◀◀COMMENT▶▶

The three most frequently raised questions concerning legal assistants are: (1) How do you define a legal assistant; (2) Who is qualified to be identified as a legal assistant; and (3) What duties may a legal assistant perform? The definition adopted by the National Association of Legal Assistants answers the first question. The Model sets forth minimum education, training, and experience through standards which will assure that an individual utilizing the title "legal assistant" or "paralegal" has the qualifications to be held out to the legal community and the public in that capacity. The Guidelines identify those acts which the reported cases hold to be proscribed and give examples of services which the legal assistant may perform under the supervision of a licensed attorney.

These Guidelines constitute a statement relating to services performed by legal assistants, as defined herein, as approved by court decisions and other sources of authority. The purpose of the Guidelines is not to place limitations or restrictions on the legal assistant profession. Rather, the Guidelines are intended to outline for the legal profession an acceptable course of conduct. Voluntary recognition and utilization of the Standards and Guidelines will benefit the entire legal profession and the public it serves.

◀◀ ▶▶

II.
HISTORY

The National Association of Legal Assistants adopted this Model in 1984. At the same time the following definition of a legal assistant was adopted:

> Legal assistants, also known as paralegals, are a distinguishable group of persons who assist attorneys in the delivery of legal services. Through formal education, training, and experience, legal assistants have knowledge and expertise regarding the legal system and substantive and procedural law which qualify them to do work of a legal nature under the supervision of an attorney.

Historically, there have been similar definitions adopted by various legal professional organizations. Recognizing the need for one clear definition, the NALA membership approved a resolution in July 2001 to adopt the legal assistant definition of the American Bar Association. This definition continues to be utilized today.

III.
DEFINITION

A legal assistant or paralegal is a person qualified by education, training or work experience who is employed or retained by a lawyer, law office, corporation, governmental agency or other entity who performs specifically delegated substantive legal work for which a lawyer is responsible (adopted by the ABA in 1997 and by NALA in 2001).

◀◀COMMENT▶▶

This definition emphasizes the knowledge and expertise of legal assistants in substantive and procedural law obtained through education and work experience. It further defines the legal assistant or paralegal as a professional working under the supervision of an attorney as distinguished from a nonlawyer who delivers services directly to the public without any intervention or review of work product by an attorney. Such unsupervised services, unless authorized by court or agency rules, constitute the unauthorized practice of law.

Statutes, court rules, case law, and bar association documents are additional sources for legal assistant or paralegal definitions. In applying the Standards and Guidelines, it is important to remember that they were developed to apply to the legal assistant as defined herein. Lawyers should refrain from labeling those as paralegals or legal assistants who do not meet the criteria set forth in this definition and/or the definitions set forth by state rules, guidelines, or bar associations. Labeling secretaries and other administrative staff as legal assistants/paralegals is inaccurate.

For billing purposes, the services of a legal secretary are considered part of overhead costs and are not recoverable in fee awards. However, the courts have held that fees for paralegal services are recoverable as long as they are not clerical functions, such as organizing files, copying documents, checking docket, updating files, checking court dates, and delivering papers. As established in *Missouri v. Jenkins*, 491 U.S. 274, 109 S. Ct. 2463, 2471, n.10 (1989), tasks performed by legal assistants must be substantive in nature which, absent the legal assistant, the attorney would perform.

There are also case law and Supreme Court Rules addressing the issue of a disbarred attorney serving in the capacity of a legal assistant.

◀◀ ▶▶

IV.
STANDARDS

A legal assistant should meet certain minimum qualifications. The following standards may be used to determine an individual's qualifications as a legal assistant:

1. Successful completion of the Certified Legal Assistant (CLA)/Certified Paralegal (CP) certifying examination of the National Association of Legal Assistants, Inc.;

2. Graduation from an ABA approved program of study for legal assistants;

3. Graduation from a course of study for legal assistants which is institutionally accredited but not ABA approved, and which requires not less than the equivalent of 60 semester hours of classroom study;

4. Graduation from a course of study for legal assistants, other than those set forth in (2) and (3) above, plus not less than six months of in-house training as a legal assistant;

5. A baccalaureate degree in any field, plus not less than six months in-house training as a legal assistant;

6. A minimum of three years of law-related experience under the supervision of an attorney, including at least six months of in-house training as a legal assistant; or

7. Two years of in-house training as a legal assistant.

For purposes of these Standards, "in-house training as a legal assistant" means attorney education of the employee concerning legal assistant duties and these Guidelines. In addition to review and analysis of assignments, the legal assistant should receive a reasonable amount of instruction directly related to the duties and obligations of the legal assistant.

◀◀COMMENT▶▶

The Standards set forth suggest minimum qualifications for a legal assistant. These minimum qualifications, as adopted, recognize legal related work backgrounds and formal education backgrounds, both of which provide the legal assistant with a broad base in exposure to and knowledge of the legal profession. This background is necessary to assure the public and the legal profession that the employee identified as a legal assistant is qualified.

The Certified Legal Assistant (CLA) /Certified Paralegal (CP) examination established by NALA in 1976 is a voluntary nationwide certification program for legal assistants. (CLA and CP are federally registered certification marks owned by NALA.) The CLA/CP designation is a statement to the legal profession and the public that the legal assistant has met the high levels of knowledge and professionalism required by NALA's certification program. Continuing education requirements, which all certified legal assistants must meet, assure that high standards are maintained. The CLA/CP designation has been recognized as a means of establishing the qualifications of a legal assistant in supreme court rules, state court and bar association standards, and utilization guidelines.

Certification through NALA is available to all legal assistants meeting the educational and experience requirements. Certified Legal Assistants may also pursue advanced certification in specialty practice areas through the APC, Advanced Paralegal Certification, credentialing program. Legal assistants/paralegals may also pursue certification based on state laws and procedures in California, Florida, Louisiana, North Carolina, and Texas.

◄◄ ►►

V.
GUIDELINES

These Guidelines relating to standards of performance and professional responsibility are intended to aid legal assistants and attorneys. The ultimate responsibility rests with an attorney who employs legal assistants to educate them with respect to the duties they are assigned and to supervise the manner in which such duties are accomplished.

◄◄COMMENT►►

In general, a legal assistant is allowed to perform any task which is properly delegated and supervised by an attorney, as long as the attorney is ultimately responsible to the client and assumes complete professional responsibility for the work product.

ABA Model Rules of Professional Conduct, Rule 5.3 provides:

With respect to a nonlawyer employed or retained by or associated with a lawyer:

a. a partner in a law firm shall make reasonable efforts to ensure that the firm has in effect measures giving reasonable assurance that the person's conduct is compatible with the professional obligations of the lawyer;

b. a lawyer having direct supervisory authority over the nonlawyer shall make reasonable efforts to ensure that the person's conduct is compatible with the professional obligations of the lawyer; and

c. a lawyer shall be responsible for conduct of such a person that would be a violation of the rules of professional conduct if engaged in by a lawyer if:

  1. the lawyer orders or, with the knowledge of the specific conduct ratifies the conduct involved; or

  2. the lawyer is a partner in the law firm in which the person is employed, or has direct supervisory authority over the person, and knows of the conduct at a time when its consequences can be avoided or mitigated but fails to take remedial action.

There are many interesting and complex issues involving the use of legal assistants. In any discussion of the proper role of a legal assistant, attention must be directed to what constitutes the practice of law. Proper delegation to legal assistants is further complicated and confused by the lack of an adequate definition of the practice of law.

Kentucky became the first state to adopt a Paralegal Code by Supreme Court Rule.

This Code sets forth certain exclusions to the unauthorized practice of law:

For purposes of this rule, the unauthorized practice of law shall not include any service rendered involving legal knowledge or advice, whether representation, counsel or advocacy, in or out of court, rendered in respect to the acts, duties, obligations, liabilities or business relations of the one requiring services where:

a. The client understands that the paralegal is not a lawyer;
b. The lawyer supervises the paralegal in the performance of his or her duties; and
c. The lawyer remains fully responsible for such representation including all actions taken or not taken in connection therewith by the paralegal to the same extent as if such representation had been furnished entirely by the lawyer and all such actions had been taken or not taken directly by the attorney. Paralegal Code, Ky.S.Ct.R3.700, Sub-Rule 2.

South Dakota Supreme Court Rule 97-25 Utilization Rule a(4) states:

The attorney remains responsible for the services performed by the legal assistant to the same extent as though such services had been furnished entirely by the attorney and such actions were those of the attorney.

GUIDELINE 1
Legal assistants should:

1. Disclose their status as legal assistants at the outset of any professional relationship with a client, other attorneys, a court or administrative agency or personnel thereof, or members of the general public;
2. Preserve the confidences and secrets of all clients; and
3. Understand the attorney's Rules of Professional Responsibility and these Guidelines in order to avoid any action which would involve the attorney in a violation of the Rules, or give the appearance of professional impropriety.

◀◀COMMENT▶▶

Routine early disclosure of the paralegal's status when dealing with persons outside the attorney's office is necessary to assure that there will be no misunderstanding as to the responsibilities and role of the legal assistant. Disclosure may be made in any way that avoids confusion. If the person dealing with the legal assistant already knows of his/her status, further disclosure is unnecessary. If at any time in written or oral communication the legal assistant becomes aware that the other person may believe the legal assistant is an attorney, immediate disclosure should be made as to the legal assistant's status.

The attorney should exercise care that the legal assistant preserves and refrains from using any confidence or secrets of a client and should instruct the legal assistant not to disclose or use any such confidences or secrets.

The legal assistant must take any and all steps necessary to prevent conflicts of interest and fully disclose such conflicts to the supervising attorney. Failure to do so may jeopardize both the attorney's representation of the client and the case itself.

Guidelines for the Utilization of Legal Assistant Services adopted December 3, 1994 by the Washington State Bar Association Board of Governors states:

Guideline 7: A lawyer shall take reasonable measures to prevent conflicts of interest resulting from a legal assistant's other employment or interest insofar as such other employment or interests would present a conflict of interest if it were that of the lawyer."

In Re Complex Asbestos Litigation, 232 Cal. App. 3d 572 (Cal. 1991), addresses the issue wherein a law firm was disqualified due to possession of attorney-client confidences by a legal assistant employee resulting from previous employment by opposing counsel.

In Oklahoma, in an order issued July 12, 2001, in the matter of *Mark A. Hayes, M.D. v. Central States Orthopedic Specialists, Inc.*, a Tulsa County District Court Judge disqualified a law firm from representation of a client on the basis that an ethical screen was an impermissible device to protect from disclosure confidences gained by a nonlawyer employee while employed by another law firm. In applying the same rules that govern attorneys, the court found that the Model Rules of Professional Conduct pertaining to confidentiality apply to nonlawyers who leave firms with actual knowledge of material, confidential information and a screening device is not an appropriate alternative to the imputed disqualification of an incoming legal assistant who has moved from one firm to another during ongoing litigation and has actual knowledge of material, confidential information. The decision was appealed, and the Oklahoma Supreme Court determined that, under certain circumstances, screening is an appropriate management tool for nonlawyer staff.

In 2004, the Nevada Supreme Court also addressed this issue at the urging of the state's paralegals. The Nevada Supreme Court granted a petition to rescind the Court's 1997 ruling in *Ciaffone v. District Court*. In this case, the court clarified the original ruling, stating "mere opportunity to access confidential information does not merit disqualification." The opinion stated instances in which screening may be appropriate and listed minimum screening requirements. The opinion also set forth guidelines that a district court may use to determine if screening has been or may be effective. These considerations are:

1. substantiality of the relationship between the former and current matters
2. the time elapsed between the matters
3. size of the firm
4. number of individuals presumed to have confidential information
5. nature of their involvement in the former matter
6. timing and features of any measures taken to reduce the danger of disclosure
7. whether the old firm and the new firm represent adverse parties in the same proceeding rather than in different proceedings

The ultimate responsibility for compliance with approved standards of professional conduct rests with the supervising attorney. The burden rests upon the attorney who employs a legal assistant to educate the latter with respect to the duties which may be assigned and then to supervise the manner in which the legal assistant carries out such duties. However, this does not relieve the legal assistant from an independent obligation to refrain from illegal conduct. Additionally, and notwithstanding that the Rules are not binding upon nonlawyers, the very nature of a legal assistant's employment imposes an obligation not to engage in conduct which would involve the supervising attorney in a violation of the Rules.

The attorney must make sufficient background investigation of the prior activities and character and integrity of his or her legal assistants.

Further, the attorney must take all measures necessary to avoid and fully disclose conflicts of interest due to other employment or interests. Failure to do so may jeopardize both the attorney's representation of the client and the case itself.

Legal assistant associations strive to maintain the high level of integrity and competence expected of the legal profession and, further, strive to uphold the high standards of ethics.

NALA's Code of Ethics and Professional Responsibility states "A legal assistant's conduct is guided by bar associations' codes of professional responsibility and rules of professional conduct."

◄◄ ►►

GUIDELINE 2

Legal assistants should not:

1. Establish attorney-client relationships; set legal fees; give legal opinions or advice; or represent a client before a court, unless authorized to do so by said court; nor

2. Engage in, encourage, or contribute to any act which could constitute the unauthorized practice law.

◀◀COMMENT▶▶

Case law, court rules, codes of ethics, and professional responsibilities, as well as bar ethics opinions now hold which acts can and cannot be performed by a legal assistant. Generally, the determination of what acts constitute the unauthorized practice of law is made by state supreme courts.

Numerous cases exist relating to the unauthorized practice of law. Courts have gone so far as to prohibit the legal assistant from preparation of divorce kits and assisting in preparation of bankruptcy forms and, more specifically, from providing basic information about procedures and requirements, deciding where information should be placed on forms, and responding to questions from debtors regarding the interpretation or definition of terms.

Cases have identified certain areas in which an attorney has a duty to act, but it is interesting to note that none of these cases state that it is improper for an attorney to have the initial work performed by the legal assistant. This again points out the importance of adequate supervision by the employing attorney.

An attorney can be found to have aided in the unauthorized practice of law when delegating acts which cannot be performed by a legal assistant.

◀◀ ▶▶

GUIDELINE 3

Legal assistants may perform services for an attorney in the representation of a client, provided:

1. The services performed by the legal assistant do not require the exercise of independent professional legal judgment;

2. The attorney maintains a direct relationship with the client and maintains control of all client matters;

3. The attorney supervises the legal assistant;

4. The attorney remains professionally responsible for all work on behalf of the client, including any actions taken or not taken by the legal assistant in connection therewith; and

5. The services performed supplement, merge with and become the attorney's work product.

◀◀COMMENT▶▶

Paralegals, whether employees or independent contractors, perform services for the attorney in the representation of a client. Attorneys should delegate work to legal assistants commensurate with their knowledge and experience and provide appropriate instruction and supervision concerning the delegated work, as well as ethical acts of their employment. Ultimate responsibility for the work product of a legal assistant rests with the attorney. However, a legal assistant must use discretion and professional judgment and must not render independent legal judgment in place of an attorney.

The work product of a legal assistant is subject to civil rules governing discovery of materials prepared in anticipation of litigation, whether the legal assistant is viewed as an extension of the attorney or as another representative of the party itself. Fed. R. Civ. P. 26 (b) (3) and (5).

◀◀ ▶▶

GUIDELINE 4

In the supervision of a legal assistant, consideration should be given to:

1. Designating work assignments that correspond to the legal assistant's abilities, knowledge, training and experience;

2. Educating and training the legal assistant with respect to professional responsibility, local rules and practices, and firm policies;

3. Monitoring the work and professional conduct of the legal assistant to ensure that the work is substantively correct and timely performed;

4. Providing continuing education for the legal assistant in substantive matters through courses, institutes, workshops, seminars and in-house training; and

5. Encouraging and supporting membership and active participation in professional organizations.

◀◀COMMENT▶▶

Attorneys are responsible for the actions of their employees in both malpractice and disciplinary proceedings. In the vast majority of cases, the courts have not censured attorneys for a particular act delegated to the legal assistant, but rather, have been critical of and imposed sanctions against attorneys for failure to adequately supervise the legal assistant. The attorney's responsibility for supervision of his or her legal assistant must be more than a willingness to accept responsibility and liability for the legal assistant's work. Supervision of a legal assistant must be offered in both the procedural and substantive legal areas. The attorney must delegate work based upon the education, knowledge, and abilities of the legal assistant and must monitor the work product and conduct of the legal assistant to insure that the work performed is substantively correct and competently performed in a professional manner.

Michigan State Board of Commissioners has adopted Guidelines for the Utilization of Legal Assistants (April 23, 1993). These guidelines, in part, encourage employers to support legal assistant participation in continuing education programs to ensure that the legal assistant remains competent in the fields of practice in which the legal assistant is assigned.

The working relationship between the lawyer and the legal assistant should extend to cooperative efforts on public service activities wherever possible. Participation in pro bono activities is encouraged in ABA Guideline 10.

◀◀ ▶▶

GUIDELINE 5

Except as otherwise provided by statute, court rule or decision, administrative rule or regulation, or the attorney's rules of professional responsibility, and within the preceding parameters and proscriptions, a legal assistant may perform any function delegated by an attorney, including, but not limited to the following:

1. Conduct client interviews and maintain general contact with the client after the establishment of the attorney-client relationship, so long as the client is aware of the status and function of the legal assistant, and the client contact is under the supervision of the attorney.

2. Locate and interview witnesses, so long as the witnesses are aware of the status and function of the legal assistant.

3. Conduct investigations and statistical and documentary research for review by the attorney.

4. Conduct legal research for review by the attorney.

5. Draft legal documents for review by the attorney.

6. Draft correspondence and pleadings for review by and signature of the attorney.

7. Summarize depositions, interrogatories and testimony for review by the attorney.

8. Attend executions of wills, real estate closings, depositions, court or administrative hearings and trials with the attorney.

9. Author and sign letters providing the legal assistant's status is clearly indicated and the correspondence does not contain independent legal opinions or legal advice.

◀◀COMMENT▶▶

The United States Supreme Court has recognized the variety of tasks being performed by legal assistants and has noted that use of legal assistants encourages cost-effective delivery of legal services, *Missouri v. Jenkins*, 491 U.S.274, 109 S. Ct. 2463, 2471, n.10 (1989). In *Jenkins*, the court further held that legal assistant time should be included in compensation for attorney fee awards at the market rate of the relevant community to bill legal assistant time.

Courts have held that legal assistant fees are not a part of the overall overhead of a law firm. Legal assistant services are billed separately by attorneys and decrease litigation expenses. Tasks performed by legal assistants must contain substantive legal work under the direction or supervision of an attorney, such that if the legal assistant were not present, the work would be performed by the attorney.

In *Taylor v. Chubb*, 874 P.2d 806 (Okla. 1994), the Court ruled that attorney fees awarded should include fees for services performed by legal assistants and, further, defined tasks which may be performed by the legal assistant under the supervision of an attorney including, among others: interview clients; draft pleadings and other documents; carry on legal research, both conventional and computer aided; research public records; prepare discovery requests and responses; schedule depositions and prepare notices and subpoenas; summarize depositions and other discovery responses; coordinate and manage document production; locate and interview witnesses; organize pleadings, trial exhibits, and other documents; prepare witness and exhibit lists; prepare trial notebooks; prepare for the attendance of witnesses at trial; and assist lawyers at trials.

Except for the specific proscription contained in Guideline 1, the reported cases do not limit the duties which may be performed by a legal assistant under the supervision of the attorney.

An attorney may not split legal fees with a legal assistant, nor pay a legal assistant for the referral of legal business. An attorney may compensate a legal assistant based on the quantity and quality of the legal assistant's work and value of that work to a law practice.

CONCLUSION

These Standards and Guidelines were developed from generally accepted practices. Each supervising attorney must be aware of the specific rules, decisions, and statutes applicable to legal assistants within his or her jurisdiction.

ADDENDUM

For further information, the following cases may be helpful to you:

Duties

Taylor v. Chubb Group of Ins. Cos., 874 P.2d 806 (Okla. 1994)

McMackin v. McMackin, 651 A.2d 778 (Del. Fam. Ct. 1993)

Work Product
Fine v. Facet Aerospace Products Co., 133 F.R.D. 439 (S.D.N.Y. 1990)

Unauthorized Practice of Law
Akron Bar Assn. v. Greene, 673 N.E.2d 1307 (Ohio 1997)
Hessinger & Associates, 192 B.R. 211 (N.D. Calif. 1996)
In re Bright, 171 B.R. 799 (Bankr. E.D. Mich.)
Louisiana State Bar Assn v. Edwins, 540 So.2d 294 (La. 1989)

Attorney/Client Privilege
In re Complex Asbestos Litigation, 232 Cal. App. 3d 572 (Cal. 1991)
Makita Corp. v. United States., 819 F. Supp. 1099 (1993)

Conflicts
In re Complex Asbestos Litigation, 232 Cal. App. 3d 572 (Calif. 1991)
Makita Corp. v. United States, 819 F. Supp. 1099 (1993)
Phoenix Founders, Inc., v. Marshall, 887 S.W.2d 831 (Tex. 1994)
Smart Indus. Corp., Mfg. v. Superior Court ex rel. County of Yuma, 876 P.2d 1176 (Ariz. App. 1994)

Supervision
Matter of Martinez, 754 P.2d 842 (N.M. 1988)
State v. Barrett, 483 P.2d 1106 (Kan. 1971)
Hayes v. Central States Orthopedic Specialists, Inc., 51 P.3d 562 (Okla. 2002)
Liebowitz v. Eighth Judicial District Court of Nevada, Nev. Sup. Ct., No 39683,
November 3, 2003 clarified in part and overruled in part Ciaffone v. District Court, 113 Nev. 1165, 945 P.2d 950 (1997)

Fee Awards
In re Bicoastal Corp., 121 B.R. 653 (Bktrcy. M.D. Fla. 1990)
In re Carter, 101 B.R. 170 (Bankr. D.S.D. 1989)
Taylor v. Chubb Group of Ins. Cos., 874 P.2d 806 (Okla. 1994)
Missouri v. Jenkins, 491 U.S. 274, (1989)
McMackin v. McMackin, 651 A.2d 778 (Del. Fam. Ct. 1993)
Miller v. Alamo, 983 F.2d 856 (8th Cir. 1993)
Stewart v. Sullivan, 810 F. Supp. 1102 (D. Haw 1993)
In re Yankton College, 101 B.R. 151 (Bankr. D.S.D. 1989)
Stacy v. Stroud, 845 F. Supp. 1135 (S.D.W.Va. 1993)

Court Appearances
Louisiana State Bar Assn v. Edwins, 540 So.2d 294 (La. 1989)

In addition to the previously referenced cases, you may contact your state bar association for information regarding guidelines for the utilization of legal assistants that may have been adopted by the bar or ethical opinions concerning the utilization of legal assistants.

BIBLIOGRAPHY

ABA Commission on Nonlawyer Practice, *Nonlawyer Activity in Law-Related Associations.* American Bar Association (1992).

American Bar Association, *Model Code of Professional Responsibility* (1969, as amended).

American Bar Association, *Model Rules of Professional Conduct* (1983, as amended).

Canon, Therese A., Legal Ethics, 2000, A NALA Campus Course, On-line Self Study Program for Paralegals. www.NALACampus.com.

Cohn, Steven, "Beyond the 'Chinese Wall,'" *Legal Assistant Today* (November/December 1995).

Emert, Laurence T., "Preserving a Client's Confidences," XIX *Facts & Findings* 5 (February 1993).

Judd, Karen B., "Beyond the Bar: Legal Assistants and the Unauthorized Practice of Law," VIII *Facts & Findings* 1 (NALA), (May–June 1982).

National Association of Legal Assistants, *Code of Ethics and Professional Responsibility* (as amended through).

National Association of Legal Assistants, *Model Standards and Guidelines for Utilization of Legal Assistants* (Annotated).

National Association of Legal Assistants, "Summary of Definitions of Terms Legal Assistant and Paralegal," XXIV *Facts & Findings* 1 (May 1997).

Voisin, Vicki, "Changing Jobs: Ethical Consideration for Legal Assistants," XV *Facts & Findings* 12 (March 1989).

Webb, Wendi, "The New Age of Electronic Discovery," *Legal Assistant Today,* (May/June 1996).

Powers, James A., "O What A Tangled Web We Weave," XXIII *Facts & Findings* 1 (May 1996).

ENDNOTES

1. *See,* for example, *Guidelines for the Utilization of Legal Assistants in Kansas,* adopted by the Kansas Bar Association and *Guidelines for Legal Assistants,* adopted by the Colorado Bar Association. Guidelines have been adopted by a majority of the state bar associations.

2. *Grant v. Thirteenth Court of Appeals* (Texas Sup. Ct., No. 94-0581, 10/6/94, *rev'g* 877 S.W.2d, 10 Law. Man. Prof. Conduct 173); *Phoenix Founders Inc. v. Marshall,* 10 Law. Man. Prof. Conduct 316 (Texas Sup. Ct. 1994).

3. *FirsTier Bank N.A. v. Buckely, State (Nebraska) ex rel.,* 503 N.W.2d 844, 9 Law. Man. Prof. Conduct 244 (Neb. Sup. Ct. 1993). *See also* Appendix 2 for a discussion of screening.

4. *In re Complex Asbestos Litigation,* 232 Cal. App. 3rd 572, 283 Cal. Rptr. 732 (1991).

5. For a thorough discussion of the considerations for a paralegal in changing jobs, *see* Cohn, Steven, "Beyond the 'Chinese Wall,'" *Legal Assistant Today* (November/December 1995); Emert, Laurence T., "Preserving a Client' Confidences," XIX *Facts & Findings* 5 (February 1993); and Voisin, Vicki, "Changing Jobs: Ethical Considerations for Legal Assistants," XV *Facts & Findings* 12 (March 1989).

6. The California Bar has issued an advisory opinion regarding the use of a paralegal employed by a law firm for appearances before the Workers' Compensation Appeals Board (WCAB). While under certain labor code sections, nonlawyers are authorized in California to represent applicants before the WCAB, the California Bar's Standing Committee on Professional Responsibility and Conduct was dealing with the effect of the representation by the nonlawyer as an employee of a law firm and on behalf of the firm's client. The committee noted the need for adequate supervision by the employing attorney and the requirement that the clients be informed and consent to the use of the nonlawyer.

7. *People v. Alexander,* 53 Ill. App. 2d 299, 202 N.E. 2d 841 (1964).

4

Judgment and Analytical Ability

4.00   INTRODUCTION

The scope and diversity of duties delegated to paralegals depends primarily upon the trust and confidence the supervising attorney accords the paralegal as an individual, not upon assumptions based solely on the title "legal assistant," "paralegal," or "certified legal assistant." This trust and confidence are earned recognitions of the personal attributes of the individual, including intelligence, a positive attitude, a willingness to assume responsibility, communication skills, ethical and moral standards, imagination, reliability, analytical ability, and good judgment.

The utility and value of a paralegal to the lawyer depend more on the last two personal skills than all the others. Weakness in analytical abilities or judgment capabilities seriously limits the duties delegated to the paralegal, for the entire legal process requires these two qualities. *Analyze* is defined as "to separate a thing, idea, and so on into its parts so as to find out their nature, proportion, function, interrelationship, and other properties." *Judgment* is defined as "the capacity to perceive, discern, or make reasonable decisions." Paralegals and attorneys work in an atmosphere of good and bad judgments. These two modifiers expand that passionless and risk-free definition of judgment into a qualitative evaluation of the action or inaction that flowed from the "formation of the opinion." That is the nature of legal work—participation and involvement, rather than uninvolved observation or comment.

Judgment is necessarily followed by a decision which sets in motion some act or causes some act not to be done. The result is then measured to determine whether a particular judgment in a particular situation was good or bad. For instance, one does not need to go to law school nor enroll in a course for paralegals to understand that if an automobile driver deliberately runs a red light, a police officer may issue a citation calling for a fine or trial. Everyone is generally acquainted with good and bad judgments and the acts, consequences, and results that can flow from them. This chapter stresses more definitive aspects of judgment and analytical ability as they relate to paralegals in large and small law offices, corporate and nontraditional paralegal settings, and in simple and complex cases.

4.01   HOW TO DEVELOP GOOD JUDGMENT

If good judgment in any given situation involved facts, statistics, or objects, each considered without self-will, opinions, biases, prejudices and preferences, tempers, egos, and feelings, then a computer could be used to sort all the factors and select the optimum decision. Reliable good judgment and productive analytical ability are developed by exercise and practice and, even more important, through mistakes. Good judgment requires the leavening of experience with analytical ability and other personal characteristics, such as compassion and flexibility, applied within a framework of the following basic guidelines:

    a. Understand the reporting system and delegation of responsibilities.

    b. Understand the scope, instructions, and authority delegated.

    c. Appreciate priorities.

    d. Honor time commitments.

    e. Recognize exceptional situations.

    f. Accept guidance, directions, and comments constructively.

    g. Enthusiastically observe moral and ethical standards.

4.011 Understand the Reporting System and Delegation of Responsibilities

Every law firm or legal department has a reporting system of personnel and delegations of responsibilities. Clearly, the librarian is responsible for the purchase and maintenance of the materials in the library. Sometimes, the office manager is the coordinator for "extra help," overtime, or other personnel adjustments and is responsible for equipment purchase, service contracting, petty cash expenditures, travel arrangements, and so on. The senior attorneys and their secretaries have certain stated, or unstated but well understood, prerogatives, while other attorneys, secretaries, and paralegals have another set of prerogatives or guidelines. It is essential that areas of authority and responsibility of the office as a whole be generally understood by the paralegal, including the avenues for inquiry, suggestions, and requests.

For example, in a firm that uses a well-established and rigidly controlled file system requiring every file to be returned to the file room daily (except with special permission), the paralegal should learn the background of the current procedure from the files supervisor before attempting to introduce changes. It is poor judgment to attempt to resurrect an old system without knowing its history and without having substantial justification and a well-founded plan or recommendation for changing it. Personal opinions and convenience simply do not qualify as justifications, even though the paralegal's suggested system may have worked beautifully and masterfully in other and even larger firms.[1]

As the paralegal becomes more and more familiar with office organization and distribution of operational authority, his or her good judgment is demonstrated by posing appropriate questions to the properly responsible parties. Learning the reporting system or assumption of roles within the office ensures that few, if any, inadvertent cases of "going over the head" of a responsible person occurs. Understanding the office dynamics gives the paralegal the proper perspective and prepares him or her to handle the other guidelines effectively.

4.012 Understand the Scope, Instructions, and Authority Delegated

Paralegals are an ambitious group who will generally accept all responsibility delegated to them and additionally create, or even usurp, other areas of responsibility. They also devise new methods and procedures not previously tried and proven, which can be effective in certain situations. That frequently becomes true but never suddenly nor without a period of gradual demonstration of reliable judgment and analytical ability. An overly aggressive or presumptuous paralegal will never achieve a high level of responsibility as a valued professional as quickly as one who proceeds with preparation, study, and deliberation.

Paralegals entering a law office or legal department must become aware of and understand the office concept of the paralegal, as well as the kinds of duties performed—who directs their work and whose work (if any) they direct; if they can spend funds and, if so, to what dollar limit; and if they can contract for the firm and, if so, what kinds of contracts (travel, document copying, photography, model-making, and so on). They must obtain information concerning how billable and nonbillable hours are recorded; who makes decisions about billable expenses; how the secretarial support system functions for the paralegal; the mail system; the docket system; and any other system that may directly or indirectly affect them.

No matter how restrictive, inefficient, or ridiculous the system first seems, the paralegal should make every effort to follow the stipulated procedures while establishing an independent level of respect in the office. Most of the poor or inefficient practices encountered in an office are the compromises of past internal struggles or "hand-me-downs" of long ago that remain through inertia. Paralegals must be flexible enough to adapt to the internal situation until they have an opportunity to make proper, thoughtful, and constructive suggestions for change to the appropriate person at the proper time.

Once the office concept and general administration procedures are understood, the paralegal seeks to understand the kinds of cases handled by the attorney as well as the preferred techniques for every procedure in which the attorney intends to involve the paralegal. The next most important area of concern is the comfortable and effective integration of the lawyer, the paralegal, and the secretary in all phases of the working relationship; this is a changing and vitally important team that requires consideration and participation from all three parties.

Becoming familiar with the attorney's schedule allows the paralegal's work efforts to be adapted to and complement the lawyer's work habits. For example, some lawyers prefer the first hour to be undisturbed for handling mail and dictation, while others prefer the last hour. Some prefer to have the paralegal meet with them once a week for a general review of all active files, while others prefer more frequent meetings for case-by-case discussions; still others are "hit it while I'm hot" advocates who are likely to say "we'll do it right now, regardless of your previous assignments." Here again, flexibility and patience are important characteristics of a paralegal.

Paralegals specializing in real estate must be familiar with the real estate laws in their state; mortgage rates; property descriptions; title information; closing statements; zoning board regulations; and local, state, and federal regulations or statutes concerning purchasing, leasing, landlord-tenant situations, and all other pertinent areas of real estate law.

Corporate paralegals must be familiar with state and federal laws concerning corporations and procedures for incorporation, including tax and other laws pertaining to different types of corporations, such as domestic, foreign, Chapter S, closed, nonprofit, charitable or eleemosynary corporations; stock splits and stock options and dividends; pension plans; minutes of meetings of shareholders, directors, and incorporators; mergers; acquisitions; blue sky laws; and certain requirements of the Securities and Exchange Commission.

Paralegals specializing in bankruptcy law must be familiar with the Bankruptcy Code (Title 11 U.S.C. and Title 28 U.S.C.) and Bankruptcy Rules and procedures, including the applicable Federal Rules of Civil Procedure and Federal Rules of Evidence, with regard to debtors and creditors.

Paralegals involved in estate planning must necessarily keep abreast of the everchanging tax laws affecting estate planning for particular clients and be familiar with proper auditing procedures, valuation of assets, preparation of federal and state tax returns, proper acquisition of bank accounts, insurance proceeds, Social Security regulations, and many other areas. The same is true in all other specialty areas—the paralegals first are thoroughly familiar with the area or areas in which they work. Then they apply judgment and analytical ability in a particular area or areas.

While there are many specialty areas in which paralegals operate, there is one area of specialization that will often encompass any one or all of the other specialty areas, and that is litigation. A litigation paralegal, of necessity, becomes involved in real estate, probate, estate planning, bankruptcy, and family law, or possibly in real estate and corporate, criminal and corporate, criminal and tax, or other combinations, depending on the case. For that reason, we shall use the area of the litigation specialist to illustrate the concept of judgment and analytical ability. The same principles can be applied in any other specialty area but can be explored in more depth in the area of litigation. Therefore, as we explore the remaining five guidelines, the illustrations we use will deal primarily in litigation.

Litigation paralegals must be familiar with the rules of federal and state courts, either criminal or civil, depending on the bulk of the office practice. If the court rules state (for civil matters) that "all law and motion matters must be filed forty-eight hours prior to the hearing," a paralegal must determine whether this means forty-eight actual hours or "no less than two full working court days before the hearing." Similarly, court rules or local interpretation give rise to such questions as: "Does the court accept pleadings on 8" × 14" paper, 8" × 13" paper, or only 8" × 11" paper?" "Will the court allow paralegals at the counsel table during trial?" "If not, what accommodations will need to be made?" Other similar questions may arise to the paralegal. The failure to resolve such questions may confound the best efforts of the paralegal, result in embarrassment to the attorney, and frustrate a tactical objective.

4.013 Appreciate Priorities

Priorities in legal assisting lie first in the court docket, including deadlines, orders, and applicable city, state, and federal rules and regulations, and then in personal preferences. Also of importance are less well-defined priorities, the most vexatious of these being the priority of work production accorded the various personalities within the firm. It is obvious that the managing partner with a job to be expedited will receive all the necessary resources to complete the assignment in a timely and diligent fashion. Less clear and compelling is the need of a junior attorney's paralegal for extra help in completing a long-term project on schedule.[2] Yet the objective merit of the situations appears to be the same. The paralegal needs to properly evaluate and predict the need for assistance before the situation becomes a panic, since he or she is in the best position to make such predictions. The occasional panic situation could be avoided by the paralegal's attention to prioritization and initiative. Such foresight is helpful not only to the lawyer, but also to the office manager, who is responsible for coping with unanticipated peaks in workloads created by "please expedite" or "panic" operations. Choosing between two necessary activities for first attention and effort is the most difficult priority judgment a paralegal makes. Pulling together a list of the pending tasks, with an outline of "pros and cons" associated with your recommendation for prioritization, should be submitted to the person(s) who assigned the tasks. It is for them to decide which task has priority. For example, develop the document control plan or assemble all the documents? Draft additional interrogatories or summarize the depositions? Thoughtful analysis can lead the way to making the decision. The work obviously cannot be predicated on the likes and dislikes of lawyers, paralegals, or secretaries, since all aspects must be done sooner or later. Ignoring logical priorities results in creating additional problems, such as doing necessary but less challenging work under inordinate and unnecessary time pressures. The usual result of panic work is often poor quality and lost time which is the result of material being improperly prepared, proofed, and/or corrected. Unreliable and incomplete material is of little or no use to the employing attorney and seriously affects the trust and confidence placed in the paralegal.

4.014 Honor Time Commitments

Time is the most important commodity of a lawyer. It determines work schedules, which may be planned many weeks in advance. In private practice, it is a primary basis for certain charges to the client. Court rulings, codes, and statutes all provide for certain periods of time to elapse in the normal course of pleadings, motions, discovery, trial, and appeal. A paralegal who is consistently and conscientiously aware of the importance of time is highly valued. It is true that many time periods may be waived or extensions granted; however, the attorney should not be forced into seeking such favors from the adversary or the indulgence of the court because of the failure or inability of the paralegal to perform. A paralegal usually knows well before a deadline whether a project can meet a specified schedule with the resources currently in use. If the schedule cannot be met, the paralegal should not hesitate to request or recommend additional help, overtime, a reshuffling or prioritization, or a combination.

Many paralegals face having too much to do in too little time. A paralegal's challenge then becomes acquiring time management techniques in order to optimize efficiency. Developing systems and starting form files are examples of how a paralegal can manage time, whether done "manually" or by computer. Computers, document management systems, desktop availability of electronic research programs, and the Internet are a few of the technological advances that have given the paralegal a set of tools to help manage the workload.

One system of time management involves establishing task lists with individual items placed in order of priority. Analyze the list for items that can be combined. For instance, when summarizing a deposition, when you receive a deposition, concurrently create a list of the names of other potential witnesses on a separate document along with a listing and description of the exhibits introduced on yet a third document. This can be done very efficiently when using a computer and working from the disk version of the transcript provided by court reporters. Another time management technique is to anticipate future needs when accomplishing present tasks.

Think in terms of working "smarter not harder." For example, in a situation of scheduling a deposition involving several parties, first review your attorney's calendar and select at least three dates and times which are convenient. Then, instead of telephoning each party (which can take an inordinate amount of time), send a letter by fax or e-mail which asks each party to respond concerning availability on the suggested dates and to provide alternate dates if not available. Go ahead and have the draft deposition notice and subpoena prepared so that when the responses are received, all that need be added is the agreed upon date and time. The resulting time savings to the paralegal can sometimes be counted in hours.

4.015 Recognize Exceptional Situations

Every paralegal, after some time with a firm or legal department, may become a secondary target (in the absence of the case attorney) for requests, questions, and demands that involve routine matters clearly within the paralegal's knowledge and functional ability to resolve. Other requests, questions, or demands may constitute serious questions involving the propriety of the paralegal to respond either affirmatively or negatively. These instances usually involve such questions as: "If I do this, will it be all right?" or "What do you think I should do?" or "If I don't know how to act on this immediately, will the chance be gone?" These all pose ethical problems regarding the unauthorized practice of law by the paralegal (*see generally*, Chapter 3, Ethics). Let us consider three basic problems in this area (commentary is provided in Section 4.04).

PROBLEM NO. 1

The client is involved in personal injury litigation resulting from injuries she received in an auto accident. She calls your office first asking for the attorney representing her on this case, but the attorney is out of the office for the day. The client states that an insurance adjuster is at her home and wants to take a written statement regarding the details of the auto accident.

QUERY: How should the paralegal handle this situation?

PROBLEM NO. 2

Preparations are nearly complete for allowing an adversary to inspect documents under a "Request to Produce" that required "each and every copy" of a specified variety of records and files. Some 3,700 pages of material, already screened, are ready. Two hundred and fifty pages of privileged material have been removed, and the appropriate list prepared, when the client reveals that a wholly owned subsidiary has nearly an exact duplicate file, plus several individual personal files reasonably responsive to the request. Seventy-five work hours have already been expended, and the inspection is scheduled for the day after tomorrow.

QUERY: What does the paralegal need to do to allow the lawyer to select a course of action? Can the paralegal suppress this information until it is too late to act on it? Should the paralegal simply throw up his or her hands and leave for the day?

PROBLEM NO. 3

A client is involved in a difficult contested divorce involving substantial assets in real estate, stocks, bonds, annuities, and other property. In the course of conducting the interview and assembling the property and asset descriptions, it becomes apparent that the client has been siphoning community property assets into a separate fund over the past two or three years. It has been skillfully done, and only the paralegal's intimate involvement and careful analysis allowed the discovery.

QUERY: Does the paralegal punish the client by advising the attorney, become a part of the client's fraud by remaining silent, or send an anonymous note to the adversary attorney to ensure that the client gets his just desserts?

These are but a few of many exceptional situations that will arise in a law office from time to time. After many such experiences, a paralegal's good judgment will become second nature, provided there is no compromise with loyalty to the lawyer and observance of good ethics.

4.016 Accept Guidance, Directions, and Comments Constructively

Paralegals need help, suggestions, guidance, and—most important—constructive criticism to improve their skills and to serve as a reminder of the legal activity they have yet to learn and master. The same can be said of attorneys and other law office personnel. Judgment often is learned through painful postmortems—the examination, after the fact, of alternatives that had not been considered. In other words, the paralegal did not appreciate all the legal issues involved; did not assemble, analyze, and evaluate all the facts or factual circumstances; or simply did not delve deeply enough into background or peripheral matters. The unsatisfactory result could be caused by a failure of the paralegal's comprehensive analytical ability. Paralegals should take initiative and responsibility for their own training and continuing legal education, whether or not their employer is supportive in those efforts.

PROBLEM NO. 4

A simple lawsuit involving the blowout of an oil well during drilling, under circumstances where an error by the drilling crew appears to be the cause, has been filed against the drilling contractor by the client oil company. The issues are simple negligence and contractual indemnity.[3] One of the officers of the drilling contractor has left that firm and lives and works out-of-state. He was not present at the blowout. His deposition is scheduled in Houston. An appropriate commission has been obtained, and one of the firm's junior attorneys is drafted into replacing the case lawyer at the deposition, for it seems to be a routine deposition. At the deposition, little was learned that was not learned from the crew. The witness clearly was not experienced, did not volunteer anything, had no personal records, did not refresh his memory prior to deposition, and relied on what he was told by others. The deposition therefore proved to be simple, straightforward, and unproductive.

QUERY: What if the witness were known before deposition to be an author of "*Blowouts and Blowout Prevention;*" taught seminars in safe drilling practices; served on the board of the American Petroleum Institute; and was sought as a technical consultant on special construction problems concerning blowout equipment?

4.017   Enthusiastically Observe Moral and Ethical Standards

Every profession that exists to serve people has recognized its obligation to provide this service within certain standards of proper conduct. Doctors follow the Hippocratic oath, lawyers follow the *Model Rules of Professional Conduct,* and pharmacists, real estate salespeople, bankers, and other professionals all create (or have created by legislation or regulatory agency) guidelines for proper and proscribed conduct. The direct beneficiary is the patient, the client, the customer, or the "civilian" who uses the offered service.

This is as it should be, and these constraints on conduct are ones that paralegals must enthusiastically endorse, accept, and observe, for the paralegal profession serves two levels of users: lawyers and clients. The first endorsed, published, and adopted code of ethics in the paralegal profession was written by the ethics committee of NALA in 1975 and is discussed in Chapter 3, Ethics.

4.02   ANALYTICAL ABILITY

Analyzing is the process of separating a thing, idea, and so on into its parts to find out their nature, proportion, function, interrelationship, and other properties. It is from this process that relevant facts are identified as being applicable to a given situation. The ability to analyze is an essential skill for the paralegal to develop. Creative thinking, imagination, and inspiration are excellent attributes; however, the routine, methodical assembly of every relevant fact or evidentiary fact is also essential. Analytical ability that cannot be demonstrated to the satisfaction of the employing attorney in direct relation to a particular case or set of circumstances surrounding a particular case has no merit or usefulness. However, when the paralegal can supply the attorney with reliable control and retrievability of the analyses of facts, testimony, or source information, then the paralegal's system and analytical ability become invaluable.

Before beginning the analysis and evaluation of facts and/or testimony in a case to determine the relevant facts, the paralegal must be aware of the essential elements of the case. For instance, a case of misrepresentation is founded on proving at least the following seven points:

1. The representation was to a material fact.
2. The representation was false.
3. The falsity was known to the party making it.
4. The representation was made with the intent to induce the other party to act.
5. The representation was relied upon by the party to whom it was made.
6. The acting party was ignorant of the falsity of the representation and reasonably believed it to be true.
7. The acting party suffered damages as a result of the act.

There may be side issues of intentional or negligent misrepresentation and oral or written contract to be considered as well. The paralegal therefore has factual categories established, each of which relates to the issues that must be proved or disproved (depending on the client's position). Otherwise, the pattern of facts assembled by the paralegal is worthless to the lawyer.

Suppose this case involved the purchase of machinery designed for a specific agricultural harvesting function and the representation involved the cost of purchase and maintenance, the speed of operation, reliability, and the capability of operation by only two people. Is it relevant that the operation damaged 50 percent of the crop? Yes! Items of proof will be necessary for the issue. Is it relevant that the machine works so slowly that the prime picking period cannot be exploited without two of the machines? Yes! Again, proof may be documentary or testimonial. Is it relevant that its dimensions prevent it from being stored in existing equipment buildings? Probably not, unless some additional representation on ease of storage can be developed. Building an additional shed may not be a supportable item of damage.

Analysis of factual situations in simple cases is often more challenging than in complex cases, for the simplicity of the case issues places a premium on identifying each relevant evidentiary fact and assigning it a value that reflects its help or hindrance to the client's case.

Consider the following hypothetical case and proceed through an interview or fact-gathering session.

> Mr. Jones called an attorney and made arrangements to be represented in a personal injury suit arising from an automobile accident. He is uninsured and has been served with a complaint as the defendant in the suit. After the initial interview with the attorney, the paralegal is the first person in the office with whom he will fully discuss the accident. He arrived by appointment, and after a few minutes of casual conversation, discussion of the case and the gathering of information begin.

The initial questions seek background information, such as name, address, telephone number, place of employment, and marital status. Since this is a case involving an automobile accident, it is essential to ask questions about his driving record; how long he has been driving; what is the model, make, and condition of his car; where it was repaired; and whether it was in prior accidents. These background questions will give insight into the client's nature. For instance, if Mr. Jones has never had a traffic citation in his thirty years of driving, presumably he is a careful driver. If his driving record discloses a number of citations, then clearly there are times when Mr. Jones has disregarded the law. Also, what kind of a car does he drive, and what color is it? Psychologists have determined that there is a link between the type and color of a car a person drives and the individual's personality; for example, a souped up red car indicates an aggressive person, while a conservative model and color suggests a conservative individual. Is the client a steady worker, or does he flit from job to job? Is he happily married, miserably married, or in the process of a divorce? The answers to these questions should be used to assist in evaluating the answers the client gives in response to questions related to the facts of the case.

> Mr. Jones admits to two speeding citations in the last eighteen months. He drives a bright yellow car with a large, modified engine with two four-barrel carburetors and is, according to him, "the fastest thing on the road." He is between jobs, and he does not approve of his wife's job. The interview proceeds into the discussion of the case.
>
> **L.A.:**   Now Mr. Jones, where did this accident occur?
> **Jones:**   In the driveway of Sam's Go-Go Bar.
> **L.A.:**   What was the date, the day of the week, and the time of the accident?
> **Jones:**   It was April 24, 1997, a Saturday, and it was just before closing time, around 1:45 a.m.

(His testimony established that the accident occurred on private property, on a weekend, and late at night. A few questions on weather, lighting, visibility, vehicle conditions, and so on should be asked.)

> **L.A.:**   Mr. Jones, had you been in Sam's prior to the time of the accident?
> **Jones:**   Yes, I had been there. My wife works as a go-go girl for Sam, and I pick her up after work.

(Now the paralegal knows why Mr. Jones was at Sam's, but the question arises, "If he picks his wife up after work, why was he leaving before closing time?")

L.A.:   According to the complaint, Mr. Smith says that you deliberately drove your car into the side of his car as he was leaving the parking lot and that after you hit his car, you left your car and attempted to pull him from his vehicle. Please tell me what really occurred in the sequence it happened.

Jones: Well, I didn't see his car in the driveway, and I only left my car to go over to him to see if he was injured.

There are now two entirely different and conflicting accounts of the same accident. The accident could have occurred as the client alleges, or it could be that he did not disclose that the plaintiff had been overly friendly with Mrs. Jones in Sam's Go-Go Bar, that Jones became enraged, left Sam's to follow the plaintiff, and in a fit of temper hit the plaintiff's car and assaulted him. With the background information about Mr. Jones along with his account of the accident, it is now time to proceed with a more detailed investigation for corroboration, identification of other witnesses, and so forth. (*See* Chapter 6, Interviewing Techniques and Chapter 7, Investigation.)

Keep in mind that clients usually tell their story in a manner that places them in the best light. They do not do this intentionally to deceive; it is a subconscious rationalization to avoid embarrassment or criticism for their actions. In the case of Mr. Jones, continue to question him to gather more facts and information to substantiate his presentation of the accident. This is done without expressing doubt and without being accusatory. If there is any doubt about the actual facts of the case, independently question the witnesses to the accident and/or to events that occurred prior to the accident. This information, along with the information given by Mr. Jones, will allow the paralegal to analyze the facts and reach a conclusion that will be helpful to the lawyer in representing Mr. Jones, including providing a basis on which the attorney can further investigate other avenues of defense or settlement. The prime rule of legal assisting is "never let the attorney be surprised by harmful information!" Find it and defuse it so the attorney can adapt to its impact.

In more complex cases, "Requests for Production of Documents" sometimes seek invoices, purchase orders, employee lists, time cards, expense accounts over a period of time, books, records, histories, and other comparative data surrounding the particular action. Responses to these requests may result in boxes and boxes of materials or may state that certain records will be available for counsel to inspect or reproduce at a particular time and place. Here, again, the ability of the paralegal to index and analyze comparative data will be of invaluable assistance to an attorney. The attorney can instruct the paralegal on the issues involved and the comparative data needed. The paralegal may then spend days or weeks reviewing statistical data, documents, manuscripts, depositions, records, invoices, or purchase orders; making comparative analyses and chronological sortings; and gathering other information. For example, perhaps the adverse party's attorney has produced computer printouts in answer to a request for certain documents or information from those documents. The paralegal must then become familiar with the computer printouts—how to read them and how to trace the source documents from which the information on the printouts came. Then, the paralegal begins comparing the printouts with the source documents to verify the accuracy of the information contained on the printouts. In performing this verification process, the paralegal may discover discrepancies between the source documents and the computer printout. This use of good judgment and analytical ability is an example of what makes the work product and effort of the paralegal invaluable to the attorney. Document cases are discussed in more detail in Chapter 9.

4.021   Basic Rules

As a legal analyst, (whether an attorney or paralegal), an established structure is required before approaching any form of analysis. Analytical ability is founded on a few basic rules with which all paralegals should be familiar.

First, you need to understand the objective of the analysis. Without a clear understanding of your objective, you will lack focus and will not be able to develop a structure to achieve the objective. If you are unclear about the objective, seek more guidance from the attorney who assigned the project to you until you feel comfortable in knowing what you are to accomplish. Many times you can review an example of a similar project that was completed in another case; this will give you a guide to follow as you plan your strategy.

Next, you will need to comprehend the resources that are available for you to utilize in achieving the objective of your analysis. Not only will you need to assemble the data which is the subject of your analysis, but you will also need a general understanding of how the data is presented and how to interpret the data. As part of your analysis, you will need to determine the function of the materials or documents to be analyzed. Knowing the purpose and function of the materials you will evaluate is paramount before performing any analysis of data. These concepts will be discussed in more detail in Sections 4.0212 and 4.0213.

Finally, after you have an understanding of the assignment and the data to be analyzed, you will need to establish the parameters of the project to develop some structure to your approach. A key element in choosing the techniques, systems, and detail, which you will utilize in establishing the structure, is the time you will take to complete the assignment. All of these make up the factors that will provide the structure to your analysis. Some possible suggestions on this topic are covered in Sections 4.0214 and 4.0215.

4.0211 Understand the Final Objective of the Analysis.

It is important to understand the final purpose of the analytical effort. Are you determining the cause and effect between two events? Are you categorizing items to illustrate their relationship to each other? Are you evaluating events to create a time line of events? These are scenarios that you may be asked to accomplish, and your understanding of the basic assignment is paramount to producing the desired result.

Initially, you need to know some basic facts before you can begin your analysis, such as the parties involved in the event, where the event took place, what motivating factors, if any, played a role in triggering the event, and what duties existed, if any, on one party to another? If you cannot answer these basic questions, begin with an overview of the facts of the case by reading case memos, complaints, and other foundational pleadings. If the facts are not clearly in focus, look to other written material which discusses the factual issues, the legal issues and/or the question of law which brought the client to the attorney you are assisting.

A different situation exists when the final objective is to provide demonstrative exhibits for use in helping a jury to understand the lawyer's case. Little learning is involved, although a testing of different mediums might be needed, such as photography, sketches, graphs, charts, maps, videotape, and models.

If the need is simply to identify and retrieve exhibits easily and quickly that were introduced in single depositions, solve that problem alone in lieu of expanding it into a casewide indexing system. Do not develop complex procedures when there is no need for them. If the utility of the deposition exhibits requires only identifying duplicates (many times several witnesses will identify the same object or document during their depositions, resulting in that one exhibit having several exhibit numbers), a detailed history or summary of each exhibit may be unnecessary. A workable, understandable, cross-reference system of duplicate exhibits would suffice. Effective analysis should fit the needs of the case.

4.0212 Comprehend the Resources Available.

Analysis can sometimes only be accomplished within the mind of one person. At other times, it requires the assembly of information, data, documents, records, photos, and other material to allow sorting, copying, indexing, and physical comparison. Large and complex tasks are sometimes better handled by breaking them into smaller, simpler tasks, which can be divided among a team. For instance, one person is responsible for creating a chronological history, while another person assembles and collates all witness statements for points of agreement or conflict, and yet another person copes with analysis and cross-referencing the data from interrogatories, requests for admission, and other discovery devices.

If only one paralegal is assigned to a large and complex task, with no extra help or funds available, then extra document reproduction, document imaging, scale model construction, and other such items may be unrealistic. Each necessary act or function must be scheduled to fit available equipment and personnel hours. A realistic approach to time estimates and dollar values is essential. The paralegal who, without protest, accepts or acquires more projects than can realistically be completed hurts the employing attorney and commits cumulative professional suicide. Effectiveness is measured by successfully completed projects.

As an example of a situation, you may be asked to analyze how an accident occurred in a manufacturing plant. This might require a broad study of a complex manufacturing process in order to comprehend the relationships of people, plans, and documents—obviously a major learning effort—before undertaking any analysis of the evidentiary material. In order to accomplish this assignment, you need a clear understanding of the answers to the questions posed previously regarding the players, event location, motivating factors, and responsibilities of each person or entity. You may need to seek educational material on the subject before you can proceed with your analysis. A trip to a public or university library may provide you with the resources you need, or you may utilize the Internet as a resource or even a retained expert to provide documentation on the process.

If you are assigned the task of coordinating an analysis of documents produced by an adverse party for use in an upcoming deposition, you will first need to make sure your work environment is conducive to doing an effective job. Select a place and time to review the documents where interruptions will be minimal and your full attention can be devoted to the task. You will need to understand the issues in the case so that you can flag documents that relate to each issue. All these steps require concentration and your greatest analytical ability. Plan your work schedule accordingly so that important details will not be overlooked.

Remember to schedule demanding projects for the time of day when you are the most mentally alert. For many people, this time will not be right after lunch. Most of us know when our peak productive time periods occur. This is the time to schedule the important task of analyzing documents produced by adverse parties. Early in the morning may be the best time for you, when you are rested and ready to tackle the day's assignments. For others who are slow morning starters, a late-morning block of time is best. Still others reach their most productive time in the afternoon, so adjust your time accordingly. Once you have the appropriate time designated for the assignment and you have identified the resources you need to help you comprehend the documents, your next step is to make some initial analysis about the function of the materials or documents to be reviewed.

4.0213 Determine the Function of the Materials or Documents to be Handled.   Paralegals do not analyze abstract philosophies but testimony, recorded events, groups of documents, production systems, material objects, and/or locations. If the material involved is evidentiary in nature, it must be preserved, protected, and prepared for production at trial. If the analytic process requires use of that object, a surrogate must be developed, a duplicate obtained, or a model created. For instance, an original evidentiary document is stored in the safe, but a photocopy is adequate for the paralegal's analytical purpose. It can be written upon, recopied (with a legend as described in Chapter 8, Pretrial Litigation Skills), or annotated. The analysis may be to summarize and simplify the utility of a document, a few documents, or all the documents, and it is important to create the proper framework to meet the need established by the attorney.

Many trial advocacy seminars bring out the fact that a good advocate does not *tell* the jury what to believe, but instead *shows* them. In order to show the jury what they need to know to render a decision, an attorney needs to have the evidence organized in a logical manner as it relates to the issues. This job is usually delegated to the paralegal to prepare before trial.

How do we ensure that our efforts contribute to a successful trial outcome? We cannot routinely prepare and answer discovery and document production requests or summarize documents without some direction in mind. This would be like driving to an unfamiliar destination a thousand miles away without using a road map. Formulate a trial plan early in the case by identifying the issues; in that way all efforts are directed toward proving those issues at trial. Armed with a clear view of the case issues, the paralegal can begin the review of documents and materials and determine their function in the case by categorizing them to the issues. One method which may be helpful in accomplishing this task is to establish issue files. Separate files can be labeled with each case issue, and then pertinent documents can be sorted into these files. This effort is the beginning of establishing the parameters of document analysis.

4.0214 Establish the Parameters of the Project.

These parameters may be the rules of law in the case by which topical breakdowns can be established; the number of hours to be dedicated to specific projects; the date of origin of the action that is the earliest date documents can carry and still be relevant to the case; the related professions that have an impact on the standards of the industry involved in the case (a general contractor may be charged with safety orders on excavation, steel work, reinforced cement, electrical wiring, heating, cooling and environmental controls, workers' compensation, Occupational Safety and Health Act regulations, and so on); or possible expert witnesses who could be utilized, for example, economists, statisticians, actuaries, psychiatrists, research analysts, and computer programmers.

If the need is to summarize depositions, then primary concentration should be placed on these summaries. Plans should not extend to cross-referencing Requests for Admission to the deposition testimony (even though it may become necessary at a later date). If the paralegal feels such a cross-reference would be a possibility, then a note to this effect could be placed on a list of possible things to do.

If the paralegal is to work on analyzing documents categorized into issue files, the first question which comes to mind may be how to identify the issues in the case. Usually, the attorney is the one to identify the issues in a case memo or in the complaint drafting. However, as a paralegal gains experience identifying documents keyed to the case issue, the next logical step is to develop the skill to identify the issues, thus providing some high-level assistance to the attorney. Entry-level paralegals may have difficulty identifying issues, but with practice, this valuable skill can be developed. By considering the factual outline of the case, the paralegal can identify the issues by asking a couple of key questions:

1. What is the controversy in this case?
2. What questions of fact will the jury have to decide?

   Wording the issues in a question form makes it easier to identify them. For example, in a construction defect case, an issue may be identified as follows:

   Did the defendant perform the work in a negligent manner?

   Did the defendant perform the work to industry standards?

   Did the defendant use proper equipment for the job?

   Did the defendant violate any statutory requirements on the job?

   Did any of the subcontractors hired by the defendant perform in an incompetent manner?

   Did the defendant follow the instructions given on the work assignment?

Another way to identify issues is to identify and review the jury instructions that are applicable to the facts of the case. Reviewing the areas of law on which the judge will instruct a jury makes it easier to formulate issue questions. This method will, in effect, work backward in trial preparation. By starting with the law and then formulating a theory of what happened, a paralegal can identify the important issues. From there, the paralegal can find the documents relating to the issues, place them in the issue files, or use another method to group the documents by issue category. At first, it may seem unusual to start at the end and work backward to identify the issues, but many trial advocates favor this approach. By first establishing what issues are to be proved, all the effort is spent in gathering evidence to support the theory of the case. Experienced trial attorneys have reported that this method is effective in focusing on the important case issues.

4.0215 Consider Time When Choosing Techniques, Systems, and Detail.   An extraordinary system that can be operated perfectly is worthless if it does not produce results on time. One of the frustrating elements of legal assisting is working within short time frames that require severely simple or incomplete solutions. It must be understood that attorneys are constantly faced with Hobson's Choice (taking what is offered or nothing at all for the lack of an alternative) in making the decision whether or not to dedicate time and money to projects that have a chance of ultimately being proven unnecessary. Sometimes, the attorney will make such a dedication based on an understanding that a certain method is "recommended by experts" in the field without attempting to adapt the method to the particular problem at hand. A prudent and efficient paralegal will become familiar with methods and devices which are both cost effective and time efficient for the attorney, as well as the client, and will evaluate and identify necessary projects from unnecessary ones.

4.022   Analytical Techniques

4.0221 Data Comprehension.   Understanding written material and data are paramount to being a successful paralegal. A critical aspect of a paralegal position involves understanding instructions given both orally and in written form and in performing the task assignment. Some questions the paralegal can go over mentally to make sure the assignment or the data is being understood include the following:

1. Do I know what I am supposed to do?
   a. Are the instructions clear? Do I understand them?
   b. Am I sure of the objectives of the assignment?
   c. Are the planned actions defensible alternatives?
2. Can I do the task?
   a. Do I see its importance?
   b. How is it difficult for me?
   c. Have I made a plan?
   d. Have I made all the necessary preparations?
3. Do I know all the steps to complete the task?
   a. Have I checked my progress?
   b. Do I need more help?
   c. Am I so confused that I have set the project aside?

4. Have I achieved the established goal?
    a. Did I include everything that is relevant?
    b. Have I made the necessary revisions?
    c. Was any portion of the assignment hard for me? Which part and why?
    d. Did the procedure work?
    e. What aspect of my accomplishment was excellent?
    f. What aspect of my accomplishment was inferior?

By using the preceding questions as a checklist to evaluate performance, a paralegal can ascertain where improvement in his or her performance is necessary. If the paralegal is unfamiliar with the case, the attorney can give a brief outline of the facts, or the assistant can read the pleadings and memos in the file before summarizing or beginning the analysis. If necessary, another meeting can occur between the attorney and the paralegal to address areas of questions that are particularly important. Armed with a clear direction and focus, the next step is to begin the factual analysis.

4.0222 Factual Analysis.   In law school, students are taught the structure of legal analysis early in their studies. Paralegals can benefit from understanding the legal analysis formula and how it applies both in analyzing legal issues and applying the facts to reach legal conclusions. The structure of legal analysis takes on the following form.

$$\text{Issue} + \text{Rule} + \text{Analysis} = \text{Conclusion}$$

Referred to as the IRAC method of studying, it begins by stating the question of law or fact raised by the client's case, such as: "Is the defendant liable for the alleged negligent construction on the plaintiff's property?" Once the issue or question of law or fact is identified, the next step is to look at the applicable rule, statute, ordinance, or other regulation and analyze the facts to reach a conclusion which will answer the issue question posed. This type of exercise is an excellent way to develop analytical skills because it requires the use of deductive and analogous reasoning and distinguishing relevant versus irrelevant data, topics which are covered in Section 4.0223 and Section 4.0224. The paralegal should feel challenged by this type of assignment, for it represents a substantive level of work which is more challenging than categorizing or indexing documents. The ability to review a document and extract factual information that is material to answering the issue being addressed is the resulting skill developed here and is one which every paralegal should strive to fine-tune. Opportunities to be challenged by taking on assignments of this nature should always be taken, even if it requires reorganizing the day's workload.
Let's look at an example of this type of legal analysis.

FACTS: A city ordinance requires all businesses operating within city limits to have a business license. A client comes into your office to determine if a business license is necessary for a proposed nonprofit operation that involves the purchase of products at wholesale prices in bulk quantities and sale to its members. No formal business location is anticipated, the president of the nonprofit organization will warehouse the products in his garage, and no profit is expected.

ISSUE: The issue raised is whether the proposed nonprofit operation constitutes a business and is required to obtain a business license to operate.

ANALYSIS: Additional information that is relevant before analyzing the situation and reaching a conclusion includes the following questions that the legal analyst must discover:

1. Is a nonprofit operation considered a "business" under the ordinance?

The legal analysis will have to review relating sections, which define the term "business" as it applies to the ordinance.

2. Is the location of the president's garage where the products will be stored within the city limits?

If it is outside the city limits, then the ordinance would not be applicable since it states that a license is required of all businesses operating *within* city limits.

3. Are members of a nonprofit organization involved in this activity considered partners, customers, or some other status?

Further review of state business and nonprofit statutes will reveal the answers to the questions posed.

4. Does the nonprofit organization have its tax exempt clearance and will it be required to collect and report state sales tax on the items?

Again, further statutory review will provide the answer to these questions.

Once the answers to the questions are obtained, the legal analyst will be able to reach a conclusion to the issue question posed. The ability to use deductive and analogous reasoning will play a key role here.

4.0223 Deductive Reasoning and Analogous Reasoning.   Being able to review facts to determine what conclusions can be reasoned or to determine whether the facts are analogous to those set forth in another source (case law or statutory language) is a challenging skill that is developed with experience. Once a paralegal develops this skill, he or she can become a valuable member of the legal team, especially in litigation matters. One method of study which can help paralegals learn to develop analytical skills is to look at the study of rhetoric and its application when preparing a legal memo that outlines the persuasive reasoning. Referring to the concept of rhetoric as taught at the University of West Los Angeles by veteran paralegal advocate, Janet Kaiser, we can see how this is helpful with legal reasoning.[4]

Rhetoric is the art or the discipline that deals with the use of discourse, either spoken or written, to inform or persuade, or motivate an audience. Classical rhetoricians dealt with the problems of selecting and arranging material in order to effect their purposes. The Latin term *dispositio* and the Greek term *taxis* refer to the study of the various parts of discourse:

1. the *exordium* or introduction;
2. the *narratio* or statement of facts;
3. the *divisio* or outline of our points/steps;
4. the *confirmatio* or proof of our argument;
5. the *refutatio* or discrediting of opposing view; and
6. the *peroratio* or conclusion.

Aristotle wrote about three types of artistic proofs, or appeals:

1. rational appeal (logos)
2. emotional appeal (pathos)
3. ethical appeal (ethos)

Quintilian, in his *Institutio Oratoria*, stated that writers needed to make judgment calls about issues such as these:

1. When should we make our statement of facts continuous, and when should we break it up and insert it *passim*?
2. When should we begin by dealing with the arguments advanced by our opponents, and when should we begin by proposing our own arguments?
3. When is it advisable to present our strongest argument first, and when is it best to begin with our weakest argument and build up to our strongest?
4. Which of our arguments will our audience readily accept, and which of them must they be induced to accept?
5. Should we attempt to refute our opponents' arguments as a whole or deal with them in detail?
6. Should we reserve our emotional appeals for the conclusion or deal with them throughout the discourse?
7. What evidence or documents should we make use of, and where in the discourse will this be most effective?

By thoughtfully reviewing these questions as we evaluate and perform deductive and analogous reasoning, one can see the evolution of legal analysis and the process that litigators go through, many without full realization of what they are actually doing as they prepare and conduct a case for trial.

As a legal memo is prepared covering the analysis, here are some thoughts to take into consideration to assist in the reasoning and writing effort.

GUIDE TO EVALUATING YOUR WRITTEN ANALYSIS[5]

1. Look at the questions presented. Are your questions written so that all necessary information is presented? For example, there is a world of difference between "What is the statute of limitations?" and "What is the statute of limitations for a negligence action in California?"
2. Look at your brief answers. Do your brief answers say the same thing as (i.e., draw the same conclusion as) your answers in the discussion section? If your brief answers are stated as "probably no" or "probably yes," do you give your reader the conditions under which the "yes" or "no" would apply?
3. Look at your statement of facts. Do you give all the facts necessary (i.e., all the facts needed to understand all the ideas presented in the discussion section)? Do you present your facts in a fair manner? Are your facts presented clearly, so that even someone unfamiliar with the matter could understand what had gone on?
4. Look at your discussion section. Check each paragraph carefully; see whether each paragraph (except, perhaps, those paragraphs that set the context of your various arguments) has the following: (1) legal principle; (2) facts; (3) analysis of how those facts relate to the legal principle; and (4) conclusion of analysis. Make sure that you never give a conclusion without having authority to back up that conclusion. Make sure that you always give proper citations for your case law; that means, for state cases, the official and unofficial citations plus the year of the decision and for federal cases, the citation(s) plus the court and the year of the decision. If you cite to statutory or regulatory law, be sure to give the name of the code or title along with the section or rule number. And remember never to cite first or only to secondary law.
5. Look at your conclusion. Is it succinct? Does it eloquently repeat the major conclusions reached in your memo? Does it give the "bottom line" (which bottom line is qualified or conditioned, if necessary)?

6. Make sure you have spelled all your words correctly. Make sure you have set forth only that which is relevant. Make sure that your legal memo has the appearance of a professionally done work product.

Some excellent points to remember when writing a memo regarding your analysis and conclusions include these four categories.[6]

1. Don't fail to explain your conclusions. You must show *how* your facts and your law relate, and you may not jump ahead to the conclusion without giving your analysis, even if you think your analysis is "obvious" to everyone.

2. Don't share irrelevant words from your quoted law. Quote only what you need. Paraphrase only if useful. Your memo won't look any better if you copy irrelevant words, no matter how eloquent those words may be.

3. Don't think that string cites will impress. Some judges think that string cites are the mark of a poor argument. While the "weight" of authority can be helpful, string cites in and of themselves—without analysis—do nothing other than make many readers suspicious of your argument.

4. Don't fail to consider opposing view. Good lawyering does not mean hiding unhelpful law. Legal memos require a full airing of all the relevant law, good or bad. Yes, you may want to discuss counter-arguments to the bad law or counter-arguments that the opposition may make to your good law.

If a paralegal can keep these thoughts in mind while performing the legal analysis, the conclusions reached about what can be deduced from the facts and how it applies to the structure of legal analysis (Issue + Rule + Analysis = Conclusion) will likely be on point. Similarly, by developing one's ability to analyze facts, causal relationships, correlations, similarities, and contrasts between two or more situations, a paralegal's analogous reasoning will be greatly enhanced. One last skill to develop is the concept of identifying relevant data from irrelevant data, which plays a key role in performing legal analysis.

4.0224 Relevant versus Irrelevant Data.

An excellent source of study in developing skill in identifying relevant versus irrelevant data is the sample tests for the law school admission test. These exercises are not only excellent for development of analytical ability, but they are also an excellent tool to utilize in preparation for the Certified Legal Assistant examination administered by NALA. Here is a sample along with some points on making the analysis.

≋ JUDGMENT AND ANALYTICAL ABILITY ≋

Each of the sets in this section contains a statement of facts, a dispute, and two rules. The rules may be conflicting. Each rule should be applied independently and not as an exception to the other. The rules are followed by questions. Select from the answer choices below the one that most accurately classifies each question as it relates to the possible application of one or both of the rules to the dispute.

A. A relevant question whose answer requires a choice between the rules

B. A relevant question whose answer does not require a choice between the rules but requires additional facts or rules

C. A relevant question that is answerable from the facts or rules or both

D. An irrelevant question or one whose answer bears only remotely on the outcome of the dispute

FACTS: Andrew had been a member of the Citizens for Sobriety Society for ten years when he decided to run for the club presidency. His only serious competition was Timothy who, for several years, had been quietly campaigning for the position. When Andrew announced his candidacy, Timothy had him closely watched. Timothy hoped to find some grounds on which he could base his claim that Andrew was not a member in "good standing," as that phrase was defined in the society's rules. Just before the election, the members held a meeting during which they were to decide if each candidate was in "good standing." Timothy chose this opportunity to attempt to establish that Andrew, in fact, was not a member in "good standing."

DISPUTE: Timothy contends that Andrew is not a member in "good standing," as this phrase is defined in the rules; Andrew contends that he is a member in "good standing."

RULES:

I. Any member who pays his dues on time each year and who attends at least 50 percent of the meetings during the course of the year shall be considered a member in good standing.

II. Any member who is convicted of a crime or who brings an alcoholic beverage into the club shall not be considered a member in good standing.

QUESTIONS:

1. If a vote is required, how many members will favor Andrew for the position of club president?

2. If Andrew paid his dues this year, did he pay them on time?

3. Assume that Andrew has attended 75 percent of the meetings each year for the past ten years and has always paid his dues on time. If Andrew was convicted of embezzlement six months ago, is he a member in good standing?

4. At the meeting, Timothy stated that Andrew has not attended any meetings for the past three years and that he brought beer to a private party that he hosted on the club premises. Would Andrew be a member in good standing if these allegations are true?

Correlate the terms, requirements, and responsibilities established by the rules with the person, institutions, and actions given in the facts.

- Do both of the rules apply to the question? Are the outcomes of the rules conflicting? If so, then the response must be A.
- Does only one of the rules apply to the question? Will the outcome resolve the dispute? If so, then the correct response will be C.
- Do both of the rules apply to the question and produce identical outcomes? If so, then the correct response will also be C.
- Can the question be answered from the facts alone? If so, then C is again the correct response.
- Does one or do both rules apply to the question but not resolve it? Would additional information resolve it? If so, then the correct response will be B.
- Does neither rule apply? Will the answer to the question serve to resolve the dispute? If not, then the correct response must be D.

(Answers to this and the following problem are provided in Section 4.04.)

Another sample of questions is the following set of facts, dispute, rules, and questions for your analysis.

FACTS: John was explaining the functions of state government to a social studies class when Albert hit Philip with his eraser. When a disruptive fistfight ensued between Albert and Philip,

John attempted to separate the two. Albert, however, resisted and, in trying to pull away from John, dislocated his own right shoulder. After the fight had been stopped, John made both boys bend over in front of the class while he struck each one five times with a yardstick. John then took the boys to the office of the principal, but on the way John tripped, accidentally bumped into Albert, and caused Albert to fall and break his left arm.

DISPUTE: Albert's parents are suing John for battery on behalf of Albert; John contests the claim.

RULES:

I. A teacher in a public school is permitted to use corporal punishment on a student when such punishment is necessary to maintain order and discipline in the classroom.

II. An intentional touching made by hand, or with an object, and without the consent of the person being touched is battery.

QUESTIONS:

1. Is John liable for battery for breaking Albert's arm?

2. Did John have the legal status of a teacher in the classroom?

3. Was Albert harmed when John struck him with the yardstick?

4. If John is a teacher in a public school and had to strike Albert with the yardstick in order to maintain discipline in the classroom, is John liable for battery for hitting Albert with the yardstick?

5. If corporal punishment may not be administered to a child less than eight years old, is John guilty of battery?

6. In the past, had John often struck students with a yardstick?

These samples are an excellent way to develop analytical skills and critical thinking, all of which will carry over into legal analysis in litigation, tort law, case law analysis, and legal research.

4.03 SUMMARY

Following basic principles aids the paralegal in analyzing factual situations. Analysis requires a good memory and the ability to link facts, testimony, or objects together in relationship to the issues of the case. Effective paralegals persevere in reading and measuring each statement, reported act, or event against others, constantly thinking, "if this is so, how can that be true?" and then proceeding to examine, study, and review to establish the answer. A good paralegal who, after examining, studying, reviewing, and attempting to establish an answer, finds nothing conclusive will not hesitate to say so. Being able to say "I found nothing" is sometimes as important as saying, "this is what I found."

Good judgment and analytical ability are developed attributes of successful paralegals. It is the result of those attributes that is noticed. Judgment improves with experience, and both good and bad judgments, when analyzed and criticized retrospectively, contribute to the improvement. Interested paralegals grasp every opportunity to make judgments in the course of their careers, no matter how small, to test the attitudes of the lawyer, their coworkers, and the firm. Such tests develop a feeling for the responsibility and authority the paralegal is permitted to exercise, expose the paralegal to others in the office, and provide the feedback that allows the paralegal to identify sources of assistance or opposition in various activities.

Judgment and analytical ability go hand in hand with prudence—careful thought in acting and planning. What is excellent for one law office may be a disaster for another. Personnel valued by one law firm may not be appreciated by another. A particular method of filing and storage of files may work fine in one office but would not meet the needs of another.

The paralegal works for people and with the problems of people. Prudence, discretion, respect, and consideration for others—coupled with a driving interest, professional pride, and the desire to perform satisfactorily—will compel the paralegal to consider each assignment, analyze it, and use the best judgment possible.

4.04   DISCUSSION PROBLEMS, COMMENTARIES, AND ANSWERS TO SAMPLE QUESTIONS

Section 4.015   Problem No. 1—Commentary

Since the client is represented by counsel, there should not be any direct discussions by the insurance company and the client. The fact that the client is represented by counsel should be conveyed to the adjuster immediately, and the interview/statement should not take place. The adjuster should then contact the responsible attorney as soon as the attorney's schedule allows.

Section 4.015   Problem No. 2—Commentary

This is not an unusual occurrence in document production cases. The obvious alternatives include: (1) instituting a priority rush program to process the additional material (and later explaining how it first was missed); (2) seeking a postponement; (3) promising future production; or (4) ignoring the documents in hope that the adversary will not discover them. Each alternative should be presented with factual data (such as hours of work involved and cost) and the paralegal's candid recommendation to the attorney. Ignoring the documents in the hope that the adversary will not discover them is not a viable alternative, since it would be ethically unacceptable and could subject the attorney and/or the client to court sanctions for discovery abuse.

Section 4.015   Problem No. 3—Commentary

There are no decisions to be made here, no matter how many alternatives can be created intellectually. The paralegal has a moral and ethical obligation to apprise the attorney of these unpleasant facts and to rely on the attorney's moral and ethical standards to guide any subsequent actions. This is not a totally unusual situation for paralegals to encounter. It may not be diversion of assets (as in this example) but some other aspect of human weakness, avarice, greed, lack of virtues, or unscrupulous business practices. It should not affect the paralegal's execution of duties for the employing lawyer.

Section 4.016   Problem No. 4—Commentary

Part of the preparation of a potential witness, such as the one described in the this scenario, requires not only factual information relative to the situation that gives rise to the pending lawsuit, but there may also be substantial information that this person could offer in a case like the one described. Advanced technology, such as the Internet, and electronic research services could have revealed this person's credentials and background, allowing for a more productive and successful deposition.

Section 4.0224   Problem No. 1—Answers

1. The application of Rule I depends upon whether Andrew paid his dues on time and attended at least 50 percent of the club's meetings during the year. Any application of Rule II depends upon whether Andrew was convicted of a crime or brought alcoholic beverages into the club. Therefore, a question that asks how many members favor Andrew for the position is irrelevant. The correct response is D.

2. This question is relevant solely to any application of Rule I since, under that rule, Andrew is entitled to be considered a member in good standing only if he has paid his dues on time. Additional information is necessary to answer this question. The correct response is B.

3. Because Andrew has attended more than 50 percent of the club's meetings every year and has paid his dues on time, he is a member in good standing under Rule I. Since he has been convicted of a crime, Rule II states that he is not a member in good standing. In this situation, both rules apply, but there are no grounds for choosing between them. The question is relevant since it deals with the central issue, Andrew's status as a member in good standing. The correct response is A.

4. If it were true that Andrew has not attended at least 50 percent of the club's meetings during the past three years, Rule I specifies that he is not a member in good standing. If it were also true that he brought an alcoholic beverage into the club, Rule II specifies that he is not a member in good standing. This question is relevant because it addresses the issue of Andrew's status as a member in good standing, and it may be answered by applying the rules to the facts. Therefore, the correct response is C.

Section 4.0224   Problem No. 2—Answers

1. This clearly relevant question can be answered from the facts given and by using deductive reasoning; we can conclude that the breaking of Albert's arm was not "intentional." The correct answer is C.

2. A review of the facts reveals the lack of a clear answer as to whether John had the legal status of a teacher or some other position. Therefore, since more information is needed, the correct response is B.

3. Whether Albert was harmed is not relevant to the outcome of the dispute since it has no bearing on the definition of the term "battery." The facts clearly reflect that John's striking of Albert with the yardstick was intentional, but the rules do not require any showing of harm to fulfill the definition of a battery. Therefore, since the answer is irrelevant, the proper answer is D.

4. This relevant question requires the choice between the two rules. The correct answer is A.

5. A review of the facts does not reveal the age of the two boys involved in the classroom scuffle. Since more information is needed, the correct response is B.

6. The history of John's striking of students with the yardstick is irrelevant and bears only remotely on the outcome of the dispute. The correct answer is D.

BIBLIOGRAPHY

Block, Gertrude, *Effective Legal Writing*, Foundation Press, New York, Ny, 1999.

Corbett, Edward P. J., *Classical Rhetoric for the Modern Student*. New York: Oxford University Press, 1990.

Fogarty, Daniel, *Roots for a New Rhetoric*. New York: Columbia University, 1959.

Koerselman, Virginia, *CLA Review Manual*. St.Paul, MN: West Publishing Company, 1998.

Koerselman, Virginia, Judgment and Legal Analysis, 2000, A NALA Campus Course, On-line Self Study Program for Paralegals. www.nalacampus.com

Reynolds, John Frederick, ed., *Rhetorical Memory and Delivery.* Hillsdale, NJ: Lawrence Erlbaum Associates, 1993.

Rombauer, M., *Legal Problem Solving.* St. Paul, MN: West Publishing Company, 1981.

ENDNOTES

1. This should not deter a paralegal from taking the initiative to promote efficiencies within the office setting.

2. Many firms and legal departments have established a less hierarchal approach and more of a team effort of prioritization.

3. *Simple negligence*—Consists of failure to exercise for protection of others that degree of care and caution that would, under prevailing circumstances, be exercised by an ordinary, prudent person.

   Contractual indemnity—A contract between two parities whereby one undertakes and agrees to indemnify the other against loss of damages arising from some contemplated act on the part of the indemnitor, or from some responsibility assumed by the indemnittee, or from the claim or demand of a third person, that is, to make good to him such pecuniary damage as he may suffer.

4. John Frederick Reynolds, ed., *Rhetorical Memory and Delivery,* Hillsdale, NJ: Lawrence Erlbaum Associates Publishers, 1993; Edward P. J. Corbett, *Classical Rhetoric for the Modern Student,* New York: Oxford University Press, 1990; and Daniel Fogarty, S. J., *Roots for a New Rhetoric,* New York: Columbia University, 1959.

5. Janet Kaiser, former professor, University of West Los Angeles.

6. Rombauer, *Legal Problem Solving* (West 1981) and Block, *Effective Legal Writing* (Foundation Press, 1992). Reprinted with permission of West, a Thomson Business.

5

Communications

5.00   COMMUNICATION CONCEPT

"Communication," as defined by *Webster's Eleventh New Collegiate Dictionary,* is "a process by which information is exchanged between individuals through a common system of symbols, signs, or behavior." Communicating is a skill each of us employs, some more successfully than others. To be a successful communicator, one must study the elements of communication and then develop the ability to use those elements that complement one's personality.

The scientific aspects of communication involve well-identified techniques that can inhibit communication or facilitate it, depending upon the circumstance.

5.01   ULTIMATE SKILL

Communication is one of the most important skills the paralegal must develop. Paralegals are charged with the responsibility of assembling and conveying facts and factual situations accurately to attorneys from the data source. This test of communication skill relies not only on the identification of a known or believed "fact," but also the effect on it of any coloration of prejudice, self-interest, credibility, and applicability to the problem. Every "fact" that comes to the paralegal originates somewhere else, not in his or her own brain. Otherwise, the paralegal would be the witness rather than the identifier of witnesses. As discussed in other sections of this book, facts may be testimonial, physical, or material. Relaying needed information to the attorney, both clearly and fully, is the paralegal's absolute duty; perhaps it is even more important than the duty to find and isolate the important facts from the unimportant or irrelevant ones.

It is true that a paralegal can accomplish this simply by flooding the attorney with every fact, inference, and circumstance relevant to the case. Doing this without attempting to provide gradations of value to these facts essentially reduces the contribution of the paralegal to little more than that of a clerk. It is important for the paralegal to use the fewest words to convey the fullest message to the attorney or, conversely, from the attorney to such other person as the paralegal is designated to contact. The paralegal's function then is not to serve as an unfiltered conduit of word flow but rather to relay clear meanings and ideas. If there is one formula for communicating that paralegals should adopt, it is the KISS formula—"Keep It Simple, Stupid." Simple words are easily understood and seldom misunderstood. Short sentences do not confuse readers or listeners, and short thoughts are more easily assimilated than long, involved sentences. Remember that one formula. It will be your salvation in all forms of communication—KISS—the minimum needed for full understanding.

5.02   METHODS OF COMMUNICATION

There are increasing numbers of communication techniques, most of which are variations or amplifications of the three most common means of communication available to each of us.

    a. *Nonverbal*, is sometimes referred to as body language. It is the associative image we project by the posture of our body, the clothes we wear or the way they are worn. The expression on our faces or the manner in which we look (or avoid looking) at others is also considered nonverbal.

    b. *Verbal*, or the process of speaking, either directly to someone or through mechanical devices such as a telephone, dictating machine, tape recorder, television camera, or a computer.

    c. *Written*, where we put our thoughts, on paper or electronically, and convey them to someone else.

Communication is also possible by use of any one of the five physical senses of sight, smell, taste, touch, or hearing. However, the message then is frequently shallow and incomplete. A combined use of these senses can afford us a fully textured communication experience with the aggregate impression triggering our "sixth sense," *instinctive reaction*.

Why people instinctively like or dislike others, trust or fear them, and are attracted to or repelled by them are questions too complex for us to study definitively. Paralegals must be aware that the total communication effort is affected by the impressions they give others, whether in the form of body image (good or bad), facial expressions, body language (we will discuss this later), voice tone, phrasing and vocabulary, or writing style and technique.

Each of these, singly or in combination, affects the paralegal's professional productivity and effectiveness directly or through stimulation of the "sixth sense."

It is not the decision reached that is critical. What is vital is that the paralegal consider, test, modify, alter, adapt, or reject concepts in establishing the technique that fits the individual's personality and contributes to strengths while minimizing the effect of weaknesses.

5.03   BASIC COMMUNICATION SKILLS

It is possible through study to improve the quality of one's communication skills. Numerous courses are available at junior colleges, community colleges, universities, private schools, or through seminars sponsored by professional associations that greatly enhance these abilities. Some of the courses that should be considered by persons entering the paralegal field are public speaking, debate, appreciation and analysis of English literature, creative writing, and spelling. All will play a distinct part in raising the communication skills of the paralegal to the highest possible level.

5.031   Public Speaking and Oral Presentations

Public speaking or acting classes, debate societies, and similar activities will assist paralegals in learning to think on their feet, select effective and persuasive words under the press of time, and listen to an adversary or partner.

Public speaking classes teach the skill of organizing a presentation into four steps:

1. The introduction
2. A bridge from the introduction to the topical matter
3. The argument
4. The closing summation

Following these four simple steps will assist the paralegal in preparing presentations to attorneys, clients, or adversaries.

The introduction (step 1) in a speech should accomplish three things: introduce the speaker to the audience; bring the attention of the audience to the presentation in comfort or ease (thus the frequent use of a suitable joke to break the tension and build a little rapport); and provide a preliminary statement of the overall topic.

The bridge to the topic matter (step 2) is a departure from the introduction and a transition to the true body of the presentation. Usually this bridge points out to the audience the timeliness, importance, or value of the material the speaker will cover.

The argument (step 3) is the presentation of viewpoint or data. It is organized in logical, progressive steps that allow the audience to follow the reasoning from a basic fact analysis, with a definition of all issues, choices, procedures, or proposals and any major alternatives.

The conclusion (step 4) is a statement of the speaker's decision, recommendation, or request. Frequently, this is presented as a recapitulation where the salient thoughts are briefly restated and a persuasive conclusion is offered.

5.032   Reading and Writing

Creative writing or literature appreciation classes increase the ability of the paralegal to write, read, and understand what is written. The ability to select words to convey the precise image desired is learned through the reading of essays, speeches, fiction and nonfiction works, and periodicals and daily newspapers.

Reading and writing legal material is a specialized activity that the paralegal must study and practice in the course of the day-to-day job. Seek critiques, discussions, and the opportunity to draft material for others to accept or reject, edit, or totally rewrite. Do not take offense; take the suggestions and criticism and modify the technique used to match the style and technique of the office. Legal writing courses may help develop these skills.

5.033   Special Problems

In communication, special problems must be overcome to accomplish a given purpose. Among those the paralegal may anticipate are communicating with people with different levels of literacy or different lifestyles and backgrounds, with people who are more fluent in a language other than English, and with those who have some form of physical handicap, such as a hearing, vision, speaking, or endurance problem. In each of these situations, it is the duty of the paralegal to find solutions to the problems. The ability to solve such problems is one measure of paralegal's value to attorneys.

With the aged and the young, where attention problems may be a difficulty, schedule a series of visits of short duration or handle only one small problem, fact, or issue at a given meeting. For a person of limited literacy, word selection and the pace of conversation must be adapted to the comprehension level of that individual. If foreign languages are a barrier to direct communication, the use of an interpreter is essential for efficiency and desirable for the interviewee's confidence. Similarly, people with special needs (i.e., those who cannot hear, see, or speak) have substitute means of communication that should be explored and used whenever possible.

5.04 NONVERBAL COMMUNICATION

This term relates to the image we create around ourselves as a matter of choice. It includes body language and sometimes is called the "associative image." It is that aura in which people clothe themselves and by which they project their self-image to others. Body language can be extremely important because the clients who visit law firms frequently differ in age, social status, levels of wealth, and backgrounds.

Law firms operate successfully on the trust of their clients, and each person who is employed by a firm to provide services to clients can reasonably be expected to contribute to that comfortable image of trust. To damage that image with whimsical or bizarre clothing or personal grooming is inexcusable and unnecessary. Each law office generally has some form of standard of dress for both men and women. It should be sufficiently flexible and comfortable so that none of the employees feels unduly constricted, nor should the attorneys feel the firm is being adversely affected or exploited by their employees' manner of dress, grooming, or personal hygiene.

5.041 Facial Expressions

A paralegal's demeanor is as important as his or her grooming. A pleasant, cheerful expression will generally elicit a responding smile from even the most unhappy or dissatisfied person.

We seldom fully appreciate the effect of the image we present to the world by the expression we wear on our faces. Actors make their living by conveying emotion, attitude, and meaning through their faces. Comedians have built their whole careers on wearing a particular expression. If the paralegal watches the attorneys' conduct in court, he or she will see that they, too, make use of the same communication techniques with the jury in trying to convey emotion, attitude, or belief to supplement or add impact to the words they are using.

Similarly, each of us conveys something about our attitude simply by looking at others and exposing our faces to their inspection. A paralegal's attitude signals to the interviewee and to everyone else whether the paralegal is serious or jocular, cheerful or sullen, interested and attentive, or bored and tolerating. Belief and disbelief often can be conveyed simply by the movement of eyebrows, and acceptance or rejection of a story can be expressed by wrinkles, motions, or lack of motions in the face. Surprise, shock, and revulsion are betrayed by facial expressions. The paralegal who does much interviewing should perform "mirror practice" so that appropriate expressions can be adopted as needed. Practice allows analysis of the effect the paralegal may create in the mind of a viewer by a particular grimace, scowl, or smile. It helps to see what the other party sees.

Remember, the most effective tool a paralegal has in a repertoire of facial expressions is that of interested, cheerful, attentive, professional concentration. It encourages interviewees to talk, it makes the employing attorney believe in the paralegal's dedication, and it assists the office manager in determining if the paralegal will properly carry out the functions delegated.

5.042 Hands and Gestures

Some gestures may be offensive to others. Be careful of such actions as pointing fingers, spearing someone in the chest or shoulder while making a point in a discussion, or touching others. Many people resent the unwanted physical contact and miss the point of the argument because they are preoccupied with the contact. A firm handshake when meeting others is an acceptable business greeting in the

United States. Most other physical contact should be discouraged in the professional environment to avoid an unfavorable impression.

5.043 Eye Contact and Body Position

These are vitally important in communication. Books are filled with descriptive terms such as "shifty-eyed liar," "darting glance of fear," and "stern gaze of righteousness," as well as "a stiff-backed rage," "trembling with terror," or "crouched in shame." These vivid descriptions engender images in our minds based on past experiences or remembered characterizations in plays, movies, and television. It is a fact that various emotional conditions produce physical changes of posture and conduct that others interpret. The paralegal is concerned with the messages given with the body or received from others. Project supportive, professional competence and avoid reflecting uncertainty, fear, confusion, irritation, or anger, unless there is a tactical need for such display.

5.0431 Nervous System.

The body's autonomic nervous system is a complex mechanism that aids it in preparing for or responding to stress. It is sometimes called the "fight or flight" condition. As stress increases, most people find their heart rate increases, their breathing rate and/or volume of each breath changes, more adrenaline is produced, and the body temperature may rise. Additional perspiration is generated, and muscle tension increases, sometimes causing trembling. The body is preparing itself for combat or escape, depending on the situation and its development.

Paralegals should observe such symptoms and try to place them in the context appropriate to the situation—normal nervousness in anticipation of a novel experience, fear of the unknown, or fear of being detected in a lie.

Common nervousness can be dispelled by accommodation to the circumstance and the establishment of a comfortable situation. Other physical manifestations should be noted, together with the stimuli that generated them. Paralegals can adjust (or record) the condition, as needed, when it is reflected. The same messages sent by paralegals may be irretrievable, and it is necessary to know, understand, and minimize the body language that adversely affects the paralegals' function. Again, note the conduct appreciated or disliked in others and adopt that preferred conduct.

5.0432 Body Language.

Among the most common types of body language with a high potential for adverse interpretation are:

a. No eye contact. Avoiding a person's eyes during conversation is very dangerous for a paralegal. It has been said that the "eyes are the mirror of the soul." Failure to look in the other person's eyes denies the paralegal an excellent means of character evaluation and may create a doubt in the other party's mind as to the honesty, candor, or interest of the paralegal. Practice looking at people when they talk. Hold their eyes and try to evaluate whether they shift their eyes because they are lying or embarrassed or just because they are nervous. Do they practice the "sincere look" when trying out a tall tale? Match the stress of the conversation with the appearance of their eyes. Stress causes the pupils to contract in some eyes; others become brighter and wetter, while others jerk back and forth. Joy, pleasure, and friendliness cause some eyes to sparkle. It is not the whole world of meanings that is most important to a paralegal professionally, but note the changes that occur during the talks and the time in the talks when the changes occur.

b. Standing too close. Most people in Western cultures want some distance between themselves and those with whom they talk. It is an outgrowth of the "territory" theory that anyone who comes too close to you is "invading your territory." Big or tall people who stand very close to smaller or shorter people create both a physical intimidation and a difficult psychological problem of submission and/or anger.

"Arm's length" negotiations imply an equality of bargaining position, physically and psychologically. Paralegals who like being close to people must gain their trust first; then closeness is tolerable.

c. Slouching, stooping, and leaning. These postures suggest carelessness, lack of interest, and lack of intensity. They are acceptable with friends but should be avoided during first meetings. Erect posture may not prove the person is alert, but its lack makes the proof more necessary.

Body language and all its elements are important to a paralegal in the employer-employee relationship as well as the interviewer-interviewee one.

5.044   The Office and the Image

Body control, personal grooming, manner of dress, and facial expressions must meet acceptable standards for the office. These standards must also extend to the order and arrangement of the desk or office. This is one place where the old adage "neatness counts" cannot be emphasized more. Neatness assists prompt location of a file when it is needed. It engenders confidence in the minds of visitors to the office, whether they are other paralegals, lawyers, or witnesses. In many ways, the office and the desk are extensions of the paralegal's self-image: organized or disorganized, neat or sloppy. Certainly for interviewees who visit the office on business, the neatness of the office and the fact that all materials relating to their case are immediately available, while the cases of everyone else are discreetly out of sight, engender confidence and the belief in their minds that they are important and that their affairs are important and confidential.

5.05   VERBAL COMMUNICATION—THE LISTENING PORTION

Verbal communication denotes dialogue, speaking, *and* listening. It requires the use of the voice and of the ear, the two essential tools in verbal communication. They function twelve to twenty hours of every day in some form or another, and of the two, the ear and its use may be the most important. It is the "inbound" half of a two-way street. Listening is not an easy skill, but it is one that should be practiced at every opportunity by every paralegal. Most people like to talk, and in talking, they expose themselves to the listener. If the paralegal will listen quietly, he or she has greater opportunity to hear what the speaker has to say, comprehend the words the speaker uses, and correlate those words with other things the speaker has said before. This allows the paralegal to accommodate himself or herself to the speaker's particular level of intelligence. The paralegal is then better prepared to phrase productive questions at the appropriate time.

5.051   Fast Mind—Slow Mouth

The mind works much faster than the mouth. As a result, many people find their minds telling them to argue, analyze, interject, question, or comment rather than to continue listening for greater and greater detail. There is nothing wrong with the mind going faster than the words of another, provided the narration is not confused by the listener's interjecting comments, thereby making the speaker reflect and fully realize what he or she is saying. The trickiest part about listening is to listen accurately and absorb what is being said, rather than allowing the mind to be distracted with comparisons, analysis, and arguments about what is being said.

5.052   Listen and Note

The preferred technique is to listen and take notes while visually observing the person doing the talking. The change of facial expression, onset of blushing, movement of the eyes, and willingness to meet the listener's eyes or the avoidance of them are all significant to the person who is watching and listening.

Whether it is an attorney giving instructions to a paralegal for the first time or an interviewee telling a story for the fourth time, it is important to listen closely to what is said.

5.053   Words—The Key to Speaking

Everyone speaks thousands of words every day. Strangely enough, the number of *different* words used among those thousands of spoken words may be small; the rest are the same words used repeatedly. It is estimated that the average high school graduate uses only 700 different words in the course of normal conversations, and that figure does not increase appreciably with a college education. Twelve hundred is a fairly common number of different words in regular use by U.S. college graduates.

By contrast, a Japanese child entering school for the first time has a working knowledge of approximately 6,000 different words. This is due in part to the structure of the Japanese language, in which verbs are combined to create conjugations reflecting tense and other grammatical elements. In English, we live through a memory course of strange rules and irrational pronunciations of certain combinations of letters. For paralegals to communicate effectively, it is necessary to learn, appreciate, and correctly use these variations to the highest degree.

5.054   Jargon

Once a person has attained a position as a paralegal, some alchemy occurs in the personality, requiring the adoption of Latin phrases and the jargon of the legal profession in that paralegal's normal conversations with peers, clients, and others. This is a serious error because people outside of the legal community may not fully understand the meaning of these words; thus, their use tends to confuse rather than clarify the meaning intended by the speaker. A paralegal needs a broad vocabulary, and toward that end, understanding legal terminology is necessary. However, legal terminology should be reserved for use in technical discussions with peers where the exact meaning of the legal terms is important.

5.055   Meanings, Words, Sounds, and Vocabulary

One of the unfortunate features of the English language is the number of words that sound the same phonetically and yet carry substantially different meanings. A different complication is words of similar sounds but different spellings. These words can pose very serious problems in the use of electronic dictating or recording equipment.

Despite the limited number of words used by the average American, *Webster's Unabridged Dictionary* modestly describes itself as containing 20,000 different words. Add to that the amazing complexity of technical languages, such as those of the legal, engineering, and medical professions, as well as the jargons adopted in business and other fields. The volume increases dramatically and so does confusion.

Since paralegals work in all of these areas, the demand for learning vocabulary is strong. However, great discipline should be exercised in the vocabulary that is used. Slang and jargon are often regional, having totally different meanings outside a given area. Learn everything but limit use to the right phrase at the right time. Do not simply exercise a specialized vocabulary to impress or awe listeners. Consider words as tools to convey appropriate meaning, not toys with which to satisfy the ego.

5.056   Ethnic Language and "Street Talk"

Complicating communication is the proliferation of slang and/or ethnic phraseology and "street talk" in modern language. Many community colleges and some universities are adopting literature classes particularly designed to satisfy the needs of ethnic language students. Whenever possible, paralegals should be familiar with these vocabularies, particularly when interviewing or contacting these ethnic populations. "Street talk" is ever changing, as is slang, and staying abreast is difficult at best. A retentive memory, inquiring mind, and patient questioning when encountering street talk can clarify the needed meanings.

5.057   Understanding Is the Object

Remember, the essence of communication is understanding, by both the speaker and the listener. The paralegal is at once a highly skilled listener, translator, and speaker. The use of profanity, slang, or ethnic stereotypes by paralegals is inappropriate. The people the paralegal will encounter may use them, and it may be necessary in the course of those conversations to be able to speak on a comfortable level with such people. The paralegal must be aware of these language dissimilarities and be able to accept their use without shock, irritation, or condescension.

5.058   Voice Tone and Implication

Perhaps more important than the words they speak is the manner in which paralegals use their voices: tone, modulation, inflection, and diction. A word correctly used but incorrectly pronounced loses the meaning ascribed to it. The paralegal often discusses matters of great importance to people in stressful situations where the listener's critical examination of the paralegal's verbal response is colored by anxiety. Many clients anticipate failure, and they expect their initial statements will be misunderstood. Support their hopes and dispel their fears as much as possible with a pleasant voice tone that is well modulated, with good diction, and with a relatively cheerful or at least neutral attitude.

5.059   Facial Expressions and Word Meaning

One delightful feature about person-to-person conversation is the ability to impute shades of meaning to another's words from the emotion displayed on the person's face and from characterizing the individual's voice tone, modulation, and diction as being helpful, supportive, confirming, or argumentative. Once the conversation is filtered through a mechanical phase, such as through the use of a telephone or dictating or recording equipment, these supplemental clues to the meaning of the speaker are lost. Often it is not possible to ask for clarification if the communication is on electronic media. Therefore, careful use of words and language and of voice tone and modulation is critical when conducting a conversation or a verbal communication through mechanical or electronic means.

5.06   TELEPHONE TECHNIQUES

The telephone is one of the most common electronic or mechanical devices in verbal communication. We seldom consider it as an extension of our personality. However, the majority of a paralegal's first contacts with people will be accomplished over the telephone, and it is very important to seriously analyze the manner in which the paralegal conducts himself or herself on the telephone.

Telephone companies around the nation offer training courses in telephone techniques for people who work in offices and use the telephone as part of their daily business. One of the things they uniformly advocate, and rightly so, is to "put a smile in your voice." There is nothing more aggravating than to call an office seeking information and be switched from one phone to another, seeking the one person who can provide the information. This is especially true if each of the people to whom the individual is transferred expresses by voice tone, inflection, or choice of words his or her lack of interest in the particular request or inability to assist the caller.

5.061   Telephone Etiquette

A quick way to alienate clients is to put a client on hold immediately after answering the telephone, according to the Telephone Doctor, a St. Louis-based training company. An overwhelming 85 percent said telephone courtesy makes "a lot of difference" in their willingness to purchase goods or services.

Answering the call: Standards should be set throughout the company for proper phone etiquette. The content should be memorized by everyone as though it were a mini commercial. The phone should be answered in two to four rings with a standard greeting, such as: "Good Afternoon, the Miller Law Firm, how may I direct your call?"

Transferring the call: Proper etiquette for transferring calls is essential. Tell the caller you are going to transfer him. ("Please hold" is unprofessional.) Be sure you are transferring to the right person. If the call is not picked up, get back to the caller.

When you are asked to screen calls: Paralegals, although they usually don't answer the phone initially, are often responsible for screening the calls for their attorneys. "I will see if Mr. Miller is available" and "Can you tell me what your call is in reference to" are common and acceptable inquiries. Make sure you get the name correct! Ask for the proper spelling and the correct pronunciation, if in doubt. Pay attention to titles.

Managing difficult clients: Difficult callers fall into a few general categories, and there are certain helpful approaches to dealing with them.

1. Those who go on and on . . . ask questions.
2. Those who are angry . . . show empathy and respect.
   a. "What you are telling me is important."
   b. Listen to understand. "Tell me what happened."
   c. Uncover the expectations. "Will you tell me what you feel needs to be done."
   d. Repeat the specifics. "Let me be sure I understand."
   e. Outline the solutions. "You have several choices."
   f. Take action and *follow through*. "I will personally check and let you know."
3. Those who speak little or no English . . . listen carefully, speak slowly.
4. When you reach a boiling point, turn the call over to a coworker, whom you have briefed, and let the client know that "perhaps Ms. Jones can answer your questions. I'll transfer you to her."

Closing the conversation: Thank the client for calling. Provide assurances that any promises will be fulfilled. Most importantly, leave the customer with a positive feeling. Although they can't see you, the client can tell whether or not you're smiling by the tone of your voice, so SMILE! A courteous closing might include, "We're happy to help," "I have enjoyed talking to you," or "If you have additional questions, please call again." Let the client hang up first, as a courtesy.[1]

5.062   Identification and Notation

When placing or receiving a telephone call, the paralegal must identify himself or herself by name and title. Notes should be taken of all calls involving clients or other office matters, and a copy of such notes should be placed in the appropriate client file. Any agreements reached or information given or received should be noted. All information should be complete and expository with date, time, and the parties identified, even if it is for the file only. Anything involving a case, the attorney, or a client should be summarized with the same elements in a memorandum to the file or to the attorney, a letter to the client, or both. A log of all telephone calls placed and received should be kept not only by the reception-ist, but also by the paralegal, particularly when he or she is accepting or placing calls on behalf of the employing attorney.

5.0621 The Telephone as an Aid.

Voice Mail: Communications through voice mail has greatly enhanced the productivity in the office. Whether busy on other telephone calls or away from the office, voice mail picks up messages while one is otherwise engaged. The caller leaves a detailed message so the person called can act on the message and then return the call with a response, without a loss of time. Of course, voice mail can only be an effective and efficient way to handle communications if the practice of reviewing all messages and returning calls promptly is adhered to.

Answering Machines: Answering machines are another tool used to record messages when the person called is away from the telephone. Taped machines or digitally recorded messages allow the communication to be delivered with the same clarity and efficiency as talking in person. Quality of equipment must be a prime consideration. Tapes that run out or digitally recorded messages that garble words are of no use in the efficient world of communications.

5.0622 Proper Use of the Telephone.   The telephone should be held so that words are transmitted directly into the mouthpiece and words emanating from the earpiece may be clearly and easily heard. Using *speakerphones* for conference calls may be beneficial if more than one person will participate on one instrument. The sound from the speakers may occasionally be eerie and distorted. The use of conference calls that interconnect several telephones so that each person can converse from his or her own office instrument may be used. In each of these cases, the participants must take turns talking.

5.063   Confirming Letters

When a telephone call involves matters of legal procedures, docketing, extensions of time to answer, arrangements for production of witnesses or documents, or other material relevant to a particular case, a confirming letter should be initiated immediately following the call. This letter should be a complete recapitulation of the discussed topics and arrangements to be included in the case file for the informa-tion and documentation of the attorney, with copies to the office docket control and each affected party in the case. Usual custom calls for the party requesting an accommodation to write the letter; however, paralegals are best advised to initiate the confirming letter immediately for the protection of their own firms and attorneys. If two letters result, redundancy will not hurt, and a difference of opinion in what the agreement was thought to be might be revealed.

5.064   Phonetics

Telephones and other mechanical or electronic equipment can alter voice tones in the normal speaking mode. As a result, the transmittal of information of any importance, particularly names, addresses, num-bers, or initials, should always be double-checked and sometimes triple-checked to insure accuracy. Let-ters, particularly, are easily misheard over a telephone or on a tape recording; B, D, F, P, S, T, and V tend to be confusing and indistinct over the telephone. Compensate with phonetic spelling. When there is doubt, use a phonetic alphabet to clarify any ambiguities. The paralegal who does not know the international alphabet must substitute his or her own, for instance, "A as in apple" and "G as in George." Numbers, too, are difficult to hear clearly over the telephone. "Fifth" and "sixth" can be confused. Therefore, when discussing an address over the phone, first be sure that the other party understands the address and that the listener reads it back to the giver precisely the way it was heard. When there is doubt, use the phonetic alphabet to clarify any ambiguities or count the numbers as in "one, two, three, four, five— fi-yiv street!"

5.065   Recording Telephone Statements

Before using the telephone to record any statements or conversations, the paralegal must first confirm with the supervising attorney that this is acceptable. If the attorney approves the use of telephone recording, the paralegal must review and observe the federal laws on the use of tape recording equipment, particularly in connection with telephone company facilities. (*See* Chapter 6, Section 6.056 Electronic Recording Decisions for a discussion on recording considerations.) Both participants must be aware the recording is being made, and both must agree to such recording. This acknowledgment should be stated at the outset of such a recorded conversation and repeated before its termination.

Do not forget to memorialize all important, nonrecorded telephone conversations with clear, written notes as previously discussed in Section 5.062. Even recorded telephone conversations can more profitably be memorialized by a concise, written summary of the call, reserving any tape recording for future reference, if and when needed, rather than having the full dialogue transcribed and edited.

5.066   Cellular Phones

Many attorneys and their staff are now using cellular phones and other hand-held electronic devices to maintain contact with their clients and firms while away from the office. The paralegal must be familiar with the proper use and etiquette of these devices. Common courtesy dictates a need to keep the ringer volume low, on vibrate, or turned off when in places such as a courtroom or in depositions. Be aware of others around you, and keep conversations brief and mindful of your duty to protect the confidentiality of these conversations. Project a professional image. The device may need to be turned off if in an area with a weak signal to avoid static interference. As a safety precaution, do not use any device while behind the wheel. Remember, the person with whom you are meeting should always take precedence over incoming messages or calls.

5.07   DICTATING EQUIPMENT

The use of dictating equipment is well established as a time-saving operation in the conduct of work for attorneys and secretaries. This dictation process now extends to a large proportion of paralegals who must convert their thoughts and notes into some less cryptic and more communicative form of preserved document. Paralegals must learn the courtesies and practices of good dictation. One of the greatest helps is to understand fully the dictating equipment to be used, both in its use and its ability to reproduce the human voice. The user's manual supplied with each piece of equipment should be studied by each user before attempting to dictate.

Every dictated communication should carry some identifying data at the outset to ensure that the material can be identified quickly and easily by the typist at the time of transcription and, if necessary, later. Among the essential items are the date, name of the dictator, dictator's phone number or extension, case or topic of the dictation, whether or not there are copies intended for other parties, and whether this effort is for execution as a draft or final form.

The use of a dictation "log" is helpful to most secretaries, whether they are experienced legal secretaries or novices from typing pools (*see* Exhibit 5-1). The log usually has a tape reference number

EXHIBIT 5-1   Sample Dictation Log

Dictator:		Date:
		Tape/Side:
		Attorney:
		Client Matter/File No.:
		Deadline:
Subject:		
To:		CC:
Special Notes: (Names, Addresses, Technical Terms, etc.)		

and identifies the dictator, the date, the type of case or topic, how many copies are needed, and the full names and addresses of all parties who are addressees or who will be mentioned in the course of the dictated material. This insures that the proper spelling of names and addresses is reflected in the final product. Including on the log any special, technical, or obscure words used in the dictation will save the dictator and the secretary/typist a great deal of time (the latter in research, the former in editing).

5.071 Voice Use

The next element encountered is how the voice is used in dictating material other people will type. The pace of dictation should approximate a normal conversational pace. However, it is necessary to use better diction and pronunciation. Slurring or the use of unnecessary words as "and," "oh," "or," and "er" are not helpful to the typist and in a long tape can be both irritating and distracting. Do not use a monotone, but use a modulated voice, as you would in conversation. If possible, place emphasis on the correct words and the usual voice inflections that reflect sentence closings, periods, or question marks.

5.072 The Outline

An outline of the material to be dictated should be prepared either mentally or on paper before beginning dictation. The entire structure of the ultimate document must be conceived ahead of time, both in content and form. Its format should be thought out and described either on the dictation log or in the introductory portion of the dictated material. Any tabulated material to be included should be referred to, and if it is in a form that can be inserted as a separate sheet or some other variety of material, it should be attached to the dictation log.

The actual dictation should proceed smoothly and quickly, with little dead space on the tape where the dictator is thinking. The speaker must concentrate on enunciating correctly so the typist can correctly understand the words and translate them into written form. Be especially cautious of using words that have unusual or irregular spelling or are technical terms, trade jargon, or of foreign derivation. Note these on the log as well.

5.073 Verbalizing Punctuation

The speaking voice has a cadence and pace that must be represented in writing by punctuation marks. Since the conversion of dictation from spoken to written form involves two people, the dictator must see the punctuation that will structure the sentence for the reader and then speak that punctuation for the typist. For example, "paragraph, all in caps, now is the time, colon, your opportunity to buy in, quote, sunshine acres, close quote, is limited, exclamation point, write for details, period, end of dictation" will look like this: "NOW IS THE TIME: Your opportunity to buy in "Sunshine Acres" is limited! Write for details."

Often an experienced secretary, listening to a familiar voice, well-modulated and speaking conversationally, can impute commas, semicolons, and capitalization. Very few typists, experienced or not, can hear a new voice and correctly punctuate for it. Typing from voice dictation is a reflex process for many typists, and they can perform only as well as the dictator dictates. The combination of modulated voice and spoken punctuation promotes efficiency through clarity and provides the maximum number of clues to the material possible.

5.074 Review, Edit, and Learn

It is not enough simply to dictate and pass the completed material over to someone to type. Paralegals must periodically review the material dictated to detect failures in dictating technique and to improve delivery. No one can learn only from reviewing his or her own tapes. Consult the experts—the typists and secretaries whose work allows them to hear and appreciate the techniques of many dictators. A "partnership" feeling between secretaries and paralegals can develop the dictating style of paralegals into one of great efficiency that is pleasant and fulfilling for the secretaries and the paralegals.

The paralegal must be critical of his or her own work and accept the suggestions and criticisms of others with a positive and constructive attitude.

5.08 USING THE COMPUTER

As with every business around the globe, computers have become the backbone of organization and efficiency for a law practice. Every paralegal must compile a working knowledge of computers. This requires a basic understanding of computer hardware, which consists of the computer itself (with choices of processors, memory capability, disk drives, networks, etc.), as well as an understanding of the various monitors, printers, modems, and other options that are available.

The type of software attorneys have incorporated into their computer systems requires paralegals to be trained and ready to perform with technical skills that cover a wide range of applications, including word processing programs such as WordPerfect® and/or Microsoft Word®; spreadsheet programs such as Lotus®, Excel®, and Quattro Pro®; timekeeping programs such as Timeslips® and TABS®; database programs such as Paradox®, MS Access®, dBASE®, and FoxPro®; and presentation programs such as Corel Presentations®, Astound®, and MS PowerPoint®.

Because computer technology is growing and changing so rapidly and because of its rapid integration into the court system and courtroom, it is important for every paralegal to stay abreast of advances and retrain when needed.

5.081 Effective Use of Computers

Drafting documents at the computer is often more effective and time efficient than dictating. By looking at the document as it is being drafted, the drafter is able to revise on screen without the necessity of reading a print copy and making manual revisions which then must be retyped into the computer.

Saving documents in a computer file for easy retrieval is a great benefit to the paralegal. Rather than reinventing the wheel each time you draft a letter or pleading, it is easy to retrieve a similar document from the computer and revise it. This saves time and guarantees consistency in the work product. Find out the forms that are used most often in your office. Investigate the use of macros, which are computer commands that perform a task automatically. For example, a macro can retrieve a file, give it a new name, and save it in another file format.

Scanning incoming documents into the computer for later use, revision, and reference is one of the most recent technology advances to find its way into the law office. Scanning software and hardware prices are now less than the costs of many printers. Scanning is particularly useful when large documents from outside sources, which would otherwise have to be retyped, are being revised. Scanning is also a time-saver when preparing responses to discovery requests, since scanning eliminates the need to type in the propounded requests which must appear in discovery responses.

5.082   Effective Use of E-mail

With the advent of networking, or connecting computers so that they share resources, the use of electronic mail (e-mail) in interoffice communications has become commonplace and in some firms and companies has taken the place of many other forms of written communication, such as phone memo slips, records of contact with clients and others, status memos, scheduling memos, and the transmittal of documents for internal review. It is important to realize that critical information that is transmitted within the office using e-mail should be saved and appropriately filed for future reference.

Electronic exchange of documents between offices or between an office and the client is also a common practice. This can be done via modem connections from computer to computer or by e-mail through the Internet. This technology combines computers with telephone lines, cable modems or wireless technology to relay messages almost instantly.

It is important that special care be taken with business e-mail. Using proper spelling, grammar, and punctuation is required, while the use of abbreviations (such as LOL for "laugh out loud" or BTW for "by the way") and emoticons (such as ;-) for smiley faces) should be avoided. Because there are potential security issues in the use of e-mail systems, the paralegal must take special care to avoid breaching client confidentiality. It is important to know whether safeguards are built into any e-mail system that you use so that security is not a question. Without the use of encryption software, data that is transmitted via modem or by e-mail is easily accessible by unauthorized persons. Therefore, to the extent e-mail may be viewed by others, it is unwise to communicate confidential information by that medium.

With the new electronic discovery rules, paralegals need to be sure they are familiar with their firm's policies regarding storage of work-related messages. E-mail messages relating to case work must be treated as any memo to the file would be treated—they have to be saved in whatever system the attorneys have set up since they are subject to disclosure.

PRACTICE TIPS

- When drafting e-mails, paralegals should be mindful that they may be discoverable and they should omit personal references and comments.
- Attorney, Client, and Work Product notations should be included on e-mail messages where appropriate.

To the extent e-mail is a written business communication, it is important that the e-mailed document clearly disclose the paralegal's nonlawyer status, just as would be done in a business letter or other external communication.

5.09 WRITTEN COMMUNICATION

This section will not include legal briefs, pleadings, formal discovery documents, or other materials whose style and form or format can be established from form books or other research material available to the paralegal and that are generally within the responsibility and editing purview of the attorney. Those elements of correspondence originated by the paralegal to the members of the law firm and those documents of correspondence originated by the paralegal, either individually or for the attorneys, from the firm to other people will be discussed.

Simple, thoughtful writing is elegant. Even complex ideas can be expressed plainly. The heart of a good writing style is the ability to write short, simple sentences. However, do not make the mistake of talking down to your readers. Search for quality vocabulary and a style that best conveys your meaning. Mark Twain once said that there is as much difference between the almost right word and the right word as there is between the lightning bug and lightning. It is worth the effort to "hunt" for the word that most accurately expresses your thought. This is particularly true for legal writing, where the wrong word can result in a mistaken interpretation, or, in the extreme case, malpractice.

Writing is easiest if you organize your thoughts before you start. Here is a successful approach to organizing legal writing, which applies to a broad spectrum of applications, from basic correspondence to intricate legal memorandum.[2]

1. Write down every idea you have on your subject, even fleeting thoughts, and in no particular order.

2. Write an introduction paragraph. You will probably rewrite it several times, even after you have completed the assignment. The purpose in writing the lead is to start you thinking about how you are going to organize what you have to say.

3. With your list of ideas and your lead paragraph, write a simple outline, checking off points from your idea list as you write. When your outline is finished, you'll discover there are gaps in your list of ideas. These are the holes this method is designed to expose.

4. Now you are ready to write. You may think of new ideas to include, and because you have an outline, these additions need not crowd out the main points.

5. Let your organization show. Let your reader understand that you know where you are, where you are going, and what conclusions you have drawn.[3]

6. Rewrite. If you are typing directly into your computer, you have help. By using your spell check, thesaurus, or grammar check (when available), you can enhance your writing quickly and easily. An excellent reference book is *The Elements of Style* by William Strunk, Jr. and E. B. White.[4] Currently, under 50 pages, of the case for cleanliness, accuracy, and brevity in the use of English, and it combines academics and insight in a short text.

7. All written materials subject to approval by a supervising attorney should be double-spaced, marked "draft," and should be submitted to your supervisor for review. Maintain all drafts for your records.

8. Reread the final version with a fresh look to see if there is anything you missed. Make sure copies are sent to the designated recipients, and without fail, file a copy of the final draft.

5.091   Internal Correspondence

The law firm's internal correspondence can take many forms, from slips of paper bearing cryptic notes to e-mail, to full-scale studies and briefing materials. Regardless of the matter to be communicated, it is important that each item of correspondence be dated, signed, and, when appropriate, directed to a specific addressee, even if that addressee is "memorandum to the file." Any correspondence originated in connection with a court action should refer to that case by suitable caption at the outset of the correspondence and should reflect the case's appropriate client and/or matter number.

The correspondence may be generated in a form established by office policy. This may include multipage materials, a typed master from which photocopies can be made, or interoffice e-mail. For correspondence within the office where an answer is requested, the use of multipage material is helpful. Many firms produce in-house memoranda forms using carbonless paper, with space provided for answering. This saves time and allows all parties to have the full text of the original communication and its answer. The electronic equivalent of this process is to use the automatic message quoting feature in e-mail which will then include the original message text when generating a reply or forwarding the message to others.

5.0911 "Tickler Systems."

Different tickler systems can be used to direct certain actions from one person to another, saving time. Tickler/suspense, docket, and calendar systems are all useful in providing reminders of anticipated due dates and/or appearances. (*See* Exhibits 5-2 and 5-3.) A handwritten tickler or suspense file system can be very inexpensive and cost effective. A 3 x 5 index card is used detailing the information and placed in a file box set up for 90 days (three months) into the future. If a response is due 30 days from the date of a filing, a tickler card is inserted in that numbered date of

EXHIBITS 5-2   Sample Tickler Card

To:	Due date:
File:	
Action taken:	
Clock starts on:	
Action needed, if no response:	

EXHIBITS 5-3   Sample Docket Card

Client:	Matter:	
File:	Timekeeper:	Manager:
Rule sets:		
Key code:		
Category:	Priority:	Location:
Due date:	Time:	
Reminders:		
Other:	Explanation:	

the month 30 days hence. As the date arrives, the anticipated reminder comes up and is handled. That numbered date is then placed at the back of the file, continuing the 90 days into new months.

Computer docketing systems are even more efficient than handwritten systems. A program is set up (or a preformatted program can be purchased) that requests the client name, matter/file number, court, due date, action required, and reminder dates for actions of paramount importance. A copy of the docket will print out what has been docketed for that specific file or case. A daily docket will list whatever is needed for a specific day or week concerning the case involved.

A 30- day calendar is also a very useful item in keeping track of actions and anticipated due dates. Recommended as a backup to any of the other systems, a large calendar (18 in. x 24 in.) can be used to write in due dates. Computerized calendars or schedulers are also very helpful.

Diligence is a must in keeping things scheduled. Any new item must be entered immediately so that any conflicts that may arise can be dealt with and arrangements made for alternative plans. Everything placed on a calendar or scheduler must be current. Any rescheduled items must update old dates to guarantee the efficiency of the system. If deadlines are missed, cases can be lost because of default, so a reliable system is a very important part of keeping track of filings in cases.

5.0912 Memos and Full Documentation.
The preparation of a memorandum to file or to an individual is an important step and should be treated as such. Do not use cryptic notes that rely on mnemonics or association with other words in order to derive the exact meaning of the memorandum. Each document should be sufficiently detailed so that its meaning and purpose are easily discernable by anyone who reads it and it is as understandable next week or next year as it is on the day it is conceived. Each document should be an independent thought. The plan of any memorandum should always follow a logical path of having an introduction, a body, and a conclusion. The extent of these three elements for a given memorandum may vary; they should be considered at the outset and honored in the execution whenever possible.

a. The introduction includes the reason for the memo—references to files, conversations, or correspondence that might be needed as background.

b. The body is the discussion of matters to be recorded, paragraphed by major thought, or a review of the elements.

c. The conclusion is the recommendation, decision, or statement of status. If any suspense date is involved, it is reflected here, and the means of observing the suspense is shown—the "writer will follow up" or "the docket clerk was notified."

5.0913 Privilege.
In those written memoranda between the paralegal and the attorney related to a given case, one of the desirable introductory sentences to be used is: "In connection with the cited case, you directed me to _____, and the following is reported." Since the paralegal addresses the memoranda to his or her employing attorney and it is in relation to a particular case, that particular document may carry the attorney-client privilege or the attorney work-product privilege. Whether the attorney at some future date may waive that privilege is not a speculation to be made by the paralegal at any time, and certainly not when conceiving the document. In each and every case, the paralegal is working for and under the direction of an attorney, and every step should be taken to ensure that the same privileges the attorney exerts on behalf of the client attaches to the work of the attorney's paralegal.

The policy and procedure of the office may or may not address this problem. If it does not, the question should be discussed with the attorney. An alternative technique may be preferred, such as the use of a stamp saying "Attorney Privilege" or "Confidential" on the top and bottom of every page of such material.

5.0914 Brevity.   Correspondence within the office should be brief. It is reasonable to believe we all work toward the same ultimate goal, and the use of excess verbiage or stereotyped language does not contribute to the communication of facts and information between members of the same firm. Simple words, clear and unmistakable, should be used whenever possible within the firm. This does not mean that in-house correspondence should not be phrased logically and persuasively. Candor, truth, and directness have greater value within the firm than in correspondence going outside the firm, which must be phrased more diplomatically and be more generalized. The paralegal can use technical phrases here or employ the jargon or acronyms commonly used by the profession. The only caveat is use them properly, spell them correctly, and, if in doubt, look them up in *Oran's Dictionary of the Law* or a set of legal *Words and Phrases* before trying to include them in an internal memorandum.

5.0915 Project Memos or Reports.   Frequently, the paralegal is directed to study, review, summarize, and make recommendations on a given problem, topic, or volume of data. Such work requires extensive analysis, often supplemented by investigation or research, as well as the submission of a detailed report. Use an outline, such as the one shown in Exhibit 5-4, to organize your thoughts before beginning to write, along with the approach detailed earlier in this section.

This format requires the paralegal to assemble the basic data; identify the assumptions (time constraints, personnel costs, task-time allocations) that will affect the conclusions; and clarify the sources of information used (whether books, documents, reports, or interviews) and the resulting dissection and analysis of the material, information, and assumptions. In applicable circumstances, an analysis of each available alternative is made and the full project then reported in terms of a conclusion or recommendation.

In the course of the analysis, footnotes, marginal annotations, or parenthetical citations should be used to refer to factual statements supporting sources or inferences that are significant in the analysis or the conclusion.

Note that this format is an adaptation of the "introduction, body, and conclusion" form. Since the study may be lengthy, it may be wise to prepare a cover letter to the attorney setting out the problem presented and the recommendation or conclusion and indicating the detailed memo attached. This allows a quick perusal of the essence of the assignment on one page, while making the full report available for more thorough evaluation if needed.

EXHIBIT 5-4   Internal Memorandum Outline

TO:		
FROM:		
DATE:		
SUBJ:		
Date of Assignment:	Assigned by:	Deadline Date:
Statement of the Problem:		
Assumptions:		
Sources of Information:		
Analysis:		
Alternative Analysis:		

5.092 Correspondence—Out-of-Office

All correspondence from the firm to persons outside the firm, whether they are clients, the courts, adversaries, or sources of information, should follow the standard established by the office in the office manual. If no office manual exists, consult with the attorney to determine the form preferred; the conventions of salutation, case citation, signature blocks; and the policies and practices honored by the attorney that are to be followed by the paralegal. Many attorneys prefer to have all correspondence go out over their signatures, while some attorneys will allow the paralegal to write and sign correspondence connected with lawsuits as long as such correspondence does not contain legal opinions or give direct legal advice and the paralegal's nonlawyer status is clear. Some attorneys mix it up. Follow the office procedures. Any questionable correspondence should be reviewed by the attorney for either his or her signature or your own.

5.0921 Style and Form.   Frequently, legal secretaries set the style and form of the correspondence. They have developed habitual forms of salutation, citation, paragraphing, signature blocks, attachment or enclosure reference, spacing, and so on and are comfortable with the established procedure. The paralegal adapts his or her writing to that style if at all possible because his or her work and the secretary's are complementary. The choice of form, provided the alternatives are equal in clarity, should be made by the secretary or the attorney. If the form is clear, direct, and acceptable to the attorney and comfortable for the secretary, the paralegal defers to their choice.

The organizational structure of letters leaving the office is extremely important, and each such letter must be composed with care. There is always the addressee identification. There may be a caption, for example, "Re: Smith v. Jones, Your file: XYZ 123, Our file: 77AB132." There may be a salutation (depending on office policy). There is always an introductory sentence or paragraph followed by the body of the correspondence, which should be limited to two or three major points (preferably one), and then a concluding paragraph in which the conclusion, decision, or request is stated and a deadline date established for any required action or response.

5.0922 Review for Impact.   Following dictation and typing, read the letter in final form to evaluate its impact. Does it fulfill the intended purpose? Is it clear? Is it concise? Is it sufficiently courteous and expository? Does it sound like you? Does it sound the way it was intended to sound?

The review will expose any clichés or stereotyped phrases that may have slipped in. Composing often is done one sentence at a time, each of which may be great standing alone but poor when combined.

5.0923 Purposes of Correspondence.   The purpose of legal correspondence, particularly that leaving an office, follows the same general principles as business correspondence. It should serve a combination of, or at least one of, the following four functions:

a. To obtain action. The letter should create action by the party to whom the letter is going. This is done by presenting a situation in which the recipient of the letter either must act or, by failure to act, accept the results of inaction. This is insured by establishing a date in the last paragraph of the letter by which an answer or response is expected and required to prevent an alternative action.

b. To provide information. The letter often is a response to an inquiry or a request by a client, adversary, court, or a source of information for information or further details. This type of letter tends to be a little longer and may be more discursive or more involved than other correspondence. Any letter whose major purpose is to provide information should contain a concluding sentence or paragraph requesting further contact if the information provided is insufficient or incomplete. It can be as simple as "please call or write if further information or clarification is needed."

c. To maintain goodwill. Goodwill should obviously be maintained with the clients, with friendly witnesses, and with sources of information. Not quite so obvious is the necessity of maintaining goodwill with opposing party's and with the court system employees. Many paralegals tend to feel that opposing party's are the enemy and, therefore, should be treated with disdain or without substantial courtesy. That attitude is wrong. Even though the opposing party may act in a discourteous, abrupt, crude, or offensive manner, there is no excuse for the paralegal's correspondence to reflect a similar attitude. Remember, the conduct of trials and pretrial discovery activity is often a complex series of maneuvers in which the advocates of the parties take on certain colorations and roles based on the factual situations with which they contend. It is foolish to allow an opposing party to force the attorney or paralegal into playing that kind of game. Correspondence reflecting discourtesy also reflects a lack of professionalism. Many times the present opposing party in a difficult and contentious piece of litigation will be a codefendant in some future action. The effect on each other of courtesy, tact, and diplomacy—or the lack of them—carries over into the next case. Paralegals are responsible for the relations between the attorney and any other person of the legal community. The correspondence should engender, not destroy, goodwill.

d. To create a record. The record to be created is one of courteous, disciplined, timely, professional, and appropriate conduct fully recognizing the rules of court. At the same time, the correspondence may create a record advantageous to the paralegal's employing attorney and his or her client regarding the opposing party's unwillingness to comply with those same rules of court. In the case of extensions of time where either side requested or agreed to a request by the other, appropriately phrased correspondence will express an attitude either of cooperation or vexatious behavior. A letter following a telephone call involving delaying tactics can be used in lieu of formal legal motions to create a record forcing the opposing party to respond appropriately or face the difficulty of explaining the letter at some future time. The letter can be courteous and effective. The more responsibility the paralegal carries in any piece of legal service and the more contact he or she has with witnesses, the court, and the opposing parties, the more important are his or her efforts to create a record in the files of the court and the parties to the case.

5.0924 Timeliness.

Correspondence should never be postponed. As soon as the need presents itself, decide what is the most efficient way to respond. Will an e-mail message be quicker and more efficient than spending time dictating a letter? If so, e-mail the person immediately, making a copy of the message to the file. That message will be taken care of in less time between the two parties involved than it would take for one person to dictate a letter and a secretary to transcribe it and prepare envelopes to mail. Always remember to save a copy of the communication for the file, which will evidence action taken on your part and that the recipient is asked to respond.

If the action taken in e-mail is setting up a meeting, deposition, or other important case matter, use an internal docketing system, if available. The docketing will be performed in a few keystrokes, showing an anticipated event in a certain case, by particular individuals, at a designated location, and for an allotted period of time. The parties involved will be alerted to the anticipated action in their daily docketing report.

If time permits, draft the letter. Ask your supervisor to check it for accuracy and to sign the letter if it meets with his or her approval. All letters confirming appointments or arrangements made over the telephone with other law offices, courts, or sources of information should be sent out immediately. If a suspense date is set in the letter, it is imperative to signal that date in the files of the attorney and the paralegal. If it affects the docket, be sure to notify or send a copy to whomever handles the docketing. Uniform understanding by everyone is the acme of communication.

If docket and calendar systems are used in conjunction, make sure all the dates are the same. If several people are calendaring (secretaries, paralegals, and attorneys), make sure everyone is counting the same days. If holidays fall during the calculation of due dates, the consensus of *all* must be the date that should be noted on all calendars and dockets.

5.0925 Stereotypes. There is a tendency among those who lack confidence in drafting letters to follow guideline books or electronic "forms" that provide examples of phrases, some of which can be adapted to the paralegal's needs. This can be a crutch of faulty strength. The paralegal does not have to create the thought, but often ends up substituting triteness for spontaneity. It also causes the paralegal to rely on the book or "forms" instead of learning the correct use of the English language and in place of creative analysis. Be certain that such "canned" letters or "boilerplate" phrases are appropriate to the situation and will fulfill the purpose of the letter before adopting their use.

5.0926 Logical Presentation and Limited Topics. Of more importance than stereotyped methods of referral is a well-organized presentation of the facts in coherent and logical fashion following the three-step structure discussed previously—"the introduction, the body, and the conclusion." Holding each letter to a minimum number of different topics will allow for easy drafting and simplicity of construction. The letter will be comprehensible if not fashionable.

Often it is better to write three letters, conveying one or two ideas in each, rather than one long letter containing five or six points. Short letters will be read promptly, while longer ones may be scanned and put aside for later detailed review. If the purpose of the letter was to generate action, its very length may postpone that action.

5.093 Grammar, Vocabulary, and Spelling

Law office correspondence, internal and external, is often the first (and many times the only) impression others have of you as a paralegal and tends to make a lasting impression. Bad grammar, poor or inappropriate vocabulary, and misspelled words combine to create the image of an incompetent, uneducated, and inept individual who need not be taken seriously. It is therefore extremely important for the paralegal to pay close attention to these basic elements of communication.

5.0931 Grammar. The composition of legal correspondence follows certain basic rules, among which are the rules of English grammar. The lack of a solid foundation in grammar will inhibit the paralegal's ability to communicate. Consequently, many paralegals find writing an onerous burden because their grammar is inadequate for the task. Those paralegals must undertake the improvement of their English grammar, creative writing ability, vocabulary, and methods of expression if they expect to advance in the profession.

In the interim, work must go on, and the easiest rule to follow in writing letters is to write as you speak. The language used in daily life sometimes may be elliptical in nature, lacking a clearly defined subject, object, or predicate, but it is a form of expression that will usually be comprehensible to the reader. A paralegal with severe problems in this area must seek and honor the advice of others and write, edit, and rewrite if necessary. In the interim, he or she should write with confidence in the same manner as he or she speaks. The paralegal is hired, in part, because of his or her ability to communicate, and the only way to improve that ability is to expose the faults to the blue pencil of critics, take note of the weaknesses thus exposed, and attempt to eliminate them in future work. The most comforting thought a paralegal can have in drafting legal correspondence is that grammar is important but generally follows the lead of everyday conversation (by a few years, unfortunately, but it does follow). If the usage in a letter is comfortable to the author, it is probably acceptable as communication and may even be correct grammatically. If it is not, critics may help and seem to enjoy doing so.

Some word processing programs contain grammar-checking programs. While these can be beneficial on some occasions, they are generally cumbersome to use and can result in a work product that is stiff and stilted.

5.0932 Vocabulary and Spelling.   The writing of letters necessarily involves vocabulary and spelling. No single skill is more important to the paralegal than the ability to use and spell words correctly. Drafting letters by hand to be typed later pinpoints the ability to spell as essential to the finished product. In dictating and proofreading the drafted material, the ability to spell is essential to insure that the material does convey the idea intended by the use of given words. Misspelled words can alter meanings and content dramatically.

The use of spell-checkers in word processing programs is beneficial in locating and correcting misspelled words. However, a word of caution is advised; most spell-checkers do not find the misused words that may be spelled correctly. One of the dangers of reliance on spell-checking is the failure to find those misused words which change the content and intent of the communication.

5.09321 Which Word Is It?   We all are familiar with the simple word "to," or is it "too" or "two"? Each has a distinctly different meaning, is spelled differently, and yet sounds the same. In dictation, each can be confused, and in handwritten notes, the necessity of spelling each of those three words properly is apparent. A great number of other questions may arise over words of similar phonetic sound. As mentioned earlier, each of the following words is spelled correctly and would not be identified as misused by a word processing spell-checker.

council or counsel	advice or advise
summary or summery	access or excess
pistol or pistil	affect or effect
chorale or corral	conscience or conscious
tear or tare	farther or further
bow or bough	all ready or already
capital or capitol	any way or anyway
principle or principal	pen or pin
imminent or eminent	their or there or they're
compliment or complement	do or due or dew

Do you recognize these words and their meanings? If not, look them up and consider the difference of meaning implicit in using one for the other. These are but a few. Watch out for the others.

5.09322 Typos and Word Meanings.   There is also the problem with words that are not pronounced the same but have all of the same letters within them, or nearly the same letters within them. Minor misspelling or transposed letters change the meaning dramatically. With the word "casual," for example, a transposition of the "u" and "s" turns it into "causal." The word "did," if misspelled, can be "dead" or perhaps "deed." More dramatic would be the word "illusive," which could be misspelled as "elusive" or, even worse, "allusive," each of which has a distinctly different meaning. Will the letter then carry the intended communication? These are all additional examples of misused words which a computer word processing spell-checker would not bring to your attention or correct.

A paralegal who cannot spell must work intensively and continuously to eliminate or minimize that basic weakness.

5.09323 Vocabulary Improvement.   Earlier we mentioned that the average range of words at the instant command of the average American is 700 to 1,200 words. The paralegal's general vocabulary must be much greater, or it will be insufficient for the normal discharge of his or her duties. There are specialized areas in the legal field that will put demands upon the paralegal's retentive and recall abilities, such as the specialized terminology of medicine and all sorts of trade terms in marketing, construction, longshoring, maritime activities, business, engineering, and so on. The ability to learn new words accurately, understand their meanings, and incorporate them into our professional lives is important. Enrolling in English classes that emphasize spelling or creative writing is certainly beneficial and offers a working professional the opportunity to improve his or her command of vocabulary and of spelling under conditions where the effort is professionally judged and critiqued. Additionally, crossword puzzles and other word games are a fun way to enlarge the paralegal's vocabulary. Each month, *Reader's Digest* contains a special vocabulary improvement section, and "Word-a-Day" calendars are a popular item at bookstores and card shops. Another method readily available to increase vocabulary is to make a habit of using the thesaurus offered by word processing programs. One's vocabulary also improves by reading good writing, such as Faulkner, Hemingway, Emerson, or Thoreau.

BIBLIOGRAPHY

Benn, Martha, *Telephone Resources*. Albuquerque, NM:, 1997.

Block, Gertrude, *Effective Legal Writing*, Foundation Press, New York, NY, 1999.

Ebbitt, Wilma and Ebbitt, David, *Index to English*, 7th ed. Glenview, IL: Scott, Foresman & Co., 1982.

Flynn, Nancy and Flynn, Tom, *Writing Effective E-Mail*, http://www.emailreplies.com.

Fowler, H. Ramsey and Aaron, Jane E., *The Little, Brown Handbook,* 4th ed. Glenview, IL: Scott, Foresman & Co., 1989.

Garner, Bryan A., "Writing for Litigation," *Scribes Journal of Legal Writing*, The American Society of Writers on Legal Subjects, Dallas, TX, 1990, pp. 66–68.

Gordon, Karen E., *The Well-Tempered Sentence: A Punctuation Handbook for the Innocent, the Eager, and the Doomed*. New York: Ticknor & Fields, 1983.

Hodges, John C., et al., *Harbrace College Handbook*, 10th ed. San Diego, CA: Harcourt Brace Jovanovich, 1986.

Kirkland, James W., et al., *Writing and Revising: Modern College Workbook*. Lexington, MA: D. C. Heath, 1986.

Koerselman, Virginia, Written Communications, 2000, A NALA Campus Course, On-line Self Study Program for Paralegals. www.NALACampus.com.

Mager, Nathan and Mager, Sylvia, *Encyclopedic Dictionary of English Usage*. Englewood Cliffs, NJ: Prentice-Hall, 1975.

Mellinkoff, David, *Legal Writing: Sense and Nonsense*. St. Paul, MN: West, 1981.

Rodale, J. I. and Urdang, Lawrence, *The Synonym Finder*. Emmaus, PA: Rodale Press, 1990.

Sisson, A. F., *Sisson's Word and Expression Locater*. Englewood Cliffs, NJ: Prentice-Hall, 1966.

Strunk, William, Jr. and White, E. B., *The Elements of Style*, 3rd ed. New York: Macmillan, 1979.

Venolia, Jan, *Write Right!* rev. ed. Berkeley, CA: Ten Speed Press, 1988.

Webster's Tenth New Collegiate Dictionary. Springfield, MA: Merriam-Webster, 1993.

Wydick, Richard C., *Plain English for Lawyers,* 2nd ed. Durham, NC: Carolina Academic Press, 1985.

ENDNOTES

1. Benn, Martha, *Telephone Resources* (Albuquerque, New Mexico, 1997).

2. Garner, Bryan A., "Writing for Litigation," *Scribes Journal of Legal Writing* (The American Society of Writers on Legal Subjects, Dallas, TX, 1990) pp. 66–68. Web site for the American Society of Writers on Legal Subjects: http://www.scribes.org.

3. Garner, Bryan A., "Writing for Litigation", *ibid.*

4. Strunk, William, Jr. and White, E. B., *The Elements of Style,* 3rd ed. (New York: Macmillan Publishing Co., Inc., 1979).

6

Interviewing Techniques

6.00   INTRODUCTION

Because each interview presents unique challenges and each interviewer has his or her own strengths, no one can script a universally applicable interview. At best, one can relate prior experiences, explain techniques that have worked in the past, point out inherent hazards, and offer potential solutions.

The ideal interviewer has a photographic memory, a broad knowledge base, a commanding yet comfortable personality, a well-timed sense of humor, is a patient and careful listener, is meticulous, is trustworthy, and is appropriately empathetic. The ideal interviewer glows with the aura of dignity.

Of course, few people meet this ideal, but we can all be effective. In the coming pages, we will learn how to adapt to certain situations and how to exploit our strengths while recognizing and improving weaknesses. By studying the work of others and applying reasonable effort, a personal interviewing style can be developed that produces desirable results and elevates self-confidence.

The concept of an interview is based on the supposition that the interviewer controls the direction and pace of the dialogue. Though not always simple or easy, this can be accomplished (and accomplished with gentleness), provided the paralegal enters the interview with predefined goals and a workable strategy in mind.

Experience is the best teacher, especially for refining skills such as interviewing. The paralegal's abilities will develop by trial and error. This is a sometimes frustrating truth that requires us to remain flexible, adjust our approach when necessary, and maintain composure through it all.

6.01   THE INTERVIEW: WHAT IT IS AND WHAT IT IS NOT

The interview is a special form of verbal exchange in which information is transferred between parties. It is not a conversation but a polite, unofficial form of interrogation. The interview seeks to separate matters of belief and/or conjecture from those which are evidentiary facts. It is also used to develop leads to other witnesses. The paralegal must control the direction and set the pace of the interview in order to successfully accomplish the task of gathering data.

We are all involved in interviews on a daily basis. Employment interviews, tax counseling, and credit applications are examples of common interviews which require the directed exchange of information. The sheer volume of interviews conducted leads to the belief that many are "canned," and in fact, many are. However, the paralegal's task of assembling evidence admissible in courts of law is too specialized to conduct according to a standard format. Because of the unique circumstances and complexities of individual cases and witnesses, each interview the paralegal conducts presents a unique set of challenges. Flexibility and imagination, combined with skilled questioning, will produce better results than any standard set of questions and forms.

Interviews are usually one-on-one conversations, but exceptions do exist. Experience shows that the amount of useful information obtained from interviews is inversely proportional to the number of people involved; the more people involved, the less information is obtained. For this reason, whenever possible, group activity surrounding the interview should be limited to the professional introduction of the paralegal by the attorney.

People are often surprised to learn that interviewing does not require a licensed attorney. Using paralegals as interviewers is a common practice for identifying potential witnesses, recreating corporate organizational histories, establishing time lines, and so forth. A thorough interview performed by a paralegal, including end report and evaluation, will provide the attorney with necessary information in a manner that is both cost-effective and efficient, which clients appreciate.

Interviewing is a learned skill requiring carefully considered, often intense preparation and responsive adaptation in pursuit of the necessary testimony which extends to a thorough evaluation of the interview and the witness. Because the findings of the interview are a critical source of information, the quality of work must be high, and the attorney is best aided by the paralegal who treats every interview as worthy of preparation, skillful execution, thorough review, and corroboration.

6.011   Obtaining Statements

Statements are used in preparation for and during trial. In preparation for trial, the written statement allows reference to all facts known by the witness. At trial, the statement, whether or not it is "sworn," can be used to *impeach* the testimony of a witness who states something different or contrary on the stand than what was stated during the interview. To impeach a witness's testimony is to damage that witness's credibility. Because juries frequently determine cases based on the perceived credibility of witnesses, the potential value of a well taken statement is immeasurable.

6.0111 Negative Statements.
Negative statements are statements made by witnesses that, in and of themselves, provide no advantage to either party. The majority of legal interviews conducted only yield negative statements. With many occurrences, such as bar fights, neighborhood disputes, and automobile accidents, there are often people who have only witnessed a portion of the event. Few will have knowledge of evidentiary value for either side in the case, but all should be interviewed because it is probable that people in the vicinity of the accident can direct the investigator to other witnesses.

6.0112 Questionable Statements.
Questionable statements are those which may or may not constitute admissible evidence because of some extenuating circumstance. For instance, the mental state of a witness could make what at first appears to be a valid statement inadmissible or not credible. Traumatic shock, whether triggered by physical or mental injury; alcohol or drug use, including some legitimate medications; psychological instability and impaired mental development—these are all conditions that can adversely affect a person's ability to accurately perceive, recall, or articulate the course of an event. How close or how far away a witness is to the event, weather conditions, time of day, the presence or absence of distractions, and the level of attention are additional factors which affect the validity or credibility of testimony. One of the objectives of effective questioning is to explore whether or not any of those factors apply.

6.012   Written Statements

Written statements are desirable for several reasons, particularly if they are in the witness's own words and handwriting and not simply a product of the paralegal paraphrasing the witness's story. If the paralegal does draft the statement, the witness should be required to correct and initial any errors, initial and number each page, and sign the last page of the statement. To authenticate the signing of the statement, having another witness the signing is appropriate. Should the witness later repudiate the signed statement by alleging that it is not his signature, the witness to the signing can testify to the authenticity. It is not unusual for the witness to request a copy of the statement, which should then be provided. It is already a requirement in many jurisdictions that a copy of the statement be provided to the witness. The purpose of this procedure is to ensure the validity of the statement, so that neither side can dispute it later.

It is essential that the statement contain the witness's full identity: name, age, home address, occupation, employer, employer's address, and work and home telephone numbers. The relationship of the witness to the case should be included and described in narrative form. For instance, describe the witness as a "witness to the event," an "accountant involved in the accumulation of records concerning project costs," or as a "party to the discussions which resulted in the agreement." A clause must be included which states that the witness has provided the statement freely and without coercion or promise of reward.

6.0121 When Not to Take a Statement.
One of the first things a paralegal should ask in an interview is whether or not the individual is represented by counsel. If the answer is yes, especially if the interview is being recorded, the paralegal must state for the record that the representation by counsel was previously unknown. The paralegal must then ask the individual being interviewed to identify his or her counsel fully, the circumstances of the representation, and whether or not the representation is related to the matter at issue. If it is, the paralegal must immediately terminate the interview and advise the employing attorney of the situation.

The paralegal should also be careful about how information harmful to the client's case is documented. Formal discovery procedures usually require the production of all nonprivileged statements when requested by the adversary. Witness statements usually are not privileged. Client statements may or may not be privileged, depending on the form and manner in which they were taken. For this reason, even if the paralegal knows or believes the witness is lying, documenting the adverse information in the statement is dangerous. If the paralegal knows the witness is lying and can prove it, that ammunition should be saved for a later time, such as when the opposition introduces the witness.

If the individual being interviewed shows evidence of incapacity, such as being under the influence of alcohol, drugs, or medications, the interview should not go forward.

6.013 Formal Statements

In addition to interviewing, there are several other more formal methods of obtaining statements from witnesses. The affidavit, the declaration, and the deposition are all examples of methods for taking testimony that is bound by oath. The paralegal should always consult the supervising attorney about what method is to be used for a given witness. Depending on what the attorney hopes to do with the testimony, different types of statements may be desired.

6.0131 Depositions.   The most solidly admissible type of formal statement is the deposition. The deposition is a recorded interrogation of the witness by counsel. The deponent (witness) is subject to the penalties of perjury, and the testimony is transcribed by a registered professional reporter and/or audio or video recorded. The witness's counsel has the opportunity to cross-examine the witness. Witnesses who are subpoenaed to provide deposition testimony can often be compelled to travel to a different location to give that testimony, although this ability is limited by the statutes of the particular jurisdictions. Depositions, while powerful, can be expensive to take, given reporting costs, possible travel costs, and witness fees.

6.0132 Affidavits.   Affidavits take two forms. They are either oral statements made under oath and transcribed by a registered professional reporter or written statements signed under oath in the presence of a notary public. Because there is no opportunity for the witness's counsel to examine the witness, the affidavit does not have the impact or admissibility of the deposition.

6.0133 Declarations.   The declaration is the simplest of the three types of formal statements to obtain. It is a written statement concerning the matter at hand, prepared and signed by its author, the declarant. It must include the explicit disclaimer that the statement was voluntarily made under the penalty of perjury.

6.02 THE PARTICIPANTS
6.021 The Paralegal

This book is written for the paralegal. In the legal interview, it is the paralegal's job to obtain pertinent information from a witness who may or may not be agreeable. This task requires disciplined communication, sound judgment, adaptability, and confidence.

6.022 The Client

Because of the wide variety of entities that employ paralegals today, the type of client encountered ranges from individuals seeking some form of government assistance to executive officers of multinational corporations. In most cases, the client is the best source of information on a matter, though this is not the rule. One interview rarely completes the paralegal's contact with the client, and each interview should be treated as a separate, important step in a well-arranged process. Clients take their problems seriously and want their perception of events taken for truth, a highly stressful situation that can make a client nearly irrational. Often this results from a deeply held faith in Murphy's Law: whatever can go wrong, will go wrong. But most clients are fine people who revert to reasonable standards of behavior on learning that the attorney and paralegal will help them succeed in their efforts so far as the facts, the law, professional ethics, and abilities allow.

6.023   Witnesses

6.0231 Friendly Witnesses.   "Friendly" witnesses are usually related to the client by blood, viewpoint, common business interests, occupation, or social acquaintance. They usually require little pressure to speak freely and fully but usually present rather biased opinions. This bias must be considered when evaluating their information. They are helpful in corroborating the client's viewpoint and can offer a means of evaluating the testimony of adversary or hostile witnesses.

6.0232 Hostile Witnesses.   The paralegal can anticipate that some witnesses will be antagonistic to the purposes of the interview, such as witnesses directly aligned with the client's opposition. Hostile witnesses do not necessarily conduct themselves in a rude manner; rather, the term is used to describe a witness who either does not wish to provide any information from the start or who during the course of the interview becomes increasingly reluctant to provide information. The truly hostile witness does exist though, and it is not always possible to know in advance which witnesses may become hostile.

If a witness becomes hostile, it is the paralegal's challenge to identify the source of the witness's discomfort because that discomfort is the reason information is not being exchanged. It is good to remember that, for a variety of reasons, interviewing can be an unnerving experience for the person being interviewed. To minimize this effect, one should give the impression of relaxed efficiency, which necessitates preparedness, smiling, appearing interested, and being focused. A sincerely interested, nonjudgmental attitude generates trust and encourages the witness to speak freely. When the hostility is not a result of the stress of being interviewed, it is important to identify other possibilities. It may relate to the case, the attorney, or the client and therefore may be significant. It may relate only to the paralegal, and that is important also, though less important than the other reasons. If the paralegal projects arrogance, superiority, or condescension, the witness may respond with hostility. It is critical for the paralegal to recognize such mannerisms and work to change them. If the paralegal cannot solve the hostility problem or otherwise doubts the validity of the information obtained, he or she must seek help from the attorney. Perhaps another interviewer will be more successful.

6.0233 Official Witnesses.   Official witnesses are crucial to many cases because of the positions they occupy. They can be municipal employees, state employees, federal employees, or officers of corporations. They can belong to associations, business groups, ad hoc citizen committees, or other organized, identifiable entities. Official witnesses are usually personally removed from the dispute, although this is not always the case. Like all witnesses, official witnesses can be friendly, neutral, or hostile. Ideally, official witnesses are impartial and objective. They neither enhance nor inhibit the development of information for either side of the dispute, but offer only those facts of which they have personal knowledge or which can be ascertained from their files, where those files are open to the public.

6.0234 Expert Witnesses.   Paralegals encounter experts in many situations. Often there is a need for an expert consultant rather than a witness. Expert consultants usually are not hostile. They have no personal stake in the outcome of the case and provide only general information, often about the expert's field. The expert witness is a different sort, providing testimony to support the contentions of one side and refute those of the other. The expert witness can usually be identified as friendly or hostile by the name on his or her paycheck, though few experts become truly hostile and attack the interviewer personally.

Expert witnesses tend to possess a narrow spectrum of information with regard to any given case and typically should not be used to develop information outside their areas of expertise. When interviewing experts, close attention should be paid to their ability to communicate so that an assessment of their potential impact on a judge or jury can be made. The degree of preparation and poise under fire also should be analyzed and assessed. The best expert witnesses are identified by their ability to cope effectively and dispassionately with attacks on their credibility and the soundness of their conclusions.

6.03 GENERAL CONSIDERATIONS FOR EVERY INTERVIEW

6.031 Language

The language, vocabulary, and communication skills the paralegal uses may not match the language, vocabulary, and communication skills of the witness. It is incumbent on the paralegal to seek a comfortable level of dialogue that will allow a thorough and effective exchange of thoughts and information. The paralegal should never adopt a superior attitude or use vocabulary that the witness does not understand. The paralegal should make the witness comfortable with the interview process using vocabulary tailored to the witness's level of understanding without sounding condescending or mocking.

6.0311 Jargon and Slang.   The language used should be comfortable for the person being interviewed. Paralegals should be careful about using legal jargon and technical terms because it may be confusing to someone with no legal background.

Professional jargon or any slang used by the witness must be identified and explained. The meaning of such words and phrases must be explored with the witness to ensure there is a common understanding. Once a common understanding of the language being used is obtained, the paralegal should explore whether that is really what the witness meant and whether the terms have meaning within the context of the case.

6.0312 Profanity and Abuse.   Occasionally the paralegal will encounter an individual who cannot speak without being profane or abusive. It is imperative that the paralegal exercise restraint, keep emotions in check, and not reply in kind. The paralegal's purpose is to obtain information. The witness should be encouraged to speak even when that speech is laced with expletives and vulgarity. The more the witness says, the more information will be revealed. The attorney may never use this particular witness at trial; however, the information obtained may be of use, leading to the discovery of a more presentable witness or source of evidence.

Offensive language, in and of itself, is not hostility. Some witnesses speak profanely, even obscenely, as a matter of habit. If such remarks are so offensive that the ability to function, control, and direct the interview is lost, then it may be an indication that the paralegal is too sensitive to interview. However, if the remarks are directed at the paralegal personally, action is required. Paralegals do not have to endure personal abuse or vilification; when it occurs, a prompt, dignified termination of the interview is appropriate.

6.0313 Body Language.   During an interview, the paralegal should observe witnesses as much as possible. Body language can be very revealing and indicative of some major or minor internal conflict. For example, during a particular line of questioning, the witness may avoid eye contact. Later in the interview, the paralegal should return to the issue that appeared to cause the witness discomfort. If the witness avoids eye contact again, the paralegal may reasonably conclude that either the witness is being dishonest or is uncomfortable with the subject matter. This would be important to note, especially in the case of perceived dishonesty, because the attorney will want to know whether or not the witness appeared to be straightforward and credible.

Arm crossing is another body language expression which may have various meanings. It may simply mean the witness is cold, or it could mean that the witness is feeling defensive in some way. The paralegal should make a notation next to the line of questioning which appeared to cause this behavior and return to it later in the interview. If the behavior is repeated when the same topic is reviewed later in the interview, it may indeed indicate that the witness is responding to an unconscious feeling of needing self-protection. If this is true, then the arm crossing may signify that the witness is withholding information.

Active listening includes the ability to observe the reactions of the witness as responses to questions are given while at the same time making note of any apparent inconsistencies between the spoken words and the body language responses. These inconsistencies can be explored at a later date in a follow-up interview.

6.032   Listening

The paralegal must listen to the witness. One of the most common mistakes made is the failure to listen. This is often perceived as insulting or condescending to witnesses. From their point of view, the interview is a unique event which may be burdensome or unfair. The paralegal who fails to listen with focused intent on what the witness is saying may be perceived as disinterested or uncaring, often resulting in the witness becoming hostile.

When a client is interviewed, the responsibility to listen attentively increases exponentially. The client is there because they are either seeking or have obtained representation. Clients are paying for legal services, and they notice when the people handling their affairs appear unconcerned or disinterested about the task at hand. Attentive and active listening is necessary to conduct a productive interview. It will allow facts and erroneous beliefs to be exposed and will enable the paralegal to recognize mistaken interpretations. Such interpretations and beliefs should be heard in context, without argument or correction, until the full account is told. Correction of even a minor but obvious error during the narration may unnecessarily create an argument. It may also unnerve the witness so badly that the interview must be terminated. Worst of all, it causes the paralegal to talk while the witness listens, a reversal of roles.

Constant interruptions during the witness's narrative disrupt the flow of the information being conveyed. The paralegal risks losing relevant facts/information, if the witness loses his train of thought. The paralegal should encourage a narrative and make appropriate notes of any inconsistencies or gaps. When the witness concludes his narrative, the paralegal's notes can be utilized for clarification of information. (*See* Section 6.04, Questioning Techniques.)

6.0321 Empathy and Interest.   The paralegal must generate a feeling of empathy and understanding as well as sincere interest in the witness. Lack of empathy by the paralegal or harsh judgment of the witness, even if conveyed by body language alone, can cause an otherwise cooperative witness to become hostile.

6.0322 Personality Clash or Lack of Rapport.   Incompatibility between the paralegal and the witness should be promptly identified. If such a personality conflict arises, a courteous inquiry should determine if the witness would feel more comfortable with a different interviewer.

The incompatibility may develop during the interview as a result of the paralegal's manner or style of interviewing. If possible, identify and modify the cause of the problem. If unsuccessful, the paralegal should consult the attorney and, if necessary, arrange for another interviewer to reschedule and conduct the interview.

6.033   Confabulation and Deception

Confabulation is a special word used in psychiatry to describe the unconscious process of replacing gaps in memory with detailed accounts of fictitious events, giving the impression of a coherent story which is more believable. All witnesses want to be believed. Frequently, when witnesses only have a disjointed knowledge of an event, they infer the connections between known facts to make the story logical and less subject to challenge. The paralegal who understands this process will carefully establish each known fact and allow the interpolated events to be established by later testimony or information from other sources.

6.0331 Correction of Erroneous Information.   It is not unusual to find that the initial statement of a witness is incorrect or incomplete. A second interview may be needed during which the paralegal can attempt to clarify inaccuracies, errors, or omissions in the account of events given by that witness. The determination of the foundation for any error along with the motivation of the witness for correcting the erroneous information is also important to the accurate assembly of facts. This will necessitate a thorough dissection of the substance of the first interview with the witness to learn what was in error and what was correct.

6.0332 Handling the Deceptive Witness.   Sooner or later, the paralegal will encounter the situation where a story told by a witness cannot be reconciled with the known facts of the case. Even tactful questioning may fail to develop explanations that account for the discrepancies. Repetition and review may convince the paralegal that the witness is deliberately telling lies, concealing the truth, or misrepresenting the sequence of events. When this happens, the interview should be concluded, and the paralegal should consult with the supervising attorney. Referring the matter to the attorney may seem to be an expression of defeat, but it is not. The paralegal's job is to assist the attorney. Knowing when to seek help is an example of using good judgment.

6.034   The Motivation to Speak

6.0341 Ego Satisfaction.   Many people derive a high level of ego satisfaction from public recognition of their knowledge and/or their willingness to testify. Sometimes this recognition is limited to that of the client, an employer, or a committee; sometimes it is even more expansive. It is the attention given by people of different professions; people who weigh the individual's words as though they are gold; and people who will rely upon those words to resolve a dispute. This motive for cooperation is rarely admitted to openly, but will be recognized if looked for.

6.0342 The Desire to Be Liked.   Some witnesses agree to be interviewed or testify because they want to please others and be liked by them. This causes the witness to look for opportunities to do or say what they believe the interviewer wants, whether that individual is the client, the attorney, or the paralegal. These witnesses do not intend to deceive or mislead, but their need to please and to be liked may interfere with, and take precedence over, their desire to be honest. A witness with this motivation will attempt to determine what the paralegal wants by paying close attention to facial expressions and the way questions are phrased. Their responses are generally calculated to provide what they believe is expected and therefore to be liked for it.

If leading questions are used, this witness type will give the answers the questions suggest. For that reason, it is important to carefully construct questions using the six basic interrogatories, "who, what, when, where, why, and how," to ensure that the witness responds with a narrative based on individual recollection and not on suggestion.

6.0343 Altruism.

Some witnesses are motivated to speak from an unselfish concern for the welfare of others and are willing to provide the facts in their possession if they think it will help someone. Others in this category are motivated by a belief that justice must be served. These witnesses are usually objective, seldom having any personal interest in the outcome or proceeding, and are often strangers to the parties involved in the case. They have the potential to be extremely credible witnesses. Official witnesses often fall into this category.

6.0344 Novelty and Excitement.

Another common motivation for some witnesses is the perception that the opportunity to testify is novel and exciting. These witnesses may actively seek to participate and become involved. They often appear to ask as many questions as they answer and are persistent in attempts to probe the interviewer for details. Despite their eagerness, these witnesses rarely possess information of evidentiary value. When they do, it is even rarer for them to present such information in a credible manner.

6.0345 Catharsis.

Some witnesses, including many clients, find that the interview is an opportunity to vent their frustrations, clear their conscience, and give voice to deeply held feelings of suspicion, mistrust, anger, and other emotions. It is a form of catharsis. These individuals relate everything they know, believe, or suspect about the matter in question. Sometimes they are so profuse that it is difficult to record all of the information they are attempting to provide. Subsequent questioning may expose the story as a fabrication woven of rumors and conjecture. The paralegal should understand and accept this as part of basic human nature, even though it can be time-consuming and frustrating. By the same token, the paralegal should not criticize a witness who suddenly recants an earlier story by confessing to exaggeration or embellishment. This effectively begins the interview process all over again, but with a new set of parameters by which to measure the credibility of the witness.

6.0346 Loyalty and Friendships.

Personal friendship or loyalty with one of the parties involved in the case often provides a motivation to speak. Witnesses motivated in this fashion often feel an obligation to provide testimony that will benefit a friend, acquaintance, employer, or coworker. Others may be driven by the desire to be part of a winning side and attempt to join it. The testimony in either case, though voluntary, is colored by these motivating factors and becomes suspect.

When the paralegal suspects that a witness may be shading the truth because of personal loyalty or friendship to a party, an explanation of the problems that can arise from reliance on questionable testimony will often cause the witness to reexamine their own testimony and offer more credible responses.

6.0347 Extrinsic Reward.

The most difficult motive for cooperation to overcome is that caused by the desire for some extrinsic reward. Although expert witnesses receive fees, there is usually little personal stake in the outcome of the case. An expert receives payment which is based on special qualifications and knowledge for research, analysis, and testimony needed by the parties, the court, and the jury in understanding a specific case issue in their field of expertise. This is very different from the witness who testifies for some perceived personal gain, such as a coveted job with an entity involved in the litigation, a portion of any money damages awarded, or a favorable recommendation by one of the parties to some other organization. A typical example would be a criminal case where one criminal testifies against another in exchange for immunity from prosecution, favorable recommendations to a parole board, or the promise of employment following release. Family disputes may also give rise to similar situations, especially if there are estates involved. The paralegal should never suggest that a witness will receive any extrinsic reward for his or her testimony.

If a witness does offer information in exchange for money or other reward, the paralegal should advise the witness that any decision concerning such an offer must be made by the supervising attorney. It is unethical to buy testimony or information. As a practical matter, the credibility of the witness suffers, the benefit to the case is questionable, and the effect on a judge and jury can be disastrous if the circumstances become known. Witnesses who sell information are perceived as amoral opportunists prepared to edit his or her story to fit with the best interests of the purchaser. Parties who pay such witnesses may be subject to criminal charges of suborning a witness.

6.035   Confirming Interviews by Letter

Every interview should be confirmed in advance in writing. This serves as a reminder to the client or witness and is an opportunity to provide written directions or maps showing the office location or interview site. Written confirmations are also an opportunity to remind the witness or client of items you would like them to bring to the interview, serving as an informal checklist. This is especially important when the items being requested from clients or witnesses are needed to meet pleading deadlines, discovery deadlines, or other deadlines established by court order.

6.04   QUESTIONING TECHNIQUES
6.041   Question Construction

The paralegal should use simple, commonly understood words and straightforward questions that do not address multiple issues. Each question should generate one answer. Use questions that require narrative answers rather than leading questions which suggest a desired response or those which require a yes or no answer.

6.0411 Narrative Questions.   Consider this question to a witness: "Were you at the corner of 15th and A Streets, Seattle, Washington, on February 12, 2007, when an auto accident occurred in which John Doe was injured?" A question constructed in this manner will usually result in a yes or no response. A negative response to this question will require five or six additional questions to find out which part of the question caused the negative response. The witness may not have been at that particular location. Perhaps the witness honestly believes the accident they saw occurred on a different date. It is also possible that the witness might remember seeing an accident at that location but did not believe that anyone was injured or that John Doe was involved. Better question construction uses the six interrogatories: who, what, where, when, why, and how. For instance, the question "Where were you on February 12, 2007?" allows the witness to answer in narrative form. It may require a series of follow-up questions to explore the sequence of acts over a span of time. Similarly, the question "While you were there, what did you see?" requires a narrative answer that can be explored and evaluated with further questions later in the interview. Questions are designed to elicit information. Well-designed questions allow witnesses to talk at their own pace, in their own language, and to create their own frames of reference concerning the time and location of an event.

6.0412 Supportive Questioning.

During the course of the interview, supportive questioning helps witnesses provide all the information they know. Words or phrases that are argumentative or indicate a lack of belief in what the witness is saying will generate anger, self-consciousness, and lack of cooperation. It is easy to alienate people by asking overly blunt questions and/or confronting them with their own inconsistencies. The goal is to frame questions that encourage a response which is a voluntary explanation in narrative form.

Supportive questioning can begin during the initial storytelling phase of the interview with such phrases as: "And then what happened?" "Who said that?" and "What did he say then?" Follow-up questions might include: "I'm a little confused now; on June first, did you write the agency or call them?" "Did this follow his letter, or did his letter follow this?" "Now that we know this, how can we prove it to the other people?" Many times the explanations to supportive questioning will clarify otherwise conflicting points. Get the witnesses to help in resolving conflicts, instead of confronting them with accusations of errors or falsehoods.

6.0413 Leading Questions.

Leading questions can make witnesses uncomfortable, turning otherwise friendly witnesses into hostile ones. A leading question suggests its own answer by often calling for a yes or no response. Questions such as "You saw the accident, didn't you?" when posed to a witness who is a friend or associate of the client may generate a sense of obligation in the witness and may cause the witness to answer the question based on a perception that the paralegal (on behalf of the friend) expects a certain answer. Instead, ask questions that allow a witness to provide a narrative answer, such as: "Where were you when the accident happened?" "How far were you from the point of impact?" or "Which way were you looking when you heard the sound of the squealing tires?" This technique will produce more reliable answers than leading questions without causing the witness to wonder what they might be expected to say.

6.042   Refining Judgment Statements

Special care must be used when a witness is asked to provide or offer judgment statements such as estimations of distance, elapsed time, or an individual's ability to carry out a certain act. For instance, consider the statement: "He was 100 feet away." Explore the accuracy of that "100 feet" by having the witness estimate distances. Use easily estimated or checked distances. Have the witness estimate distances at the scene if possible, or have the witness mark the important reference points on a witness sketch and then measure the distance in reality. Do not let an important witness testify concerning a distance or length without first checking its reasonableness.

Understandably, time estimates can also be dangerous. "It just took a minute" must be explored to determine if "a minute" was sixty full seconds, a split second, or a figure of speech. Ask the witness to recreate the time by saying: "I'll time a full minute; you tell me if it is too long." Use a watch or clock with a sweep second hand or a stop watch, and sit quietly through the full period estimated by the witness. Seldom will it feel correct. Have the witness reenact or "role play" the time period as originally experienced while discretely marking the actual time. Record the actual elapsed time period and discuss this with the witness.

Initial descriptions can be treacherous if they are accepted at face value. Have the witness provide a description, and then check its salient points. Remember, people are identified by race, sex, age, height, weight, general physical build (slim, stocky, stout, fat, etc.), hair color, eye color, and outstanding physical characteristics or distinguishing marks. These latter two characteristics include scars, disfigurements, hairstyles, glasses, limping, the use of crutches or braces, tattoos, cosmetics, wigs, jewelry, and watches.

Physical objects often require a description. Vehicles and colors can often be troublesome elements. For example, red does not mean quite the same thing to everyone. It could be "tomato" red, "fire engine" red, or "beet" red. An artist's color chart is a good aid for defining colors. Vehicle makes, models, and production year are difficult for most witnesses to quickly identify. A good method for aiding vehicle identification is to visit new and used car lots with the witness to locate similar or identical cars.

Conduct is another judgment element which often needs additional description. If a witness says the plaintiff or defendant was "acting strangely," follow-up questions should be used to add specifics. What do you mean by strange? Glassy, unfocused eyes? Staggering? Unresponsive to direct questions? Grimacing from pain? Sorrow? Shock? It may be difficult for the witness to put into words, but it is easier to do so in an interview than in a deposition or on the witness stand during cross-examination by opposing counsel.

Occasionally, a witness will have a solid factual foundation on which to base a statement. A time estimate may be based on an event occurring at the same time a favorite television show was starting. A vehicle description might be based on the fact that a relative "owns one just like it." A time period might be correlated to a timed activity: "I had just put a dish in the microwave and started it on high for thirty seconds when I heard the sound and looked out the window. The timer went off at the same time the police were driving up, and I noticed a man running down the alley in the opposite direction." Ask questions designed to help the witness remember any details which will help frame or define a judgment statement.

6.043 Recapitulation

Another important questioning technique in an interview, called recapitulation, is to go back through the major details of testimony with the witness. This is done after the witness has provided narrative testimony and the paralegal has asked follow-up questions. This is accomplished by restating each major element of the testimony. This process should be repeated until the witness is satisfied that the paralegal understands what has been said.

6.05 INTERVIEW PRELIMINARIES
6.051 Scheduling Considerations

When a person is known to have information that the paralegal wants to document, a statement should be taken via interview. But first, the paralegal must decide whether to contact the individual in advance to schedule an appointment or approach the individual unannounced. This first decision can be very important because each method of approach has its particular drawbacks and advantages.

Scheduling the interview in advance gives a witness time to prepare. The witness can gather and review documents, notes, memorabilia, and/or other materials for the coming interview which serve to refresh memory. While this process may help the interviewer's search for truth, it also has the disadvantage of giving the witness time to prepare mentally, to compose responses that provide minimal information, obscure important facts, or limit the information to only those facts the witness chooses to reveal.

Although approaching the witness unannounced generally prevents the kind of mental preparation which inhibits spontaneous production of the desired information, surprising the witness can backfire. When confronted by unknown individuals about potentially volatile matters, people may experience fear.

Fear often causes witnesses to employ delay tactics and may trigger aggressively defensive behavior, both of which hinder the interview's progress. Try to get as much information in advance as possible about the intended witness and his or her relationship to the matter at hand; it will help in planning the correct method of approach.

6.052   Review of Law and Facts

It is important to have a basic understanding of the general areas of law which are applicable to the client's case. If time allows, research and review those general areas of law expected to arise in the case, particularly those with which the paralegal is unfamiliar or has not worked with in some time. The paralegal should never hesitate to seek the advice of the supervising attorney when approaching a new or unfamiliar area of activity and must develop the confidence to face the attorney and say: "What do you recommend I read or study to prepare?" or "I'm not familiar with this type of case; can you brief me or point me toward reference material I can study?"

In addition to having a basic understanding of the law which may come into play, a thorough review of all available factual information is essential in preparing for an interview. This review should include all documents in the file, including internal notes and memoranda, which concern or relate to the matter to be discussed in the interview. This review may involve a multitude of facts in the form of documents, statements, and/or citations of code, statute, or case law. Because of this, the paralegal needs to develop a method of coordinating existing facts with supporting references. Each fact can be listed chronologically, with its corroboration, on the left side of a piece of paper, with questions needed to develop, corroborate, or attack the information listed to the right. For instance, if the dispute involves a contract and the client seeks specific performance, the contract may be the physical fact, and a client statement may corroborate it. The questions on the right side might include: "Novation?" "Rescission?" "Consideration made?" "Is the contract capable of performance?" or "Who drafted the document?"

6.053   Gathering Checklists and Forms

The law office should have checklists and forms concerning the type of legal services performed. The paralegal's use of the appropriate forms during interviews will expedite parts of the interview but should not replace the paralegal's good judgment. The paralegal should take all forms that could apply to the given situation to the interview. It is better to have more forms and checklists on hand than will actually be needed; they can be returned to stock more easily than the interview can be interrupted to obtain them. Many jurisdictions have standard forms which have been approved by the courts or the legislature, such as living wills, powers of attorney, and probate declarations. Using these forms contributes to the smooth, efficient management of the case. For example, in a personal injury case, the names and addresses of doctors, hospitals, insurance companies, employers, and witnesses, among others, will be needed. Using a form for gathering the information increases efficiency and ensures that nothing is forgotten. Other types of standardized forms commonly used are those to be signed by the client which authorize the release of medical records or other privileged information from doctors, hospitals, therapists, accountants, and employers. Whenever possible, the paralegal should develop forms for gathering the basic information used in specific kinds of cases to maximize efficiency. Think ahead, save time, and be professional.

6.054   Planning the Interview Site

Selection and arrangement of the interview site may be a problem unless adequate notice is given. Ideally, the interview should be in an uncluttered conference room of an appropriate size, comfortably furnished and arranged to avoid distraction or uneasiness. During the interview, the paralegal needs to keep the witness focused on the issues at hand. Eliminating unnecessary files and materials not related to the interview will help the paralegal with this task. The room should also be equipped with all necessary miscellaneous supplies, such as scratch pads, pencils, a carafe of water, and glasses. Arrange the chairs and tables so that the paralegal sits alongside the witness or at the corner of the table. (*See* Exhibit 6-1.) Placing the table directly between the interviewer and the witness creates a physical barrier and the classic posture of confrontation: eye-to-eye. Barriers and confrontation, whether actual or implied, physical or psychological, are not conducive to the feeling of rapport the paralegal needs to cultivate in order to uncover the true facts.

If the interview cannot be conducted in an ideal setting, such as the conference room previously described, but occurs at the paralegal's desk, clear the desk of all other materials. Put away correspondence, files, and reference materials. Create the impression that the interview is the most important thing occurring at that time and place. Arrange for the telephone to be answered elsewhere. Not every interview can be conducted under ideal conditions, but they should always be controlled to the largest extent possible. Interviewing is difficult enough without allowing distracting influences to inhibit or interrupt the dialogue between the interviewer and the witness.

Sometimes the interview must be conducted in an uncontrolled environment. Special problems arise when this is the case. Frequently, time pressures exist because the interview is being fit into the witness's schedule. Distractions, such as windows and telephones, throw the interview off course. Courtesy, sincerity, and a dogged willingness to adapt the interview to the situations encountered will serve the paralegal well. Occasionally, the paralegal can arrange to interview the individual at lunchtime or during a work break or sometimes immediately after work, sitting in a car. These conditions are not conducive to the contemplative, thorough, and deep-ranging discussions paralegals prefer, but situations are not always perfect.

Regardless of the interview setting, the paralegal must be alert and sensitive to any special needs the witness may have. For example, someone may be hard of hearing in one ear and may ask that the paralegal sit on a particular side so that the witness can hear better. Others may be uncomfortable if the paralegal happens to be sitting too close. Be observant and do whatever needs to be done to put the witness at ease.

6.0541 The Young and the Old.

Children should never be interviewed without the consent of their parents. They usually speak more easily if their parents are with them. However, the presence

EXHIBIT 6-1 Arranging the Interview Room

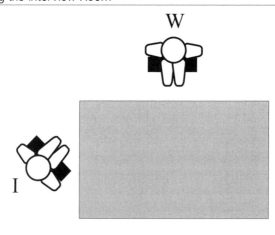

of a parent complicates the interviewing process because children often look to parents for guidance or approval when speaking. Preparing parents properly for involvement in such interviews, teaching them not to coach the child by word or gesture, presents an interesting challenge to the paralegal. One possible remedy is to arrange the chairs so that the paralegal and the child are sitting side by side at the table or desk and the parent is to the rear of the child and out of sight. However, this does not prevent the parent from speaking to the child.

It may be necessary to conduct interviews of older persons under circumstances that are a little unusual for the paralegal. Many times the interview will be conducted in the home of the witness. Interviewing an aged person in his or her own environment may be more advantageous than putting that person through the difficulty of traveling to an office for an interview. This possibility should be given serious consideration if a very aged or infirm person must be interviewed.

6.0542 Telephone Interviews.   Telephone interviews can be a cost-effective method of identifying witnesses or obtaining basic facts from a client. They allow the paralegal to make many contacts in short periods of time, to terminate the interview quickly if it appears unproductive, or to be expanded if the interview is going well. During a telephone interview, the paralegal should work to establish rapport with the individual, with the goal of making a face-to-face interview easy to schedule if the witness has, or contends to have, information bearing on the facts of the case. As discussed in the section on body language, people exhibit certain tendencies during an in-person interview which are an aid in determining credibility. A disadvantage of using a telephone interview is the inability to make personal observations of the witness's behavior and body language.

6.0543 Other Special Cases.   In addition to the problems associated with interviewing children and older people, other types of witnesses will make the arrangement of an interview site difficult. These include people who are hospitalized or under medication at the time of the interview, prisoners in correctional facilities or jails, and people who are willing to provide information but who are unwilling to be identified as the source of that information.

This last category of witnesses, also known as anonymous or confidential sources, may volunteer information that is actually available publicly but which would not be requested in the course of a normal investigation because of its relative obscurity. These individuals may offer contacts who, because they are aware of the paralegal's particular interest, generate more information than would be obtained by a routine request. The identity of these contacts and confidential sources must be protected if the paralegal agrees to accept their information. The major danger in using confidential sources is the inadvertent exposure of them to others involved in the case.

The paralegal who develops confidential sources, whether they are neighbors who volunteer information of a private and personal nature regarding the adversary or government officials who have provided special information from their own and other departmental files, must keep these sources strictly confidential. Their value in assisting the paralegal and lawyer in other phases of formal discovery cannot be measured because it places the attorney in a superior position with regard to knowledge of facts.

6.055 Notetaking

The paralegal conducting the interview should always make notes during its course, even when consent is obtained to record the interview electronically. These notes should not be transcriptions. They should be succinct, reflect relevant portions of the interview, and include physical observations and mental impressions about the witness. Take the notes in such a manner that the witness cannot read what is being written; this prevents the witness from being distracted or influenced by the notes and modifying behavior as a result. After the interview, use the notes to prepare a quick summary of events, saving both documents for permanent storage in the case file. Remember, notes are not transcripts; they are meant to aid the paralegal's recollection of the interview. Keep them short.

6.056   Electronic Recording Decisions

The decision whether or not to use recording equipment to memorialize the interview depends on several things, including the opinion of the attorney, the attitude of the client or witness toward the recording device, and the circumstances or purposes of the interview. While electronic recording of interviews by paralegals is not common in many jurisdictions, it is important to understand the concepts and procedures.

First, as we have seen, interviews are conducted for a wide variety of purposes, some of which do not necessitate recording. Second, because recording the interview can be costly, it is a good idea to limit the number of recorded interviews to include only those expected to generate critical information; for this reason, it may be advantageous to conduct a preliminary oral interview or document review to determine the extent of the witness's pertinent knowledge. Finally, even though the ultimate decision to record the interview must be cleared with the supervising attorney, unless the interview is a formal deposition, the witness may prevent the interview from being recorded by refusing to give permission.

The recordings serve a second purpose, beyond that of data storage; they are a wonderful teaching aid for the paralegal trying to perfect the art of interviewing. There is no better cure for backward mannerisms like watching yourself do them or hearing yourself say them. If you are allowed to record any interviews, review them with a critical eye and ear, noting areas that need improvement as well as those that do not.

6.0561 Special Considerations for Audio and Video Recording.   If audio, video, or other electronic devices are used to record an interview, there are some conventions that should be observed.

a. The paralegal (or investigator) introduces himself or herself; gives the date, location, and purpose of the interview; and provides the case reference or title. For example, "This is Robert Smith, a paralegal employed by Jane E. Jones, attorney for Alice S. Brown, who is the Plaintiff in Brown vs. ABZ Corporation. The following will be a (audio/video) recorded interview with Ms. Brown conducted in the law offices of Jones, Jones, and Day at 1655 North Street, Jonesville, Ohio. Today is April 3, 2007; it is now 10:05 a.m."

b. The witness to be interviewed should be introduced; for instance, "Ms. Brown, please state your full name and spell your last name." Allow the witness to answer. Then ask: "Ms. Brown, will you allow us to record the discussion we have planned to have today?" The next question may be: "Our discussion will deal with the events that gave rise to this legal action. Will you freely and voluntarily relate your best knowledge and recollections of this matter?"

c. Each person present in the room must also be introduced and asked to state their identity, relationship to the case, and willingness to have the session recorded.

d. If a log or counter is used, the recording identification should be spoken early (during the initial introduction preferably) and at the conclusion of the recording.

e. All interruptions of the recording should have the time (hour and minutes) and the reason for stopping read at the point when stopped. The date, time, and a brief restatement of the people present should be made when the recording is resumed.

f. Some jurisdictions require that witnesses be supplied with copies of their statements when preserved in writing or by recording. Some witnesses will agree to make a statement only if they can have a copy of it.

g. At the conclusion of an interview, the paralegal should have the witness reaffirm that the statement was recorded knowingly and voluntarily and ask whether the witness wishes to add, delete, or clarify anything discussed during the interview.

If audio equipment is used and more than two people are present for the interview, it is important that microphones be positioned to pick up each voice equally. If various people speak intermittently during the interview, each person should state his or her name before injecting comments. This allows a more accurate transcription of the recording.

When video equipment is used, it is important that the camera(s) and any microphones, if separate, be positioned so that all of the participants can be seen and heard. To facilitate this, the chairs should be arranged so that no one's back is to the recording device.

6.0562 Drawbacks and Benefits of Audio Recording.

Audio recording an interview, while a way to guarantee total recollection of the dialogue, does have its drawbacks. The first is the general problem associated with any means of recording an interview; the recorded interview will almost certainly be subject to discovery by the adverse party. If favorable testimony is expected, the recording may be helpful, but if it is anticipated that the testimony will not be helpful or perhaps even harmful, the interview should not be recorded. Instead, a preliminary interview should first be done orally, with the interviewer's notes serving as the only record. Then, if the information is not harmful, a second interview can be conducted which may be recorded or a written statement may be prepared for signature by the witness. The attorney directs which method is preferred.

The second drawback to recorded interviews is that it adds a significant number of procedural steps that must be followed during the course of the interview. For this reason, it is generally a good idea for paralegals with relatively little interviewing experience to avoid recording their sessions. Additionally, recording itself is a distraction that may adversely affect both the interviewer and the witness.

Finally, many witnesses are intimidated by recording devices and may not speak as freely as they would during an unrecorded interview or may refuse to speak at all.

6.0563 Drawbacks and Benefits of Video Recording.

The drawbacks that applied to audio recorded interviews apply equally to video recorded, although the procedural complications are lessened by the fact that on a video there is no need for constant verbal identification of the speaker. The nature of a video presents its own special circumstance; some individuals, while entirely honest, give the appearance on video as shifty or crooked, while some individuals who are completely crooked look like saints. Videos allow the personality of a witness to affect the testimony, whether or not the witness is conscious of that fact. For this reason, a video should not be used to record an interview until the subject has been contacted in person and an assessment made of that subject's dynamic effect.

It is worth noting that video record's greatest potential drawback, its ability to either subdue or enhance certain aspects of the individual, is also its greatest potential strength. A client whose image to a judge and jury is positively enhanced by video recording will be very appreciative; that same client will also appreciate the video that reveals the nervous nature of an adversary. Video recording is a two-edged sword with no handle; do not pick it up until it has been thoroughly examined and all caution is employed.

6.06 THE INTERVIEW PROPER
6.061 Introductions

The introduction of the paralegal to the involved parties is extremely important because it puts the relationship of the paralegal to the attorneys, the client, and the witness in proper perspective. The introduction to the client should be performed by the attorney. The introduction should be professional and reflect the attorney's full confidence in the paralegal's capabilities. Ideally, the attorney will discuss the paralegal's role in the case with the client before this formal introduction occurs.

If the lawyer is not present when the paralegal first meets the witness, it is the paralegal's duty to clearly delineate the differences between lawyers and paralegals and to explain the paralegal's role in the coming interview. The witness must be made fully aware of the object and purpose of the interview, the parties involved, and the paralegal's connection to the matter. It is not uncommon for a witness to refer to the interviewer as an attorney during the course of an interview, even when the status and role as paralegal has been previously explained. When this occurs, the witness must be immediately reminded that the interviewer is a paralegal conducting the interview at the request of an attorney for the benefit of the client.

6.0611 Walk-Ins.   In many law offices, particularly those of solo practitioners and small firms, the paralegal will be the first to encounter the walk-in person seeking aid or advice. In these instances, while there is little or no opportunity to prepare for the interview, the paralegal must be well acquainted with the ethical considerations and requirements as well as the predefined limits of authority and responsibility (*see generally,* Chapter 3, Ethics). The paralegal must also be knowledgeable concerning the various types of inquiries which are likely to be received in this situation. Checklists, forms, and resource material covering the routine problems the paralegal will generally encounter with walk-in clients must be kept at hand for immediate reference. When the paralegal is asked for information not routinely handled or outside the scope of authority, responsibility, or ethical restraints, it is best to make a clear explanation to the client that the information requested needs to be provided by the supervising attorney.

6.062   Establishing the Purpose of the Interview

The purpose of the interview should be one of the first things established. For instance, a common purpose for the initial interview of a client is to prepare for or respond to litigation. Such preparation may develop enough information to clarify the issues and lead to a settlement of the dispute that first brought the client to the office. To most clients, a quick resolution to their problem which avoids litigation is preferable to a lawsuit filed, fought, and won at some uncertain future date.

Legal services which do not involve litigation may also require the use of interviews to develop the necessary information for successful completion. These include such tasks as researching corporate organizational structures, estate planning, probate, difficult and complex commercial transactions, business mergers, applications to governmental agencies, drafting contracts, and employer-employee matters.

6.063   The Meeting and the Establishment of Rapport

From the moment the paralegal meets the witness, a rapport should be cultivated. As the witness is being escorted to the interview site, the paralegal should make every effort to put the witness at ease. It helps to engage in casual conversation, during which the paralegal may gain insight into the personality of the witness. The exchange of pleasantries, comments on the weather, inquiries into the traffic situation, or how the ball team did are opportunities for the paralegal to determine the presence of any hostility in the witness as well as the level of communication skills. It also allows the witness to evaluate the paralegal and to some extent overcome any initial apprehension they may have concerning the interview.

Coffee, tea, or a glass of water should be offered at this time. It allows witnesses to do something with their hands and helps to establish a connection with the paralegal. Rapport is the establishment of a harmonious relationship based on mutual trust and respect between people. The paralegal's appearance, sincerity, cheerful attitude, and demonstrated courtesy will aid in dispelling any fears and will help to generate rapport and the feeling of working together toward a common goal. If a decision to record the interview has been made, the paralegal should take the opportunity at this time to learn how the witness feels about the use of recording equipment, whether the idea makes them nervous and uncomfortable or is objectionable for other reasons. This inquiry should be done tactfully and discretely to avoid destroying the rapport which has been established to this point. If the witness is obviously uncomfortable with the idea of being recorded, the paralegal should not go forward with recording plans at that time. It is possible that as more rapport is established, the witness will become more comfortable with the idea.

6.064 Beginning the Interview

Following the introduction and attempt to build rapport with the witness, the paralegal begins taking down preliminary data. This process serves to calm emotions in most witnesses because these things are routine, well-known, not in dispute, yet essential to the identification of the people involved in the case, the dates at issue, and the establishment of the purpose of the interview. If permission has been obtained to record the interview, the requirements discussed in Section 6.056, Electronic Recording Decisions are followed.

Once the preliminary information about the witness has been noted, the paralegal should ask whether the witness has brought any documents, photographs, sketches, drawings, or other items to the interview. Each item brought by the witness should then be described and physically identified. The witness should be asked for permission by the paralegal to take custody of the items. In the event the witness refuses to allow the paralegal to keep any originals, permission should be obtained to have copies made of any documents or computer disks and photographs taken of any physical objects. It is also a good idea at this time to have copies made of any documents so that both the witness and the paralegal can refer to them during the interview.

6.065 The Body of the Interview

Usually a witness has a preconceived idea or sequence of thoughts to present. The most effective way of gauging the value of a witness is to begin by encouraging a general narration of what the witness knows. Meanwhile the paralegal should take notes of points that need corroboration or further detail, information which is in conflict with other known facts, or information which appears difficult for the witness to have obtained firsthand. During this stage, the paralegal encourages the narration by using supportive questioning techniques and body language, such as nodding the head, empathetic facial expressions, and extensive eye contact. Many people, once they begin talking, like to talk. One of the difficulties the paralegal may have is keeping the focus and direction of the witness away from peripheral issues or irrelevant matters.

Once the paralegal has heard the story offered by the witness, the next phase of the interview begins. The points and facts raised by the witness are categorized through gentle but focused questioning as either arising from personal knowledge, inference, or supposition. Search for corroboration of every point of the story through skillful questioning which invites additional narrative, refines judgment statements, and recapitulates what the witness has said. Determine whether the witness knows of other potential related parties, remembers any photographs being taken, recalls the existence of maps, or can identify any other documents or objects from the case file.

Another final essential topic to be explored in the interview is whether the witness has previously provided any written or recorded statement to anyone about the case. The firm's policy will determine what advice or instructions should be given to the witness who may be approached by an adversary for an interview. The policy may be to cooperate or to decline to give another statement, but in either event, the requesting party should be referred to the client's attorney. The goal is to avoid an inconsistent statement, which can cause an otherwise competent, honest witness to lose credibility.

6.066   Concluding the Interview

The interview should be brought to a close politely with an understanding that additional information may be needed in the future. Obtain an agreement about a completion date of any checklist, form, or other document or information that the individual has agreed to provide. The paralegal should remember to calendar that date for follow-up at the appropriate time.

The paralegal should escort the witness and any other participant back to the door of the office or, if an appointment has been scheduled with another individual in the firm, to the next person the witness is to see. Never abandon a witness, client, or other participant after completing this first interview. Keep in mind that rapport is to be nurtured throughout the case, not just during the first meeting.

6.07   SUMMARIZING THE INTERVIEW

As soon as possible after conclusion of the interview, the paralegal should prepare a summary for the attorney which contains a succinct description of the interview and its basic facts. If the interview was recorded, it may be necessary at some future time to have a full transcription prepared. In addition to a recapitulation of the important facts both supporting and refuting the client's position, the summary should include an evaluation of the witness and the elements of proof provided in the testimony, a listing of potential additional witnesses, evidence or other documents, and descriptions of any documents or objects received from the witness.

6.071   Evaluation of the Witness

The opportunity to evaluate a witness, in terms of potential impact on a jury or the likelihood of changing testimony under the pressure of cross-examination, is one of the major benefits of the interview. The attorney will want the paralegal's general impressions of the witness, such as the witness's overall appearance and image, whether they appear sincere or deceitful, whether they have mannerisms which would affect their ability to communicate with a jury, and so on.

These opinions should be based on any perceived inconsistencies in the story, knowledge the witness could not have but claims to know directly, and any physical mannerisms or other observations the paralegal observed during the course of the interview. This evaluation and its foundation are important for supplementing the attorney's opinion about the witness and for alerting the attorney to areas requiring special consideration.

6.072   Elements of Proof

What evidentiary value does the story have on its own? What other evidentiary facts does it corroborate or refute? What conflicts in fact, opinion, or allegation does it create? Facts provided by a witness's testimony should be evaluated in terms of use as an element of proof. The evaluation should also differentiate testimonial proof from documentary or demonstrative proof. Points of corroboration or points of refutation should be outlined for each statement that could have a bearing on the factual issues relevant to the case. Additionally, testimonial proof needs to be identified as "inferred," "deduced," "hearsay," or "firsthand, personal" knowledge. This information will also be used by the paralegal to assist the attorney in preparing for trial by incorporating it into a master index of the facts and proofs for each issue of the case along with a listing of the witnesses who can offer testimony on those points.

6.073   Possible Remedies, Responses, and Additional Potential Defendants

Some matters discussed by the supervising attorney and the paralegal, such as potential remedies, strategy, or planned courses of action, are items which the paralegal should not discuss with either a witness or a client.

During client interviews, the paralegal always seeks to have the client articulate as many acceptable remedies, solutions, or recourses as possible. Identification of potential additional defendants or other interested parties is always important whether the client is a plaintiff, defendant, or other interested party. Equally important is the investigation, discussion, and possible mediation of disputes, which can often resolve the issues without the need to file suit. In some cases, the client's position can be advocated for him or her in a forum that has not already been considered.

The paralegal should not suggest or comment on the probability of success or propriety of pursuing any potential resolutions to the client. Such comments or suggestions to a client may be interpreted as the practice of law because they have the appearance of being independent legal opinion or advice. The paralegal should voice any such comments or suggestions to the attorney, since they are often an important element in the attorney's process of reaching a conclusion on those issues.

6.074   Leads to Additional Witnesses, Evidence, or Documentation

The interview summary should include a list of additional potential witnesses or interested parties as well as a list of documents or objects which need to be obtained. Time, location, the technical nature of the matter, or other impediments should be identified. The paralegal should make a note to discuss with the supervising attorney the arrangements which will need to be made to meet with these additional witnesses and obtain the additional documents or objects.

BIBLIOGRAPHY

"*Investigation*" presentation to Paralegal Association of Santa Clara County—Litigation Section, May 23, 1996 by Ken Edick, P.I., ACTION P.I., San Jose, CA.

GENERAL REFERENCES FOR FURTHER STUDY

California Legal Assistant Handbook, 1st ed. James Publishing, Inc., 1996.

Dwight, Jennifer, *The Nuts and Bolts of Civil Litigation Practice.* Clark, Boardman, Callahan with Estrin Publishing, 1994.

Koerselman, Virginia, *CLA Review Manual.* West Publishing Company, 1998.

Weinstein, Mark, *Introduction to Civil Litigation,* 3rd ed. The Philadelphia Institute, West Publishing Company, 1993.

7

Investigation

7.00 ROLE OF THE INVESTIGATOR

An investigator is the gatherer of facts in a situation where a client is seeking services or advice from an attorney. The attorney clearly has the first responsibility of gathering sufficient facts on which to base his or her opinion as to the proper course of action to pursue. Since the attorney is not an expert in many other fields, he or she will often employ the services of accountants, engineers, doctors, real estate appraisers, or other professionals to provide the special type of information required. In cases where litigation or advocacy may be required, the employment of an investigator may be necessary. Investigators may be called "private investigators," "insurance adjusters," "police officers," or "paralegals." These people are all alike in their purpose. They take directions from an attorney to follow the legal theory to support or refute that theory through careful and thorough assembling of pertinent and relevant evidentiary facts within their ability to locate, identify, corroborate, and report.

The primary goal of conducting an investigation is to effectively uncover the key factual data and information that will directly support and corroborate the ultimate legal issue(s) of the client's case. For example, when conducting an investigation into an alleged product defect which caused injury to a client, the key evidence that may be needed will include the actual physical product at issue, the manufacturer's knowledge level of the alleged product, associated recalls and technical bulletins, and past incidences of product failure due to the alleged defect. The investigator or paralegal must keep in mind that the legal elements of proof must be satisfied, and these elements must be integrated as the guiding light of the investigation efforts. Identification of the legal issue(s) in dispute will ultimately be determined by the attorney in charge of the case. Key facts will be gathered through an initial (and perhaps, a follow-up) interview with the client and/or key eyewitnesses, reports, documents, data, and evidence.

Burden of proof standards must also be taken into consideration when planning and conducting the investigation. In criminal proceedings, the standard of proof is "proof beyond a reasonable doubt." In most civil matters, the standard of proof is "by a preponderance of the evidence." In some civil cases, such as product liability, some employment discrimination cases, and medical malpractice, the standard of proof is "clear and convincing evidence."

A thorough investigation, prior to the filing of a lawsuit, can change not only the decision as to whether to file a case, but also the end results of the case. The rule-of-thumb is if a case is filed today, be prepared to start trying the case tomorrow. The investigation prior to filing a suit must be thorough, and the information gathered must answer the ultimate legal question(s) being investigated. The attorney will have a distinct advantage of thorough preparation and command of evidentiary facts which will greatly enhance his or her ability to provide the client with the best representation.

Investigation involves a variety of activities, such as research, collection and analysis of specific information that substantiates the facts in determining whether or not a cause of action exists, and collecting evidence that supports the client's case. The main activities of an investigation include:

a. Searching official records, unofficial records, or quasi-official records of any form, type, or nature.

b. Obtaining the statement or testimony of witnesses and other people who have direct, peripheral, or hearsay information bearing on the matter at issue.

c. Creating or uncovering existing evidence in the form of photographs, drawings, reproduction of documents, models of places, things, and conditions.

d. Collection and preservation of physical objects and other forms of evidence for later use.

All tasks associated with the conduct of an investigation should be done in a professional and efficient manner. Always supply the attorney with reliable factual information on which to base his or her legal conclusions and advice to, or advocacy for, the client. The investigator must be thorough in this fact-finding process, so that the attorney can then select and rely on the information he or she deems important and further be aware of both supporting and damaging information. Investigations should be conducted in an impartial manner to assure that witnesses are willing to submit to follow-up interviews by either the investigator or the attorney. The idea behind any investigation is to find the truth. The investigator should take all precautions not to make the appearance of harassing anyone, even if there may be cause to suspect something irregular.

Paralegals should be aware that most public and private investigators pursue an investigation with a "micro" view; that is, they focus only on the scope and parameters surrounding the investigation and not on the peripheral matters that the law firm will handle. They rely on the attorney and his or her support staff to handle the legal-related matters. They will not often conduct, nor gather, any formal legal research. They look to the attorney for legal and procedural advice. It is both practical and wise to develop a good working relationship with the investigator and, if possible, with his or her staff. The paralegal may need to rely on the investigator's findings when going through the informal discovery process in anticipation of litigation or when a formal lawsuit is being prepared for filing.

The paralegal who is acting as the investigator, on the other hand, will often take a "macro" approach when conducting an investigation. In addition to conducting the investigation, the paralegal will ultimately follow all facets of the case, from initial client interview through the formal lawsuit to trial and, if necessary, appeal. Being actively involved in the investigation of a legal matter will give the paralegal a distinct advantage of understanding the case and its development, as well as efficiently assisting the attorney throughout the lawsuit, since the paralegal has been directly involved since the outset of the case.

7.001   Basic Elements of Investigation

Investigation is "informal discovery." It is a unilateral collection of facts and evidence ordered by the attorney and without specific notice to the adversary.

The investigation plan must consider all possible theories and applicable legal actions the attorney contemplates handling and proving throughout the life of the case. From these theories, the essential elements of proof can be identified and serve as guidelines to the investigator in seeking out the factual support for proving the elements. The elements of proof can be found in most jurisdictions by consulting the approved jury instructions, the appropriate code or statute to be litigated (or the standards to be met in applications), or the texts and commentary that define the common cause actions. Identities, locations, and physical evidence are always crucial for the investigator to consider, examine, obtain, and preserve.

Whether the investigation consists of a brief gathering of facts by one investigator or a full team of field investigators investigating multiple issues, the basic principles of an investigation are the same:

a. Define the issues in dispute.

b. Identify the essential elements to be proven.

c. Identify the facts needed to prove each of the elements.

d. Analyze the potential sources and locations of evidentiary factual data and/or witnesses that may contribute or impede the establishment of the facts.

e. Elect the method of investigation most likely to produce timely, reliable results commensurate with time, distance, economy, and the importance of the data to the case.

f. Find, preserve, and present both the evidentiary facts (with foundation) to the attorney and an explanation for the lack of availability of those facts that could not be obtained or established.

g. Reevaluate, reinvestigate, and redevelop data needed and/or revealed right up to conclusion of the investigation and, ultimately, the case.

7.002   Judgment, Ethics, and Investigation

An investigator is required to exercise a great amount of judgment when gathering the facts during the conduct of an investigation. Impartiality is key to conducting an effective investigation. The idea is to uncover the truth in support of proving the facts in dispute. The investigator must be prepared to report both the positives and negatives about the facts uncovered and do so in a nonbiased fashion. If the investigator is called to testify at trial, an unbiased, impartial attitude will hold greater weight with a judge or jury. The investigator's role in both the conduct of the investigation and in providing testimony is to tell the truth. If the investigator appears to have a personal interest in the outcome of the trial or is perceived to be unprofessional in his or her demeanor, the investigator's credibility will suffer greatly in the eyes of the judge and jury.

Witnesses are often interviewed, statements are taken, and scene inspections are conducted. Thorough analysis and sound judgment about the facts and circumstances surrounding the investigation must be completed with due diligence, objectively and ethically. The integrity of the investigation can never be compromised by subjective judgment, stretching the rules, or personal opinion. It is imperative that the investigator be able to ensure that all facts and circumstances have been fully gathered and investigated and that final opinions and determinations have been made based upon the evidence and investigation record. The investigator must ultimately be able to go to court with clean hands and defend both facts and opinions with honesty and integrity.

Established protocols and standards for the conduct of an investigation, as well as the identification, collection, and preservation of evidence, must always be followed. During the conduct of an investigation in anticipation of a civil lawsuit, the investigator must take every precaution to preserve evidence in an unaltered condition and give all involved parties the opportunity to examine the evidence. Evidence must be preserved with ultimate care and with all due respect for ethical guidelines and established protocols. For example, the standards for conducting fire scene investigations are outlined in the National Fire Protection Association's industry standard, *NFPA 921 – Guide for Fire and Explosion Investigation* (current edition, 2007; updated every three (3) years). The investigation should ensure that the applicable version of a standard is applied when conducting the investigation.

Both public and private sector investigators receive formal training in conducting a proper and thorough investigation, along with training in the collection and preservation of evidence. Many private investigators are retired law enforcement officers. Other private investigators may be licensed engineers, university professors, or licensed professionals with advanced degrees. Private investigators are usually regulated by state law or licensed by a state agency. They are usually required to be insured and be bonded. Unethical or illegal conduct of any sort on the part of an investigator will jeopardize their own businesses, as well as their professional licensure and reputation. Illegal or improper conduct reflects adversely on the attorney as well and may jeopardize his or her right to practice law. Careful selection of a private investigator, including a background check, should be conducted before simply retaining a private investigator based on marketing materials or a for-profit referral service.

The investigator and particularly the paralegal who is acting as an investigator work under the direct supervision of an attorney. The scope of investigation will be clearly defined by the attorney, and discussion about the particulars of the investigation will take place so that the attorney can get the investigator's viewpoint. Checkpoints should be established during the conduct of an investigation so that the attorney can review the work completed to date and evaluate the proper course of action, especially if unexpected leads or information are uncovered which could have a direct impact on both the investigation and the case in general. . .

Because of increased scrutiny and formal challenges that investigators can face or may be raised by the opposing party at a later time, the paralegal should not assume the role of evidence gatherer. This is not to suggest that the paralegal is unqualified or incompetent, but rather to safeguard the paralegal against any civil sanctions, loss of employment, or loss of credentials due to what may be an otherwise simple mistake or lack of experience. Simply put—when in doubt, let the more experienced collect the evidence and do the things in which the paralegal lacks the requisite training and experience.

7.003 Privacy and Civil Rights Considerations

The preservation of individual privacy plays a pivotal role in the conduct of an investigation. Although investigation is an informal discovery process, the investigator or paralegal must always consider state and federal privacy laws and civil rights issues while conducting an investigation. The investigator or paralegal should carefully examine the facts of the case to determine whether or not authorization forms will be needed to obtain certain information covered under state or federal privacy laws. The client may be readily agreeable to authorize requests, such as for medical records, but other potential witnesses and parties are under no obligation to sign any release or authorization forms or even speak with the investigator. In criminal investigations, certain guidelines exist which permit the investigator to obtain information that would otherwise be subject to the consent of the individual in a civil investigation. Consumer protection laws protect individuals from unauthorized release of information. Protection of individual privacy rights, including that of the client's, must always be at the forefront when conducting an investigation prior to the commencement of a lawsuit.

Privacy considerations must always be factored into the investigation plan. Information can be obtained from various sources, such as the Health and Human Services web site (www.hhs.gov). This includes information about the Health Insurance Portability and Accountability Act of 1996 (HIPAA) (http://www.hhs.gov/ocr/privacy/hipaa/understanding/). The Electronic Privacy Information Center (http://www.epic.org/privacy/consumer/states.html) is also a helpful site.

7.01 THE INVESTIGATION PLAN

The first order of business upon receiving an investigation assignment is to develop an investigation plan. The overall goal of developing this plan is to determine the actual steps and associated tasks that must be completed to generate the information needed for the attorney's review and consideration as to whether or not a cause of action exists and how the attorney can properly advise the client. The development of an effective investigation plan is invaluable to the investigator as the first step in examining the legal issue or problem. This plan is presented to the attorney with the considerations to be made in determining the work to be done by the investigator or the paralegal to generate the information needed to provide the service to the client.

Among the major considerations to be discussed at the outset is whether or not the firm is acting on behalf of the plaintiff, the defendant, or an applicant. The needs are different, and the time element involved varies widely according to the circumstances under which the investigation is made. If the client is the plaintiff, the investigation can be made before the complaint is served, often before a claim is presented to the potential defendant. The plaintiff's attorney has a tremendous advantage since the only time deadline that needs attention is that the claim or case is filed prior to the expiration of the applicable statutes of limitations. This usually provides ample time in which to perform the investigative tasks necessary to firmly establish the factual foundation of the client's rights to the remedy sought. Another advantage is that the client usually has a substantial number of facts readily at hand. As the injured party, the client has personal knowledge of the circumstances that caused the action to arise, names of witnesses, types of documents involved, and potential issues. This is a major head start for an investigator in assembling the evidentiary facts necessary to proving the case.

The defendant has a different set of challenges. Time frequently is a handicap if the action is one that began some time ago and a response is required by statute within a short period of time or the statute of limitations is about to expire. While the plaintiff's investigator could speak freely to each person in seeking witness statements, the defendant is precluded from talking to the adverse party (or the party's employees) without the agreement of plaintiff's counsel. As a result, a substantial source of testimonial fact is not available to the defendant until a formal legal action has been commenced.

Once the final investigation plan is developed, it must be presented to the attorney for review and consideration of the work to be done by the investigating party, the information required to be generated, estimated costs, and to weigh the strengths and weaknesses of the case. The investigation should be developed expediently, particularly if time constraints are a major consideration.

7.011   The Investigation Plan

The investigation plan covers a wide variety of tasks, depending on the scope and type of investigation to be conducted. There is a definite, systematic approach to developing an investigation plan—from the events surrounding the incident to the loss, injury, or destruction incurred as a result; to securing information and data from public and private investigators: to eyewitness accounts, conclusions reached, and evidence preserved as a result of the investigation. The outline should always include the following steps:

a. What facts are believed known? How can they be proved? Supported?

b. What facts must be corroborated?

c. What evidentiary facts must be proven?

d. How do we locate and establish them?

e. Where will the needed evidentiary facts or information be found?
   - Federal, state, local governments, agencies, and commissions
   - Business, trade, and professional associations
   - Private firms' or businesses' records
   - Industry groups
   - Public domain sources (libraries, newspapers, television stations)
   - Individuals' files, memories, and knowledge

f. How best can the inquiries be made?
  - By telephone
  - By letter
  - FOIA or state right-to-know requests
  - Electronically (e-mail, computer-assisted research, etc.)
  - Need for subpoena to obtain certain reports and other documentation
  - By physical contact, examination, or interview
  - Through employment of associated investigators who will perform informal discovery tasks
  - By formal discovery methods

g. Who will complete the review?
  - Private investigator
  - Temporary employment of special staff
  - In-house staff
  - Paralegal

h. Which entity or person has custody of key evidence?
  - Identity
  - Location
  - Opportunity to obtain copies
  - Opportunity to examine/inspect/photograph

i. What privacy considerations must be taken into account?

j. What are the time constraints and possible obstacles/challenges?

k. In what format should the findings be presented to the attorney?

7.012   Inhibitors of Investigation

The investigation may be inhibited by a variety of factors, such as cost, the geographic location where the investigation must take place, document volume, or the time available for the work. Be sure to complete an analysis of these factors before commencing the investigation and present them to the attorney for review and consideration. This could make all the difference in whether or not the investigation will be a productive use of time and resources.

7.0121 Comparing Cost versus Benefit.   The method of investigation has a tremendous impact upon its economics. Before an investigation is undertaken, a cost/benefit analysis should be conducted. Investigation can demand an extensive outlay of up-front costs and human resources, especially when contingency fee cases are being developed. Consultation with the attorney regarding cost parameters should take place in order that precious time and money is not wasted.

Modern technology, such as desktop computers, scanners, digital imaging, fax machines, computer-aided research software, e-mail, high speed Internet access, and Web-based research provide vital investigative tools available to most investigating parties. These tools allow the paralegal or investigator to conduct an investigation primarily from the office, thereby minimizing the costs and providing ready access to information. If the paralegal has access to a laptop computer and Internet/e-mail capability, the ability to perform tasks such as generating information, taking and recording witness statements, completing investigative notes, and transmitting the information back to the office from a remote location is expedited, particularly when time is of the essence.

7.0122 Geography.   Geography may be a barrier to investigation if time and/or cost are major elements in the choice of investigative technique. Many of today's cases cross state and, possibly, international lines. The use of online services or private investigation firms can help narrow the geographical search for witnesses and other individuals who have key information that may have a direct impact on the outcome of the investigation. For example, the use of "skip trace" software will assist in locating witnesses. Sometimes witnesses are located in remote areas, and the only way to reach them may be by going there in person. It may be necessary to travel to remote areas to examine records and directories. On occasion witnesses can be located by telephone or letter. Locating relevant documents from large volumes in diverse locations requires time and experienced eyes and may be best accomplished by an investigator fully versed in the case background and issues. Telephones and letters can be weak substitutes for physical examination. It may be necessary to actually travel to the location to conduct what is known as a "field" investigation. All of these things take time, resources, and expense.

7.0123 Volume of Material.   If the case involves large volumes of documents for review and analysis, alternative means of accomplishing that task should be explored. These alternatives include the temporary employment of a special staff for the particular project or the use of the client's own personnel under the supervision of a paralegal. (*See* Chapter 8, Pretrial Litigation Skills, and Chapter 9, The Paralegal and Document Discovery Cases.) In any case, the investigation must be pursued within the parameters established by the attorney and as fully explained to the investigator, paralegal, or other party assisting with the investigation activities.

7.0124 Time Considerations.   Conducting a thorough investigation is vital to a most favorable outcome to the client, and a thorough investigation prior to a suit being filed is imperative to uncovering the key facts, through the gathering and review of documents and evidence of the case. A thorough investigation requires a dedication of time. Once an action has begun, time is no longer under the control of the attorney. The attorney must maintain a distinct, knowledge-based advantage over the opposing side by having a thorough command of the case, including the issues involved and the documents to be presented as evidence, in order to provide the best representation to his or her client. Completing a thorough investigation, especially in contemplation of litigation, is necessary to insure that no step in the investigation is missed or skimmed over as being mistakenly unimportant to the case. The rule-of-thumb is that when the complaint is filed, the attorney should be ready to try the case tomorrow. When a formal action is begun, court rules, procedures, schedules, and deadlines are the controlling factors.

Time may also be an issue in matters involving the application for licenses or permits. Accuracy and completeness are pivotal factors in conducting the investigation. For example, there may be occasions when the investigator or paralegal may need to attend or intervene in an administrative hearing to gather data on an applicant's objective. This is particularly common where environmental considerations are involved. These interventions can be a quick learning experience that aid in the development of information to counter unanticipated allegations of the intervenor.

Time can also be a major element when criminal prosecutions are involved because of the time constraints involved throughout the life of a criminal matter. For instance, in federal criminal prosecutions, where a plea of not guilty is entered, the trial usually commences within 70 days from the date of filing, 18 U.S.C. § 3161(c)(1) (2001). This does not allow much time to secure documents from the government, experts to review the documents, meet with witnesses, research the law, and prepare for trial. When a client indicates that he or she has been contacted by the government or that business acquaintances are getting subpoenaed regarding the client's business and/or activities, it is essential to begin gathering information and preparing for trial. The government has a "heads up" because they have been conducting their investigation for months. The defense attorney should not wait until the indictment is filed to begin preparation on the case. By conducting a thorough investigation prior to indictment, it may possible to avoid an indictment altogether.

7.013   Formal and Informal Discovery and Privilege

The term "investigation" reflects the work that is performed by an investigator or a paralegal during the informal discovery phase of the case. Investigation covers a wide range of tasks, such as going out to the scene of an accident to take photos and measurements, interviewing witnesses (also known as a "field" investigation), requesting documents for review, creating a time line, or conducting research. Each investigation will have its own unique scope and parameters. This is why it is important for the investigator or paralegal to obtain specific instruction from the attorney before undertaking any investigative task.

Investigation is distinguished from the formal discovery process available through the code sections of the jurisdiction and the rules of the court. Formal discovery procedures include interrogatories, depositions, requests for admission, requests for production of documents, and all of the related law and motion matters associated with those functions (*see generally,* Chapters 8 and 9). Informal discovery, or investigation, is conducted by the attorney's staff or outside parties retained, without the need to consult with opposing counsel. Much of the information obtained in this manner is covered under the "work product" privilege, since it is obtained "for and by direction of an attorney in contemplation of litigation." The paralegal and investigator must insure the material obtained, as well as any reports prepared, is handled in a manner that will not breach or waive that privilege. The assertion of the "work product" privilege is exclusively the right of the attorney. Ruling on whether the privilege applies or has been waived is the duty of the court.

In today's litigation arena, physical evidence, photography, documents, and statements of witnesses (if written or recorded) will not usually be considered as privileged information and will be available to the adversary through formal discovery. This lack of privilege and the potential for discovery is considered by the investigator or paralegal when locating information adverse to the attorney's client. In many cases, a confidential memorandum or report of examination to the attorney may be the best method of alerting the attorney to the adverse data without creating a discoverable windfall for the adversary.

7.0131 Investigator Notes and Reports.   The paralegal or investigator must take detailed notes to ensure the attorney receives a complete, accurate, and clear factual account of the information learned. For example, it is often necessary to interview witnesses about their recollection of the facts and circumstances surrounding an incident. The private investigator or paralegal will normally jot down information in an abridged fashion when interviewing a witness. There is a danger in this from a practical standpoint. If some time has passed between interviewing the witness and creating a formal written record, some key information may be forgotten, or misinterpreted, or even missed. The best courses of action are (1) have the witness complete a handwritten statement at the time of the interview; (2) tape-record the statement (always get the witness's permission before making an audio recording); (3) if the investigator is equipped with a laptop computer, the statement can be typed as the statement is being given; or (4) if the witness will not agree to a written or audio statement, the investigator or paralegal must take copious notes to ensure the information presented is as accurate as possible. The notes should be transcribed as soon as possible to ensure the best possible recall of the witness's account. The investigator or paralegal should ensure that key information is included in the statement, such as:

   a. Date, time, and location of the interview

   b. Permission granted by the witness for interview

   c. Accurate and correctly spelled names, addresses, and other demographic information

   d. If a handwritten statement is executed, that the witness is preparing the statement at the request of the investigator/paralegal

   e. If recorded, questions at the end of the interview asking if there are any other facts that the witness can recall or wishes to share; that the witness has given the statement to the best of his or her ability to recall the information contained in the statement

   f. A concluding statement by the investigator or paralegal as to the time that the interview was concluded and identification of the investigator and witness.

An investigator or paralegal may also have the need to take measurements, draw freehand sketches for referral when constructing a scene diagram, or use handwritten notes or other abbreviated methods when recording initial observations. It is important for the investigator or paralegal to accurately list dates, times, places, persons, things, and especially evidentiary considerations, when conducting the investigation.

Opinions differ on how such notes ought to be preserved and maintained. One viewpoint is that notes are only a temporary account of details that need not be maintained or preserved once the details have been included in a confidential memorandum to the attorney. In the past, handwritten notes were the primary means that the investigator or paralegal used to create their final account of all investigation activities. With the availability of computers in the workplace today, most investigators or paralegals may transcribe their notes onto typewritten documents through word processing software, or they may have a laptop computer right at the scene to record the data collected. Also many may use a microcassette recorder, photographs, and/or videotape when creating a narrative record of activities. Many investigators now use three-dimensional or computer-aided drafting programs to prepare scene sketches. Digital cameras have become a norm for the investigator. There has been a great debate about the use of a digital camera due to the potential for alteration of a photograph, although the astute investigator would not resort to such tactics in "skewing" the facts in favor of a client.

In most cases, a confidential memorandum, note to file, or confidential report of examination to the attorney may be the best method of alerting the attorney to both favorable and adverse data without creating a discoverable windfall for the adversary. It is important to remember that memoranda, whether informal or formal or assumed to be confidential, could be subject to discovery, especially if the investigator is subsequently designated as an expert consultant or witness on behalf of a party in litigation. When expert discovery is conducted, most attorneys will issue a *subpoena duces tecum* with a comprehensive request for all documentation associated with the expert's determination of his or her opinions and conclusions.

Today an investigator will often be called to testify at trial or deposition. Their testimony will include explanation of photos that were taken, sketches that were made, or a physical examination made of the scene or of document files. There are many factors associated with the investigator being called to testify, such as if the investigator was on staff or was retained to conduct the investigation, the ultimate role, or scope, of activities associated with the investigation, and the standing of the investigator in his or her field of expertise. In the case of the paralegal acting as an investigator, the supervising attorney will take every precaution to ensure the paralegal's investigatory activities will remain under the privilege of attorney work product. There could be the rare occasion when the paralegal will be called to testify, depending on the depth and scope of the role the paralegal played in the investigation. If a subpoena is issued, the attorney normally will petition the court to have the subpoena quashed under the principle of work product and/or attorney/client privilege.

In any case, the natural reflex of the investigator or paralegal is to review all the documents available to prepare for the proceeding. Talk to the attorney first. Anything personally reviewed to refresh a memory may have to be made available to the "noticing" or cross-examining attorney. The most effective procedure is for the attorney to review the memoranda and discuss the matter with the paralegal or investigator. The attorney can refresh the memory of the paralegal or investigator with questions while preserving the privilege of a specific report or memorandum or other evidentiary documentation.

7.02 ESTABLISHING AND MAINTAINING PROFESSIONAL CONTACTS

Investigative activities create contacts between an investigator or paralegal and a wide variety of people in private and public roles. The investigator or paralegal should always keep in mind that he or she is a representative of the attorney and the law firm for whom he or she works or has been retained. The manner in which the investigator or paralegal conducts business and interacts with other people will indeed make an indelible mark in the minds of the people with whom the investigator or paralegal are interacting. The manner of speech and dress, arrangement and honoring of appointments, and efficiency displayed in the conduct of the business, particularly in public offices, are all contributing factors to the public image and impression made by the investigator or paralegal and the attorney's office. The rule is: "Be pleasant, be cooperative, and be firm, but be reasonable." Confrontational or rude behavior should never be displayed, even if seemingly warranted.

Clear and concise communication with busy professionals will serve both the investigator and paralegal well. A request for information that is clear, concise, and easily understood will most likely result in a positive, expedient, or accurate result. Before asking others for assistance, the investigator or paralegal must have a clear concept of the kind of help needed and the appropriate office, agency, or department in which the request for assistance can be honored. For example, asking for real property assessment information from the city planning office will waste the time of the city employee, as well as the paralegal, since that kind of information is not maintained at that public office.

The investigator or paralegal should carefully plan and prepare visits and associated requests for information in advance. Work efficiently and in concert with others. When pursuing information from both public and private agencies, follow these guidelines:

a. Make every effort to ensure that requests are reasonable.

b. If multiple requests for information are necessary, be sure to break them down by individual request.

c. Be prepared for delays with both public and private agencies. Ask for an estimate of time that it will take to have the request(s) filled and what fees, if any, apply in honoring the request.

d. Research the agency's public information and privacy procedures before making requests for sensitive information. There may be a restriction on obtaining such information.

e. Review, understand the parameters of, and then prepare Freedom of Information Act (FOIA) or state right-to-know requests. Be aware that these requests often take time to review and process. Be prepared for a rather long wait depending on the agency.

f. Avoid "panic" searches, last minute certifications, and/or "rush" filings.

g. Understand that there may be at least one opportunity that the agency may need clarification as to what is being requested and promptly respond to these requests.

Be familiar with the county clerk's office and know what kinds of records are kept there. Make at least one trip to the courthouse in the company of a more experienced person who can explain the offices in the building and detail the files that are kept there. Knowledge of how recording and retrieval are accomplished in the ordinary course of business, along with names and telephone numbers of contact personnel, will be a valuable resource. Government phone numbers may be found in local telephone book and on the Internet.

The investigator or paralegal can expect to see the staff in public offices again in other cases. Custodians of Record for public agencies and offices are the "official witnesses" who have custody and control of documents and files. It is essential to demonstrate a working appreciation for the information they possess, their expertise in locating and producing data, and their willingness to assist, even when those efforts may seem feeble, inefficient, or untimely. The successful investigator hides irritation and accepts help cheerfully, graciously, and with sincere gratitude. Future trips to that same office will likely result in the investigator or paralegal being greeted positively and receiving timely assistance. Cooperation is the essential element. The way to obtain cooperation is to be cooperative and considerate of the staff in public offices.

7.03 IN-OFFICE INVESTIGATIONS

The days of pounding the sidewalks and driving the streets to conduct an investigation are, for the most part, in the past. Although there are certain activities, such as in-person interviews, that may need to be conducted, the overwhelming majority of investigative activities can often be completed without the need to leave the office, thanks to modern technology.

7.031 Technology and Investigation

Technology available in today's law office includes desktop or laptop computers, computer-aided legal research programs such as LexisNexis and Westlaw, scanners, digital imaging equipment, and dial-up or high speed Internet Access. The availability of such technology depends on the particular law office. This technology allows the paralegal, who cannot leave the office, to conduct many investigative activities with ease, convenience, and quickness. Most often, private investigation firms have purchased specialized software, such as skip tracing (or "people finder") programs, computer-aided design, or other types of software, that assist the investigator with ease and convenience. Technology can also be instrumental in managing the cost of an investigation.

In addition to resources available online, many private firms perform research functions for clients within the files of state and federal agencies. Using these resources allows the paralegal to verify or obtain a variety of information from such things as drivers' licenses, car titles, and official government or agency filing forms to copies of proposed legislative bills and other government documents or reports. Search inquiries must be clearly defined as to topic, scope, and acceptable costs before they are initiated. Costs may become prohibitive.

Another resource for information compiled by government agencies accessible by the internet is a subscription to periodic reports. For instance, monthly climatological data segregated by specific location is available from the National Oceanic and Atmospheric Administration, Environmental Data Service, National Climatic Center, in Asheville, North Carolina. A listing of all such available subscription services, as well as a listing of all government publications, can be obtained from the U.S. Government Printing Office.

Establishing personal and direct contact with the people who staff government agencies, on any level, and building a relationship of mutual trust and respect with those individuals will make it possible to call a person by telephone and ask for a timely search, photocopying, mailing, and billing of specific information. Asking others to search records in this manner is acceptable, efficient, and reliable when the volume of material to be screened is small and the facts or issues are clearly defined and easily recognizable. If the issue or fact is affected by the context of the documents, personal examination is required, and the telephone inquiry should be avoided.

7.032   Sources of Information

Federal, state, and local government offices, such as agency records offices, public defender, law library, corporation filings office, clerk of courts, and others, have tremendous amounts of information that may be accessed by telephone or Internet access if the paralegal is familiar with the right questions to ask and the protocol needed to obtain such assistance. Many directories are also available at nominal or no cost on the Internet or are incorporated in CD-ROM programs available for purchase. Most, if not all, governmental agencies publish special directories of telephone numbers (at nominal cost). General information numbers to assist in locating the correct source for particular kinds of data are usually available from the telephone company directory assistance or are published in the local telephone books in the government sections (often known as the "blue pages").

The Internet is a readily accessible tool for the investigator or paralegal to determine the correct agency which may have the information being sought. In addition to resources available online, many private firms perform research functions for clients within the files of state and federal agencies. Using these resources allows the investigator or paralegal to verify or obtain a variety of information, such as drivers' licenses, motor vehicle titles, official government or agency filing forms, copies of proposed legislative bills, and government documents or reports. Search inquiries must be clearly defined as to topic, scope, and acceptable costs before they are initiated. It is necessary to work within the parameters of the investigation budget, especially if the firm or client has only limited financial resources.

7.033   Telephone

The telephone was once the primary tool for the investigator to gather information from various sources. Use of the telephone in conducting investigation-related activities is still considered valuable if other, more efficient means are not available. Telephone-related investigation activities will not typically provide the ease of locating information as do online searches. Using the telephone when conducting an investigation is now considered to be a secondary source of contact and information gathering. Today the telephone is primarily used to set up appointments, establish some remote contacts, obtain logistical information, and other peripheral activities.

The telephone can still be used to locate witnesses, contacts, and other parties that may be involved or have knowledge of the facts and circumstances related to an investigation. Today's telecommunications-related enhancements can make it difficult for the investigator or paralegal to make successful contact with respective individuals. It is very easy to avoid any contact with an investigator or paralegal by simply screening the Caller ID option on the telephone. In addition, two major drawbacks of using the telephone in locating information and people are (1) the difficulty to evaluate the credibility of the person on the other end of the line solely by voice tones and words and (2) the time-consuming nature of locating the appropriate office and contact when only general numbers are available as a starting point. The investigator or paralegal may also find that he or she may spend valuable time being placed "on hold" for extended periods of time, which may prevent the paralegal or investigator from attending to other pressing matters.

7.034   Correspondence

Correspondence is another investigative tool that can be effectively utilized to gather information. The key advantage of using correspondence is that a written record can be created which makes follow-up easier to track. Most offices have form files, which contain letters of inquiry for basic types of information relating to particular kinds of cases. These letters may include requests for medical records from doctors and other care providers; authorization forms; employment records from employers; accident reports and other reports of investigation from law enforcement, fire, or regulatory bodies; or studies from governmental agencies. The paralegal or investigator should keep in mind that most, if not all, law enforcement agencies require a subpoena before a request for official agency documents or reports are honored. Governmental and court offices, in most cases, will honor requests for information without a subpoena but will require a formal written request to be made to the agency or court for determination. Fees often apply for services such as photocopying. The investigator or paralegal should contact the agency or court or conduct research into the respective agency or court to determine fees, costs, limitations, and other considerations prior to transmitting a request. Again, there could be a significant time gap between the date of transmittal and receipt of the requested information.

Potential witnesses may be contacted by a letter. The letter should include "form" questions that serve to identify those with helpful information, as well as specific questions that will generate key facts and other important feedback from the potential witness. Having a written record of the contact will verify that the potential witness has, in fact, been contacted, and the level of cooperation can be determined simply by the tone or lack of response. Enclose a self-addressed, stamped, envelope for more enhanced chances of obtaining the information requested. Assuming the potential witness cooperates, this makes it easy for prospective witnesses to provide the information needed and for the investigator or paralegal to determine whether or not the potential witness should be contacted personally for further details. This technique is relatively inexpensive to use. The investigator or paralegal should avoid using this technique for important or complex cases where solid evidentiary representations by each potential witness are required.

7.035   Computer Resources

The Internet provides a swift means of accessing information for the legal professional. Many court records are now available by electronic access using a computer with Internet access dial-up, or broadband capability.

Most federal and many state courts have established electronic access to records to obtain case information. Internet access to court information has expanded dramatically since the turn of the century. This information is managed at the federal level by the Administrative Office of the U.S. Courts, including the judiciary's internet website. General information on the judiciary, publications, and proposed rules for comment are included on the website. In addition, several individual courts have also established internet websites and offer court-related information, opinions, and court rules. All of these services provide the public, and especially the investigator or paralegal, with greater and more rapid access to court-related information. The Web-related services provide flexible options to meet the needs of the individual user. The services also reduce the barriers to the public's ability to access court-related information.

There are a number of other internet websites that can provide information concerning the courts and its business. For example, a consortium of law schools (generally, one from each circuit) provide free access to appellate slip opinions through the school's internet websites. The member law schools have complete responsibility for retrieving information and uploading them on their Web sites. Some law school Web sites, such as that of Cornell University School of Law (http://www.law.cornell.edu), provide a wealth of court information by type of law, jurisdiction, and the like.

7.036   Court Records

7.0361 Public Access to Court Electronic Records (PACER). PACER is a system that allows any user with a personal computer to access federal district or bankruptcy court information and to retrieve official electronic case information and court dockets simultaneously. PACER is predominantly used by attorneys and paralegals. The main advantage of PACER is that it eliminates

the need to travel to the courthouse to retrieve routine information. Technical requirements to access PACER are a Javascript enabled Web browser and Internet access. The official website address is http://pacer.uscourts.gov.

Each court controls its own computer system and case management database, which results in variations among jurisdictions as to the informational offerings. Information currently available through PACER includes basic case, docket and index information, and opinions. Many jurisdictions offer toll-free lines. The toll-free number for PACER is 1-800-676-6856. PACER service hours are 8:00 A.M. – 5:00 P.M. Monday through Friday, Central Standard Time.

Cases can be searched by party name, case number, or by a list of cases before a specific court. Information available includes causes of action, nature of the lawsuit, parties and participants, filing deadlines, and hearing dates. Information is usually current as of the previous day's filings. Many courts allow users to download and print copies of filed documents for a current fee of $.08 per page.

7.0362 Case Management/Electronic Case Files (CM/ECF). CM/CEF is a case management system that allows attorneys to file petitions and other documents electronically over the Internet using a standard Web browser. This results in an electronic "case file." Case information, including images of documents, is available for examination electronically from any location using Internet access. All cases and adversary proceedings filed on or after January 1, 2003, have been assigned to the system. Chapter 11 bankruptcy cases and related adversary proceedings filed on or after April 1, 2002, are also available on the system.

As of February 1, 2007, nationwide implementation of the federal judiciary's CM/ECF is complete in 98 percent of the federal courts: 92 district courts; 93 bankruptcy courts, the Court of International Trade, the Court of Federal Claims, and the Bankruptcy Appellate Panel for the 8th and 10th Districts. Implementation is advancing in the federal appellate courts. CM/ECF replaces both the courts' electronic docketing and case management systems. It also provides the courts with the option to have case file documents in electronic format and to accept filings electronically. The Judicial Conference on Court Administration and Case Management oversees the continued implementation and public access recommendations.

CM/ECF uses standard computer software, an Internet connection, and browser. The system accepts documents in Portable Documents Format (PDF) via Adobe Acrobat. Adobe Acrobat Reader may be downloaded for free at http://www.adobe.com. The system is easy to use; documents using conventional word processing software are prepared and then saved as a PDF file. There are no added fees for filing documents over the Internet using CM/ECF, but existing document filing fees do apply. Access to court data is available through PACER.

Over 27 million cases are located on the CM/ECF system. Practitioners have found the ease of filing documents electronically to be a distinct advantage in making timely filings and having an instant record of the filing. Another advantage of the CM/ECF system is the ability of the courts to make their documentation readily available for public access.

The judiciary has set the fees at the lowest possible level sufficient to recoup program costs. Litigants can receive one free copy of documents electronically filed in their cases. Additional copies are available to attorneys and the general public for viewing and downloading at $.08 per page, with a maximum cost per document of $2.40, except for access to transcripts filed with the court. As of February 1, 2007, all district and bankruptcy court CM/ECF filers who pay fees online via credit card will be required to enter a security code to complete the transaction. For more information, log onto http://pacer.psc.uscourts.gov/announcements/general/cc_code.html.

To register for a CM/ECF access account, contact the applicable court. Further information on the CM/ECF system, including the courts that are operational on the system, can be found at http://www.uscourts.gov/cmecf/cmecf_about.html or by calling the Office of Judges Programs at 202-502-1862.

To file a document, the user logs onto the court's Website with a court-issued password, enters basic information relating to the case and document being filed, attaches the document, and submits it to the court. A notice verifying court receipt of the filing is generated automatically. Other parties also receive an automatic e-mail notification of the filing.

7.0363 U.S. Supreme Court.   The U.S. Supreme Court offers two electronic access services to the public.

a. The Electronic Bulletin Board System (BBS) provides online access to the Court's automated docket, argument calendar order lists, slip opinions, rules, special notices, and general information. The automated docket posted on the BBS is current as of the preceding day's business. Slip opinions and orders are posted within a few days of release. The system contains opinions issued during the October Terms of 1993 through 1995. Access to BBC is presently provided at no cost. To access the BBS system, log onto http://www.pacer.psc.uscourts.gov/phone_access.html or by calling 202-554-2570.

b. The U.S. Supreme Court Clerk's Automated Response System (CARS) permits a caller using a standard touchtone telephone to obtain the status of cases on the U.S. Supreme Court automated docket from an automated voice synthesizer response system. Callers may receive case information or speak directly to a clerk. The access telephone number is 202-479-3034.

7.0364 Appellate, District and Bankruptcy Courts.   These courts offer several electronic public access systems.

a. Voice Case Information System (VCIS) uses an automated voice response system using a touchtone telephone to read a limited amount of bankruptcy case information directly from the court's database. The caller can obtain information about a bankruptcy case quickly and easily by simply making a telephone call. The service is operating in approximately 75 bankruptcy courts and is currently free of charge. A listing of VCIS telephone access numbers can be found at http://www.pacer.psc.uscourts.gov/phone_access.html

b. Appellate Voice Information System (AVIS) is comparable to the VCIS but focuses on obtaining appellate case information through the use of a touchtone telephone. The service is currently free of charge.

c. Appellate Bulletin Board System (ABBS) is available in all but one federal appellate court. The system offers electronic access to court decisions (slip opinions) and other court information such as calendars, case dockets, local court rules, notices, reports, and press releases. Most of the appellate courts have upgraded their systems and now offer both slip opinions and case dockets on the same public access computer and telephone number. Information can be viewed online and can be automatically downloaded. Most appellate courts charge a user fee for this service.

d. Public Access Terminals provide a quick and easy way to obtain pertinent case and docketing information in all appellate, district, and bankruptcy courts. This service is currently free of charge; however, access is limited to the clerk of courts offices. The paralegal wishing to use this service will be required to physically go to the applicable clerk of courts office to research and access information.

7.0365 State and Local Courts.   Each state and various local courts have their own individual computer-generated information systems. These include state supreme courts, state appellate courts, and county or local courts. For information concerning access, fees, specific information available online, and other information, consult the particular court of jurisdiction.

7.0366 Additional Considerations.   It is important that the paralegal verify court rules and procedures and determine which specific services are available from a particular jurisdiction. The paralegal should obtain and record the necessary log-in and passwords and keep them in a safe place. The paralegal should also check the applicable procedures and guidelines established by law or regulation for government oversight agencies, corporations, business, and nonprofit organizations to gain a better understanding of how things such as a request for information or inspection of records can be accomplished with minimum or no difficulty.

7.0367 Web-Based Information and Research.   The Internet contains a wealth of information that is instantaneous and, in the majority of instances, free. Independent companies, individuals, legal publishers, universities, and local, state, federal, and foreign governments provide free access to all manner of information and data using the Internet. The information does change frequently and should only be used as a stepping stone or supplemental source of information or legal research. Information and data on the Internet should always be verified for accuracy and completeness. For example, check the home page or link page of the particular Website for the date that the Website's information was last updated. Especially if information is contained on the Website which reflects court decisions or government agency actions, a good rule to follow is that if it is more than a month or more old, check the official Website of the agency or jurisdiction for the most up to the minute information.

The Internet is an invaluable tool for obtaining scientific, corporate, and other kinds of information. There are many methods of searching on the Internet. Two of the most widely used "search engines" are Yahoo® (http://www.yahoo.com) and Google (http://www.google.com). These are just examples. Do not expect these to open. These search engines provide fast links to newspapers and magazines that publish online editions, as well as links to specialized indices such as nationwide telephone books, people and business directories, digital maps of cities in the United States, thesaurus and dictionary, and other reference services. To begin a search with these tools, type in a key word or phrase. To narrow the focus of the search, use special terms and connectors, such as an asterisk (*) after the key word or phrase.

See Chapter 2, Legal Research, for information on how to properly cite an information source from the Internet. A listing of useful search engines and other websites can be found in Section 7.11.

7.0368 Computer-Aided Research Subscription Services.   The overwhelming majority of law offices today have some type of subscription to computer-aided research services, such as Westlaw and LexisNexis (see Chapter 2, Legal Research). These services provide a direct gateway to very sophisticated investigation programs and legal research tools. The most widely used computer-aided software programs in the law office are LexisNexis and Westlaw. Both programs are subscription-oriented and provide a cafeteria style where the subscriber can pick and choose what subscription is most suitable for the type of law practiced and the firm's clients. Offerings include state and federal law and regulation, court decisions, court rules and procedures, and numerous other offerings, such as people searches. The programs are updated daily. A notable feature of Westlaw is the ability of the paralegal to customize their research page to a total of six specific links. This is particularly useful for the paralegal who works in a specialty area or only deals with a specific court jurisdiction, such as bankruptcy. LexisNexis provides similar services. These services are under constant development, improvement, and expansion to provide the subscriber with ease of access and understandability. For example, LexisNexis now offers a wide range of subscription services for the full service law firm, the specialized firm, and firms serving individuals and small businesses. A subscription and a password are necessary to gain access to computer-aided research systems. For more information on subscriptions and offerings, log onto http://www.lexisnexis.com or http://www.westlaw.com.

The paralegal who has a computer-aided legal research subscription service at his or her fingertips should utilize it to its maximum capability. These services are a type of "mini Internet" for the legal professional, and depending on the type of subscription contract, the service can be easily utilized to complete a large portion of the investigative work being undertaken. To find an investigative database suitable to the investigator or law firm's needs, scan legal periodicals for advertisements pertaining to investigative research or follow the links when searching on free online directories.

7.04 LOCATING WITNESSES

Chapter 6, Interviewing Techniques, discusses many of the problems associated with interviewing prospective witnesses. The chapter does not discuss the difficulty of locating the witnesses. There is a distinct advantage to identifying and locating witnesses and interviewing them in the informal discovery process of investigation. This offers an opportunity to determine the extent of the person's knowledge and whether it is helpful or damaging to the client's position. The formal discovery process of deposing a witness requires notice to the adversary counsel of the existence of the person and the possibility that his or her testimony is important to the case. It is also very expensive. The informal discovery process bypasses many of the formalities involved in deposing a witness.

7.041 Locating Lay (Fact) Witnesses

The first step in locating potential witnesses is to identify those persons who are essential to obtain facts, authenticate other forms of evidence, and provide leads to other testimony and evidence. Potential witnesses are identified in many ways. Some are directly revealed by their names on official records and reports, news and media accounts, or within private documents that comprise part of the evidence gathered during the investigation process. Often the client, friendly witnesses, or hostile witnesses will refer to other people who they believe have knowledge of the circumstances surrounding an incident. Whenever a person is mentioned in oral or written form, the investigator should note the name and source(s) that identify the name, address, and other useful information about the potential witness, such as date of birth (DOB), social security number (SSN), and place of employment, if applicable. Not all persons named as potential witnesses will become fact or expert witnesses if a formal cause of action is subsequently filed.

After identifying various persons associated with the case, the next task is to determine how to locate them. This stage of investigation requires the qualities of persistence, assertiveness, and patience. The search commences by concentrating on any information that has already been gathered about the person's residence, whereabouts, occupation, and/or place of employment. Traditional sources for locating addresses include accident and crime scene reports, local telephone directories, voter registration records, the city directory, driver license records, vehicle registration records, and public utility registers. Each of these resources contains addresses. As these resources are used, the paralegal should consider different spelling of names, especially those received from statements or oral testimony, nicknames, maiden names, and misspelled names on documents.

Computer-aided subscription services or per-search programs provide direct gateways to very sophisticated investigative or "skip trace" types of services. LexisNexis, for example, has added a subscription service entitled Company & People Intelligence Gathering. There are other investigative database providers on the market that permit the public to directly link to their computers for nominal fees. Providers such as Iqdata (http://www.iqdata.com), Civil Records (http://www.civilrecords.org), and Intelius (http://www.intelius.com) will provide detailed information about a potential witness's current address and other personal information for a reasonable fee. Unfortunately, the days of free people searches are a thing of the past, except for the very basic information, which is often only a starting point in identifying and finding potential witnesses.

Crime or accident scene photographs may identify business logos or license plate numbers that can be used to trace individuals. Business and governmental organization rosters and in-house telephone rosters are also helpful in directly identifying witnesses when a person's position is known but their name is unknown.

If none of these sources yields results, inquiry should be made of persons who can reasonably be expected to be acquainted with the person. This may include all of the other potential witnesses previously interviewed on matters relating to the case and during which discussion they did not mention the person's name. Questions as to the identity and location of the new potential witness may reveal that the name is misspelled or mispronounced, that it is a nickname, or that it is only a diminutive of the real name. When interviewing any witness, it is a good habit to ask near the end of the examination: "Do you know anyone else who has knowledge of the events that we have been discussing?" As an interview progresses, many persons develop recall of names, descriptions, or work addresses through the process of talking about the events. Show photographs or diagrams of scenes to enhance witness memories.

The paralegal can personally access nontraditional methods of locating prospective witnesses. Computers with Internet connections are now a mainstay in law offices, public libraries, educational institutions, and homes. A computer with Internet access provides several easy-to-use address directories with nationwide access, and it is possible to readily program an electronic address book to automatically dial these nationwide address directories. The paralegal should not pass up the opportunity to learn and acquire skills using this vital research technology. Some Internet addresses that permit the user to input a name and location and retrieve the corresponding street address and existing telephone number are Switchboard® (http://www.switchboard.com) and Bigbook® (http://www.bigbook.com). These online directories are useful and are the equivalent of having a white pages telephone directory for the entire nation, but they are limited to information published in those directories, which are usually published only on an annual basis and do not contain information of those who maintain unlisted telephone numbers. Some Internet directories even provide street maps to business addresses. Free of charge Internet websites such as Rand McNally (http://www.randmcnally.com) and MapQuest (http://www.mapquest.com) can provide street maps and driving directions to both personal and business addresses. An online search utilizing search engines such as Google® or Yahoo® can also be utilized to locate witnesses. This can be accomplished by typing in the name or names of the individual witness in the "search" bar of the search engine. There are many nontraditional websites available which may be a source for finding potential witnesses. For example, MySpace (http://www.myspace.com), UTube (http://www.utube.com) and Facebook (http://www.facebook.com).

Once an initial address or telephone number is located, attempts to make contact with the witness will be pursued. If the address is not current, the possibility always exists of seeking the assistance of the post office for a forwarding address. The U.S. Postal Service provides forwarding address data when requested in writing, but only on their form entitled *Request for Change of Address or Boxholder Information Needed for Service of Legal Process.* (*See* Exhibit 7-1.) The Postal Service is required only to forward mail to new addresses for one year.

Neighbors and coworkers may also be able to provide clues as to the location of witnesses that have moved or transferred from the area. Once an accurate name and at least one address for the witness is obtained, the credit bureau of the community may provide a reliable source of identifying past and present addresses. Under current laws regarding fair credit reporting, the credit bureau may be required to reveal the paralegal's interest to the individual, but such disclosure is not of particular concern in most cases. Motor vehicle and vehicle operator license bureaus often can furnish reliable data directly or through private services at nominal cost. If the residence cannot be determined, the paralegal may have to work through the

EXHIBIT 7-1   United States Postal Service Change of Address Form

---

(LETTERHEAD OPTIONAL)

Postmaster   Date _____

_____
City, State, ZIP Code

Request for Change of Address or Boxholder
Information Needed for Service of Legal Process

Please furnish the new address or the name and street address (if a boxholder) for the following:

Name: _____

Address: _____
NOTE:The name and last known address are required for change of address information. The name, if known, and post office box address are required for boxholder information.

The following information is provided in accordance with 39 CRF 265.6 (d) (6) (ii). There is no fee for providing boxholder information. The fee for providing change of address information is waived in accordance with 39 CFR 265.6 (d) (1) and corresponding Administrative Support Manual 352.44a.

1.   Capacity of requester (e.g., process server, attorney, party representing himself):
     _____

2.   Statute or regulation that empowers me to serve process (not required with requester is an attorney or a party acting *pro se*—except a corporation acting *pro se* must cite statute):
     _____

3.   The names of all know parties to the litigation: _____

4.   The court in which the case has been or will be heard: _____

5.   The docket or other identifying number if one has been issued: _____

6.   The capacity in which this individual is to be served (e.g. defendant or witness): _____
     _____

WARNING

THE SUBMISSION OF FALSE INFORMATION EITHER (1) TO OBTAIN AND USE CHANGE OF ADDRESS INFORMATION OR BOXHOLDER INFORMATION FOR ANY PURPOSE OTHER THAN THE SERVICE OF LEGAL PROCESS IN CONNECTION WITH ACTUAL OR PROSPECTIVE LITIGATION OR (2) TO AVOID PAYMENT OF THE FEE FOR CHANGE OF ADDRESS INFORMATION COULD RESULT IN CRIMINAL PENALTIES INCLUDING A FINE OF UP TO $10,000 OR IMPRISONMENT OF NOT MORE THAN 5 YEARS, OR BOTH (TITLE 18 U.S.C. SECTION 1001).

I certify that the above information is true and that the address information is needed and will be used solely for service of legal process in connection with actual or prospective litigation.

_____   _____
Signature   Address

_____   _____
Printed Name   City, State, ZIP Code

FOR POST OFFICE USE ONLY

____ No change of address order on file.   NEW ADDRESS or BOXHOLDER'S POSTMARK
____ Moved, left no forwarding address.   NAME and STREET ADDRESS
____ No such address.
                                                                    _____
                                                                    _____
                                                                    _____

potential witness's occupation, and the problem becomes much more complex. If the occupation can be linked to a particular company, it sometimes is possible to obtain the address from the personnel department of that company. However, this possibility is diminishing with the right-to-privacy laws inhibiting the release of information. If the paralegal does not have the time or ability to locate witnesses or if all direct investigation fails, there are private investigation firms that specialize in "skip-tracing." When a witness is critical to the case, the cost to hire an outside investigator to locate that witness is well spent.

If all other methods fail, attempt to contact others with the same last name listed in the local telephone book. It is possible that the person is related to the witness being sought. This can be a lengthy and unproductive process, depending on the commonality of the surname of the witness being sought.

7.042   Opinion Testimony by Lay Witnesses

Normally, lay or fact witnesses testify according to the five senses: what they saw, heard, touched, tasted, or smelled. They are normally not considered in any way as an expert witness, and their testimony is most often limited to factual matters surrounding a case.

One of the ways the court ensures that testimony is reliable is to require the witness to have firsthand knowledge, as set forth in *Federal Rule of Evidence* (FRE) 602. In essence, the process of establishing a witness's personal knowledge to the facts in which the witness will testify is called "laying a foundation." This requirement affects the attorney, investigator, and paralegal.

During the course of an investigation, information can be obtained from a witness that could uncover the need for the witness to testify as to their lay opinions and conclusions. Federal Rule of Evidence 701 contains a provision regarding when a lay witness can offer expert testimony. Specifically, the rule provides that a lay witness can testify about their opinions but only if the opinion or inference is rationally based on the perception of the witness and helpful to a clear understanding of the witness's testimony or documentation of a fact at issue. Before a lay witness can state an opinion, a foundation must be laid establishing the fact that the witness has personal knowledge of the event that forms the basis of the opinion. This requirement meets both the relevancy requirement of FRE 701 and the personal knowledge of the facts requirement under FRE 702. The primary goal is to question the witness to determine whether their opinion meets the requirements that make opinion testimony possible.

The investigator or paralegal that interviews or reviews statements or other information that a lay witness provides should be careful in simply considering a lay opinion of a fact at issue as being one which will automatically meet the requirements under the FRE. The best judges of whether or not a lay witness may be qualified to render opinion testimony are the attorney and/or the courts.

7.043   Consultants and Expert Witnesses

Investigations of areas beyond the expertise or personal experience of the legal team will often require consultation with an expert witness. Until an individual is designated as an expert witness, he or she will only be considered as a fact witness or as a factual consultant. During the investigation (informal discovery) phase, a potential witness does not have to be disclosed to the opposing party.

The complexity of today's lawsuits will often require the services of a consultant or expert witness. Most often, those first retained as consultants may ultimately become an expert witness at trial. To that end, the consultant or expert should be integrated as part of the legal team as soon as he or she is retained.

a. **Identify the need for expert help.** Most cases require help to identify the theory of liability, to distinguish evidentiary facts, to prove some of the evidence involved in the case, or to refute the testimony of expert witnesses on the opposing side. Medical malpractice, products liability, and vehicle accidents are but a few of the types of cases requiring insight into the standards of medical care, design and manufacturing practices, the maintenance principles for vehicles, and so forth. Surgeons, engineers, physicists, industrial hygienists, economists, and vocational placement counselors are among the experts the paralegal must consult to establish a framework from which the attorney may deduce the productive course of legal action. Thereafter, damages, compensation, or recourse may compel the use of other experts to provide insight into the fairness of proposed settlements or to prove those elements to a judge or jury.

b. **Expert witness qualifications.** Expert witnesses need to be authorities in their particular field, effective communicators, and credible. Although expert witness opinions often influence settlement of cases prior to trial, an expert in a particular discipline should be selected with the intention of using him or her in trial. Accordingly, the expert should speak clearly and comfortably in front of an audience and present an image of a confident manner without being overbearing or gratuitous. Gauges of credibility include prior expert testimony on the subject, publications of articles or textbooks, educational background, training (continuing professional development), instructional experience in the area of expertise, and length of time as a practitioner in the subject field of expertise.

c. **Locating experts.** Law firms often have a list of experts, some for consultation and some for both consultation and use as expert witnesses. Not all experts are suitable for both purposes, and not all expert witnesses are the most knowledgeable people in their field. When seeking an expert's information, the best expert available should be utilized since the expert will contribute to the understanding of the technical material of the factual issues. The paralegal should be cautioned that the "best expert" does not necessarily mean the highest paid or most utilized expert in a particular field. Expertise comes with a high price, and many well-known experts can charge anywhere from $200 to $400 per hour for providing that expertise. The price tag of an expert witness does not mean, in all cases, that the cost will be offset by an automatic win at trial, nor should it guide the decision of choice. There are many expert witnesses who are exceptionally knowledgeable and successful on behalf of a client who are not financially impossible to reach.

If the paralegal must locate an expert without the benefit of an office expert file or recommendations from a knowledgeable source, a thorough background search should be conducted to determine what expert witness will fit best with the legal issues of the case. Alternatives to the office file or recommendations include the following:

(1) The *Lawyers Desk Reference* lists expert firms and individuals by their specialty and basic services offered (analysis, examination, exhibit preparation, testimony, and so on), together with addresses and telephone numbers.

(2) Research publications or home offices of attorney associations and specialty groups, state bar associations, Defense Research Institute, American Association for Justice (fka American Trial Lawyers Association), and American Board of Trial Attorneys are but a very small sampling of organizations that may have expert witness information files or listings.

(3) There are numerous for-profit organizations that serve as clearinghouses for experts. TASA (Technical Advisory Service for Attorneys) is an example of this type of service. The Internet has become an increasingly valuable source for locating authorities and witnesses. Generally, a keyword search of "expert witness" or Internet research in the many legal websites will result in useful leads.

(4) Experts frequently are authors and reviewing professional journal articles and textbooks in the area of expertise will yield an author's name and business address. Larger public and university libraries have reference sections where trade or specialty publications can be

perused, or they may be accessed over the Internet. Also, many expert witnesses have their own websites which will contain a listing of their specialties and may even include a detailed biographical sketch as well as an abridged listing of textbooks and articles authored.

(5) Review jury verdict publications or online services to identify experts used in particular cases. For example, Westlaw offers searchable jury verdicts in the "LRP" database. If the paralegal were to conduct a Westlaw search using the terms "'automobile accident' & Maryland," the result would identify experts involved in a sampling of Maryland state auto accident cases. LexisNexis also offers an expert witness database.

(6) Trade libraries are excellent sources for locating knowledgeable authors. Utility companies, oil companies, merchandisers, contractors, and others often have professional associations or societies that maintain libraries and may allow nonmembers access to these resources.

(7) Professional, academic, trade, and industry associations and societies maintain membership lists that may serve as a starting point in seeking comments on the reputation of their individual members, a beginning in establishing the qualifications of an expert. The paralegal can start the inquiry by contacting the membership secretary or by seeking the "best known" member in that organization.

(8) Searching courthouse case files for similar cases can provide the identity of expert witnesses who have been used in local actions. When reviewing the case files, you may even be able to find a deposition of the named experts.

(9) Word of mouth can reveal not only the identity of an expert, but also the referring person may have developed an information file on the expert which includes a curriculum vitae and transcripts of prior testimony.

d. **Retention.** When the decision has been made to retain an expert and the initial verbal contact has been made, an engagement letter should be prepared. The letter should: confirm the expert's fee schedule, describe the nature of the case, define the scope of work and/or testimony required from the expert, applicable deadlines, whether a written report will be required, and define the type, form, and manner of the report. At some point in the working relationship, material and evidence will be made available or provided to the expert.

Prudent practice and professional courtesy dictate that all material provided to experts should be done under cover letter, with a complete description of the material provided. Be sure to include any court-designated or internal deadlines so that the expert will have advanced notice of these days and can supply a timely response. Eleventh hour requests for information or documentation (such as an expert report) will not fare well with the expert and will most likely result in a rushed response with the potential for incomplete, unverified, or incorrect information being supplied.

One important caveat that must be considered with respect to an expert witness is that any document or evidence produced by the expert witness could very well be subject to discovery by the opposing party. This can include e-mail transmissions or even a written telephone message. Before providing confidential, privileged, or sensitive documents or making a request for same, check with the attorney prior to completing the transaction to avoid discovery land mines.

Follow up with an expert concerning informational needs, transmittal of documents, preparation of reports, and other needs is most often conducted by the attorney, unless the responsibility is directly delegated to the paralegal. Be sure to get all of the details from the attorney before contacting the expert witness. If an expert witness asks for certain information, do not transmit it without first consulting with the attorney.

7.044 Opinion Testimony by Expert Witnesses

When an expert is retained, the paralegal should keep in mind that the expert will undergo intense scrutiny by the courts and opposing parties. This is why it is important to conduct a thorough background investigation prior to expert retention. Expert testimony is guided by evidentiary rules or state common law regarding admissibility. Normally, both the plaintiff and defendant will retain experts that will testify at deposition and trial. In many cases (especially those in which one party has a weak case), one party may seek ways to disqualify the other party's expert witness through the use of standards for admissibility espoused in a trilogy of cases decided by the U.S. Supreme Court (for federal and some state courts). These cases are all based upon the FRE 702 (Testimony by Experts), FRE 703 (Basis of Opinion Testimony by Experts), and FRE 704 (Opinion on the Ultimate Issue).

   a. In the federal court system, the admissibility of expert testimony is guided by the *Daubert* standard. This standard is based primarily on the relevancy test and FRE 702 and was established in the landmark 1993 decision by the U.S. Supreme Court in *Daubert v. Merrell Dow Pharmaceuticals, Inc.,* 509 U.S. 579 (1993). In this case, the Court established the standard regarding the admissibility of scientifically related expert testimony, with primary focus on the reliability of testing and data, and relying on relevance and reliability as baseline measures. Expert witnesses must be able to satisfy the *Daubert* standards before their testimony can be admitted in all federal and some state courts. A foundation must be first established, including the expert's qualifications, expertise and specialty, prior testimony over the past five years in the area of expertise, peer review of publications and other authored documents by the expert, and whether the expert's theories are accepted by the scientific community. This, again, emphasizes the need for the conduct of a thorough background investigation into the expert's qualifications, expertise and specialty prior to retention, and continued oversight with regard to expert witness activities and testimony by the attorney, during both the conduct of an investigation and during the course of a lawsuit.

   b. The U.S. Supreme Court's 1997 landmark decision in *General Electric v. Joiner,* (522 U.S. 1997) clarified two points of law left unclear after *Daubert* with respect to the admissibility of expert testimony: (1) that the courts should apply the "abuse of discretion" standard in reviewing a trial court's decision to admit or exclude expert testimony under *Daubert* and (2) that a trial court must examine the conclusions of expert witnesses (FRE 704 – Opinion on Ultimate Issue) and ensure the conclusions logically connect the facts of the case to the science or tests upon which the expert relies.

   c. Initially, *Daubert* applied only to scientific expert testimony. It did not extend to experts who were not, per se, scientists but whose expertise or testing involves technical or specialized knowledge based on years of experience. The U.S. Supreme Court's 1999 landmark decision in *Kuhmo Tire Co. v. Carmichael* (526 U.S. 137 (1999)) extended the *Daubert* standard to the admissibility of technical expert witness testimony. The effect of the *Kuhmo* decision, according to the Court, made no distinction between scientific and technical or specialized knowledge.

Prior to *Daubert,* the federal court system applied only a "general acceptance" test for the admissibility of expert testimony. This test, known as the *Frye* standard, was based on the U.S. Supreme Court's 1923 landmark decision in *Frye v. United States,* (293 F. 1013 (D.C. Cir. 1923)). The *Frye* standard allows for the results of scientific testing to be admitted if the test has gained general acceptance in the particular field in which it belongs, or as the Court termed it, the "scientific community." Certain state courts (such as Pennsylvania) still apply the *Frye* standard for the admissibility of expert testimony. The particular state court should be researched to determine which standard is applicable.

7.045 Physical Examination

The ability to make a physical examination of the evidence is usually the best form of inquiry by an investigator or paralegal. Personal observations allow reliable comprehension of related testimony, perception of related exhibits, and quick recognition of error, confusion, and mistake. However, many legal procedures and other protocol now apply to physical examination of evidence which must be followed to avoid any potential for impropriety or accusation of evidence tampering or spoliation.

The paralegal must use extreme caution and diligence when conducting a physical examination of artifacts, documents, and other potential sources of evidence (*see,* Evidentiary Considerations, following). The paralegal should note, particularly with respect to physical evidence, that permission must, in most cases, be obtained from the owner, custodian, or other entity to gain access to physical evidence or even to a scene. The paralegal should have a full working knowledge and appreciation of the standards and rules regarding the chain of custody and preservation of evidence to avoid unintended alteration or destruction of the evidence so as to eliminate any potential for dismissal of a case based on evidence spoliation.

7.05 TIME LINES AND CHRONOLOGIES

Establishing a time line of events, facts, and circumstances is one of the most crucial aspects of investigation. Events happen in sequence, by consequence, and at specific times. In any incident or occurrence, human being are involved, and along with that comes excitement, uttered statements, actions, and other things that happen at certain times before, during, and immediately after the incident or occurrence. Developing a time line or chronology of events can present a difficult challenge to the investigator or paralegal during the conduct of an investigation. Time-related challenges will be the norm since many facts and witnesses are involved in the time frame of the incident or occurrence.

Depending on the circumstances and involvement of witnesses, time-related challenges will abound. Statements such as "it seemed like forever," "it was maybe 15 to 20 minutes," or "it was more like 30 minutes to an hour before" will often be heard when interacting with eyewitnesses and bystanders. Especially when it relates to the victim(s) or survivors of an incident, time-related recall may, at best, be only a guesstimate of time line or chronology surrounding the event. Keeping this in mind, the investigator or paralegal conducting the investigation should be prepared for much ambiguity and sometimes incomplete or inaccurate accounts with respect to time when interviewing victims and witnesses who have suffered catastrophic physical, emotional, or financial loss.

There are many sources of information that can prove to be both valuable and, to the extent possible, reliable when developing a time line. These sources include, but are not limited to:

a. Police reports (subpoena may apply)
b. Fire investigation reports
c. Ambulance (EMT) records
d. County or metropolitan 911 communication center tapes
e. Medical records
f. Public records (restrictions and fees may apply), including birth and death certificates and motor vehicle records
g. Criminal records (restrictions may apply)
h. Photographs
i. Recorded statements
j. Insurance records

In many cases, the investigator or paralegal will establish a time line or chronology based on approximate times. The approximate timing will also include between a particular time frame, such as "between X hours A.M. and X hours P.M." This is perfectly fine to do as a first step in creating the initial version. It is important to note that the time line or chronology is an ongoing document that should be updated as new information or clarification of time based upon newly discovered information, facts, or documents is obtained during and after the investigation phase.

It is important to note that many public official reports, such as 911 communication tapes and police reports, incorporate the use of military time. Time is recorded by the hour (example: 11), minute (example: 32), and seconds (example: 48). Putting together the example, the military time would be 11:32:48. The timing is down to the second, especially for incidents involving the dispatch of public sector or emergency personnel. To convert military time to "civilian time," use the following method. From 0000 through 1159 hours, the time in civilian hours is 12:00 A.M. – 12:59 P.M. From 1300 hours through 2359 hours, the time in civilian hours is 1:00 P.M. through 11:59 P.M. This can be done by adding the civilian time hour number (example: 3) to 12, or 3:00 P.M. Hospital emergency rooms normally use civilian time when logging in the time of arrival of a patient into an emergency room or calling the time of death in a hospital setting.

When creating the time line, use these four categories to ensure completeness:

a. Day, date, and year (example: Monday, January 1, 2007)

b. Exact, or approximate, or "between" hours (example: approximately 12:45 hours)

c. Brief summary of the fact corresponding to the time (example: a structural fire occurred at the home of John and Mary Doe, 123 Anywhere Avenue, Anytown, USA 00000)

d. Source of information from whom or where the information was obtained (example: statement, Investigation Report, Anytown Fire Department, page 2, paragraph 3)

Other information may be added in other categories depending on the incident, investigator's style, and other factors.

7.06 EVIDENTIARY CONSIDERATIONS

Evidence is that testimony or material that proves, or tends to prove, a specific fact. The first action of an incident or occurrence begins the generation of various forms of evidence, depending on the incident or occurrence. The key to proving the elements of a cause of action is obtaining and preserving key evidentiary objects and artifacts. Evidence generates suspicion, key facts, and proves or disproves the elements of a case. It begs the questions of what the evidence is telling the investigator, that is, how does it speak to the investigator, and what story is the evidence telling the investigator about the incident or occurrence.

Judges, attorneys, and paralegals consult the rules of evidence of the particular jurisdiction in determining whether a piece of evidence is admissible. Trained investigators will normally follow the lead of the attorney or will have firsthand knowledge based upon their experience. Normally, the attorney will supervise evidentiary considerations in the course of an investigation in a civil or criminal defense case. The district attorney supervises evidentiary considerations in criminal prosecutions.

Evidentiary considerations are addressed in both the Federal Rules of Evidence (Title 28, *United States Code*) as well as in state and local rules of evidence. Most states have adopted evidentiary rules similar to that of FRE. State and local rules may vary throughout the respective jurisdictions and must be consulted to determine applicability to a particular case. Because of the potential of differentiations between state and federal rules of evidence, only the FRE are addressed in this section, unless otherwise noted. All evidentiary rules must be considered during the conduct of an investigation to ensure that the evidence is relevant, reliable, and, ultimately, admissible at trial. Constitutional considerations will apply in the case of criminal prosecutions.

7.061   Obtaining and Preserving Evidence

During the conduct of an investigation, one or more forms of evidence can be discovered:

   a. Physical evidence, in the form of a tangible object, such as a broken mechanical part, skid marks on the road, an appliance that did not work correctly or failed to work at all, or the tools or devices used to commit a criminal offense that is the subject of an action.

   b. Testimonial, in the form of the personal recollections of a person with firsthand knowledge of the matter, either obtained voluntarily through written statement or record, or taken under oath at deposition and trial, or by affidavit.

   c. Documentary evidence, in the form of letters, notes, signature, memoranda, tape recordings, photographs, movie strips, videotape, microfilm, or other recorded data and retrievable information.

   d. Demonstrative evidence, which includes sketches, diagrams, maps, models, reconstruction, tests, computer simulations, or exemplars of equipment identical to the item involved in the case.

7.062   Identification

Identifying potential evidence is perhaps the most difficult aspect of the investigation. For example, an investigator at a fire scene works under certain time constraints, weather, and lighting conditions before the cleanup activity begins. There can be a substantial amount of confusion regarding the circumstances of the event, as well as the number and variety of people interested in or investigating the matter. Police, fire department, and public safety personnel all have responsibilities in any accident involving property damage, injury to life, or fatality. These entities will maintain custody of the scene until their investigation is complete. In the case of police and fire departments, if the outcome of the investigation is ruled accidental in nature (that is, no criminal activity has been determined), the respective investigating agency will release the scene to a private custodian or other designated party, such as an insurance investigator.

The private investigator (and in some cases, the paralegal if he or she is the investigating party) often arrives at the scene after the evidence is shifted or removed. In these situations, the investigator or paralegal will have to rely upon the investigating agency for diagrams, photographs and reports. Such documents may be obtained from the respective public or governmental agency for use in producing additional diagrams or for a variety of other reasons, such as for client review and confirmation as to the accuracy of the information contained in the documents. Depending on the agency, some documents will be made available for a reasonable cost and/or by subpoena.

As previously noted, evidence comes in various types and shapes. Identification of evidentiary objects and artifacts will depend on the type of investigation being conducted. It is very important to narrow down, to the extent possible, the nature and type of evidence to be sought to be identified before requests are made. For example, when the investigator or paralegal conducts an investigation, he or she should obtain reports prepared by responding fire departments, public safety agencies, and/or emergency medical organizations. Scene photographs can be obtained by formal written request for a nominal cost of reproduction per photo. Other sources of information, such as motor vehicle records, insurance records, or medical records, can also be obtained by subpoena or in some cases by client authorization. Fees and charges will most likely apply. Contact with the respective agency should be made to determine the appropriate protocol for requesting documents, as well as associated fees, costs, and time frames for responding to the request for documentation.

7.063 Physical Evidence

Physical evidence, also known as physical artifacts, is the actual physical object(s) that can be directly linked to the cause of an incident, accident, or other occurrence. It is something that can be seen, touched, heard, smelled, or tasted. Every time an object is identified as potential evidence, the investigator must follow a formal protocol, or chain of custody of evidence. This is normally completed in a potential civil action by a trained investigator on behalf of the victim, injured party, or insurance carrier. In a criminal matter, the chain of custody of evidence is normally established and maintained by the respective law enforcement agency.

The protocol for the collection, preservation, and, ultimately, the full chain of custody of evidence is very involved and requires the investigator to: (1) acquire, preserve, and identify the evidence and make a complete photographic record of its location before and after removal; (2) properly pack and tag the evidence for shipment; (3) complete an evidence custody inventory; (4) ensure the safe transportation of the evidence or the storage facility for safekeeping, retrieval, testing, inspection, and return to the facility; (5) ensure the integrity of the chain of custody of evidence is maintained; (6) produce the evidence for introduction at trial; and (7) create the foundation for its admissibility. Simply put: ensure that the physical evidence is kept as found in its discovered state.

In recent years, the courts have scrutinized many evidentiary matters. Included in this scrutiny is what is known as "spoliation of evidence." Spoliation of evidence refers to the loss, destruction, or material alteration of an object or document that is potential or actual evidence in a legal proceeding by one who has the responsibility for its preservation. Spoliation of evidence can occur when the movement, change, or destruction of evidence or material alteration of a scene impairs the ability of other interested parties to obtain the same evidentiary value from the evidence as did any prior investigator. Remedies for evidence spoliation employed by the courts include discovery sanctions, monetary sanctions, application of evidentiary inferences, limitations under the rules of evidence, exclusion of expert testimony, dismissal of a claim or defense, independent tort actions for the negligent or intentional destruction of evidence, and even prosecution under criminal statutes relating to obstruction of justice or tampering with evidence. This is why investigators must conduct their investigation and evidentiary collections carefully so that loss or destruction of evidence or accusation of spoliation can be minimized.

If a client's case is lost due to evidentiary issues that were known or should have been known by the attorney and his or her legal team, the client could have standing to sue both the attorney and the investigator for malpractice. The attorney and members of the legal team could all be subject to sanctions and loss of professional licensure or certification. Investigators, in particular, have been disqualified by the courts for questionable or even unethical mishandling of evidence. It is not uncommon for a moving party's motion for summary judgment to be granted by the court for challenges to the validity, violations of protocol, or outright spoliation.

In a criminal prosecution, evidence that is taken into custody by questionable or unconstitutional means or without a warrant could be rendered inadmissible through the application of the exclusionary rule under the Fourth Amendment. Criminal prosecutions are supervised and conducted by the district or state's attorney's office. The private investigator acting on behalf of a defendant may get the opportunity to view and visually examine the evidence at the discretion of the prosecutor's office, prior to formal discovery. However, evidence inspections are normally limited to the formal discovery process.

In many cases, the investigator does not have exclusive legal title to the evidence he or she wishes to take into custody. For example, there may be occasions when the ownership of an evidentiary item is called into question, and the property of taking custody of the evidence calls for sound judgment on the part of the investigator. Any investigating party will need to obtain formal permission by the rightful owner or custodian prior to conducting the investigation and/or before entering the premises or scene. The private investigator should touch base with the appropriate public agency to determine what evidence the agency may have taken into custody. The investigating party should *never* assume that entry to a premises or scene is automatic, nor should the investigation party assume there is an entitlement to physical evidence without the necessary consent. Every attempt should be made to protect and preserve both the scene (if available) and ensure the evidence remains as intact and undisturbed as possible. A rule of thumb followed by the investigation community is that the entire scene should be considered physical evidence until a final determination as to actual cause, origin, and responsibility has been made.

When the paralegal is conducting an investigation, the same protocols and considerations apply as those imposed upon an investigator. More importantly, the *paralegal should never undertake the collection and preservation of evidence without formal training and experience.* Inexperience or lack of training will not, in most cases, be an affirmative defense, even if the paralegal unwittingly collected evidence in what may be considered an improper fashion or contrary to evidentiary protocol.

In case of doubt, the investigator or paralegal should not take evidence of any form into custody until further inquiry is made, nor should the investigator or paralegal simply leave a receipt indicating their name and identity and the means by which people can contact them if they wish to exert ownership rights. This is a surefire prescription for disaster, not to mention the problems, sanctions, and other penalties that could arise as a result of unauthorized evidence collection. In cases where public sector investigators are on the scene, a private investigator will not be permitted to enter the scene until the public sector investigation is complete and the scene has been released.

7.064 Documentary Evidence

Documentary evidence is evidence that is written or recorded, including letters, typewritten documents, wills, deeds, prints, photographs, or recordings. Documents are one of the most valuable tools in an attorney's case. How the documents are acquired is just as important as their safeguarding, and both must be preserved by the investigator. As with physical evidence, the proper foundation must be laid through a witness who can testify to the document's authenticity. *See* Chapter 9 for a discussion regarding discovery of electronically stored documents (ESI).

The investigator or paralegal must be careful to ensure that each step of locating and acquiring documents is carefully documented to create a foundation for the attorney's later use. The "best evidence rule" as set forth in the *Federal Rules of Evidence* requires the original of a given document to be offered in evidence (FRE 1002). Only when the original cannot be located may copies be substituted (FRE 1004). Sometimes copies may be admissible under exceptions to the "hearsay rules" (FRE 803). Neither the paralegal nor the investigator should make assumptions as to the document's admissibility or expect the attorney to rely on documents collected without some foundation. Foundation can be established by the answers to such questions as: Where was the document located? Who was the custodian? Why was the document in the file? If a copy, is it a notarized or certified copy? Where is the original? Where is a duplicate original? Who else might have one?

The attorney will also need the investigator's or paralegal's opinion of what evidentiary fact the document establishes. Perhaps in a contract case, it represents a contemporaneous memorial of the requisite "meeting of the minds," or acknowledges the tender of the consideration, or perhaps it is persuasive that the defendant's defense of "mistake of material fact" was not a mistake at all but a well-understood gamble. In a matter in probate, the document might represent support for a contention that the decedent had made a true gift *inter vivos* that should allow an asset to be exempted from the estate.

Each document in a case can be more than informational if the paralegal continually seeks to locate and preserve the documents that, with proper foundation, constitute evidentiary facts proving or disproving the essential elements of the case, corroborate or refute testimonial evidence, or support or refute the credibility of the witnesses. The foundation may be established easily at the time the document is found by any of several methods:

1. Certified true copies of public records should be obtained.

2. Records of private firms may be obtained with a short statement from the custodian identifying the document, file, firm, and custodian with a notarization of the statement and document by a notary public.

3. Client records should be fully identified by file, location, and identity of the person who will testify as to how, why, and where the document was kept.

4. When certification or notarization is not possible, obtain full details of the document—identity, custodian, file identity, and purpose—for a formal discovery proceeding.

Documents pose a special identification and storage problem for all parties concerned. Documents are most valuable to the attorney in their unaltered state. The investigator usually must describe the document and provide a foundation for its use, for both report and testimonial purposes. When the document is a letter, written memorandum, or pamphlet, many investigators mark the document "EXHIBIT" or "ATTACHMENT" and staple it to the report. This is a technique that should be avoided since the attorney now has an altered document, although not substantively altered, and the convenient title "EXHIBIT" or "ATTACHMENT" may have to be explained in the future. The acceptable and most pragmatic technique is to provide a copy of the document, if it is to be attached to the report, and place the original document in a transparent or opaque envelope and apply the "EXHIBIT" or "ATTACH-MENT" label to the envelope, together with a thorough description of the document (date, document type, author, addressee, topic or title, number of pages, and any attachments), as well as a short statement of the source of the document, custodian, and relevance of the document to the case. Alternatively, a "face sheet" can carry this information. The photocopy of the document can be used as a "work copy" during preparation of the case. Never add underlining, marginal annotation, or writing on the document on the original document (whether the true original, a duplicate true copy, or a photocopy). This could very well render the document as being "spoilated" and thus could render the document inadmissible in a court of law.

All documentary evidence, to the extent possible, must be preserved in the discovered state. If a copy is made, it should be marked as a copy, preferably with a marginal label "Copy of a document in the file X vs. X." This avoids the problem of creating yet another piece of evidence that could confuse the future admissibility of the original document at the trial. Other forms of documents such as, videotapes, CDs, DVDs, tape recordings, and even photographs are not quite so susceptible to contamination as paper documents. Safeguards should be considered for any item that may become evidence at trial through appropriate and established methods of preservation and storage.

The FBI system of marking original documents with alpha-numeric or "bates" stamped numbers or initialing the document with the date received and file number is not considered by courts as an "alteration" of the original document. As long as the substance of the original document is not altered, some form of identification is allowed.

7.065 Control and Retrieval

Investigators need to properly manage physical evidence to ensure its identification and legal status. Attorneys and the court will require assurance that an object is genuine to ensure its admissibility at trial and to avoid a charge of evidence spoliation. A broken bolt, for example, has no significance in the courtroom unless it can be positively linked to a cause of action.

Preservation, control, and retrieval of evidence are tantamount to linking facts and relevance of the evidence to those facts. When the investigator takes evidence into custody, its later identification can be recreated by recording the "five Ws": Who, What, Why, When, and Where. Establish the name(s) of Who takes custody of the evidence. Describe What the evidence represents. Note Why the evidence is obtained. Register When the evidence is taken into custody, and state Where the evidence will be stored or located for later retrieval. Record these five essential information elements in writing, with a hand-held tape recorder (and transcribed into a written document or report), through photographic documentation, and/or by video camera. In addition to recording facts pertaining to the material, objects may require minor but unique marking to allow absolute, positive identification of that particular object as being the one taken into custody on the date and at the time involved. A forensic investigator kit commonly includes copper wire, paper tags which can be used to identify key information (such as the date, time, and place in which the object was originally located, personal identification of the custodian, company logo, and a complete description of the object), paper bags or opaque envelopes, marking pens, plastic wrap, and other types of materials used to collect evidence. The means by which the evidence is preserved will vary by the type of evidence presented.

The system used can vary, but it must provide (1) a means of distinguishing that one object from all others similar to it; (2) a credible basis for testifying that the object is the one collected as evidence on a given date; and (3) that the system satisfies established protocol for the collection, preservation, control, and retrieval of evidence. From the time that object is identified as potential evidence, its custody must be substantiated by a document trail showing every transfer of custody from the point of the incident or event to the trial. That chain is based on the investigator or paralegal creating that first step in a proper, ethical, and careful manner and recording each subsequent transfer in detail. When physical evidence has been gathered, it is good practice to create a computer database or written (preferably typewritten) log for incorporation in the case file.

The investigator should physically check on the status of physical evidence that has been placed in storage or entrusted to the custody of others. The week before trial is a poor time to discover that important evidence has been lost or deteriorated into a useless form. A procedure should be in place which provides time frames, conditions, and return of physical evidence. The procedure should be clearly understood by all parties. This is particularly important for the custodian who initially took the evidence into custody and will be relying on that evidence to prove material facts at issue during trial.

7.066   Storage

Once the document or object is in custody, it should be placed in a controlled environment with restricted access to prevent it from being removed, altered, or damaged. Each time the evidence is examined, between the time of taking custody and its introduction to trial, it should be recorded in detail to include the date and time, person authorizing the particular examination or movement, person benefiting from such activity or movement, duration, and date and time of the return of the object to the place of storage. This process ensures that the chain of custody has not been broken between the time of initial custody up to the time of its introduction at trial. Anyone taking possession of the object must sign for it with a pledge that it will be safeguarded and returned or preserved in the exact same condition. Digital or 35 millimeter photos are appropriate for memorializing the transfer. A suitable form for controlling evidence is shown in Exhibit 7-2.

7.067   Testing and Examination

Physical evidence must be tested, examined, or disassembled to validate its evidentiary value in supporting or challenging the ultimate legal issue(s) at trial. The purpose of the examination and method

EXHIBIT 7-2   Example of an Evidence Log

Case:		Event:		
Description of Evidence:	Date Acquired:		Acquired by:	How Acquired:
	Identifying Marks:		Marked by:	Date Marked:
Storage Location:	Custodian:			Date:
Released to:	Date/Purpose:			

in which the examination will be conducted (also known as the "protocol for examination") should be planned, and the protocol which applies to the testing or examination should be clearly outlined, including instruments that will be used (such as scanning electron microscopic (SEM) devices). On many occasions, destructive examination, disassembly, or testing which will damage or destroy the object will take place. When this situation arises, the attorney should ensure that the adversary and all other parties to the action have an opportunity to have representatives present to observe and participate in the examination. Normally, an exemplar of a physical object in evidence will be secured well in advance of the destructive testing as a comparison object for both examination and testing.

The investigator who took the evidence into custody is responsible for, among other things, removing the evidence from storage and transporting it to the place of examination. The investigator should document each step of transmittal and the entire course of the examination. All parties to the action should receive formal notice in timely fashion to allow them or their experts to participate or observe the necessary examination. The entire process should be recorded through photographs, documentation, and videotape. Each party is responsible for documenting the steps included in the examination and testing process. The investigator records the presence of all witnesses, including their full identification and their association with their respective parties in the action on what is commonly known as an "Evidence Inspection Log." All experts and other official representatives of the parties to the action must be fully identified as to name, address, and party represented. Any examination, testing, or disassembly of the item that destroys or changes the physical characteristics of the item and is not accomplished with the knowledge, consent, and participation of all of the parties will not prevent the admissibility of the evidence at trial and could result in a successful motion to exclude evidence due to spoliation, motion for summary judgment, sanctions, dismissal of the case, or other adverse action.

7.07   SURVEILLANCE AND ACTIVITY CHECKS

Occasionally, there will be a need to verify the activities of certain parties to a lawsuit. One example of this type of investigation is done when plaintiffs or claimants are alleging disabilities that either preclude them from certain activities or limit abilities to perform particular tasks. Sometimes the alleged disabled party is observed working around the yard or involved in sporting activities with little or no sign of physical limitations. A serious limp that was quite obvious in the doctor's office sometimes can miraculously disappear. Videotaped proof of these activities may be used in the courtroom to raise questions of truthfulness in regard to the alleged disabilities.

Divorce and child custody disputes may require "domestic" surveillance. In states where grounds for divorce are required, surveillance may be used to establish the evidence to determine certain grounds, such as adultery. Surveillance in child custody cases may yield helpful evidence regarding the fitness of the adverse parent.

Activity checks are usually conducted by talking with neighbors or other persons who make frequent observations of the plaintiff or claimant. Though these checks may provide helpful information, they will often alert the plaintiff or claimant that an investigation is being conducted. For this reason, activity checks should be done near the end of the investigation.

Only trained, licensed investigators with the expertise and equipment to properly perform this type of investigation should conduct surveillance. The purpose of the surveillance, activities associated with the conduct of the surveillance, time considerations, and costs should be discussed with the attorney prior to commencing any surveillance activity. It should be noted that this kind of investigation may be expensive and may ultimately yield no useful information.

Obtaining a qualified investigator to conduct surveillance activities is not just a matter of simply looking under "Private Investigators" in the yellow pages. The investigator should be reputable and known to do the job professionally. Qualifications to be considered when searching for a surveillance investigator include:

a. License and bonding information (not all states specify such requirements).

b. A current copy of the investigator's Curriculum Vitae (CV) or resume.

c. A list of credible references (recent job contacts or clients since anyone can look good on paper).

d. A list of testimony to determine if the investigator ever has testified in court and if the investigator ever has been qualified as an expert.

e. Appearance and demeanor (the investigator may have to appear in court). The investigator must be likable, believable, and gain the jury's confidence as an investigator who is honest and has integrity.

f. Association affiliation. Many investigators belong to state affiliations; this can show a dedication to their career and a willingness to keep up-to-date on new developments in the field of surveillance.

g. Local law enforcement registration/endorsement/consultation. In many states or local jurisdictions, investigators have to register with local law enforcement or county sheriffs and possess a valid private investigator's license. In some states, the investigator must obtain the endorsement of both the sheriff and prosecutor in their principal residence county with their initial application and with renewals. Local law enforcement may also know if any complaints have been made against the investigator or if he or she has exhibited unprofessional or illegal methods of investigation. The licensing agency may have background information regarding the investigator that could be obtained under the Freedom of Information Act.

7.08 DEMONSTRATIVE EVIDENCE

Demonstrative evidence is evidence that demonstrates, illustrates, or recreates evidence that has already been presented in another form, such as sketches, drawings, or surveys created as a means of preserving transitory physical evidence in retrievable form. For example, engineering design drawings of a product assist a technical or expert witness in providing testimony in support of their opinions and conclusions. Investigators will often require a certain amount of documentation for use at future times, such as a diagram of a fire scene to demonstrate the layout of the scene and the particular point of origin. The means and method of making the measurement represented in the drawing will be subject to question and must be supported by the proper foundation. The presence of a scale and the date and the name of the person who rendered the drawing are essential. The date of the examination and measurements is essential, particularly if it is different from the date of the event in question. It is important to support these drawings with photographs of the same area, especially when only estimated measurements could be taken based upon the destruction of the scene or when time has passed and the scene has been cleaned up or rehabbed. In this case, the investigator or expert will offer an approximate, not to scale drawing.

Demonstrative evidence that is a model, replica, reconstruction, computer-aided simulation, or an exact duplicate of the object involved in the case requires the same establishment of the dates, times, scale (or approximate scale, depending on the circumstances), methods of calculation, sizes, and measurements. The accuracy of the representation probably still will be subject to questioning. Many of these demonstrative evidence procedures are very expensive, particularly in the case of a computer-aided simulation and should be discussed with and authorized by the attorney before they are undertaken.

7.081 Scientific or Technical Illustrations, Drawings or Exhibits

Certain injury litigation cases and regulatory agency actions benefit from the use of renderings by various graphic artists. Medical illustrators are talented at clarifying what otherwise might be very difficult explanations of X-rays (even if produced as positives) by converting them into easily understood colored drawings at relatively little cost. If a general medical illustration is all that is desired, many programs are now available on CD-ROM which allow the user to print standard depictions of human anatomy and disease. Graphic illustrators can show a proposed development or project in simplified form to assist the presentation for permits, zoning actions, and so forth. Any witness who plans to use scientific or technical illustrations should be prepared to explain them in understandable, laymen's terms so that both the judge and the jury can fully understand the introduction of this type of evidence and the relevance of the evidence to the facts and legal issues of the case.

7.082 Photography

Almost any photograph related to an event is potentially admissible at trial, and almost any photograph may be subject to argument over its admissibility. The judgment of the person taking the photograph and his or her expertise is often subject to question. The average investigator or paralegal who chooses to take his or her own pictures, if inexperienced at forensic photography, must be prepared to defend the representations in the photographs. For this reason, law firms may sometimes employ the services of a professional photographer. Most experienced investigators and experts understand the use of adjustable lens cameras that allow shooting wide-angle, normal-angle, and telephoto views of the same scene and the fact that using such lenses may alter a photograph's perspective as focal length changes. Today, most investigators and experts use digital cameras with at least a 5x zoom lens or the traditional, professional 35 millimeter camera. There has been debate in the past about the use of digital cameras, primarily because of the ability to easily alter or enhance the photo's original depiction.

To ensure that the investigator maintains an accurate recall of the photographic representation, he or she normally prepares some form of photo log. The photographic log will normally note the date of each photograph taken, type of camera (digital or 35 millimeter), film speed, film type (if using a 35 millimeter camera), filters, and whether or not artificial lighting equipment was used. If possible, each photograph should be related to a sketch indicating the location of the camera and the direction it was pointed to get the view in the photograph. (*See* Exhibit 7-3.)

EXHIBIT 7-3   Example of Photo Log

Case:		Photographer:				
Camera/Equipment Used:						
#	Date	Time	Place	Details of shot	Notes	3

     The skilled investigator or expert should consider the evidentiary value of each photograph that he or she intends to take, as well as its detriment. Photographs are discoverable. Honesty and integrity in taking and producing photographic evidence must override the desire to withhold potentially detrimental photographs from the opposing party during discovery. If this is the case, the photograph(s) that are withheld will not be admissible at trial, and the actions of the person who withheld the photographs, including the attorney, could be brought into question.

     At no time should photographs be destroyed until the case has concluded and the case file retention period has passed. Today, photographs taken during the course of an investigation are preserved in both hard copy and on a CD-ROM, digital memory card, or memory stick. The hard copies should be stored in protective sleeves, preferably in a notebook, with a copy of the photographic log which describes the particulars of the photos included.

     The type of event which resulted in an investigation being conducted and/or a formal action being filed will help the investigator or paralegal to determine what types of photographs must be taken. For example, photographs taken of bodily injuries are shockingly persuasive to the jury to demonstrate the obvious pain and suffering caused by the injury. If the client is a plaintiff and the accident investigation involves a motor vehicle with injuries, photographs of the amount of blood spilled, tire marks on the street pavement, and photographs of the specific road intersection, entry or exit ramp, and road signs may be necessary to corroborate the facts and testimony of eyewitnesses and investigators.

     The use of lighting has a distinct effect on the utility of a photograph. Daylight provides one form of reflected light, while incandescent light tends to throw a warmer red-toned color on the same object. Fluorescent light tends to provide more yellow-green, and flashbulbs, depending on their size and nature, affect the color quality of the image produced. Infrared film can be highly informational in cases involving vegetation growth, decline, and death or in heat gain and loss disputes.

     When an investigation begins some time after the incident, a wide variety of sources of photographs should be explored. The police often take photographs, as do fire departments, coroner's officers, newspapers, wire services, and freelance photographers. The more important, dramatic, and long-term incident produces a veritable flood of photographs to which the paralegal can obtain access. Occasionally, a neighborhood canvass will also locate snapshots of the immediate area or general location.

     It is often desirable to employ a professional photographer to take selected photographs for specific purposes. Such photographs are relatively expensive, but professionals can usually qualify their photos for introduction as evidence. Be specific in the request for the number, sizes, type of film, and views desired. Every photograph should benefit the understanding of both the judge and the jury about the meaning, relevance, and interpretive value of the photographic depiction.

In some cases, overhead views obtained through aerial photos can be obtained from a wide variety of sources. Google is a good online source for aerial photographs. Also, the U.S. Coast and U.S. Geologic Survey have a tremendous collection of recent and historical aerial photos in different scales. The U.S. Department of Agriculture uses aerials in its studies. Forestry departments, state and federal highway projects or departments, city and county public works, and planning departments turn more and more to aerial photographs for planning, zoning, and traffic study work. Many have aerial photographs of diverse locations. Any area subject to land management or reclamation probably has been photo-mapped by the U.S. Department of the Interior. These governmental sources generally provide fine, full-frame prints at nominal cost but often with a bureaucratic time delay problem. Using private aerial photograph sources often permits enlargements of all of a negative or a portion of it, at the lawyer's election. The cost is a little more for the custom work but often is well worth the extra expense. Individually, photographs from an upper-story window or rooftop can be helpful. A photograph from a chartered airplane may be desirable. It is difficult for these photographs to be used to scale, and that is one of the major benefits of professional aerial photographs—the exact determination of scale.

7.083   Videography

The video camera is a valuable investigative tool. It is useful in illustrating accident scenes, roadway views taken from a vehicle traveling on the roadway, statements of witnesses, depositions of expert witnesses not available to testify at trial, and "day-in-the-life" videos of disabled plaintiffs. Videography should adhere to the same standards required of still photographs. When illustrating roadway views, the camera operator should be prepared to testify about the position of the camera and the general speed of the vehicle while the recording was being done.

"Day-in-the-life" videos should be recorded in the natural environment where the disabled plaintiff illustrates daily routines. The video should, in a discrete manner, show the plaintiff in general daily routines, such as getting out of bed in the morning, taking care of personal hygiene, preparing and eating meals, and doing other chores. These videotaping sessions should not be rehearsed. Opposing counsel should generally be given notice that such videotaping will be done. These "day-in-the-life" videos can be very instrumental in representing to a jury the plaintiff's life in terms of pain and suffering and his or her general loss of enjoyment of life. While the scenes may be unpleasant, so are the injured party's injuries.

Although a paralegal or investigator may be familiar with the operation and functions of camcorders and video cameras, indispensable videographic evidence is generally best preserved by professional videographers. Professionally trained videographers can, under the guidance and direction of paralegals and attorneys, determine the cinematic angles, lighting, and distance to most effectively depict the intended video impression. Videographers typically possess sophisticated equipment and tripods that stabilize their camera and reduce jerking, vibrating scenes. A videographer also is skilled in the art of accurately capturing sounds and dialogues that enhances the video record. The cost of a videographer is usually well worth the investment for vital evidence, including copies of the videocassette or CD-ROM for long-term preservation.

7.09   PRESERVING DIGITAL, ELECTRONIC, AND PHOTOGRAPHIC DOCUMENTS AND OBJECTS

As discussed throughout this chapter, investigative evidence comes in many forms. Audio evidence may be created in several cassette sizes, on CD-ROM, or on videocassettes. With the recent proliferation of software and audio computer files, it is possible for an investigator to store audio evidence on computer

EXHIBIT 7-4   Log for Digital, Electronic, and Photographic Evidence

ID No.	Destruct Date	Case Name	Description of Evidence
97001	01/05/11	Jones v. Martin	Microcassette recording of interview with Bob Marley.
97001	01/05/11	Jones v. Martin	Microcassette recording of interview with Sarah Beechnut.
97003	01/05/11	Jones v. Martin	Photographic negatives of Marvin Jones's early childhood.
97004	09/25/16	Niles v. Mitchie	3.5″ diskette of Mitchie Inc. quality assurance inspections during 2006 for the Whupmobile production line.

floppy disks or CD-ROMs. A quick search of the Internet reveals numerous downloadable audio files and audio file "readers." Photographic evidence also comes in numerous formats such as videotapes of various sizes, photographs, undeveloped film, pictures from news articles, and computer graphic files. Electronic and digital data can now be readily obtained in computer disk or CD-ROM form.

The preservation of digital, electronic, and photographic evidence is a challenge requiring foresight and planning. Some forms of this type of evidence are sensitive to environmental factors. All of the aforementioned evidence is susceptible to physical hazards such as crushing, tearing, or damage from being carelessly placed into case files. Computer disks and audiotapes are prone to destruction from exposure to magnetic fields, fluid spills, or humidity. Excessive heat may warp videotapes or CD-ROM disks. All forms of storage should comply with the particular media's storage requirements, which includes storage in a cool, dry atmosphere or at room temperature. Digital evidence may also be uploaded to online depositories to minimize the effects of environmental factors.

A special storage facility for recorded evidence should be maintained, along with a system to identify the evidence for later use. A log for digital, electronic, and photographic evidence typically would include an evidence identification number, a description of the evidence, a cross-reference to the case file, and a suspense date to dispose of the evidence following resolution of the case. An evidence identification number might consist of the last two digits of the year, the initials of the investigator, and the number of the tape (an increasing sequential series) to be affixed to the tape. (*See* Exhibit 7-4.) Maintain the evidence log on a computer database or word processing program to enhance the retrieval capabilities of pertinent items.

7.10 DISCOVERY THROUGH INVESTIGATION

The primary purpose of the informal discovery (investigation) is to assist the attorney in developing lines of inquiry to be explored in formal discovery and also in evaluating the responses of the opposing party to the questions and motions posed in the formal discovery.

The investigation provides a fountain of knowledge to assist the attorney in creating the deposition plan. Statements that might otherwise be overlooked when taken of opposing party witnesses often can be used in preparing the attorney to generate sworn testimony. Such statements may reveal motivation, relationships, background, and post-incident activities of immense interest to the attorney. The basic rule is to know as much about the witness and what he or she is going to say as it is possible to know prior to trial. The use of testimonial statements, physical evidence, and photographs are essential to proper preparation of the attorney for the confrontation in the deposition procedure.

No item of evidentiary fact will stand alone at trial. Each fact must be corroborated. One of the best ways of corroborating a fact is to ask questions of the opposing party under oath at deposition or through interrogatories, requests for admissions, statements, and affidavits. Each tool is effective. Investigation provides the basis for specific and explicit questions to be posed to the opposing party. Investigation changes broad-based or generalized questions into specific, detailed, and pointed inquiries of special interest.

A thorough, effective investigation is the integral cog in the wheel of obtaining a wealth of knowledge about the legal issues, the parties, the circumstances, the facts, and the evidence. Finally, the investigation gives a real "heads up" for the legal team in providing the best possible client representation, from the initial contact through trial.

7.11   WEBSITES

Address	Description
Government	
http://www.usa.gov	Official Web portal for the U.S. government; includes agencies, Congress, and government information by topic
http://www.recalls.gov	Official Web portal for six federal agencies overseeing recalls of products, and so forth
http://www.loc.gov	Official Web ports for the Library of Congress
http://catalog.loc.gov	Library of Congress online catalog; includes basic and guided searches; Library of Congress authorities
http://www.glin.gov	Global Information Network (GLIN)—public database of official texts of laws, regulations, judicial decisions, and other complementary legal sources contributed by governmental agencies and international organizations
http://www.gpoaccess.gov	GPO Access—Excellent source for the three branches of the federal government
http://www.law.upenn.edu/library	University of Pennsylvania Law Library—uniform/model state laws
http://www.usdoj.gov/oip	Official link to the Federal Freedom of Information Act via the U.S. Department of Justice and associated federal agencies
http://www.house.gov	Official portal for the U.S. House of Representatives
http://www.senate.gov	Official portal for the U.S. Senate
http://www.loc.gov	Library of Congress—comprehensive legislative information
http://www.usa.gov	Official Web portals for state governments
General Search Engines	
http://www.ixquick.com	IXQuick metasearch engine
http://www.google.com	Google
http://www.dogpile.com	Dogpile
http://www.allsearchengines.com	Compendium of search engines, including law-related

(continued)

Address	Description
Law-Related Search Engines	
http://www.hg.org	Hiero Gamos
http://www.findlaw.com	Find Law
http://www.ilrg.com	Internet Legal Research Guide
http://www.megalaw.com	Megalaw
http://www.alllaw.com	All Law—research, cases, government forms, and more
http://www.infolaw.com	InfoLaw
The Courts	
http://www.ncsconline.org	National Center for State Courts—link to "site map" for extensive listing of CourTopics resources
http://www.supremecourtus.gov	Official Web portal for the United States Supreme Court
http://www.uscourts.gov	Official portal for the federal judiciary system
Law-Related	
http://www.law.cornell.edu	Cornell University, Legal Information Institute—includes links to federal and state law, regulation, court rules, and law by topic
http://www.law.harvard.edu	Harvard University School of Law—national/international research guide
http://www.lpig.org	Law and Policy Institutions Guide—comprehensive repository of legal resources, law articles, legal practice information; legislative and judicial resources for U.S. and international legal professionals
http://www.abanet.org	Official Web portal for the American Bar Association; includes an A–Z topical index
http://www.freeadvice.com	Free Advice—law and legal advice on select topics; link to "view all law topics" for expanded index
http://www.lexisone.com	Lexis One—free legal forms and case summaries; use for general searches (fees apply to expanded searches)
Medical	
http://www.media4u.com	Medical abbreviations
http://www.eicd.com	Medical diagnosis codes
http://www.medlineplus.gov	Medical terms and encyclopedia
http://www.rxlist.com	Prescription drug information
http://www.thebiotechdictionary.com	Short, simple explanations to biotech terms

Address	Description
People-Related	
http://www.ancestry.com	Social Security death index
http://www.superpages.com	Superpages—Name, address, telephone #; reverse searches
http://www.workpermit.com	Work Permit—Work visa, immigration, naturalization services
http://www.crimcheck.com	CrimCheck—data from over 10,000 local courts and 3,500 county courts in all 50 states. Listing of free public records and criminal (individual states), land, bankruptcy and other records for people and legal actions
Expert Witnesses	
http://www.idex.com	All-inclusive website providing information on experts, including background, *Frye/Daubert* challenges, and state licensure discipline search
http://www.lexisnexis.com/analyzer	LexisNexis—includes expert witness search link
http://www.jurispro.com	Juris-Pro—listing of expert witnesses; can be somewhat limited in usage.
http://www.atla.net	American Association for Justice (formerly American Trial Lawyers Association); must be a member to use
http://www.dri.org	Defense Research Institute—link to "Expert Witness Database"
http://www.ama-assn.org	American Medical Society—includes information on medical experts
Reference Materials	
http://www.ipl.org	Internet Public Library—includes law and government, newspapers, journal, and other information; search site and tips for searching links
http://www.infoplease.com	InfoPlease—includes dictionary, encyclopedia, almanacs, free online references, research, and more
http://www.legal-definitions.com	Explanations for common legal terminology
http://www.iii.org	Insurance Information Institute— compendium of insurance industry-related information, including glossary, insurance tools, latest developments/news; link to "Researching and Insurance Issue?"

(continued)

Address	Description
http://www.kbb.com	Kelly Blue Book—information on valuation of new and used automobiles and other useful information
http://www.naca.net	National Association of Consumer Advocates—link to "NACA index"; includes information on association activities, latest developments, consumer rights, consumer resources, and other useful information
http://www.usps.com/zip4	Zip code +4 directory

BIBLIOGRAPHY

Buchanan, John C. and Bos, Carole D., *How to Use Video in Litigation: A Guide to Technology, Strategies, and Techniques.* Englewood Cliffs, NJ: Prentice-Hall, 1986.

Buckles, Thomas, *Laws of Evidence.* NY: Thomson-Delmar Learning, 2003.

Criminal Justice, 12 ABA *Journal* 1 (Spring 1997).

Dudnik, Robert M., *Anatomy of a Personal Injury Lawsuit,* 2nd ed. Washington, DC: Association of Trial Lawyers of America, Education Fund, 1981.

Federal Civil Judicial Procedure and Rules. St. Paul, MN: West, 2008.

Federal Rules of Civil Procedure, St. Paul, MN: West, 2008.

Federal Rules of Criminal Procedures. St. Paul, MN: West, 2008.

Kinzie, Mark A, and Hart, Christine E., *Product Liability Litigation.* NY: Thomson-Delmar Learning, 2002.

Kirk, Paul L. and Thornton, John I., *Crime Investigation.* New York: Wiley, 1985.

"Legal Research in the Information Superhighway," *Legal Assistant Today* (March/April 1997).

Legal Secretary Federal Litigation, 4th ed. Costa Mesa, CA: James Publishing, 1996.

Magarick, Pat, *Casualty Investigation Checklists,* 3rd ed. New York: Clark Boardman Co. Ltd., 1985.

Philo, Harry M., *Lawyers Desk Reference,* 7th ed. Rochester, NY: Lawyers Cooperative Publishing Co., 1987.

1997 Wiley Expert Witness Update: New Developments in Personal Injury Litigation. John Wiley & Sons, Inc., 1997.

8

Pretrial Litigation Skills

8.00   INTRODUCTION

Litigation is the focal point of our American legal system. Regardless of area of practice, attorneys are either working to prepare a legal dispute for trial or to avoid a dispute that could lead to litigation, allegations of malpractice, or other antagonistic situations. A basic working knowledge of the litigation process is an essential component of the skills a valuable paralegal should possess. This chapter explores paralegal duties in suit preparation and discovery practice.

The duties of a litigation paralegal may include interviewing clients and witnesses, searching public records and locating potential documentary evidence, performing legal research, and drafting pleadings and discovery documents. These tasks require extensive training and practice. Attention to detail, critical analysis of statutes and court opinions, and superior written and verbal communication skills are essential. While many pleadings, such as notices, are fairly simple and routine, others require creativity, as well as considerable familiarity with substantive and procedural law.

A paralegal in an active trial practice makes substantial contributions in the area of discovery. All discovery requires a manager to oversee its organization, systematize it, and monitor its implementation. The paralegal may draft interrogatories and other discovery requests, assist clients in preparing responses to discovery requests from opposing parties, prepare summaries and digests of discovery documents as the case progresses, and perform other tasks as delegated by the supervising attorney. The paralegal plays a valuable role in developing outlines of questions to be used at depositions, taking notes and tracking exhibits during depositions, and generally serving as another set of eyes and ears for the attorney.

As the trial date approaches, the paralegal attends to crucial details, such as keeping in touch with witnesses, having subpoenas issued, and organizing the trial notebook. At trial, the paralegal tracks exhibits, take notes, and performs other tasks delegated by the attorney.

Paralegals cannot represent clients in court. They may represent clients before an administrative agency if the rules governing that particular agency permit nonlawyer representation. Assuming that nonlawyer representation is permitted and that both the attorney-employer and the client consent, it is critical that the paralegal in this situation master the necessary advocacy skills and have a strong working knowledge of substantive and procedural law.

8.01   THE ADVOCACY SYSTEM AND THE PARALEGAL

Clients, as consumers of legal services, are driving the legal market to become more competitive. As clients become more knowledgeable of the value of paralegals, they are seeking firms who utilize highly educated, trained, and credentialed paralegals. Terms such as cost-effectiveness and cost-benefit analyses appear frequently in corporate memoranda. Competition for clients, particularly corporate clients, is intense. Law firms must streamline procedures and computerize operations if they are to compete in today's world. Low and moderate income families cannot afford to pay high prices for legal services and often must resort to poorly funded public assistance programs. More attorneys now recognize their ethical duty to serve all phases of society and seek to deliver those legal services more efficiently.

As a direct result of increased emphasis upon efficiency and economy, many tasks previously performed solely by attorneys are now delegated to paralegals. Discovery is one of these areas that have become more encompassing for members of a litigation team. Attorneys are becoming more skillful in identifying possible sources of evidence and information. The skilled paralegal who accumulates, analyzes, collates and cross-indexes factual information, and drafts discovery requests ranging from the simple to the complex increases firm productivity. Generally firms not using paralegals are at a serious disadvantage. Without paralegals the attorney is forced to devote a higher percentage of time to factual matters in the case. Opposing counsel, reinforced by paralegals, can perhaps spend more time on the law, tactics, and trial strategy.

As every new case is commenced, the paralegal should consult with the attorney and review the substantive law and court procedures and practices. Of course, this review should be incorporated into the paralegal's ongoing continuing education habits. This ensures the paralegal's place as an effective litigation team member. It further allows the paralegal to anticipate the needs of the case, specifically the time elements, forms requirements, and policies that will affect its outcome.

The beneficiaries of the paralegal's work are simultaneously the client, the attorney, and the legal system as a whole. The paralegal, by performing many tasks formerly performed by the lawyer, accelerates the pace of discovery, leading to the ultimate resolution of the case in a timelier manner. The paralegal improves the attorney's perception of the factual information developed in discovery by organizing and digesting it into compact summaries that are cross-referenced to exhibits. The attorney then applies the result to produce cogent, concise, and persuasive presentations. It allows thoughtful consideration and evaluation of the facts, law, timing, and suitability of settlement, along with evaluation and selection of the settlement options.

8.02 SPECIFIC LITIGATION SKILLS

The benefits an attorney gains from utilizing a paralegal increase incrementally as enhanced knowledge of legal procedures, exposure to different situations, and awareness of the techniques and strategies preferred by the supervising attorney increase. Those skills include drafting complaints, subsequent pleadings, motions and related documents, discovery requests and responses, performing legal research and investigation, analyzing discovery responses from opposing parties, conducting interviews, and managing the information accumulated in the case file. Each of these activities enhances the value of the paralegal to the attorney and clients.

As a case progresses, facts may develop that clearly indicate the case should not be tried, either from a plaintiff's or a defendant's point of view. The paralegal, by carefully monitoring the factual development through discovery efforts, is in a unique position to identify such a potential situation, refer it to the supervising attorney, and assist in a quick resolution of the dispute.

8.03 PRELIMINARY CONSIDERATIONS IN LITIGATION

Long before the pleadings are prepared and filed, the supervising attorney and other litigation team members must make some basic decisions about the case that will have long-reaching effects. During, or very shortly after the client's first interview, the facts of the case must be analyzed to determine whether the client has a valid cause of action. The legal theories and remedies that may be available to resolve the client's claim must be explored, and potential defenses that may be raised by the opposing party should be identified. A preliminary calculation of the damages or other relief to which the client may be entitled must be analyzed.

The attorney must develop the legal theories that will provide the framework for all that follows, from drafting the complaint through the trial itself. To avoid overlooking important details, experienced trial attorneys use checklists of the requirements for each legal theory of recovery and for each defense that

EXHIBIT 8-1   Examples of Legal Theories for Checklists

A. Law Action Theories
   1. Contract
   2. Personal Injury Torts
      a. General Negligence
      b. Products Liability
      c. Premises Liability
      d. Professional Liability
      e. Governmental Liability
      f. Worker Compensation Claim
   3. Other Torts
      a. Intentional Torts
      b. Defamation (Libel/Slander)
      c. Fraud/Misrepresentation

B. Equity Action Theories
   1. Mandamus
   2. Injunction
   3. Rescission
   4. Reformation
   5. Specific Performance
   6. Equitable Trust

C. Damages Recoverable
   1. Compensatory Damages
   2. Restitution Damages
   3. Punitive Damages
   4. Liquidated Damages
   5. Lost Profits
   6. Diminished Earning Capacity (reduced to present value)
   7. Future Medical Expenses (reduced to present value)
   8. Interest
   9. Attorney Fees

D. Defenses/Limitations to Recovery
   1. Performance
   2. Satisfaction/Accord and Satisfaction
   3. Statute of Limitations
   4. Statute of Frauds
   5. Privity of Contract

   6. Prior Breach (of contract)
   7. Duress
   8. Impossibility of Performance
   9. Illegality of Purpose
  10. Laches
  11. Agency/Independent Contractor Status
  12. Contributory Negligence
  13. Comparative Negligence
  14. Assumption of Risk
  15. Indemnity/Contribution
  16. Economic Waste
  17. Statutory Limitation of Damages
  18. Governmental Immunity
  19. Third-Party Liability
  20. Exhaustion of Remedies (administrative)

A portion of the legal theory checklist is reproduced below to demonstrate how it might be expanded.

   3. Other Torts
      a. Intentional Torts
         (1) Act by Defendant
         (2) Intent
         (3) Causation
         (4) Damage
      b. Defamation (Libel/Slander)
         (1) Defamatory Statement (Written/Oral)
         (2) Plaintiff Identified or Identifiable
         (3) Publication to Third Party
         (4) Plaintiff's Reputation Damaged
         (5) Calculation of Loss to Plaintiff
      c. Fraud/Misrepresentation
         (1) False Statement/Misrepresentation of Fact
         (2) Knowledge of Falsity by Defendant (for fraud only)
         (3) Intent that Plaintiff Rely
         (4) Plaintiff's Reliance Justified
         (5) Damage to Plaintiff

may be used. As each requirement is drafted into the complaint or presented at trial, it is checked off the list. For each element on the checklist, supporting facts must be outlined, along with all sources that prove such facts (which make it more likely than not in civil cases or cause a reasonable doubt in criminal cases). The checklist will serve as the paralegal's constant companion when reviewing and processing documents obtained during the discovery process. Supporting facts may be in the form of one or more witnesses and/or one or more exhibits.

The checklist will be expanded, contracted, summarized, and cross-referenced as the case progresses. At the preliminary stage, the checklist is crucial more *because it exists* than because of what it contains. It provides the foundation for constructing appropriate legal theories that will result in a purposeful and thorough litigation plan. *See* Exhibit 8-1 for examples of possible legal theories that might be used in preparing such a checklist.

8.04 PLEADINGS AND PRETRIAL MOTIONS

8.041   Rules of Procedure

In addition to the substantive legal theories and rules, the litigation team must be familiar with the procedural rules that govern a particular case. At the federal level, all courts are governed by the *Federal Rules of Criminal Procedure* for criminal cases and by the *Federal Rules of Civil Procedure* for civil cases. Federal trial courts (U.S. District Courts) are permitted to adopt local court rules to supplement the federal rules; however, they may not replace the federal rules or materially change the character of the federal rules.

As an example of this interaction, Rule 12(b) of the *Federal Rules of Civil Procedure* permits certain motions to be filed to test the sufficiency of the complaint. The rule lists specific bases that can be included in such motions, such as: (1) lack of jurisdiction over the subject matter, (2) lack of jurisdiction over the person, (3) improper venue, (4) failure to state a claim upon which relief can be granted, (5) insufficiency of process, (6) insufficiency of service of process and (7) failure to join a party under Rule 19. Under Rule 83, a particular federal district court would be permitted to adopt a local court rule requiring all Rule 12 motions to be filed in triplicate. This type of local rule does not change the character of the federal rule, but it does add another requirement. However, Rule 83(a)(2) states "A local rule imposing a requirement of form shall not be enforced in a manner that causes a party to lose rights because of a nonwillful failure to comply with the requirement."

State court systems also have procedural rules, many of which closely resemble the *Federal Rules of Civil Procedure.* These state rules of civil procedure are adopted either by the highest court of the state or by the state legislature. As in the federal system, many local courts are also permitted to adopt local court rules so long as the local rules do not supplant state rules of procedure. The discussion that follows uses the *Federal Rules of Civil Procedure* as its general basis.

8.042   Pleadings

Rule 7 states what documents constitute pleadings: the complaint, the answer, the reply to a counter-claim, an answer to a cross-claim (if the answer contains a cross-claim), a third-party complaint, and a third-party answer, if applicable. The pleadings inform the court of the allegations or contentions of each of the parties by outlining the claims of the plaintiff(s) and the affirmative defenses of the defendant(s). Pleadings also assist the court in formulating the issues.

The general rules of pleadings are found in Rule 8. With regard to claims for relief, the pleadings:

1. Establish the court's jurisdiction or authority to adjudicate the controversy
2. Briefly state the facts, circumstances, or theories that provide the basis of the claim for relief
3. Briefly state any affirmative defenses that the defendant claims against the plaintiff
4. Include a demand for relief, remedy, or judgment sought by the pleader.

General rules of pleadings and language should be followed consistently. One should avoid expressions that are trite or redundant, such as: each and every, due and owing, or null and void. A proper pleading must be able to stand alone, must state facts, and must not simply allege evidentiary matters. Often the pleadings will refer to a statute or authority under which the plaintiff bases his claim for relief. *See* the Appendix of Forms attached to the *Federal Rules of Civil Procedure* for sample summons and complaints.

The key to drafting effective pleadings is to include only those matters that are absolutely necessary, stated in a simple, concise way. One should never admit unnecessary facts that may later become embarrassing obstacles in the proper presentation of the client's case. One should save legal arguments for the trial brief, since these have no place in pleadings.

8.0421 Complaints, Answers, Motions.

In a complaint (sometimes called a petition in state courts), the plaintiff formally notifies the court and the defendant of the basis for the plaintiff's claim. It is filed with the clerk of the court and served upon the defendant, along with a summons notifying the defendant that an answer must be given within a specified period or a default judgment will be entered. Rule 79(a) governs the manner in which the clerk of court assigns the civil docket number to each case. Actions are assigned consecutive file numbers and each document filed subsequent to the initial summons and complaint is assigned a folio number within that initial file number. The clerk maintains a chronological listing of all documents in the case.

When the complaint is received, the defendant's attorney analyzes it for legal sufficiency in an attempt to weed out claims and defenses that are without merit. The defendant may challenge the legal sufficiency of the complaint by filing a motion to dismiss (called a demurrer in some state courts, but abolished by Rule 7(c) of the *Federal Rules of Civil Procedure* in federal courts) and by serving a copy of the motion on the plaintiff's attorney. In a motion to dismiss, the defendant asserts that the case should be dismissed because of a specific defect. The defect, as described previously and in Rule 12(b) may be lack of subject matter jurisdiction, lack of personal jurisdiction, improper issuance of summons, improper service of summons, or a failure to state a claim upon which the relief can be granted. The motion to dismiss and all other pretrial motions are set for hearing by the judge assigned to the case.

Depending on the jurisdiction, other pretrial motions may be used to refine the allegations contained in the pleadings. Among these are a motion for a more definite statement, a motion to strike (referring to statements in a pleading that are redundant, immaterial, or scandalous), and a motion for judgment on the pleadings (also called a motion for summary judgment in many state courts).

If the complaint survives the preliminary motions designed to test its sufficiency, the defendant must then file a written answer. The answer strives to minimize the damage and potential exposure to the client, not only monetarily, but also to the client's business and/or personal reputation. The attorney will usually follow an issue analysis approach, seeking to separate known facts from those that must be proven by the plaintiff. The answer may contain admissions, denials, affirmative defenses, and counterclaims. If the defendant admits a particular allegation, there is no need to prove that fact at trial. If the defendant denies a particular allegation, a factual issue is created, and the plaintiff must then prove the fact at trial, unless he or she is able to do so before then.

After the defendant's answer has been filed, the plaintiff must file a reply if the defendant asserted any counterclaims in its answer. Some state jurisdictions also allow a reply to any affirmative defenses listed in Rule 8(c). In the reply, the plaintiff responds to the causes of action asserted (or any affirmative defenses stated when allowed) by admitting them, denying them, or stating any affirmative defenses, if applicable.

8.0422 Affirmative Defenses.

Allegations contained in the answer that may prevent the plaintiff's recovery are called affirmative defenses. They describe acts or circumstances which may have occurred before, after, or concurrently with those alleged by plaintiff in the complaint. Just as the plaintiff is required to prove the allegations contained in the complaint, the defendant must prove the elements of the affirmative defenses raised in the answer. Rule 8(c) lists affirmative defenses as the following, along with very brief explanations:

1. Accord and satisfaction: payment in full or completion of obligation
2. Arbitration and award: prior agreement to arbitrate matter

3. Assumption of risk: plaintiff assumed risk and should accept consequences
4. Contributory negligence: plaintiff failed to exercise due and ordinary care
5. Discharge in bankruptcy: debt discharged or matter adjudicated by bankruptcy court
6. Duress: defendant's action caused by plaintiff's threats or inducements
7. Estoppel: plaintiff's action or silence in failing to assert a right
8. Failure of consideration: consideration for a contract no longer exists (i.e., house destroyed by fire, etc.)
9. Fraud: false representation, failure to disclose
10. Illegality: unlawful act
11. Injury by fellow servant: negligence by another employee was cause of plaintiff's injury
12. Laches: neglect in asserting right or claim
13. License: permission granted by law
14. Payment: prior discharge of obligation and acceptance by plaintiff
15. Release: relinquishment of a right
16. *Res judicata:* matter previously decided by court
17. Statute of frauds: agreement must be in writing to be valid
18. Statute of limitations: if applicable, and if expired, action may not be pursued
19. Waiver: intentional or voluntary abandonment (differs from estoppel in that it is a "knowing" abandonment, rather than estoppel where intent is immaterial)
20. Any other matter constituting an avoidance or affirmative defense.

8.0423 Counterclaims, Cross-claims, Third-Party Pleadings.   In a counterclaim, the defendant states a cause of action against the plaintiff. If the defendant's cause of action arises from the same facts as plaintiff's cause of action, the defendant's counterclaim is compulsory, that is, the defendant *must* file the claim against the plaintiff in the existing action, or the claim is barred. If the defendant's cause of action against the plaintiff is based upon a different occurrence or a different set of facts, the defendant has a permissive counterclaim which may be filed in the same case, but the defendant is not barred from bringing a separate action for the claim. A counterclaim is usually included as part of a defendant's answer.

A cross-claim is a cause of action by one defendant against another defendant and is also often included with an answer. Cross-claims are governed by Rule 13 of the *Federal Rules of Civil Procedure.* They must arise out of the same transaction or occurrence stated in the complaint or a counterclaim or must relate to any property that is the subject matter of the complaint.

Rule 14 governs the procedures allowing third-party practice. In a third-party complaint, a defendant alleges a claim against a party not previously included in the lawsuit. In general, permission from the court must be obtained before a defendant is allowed to become a third-party plaintiff. The party against whom the third-party complaint is filed becomes known as a third-party defendant.

An additional kind of "third-party" pleading occurs when an outside party seeks permission from the court to intervene in a lawsuit. Rule 24 of the *Federal Rules of Civil Procedure* governs interventions. The motion to the court applying for intervenor status must contain an assertion that the right to intervene is: (1) conferred by a statute, *or* (2) based on an interest relating to the transaction or property which is the subject of the lawsuit, *and* (3) the party will be unable to protect its rights unless allowed to become a party to the lawsuit.

8.043   Administrative Controls

Administrative controls include all calendars, lists, document logs, and numbering systems that are created and maintained throughout the case until the time of trial. At that time, these items are incorporated into the trial notebooks. Keeping tickler files, case calendars, and to-do lists should be a daily ritual for the paralegal. Methods for maintaining such controls vary based on resources and size of the case. Deadlines for responding to pleadings and discovery requests are an inherent part of each case. The court does not appreciate excuses for missed deadlines. Such failure to adhere to deadlines may result in staff dismissal and attorney disciplinary proceedings. The paralegal should carefully review the rules governing time allotted for response to pleadings and discovery requests. It is important to avoid potential scheduling conflicts.

Calendaring and docketing software is usually used, and often recommended by malpractice carriers, to assure that no deadlines are missed and any scheduling conflicts are resolved. As with any software application, the results of its use are only as good as the information input into the computer. The responsibility for overseeing such tasks often belongs to the paralegal member of the litigation team.

8.0431 Pleadings and Documentary Files.

In complex litigation, particularly multiple party actions, simply maintaining pleadings, discovery motions and orders, trial testimony, transcripts, evidentiary material, and other documents may prove cumbersome. Case documents are usually stored in chronological order. The paralegal should formulate a cross-indexing system to facilitate reference and retrieval. This is no small or insignificant task; however, it may be accomplished manually or by computer. Filing and indexing systems should also include categories for all pertinent documents in the case, including lists of parties and witnesses. Such systems should be standardized and as succinct as possible, utilizing color-coded labels or whatever devices may be effective for the firm and the needs of that particular case.

It is essential to have indexed copies of all the pleadings, including the date filed. This index supports a file containing copies of these pleadings marked by a numbered tab on each pleading, corresponding with the number listed in the index of pleadings. The index includes a description of the pleading filed, date it was filed, pleading number assigned and tabbed on the pleading, and any other desirable information. (*See* Exhibit 8-2.) A cross-index arranged by topics should also be prepared.

In the case of a multiparty suit, it may be desirable to prepare separate files to contain the following, all properly tabbed and indexed: (1) correspondence, (2) notes, (3) pleadings (with subsections for complaints, answers to complaints, counterclaims and cross-claims, if separately filed, court orders and notices, proofs of service, subpoenas, etc.), (4) discovery (interrogatories, answers to interrogatories, plaintiff or defendant objections, requests for admissions, requests for production of documents, motions to compel responses, etc.), (5) documents (arranged by sources/parties), (6) witness files (including expert witnesses), (7) exhibits for trials, notebooks, and other files as needed. For the most effective retrieval, the index should be established in both chronological and topical format. Throughout this process, the goal is to retrieve any document on a moment's notice.

8.044   Using Computer

A paralegal should acquire and maintain his or her computer skills. Today, the computer is used in all aspects of litigation – from pretrial through trial and appeal. Computerized databases to manage indexing tasks are available commercially and their use should be considered. Chapter 9, The Paralegal and Document Discovery Cases, discusses use of the computer in the area of discovery and document

EXHIBIT 8-2   Sample Pleadings Index

Index to Pleadings
Filed in Case 70-823

Doc. #	Vol. #	Date Filed	Description
8	II	7/11/06	Plaintiff's Rule 34 Request for Document Prod.
9	II	7/16/06	Order on Preliminary Pretrial Conference
10	II	7/15/06	Withdrawal of Appearance of Danny J. Jones
11	II	7/16/06	Order Consolidating Cases and Adding Counsel
12	II	8/09/06	Answers of the Lean Co. To Pl.'s Interrogs. #1
13	II	8/09/06	Answers of Pipe Corp. Pl.'s Interrogs. #1
14	III	8/09/06	Answers of Clamor Co. To Pl.'s Interrogs. #1
15	III	8/09/06	Answers and Objections of U.S. Co. To Pl.'s Interrogs. #1
16	III	8/09/06	Def's Response to Pl.'s Rule 34 Req. For Prod. of Docs.
17	III	8/09/06	Answers of ASCO to Pl.'s Interrogs. #1
18	III	8/09/06	Def's Objections to Pl.'s Interrogs. #2
19	III	8/09/06	Answers & Objections of Clamor to Pl.'s Interrogs. #2
20	III	8/09/06	Answers of OUTGO to Pl.'s Interrogs. #1
21	III	8/12/06	Arno's Ans. & Objections to Pl.'s R. 34 Req. for Doc. Prod.
22	III	8/12/06	Arno's Ans. & Objections to Pl.'s Interrogs. #1
23	III	8/12/06	Answers of Met. Gov't. Of Anywhere to Def's Joint Ints. of June 25, 2006
24	III	8/12/06	Joint Response of Plaintiffs to Def's Joint Int.
25	III	8/12/06	Answers of CA to Def's Joint Int. Of June 25, 2006
26	IV	9/17/06	Def's Memo R. 37 to Compel Ans. by Pl.'s to Def's Joint Int. and Other Relief
27	IV	9/18/06	Pl.'s Motion & Memo. in Support of Class Actions
28	IV	9/20/06	Memo of all Def's in Opposition to Cl. Action
29	IV	9/20/06	Arno's Reply to Pl.'s Rule 37 Motion
30	IV	9/23/06	Def's Memo In Opposition to Pl.'s Motion for Order Pursuant to Rule 37
31	IV	9/23/06	Pl.'s Response to Def's R. 37 Motion & Memorandum
32	IV	9/23/06	Agreement Ltr. Between Met. Gov't. of Anywhere 7 Messrs. Brown & Moulder dated 1/21/2006

production, and the paralegal could apply much of this discussion to the case management file. Other sources to investigate include the firm's computer systems analyst and/or firm administrator, specialty vendors, and serial publications for attorneys and paralegals. Some paralegals possessing strong computer skills have designed their own databases utilizing commercially available software. Of course, the paralegal should elicit support from supervising attorneys before commencing such tasks.

8.05 DISCOVERY AND PRETRIAL PREPARATION

While the issues are being joined through the process of written pleadings and pretrial motions, formal discovery may also be undertaken by the parties. Formal discovery includes interrogatories, depositions, requests for production of documents and other things, and requests for admission. The ability of the parties to go forward in federal court with formal discovery is controlled, and may be limited, by Rule 26(a) and (f).

The purpose of discovery is to learn what the other party knows, what the party will argue in answer to your client's contentions or defenses, and the strength or weakness of those arguments. It will also reveal those facts about which the parties have no argument. This, in turn, will eliminate the necessity for court adjudication of undisputed facts. Also, discovery will reveal the legal issues that the court can determine without a jury, since the jury considers and renders verdicts only on the facts of a case and the court (judge) decides issues of law and instructs the jury.

In the federal courts, Rule 26(a) requires that certain disclosures be made to the opposing party, without awaiting a discovery request and within a specified time period. These required initial disclosures may be waived or altered by order or local rule of the district court. Therefore, the paralegal must check local rules when a lawsuit is filed in federal court to determine whether the initial required disclosures have been adopted or waived by local court rule or court order. If the initial disclosures are required, they must include information concerning:

- Identity of persons/entities having discoverable information about the claims and defenses in the lawsuit
- Copies or descriptions (by category and location) of documents, data compilations, and tangible things in the possession of the party that are relevant to the claims and defenses in the lawsuit
- A computation of damages claimed by the disclosing party and the availability of copies of documents and materials, not privileged or protected from disclosure, on which the computation is based
- Any insurance agreements under which any insurer could be liable for all or part of a judgment entered in the case
- E-discovery and related issues must be discussed.

Identity of expert witnesses who will be called to testify at trial, as well as a report from any such expert containing the expert's opinions, the facts considered in formulating such opinions, exhibits to be used by the expert, the qualifications of the witness, including a list of all publications the witness authored for the previous ten years, the compensation to be paid for the expert's work and testimony, and a list of other cases in which the witness has testified as an expert at trial or by deposition within the previous four years.

A party must also provide the other party with a list of potential witnesses, designating which witnesses will testify live and which by deposition, and a list of documents the party will introduce as exhibits at trial. Each category of these disclosures has different time periods assigned within which the disclosures must be made. Rule 16(b) sets forth guidelines and requirements for pretrial conferences in which parties schedule time limits for completing discovery and various pretrial motions. Rule 26(d) provides that, absent court order or by agreement of the parties, no party can institute written or other discovery from another party before the parties have met, prepared a discovery plan, and submitted it to the court. The Rule 26(f) meeting of the parties must be accomplished and the report generated as a result of the meeting must be filed before the first scheduling conference is held or a Rule 16(b) scheduling order is due to be issued.

The rule outlines what matters must be discussed at the Rule 26(f) meeting, but the overall thrust of the meeting is to plan the discovery phase of the case in as much detail as is possible at that early stage in the case. Rule 26(a)(5) provides that parties may pursue discovery by more traditional methods as well: oral depositions, depositions by written question, written interrogatories, requests for production of documents or things or permission to enter upon land or property, requests for physical and mental examinations, and requests for admissions. Rule 26(d) provides that these traditional discovery methods may not be commenced until after the meeting of the parties unless the local court in which the case is filed has opted out of the Rule 26(f) requirements.

Other than those facts withheld for impeachment purposes and those facts that are privileged, the underlying philosophy of the *Federal Rules of Civil Procedure* and their state court counterparts is that all relevant facts should be available to all parties prior to trial, provided that the party has properly requested this information. If each party honestly and adequately responds to discovery requests by the other parties in the case in sufficient time prior to trial, the presumption is that many cases will be settled. This presumption is probably correct, since only a very small percentage of cases result in a full trial on the merits. The formal discovery process lends itself especially well to the skills of the paralegal member of the litigation team.

The scope of discovery described in Rule 26(b) reflects this underlying philosophy. It provides that parties may discover any matter, not privileged, that is relevant to the subject matter of the action. Discovery may even be had of any information that is not admissible at trial, as long as it appears reasonably calculated to lead to the discovery of admissible evidence.

The most common privileges asserted in objections to discovery are attorney-client privilege, opinion work product (also known as the mental impressions, theories, and opinions of the lawyer), and material prepared in anticipation of litigation. Generally, information protected by the attorney-client privilege and the opinion work product privilege may not be obtained under any circumstances. Only if a party waives one of these privileges is such information usually made discoverable. The third category of privilege is more of an immunity than an absolute privilege. Rule 26(b)(3) provides that such material is protected from discovery unless the party seeking discovery can show that he or she is unable, without undue hardship, to obtain the substantial equivalent of the materials by other means. If such a showing can be made, the court may order that the material is to be produced to the party seeking discovery, but must protect against disclosure of the mental impressions, conclusions, opinions, or legal theories of an attorney or other representative of a party about the litigation.

Any party to the lawsuit and any person not a party to the lawsuit may obtain copies of statements they have previously given concerning the subject matter of the litigation, without any necessity of showing "good cause," or indeed any cause at all, and may move for an order compelling production of such statements if the party holding the statements refuses to provide it to the requesting party.

8.06 INTERROGATORIES

Interrogatories are a discovery device consisting of written questions submitted to another party and answered by that party in writing and under oath. The primary purpose is to provide a relatively inexpensive way to gather information from the opposing party. They are authorized in the *Federal Rules of Civil Procedure* under Rules 33 and 37 and parallel state rules. Rule 33 provides that any party may serve any other party in a lawsuit with written interrogatories that must be answered within a specific time limit. Rule 33(a) also limits the number of interrogatories allowed to be served to no more than twenty-five, including subparts. The number limitation is not absolute. If you can demonstrate to the court what information is required from additional interrogatories and that the information is necessary to properly and to fully prepare the case for trial, the court may grant an order giving permission to serve additional interrogatories.

Always check local rules when preparing interrogatories. State and local court rules may also impose conditions or limitations. These generally pertain to the form of the interrogatory and the number of interrogatories that may be propounded to an opposing party. Generally, these number limitations (ranging from 15 to 50, depending on the jurisdiction) include subparts of each interrogatory as part of the total allowed.

Interrogatories are self-executing discovery devices; each question must either be answered by the party served or for entity/corporate parties by an officer or agent of the corporation, partnership, association, or governmental agency. Interrogatories must be answered under oath, in writing, and signed by the party who provides the answers. Should objections be lodged to some or all of the interrogatories, the attorney for the party must also sign the answers. Objections must be detailed and must be made within the time limit permitted for responding.

Interrogatories and the answers or objections to interrogatories may be contained in separate documents. Many jurisdictions have court rules that require the *engrossment* of the question and the answer to interrogatories in the interest of clarity. Simply put, this means that when answering an interrogatory, the entire question must be restated as propounded prior to the answer. With today's technology, the scanning of an opponent's interrogatories into your computer allows you to include your answer directly under the question. If you cannot do this, you may be able to use the "cut-and-paste" method, or the interrogatory format may provide sufficient space between questions to permit the insertion of appropriate answers. These practices allow the court and the parties to look at one document and find, in successive order, question and answer, question and answer, and so on. Few courts have solved the problem of supplemental answers, and few require engrossment of supplemental answers with the original questions and answers.

Under the federal rules, a party may serve more than one set of interrogatories but may be required to number the interrogatories sequentially in order. In other words, "Set one" may include questions from 1 to 15, and "Set two," filed at a later date, begins with question 16 and extends to the completion of that set. It allows quick and easy reference to questions from the beginning of discovery in the case to its conclusion and is a desirable system since it allows easy collation of one answer to another on a related point.

8.061   Interrogatories as Part of the Discovery Plan

Interrogatories are only one part of the overall discovery plan and can be extremely useful if carefully planned and drafted. In interrogatories, almost anything can be asked. Relevance to the issues or the possibility of leading to relevant, admissible facts are the only tests, and these tests are liberally construed. The only other possible limitation is the privileged status of the information being sought, but sometimes even a privilege may be breached and the information obtained from the opposing party.

The timing of written interrogatories in the discovery process must be coordinated with depositions, requests for production, requests for admission, and the other discovery devices to ensure the maximum return for the effort. Similarly, many items may be better developed by independent investigation (informal discovery) or by using a different discovery method.

The resulting benefit of informal discovery is the ability to conceal the attorney's specific interest from the opposing party. The number limitation placed on interrogatories by the federal rule or a local rule may make it more advantageous to convert an interrogatory that asks *about* a certain document or tangible evidence into a request *for* the document or tangible evidence.

A paralegal should never serve interrogatories without a plan, since this can be unprofessional, unproductive and usually yields only minimal discovery of relevant information. When such a set is received, the paralegal and lawyer can easily recognize that the opposing party is far behind in case planning and analysis, which gives them a tactical advantage over the opposing party.

8.0611 Forcing the Opposing Party to Prepare the Case.

The untimely submission of extensive interrogatories may force the opposing attorney to prepare his or her case much earlier than otherwise. In the early development of the discovery plan, the merits of the case must take into account the effect that extensive and detailed interrogatories may cause. It is a fact of life that many lawsuits are filed on "bare-bones" allegations and seldom with a full set of supporting facts. Often both sides have strengths and weaknesses in their positions. Discretion in drafting and answering interrogatories is appropriate and necessary.

8.0612 The Paper War.

Serving extensive and unnecessary interrogatories may spur the opposing party into a similar response and create a "paper war." This is harassing and nonproductive in that it requires the expenditure of extensive blocks of both paralegal and attorney time with little benefit to the client.

Federal Rule 26(g) requires that discovery requests be signed by an attorney and provides that such a signature certifies that the discovery is: (1) consistent with the federal rules and warranted by existing law or a good faith argument for a change in existing law; (2) not propounded for any improper purposes such as harassment, delay, or increasing the cost of litigation; and (3) not unreasonable or unduly burdensome or expensive. If discovery is propounded in violation of these principles, the court is required to impose an appropriate sanction, usually monetary in nature, upon the party and/or the attorney who violates them, or both. These potential problems can be minimized by asking only cogent and relevant questions with obvious and focused purposes and by avoiding the trap of using reams of pattern or canned interrogatories of a general nature (sometimes called "boilerplate interrogatories").

8.062   Objectives and Purpose

The primary objectives of interrogatories are to identify people and entities that have information concerning the subject matter. Interrogatories also identify and locate documents or tangible evidence, discover and establish facts that are relevant to claims or defenses raised by the parties, identify contentions of fact, and narrow the issues for trial. Interrogatories are also used as tools to pierce the corporate veil, to establish *res ipsa loquitur,* to overcome language problems, and to provide a foundation for summary judgment. Each of these objectives will be explored in some detail.

8.0621 Identify People or Entities.

In order to prepare a comprehensive deposition plan, it is necessary to obtain personal and employment information about individuals (whether parties or nonparties), their relatives, experts, or principal officers and directors of corporate bodies. Identifying "people" also involves identifying legally fictitious or jurisdictional entities, such as partnerships, corporations, or associations. Exhibit 8-3 lists interrogatory topics that seek to meet this objective.

8.0622 Identify Documents and Objects.

In relatively simple cases, relevant documents may be very limited in nature. They may be easily characterized by the responding party through date, author, addressee, type of document, subject matter of the document, and/or file number. In other cases, it may be necessary to identify the size and character of the file, describe the filing system and method of identification of files, and describe the storage location for subsequent examination and/or production.

Interrogatories may also be used to request information about tangible things that may or will be used as evidence at trial. For example, in a products liability case, one or more parties may propound

EXHIBIT 8-3 Topics for Identification of People or Entities

Identities of Parties. Identity and physical description to include full name, date of birth, and Social Security number. Depending upon the circumstances of each case, interrogatories may ask about nicknames, maiden or adoptive names, aliases, professional names, pen names, citizenship status, naturalization dates, immediate family, and immigration sponsor. In any event, the thrust of these "identification" interrogatories should be used to gather necessary personal information about persons who are opposing parties.

Identities of Witnesses. It is essential to seek the identity of any witnesses known to the other party.

Note: If the matter is in federal court, and the federal district court in which the lawsuit is filed has not opted out of the requirement for initial disclosures required by Rule 26(a), FRCP, this interrogatory will not be necessary, because this information must be given to opposing parties under this rule. However, if the district court has opted out of the provisions of Rule 26(a), or the case is filed in a state court which does not require a similar disclosure, use the same language found in 26(a)(1)(A) to structure the question.

Official Identity of Fictitious Persons. If the defendant, or sometimes the plaintiff, is a business, a fictitious person, or a person doing business under a title not linked with his or her own name, interrogatories can be used to inquire into the identity of the organization, structure, officers, or managerial personnel of the business entity. Similarly, the authority under which the organization operates, such as articles of incorporation, partnership agreements, or the filing of the fictitious name with the appropriate regulatory agency are all suitable areas of inquiry. Distribution of stock; identity of agencies that regulate or license the business; identity of reports that must be filed with regulatory agencies; the identity of the agency or association that writes, adopts, and promulgates industry standards; and the actual standards that have been adopted by the industry are also proper areas of inquiry.

Identities of Experts. Ask opposing parties to identify experts who will be called to testify at trial, the expert's area of expertise, the facts upon which his or her opinions are based, what those expert opinions are, and ask for production of the expert's curriculum vitae. It may even be necessary to ask for a list of articles or publications authored by the expert and/or a list of cases in which the expert has given deposition and/or trial testimony. This latter information may be necessary to attack the expert's opinions and credibility. This can be done by checking the contents of the articles or publications authored by the expert to see whether they contradict his or her opinions in the current case, and to check the expert's testimony in previous cases to see whether, given the same or similar facts, his or her opinion was different enough in the previous case to erode or eliminate his or her usefulness to the opposing party.

Note: If the matter is in federal court, and the federal district court in which the lawsuit is filed has not opted out of the requirement for initial disclosures required by Rule 26(a), FRCP, this interrogatory will not be necessary, because this information must be given to opposing parties under this rule. However, if the district court has opted out of the provisions of Rule 26(a), or the case is filed in a state court which does not require a similar disclosure, use the same language found in 26(a)(2) to structure the question.

Addresses. Addresses, both residential and business, should be obtained through interrogatories. Normally, questions on current residence and business addresses present few problems; however, the same may not be true regarding prior residences and prior employment. Interrogatories require the responding party to consult records and give complete and thorough answers; at deposition, the party may not recall this information and decline to speculate or guess, thus yielding no information.

---

interrogatories asking for identification of the object by asking for a physical description of the object, as well as information about each and every person who has had custody of the object since the time of the incident at issue up to the present time. This will enable the requesting party to check the chain of custody of the object in order to determine who has had the opportunity to inspect and test the object subsequent to the incident. This, in turn, may lead to the addition of names to the deposition and/or overall discovery plan.

Remember that if your interrogatories are growing too large for the number limitation placed on you by either the federal or local rules, you should consider converting interrogatories that ask *about*

EXHIBIT 8-4   Interrogatory Topics for Identification of Documents or Objects

Documents.   When asking about the existence of documentary items, request each item be identified by date, author, addressee, type of document, subject matter of the document, and/or file number. Other identifying characteristics could include the size and character of the file, the filing system, method of identification of files, whether the documents exist in electronic format (computer disks, e-mail, databases, etc.), and storage location for subsequent examination and/or production. When document identification is requested, the identity of the current custodian of each category of documents also is necessary, and should include a request for the name, business position or title, business address, and business telephone number. Identification of the document custodian at the time of the event at issue, if different from the current custodian, should similarly be requested and should include all of the above information.

Existence of Tangible Evidence, Photographs, Videotapes, Maps, Sketches, and Models.   In certain circumstances, photographs, videotapes, maps, sketches, and/or models will be made specifically for use at the trial by one party or the other. Appropriate interrogatories will reveal whether such items exist, their current location, the types of such presentations, and the name, address, and qualifications of the person who prepared them. In addition, a description of the facts and/or assumptions upon which the maker of the item based his or her finished product is necessary in order to test whether the maker's understanding of the facts and/or the assumptions made were accurate or appropriate. If the maker of the item had a poor understanding of the facts of the incident or made erroneous or inaccurate assumptions in making the item, the discovery of that fact will assist your attorney in attacking the opposing party's ability to use of the item in discovery or at trial, and may even lead to the item's exclusion.

Existence of Physical Evidence.   Similarly, physical evidence may play a part in the case, and appropriate questions should be propounded to determine whether such physical evidence is held by any party or by his or her counsel. The propounding party is entitled to inquire into the nature of each item of evidence, the time and place the evidence was obtained or acquired, and the name, address, telephone number, and place of employment of the person who is custodian of the evidence at the current time. Follow-up requests for production for purposes of inspection and perhaps even destructive or nondestructive testing of the evidence may be essential in order to provide your own expert witness(es) with pertinent factual information upon which their opinions may be based.

---

documents or things to a request *for* the documents or things. If you really want to obtain or inspect or test the document or thing, perhaps a request for production is the proper discovery tool to use. Exhibit 8-4 lists interrogatory topics that seek to meet this objective.

8.0623 Establish Facts.   Many incident cases are tried on facts solely in the personal knowledge of witnesses. Some witnesses are parties; some are not. Because interrogatories can be served only on parties, they may be used to elicit all discoverable information within the parties' knowledge. Often the questions are designed to elicit identification of sources of facts beyond the personal knowledge of the parties. Those sources (usually witnesses, documents, and tangible things) can then be explored. Witnesses can be interviewed regarding their knowledge either by informal discovery or by deposition; documents and tangible things, if in the hands of nonparties, may be obtained through informal discovery means or by deposition in which the nonparty's knowledge of the document or thing may be explored. If they are in the hands of a party, they can be requested by a subsequent request for production.

A major benefit to using interrogatories is the fact that the answer of the responding party must be verified under oath and may be used at the trial if the testimony is later changed. This advantage minimizes the chance of loss of memory or a change in testimony by parties during the life of the lawsuit and reveals at least the sources of facts within the opposing party's knowledge as early in the lawsuit as possible, if not the factual information itself, depending on whether it is protected by a privilege. Even if the factual information itself is protected by a privilege, the information *about* the sources used by the opposing party to gather the information will be available to the requesting party. Exhibit 8-5 lists interrogatory topics which seek to meet this objective.

Educational Background.   It may be relevant to inquire into the educational background of the witness. Issues that might not have been apparent can be discovered, depending upon the level and type of education of the party.

Marital and Parental Status.   The party's marital and parental status may be significant, as well as the status of the marriage (common domicile, legal separation, pending interlocutory decree, reconciliation, and/or child custody). The number of children and the quality of the family's relationships should be explored.

Employment History.   Information about current and past employment, including names and addresses of employers, dates of employment or self-employment, hours worked in a typical week, job titles and descriptions of work performed, rate of pay, and monthly and/or annual income received, and reasons for termination of employment should be requested.

Military History.   If a party has a history of military service, a search can be made of the military record to discover whether any facts or circumstances in that history have a bearing on the litigation, even if only to attack the party's credibility.

History of Crimes or Citations.   Any criminal history of opposing parties should be explored. Sometimes criminal convictions have a direct bearing and effect on the litigation. Perjury is highly significant in any case. Violations involving alcohol or drugs and driving records could be significant.

History in Civil Litigation.   Ask about any past claims or lawsuits of any kind in which the party may have been involved.

Compliance with Regulatory Rules.   Compliance with, or citations for violations of, administrative rules, building codes, standards of health and hygiene, or environmental rules and regulations may be a proper area of inquiry, depending on the case and the identity or status of the opposing party.

Ownership Interest in Real Property.   Ownership interest, or leasehold interest in real or chattel property, may be highly relevant and pertinent to the case.

Insurance Coverage.   The types of insurance coverage for the matter, incident, or accident giving rise to the litigation, the identity of the carrier, and the limits that are applicable to the subject matter of the litigation are all basic areas of inquiry. Ask whether the insurer has raised any coverage defenses; whether the accident occurred in the course and scope of the defendant's employment; and whether any subrogation rights are claimed by an insurer.

Consumption of Alcohol or Drugs.   In accident cases, questions regarding the events prior to the accident are appropriate. Such questions should specify a particular time preceding the event and explore the frequency and quantity of consumption, the place and location where the alcohol or drugs (whether legal or illegal) were ingested, the identities of witnesses who were present during the consumption, the quantity, quality, dosage, and name or type of drug, medicine, or alcoholic beverage taken, whether any of these were by doctor's prescription, the physician who prescribed the drugs, and the pharmacy providing the medication.

The Accident Scene and Conditions.   Interrogatories requesting a description of the accident scene should include the date, time, and exact location of the accident, weather conditions, visibility, physical makeup of sidewalks and street surfaces, presence or absence of curbs, presence or absence of shrubbery, fences, street lights, holes, posts, traffic signals, warning signs, crosswalks, guards, or custodians, floor condition, presence of foreign substance/object, and efforts to clean up foreign substances/objects.

How the Accident Occurred.   Ask for a description of how the accident/incident occurred, including each element that contributed to the accident. Follow-up questions ask the responding party to identify any documents, reports, photographs, or other records of the accident, the conditions, and circumstances surrounding it.

Plaintiff's Damages and Lifestyle.   Ask about the injuries allegedly sustained by the plaintiff and damages being claimed as a consequence. Ask for bills, estimates, expert appraisals, financial records, hospital records, doctors' reports, medical bills, bills for miscellaneous out-of-pocket-costs, and indirect but consequential costs.

Knowledge of the Statements and Conversations with Others.   Ask whether opposing parties have *taken* a statement from, or talked with, any other party or nonparty witnesses concerning the lawsuit. Ask whether they have *given* any statement to, or talked with, other persons about the lawsuit. Ask to identify the person, the date, time, and place of the conversation, and the substance of the conversation. Ask for the location of any written statement or other record of the dialogue, the identity of the custodian, and how it can be obtained.

8.0624 Identify Contentions.   Properly timed and phrased interrogatories require the adverse party to state the contentions on which he or she relies in advancing his or her claims, or defenses, damages, or refutation of damages. From these responses, the merits of the adverse party's position may be deduced or weaknesses identified. Contention interrogatories usually are followed by questions requesting identification of the specific facts upon which the party's contentions are based.

The contentions may deal with whether the issue is one of law or fact. If it is a factual issue, the contentions will seek evidentiary facts on which the party relies, the source of the evidentiary facts, whether corroborated by documentary or physical evidence, and so forth. If the contention is not based on evidentiary facts, the attorney may then prepare to contest the issue based perhaps on the absence of facts or on the law, or both, and may attempt to have the matter decided by motion, that is, to have the matter either established or dismissed prior to trial. This eliminates the necessity of the court's having to adjudicate the issue later on, either by motion or at trial on the merits.

When drafting a response to such interrogatories, the paralegal must know the contents of previously filed answers to the complaint and answers to prior written discovery, as well as prior deposition testimony. Familiarity with these documents will help prevent the providing of an answer that was already admitted in the previously filed answer to the complaint or in deposition testimony or prior answers to interrogatories.

8.0625 Narrow the Issues for Trial.   Timely interrogatories will force the exposure of information from the opposing party under oath and thereby identify all issues. Some of these issues may be disposed of before trial, and some may be disputed matters in court.

8.0626 Pierce the Corporate Veil.   The plaintiff suing a corporation can, through interrogatories, gather information that can be used to "pierce the corporate veil" as well as to identify that particular person, file, or policy most important to the establishment of the essential facts of the client's case. The corporation must provide all the information and facts available to it (and to its counsel and any other entity over which it has control) in response to any given question. Thus, the interrogatory is a highly effective tool for the individual plaintiff against an economically superior opposing party.

The careful, methodical creation of appropriate interrogatories and analysis of the responses can provide a factual foundation for productive depositions and requests for production of documents by establishing such information as organization, chain of command, policies, practices, standards of the industry, applicable regulations, file systems, and other information concerning the corporation(s) that are the object of the effort to "pierce the corporate veil."

8.0627 Res Ipsa Loquitur.   If a diligent discovery effort has been conducted to identify the cause of an accident, but the discovery has not elicited satisfactory or sufficient explanation of the event from the parties or witnesses, and if independent investigation and expert witnesses have developed theories rather than facts, yet the accident could not have occurred if everything and everyone operated reasonably and properly, the attorney may have the data to support a plea of *res ipsa loquitur,* a Latin phrase meaning "the thing speaks for itself." This legal doctrine holds that there is a rebuttable presumption or inference that the defendant was negligent, which arises when proof is given that: (1) the instrumentality causing injury was in defendant's exclusive control and (2) the accident was one which ordinarily does not happen in the absence of negligence. If proof of these two elements can be identified in interrogatories or answers or other discovery responses, there is no need for the plaintiff to provide further explanation of the accident and the circumstances surrounding it; the burden shifts to the defendant to disprove the elements of the *res ipsa loquitur* doctrine.

8.0628 Overcome Language Problems. Written interrogatories are an excellent means of surmounting communication obstacles of the adverse party. It matters little whether the obstacle is illiteracy or lack of English facility (sometimes a deadly problem in depositions), blindness, deafness, senility, incapacity due to illness, injury, or the side effects of medication. The written interrogatory must be answered by the party through whatever assistance is necessary. The opposing counsel has the burden of obtaining responsive answers from the client, the client's agents, or from the file and must submit the answers in a timely fashion. The questions and answers are in English, verified and under oath or, if in a foreign language, accompanied by an English translation.

8.0629 Foundation for Summary Judgment. The correct and timely use of interrogatories often will elicit sufficient information so that, because they are given under oath, they can be used by the lawyer in support of a motion for summary judgment when that action is appropriate. Cogent, pointed, and extensive interrogatories are a legitimate and effective means of exposing a party who files an exaggerated or specious lawsuit or asserts improper, unfounded, or frivolous defenses. The objective here is to force quick and timely resolution of the matter without extensive legal proceedings and their attendant cost.

8.063 Drafting Interrogatories

Drafting interrogatories is a duty frequently assigned to paralegals. To be done effectively, the paralegal should be familiar with the facts, the pleadings (complaint, answer, and reply), and the elements of the causes of action involved. The type of case will often dictate whether the paralegal must draft all new interrogatories or whether "form" or pattern interrogatories may be used to find questions that have worked well in the past. Incident or accident types lend themselves to certain patterns of questioning. Contract disputes generate another set of typical questions. Product liability and antitrust cases often require extensive questions with different thrusts in several sets of interrogatories.

Previous sets of interrogatories used within the law firm on similar cases may be a great asset in learning certain preferences, information categories, and phrasings from past. Commercially published "form books" containing pattern interrogatories are very helpful to the paralegal. Neither should these pattern or "form" interrogatories serve as the sole source of information for the creation of questions. The use of these form interrogatories may be helpful in saving time, but they must be edited to conform to the needs of the individual case. Additional specific questions are also necessary.

A paralegal should not just use form interrogatories, insert the proper captions and certificates of service, and mail them out to the opposing party. The danger of this practice is that a number of the questions may be inappropriate, and the opposing party may object to the entire set as inappropriate, unintelligible, irrelevant, and unjustly burdensome. An example might be a car-pedestrian accident where the questions sent to the plaintiff (pedestrian) seek data about "the other car" or "plaintiff's automobile's speed at the time of the collision," "its mechanical condition," or "its maintenance record."

Early in the case, it is important to identify people, locations, sources of information, documents, and things. By tapping into the opposing party's bank of information in these areas, the propounding attorney will then have a more complete picture of the people, locations, sources of information, documents, and things, so as to be able to prepare a more complete discovery plan. It is not so important at this stage to seek the contentions of the opposing party.

Interrogatories submitted to the opposing party late in the case can concentrate on contentions and on the facts on which they are based. Questions regarding identities (late in the case) may be used to check on whatever informal discovery the opposing party may have conducted since the case began, identify expert witnesses, or focus on the discovery of significant documents that have been revealed during discovery.

8.0631 The Introductory Paragraph.

Every set of interrogatories has an introductory paragraph in which the propounding party should state that the responding party is directed to answer the questions that follow. In multiple party cases, this introductory paragraph may be directed to each opposing party separately, or to the parties jointly, with instructions that each must answer separately, in writing, under oath, and within the time limitation provided by law. This paragraph usually contains reference to the specific rule of procedure or code that governs interrogatories in the jurisdiction.

8.0632 Definition of Terms.

Following the introduction may be a definition of terms used in the interrogatories. The definitions will include the identities of individuals or corporations, fictitious names, and so forth, which may be abbreviated or reduced to a one-word representation or acronym.

For instance, if the suit happens to be against the U.S. Bureau of Reclamation of the Department of the Interior, a definition might state that the acronym "USBR," when used within those interrogatories, refers to the U.S. Bureau of Reclamation, Department of the Interior. Use of that same definition throughout the interrogatories eliminates ambiguity, reduces the length of the interrogatories, and eliminates unnecessary words. Similarly, if the defendant in the case is the (fictitious) firm, the National Textile Corporation of the North American Continent, a single-word identification such as "National" or an acronym such as "NTCNAC" may be used in the definition and then throughout the interrogatories to refer to that firm. Words that will be used repetitively in the set of interrogatories may also be defined at this time for accuracy, clarity, and understanding. For example, the word "documents" may be defined as "all writings, records, letters, memoranda, notes (whether handwritten or typed), studies, reports, books or volumes (bound or unbound), photographs, tape recordings, belt recordings, disc recordings, computerized or other electronic recordings, or other forms of recording, however produced or reproduced, whether a draft or final version, whether signed or unsigned, whether approved, sent, received, redrafted, executed, erased, or otherwise defaced or mutilated, from wherever obtained, which are in your possession, custody, or control."

The term "identify" may be used to shorten and make interrogatories clearer by defining it as the following: "'Identify' when requested in relation to a natural person in these interrogatories requires the full name, age, home address, home telephone number, business or occupational title, place of employment, address of employer, business telephone number, date of birth, and Social Security number as minimum elements when available. 'Identify' when referring to documents requires the following minimum information to be provided: date, type of document, author, addressee, major topic or title of the document, the number of pages comprising the document, and a description of any attachments or exhibits incorporated by reference therein." Another example of providing a useful definition is establishing what is meant by *accident.* "'Accident' when used herein refers to that incident which occurred on the 10th day of June, 2006, in which two vehicles collided at the intersection of "A" Street and "B" Avenue in the town of Clearview, Arkansas, and is the focus of this lawsuit, unless otherwise specified."

Definitions of this general type allow the subsequent questions to be phrased with a minimum of words and a maximum of meaning. Proper use of such definitions requires productive answers. In very complex or technical litigation, there is a tendency to expand the definition of terms to such an extent that they become unwieldy and difficult to remember by any of the parties. When this occurs, the definition of terms has lost its purpose and may create a situation where the answering party may respond with an objection on grounds that the definitions, and thus the interrogatories themselves, are burdensome, oppressive, and confusing and thus cannot be properly and accurately responded to by the objecting party.

8.0633 Numbering System.

At the outset of drafting the interrogatories, it is important to establish the numbering system to be used and then to follow it consistently. Whether each question will receive a separate Arabic number, or whether a decimalized system (a parent question with pointed numbers for each subsection), or an Arabic number with alphabetic subparagraphs is to be employed is immaterial, so long as the decision is made early in the process and strictly followed. In many federal courts, it is necessary to number all questions sequentially in order, even when moving from one set of interrogatories to another, for the convenience of the parties and the court. This is a technique that may also be required in some state courts and is a great convenience to the paralegal. If it is not required but permitted, use of the sequential numbers through several sets of interrogatories is a great help later on in collating answers and evaluating them in light of issues of fact and allegations.

8.0634 Question Construction.

8.06341 Format.   While "interrogatories" seems synonymous with "questions," in practice it is not unusual to find those that begin with terms such as "Please state.." The better and more professional practice for the paralegal is to construct interrogatories in question format to avoid the possibility of creating a statement that does not require a response. Here is an example:

> "If you will do so without a motion to produce, attach copies of the above documents to the set of interrogatories."

This statement requires no answer; it requires no attachment of interrogatories and is a useless, wasted statement. The better practice is to include this request as a subpart to a series of questions regarding documents, such as:

> "3(a). Describe all the documents prepared by George Jones in response to requests by his supervisors for a justification of the research and development expenditures on the XYZ Widget during the time period January 1, 2000 through January 1, 2007.
> 3(b). Will you attach copies of the documents identified in response to 3(a) above without the necessity of a request for production or motion to produce?
> 3(c). If your answer to 3(b) above is 'yes,' please attach such copies to your answers."

Using this technique, the answering party must either provide a listing identifying all the responsive documents or attach copies of the documents to the interrogatories; in either case, the party must respond.

Under the *Federal Rules of Civil Procedure,* and in many state and local jurisdictions, Rule 33 allows the answering party to produce business records when the answer to an interrogatory may be derived or ascertained from those records. For that reason, it is usually not necessary or effective to add a section to the "Definitions" which provides an option to attach the document or to require the responding party to identify the document, the storage location, and the custodian with sufficient specificity to allow serving an appropriate request for production. In addition to being unnecessary and redundant, there is a risk that the "definition" will provide the opposing party with room for "inadvertent omission" or an objection to "complex, confusing, and oppressive instructions" if it is not clear and specific and within the bounds of that which is stated in the rules as allowable.

8.06342 Relevant Time Span.   The time span to be covered in each interrogatory must be relevant to the matter being litigated. No matter whether the case arises out of an accident, business transaction, or alleged antitrust activity, many of the records, conduct, and actions of the party prior to the event giving rise to the litigation are important. Seeking information preceding the event that gave rise to the action may also be relevant.

It is important that the inquiry into past events, documents, and conduct be sufficiently comprehensive to discover anything that is relevant or is capable of producing leads to admissible evidence in the case. It is also important to balance that need with the practical reality that a shorter period of time will involve a smaller volume of material and will be less likely to give rise to objections based on the burdensome nature of the interrogatory. A short, relevant period may encourage the opposing party to respond to the request rather than to stonewall, object, or provide partial or incomplete answers. This type of decision can be made only by the attorney. A careful analysis should be made. The paralegal should be prepared to recommend a time period that would encompass the various kinds of material sought. Some records have a reasonable life of only one year and some for three years. Some financial data must be preserved for seven years, and some corporate data may be permanent and/or perpetual (life of the corporation plus a statutory period).

8.06343 Tense in Questions.

Lawsuits concern matters in the past, and the phrasing of interrogatories in the proper tense is extremely important. If the current practice of a party is sought, the question must ask: "What is the practice…?" If past practice is important, then the question must ask: "What was the practice of the company…?" Consider only the pertinent time. The use of wrong verb tenses can result in a truthful but useless answer and wastes time.

8.06344 Simplicity.

Keep the question simple. Use the definition of terms described previously and restrict the use of adjectives and adverbs. For instance, if the case involved an excavation by the defendant in which a pipeline was struck and damaged, there may be a tendency to ask a question such as the following:

> "Did an employee of the defendant during excavation on June 12, 2007, strike, damage, and sever a five-inch cast-iron water pipeline three and one-half feet below the surface of Jackson Street, Oklahoma City, Oklahoma?"

The question is capable of easily being answered by the defendant with a "No." It is possible the defendant did not know whether it was a "cast-iron pipe;" it is possible he did not know he had "struck, damaged, and severed" the pipeline; and it is possible he did not know how deep it was. It is far better to request the information in several questions:

> "1. Did an employee of the defendant strike a buried pipeline on June 12, 2007?
>
> 2. How deep was the pipe buried at the point of contact?
>
> 3. Where did the defendant's employee report the contact to have occurred? (Please provide street, location, distance laterally from the south side of the road, distance from the nearest intersecting street, or alternatively, provide photographs and sketches that may have been made regarding this event.)"

Trying to write one clear but complex question, rather than a related pattern of simple, specific, clearly focused questions is dangerous. It may also be unproductive, a waste of time, and may require additional questions in order to clarify the exact extent of the defendant's knowledge.

8.06345 Belief Questions.

Such questions as "Why did he do…?" or "Why did he say…?" are particularly unproductive, especially in the early stages of the case. Almost every such question will produce answers such as "He believed he had a right to…" and "He said it because he believed it to be true." Depositions are usually far more productive than interrogatories for this type of question.

After drafting a question or a series of questions test them by answering them as unresponsively as possible. If the propounding party can answer the question unresponsively, a responding party should have no difficulty in providing the same unresponsive answers.

8.06346 Spelling.   Good spelling is essential in writing interrogatories. Misspelling the name of the party or of any witness, the street, town, or any other identifiable feature, document, or matter of inquiry will result in an answer that negates the value of the question. The parties may enter into a stipulation to correct the spelling, if necessary. Professionals should be able to draft and proof documents.

8.0635 Contention Interrogatories.

Among the types of questions that may be asked in interrogatories, usually late in the case and shortly before trial, are interrogatories in which the attorney asks the opposing party for an explanation of his or her legal and factual contentions. These may be phrased in very simple terms, such as in Exhibit 8-6.

Other alternatives are to pose a pattern of interrogatories based on a specific factual allegation which require the opposing party to agree with the truth of the statement, to specifically deny the truth and expansively detail the grounds for the denial, or to admit the denial is not based on factual or evidentiary grounds. The format might appear as shown in Exhibit 8-7.

EXHIBIT 8-6   Sample Contention Interrogatory

9. Do you contend that Plaintiff did not violate the right-of-way of the Defendant in the accident that is the focus of this lawsuit?

  A. If no, please state:

    1. Each fact on which you base your contention.

    2. The identity of each person who has supplied you with information or testimony on which you base your contention. Identification requires names, addresses, telephone numbers, and relationships to plaintiff, at a minimum.

    3. The location and description of any documents, objects, or other evidentiary facts or materials that you believe support your contention.

    4. The name, address, telephone number, and name of employer of the custodian of any documents, objects, or other evidentiary facts or materials identified in (3) above.

EXHIBIT 8-7   Sample Pattern Contention Interrogatories

13. Do you contend that the following statement, or any portion thereof, is not true?
    (Here set out the statement.)

14. If your answer to No.__ is in the affirmative, state which portion thereof you contend is not true.

15. Is your contention, described in No. __ above, based upon or supported by any facts known to you that are contrary to or inconsistent with the claimed truth thereof?

16. If your answer to No.__ is affirmative, state:

    a. The evidentiary facts that support or tend to support your contention.

    b. The identity of each person who has supplied you with information or testimony on which you base your contention. Identification requires names, addresses, telephone numbers, and relationships to plaintiff, at a minimum.

    c. The location and description of any documents, objects, or other evidentiary facts or materials that you believe support your contention.

    d. The name, address, telephone number, and name of employer of the custodian of any documents, objects, or other evidentiary facts or materials identified in (3) above.

17. If your answer to No. __ is negative, state whether you have conducted any investigation or inquiry as to the truth or falsity of said statement.

18. If your answer to No.__ is negative, state with particularity all bases, reasons, and grounds for your non-factual contention contrary to, or inconsistent with, the claimed truth thereof.

With the pattern established, statements can be inserted to force the opposing party into admitting their truth, or alternatively, pinpointing areas of disagreement and the factual foundation on which he or she relies. Examples of the type of statement that can be inserted into these pattern contention interrogatories are: "Defendant was driving his own automobile in the proper traffic lane, at a lawful rate of speed immediately preceding the collision with plaintiff's car" or "There are no independent witnesses who have expressed the belief that plaintiff violated defendant's right-of-way."

Such statements, if handled correctly, can dispose of many issues that otherwise would be tried in court. If the statements are contested, the patterned subparts and subsequent questions elicit an identification of the areas of disagreement, factual bases for the opinion, witnesses, disclose whether an investigation was conducted, and generally determine the sources of the contentions. This in turn assists the attorney in making further discovery plans, if there is still time to accomplish discovery prior to trial. At the very least, the attorney is made aware of the sources of the information on which the contentions are based and is better able to prepare to controvert or disprove the contentions at trial.

The execution of a few critical statements in contention interrogatories, which must be answered under oath, may eliminate a substantial number of issues from the trial, particularly if the submission of the interrogatories and the answers are very close to the trial. They are far more beneficial than requests for admissions, since they provide the opportunity for follow-up questions that explain a denial of the base question.

If contention interrogatories are used early in the case, the attorney is attempting to determine a better foundation for vague or uncertain allegations and forcing the opposing counsel to state the issues with specificity. It is difficult to elicit much data supporting the opposing party's contentions until the discovery process has matured. Often contention interrogatories used early in the history of the case elicit answers indicating that discovery and investigation are not complete, and thus the question cannot yet be answered by the responding party.

8.064 Answering Interrogatories

The party responding to properly served interrogatories has a duty to answer each question in writing, separately, fully, responsively, and under oath; the only limitation is that the information requested must be relevant to the subject matter of the action and reasonably calculated to lead to the discovery of admissible evidence. The exceptions are where the information is privileged because it is protected by the attorney/client privilege, or the work product of the attorney, or is material prepared in anticipation of litigation, or when answering would be an oppressive burden on the responding party. Failure to answer a properly phrased, relevant interrogatory within the time allowed may result in an order to compel answers. Worse than that, the failure to respond on time may waive the attorney's right to object to answering any interrogatory for which a proper objection could have been made if responses had been served within the deadline for answering.

Providing the information necessary to answer interrogatories, particularly personal information, is usually the duty of the client, with the help of the paralegal, whose primary task is to assemble the factual data and provide draft answers from which the final responses are created.

"Responding" to interrogatories is the responsibility of the client's attorney. "Responding to" and "answering" interrogatories are not necessarily the same. "Answering" interrogatories includes expository answers, fully complete as to all relevant, known data; such answers may also include "volunteered" information that is beyond the scope of the specific question asked or may be public information equally available to both sides. Such an answer may include the attachment of documents responsive to the question in lieu of a detailed, written response. On the other hand, a "response" to an interrogatory may consist of a complete refusal to answer stated in the form of an objection or consist of an answer to the nonobjectionable portion of an interrogatory combined with an objection. This imposes a special responsibility on the paralegal to ensure that all sources of information readily available to the client or the attorney are carefully searched and that properly inclusive responsive answers are drafted for the consideration and editing of the attorney. It requires a careful analysis and full understanding of the interrogatories received and the issues in the case.

For instance, a question may seek a listing of "any and all evidence in your possession." This is not a well-crafted request. The word "evidence" is one with a specific legal meaning. Whether or not something qualifies as evidence is usually determined by a judge unless the parties stipulate to that fact. Therefore, the responding attorney could completely object to answering that interrogatory on the grounds that only a court may rule whether items or exhibits qualify as "evidence" or could object in part and answer in part: "We object to that portion which calls for a conclusion that all items in the possession of the party qualify as evidence; notwithstanding that objection, the party does possess the following items which may be offered as evidence at the trial of this case." The latter response is better practice, for it is in keeping with the spirit of the federal rules on discovery.

The paralegal is responsible for making certain the responses to interrogatories are prepared and served within the established deadline. Making certain that the due date of the interrogatory answers, with appropriate warning dates, is recorded in the firm's or attorney's calendaring system is the best way of ensuring that the interrogatories are answered on time.

8.0641 Time to Answer.
Every jurisdiction, whether federal or state, provides a specific period of time within which answers and responses to the interrogatories must be served. Any response that asserts an objection must be made within the applicable time period for answering. Unstated or untimely grounds for objection may be considered waived.

If additional time is needed to answer interrogatories, an informal request to the propounding party for an extension may be made by telephone or by letter; in most cases, one will be granted. There is no particular rule on the period of time to be granted as an extension. This is negotiated between the lawyers or their representatives under the provisions of Rule 29. Precision in language is important when requesting extensions. An agreement that allows additional time to *answer* interrogatories, but does not include additional time to *respond* may have the effect of responding party waiving the right to object. The better practice is for the responding party to include language which "extends the time to answer and/or otherwise respond to the interrogatories."

When either a full or a limited extension of time to answer or respond is given, that agreement should be confirmed in writing with the other party the same day it is granted. It is not good practice to give or receive verbal extensions of time to answer or respond to interrogatories without written confirmation. Often the attorneys for both parties will send letters confirming the terms of the agreement. When the other attorney's letter arrives in the office, the paralegal or the lawyer should check it to make certain the terms of the agreement are accurately recorded in the letter. This alleviates future confusion and misunderstandings. If the opposing party will not grant an informal extension of time and the attorney believes he or she has sufficient grounds to do so, a formal motion for extension of time may be filed. Often the requesting party will not contest this formal motion, even though he or she would not grant an informal extension of time. But the responding party should be able to provide specific and valid reasons for the requested extension of time.

8.0642 Initial Review.
The interrogatories should first be read immediately on receipt, not analytically or argumentatively but from beginning to end, as a novel would be read. This allows an appreciation of the flow and scope of the interrogatories and suggests the approach of the opposing party and the overall thrust of the set of questions: Does the opponent seek facts or identities? Does

it seek contentions of the responding party? Are the questions specific or generalized and broadly in-clusive? Does the requesting party aim at clarifying proximate cause or the affirmative defenses being asserted by the defendant?

Following the initial reading, a careful question-by-question reading of the set should be per-formed by the paralegal independent of the attorney. Some questions are of a straight factual nature, while other questions appear to be mixed questions of fact and law, particularly susceptible to interpre-tation by the attorney; others ask for pure legal interpretation. The paralegal should make notes during the analysis to include the probable responding responsibility as "paralegal," "attorney," or "client," or any combination thereof.

8.0643 Attorney and Paralegal Conference.   The third reading occurs during a planning meeting that the paralegal should schedule with the attorney to formalize the answering procedure. The attorney probably will have read the interrogatories (or may read them during the course of the meet-ing), and decisions then can be made about how to proceed in the case. The responding responsibilities noted by the paralegal are confirmed or modified, and decisions on how to handle the "client" answers can be made, that is, whether to call the client to the office, mail a set of the questions with instructions to return the answers by mail, mail a set of questions and then record the client's answers in a telephone conference, or coordinate with the client other means of obtaining the information within the client's knowledge and control necessary to prepare proper responses.

When the potential answer depends partially on a legal interpretation by the attorney, the parale-gal should assemble, in draft form, the factual data called for by the question. The paralegal should then schedule a meeting with the attorney to discuss how best to respond to the interrogatory.

8.0644 Source of the Answer, Responsibility, and Control.   Following the attorney's and paralegal's review of the interrogatories, the paralegal should decide on the best source(s) of the information from which to obtain answers to the questions the attorney delegated to the paralegal to answer. If the information is in the case file, the paralegal can simply extract it, draft the answers, and submit them for approval, editing, or rejection by the attorney.

If the client is a corporation, the paralegal can establish a contact person in the corporation to coordinate the distribution of the interrogatories (or portions) to appropriate personnel within the cor-poration and to establish deadlines well in advance of the answer date for the return of appropriate information. It is essential for the paralegal to have a follow-up procedure for contacting the contact person prior to the established deadline, so that the information gathered by the client will be received on time. This is particularly important when the client decides that objections to certain interrogatories should be made instead of answering them. The attorney will not be in a position to agree or disagree with this conclusion until the client's information is received and reviewed.

When questions will be answered using information and material from a variety of sources, it sometimes is helpful to photocopy the entire set of interrogatories and supply each source with those questions he or she is being asked to answer. A long or complex series of pattern interrogatories (one ba-sic question followed by related subsections based on alternative anticipated answers) can be effectively controlled by photocopying the full set, then cutting and pasting each question onto paper punched for three-ring binders. As the source's material is received, it can be filed behind the question until it is time to draft answers. This system is helpful for the process of engrossing answers, if the material is carefully prepared and organized.

Various alternatives exist on organizing interrogatories and responses. One method is to make an extra copy of the interrogatories and mount them on the left-hand side of a file folder and then collect and file the data and draft answers on the right. Another method is to place the interrogatories (without cutting and pasting) in a three-ring binder and then collect and file behind separate, labeled divider tabs the information and draft answers corresponding to each question. Creating online folders and files or establishing a standard protocol for naming saved documents (i.e., "plaintiff's responses to 1st set of def's. interrogatories") is also recommended. These organizational methods assist everyone in keeping track of the collection of the information by providing one place where that material can be stored until it is time to begin preparing the draft and, ultimately, the final answers and responses.

8.0645 Format and Form of Answers.

As mentioned in Section 8.063, Drafting Interrogatories, the *Federal Rules of Civil Procedure* require the question and the answer to be engrossed in the final version of the answers, which means that each interrogatory appears first, followed immediately by the answer to that interrogatory. This practice is very helpful to all parties and to the courts and jury in the conduct of a case, whether that is a court rule or not. Many state courts have adopted the same or similar rules.

With the advent of scanners into the legal world, this procedure has become easier to accomplish. Each set of interrogatories is scanned into a computer and converted into the appropriate word processing program, and answers can then be inserted after each interrogatory. When a scanner is not available, the alternatives are to have the questions retyped, or to cut-and-paste the interrogatories, one to a page, to provide sufficient space for the answers, or to simply use addendum pages onto which the "overflow" of the longer answers can be typed.

The attachment of exhibits to answers to interrogatories can be a very useful and inexpensive way of providing (and receiving) relevant information. For instance, when an interrogatory asks you to explain the terms and conditions of the warranty on the product in question, you can attach a copy of the actual warranty and reference in your answer to see the attached document.

8.0646 Content of an Answer.

The *Federal Rules of Civil Procedure* places the responsibility on the responding party to provide full answers to the extent the interrogatories are not objectionable. If one question is objectionable on the grounds that it is too burdensome, it does not relieve the responding party of answering a similar question on a related topic or issue that asks for smaller amounts of information. Also, the fact that the responding party may need additional time to respond to some questions (or portions of some questions) does not justify a delay in responding to those questions (or portions of questions) that can be answered within the applicable time period.

Once a party decides to answer an interrogatory, the answer should be clear, concise, and directly responsive to the question. It should be based on information that the responding party has at hand. It is not necessary to provide information that is unavailable to the client or over which neither the client nor the attorney has possession, custody, or control. When answering an interrogatory based on lack of knowledge, the attorney, the paralegal, and the client must be sure there is no access or control question that can be raised by the requesting party in a motion to compel.

A corporate client is very susceptible to a strict interpretation of the duty to answer in this situation because all information available to any employee of the corporation is considered equally available to the corporate entity and its counsel. If a court finds that the search made by the corporation was insufficient and the corporation had control of, or access to, the information through a subsidiary, branch, or other related entity, it may uphold the motion to compel and apply sanctions which may not only be monetary, but may also result in answers being stricken or matters being deemed admitted. Therefore, clients must be warned that a thorough search of all potential sources known to, or in the control of, the corporation must be made in gathering information with which to answer interrogatories. Additionally, lengthy answers that evade the question should be avoided since they will also often result in the filing of a motion to compel by the propounding party and may also result in sanctions against the answering party if successful. These activities create mistrust between the parties, waste time and money, and do nothing to favorably advance the client's position.

The final draft of the answers must be proofread for form as well as content. Each answer should be checked to make sure it properly answers or responds to the question asked. All typographical errors should be corrected and the overall answers checked for compliance with form requirements. In addition, the paralegal should check to make certain that any documents to be attached to the answers are copied and properly labeled to correspond to the number of the interrogatory to which they respond. All the answers should then be checked for internal and external consistency one last time.

8.0647 Grounds for Objection.

Prior to objecting to an interrogatory, the paralegal should be familiar with the *Federal Rules of Evidence* and which objections are allowable. If the paralegal finds the interrogatory extremely complicated, difficult to understand, or that it requires excessive amounts of effort, research, assembly, collation, and reporting of information to enable the attorney to properly and fully answer the interrogatories, objection to those particular interrogatories (or the entire set, if appropriate) should be considered. In this situation, the grounds for objection are essentially those of injustice. For instance, it is immaterial that the information requested may require hearsay, since interrogatories have a much broader range than admissible evidence at trial. The purpose of discovery in general and interrogatories in particular is to learn about evidence that is admissible at trial or that may lead to the discovery of admissible evidence, not necessarily to provide the evidence itself, although any answer given may be used against the respondent. If this type of objection is raised, it must be couched in phrases the court will honor, and those always must include a showing of some form of injustice to the responding party.

The grounds for objecting on the basis of privilege or protection should also be stated specifically. Federal Rule 26(b)(5) requires a responding party to notify all other parties if it is withholding materials that are otherwise discoverable when the grounds for objection relate to any type of privilege or protection, including attorney work product and materials prepared in anticipation of litigation. Withholding such materials without notice violates Rule 26(b)(5). Such action could be the subject of a motion for sanctions under Rule 37(b)(2), and the privilege could be deemed waived.

This rule also requires the responding party to provide enough information about the withheld materials to enable the other parties to evaluate the validity of the privilege or protection that is claimed. The other parties may believe that the privilege or protection invoked by the responding party is not valid and may challenge the claim by motion to compel, in which case it is the court's duty to decide whether the privilege or protection applies to those materials. The type of information that should be provided by the party invoking the privilege concerns such things as general subject matter of the materials, applicable time periods, identity of persons who prepared, read, or received it, and so forth. If the materials being withheld are voluminous, the better practice might be to describe the documents by category instead of the more specific information.

The attorney is the authority on objections and whether to assert them. The paralegal may find at the conclusion of the meeting, in which the decision has been made to object, that the attorney will say: "Give me the draft answers and objections by tomorrow at ten, please, so they can be typed and served by four." Because paralegal s often work on such short deadlines, familiarity with some of the language of objections can save substantial time and reduce the necessity for rewriting.

8.06471 Continuing Answers.

For interrogatories that require "continuing answers," the objection may say: "Plaintiff objects to this entire set of interrogatories on the grounds that the request to treat these interrogatories as a continuing obligation is not required under *Federal Rules of Civil Procedure*

26(e) or 33 and would constitute an unjust, oppressive burden." While the *Federal Rules of Civil Procedure* provide for certain circumstances when discovery answers and responses must be supplemented, there is no requirement that discovery responses be treated as "continuing." A party that seeks to obtain "continuing interrogatories" must petition the court specifically to be given permission to place such a burden upon the responding party and must show good cause why it should be allowed to do so.

8.06472 *Confusing Instructions.*

If the propounding party includes instructions that are confusing or which contain confusing subinstructions, this may constitute a basis for objection by the responding party that may be phrased this way: "Defendant objects to the form of the instructions controlling these interrogatories on the grounds that the instructions are so complex and contain so many subinstructions and are so detailed that they require the respondent to spend unnecessary, extra, and unjustified time and effort to ascertain the impact of these instructions on succeeding interrogatories, and the instructions are therefore unjustly burdensome and oppressive."

This should serve as a warning that if instructions are going to be included in interrogatories, whether simple or complex, they should be relatively few and clearly and reasonably phrased. If not, the answering party will have grounds for objection on the basis that it will have a difficult time in either obtaining an answer or expressing its position in a motion to compel.

8.06473 *Public Records.*

Public records and documents are often sought by the propounding party and resisted by the responding party. The mere fact that the documents are a public record, equally available to both sides, is not necessarily a legitimate objection. However, if the objection is phrased in the proper way, the objection is more likely to be upheld. Here is an example: "Plaintiff objects on the grounds that the requested information is a matter of public record contained in public documents which are not in plaintiff's possession or control and that this information is equally available to Defendant, such that requiring Plaintiff to locate, copy, and furnish such information would be unreasonable, unjust, burdensome and oppressive."

8.06474 *Irrelevancy.*

Some interrogatories go far afield and may intrude on areas not relevant to the issues raised by the claims and defenses in the lawsuit. In such a case, an objection may stand on the ground of irrelevance, but the objection must be combined with a statement that the question "is not reasonably calculated to lead to the discovery of admissible evidence." The burden then shifts to the propounding party to file a motion to compel and show the relevance of the requested information to the subject matter of the lawsuit, the rationale behind the question, and in what manner the information sought would lead to the discovery of admissible evidence.

8.06475 *Uncertainty and Ambiguity.*

If an interrogatory is written in a vague and ambiguous manner, to the extent that the attorney and paralegal must impute meaning to the request, there is a basis for an objection on those grounds. This objection may be phrased in this fashion: "Interrogatory No. 2 and particularly the phrase 'riding lawn mowers like the one involved in the accident sued on' is so ambiguous, uncertain, and unintelligible that defendant cannot frame a meaningful reply and therefore objects to the form of the question." Usually, the propounding party will rephrase the question in a more intelligible fashion and serve it again. Alternatively, the responding party could object in part as stated above and answer in part by imputing to the interrogatory the meaning most favorable to the client's case and then provide an answer consistent with that view. This places the propounding party on a double hook. It is difficult to argue in a motion to compel hearing that you are entitled to the information that is sought by a poorly worded, vague, or ambiguous question when a free and willing offer of some information has been given by the responding party.

8.06476 Burdensome and Oppressive Questions.   Sometimes interrogatories impose severe burdens on the responding party to obtain the information upon which to base answers or responses. Lack of time, money, available employees, and the necessity of travel are some of the reasons why such interrogatories may be burdensome or oppressive. In such a situation, the attorney will consider objecting to the interrogatories on those grounds.

Usually, the paralegal is the person with the best command of the facts of the case and the sources of information that interrogatories of this nature will require. If it is anticipated that the search for the information required by interrogatories will be—or may become—"burdensome and oppressive," the paralegal must assemble factual data on the nature and extent of the burden to assist the attorney in deciding whether to object to the interrogatory or to assemble all or a portion of the information for the answers. The foundation for such an objection will require calculation of the amount of time and the overall expense, including any necessary travel, cost of use of employees, or of hiring additional employees to perform the research, copying costs, and other such expenses. The paralegal should confer with the client to ensure that all expense and time-related factors are included in the calculations and that the calculations are as accurate as possible.

8.0648 Additional, Supplemental, or Correcting Answers.

Frequently, not all the information necessary to properly and fully answer or respond to interrogatories is available within the applicable time limit. In such cases, it is appropriate to say in the response that "supplemental information will be provided," or "will be supplied," or "documents will be supplied in a timely manner that respond to this interrogatory," or to use similar phrasing indicating that the information is not being provided, that no objection to the interrogatory is raised, and that it will be given to the requesting party when it is available to the responding party. When such commitments are made, it is important to record the promise and to follow up on fulfilling it.

When it is learned that information previously supplied in an interrogatory answer is incorrect, an amended answer correcting that information should be provided in order to clarify the record. It is extremely difficult to correct such errors at trial without doing serious harm to the client's credibility or the overall case. The paralegal should constantly keep track of facts developed in a case and, as factual conflicts are identified, bring them to the attention of the attorney. The paralegal can prepare drafts of amended answers or stipulations to correct and clarify the information previously given.

8.0649 Analysis and Use of Interrogatories.

The paralegal is usually charged with tracking and analyzing all interrogatory responses given by or on behalf of the client. It is necessary to accumulate both the questions and the answers and to relate them in some collated form to the issues or the elements of proof in the case. The plaintiff's claims must be outlined, detailing the elements of each type of claim for both liability and damages. The defenses, affirmative or otherwise, of each defendant must also be outlined. In addition, the elements of proof for each affirmative defense should be included in the outline. The paralegal then reviews each interrogatory and answer to determine its bearing on the various claims and defenses.

Analysis of the other party's answers is extremely helpful to the attorney, particularly where the interrogatories included documents attached as exhibits and answers were obtained that specifically or impliedly affirmed the documents as true or correct copies of originals. If the originals cannot be found, a foundation has been laid to introduce the exhibits as "secondary evidence" at trial.

Any other party, as an admission against the interests of the client, may use any information contained in another party's answers to interrogatories but not their own answers. In other words, a party cannot use his or her own answers to another party's interrogatories as proof of the fact in issue. Any other party may be able to use those answers (because they are given under oath) as proof of a fact against the responding party. This emphasizes the importance of knowing the foundation of each answer supplied and that the answers are as factually correct and consistent as possible.

8.065 Opposing Party Answers to Interrogatories

It is important for the paralegal to carefully analyze, immediately on receipt, the answers provided by the responding party to the client's interrogatories. Evasiveness in answering any interrogatory should be discovered immediately because there is a very short period between the time when the answers are served and the date by which any motions to compel further answers can legitimately be made. Occasionally, interrogatory answers are incomplete or unresponsive, but without determining a pattern of obvious deception or intent to deny the information called for by the interrogatory, it is difficult to win a motion to compel.

PRACTICE TIP—CASUAL HANDLING

Clients often do not understand the legal or factual import of some interrogatories, or they may misunderstand or misconstrue a word or phrase in an interrogatory. Using their unedited answers to interrogatories can therefore be damaging to the client's case. Preparing answers using information from the attorney's work file may inadvertently waive a discovery privilege or immunity. It is imperative that the attorney and/or paralegal carefully peruse the questions that are posed and decide the best source of an answer, if any answer is to be given. Further, the answers should be checked for consistency with answers to pleadings, prior statements, prior deposition testimony, and prior responses to written discovery. Before the answers are finalized and submitted to the requesting party, they should be reviewed by the supervising attorney.

8.0651 Incomplete or "To Be Supplied" Answers. It is best to compare exactly what is requested by the interrogatory with the information provided in the answer. Where the relationship between the question and answer is reasonable, sometimes the matter can be resolved by communicating with the opposing counsel's office, informally asking if the incomplete answers were inadvertently provided, and offering to grant an extension of time in which to answer. Of course, such an inquiry and offer should only be made by the paralegal with the approval and the authority of the supervising attorney. The extension should be confirmed in writing to the other party and contain a provision that the other party agrees to have the time limit for filing a motion to compel tolled until the receipt of the supplemental or corrective answers or notification that the party will let the original answers stand.

Incomplete or "to be supplied" answers are very dangerous for the responding party. The propounding party has a right to complete answers. Any indication by the responding party that the answer is incomplete or will be supplied at a later date creates a burden that the responding party must honor in the future. It also places an additional burden on the propounding party to follow up such a response to ensure the answer is actually supplied. The paralegal for either party should calendar the matter properly and be prepared, before discovery comes to a close, to remind the attorney to resolve such incomplete answers in a timely fashion.

Consider the effect of a plaintiff trying to move the case along to trial who, during discovery, serves a "to be supplied" answer to an interrogatory propounded by the defendant. Discovery reaches the closing stages (usually about 30 days prior to the trial) when the defendant discovers that the plaintiff has not completely responded to the defendant's discovery. In many jurisdictions, the case may be removed from the trial calendar until discovery is completed. This can result in the case not being rescheduled for trial for a period of up to a year or more, depending on the size of the court's docket. The plaintiff's attorney has provided the defense attorney with a perfect opportunity for delaying a trial, which can be an effective method of delaying the financial burden of a judgment. Provided the defendant's actions are not obviously the grounds for the postponement, this kind of delaying tactic is seldom subject to sanctions by the court.

The lawyer and paralegal should be a team that effectively moves the case forward and denies the opposing party adversary these types of "sitting duck" grounds for postponements and delays.

8.0652 Unresponsive Answers.   Unresponsive answers are fairly common. Though they may appear on the surface to be a proper response, closer inspection may reveal that they have not answered the question asked. The propounding party's responsibility is to review the answers and determine whether or not they are acceptable and fully responsive to the question asked. If they are not, there is usually a limited period of time in which to compel responsive answers because of the deadlines set in the court's scheduling order. Because of the self-executing nature of interrogatories, an attorney who allows that period to pass without action waives the right to have the unresponsive answers corrected, which means they may not be used at trial or that their use may be severely curtailed.

PRACTICE TIP—UNVERIFIED ANSWERS

Unverified answers, though not proper, often occur through failure (inadvertent or deliberate) of the responding party to execute the verification to which the propounding party is entitled. This failure on the part of the answering party can be caught if the propounding party checks the answers to determine that they were submitted in verified form. Unverified answers are not under oath. They do not have the same force and cannot be used in the same way as verified answers. Due to the self-executing nature of interrogatories, the failure to detect the unverified answers and to move timely and appropriately to compel verification in timely fashion may require resubmission of the interrogatories to the opposing party in order to obtain the verification. If the party refuses to submit the appropriate verification the attorney and paralegal may have to file a formal motion to compel if they are unable to obtain the proper verification informally.

The attorney who uses paralegals will usually designate either the paralegal or the legal secretary to check incoming answers for verifications. The paralegal recognizes that errors can occur and should double-check each set regardless of office procedure or custom and immediately call the lack of proper verification to the attention of the attorney.

The paralegal who reviews the answers as they arrive can be of great assistance to the lawyer on this point alone. Analysis of the question and its answer may reveal the question to be unclear, ambiguous, or capable of various meanings. The answer may be an obvious evasion, misunderstanding, typographical error, or inadvertent misstatement. Such an analysis will suggest the corrective action needed: a motion to compel, a phone call to the opposing party to informally request that the answer be supplemented, or the submission of more specific and clarifying interrogatories.

In cases where the answers are obviously nonresponsive or appear to be deliberately incomplete, the same procedure for informally contacting the opposing party to request that the answer be supplemented as outlined in Section 8.0651, Incomplete or "To Be Supplied" Answers may be followed. In this situation, the offer of additional time is made in writing to the responding party as follows:

> "This will confirm the telephone conversation between my paralegal, Mr. Jones, and Ms. Smith of your office regarding your incomplete Answers to our Interrogatories, Set No. 2, in which we offered to extend the time for your answers for an additional 15 days from date of this letter. The time for us to file a motion to compel further answers will be tolled until we are notified that your answers will stand as submitted or we receive the full, complete answers."

This action places the burden on the responding party to decide whether to stand on the answers or provide additional information. At the same time, it protects the right of the propounding party to initiate a motion to compel further answers, yet shows cooperation and courtesy. This method may elicit the requested information in the 15-day period, which would eliminate the need to spend time preparing a motion, filing and serving it, and having it set for hearing, as well as the other potential delays in obtaining the information itself.

8.07 DEPOSITIONS

An oral deposition is one of the best discovery methods for obtaining information within the personal knowledge of a witness or party to the action. It also affords an opportunity for counsel to evaluate the appearance, credibility and communication skills of parties and witnesses. Depositions should be part of a carefully scheduled, timed and executed discovery plan, and paralegals play an important part in making physical arrangements for the deposition as well as preparation for interrogating the party or witness. It is not necessary to obtain court permission for depositions unless the proposed deponent is in prison; has already been deposed in the case; would result in more than 10 depositions being taken by plaintiffs, defendants, or third-party defendants in this case; or when a party seeks to take a deposition before the meeting of the parties required by Rule 26(f) of the *Federal Rules of Civil Procedure*.

Depositions are an important part of the discovery process. The testimony which a party or witness gives under oath may be used for impeachment purposes at trial, and if the deponent is unavailable, it can be read into the record under certain circumstances. Depositions are taken in the presence of counsel for all parties. The testimony is recorded by a person who is authorized to administer oaths by the laws of the United States or of the place where the deposition is taken or before a person appointed by the court where the action is pending. Sometimes it is simultaneously videotaped. Applicable rules also provide for depositions to be taken by telephone or upon previously submitted written questions.

Depositions in federal cases are governed by Rules 28, 29, 30, and 31 of the *Federal Rules of Civil Procedure* as well as any local district court rules (which could modify or enhance those rules). State courts generally have similar provisions within their codes, statutes, and/or court rules, and some state courts also have their own local rules. It is important to consult and follow *all* applicable rules in making arrangements for depositions and issuing notices. Rule 45 of the *Federal Rules of Civil Procedure* should be consulted and followed if it is necessary to subpoena the witness.

Depositions taken by telephone or other remote electronic means (such as video conferencing) are governed by Rule 30(b)(7) of the *Federal Rules of Civil Procedure*. A written stipulation signed by all parties or a court order is required. Arrangements must be made for a court reporter or officer authorized to administer oaths to be at the place where the deponent will be answering the questions.

Depositions upon written questions must be scheduled pursuant to Rule 31 of the *Federal Rules of Civil Procedure*. It is important to note the time requirements for the parties to submit written questions in advance. At the very least, that process would take at least one month. Usually, parties resort to this procedure when the subject of the deposition is very limited or routine (such as authentication of medical records). This type of deposition also requires engaging a court reporter to be at the place where the deponent will answer the questions. In fact, the court reporter actually reads the questions to the witness before recording the answers. Transcripts of depositions taken pursuant to this rule are lodged with the court close to the beginning of trial.

It is not always necessary that you know the name of the person who will testify at the deposition. If you want to depose a public or private corporation or a partnership or association or governmental agency, you can notice the entity for a deposition and describe in the notice the matters on which examination is requested. In such instances, consult Rule 30(b)(6) of the *Federal Rules of Civil Procedure*. After the organization receives the notice, it must designate one or more officers, directors, or managing agents or other persons who will testify on its behalf. A subpoena is required to advise a nonparty organization of its duty to make such a designation.

8.071 Making Arrangements for Depositions

Professional courtesy usually dictates coordination of the desired date and time for the deposition with counsel for all parties before the official notice is issued. This requires communication with attorneys or their assistants to check available dates. The first such communication should be made to the attorney for the party whose witness is going to be deposed. As a general rule, most attorneys prefer that their own client and witnesses be deposed in their office. If this is a practice in your area, you should also check the availability of a conference room or other suitable place for the deposition as part of your communication process. After you achieve a general consensus for the deposition date, be sure to engage a court reporter or other officer to take the testimony. If you are taking the deposition in an unfamiliar town or city, you need to remember to identify the witness, all parties, and all attorneys involved in the case to the reporter to avoid any possible disqualification for interest. Rule 28(c) of the *Federal Rules of Civil Procedure* provides that no deposition shall be taken before a person who is a relative or employee of any of the persons involved. If the deposition is taken in another location, you may also need to make physical arrangements for the deposition. Usually arrangements can be made to use a conference room at a law office, a room at the local courthouse, or a hotel or motel room. Contacts with paralegals in other areas can come in handy in such circumstances.

Sometimes local practice or the number of parties and counsel in a case does not make courtesy calls in the preliminary arrangements for depositions practical. In such cases, select a date, time, and place for the deposition which meets the notice and location requirements of the applicable court rules and fits the schedule of the supervising attorney and the attorney for the party or witness who is going to be deposed. In some jurisdictions, a specific number of days' notice is required; others merely state "reasonable notice," which is usually interpreted to be five or more days. Local court rules often give more specific information in this regard than the civil rules of procedure.

8.072 Formal Notice for the Deposition

Rule 30(b) of the *Federal Rules of Civil Procedure* contains a road map and the requirements for the formal notice of deposition. Refer to this source every time you prepare a notice and comply with the requirements to the best of your ability. Besides the obvious information (name of witness or party, date, address, etc.), it is important to note and remember that if you are serving a subpoena on the proposed deponent, the description or designation of the materials to be produced must be included in the notice or attached thereto. A copy of the formal notice of deposition must be served on all counsel (or parties if they are not represented). Some jurisdictions require that the original notice be filed with the court; some do not. Always check your local rules.

Deposition arrangements are often subject to change for various reasons—attorneys get called to court on other matters, parties and witnesses get sick, expert witnesses get called to other jurisdictions, and so forth. When it becomes necessary to reschedule a deposition, an Amended Notice of Deposition must be prepared and served on counsel, and an Amended Subpoena must be prepared and served on the deponent.

8.073   Subpoenas

Rule 30(g)(2) of the *Federal Rules of Civil Procedure* states that if the party noticing the deposition of a witness fails to serve a subpoena upon the witness and the witness fails to attend, the court may order the party giving notice to pay the reasonable expenses, including attorneys' fees, of all other parties who showed up for the deposition. Therefore, it is good practice to subpoena all nonparty deponents. It is not necessary to subpoena parties—notice of their deposition served on counsel is sufficient.

Rule 45 of the *Federal Rules of Civil Procedure* governs the issuance of subpoenas. In federal court you cannot compel the attendance of a witness for deposition if the witness is required to travel more than 100 miles from the place where he resides, is employed, or does business. Similarly, most state courts impose limitations on the distance a nonparty witness must travel. In federal cases, a check for one day's attendance and the mileage allowed by law must be delivered to the witness with the subpoena. The attendance (or per diem) fee is set by statute and changes at various times, usually at the beginning of a calendar year. Check the rules for the current per diem and mileage rates. Remember to double the mileage from the witness's starting point to the location of the deposition—witnesses are entitled to round-trip mileage.

Federal subpoena forms can be obtained from the Internet. The subpoena may be issued (signed) by the clerk of the court where the witness will be deposed or by an attorney who is authorized to practice in that court or the court where the action is pending. The witness can also be required to produce documents or records at the deposition. Do not forget to fill in the appropriate blanks on the form and to serve a check for the required fees along with the subpoena. In the rare event of issuing a document subpoena to a party for his deposition, note that you cannot circumvent Rule 34 of the *Federal Rules of Civil Procedure*. A party is entitled to 30 days to produce documents or records whether the request is made via a request for production of documents or a subpoena.

A subpoena in a federal court action may be served by any person who is not a party and who is not less than 18 years of age. It is recommended that you check your local district court rules to determine if they have any additional requirements. Some districts require that a process server must be registered with the clerk's office. Check the local rules to ascertain whether subpoenas with endorsed returns of service need to be routinely filed.

8.074   Preparing the Deposition Outline

Depositions are an opportunity for the paralegal to make effective use of case knowledge, organizational skills, judgment and analytical ability, and creative thinking. Ideally, the paralegal's contribution to the substantive deposition process should begin with preparing a topical outline of the desired or expected testimony. If possible, this should follow a conference with the attorney to identify his or her goals with regard to the deposition. Before beginning any outline, make sure that you understand the legal and factual issues and how the deponent might relate to your burden of proof. The format of the outline should provide space for the attorney to make notes in preparing for or during the deposition—triple or quadruple spacing is good between topical references. Refrain from formulating specific questions unless your attorney has requested you to do so. Most attorneys want topical reminders but prefer to pose their own questions.

In a document intensive case, start your outline process by going through the documents and re-cords that you have on hand (or start with the document indices—let your fingers do the walking). Iden-tify and tag anything you think might be helpful. Then put the documents in chronological order, and you will probably find that the outline practically writes itself. You will find that you end up with two types of documents—those that can be used as exhibits at the deposition and others that can be used by the attor-ney for reference or reminders of the witness's actions or knowledge. Proposed exhibits should be noted on the outline—either adjacent to the topics they relate to or in a separate list. After the exhibits are deter-mined, it is recommended that you make a minimum of four copies of each proposed exhibit. That will enable the deposition to flow better because the witness can use a document, his or her attorney can do likewise, your attorney has the third copy in hand, and one copy for the court reporter. Clip the copies to-gether and put a deposition exhibit sticker on the "original," but do not number the exhibit until it is used at the deposition. Often one topic on the outline might lead to one on another page, and the natural flow of questions might change the anticipated order of introducing the exhibits. Lastly (but not last minute), go over the outline and proposed exhibits with your attorney and revise the deposition plan if necessary.

8.075   Preparing Your Client or Witness for Deposition

It is important that your client or witness be made to feel confident and comfortable prior to being deposed. Many attorneys prefer to work directly with the client in this regard, but some like to delegate the routine testimony instructions to paralegals. Ideally, the attorney and paralegal will prepare the cli-ent together.

In case you are asked to handle this phase of the deposition preparation alone, the basic rules for testifying are:

a. Give only honest, responsive answers to questions in as few words as possible.

b. If you can answer "Yes" or "No," do so.

c. Do not volunteer any information.

d. Listen carefully to the question and do not be afraid to say you do not understand it.

e. Allow the attorney to finish the question and then hesitate a minute before responding—in case your attorney wants to assert an objection.

f. Do not guess or speculate! If you do not know, say that you do not know or do not remember.

g. Be aware that the "friendly" attitude of opposing counsel is for a purpose. Never forget that that attorney represents the opposing party.

Professional videotapes are available for preparing witnesses to testify. They are available through bar associations and legal publications. Some of the tapes illustrate the traps that witnesses can get themselves into when they do not follow the basic instructions. Use of such tapes frees the paralegal and the attorney to do other work while the client views the videotape. Then the attorney and/or the paralegal can meet with the client to go over case-specific information necessary to fully prepare the client for the deposition. Most witnesses are reassured to be told that they need only tell the truth as best as they can recall it.

8.076   Attending Depositions

Attorneys have found that it is beneficial for paralegals to attend depositions whenever possible. They can help the flow of introducing and processing exhibits, take notes to assist the attorney, and monitor coverage on the topical outline. Be sure to have a copy of the case caption and listing of counsel to give to the reporter when he or she is setting up. If you will be attending the deposition, you should inform the court reporter of your name and title and specifically request that the reporter shows you as "Also Present" for the party your attorney represents. This helps to avoid any inadvertent listing as an attorney on the transcript. Also tell the reporter if you have premarked the exhibits or if you will be numbering them as they are introduced. Generally, reporters appreciate this assistance so that they do not have to stop and number the exhibits. At the end of the deposition, assemble the "original" exhibits (usually the copies which were shown to the deponent) and give them to the reporter to include in the transcript. Be sure to get the reporter's business card. Sometime it helps to ask when you can expect to receive the transcript.

8.077   Tracking Deposition Exhibits

Deposition exhibits may include photographs, documents, or other objects that were obtained prior to the deposition or produced at deposition in response to a subpoena, as well as documents created during the deposition such as sketches, diagrams, or drawings. The purpose of introducing these exhibits at a deposition is: (1) to have their nature, origin, content, and identity established under oath or (2) to attempt to provide clarification of matters which are difficult to describe verbally.

In the absence of other directions by the parties, court reporters will mark exhibits in numerical sequence from the first exhibit introduced at deposition through the last, usually noting the name of the deponent and often using the traditional yellow or blue exhibit stickers to indicate the party which introduced the exhibit. Because there are a variety of methods used to mark deposition exhibits, it is important that the paralegal develop a method of tracking all exhibits introduced during the various depositions throughout the course of discovery.

In complex cases, where there are multiple parties and the potential for large numbers of exhibits exists, counsel often agree at the outset of the deposition phase of discovery to maintain a continuous system of exhibit identification to avoid duplication and resulting confusion. Establishing and maintaining the integrity of this system throughout the lawsuit is a task usually delegated to paralegals and often requires coordination with paralegals working for counsel representing other parties. When a sequential numbering system is adopted, it is absolutely essential to maintain an ongoing index of deposition exhibits in a system that is easy to access and use. It is also important that all court reporters be aware that the sequential deposition exhibit numbering system has been adopted. Coordination and cooperation among the parties is vital. If you are in charge of maintaining a deposition exhibit index or register, be sure to check with all court reporters immediately after each deposition so that you can identify and index new exhibits. A sample deposition exhibit register is shown in Exhibit 8-8. Records of this type, which track chronologically and describe all deposition exhibits in the case, simplify the process of retrieval and identification in preparation of briefs and trial exhibits. Reliable identification, control, and retrieval are the prime functions of paralegals in litigation.

8.078   Summarizing Depositions

Deposition transcripts, by the very nature of their question and answer format, generally involve many, many pages of testimony recorded in the order it is obtained from the witness. The transcripts are often bulky and difficult to use in the courtroom. Because of this, depositions are usually summarized for use in final trial preparation and to act as a quick guide to specific testimony during the trial. There are several methods of summarizing depositions, which include the chronological summary, the index or digest method, and the topical summary. The method or format will vary according to the attorney's need or preference as well as the scope and extent of the case and the issues involved. Sometimes it will be necessary to prepare more than one type of summary.

EXHIBIT 8-8   Deposition Outline—Plaintiff

I. Background Information
   A. Personal
      1. Full name
         a. Any other names used in past 10 years
      2. Birth date
      3. Marital status
      4. Children
         a. Names and ages
      5. Social Security No.
   B. Education
      1. High school
      2. College
      3. Other
   C. Employment History – past 10 years
      1. Employer's name and address at time of accident
      2. Position held
         a. Duties
II. Plaintiff's Activities for 24 Hours Prior to Accident
   A. Describe all activities
      1. Food consumed
      2. Beverages consumed
         a. Alcoholic?
      3. Prescription medicines?
      4. Nonprescription pills or liquids consumed
   B. Amount of sleep
   C. How long driving prior to accident?
   D. Destination
   E. Identify any passengers
III. The Accident
   A. Describe events immediately preceding
      1. Using cell phone?
      2. Smoking?
      3. Consuming water or beverage?
   B. What done to try to avoid collision?
   C. What happened after collision?
      1. Who did you talk to?
         a. Identify each person
            i.   What did you say?
            ii. What did they say?
      2. Where did you go?
      3. How did you get there?
IV. Claimed Damages
   A. Medical expenses
      1. Identify all care providers
      2. Describe their services or area of expertise
      3. Itemize all charges for their services
   B. Lost wages
      1. Dates unable to work
      2. Lost income
   C. Expense for home health care or assistance with household duties
      1. Identify caregivers
      2. Itemize expenses
   D. Property Damage
      1. Vehicle
      2. Other

The first and most important rule for paralegals in summarizing depositions is to know and understand the legal and factual issues in the case. At the very least, this involves reading the most recent complaint and all responses from defendants. You must know the players and have some idea of each party's burden of proof in order to recognize important and relevant testimony. Do not hesitate to ask questions if you do not fully understand what the case is about.

The second rule is to ensure that you do not have the original deposition transcript in hand. Most state and federal courts now require that the party taking the deposition maintain custody of the original transcripts for use at trial rather than filing them with the clerk of court. Some jurisdictions prefer or require that the original transcripts be kept in sealed envelopes that can only be opened at trial. Most attorneys still order a copy for their use throughout the case. Chances are that no one will hand you an original transcript to summarize, but it never hurts to make sure! Ideally you will have a photocopy of the transcript or a miniscript (with four or more pages on one page) to work with.

There is no one prescribed method for summarizing deposition transcripts. Some people start out at page one and summarize each page as they go while sitting at the computer. Others read through the entire deposition before attempting to begin the actual summary. The writer prefers to read through with yellow highlighter in hand to mark first impression important items. The important thing is for each paralegal to find the procedure that works best for him or her. If at all possible, it is best to avoid interruptions when you are trying to identify important and relevant testimony.

It is important that you know before you start the summary how and when it may be used. If the attorney routinely relies on a deposition summary for use at trial in quickly locating specific testimony, it is vital that you summarize only one page of relevant testimony at a time because the pace of the courtroom prohibits searching multiple pages of the actual transcript. If the attorney anticipates using the transcript to identify and cite specific facts or testimony for a brief, you should also include reference to line numbers. If not, it is much quicker to prepare the summary with reference only to page numbers. Deposition transcripts contain only 25 lines, and it is not that difficult to locate key testimony.

8.0781 Chronological Summary.

A good rule of thumb for efficient chronological summaries is averaging 10 pages of transcript to one page of summary. This is the most common form of deposition summary, which is simply a page-by-page paraphrasing of the deponent's testimony. In essence, this is just a reduction of volume, both in number of pages and amount of material that eliminates rhetorical verbiage, colloquy of counsel, and the "fencing" or "game playing" dialogue employed by some witnesses and/or attorneys. It is the fastest method of summarizing a deposition. The drawback to this method is a lack of order or organization of subjects. Following the progression of a particular deposition does not necessarily result in all the data on any one issue being developed in one set of questions and answers. A deposition is an interrogation with all the problems of memory refreshment and afterthought that occur from the witness's detailed retelling of a story and/or the accidental revelation of a fact the attorney had not previously known or considered. Because of these factors, the subject matters that are covered in the deposition are mixed in the transcript. On the other hand, in a relatively small case with uncomplicated factual and legal issues, this may be the better or more efficient method of summarizing testimony. (*See* Exhibit 8-9.)

8.0782 Index/Digest Method.

The index or digest method of summarizing a deposition lists the main topics covered in the deposition with page and line references "indexed" under each topical heading. Just as the index of a book is the quickest means to find where information on a word or phrase appears, this provides a quick reference to exactly where testimony on each major topic is located. It can be used alone or as an accompaniment to the chronological summary. The drawback to this method is that, by itself, it does not provide any detail about the testimony. (*See* Exhibit 8-10.)

EXHIBIT 8-9   Summary of Deposition of Mary Kosko Taken September 10, 2007

Page #	**Summary of Relevant Testimony**
3	Plaintiff's name is Mary Margaret Kosko. She was born on 05/23/75 and has been married to David J. Kosko for 5 years. They reside at 543 Cherry Street in Bishopville. She had a brief previous marriage to John Cook – in 1994. They were divorced in December 1995.
4	MMK's Social Security # is 123-45-6789. She and David have one daughter named Susan, who is three years old. MMK was pregnant with their second child at the time of the accident.
5	MMK graduated from Bishop High School in 1993 and then attended Coastal Technical College. She completed the nursing program there in 1996 and subsequently passed her licensing exams on her first attempt.
6	MMK testified that she worked as a waitress at John's Steak House while she was going to CTC. Her first nursing job was with Dr. Phil Hurd, assisting him in his office on Front Street. She worked for him about 3 years.
7	MMK stated that she starting working at Metropolitan Hospital after her daughter was born, mostly on the evening shift. That way, David could be home with the baby and they did not have to pay for child care. MMK was employed at Metropolitan at the time of the accident. She was a floor nurse and usually worked 12 hour shifts 4 days per week.
8	Plaintiff testified that she had worked all night just before the accident. She was on her way home from the hospital and had just dialed her home number on her cell phone when Defendant's car crashed into the driver's side of her SUV. MMK was on Main Street, and the traffic light was green.
9	She doesn't know what happened immediately after the accident. She has been told that the impact rolled her vehicle over and that the paramedics had to use the Jaws of Life to get her out. She lost the baby she was carrying after she got to the hospital. Both of her legs were broken.
10	MMK's right arm was also broken in the accident. She was right handed. She doesn't remember much for the first few weeks after the accident occurred. She has been told that she had to have two operations then.

EXHIBIT 8-10   Sample of Index/Digest Summary Method

Deposition Summary	
Testimony of Albert Jones	
Date of accident	**Description of vehicles**
p. 7, l. 4	p. 10, ll. 1–13
	p. 11, ll. 17–18
	p. 33, l. 9
Place of accident	p. 62, l. 25
p. 7, l. 14	
p. 43, ll. 6–12	**How accident occurred**
	p. 17, ll. 3–24
	p. 18, ll. 7–19
	p. 61, l. 9–p. 62, l. 22

8.0783 Summary by Topic or Category.

This is the most detailed and most time-consuming method of summarizing depositions. There are several ways to proceed with this type of summary:

a. First create a detailed chronological summary of the deposition, and then cut-and-paste statements from the summary about particular subjects into a group with page and line references.

b. Create an index/digest summary and then, using the page references under each topic as references to all the testimony in the deposition about that one topic or category of information, dictate or type a summary of the testimony about each topic or category with page and line references.

c. Label separate sheets of paper with headings for each important topic and write summaries of the testimony, with page and line references, while reading through the deposition.

d. Photocopy the deposition transcript, and then cut the various statements pertaining to each topic from the copy and paste them together to make the summary. You may need to duplicate parts of the transcript more than once if testimony on the same page pertains to more than one category.

Many specialized computer software programs are available which perform much of the manual work described in this section. Generally, these programs allow a deposition transcript which is on a computer disk (which are generally provided free or at a nominal charge along with the written deposition transcript by the reporter) to be loaded into the software program for processing. The paralegal can then create specific case related issues and tag or code specific testimony to the issues or insert notes or comments directly into the program without changing the deposition transcript. The program also allows one to easily and quickly locate portions of the transcript that refer to discrete topics which have been identified by the paralegal and the attorney and provide page and line references to transcript testimony containing the topic word(s) or phrases no matter where it appears in the transcript. The software and all depositions taken in a case may be loaded on a laptop and transported to trial and other depositions or hearings. Locating specific testimony can be done almost instantaneously.

In addition to the specialized software programs, many paralegals use word processing software to perform the methods listed in (a) through (d) to cut, paste, and copy electronically from deposition transcripts on computer disks provided by court reporters. Some programs have the added benefit of being electronically "searchable" for words and phrases. Specialized software programs are cost-effective because they are available within the office.

8.08 REQUESTS FOR ADMISSION

Among the discovery tools available, requests for admission are relatively inexpensive, considering the amount of court time usually devoted to resolving discovery disputes. The purpose of requests for admission is to limit the number of disputed issues and material facts to be argued and proven at trial or to create a further foundation for the introduction of evidentiary materials and documents. The paralegal working with requests for admission should be familiar with Rule 36 of the *Federal Rules of Civil Procedure,* which governs their usage. The scope of the requests, as set forth in Rule 26(b)(1) governing discovery, is far-reaching: "any matter, not privileged, which is relevant to the claim or defense of any party, including the existence, description, nature, custody, condition and location of any books, documents or other tangible things and the identity and location of persons having knowledge of any discoverable matter." Requests for admission are therefore founded on matters developed from previous discovery mechanisms, including interrogatories, depositions, and requests for production of documents.

Requests for admission are directed solely to parties and are for purposes of the pending action only. Admissions or denials are binding only upon the answering party and may not be used in any other litigation. The paralegal is reminded that federal, local rules, and state practices vary. They may restrict the number of requests for admission that may be served and should always be consulted as to limitations and provisions for exceeding such limitations (which is usually upon consent of the parties or motion to the court).

8.081   Timing

Without leave of court or by written stipulation, requests for admission may not be served prior to the scheduling conference required by Rule 26(f).

The paralegal contributes to the creation of effective requests for admission by assembling from previous discovery responses those facts and documents important to the case that have not been specifically acknowledged by the other parties. This may include documents introduced at depositions and requests for admission propounded by the other parties to obtain reciprocal admissions to the fact, document, or thing, since answers to requests for admission are binding only on the answering party.

Rule 36 provides for a 30-day response time. For the party on whom the requests for admission is served, action must be taken immediately. The paralegal should circulate a copy of the requests to the supervising attorney and should calendar the response date at once. If no responses are served, the matters are considered admitted and conclusively established.

Usually, when a foundation has been developed, the answering parties will admit the truth of the facts or the genuineness of the documents, but there is no compulsion to do so. They may put the propounding attorney "on strict proof." When such proof is forthcoming at trial, the propounding party may ask the court to award the costs of the proof, such as the transportation of a witness or the expert witness's fee.

Responses to requests for admission are limited. Parties may admit, deny, refuse to admit or deny, or object. Admitting has the force of a judicial admission and may be used as evidence in court. Denying can be costly if the matter is later proven true at trial. Refusing to admit or deny has the effect of admitting by default if the request is not also objected to. It is difficult for a party to prove an objection to a request because it must establish lack of personal knowledge to the satisfaction of the magistrate or judge.

The propounding party in such instance should serve notice by registered or certified mail that it is deeming the answers to be admitted based upon Rule 36. The propounding party may also move the court for an order compelling further responses, if it believes a response is incomplete or evasive or an objection is to be without merit.

Parties may also amend their responses upon motion to the court, which may grant such motions if timely made and if such amendments will not prejudice the propounding party.

8.082   Form

Requests for admission are usually posed in positive statements to which the answering party answers with "admitted" or "denied," as shown in Exhibit 8-11 and Exhibit 8-12, respectively. Objections or other answers may be provided, such as "Defendant can neither admit nor deny the truth of the matter because…" Requests for admission may be propounded as one set or several sets, and federal court rules usually require sequential numbering for purposes of clarity and control.

8.083   Collation of Denials and Costs of Proof

Because Rule 36 allows the party who serves requests for admission to collect any costs from the responding party who denies a request later proven to be true, the paralegal collates all *denials* of requests for admission and coordinates with the supervising attorney as to the necessary method of

EXHIBIT 8-11   Sample Request for Admission under Rule 36

Plaintiff AB requests Defendant CD within ____ days after service of this request to make the following admissions for the purpose of this action only, and subject to all pertinent objections to admissibility which may be interposed at the trial:
1.   That each of the following documents, exhibited with this request, is genuine:
     (Here list the documents and describe each document)
2.   That each of the following statements is true:
     (Here list the statements)

EXHIBIT 8-12   Sample Response to Request for Admissions Under Rule 36

Defendant CD responds to Plaintiff AB's Request for Admissions as follows:

Response to Request No. ___: Defendant CD admits that . . . *(here repeat the information)*

Response to Request No. ___: Defendant CD denies . . .

Response to Request No. ___: Defendant CD has no information with which to admit or deny this request. Defendant CD has made reasonable inquiry and the information known or readily obtainable by the party is insufficient to enable the party to admit or deny and, therefore, on the basis of this lack of information, denies the request.

Response to Request No. ___: Defendant CD objects to this request on the groups that it seeks information that is privileged under the attorney/client privilege *(or state the grounds for objections)*.

proof. Once the plan of proof is selected, the paralegal establishes a record of the costs associated with the proof of each disputed fact or document to serve as the foundation for seeking recovery of those costs, if deemed appropriate by the supervising attorney.

8.09 REQUESTS FOR PRODUCTION OF DOCUMENTS

Production of documents and things is used to discover what evidence the other side has and to locate evidence that may be beneficial or damaging to your case. The request for production and inspection can be extremely beneficial in terms of expert witnesses by allowing you to obtain copies of any tests performed by the expert or by allowing you to actually watch the tests as they are performed.

Federal Rule of Civil Procedure 34, entitled "Production of Documents and Things and Entry Upon Land for Inspection and Other Purposes," permits any party to serve on any other party, including a person not a party to the action (by *subpoena duces tecum* under Rule 45), a request to produce and permit inspection of designated documents or any other tangible items and to permit entry upon designated land in possession or control of the parties. The documents or any other tangible items to be produced or inspected are itemized in Rule 34 as: "writings, drawings, graphs, charts, photographs, phone records, and other data compilations from which information can be obtained." Procedures for parties to follow to respond to such requests are set forth in Rule 34. Rule 34 also requires that documents are to be produced as they are kept in the usual course of business. With many records now stored using technology, this phrase, the "usual course of business," has evolved to mean every sort of print, film, computer disk, and audio and visual media. Business records once kept in dusty archives and cumbersome ledgers are now stored in the "usual course of business" on microfilm, microfiche, computer disks, tapes, CD-ROMs, and so forth. This is another area where the paralegal's enhanced computer skills and awareness is invaluable.

It sounds trite to state that this is the "age of information," but we are in the midst of it! Each day brings technological advances only dreamed of a few short years ago. The paralegal should be aware of new technology and know how to utilize it and/or where to find vendors and specialists who may assist in utilizing it. Discoverable evidence can be found in clients' computers (and opposing parties' computers) in the form of correspondence, memoranda, spreadsheets, reports, databases, calendars and other forms of schedules, accounting records and data, and e-mail—both saved and deleted. A trained technician or "computer detective" is capable of retrieving smoking guns from computer disks and computer tape backups. E-mail can be especially dangerous since it brings a false sense of privacy to the user, often revealing the user's unguarded thinking. Throughout the following discussion, the paralegal should keep in mind that the procedures also apply to all electronic data.

8.091   Basic Considerations

Whether the volume of documents is relatively small and manageable or large and cumbersome, there are certain basic considerations that apply. When reviewing documents to be produced by the client, consider the following:

a. The opposing party is entitled to those documents that can be described with sufficient specificity to allow the client, the client's counsel, and the paralegal to identify them, provided the *scope* of the request is not burdensome and oppressive, the material is not privileged, and the documents are actually in the possession, custody, or control of the client.

b. The attorney and the paralegal must review each document page before allowing the opposing party to see it in order to ensure that no privileged documents, trade secret material, or documents not responsive to the specific request are included.

c. Client documents should be received and reviewed as they are kept "in the ordinary course of business" as well as in chronological context to determine whether the documents and records are complete. A chronological review helps detect files or documents that have been lost, misfiled, retired, or destroyed. These events must be explained.

d. It is important to establish and maintain the source of each document, or sets of documents, produced during litigation. Source origination is very important as part of the foundation for offering a document as an exhibit at trial.

When reviewing documents obtained from other parties or nonparties, these are the considerations to bear in mind:

a. Are the items produced responsive to the request?

b. If an objection was made, was it reasonable, or will it be necessary to prepare a motion to compel?

c. If documents are being withheld subject to a privilege, has a list been provided with enough information to determine whether the privilege should be challenged?

d. Is the pertinent time period covered?

e. Do the records deal with the person, company, or entity directly or only by reference?

f. Do the records deal with the issues in the case?

g. Do the records refer to other records neither attached nor already obtained?

h. Do the records require expert help in interpretation or understanding?

8.092   Form

Requests for production have the same general format as interrogatories. A "Definitions" section may be used to identify common terms, words, and phrases. Each request is set forth in a separate sequentially

EXHIBIT 8-13   Sample Request for Production of Documents and Related Items under Rule 34

Plaintiff AB requests Defendant CD to respond within _____ days to the following requests:

1. That Defendant produce and permit Plaintiff to inspect and to copy each of the following documents: *(Here list the documents either individually or by category and describe each of them, and state the time, place, and manner of making the inspection and performance of any related acts).*
2. That Defendant produce and permit Plaintiff to inspect and to copy, test, or sample each of the following objects: *(Here list the objects either individually or by category and describe each of them, and state the time, place, and manner of making the inspection and performance of any related acts.)*
3. That Defendant permit Plaintiff to enter (here describe property to be entered) and to inspect and photograph, test, or sample the following: *(Here describe the portion of the real property and the objects to be inspected, photographed, tested, or s ampled and state the time, place, and manner of making the inspection and performance of any related acts.)*

---

numbered paragraph. The request must state the specific date, time, place, and manner of inspection, copying or testing, which may not be any sooner than the time within which the opposing party may respond under Rule 34 or its jurisdictional equivalent. Each requested item or category of items should be identified specifically enough to allow the opposing party to be able to determine what to produce. The terms used should be general enough so that all potentially responsive documents are included. For instance, the type of documents sought might be a company's internal policy and procedures manual for employees. Because the company might have internal policy and procedures, yet may not have them assembled in a volume called "policy and procedures manual," a request to obtain the equivalent information might state: "Produce all documents which detail, discuss, or relate in any manner the policy and procedures the company follows in regard to employees or expects the employees of the company to follow, including but not limited to reports, manuals, memoranda, statements, e-mail, or any other document whether written or recorded, for the period 2000 to 2007." It is good practice to state a reasonable and relevant time period. Failing to do so could result in the production being so large that it is overwhelming as well as significantly more expensive for the client in terms of both costs and fees. Stating a relevant time period also eliminates a reason for objection by the opposing party. An example of a Request for Production of Documents is contained in Exhibit 8-13.

8.093   Requesting Documents from Nonparties

Federal Rule of Civil Procedure 34 provides that the method of obtaining documents from nonparties is by issuing a subpoena pursuant to Rule 45, on a form provided by the local clerk of court. As previously mentioned in Section 8.07, Depositions, this is called a *subpoena duces tecum,* which is a Latin phrase meaning "under penalty you shall take it with you." These types of document requests are most often issued to the custodian of record for a business or other entity to appear together with the records and be prepared to discuss the manner of origin and filing of the documents. If all that is sought is the records production, and not a deposition, the records custodian may be given the option of providing copies of the records in lieu of actually appearing. As a practical matter, many of the documents requested from nonparties are routine business records generated by neutral parties, and no dispute over the admissibility of the records exists, for instance, medical records of a plaintiff in a bodily injury lawsuit or employment, education, or military service records. It is common practice (on mutual agreement) for such subpoenas to be issued to a firm specializing in attorney's legal services to serve the subpoena on the custodian, take custody of the records, copy and notarize the relevant documents, deliver the copies to the attorneys, and return the originals to the custodian. In those cases where a dispute over admissibility of the records may exist, the custodian of record will be required to appear and give testimony concerning the records produced. When this occurs, the procedures discussed in Section 8.07, Depositions should be followed.

8.10 MOTIONS TO COMPEL DISCOVERY

Motions to compel discovery are generally looked upon with disfavor by the courts. However, Rule 37 provides a method to force a party who has failed to answer interrogatories to answer them fully, completely, and responsively. A motion to compel under Rule 37(a) may be accompanied by a request that the party who failed to answer be ordered to pay the costs of making such motion (sanctions), including attorney's fees. Corresponding state rules or code sections allow substantially the same motion.

In every case, the rules of court outline the requirements necessary for filing such a motion. In almost every case, the moving party must submit several documents. There may be a requirement for a notice of the hearing date on the motion, the motion itself, a memorandum of points and authorities supporting the motion, and a declaration by the attorney as to the legitimacy of the motion. Local rules should always be consulted before drafting a motion to compel. Some courts have local rules that require either an allegation in the motion or a separate certificate by the attorney for the moving party that the parties have met and made an effort to solve the discovery dispute, but have been unsuccessful in doing so.

One of the most common errors made by parties filing discovery motions is the general nature of stating the allegations that the responses to the discovery were unacceptable. Most courts require the moving party to state specific reasons why each disputed response is unacceptable. Most courts have adopted rules that require the following contents in the motion:

a. State the full text of each interrogatory that is not fully answered.

b. Immediately follow with the full text of the response given by the answering party and/or the objection thereto, in full.

c. Provide a short statement of the moving counsel's contention that the interrogatory is not fully answered and/or the reasons why the responding party's objection should be overruled. The attorney may cite any legal and factual points and authorities applicable to his or her position.

d. The moving party must serve the documents, along with the notice of the motion (if required by local rule) and any other papers required by law or local rules, upon the party or parties against whom the motion is directed, within the time period prescribed.

The burden is upon the party receiving the answers to interpret them correctly as being responsive or unresponsive, to determine whether the objections have merit or not, and to initiate such appropriate action as he or she feels appropriate and legitimate. Allowing any applicable time period to pass without action will waive the right to file a motion to compel further answers on that set of interrogatories. The moving party must show that the information is reasonably believed to be available to the responding party and that the information sought is relevant to the proceedings and/or calculated to lead to the discovery of admissible evidence. Further, there must be a statement denying that answering the interrogatory will be burdensome, a harassment, or oppressive, if the responding party used those terms in objecting to the interrogatory.

The courts will often instruct responding parties to respond to the questions correctly and fully on an individual basis so long as there is not an extraordinary burden and so long as the questions do not constitute oppression. Oppression can mean inordinate expense for the value of the information provided or excessive work effort necessary to locate the information or determine the existence of information over long spans of time or through huge masses of paper with little or no probative value to the case. The court may deny the motion to compel on these grounds if it finds the oppression or burden is too great on the responding party. If the responding party has created an unreasonable burden (that is, the necessity of filing the motion to compel) on the propounding party in order to obtain the requested information, sanctions (the costs of the motion and attorney's fees for appearing in court for the motion) may be sought and obtained against the responding party. As a general and practical rule, courts are hesitant to grant sanctions early in a case or for failure properly to respond only to one set of interrogatories. A pattern of obstructive behavior or unwillingness to participate fairly and cooperatively in the process may result in the court assessing financial sanctions against the noncooperating party.

If an order is issued as a result of a motion to compel commanding the responding party to answer the discovery and the responding party violates the court's order by failing to respond or failing to fully respond, as required by the order, Rule 37(b) provides that, in addition to monetary sanctions similar to those provided in Rule 37(a), the court may issue an order striking claims or defenses or other matters from the pleadings, order designated facts to be taken as established for purposes of the case, or to hold the party and/or its attorney in contempt of court.

8.11 DISCOVERY AND EXHIBIT CONTROL SYSTEMS, DAMAGE CALCULATIONS, AND SETTLEMENT OFFERS

8.110 Discovery and Exhibit Control Systems

The documents collected and reviewed during the discovery and investigation phases must be organized in a manner that allows for easy access. This system is essential for the efficient use of the information and reduces the possibility of lost documents. Without good planning for identifying, indexing, controlling, and retrieving the documents, their contents will be of little or no value to the attorney in future discovery, in settlement negotiations, or at trial.

Original documents must be preserved with care to avoid changing their character from the "as found" condition. Marking the original documents with a unique identifying number is a generally accepted practice which is not considered to have the effect of changing their character, just as placing an exhibit identification number on a document does not change its character. Marking documents in such a manner simplifies the process of accounting for those documents as the case progresses and makes subsequent retrieval and use much easier. When marking documents for identification, care must be taken not to obscure or obliterate any writing or other marking which appears on the document's face. It is suggested that the marking be placed consistently. For example, the number always appears in the lower right-hand corner, or if that is not possible, then at least on the right side of the document.

When documents and other items are assembled to be produced or when they are received or inspected in response to a request, the paralegal should prepare an index containing basic identification data which includes any identification number which has been assigned, type of document, date, author, addressee, number of pages, and attachments. If there are characteristic file numbers or subject titles, they may be included. Chapter 9 covers document production in more depth and detail, and although it refers to large document cases, the same general principles apply to the management of small and medium cases as well.

From the beginning of the discovery plan, a general estimate of the number of documents pertinent to the case should be made and a system chosen. This system should be organized to identify, index, number, and control documents received from the client, from investigations conducted by the firm, and from opposing parties throughout the discovery phase of the case. Once the control procedure is in place, it should be strictly adhered. Every document that is received during discovery

EXHIBIT 8-14   Sample Case Exhibit Control Log

CASE: *Howard Jones v. Holiday Inn*
ATTORNEY: Jack Bonin
CLIENT: Howard Jones
DATE LAST POSTED: 7/19/06
LEGAL ASSISTANT: Jan Harlow

Pltf	Deft	Other Party	How Submitted	Description of Exhibit
X			Complaint—Ex 1	Holidady Inn Annual Report—2003
	X		Interrog. Answer #5	Financial Audit—Holiday Inn—2003
		X 3dp Def Comfort Inn	Depo.—30(b)(6)— Comfort Inn	Comfort Inn Annual Report—2002

EXHIBIT 8-15   Discovery Exhibit Log

CASE: Benjamin Jackson   ATTORNEY: Ford Mason
CLIENT: Aimes Alabaster
DATE LAST POSTED: 3/27/2006
LEGAL ASSISTANT: Marilyn Afeman

Doc #	Who Submitted	Discovery Event	Description of Document
1	Def.—Aimes Alabaster	Pl. B. Jackson Int.Ans.	10 Photos of accident site
2	Def.—Aimes Alabaster	Pl. B. Jackson Int.Ans.	13 Photos of automobile
3	Def.—Aimes Alabaster	Pl. B. Jackson Int.Ans.	2000–2006 Income Tax Returns
4	Def.—Aimes Alabaster	Pl. B. Jackson Int.Ans.	Johns Hosp. record 2/9/99–3/17/99
5	Pl.—B. Jackson	Def.—Ames Int.Ans.	Videotape of accident site
6	Pl.—B. Jackson	Def.—Aimes Depo.	Sketch w/measurements of skid marks
7	Pl.—B. Jackson	Def.—Aimes Depo.	Photos of 18-wheel truck & trailer

should be entered into the system immediately upon receipt. This should result in the ability to easily and quickly retrieve any document produced in the discovery phase of the case. The system used will depend on the size of the case and the preference of the supervising attorney and/or paralegal. How you track and organize discovery documents and potential exhibits is not nearly as important as the fact that you do so!

One effective system for controlling exhibits introduced from the outset of the case is the use of a Case Exhibit Control Log. This type of log identifies every exhibit introduced by each party, in chronological order. It permits the attorney to track his or her own and other parties' exhibits in numeric or alphabetical or sequential order, no matter whether they were attached to the complaint, answer, discovery responses, or motions. (*See* Exhibit 8-14 for an example of a Case Exhibit Control Log.)

The Discovery Exhibit Log allows you to maintain an integrated exhibit log for all exhibits produced with discovery responses. (*See* Exhibit 8-15.) It permits the attorney to track his or her own and other parties' answers to discovery requests.

If the discovery and exhibit logs are to accomplish their purpose, some sort of sequential numbering system should be used. The numbering system used will depend on firm practice, the supervising attorney's preferences and/or the paralegal's preferences. Documents can be placed behind numerical tabs (e.g., 1, 2, 3, …) or by using the Bates numbering system (00001, 00002, 00003, etc.). It is much simpler to refer to 20 exhibits introduced from various sources if they are numbered sequentially with cross-references to the identity of the party who submitted it, in connection with what pleading or discovery event it was introduced, and a description of the document. The attorney may refer to the log and request Document #2 or Document #00105 to #00117, rather than requesting Exhibit D2 in the deposition of John Albert Thomas, taken by defendant on June 22, 2007. Using a sequential numbering system requires close cooperation and discipline by the members of the litigation team, and if the case has more than one attorney assigned to it, it becomes even more complicated. There is a need for clear understanding of the procedure from the beginning of the lawsuit, so that each person who is involved in the logging process understands the process and the necessity for uniformity in maintaining the log.

8.111   Damage Calculations

The plaintiff is the primary source of the documents necessary to prove the damages portion of the case, although such documents may also be collected from their originating source. These documents may include medical bills, checks, receipts, vehicle repair estimates and bills, invoices, financial statements, general ledgers, and any other document that supports an amount for any type of damage being claimed. The paralegal should ensure that only legitimate and relevant amounts are included in the calculation. The bills should be assembled first into categories and then in chronological order.

Generally, computing a party's damages involves more than totaling the amounts in invoices, receipts, and estimates. For example, in a complex litigation, a plaintiff may claim that the actions of the defendant were the proximate cause of the plaintiff declaring bankruptcy, during which the plaintiff's business loses its entire inventory to creditors, although a portion of the original business remains. In this situation, some creative thought must be given to the various things that the plaintiff has lost, as well as a method of placing a value on those items. Is the value of the lost inventory the amount owed the creditors, the original purchase price, or the amount the plaintiff would have received if the inventory were sold in the ordinary course of business? Did the plaintiff lose accounts or customers because there was no inventory to sell? If so, how is the value of that loss to be determined? The paralegal working on damages in a lawsuit, whether for the plaintiff or the defendant, must be aware of circumstances where routine measures of the value of damages make little contribution to the lawyer's efforts. Flexibility and imagination are necessary. Every case has a unique set of facts that bear on the damage elements of the case. The paralegal and the attorney must analyze the basis of the damages sought, seek expert help in valuing the claimed losses, and explore alternative methods of settlement where appropriate. (*See* Exhibit 8-16.)

8.1111 Damage Analysis.   In cases involving injuries or other damages for which the services of medical professionals were utilized by the plaintiff, a detailed examination of the medical bills should be made to separate bills related to diagnosis from those of treatment—whether the case is medical or not. Only amounts in medical bills related to diagnosis and treatment of injuries, illnesses, or conditions that are the subject matter of the lawsuit should be included in damage calculations. This requires a careful reading of each medical bill to eliminate those charges that are for routine checkups or other nonlawsuit-related treatments. Careful comparison of the medical history notes against the doctor's office or hospital billing may reveal that the bills include charges for medical treatment totally unrelated to the incident at issue, and that should be deleted from the damage total. For instance, a man suffering

EXHIBIT 8-16 Factors Considered in Assessing Settlement Values

1. The ease or difficulty plaintiff will have in proving all elements necessary to prove defendant's liability;
2. The ease or difficulty plaintiff will have in proving the damages claimed;
3. The nature of the injury, that is, whether the injury is a relatively common one or has a "horror factor," such as serious burns and resulting scarring or the loss of a limb or eyesight or hearing;
4. Prior medical history (e.g., preexisting back problems) that the plaintiff is suffering from due to current injury;
5. The credibility of the lay witnesses and damage witnesses whose testimony is critical to proving important elements of liability or damages, or both;
6. The amount of the defendant's insurance coverage or the ability of the defendant to otherwise pay the judgment;
7. The plaintiff's financial status—that is, if the plaintiff's financial status will support him during the time the case is pending;
8. The past record of the trial forum for large or small verdicts, including the known propensities of the judge and of past juries in similar cases; and
9. The experience and ability of the opposing lawyer(s).

---

a minor knee injury who is treated by his family doctor may also be treated for allergy problems on a repetitive basis before and during the knee injury episode. All office visits, treatment, lab work, and other procedures related to the allergy condition can be identified by comparing the doctor's office notes or the treatment notes in the hospital record to the bills from these health care providers. Once they have been identified as unrelated to the plaintiff's claims in the lawsuit, they can be deleted from the list of damages.

In cases that are not medical, the value of estimates by professionals may be included. For instance, estimates and bills can support the damage to a home, but not all proposed or actual repairs may be necessarily related to the actions or inactions of the opposing party. In business claims for lost earnings or profits, the accounting documents that support each amount must be verified. Where calculations are based on time periods, the validity of the time period as supported by documentary or testimonial evidence must be checked. If an interest rate is used, it must be verified that the use of that rate has a basis. These types of documents must also be examined carefully to identify items that do not relate to the matter that is the subject of the litigation.

Along with reviewing the documents for accuracy, foundation, and relevancy, every effort must be made to ensure that an item or amount is only counted once. Remember not all bills will be of the same type. In a bodily injury case, there will be bills (some paid and some still owed), some vouchers showing insurance payments, some receipts for cash payments, canceled checks, charge account or credit card purchase slips, cash register tapes with handwritten notes identifying a purchase, and so on. These documents will come from different sources, and some may be duplications of others. Sometimes the duplication occurs when using one item as an element in arriving at the total for more than one category of damage. Such duplications may be innocent and thoughtless, or they may be preconceived and deliberate. The plaintiff's paralegal must carefully examine all these documents and, where they are being used to support a total or subtotal, avoid placing the supervising attorney in an embarrassing situation. By the same token, the defendant's paralegal can prevent inflated damage totals by identifying such duplications and calling them to the attention of the supervising attorney.

The paralegal's services in checking and rechecking all types of documents that support damage claims in order to make certain that only the damages caused by the alleged actions or inactions of the opposing party are included in calculations and that there is no duplication or overlapping of claimed items or amounts is invaluable. This type of work by the paralegal ensures that only valid claims are made and paid for injuries or damages (whether bodily injury or property damage) that were caused by the incident or accident that forms the basis of the litigation.

8.1112 Death Cases.

How can a death be valued? How can money restore the survivors to the position they were in prior to the death? Actuaries can tell us the expected life span of an individual; economists and other experts can postulate that certain statistical methods provide an accurate estimate of the earning capacity of people of "X" ethnic groups, according to sex, age, education, and fields of endeavor. The U.S. Census Bureau has compiled figures considered reliable in making such calculations. With this basic data in hand, the application of a norm to the case at hand can be undertaken. Local statutes or jury instructions should also be consulted since some states have their own actuary tables.

For example, an economic expert may calculate that a 25-year-old man who has a college education and a job in a progressive company can be expected to earn not less than $750,000 over his working life. This is calculated by creating a facsimile of the specific individual's career in the company, with normal advancement, from date-of-death to retirement. Then a separate calculation is made for income from retirement and Social Security benefits.

A housewife's damage includes her marital interest in the earnings of her deceased husband (including retirement benefits), her loss of consortium and companionship with her husband, her loss of her husband's support in rearing the children, and out-of-pocket costs connected with the injury and death, such as funeral and related expenses.

A decedent's child is entitled to the value of the support the child would have had if the deceased parent had lived, loss of parental companionship, and loss of the parent's services. The paralegal must consult with the attorney to determine the factual information that is necessary to make these calculations, convey them to the economic expert, and assist the expert in obtaining whatever other information may be necessary to make proper calculations of this nature.

8.1113 Continuing Damages.

Some cases involve a situation that cannot be remedied or has not been resolved by the time of trial, and the damages are continuing or cumulative in nature. For example, the contamination of an underground water source, or the accidental industrial poisoning of a person, where the poison's damage is a function of time of exposure and the material is slow to be expelled from the body, or a medical condition caused by an accident or injury that will require continuing medical treatment into future. These circumstances require the lawyer and paralegal to explore every available recourse for means of proof or refuting such proof. They will need to gather expert or lay testimony upon which calculations that are required to estimate duration and effect may be based, and to identify measures to correct, mitigate, or minimize the situation or circumstance.

8.1114 Alternative Recoveries.

Damages usually are seen as a one-time cash payment placing the injured party where he or she would have been, but for the injury. In many cases, the aggregate dollar amount is so great that the defendant is incapable of paying such a judgment even when it is fair and reasonable. Bankruptcy may be the outcome of this type of situation, and the plaintiff may not be compensated if the defendant declares bankruptcy. In other cases, a large cash settlement may be insufficient to cover the rapidly expanding cost of future necessary medical care. An alternative method of settlement is necessary to address the needs of all parties in these situations. In the death case cited previously, annuities or endowments to guarantee the children's education as a part of the settlement might be considered. The mother might consider an investment portfolio with a projected or guaranteed annual income as a part of the settlement. Discharge of a mortgage, prepaid medical care plans, or real estate investments—all are possible alternatives to be explored to avoid destroying the defendant while justly compensating the plaintiff.

8.1115 Present Values of Future Amounts.   When considering lost wage or lost earnings damages in any kind of lawsuit, the parties always begin with a calculation of all the dollars lost, including future lost dollars. Future dollars are always adjusted, first upward to reflect the impact of inflation and then downward to reflect the benefit if receiving all the money at one time, rather than in a piecemeal fashion over a number of years, as most of us do by earning our salary. Clearly, the death case previously mentioned points out that the $750,000 the decedent would earn over 40 years would not have the same value as that amount invested now and returning 10 percent per year to the survivors. In effect, the survivors would receive an amount greater than what they would have received had their loved one lived, a "windfall" to which they are not entitled. Here are the calculations using that example: 10 percent of $750,000 times 40 years equals $2,000,000. There are economists and investment experts who can and do provide reliable foundations for calculating such adjustments. There are also computer software packages available commercially that have all of the basic assumptions, such as the U.S. Department of Labor's life expectancy and work life expectancy tables built into the program. The paralegal and/or lawyer enters information on variables into the program, such as the principal amount recovered or to be recovered, the inflation rate, and the rate by which it must be reduced in order to allow for the party's having received all the money in one lump sum, the time period over which the money would have been earned (i.e., the work life expectancy or life expectancy), and any provable raises or increases in salary and/or benefits over the term of the person's life or work life. The program then makes all the necessary calculations and arrives at the present value of the total raw-dollar sum. These calculations, whether made by an economic expert or by a computer program used in the office, provide the basis for calculating future lost earnings that can be claimed in any kind of lawsuit where lost earnings is an element of the damages claimed. The paralegal should become familiar with the principles behind such calculations and the factual information upon which such information must be based, so as to be able to locate that information and either provide it to the expert or use it himself or herself in making these calculations.

8.1116 Arithmetic.   Because every damage claim involves some calculation of the value of a party's loss, the paralegal can assist the attorney by checking the arithmetic used in the calculation process and, more importantly, the actual numbers supporting each subtotal and total. The paralegal can pull all documents that provide a basis for each amount claimed by the party, double-check that each amount has been properly entered in the list of damages, and assemble copies of the documents that support the recapitulation of each category of damages. Although this is often a tedious and time-consuming task, it is one that is critical. Errors in numbers and calculations can cause the credibility of the damages to be weakened, both during settlement negotiations and when presented at trial.

8.112 Personal Injury Settlement Offers and Associated Events

Settlement offers are usually tendered by the plaintiff to the defendant, although sometimes defendants invite such offers and, on occasion, make the first offer to settle. The subject of settlement status and negotiations is mandated by Rule 16(c)(9) of the *Federal Rules of Civil Procedure*. Most courts require that the parties participate in mediation or settlement conferences and/or other alternative dispute resolutions prior to trial.

The most common method by which a plaintiff initiates a settlement offer or demand is by a detailed letter directed to the defendant's attorney. Paralegals for plaintiffs' attorneys are usually involved in drafting settlement letters and in locating and organizing any supporting documentation or other materials. The settlement letter should outline, in as much detail as necessary, the facts developed by the plaintiff that support plaintiff's settlement demand. (*See* Exhibit 8-17.)

EXHIBIT 8-17   Sample Settlement Letter Outline

1. An introduction of the plaintiff and his/her family, including personal statistics;
2. Statement of the facts of the accident/incident giving rise to the litigation;
3. Summary of plaintiff's theory of liability;
4. Summary of the law applicable to the case, with emphasis on how and why liability can and will be proven if the matter is tried;
5. Description of the nature and extent of the damages plaintiff suffered, and the prognosis for partial and complete recovery;
6. Review of the different damage elements the plaintiff is claiming, such as:
   a. a review of jurisprudence that has made awards for damages similar or identical to those of the plaintiff;
   b. a demand for reimbursement for all past medical expenses incurred, with reference to the supporting medical recapitulation and supporting medical bills (all of which should be attached as an exhibit);
   c. a demand for reimbursement for future medical expenses that plaintiff's treating physicians have testified are necessary (if any), in a specific sum, with reference to the basic list of necessary treatments, drugs, equipment, etc., and the economic expert's calculations of the present value of such treatment (both of these documents should be included as supporting materials);
   d. a demand for reimbursement of past and future lost earnings, with reference to the economic expert's report (which should be included as an exhibit);
   e. a review of any other damage claims the plaintiff may have;
7. An offer to settle in a specific amount, along with a statement of any conditions, such as time limitations, who is to pay court costs, etc., that are a part of the offer to settle;
8. Supporting documents or materials:
   Examples for a personal injury case: accident or incident report; documents generated through discovery that demonstrate the manner in which the defendant was at fault, and the relationship of that fault to resulting damages; excerpts of deposition testimony supporting plaintiff's claims (as to liability or damages or both); photographs of the plaintiff, both before and after the accident; excerpts from hospital records and/or doctors' reports detailing the nature and extent of plaintiff's injuries and the treatments plaintiff was given to cure them, as well as the prognosis for plaintiff's partial or complete recovery from the injuries; excerpts from treating physicians' depositions describing the nature and duration of the treatment plaintiff required; information detailing plaintiff's work history and the nature of the work plaintiff was performing at the time of the accident; a recapitulation of the medical and related expenses plaintiff incurred while undergoing medical treatment; if appropriate, a list of expenses plaintiff can be expected to incur for medical treatment (or other items) in the future; information relating to plaintiff's earnings at the time of the accident; and a report from the economics expert detailing plaintiff's past and future lost earnings (or income and profits).

In cases where the potential monetary return justifies the effort and expense, consideration should be given to preparing a videotape and/or settlement brochure to accompany the settlement letter. The attorney may want to introduce himself and the client (or the client's decedent), give a short personal history of the client (and/or the client's decedent), and then proceed to verbally summarize each element of the settlement demand. Photographs or videotapes of family gatherings or activities can be included in the settlement video and will demonstrate more clearly than any words the impact the evidence about the injury or death will have at trial. Short presentations by key expert witnesses can also be included in the video. The paralegal can be of great help to the attorney in assisting with the preparation of a settlement video in many ways including, but not limited to, tentative selection of photos, preliminary interviews with client and family members, conferences with expert witnesses, and participating in the final editing process.

A well-prepared settlement demand letter that outlines all the elements of proof necessary for the plaintiff to prevail at trial, supported by documents and other evidence that will be used at trial to prove each element, generally carries great weight with a defense attorney and the defendant's insurer. Often, this type of settlement proposal opens the door to negotiations with a realistic view toward settling the case.

8.1121 Statutory Offers to Settle.

The codes of civil procedure (or the equivalent) of some states provide for formal offers of settlement to induce the parties to make reasoned, good faith settlement offers to the opposing party. The inducement to act in good faith lies in allowing the proponent to recover the costs of trial from the opposing party who refuses the settlement proffer if the ultimate jury award equals or exceeds the offer. For instance, if the plaintiff makes a formal offer to settle as provided by statute for $14,000 and the defendant declines and if the jury then awards $15,000 at trial, the plaintiff may seek recovery of trial costs from the defendant. These statutes or code sections usually have a time limit within which both the offer and acceptance must be conveyed. This procedure is particularly effective when a defendant is represented by an insurance carrier with undisputed coverage, the offer made by plaintiff is within policy limits, and a prospective jury award may exceed the policy limits. The insurance company must weigh the merits of the case itself along with its responsibility to the insured defendant to act in "good faith" in indemnifying the insured, while representing the insured's and its own interests.

8.1122 Settlement Conferences.

Settlement conferences have been held in federal courts for many years. The procedure was somewhat voluntary at first, but it has become mandatory in many district courts over the past several years and is often included in the order that is entered by the judge at the first scheduling conference in the case. *See* Rule 16(a)(5), *Federal Rules of Civil Procedure.* In federal court, it is generally the practice to assign a U.S. magistrate or a U.S. District Court judge who is not involved in the case to conduct the settlement conference. All parties and their counsel must participate. If an insurance company is ultimately liable, a representative with settlement authority must be in attendance.

Nothing appears in the court record except the order approving or ordering the scheduling conference. All parties are required to prepare a position paper or settlement statement and deliver it in advance to the magistrate or judge who is going to conduct the settlement conference. This paper is not filed, nor are copies served on opposing counsel. There are set topics to be addressed in this submission, which are usually set out in the order for settlement conference. Generally, they direct each party to state the claims of the parties, the legal and factual issues, actual or expected testimony, and applicable case law.

Settlement conferences usually begin with introduction of the parties, followed by brief statements of their claims made by counsel. During these presentations, it is not unusual for counsel to describe or present persuasive exhibits. Caution must be exercised in this regard—a settlement conference is not a trial, and there is no procedure to receive or handle exhibits. Charts, photographs, diagrams, or other forms of demonstrable evidence are good examples of the type of exhibits that would be used at this time. Following the initial presentations, each party and their counsel would be directed to a different room, and the settlement official would commence private discussions by making the rounds. Often, the first round would include some direct questions to one or more of the parties as well as counsel. Subsequent rounds eventually involve the settlement official pointing out strengths and/or weaknesses of each party's claim and perhaps a preliminary assessment of a realistic settlement range as well as a party's chances of prevailing at trial. The next step is conveying settlement offers and counteroffers to each of the parties involved. Sometimes the magistrate or district judge calls all the persons involved back into the main meeting room for a pep talk or admonition, and at other times the parties and counsel stay in their assigned rooms until the end of the conference. If the parties are able to realistically assess the strengths and weaknesses of their claims and are willing to compromise to some extent, the settlement judge can usually find that bargaining range and get the parties to agree to a settlement. Only the end result of the conference is reported (usually orally) to the judge handling the case. All facts, figures, and theories expressed at the conference are kept confidential.

8.1123 Mediation.

Another method of entering into settlement negotiations is voluntary or mandatory mediation. Many state courts now require mediation before trial if the amount in controversy exceeds a stated amount. Check your state rules of civil procedure as well as the local court rules.

The mediation process is similar to the settlement conference procedures outlined herein, except that the parties are required to hire a mediator and pay their respective shares of the mediator's fees. Generally, mediation is held at the mediator's office unless the number of parties involved requires rental of a commercial facility such as hotel meeting rooms. Like the settlement conference, each party needs to have a separate room available to confer with the mediator and confer with their own counsel. Corporations, partnerships, insurance companies, and other business entities who are parties to the lawsuit generally send representatives who have authority to negotiate on behalf of their principals and enter into settlement agreements.

8.1124 Court Approval.

Some settlements require approval of the court and may also require the appointment of a guardian or trust administrator. Such procedures are most common in cases involving minors or those who have been adjudged incompetent to handle their own business and personal affairs. The procedures and requirements differ from state to state, but where encountered, the paralegal should review the current requirements of the jurisdiction and make certain that all necessary documents are prepared and all requirements are met so that settlement can proceed smoothly and correctly.

BIBLIOGRAPHY

Federal Civil Judicial Procedure and Rules. St. Paul, MN: West, 2008.

Federal Rules of Criminal Procedures. St. Paul, MN: West, 2008

Federal Rules of Civil Procedure, St. Paul, MN: West, 2008

Koerselman, Virginia, Civil Litigation, 2000, A NALA Campus Course, On-line Self Study Program for Paralegals. www.NALACampus.com.

Koerselman, Virginia, *CLA Review Manual.* West Publishing Company, 1998

National Association of Legal Assistants, Advanced Paralegal Certification (APC) Course – Discovery, (Introduced July 2006), http://nala.org/apcweb/index.html

National Association of Legal Assistants, Advanced Paralegal Certification (APC) Course – Trial Practice, (Introduced January 2007), http://nala.org/apcweb/index.html

Oran's Dictionary of the Law, 4th ed. Albany, NY: Delmar Cengage Learning, 2008.

9

The Paralegal and Document Discovery Cases

9.00 INTRODUCTION

Document production is a critical part of the discovery process. Generally, paralegals are more involved than attorneys in requesting, reviewing, inspecting, and/or producing papers and records relating to the subject of the controversy. Therefore, it is important to learn the rules and general procedures for production of documents and things and inspection of land.

As discussed in Chapter 8, the document inspection phase of formal discovery is governed by Rule 34 of the *Federal Rules of Civil Procedure.* Many states have adopted a similar or identical rule which outlines the procedures in the state court system, but one should not assume that to be the case. It is important to locate and compare the applicable state rules regarding document requests and production and to note the variances. It is also important to review existing local rules for any court in which your action is pending.

The request for production of documents and things, whether initiated by the client's attorney or by the opposing party's attorney, whether large or small, is designed to make available all the relevant facts in the case that have been memorialized in documents or things which can include writings, drawings, photographs, and, most recently, electronic data in various forms. The larger the volume of documents to be produced, the more difficult, time-consuming, and costly the effort will be. The basic concepts of document production apply to all cases, whatever the size, and should be followed to obtain the most cost-effective and efficient results for the client.

The attorney and the paralegal must consider and analyze the value, need for, and utility of the discovery plan. They must weigh the time and cost against the anticipated benefits. It does little good to expend time and money designing and implementing a system that does not substantially contribute to reaching the goal in the case. One must also keep in mind that many courts now have technical requirements that must be met with respect to how documents will be presented and used in court. Many courts are now leaning toward requiring "paperless" trials, which will enable the paralegal to use or learn different skills to facilitate these requirements.

Document discovery and the systems developed to handle them require intensive thought and consideration early in the case to produce effective and reliable results as well as giving thought to their ultimate use in court. Once committed to a given course, it can be difficult and expensive to change directions. For that reason, it may be necessary to convince the client that monies expended up front will save them in the long run. Because the majority of the work with documents is a physical task, time is a critical element. The best work is conducted with intensity but not panic in a consistent and reliable manner.

9.001 The Discovery Plan

The initiation of discovery requires the attorneys and the paralegals to consider jointly the problems anticipated in implementing any discovery plan for documents. There are two sides to this consideration: the client's documents and how to handle them and the opposing party's documents and how to handle those. Decisions on the system to employ and the staff required will vary according to a number of factors such as the following.

9.0011 Plaintiff or Defendant.   Whether the client is the plaintiff or the defendant in the case will play a part in staffing choices. If the client is the plaintiff, usually there is adequate time before filing the complaint to locate all of the client's documents and to arrange them in a reasonably ordered fashion. In this case, it is possible to work with a much smaller staff than when the client is the defendant responding to an aggressive plaintiff and suffering from the constraints of time created by court orders. In this electronic age, serious consideration should be given to utilizing coding and/or imaging of the documents. This is an exercise that may be costly initially but will save the client throughout the case and, most importantly, in trial preparation and at trial.

9.0012 Time Problems.   Time constraints may arise from many sources. The statute of limitations effective in the case may have a bearing on the organization of personnel and equipment. The service of a request for production of documents with a statutory period in which to respond may present timing problems. It is axiomatic that the shorter the period of time in which to accomplish the production, the larger the staff needed and, generally, the more limited the choices of the manner in which the production will be performed. Once again, the coding and/or imaging of the documents could be quite helpful not only in the organization of the documents, but also in the review and ultimate production.

9.0013 Volume.   Documents in business litigation, product liability, and antitrust cases may vary from 1,000 pages of material to 500,000 or more pages of material. It is not uncommon for documents in mass tort, complex, class actions, and multidistrict litigation to number in the several millions. Document volume has a major effect on the difficulty of production and will make demands both on the attorneys and the paralegals in terms of the system employed and the manner of handling the documents (which will be discussed later). Generally, 1,000 to 2,000 pages can be handled easily using searchable lists of documents as a control device; although with the proliferation of computer databases on the market, it is not recommended as the most time-or cost-effective way to go. If monetary constraints drive the document production, a small team of one or two people can be used. This team quickly becomes very familiar with the individual documents. Control and retrieval of the documents can then be simplified.

As the volume of documents increases, the ability of the team to recall the important documents with certainty diminishes, regardless of the size of the team. If time is a problem, the team may be larger, and consequently, the number of "duplicate documents" that exist in all files may not have the same impact on the discovery team as they would if only one or two people worked on them. Generally, with a volume over 2,000 pages, document databases (which are discussed later) become necessary to handle the files properly. The "rule" in document discovery is the smaller the crew, the better. A small team gives each person a high degree of familiarity with the file, but it also means the routine tasks of numbering, indexing, designating, and reviewing will take longer, and there is a greater impact on the effort if the team loses a member. There are outside vendors who can provide the electronic numbering and designating with appropriate instruction. This decision may save valuable review time.

9.0014 Special Document Considerations.   Routine correspondence, contracts, drafts of contracts, letters and memoranda, and so on can be handled by paralegals with reasonable training, time, and familiarity with the subject of the lawsuit. When the documents contain extensive and technical engineering reports or highly complex studies and mathematical calculations related to those studies, the use of an engineering-qualified paralegal or an engineer on loan from the company department in which the lawsuit originated may be absolutely essential. It is often a rule of thumb to initially collect all technical documentation for later review by experts to determine what is relevant and/or responsive for the production.

Other special document problems can arise involving economic data, tax matters, or accounting documents peculiar to a large firm in which computer printouts and/or prenumbered forms might be adapted directly into the system without "special" or additional identifying data.

9.0015 Locating Responsive Documents.   Among potential discovery production problems is the location and production of all responsive documents as opposed to the production of a representative copy of a particular type of requested document. The attorney must be consulted in determining whether all copies should be produced or whether a single copy will suffice. An example is a personnel manual. It is probable that only one manual need be produced unless there is more than one version, in which case all versions may need to be produced. When the client is the plaintiff, thought should be given to identifying all categories of documents which have any relation to the issues in the lawsuit, including the proof of damages, with the idea of anticipating the documents which the adversary is most likely to request. Once through the files is difficult, but twice through is very expensive and time-consuming. The search must be thorough to identify all the documents within the guidelines established. Additionally, it is important to maintain the files "as kept in the ordinary course of business" unless the attorney makes a strategic decision not to do so. In any event, production of complete files is essential. Files of a fragmentary nature are extremely difficult to explain in discovery proceedings and will create many difficulties for the discovery team later in tracking the normal handling of such documents. Any gap in the numbering or the appearance of incomplete files may trigger questions including inclusion in a privilege log. Alternative numbering exercises will be discussed later.

9.0016 File Location.

One of the most difficult problems to overcome in document production is that of physical location. Files are often spread out among offices of a large corporation or the departments of small companies based on their duties, functions, and responsibilities. Sometimes the relationship between a file and an office or department is so tenuous that it is difficult to anticipate all the locations where the documents might be; this poses a substantial problem in the identification and location of those documents. The paralegal's imagination should be pushed to its limits in considering the possible resting places of potentially responsive material. It may be in a central file room, in one or more offices of individuals, or in storage. Consider each possibility, and then during the physical search, ask each person: "Who else might have copies of this?" "Who do you send material to?" and so on. A checklist of questions to ask may be helpful to verify that a diligent search was made. Clear and concise communication with the client is critical in soliciting their assistance in the location of all documents.

9.0017 Work Space, Equipment, and Budget.

The space in which the work is performed, the equipment with which to conduct the effort, and the budget within which the discovery team attempts to operate all effect the team's ability to produce results in a timely manner. It does little good to rage against problems beyond one's control, and the paralegal's flexibility in adjusting to any limitations will assist the discovery effort and present a positive and effective attitude.

9.0018 Documents—Evidence and Company Operation.

The need to produce documents in a suit requires the attorney to take custody of potential documentary evidence. The client's daily work must continue with as little disruption as possible. Depending on whether or not it will be possible to remove the documents from their location for any period of time will drive how you recover the potentially relevant documents for review and possible production. If it is imperative that the documents remain where they are, you may just want to flag or slipsheet (in the case of large continuous relevant documents in file folders or entire drawers) the documents for copying. Depending on the volume of the flagged or slipsheeted documents, you may want to bring in an outside copy service, possibly with their own equipment so as not to further interrupt the ongoing operations of the company. The paralegal must oversee all aspects of this reproduction from the removal of documents to the copiers and the immediate return. Indices must be kept of which documents came from where.

Although an initial thorough search is preferable, it is sometimes unavoidable to have to return to the company or warehouse for an additional review of original documents. In order not to duplicate the reproduction of documents previously reviewed, leave a paper trail of what was reviewed and/or copied, when, by whom, and for what purpose.

9.0019 To Number or Not to Number.   Once the potentially responsive and relevant documents are identified, the problem of future reference to each one must be addressed. The documents may be marked with a unique identifying number, alphabetic character, or an alphanumeric combination before any photocopying, sorting, or other handling is undertaken. Tactical or strategic considerations or the personal preference of the attorney may dictate otherwise. Many clients prefer that their original documents not be marked so copies are made of the originals, the originals are either returned to the client or safeguarded until the disposition of the case, and the copies are marked. This set can be referred to as the "organizational" or ORG set. The integrity of this set should be maintained by keeping it in numbered order. Early numbering establishes control over the documents and minimizes the chances of a document becoming lost or misfiled. It also has the benefit of dealing with a laborious job in the beginning of the case, simplifies the recognition of individual documents and their subsequent copies and the comparison of apparent duplicates, and facilitates the use of file indexing, databases, or other techniques. Some attorneys prefer not to number the documents until after the opposing party has reviewed and inspected them. This creates difficult control and identification problems for the paralegals (and ultimately for the attorney). Its worst feature is that it delays the labor of numbering until after the inspection by the opposing party. This often means that a huge volume of documents must be numbered and potentially designated under a time constraint, as opposed to the more comfortable system allowed by the technique of numbering them after review for relevance. Even with the ability to electronically number documents, it takes time. Note that when the documents are electronically numbered, you do not have the tactile label to ascertain the original numerically labeled document. This inability is actually of no consequence, and the dependence can be overcome. An additional drawback of unnumbered documents it that when the opposing party later in the case uses that document, it may not be possible to know whether or not it originated from the client's production. It is also impossible to know whether any documents were removed from the document production area if no tracking numbers are used. When the documents have been numbered in advance, there is no doubt of their source. The use of the Document Tracking Inventory (DTI) plays a role in documenting the genesis of the documents and later tracking their review, coding, imaging, and/or production. (*See* Exhibit 9-1.) This becomes even clearer when both sides may produce the same document, and it is sometimes preferable to use the adverse party's numbered documents as exhibits to Declarations or at Depositions and so forth because of possible authentication for genuineness issues.

9.00110 Document Control Methods.   Since the documents may range in volume from 1,000 to several million pages, the choice of control methods must be one of the first decisions made. Failure to do this will result in duplication of work, additional labor, and added cost and may result in documents being lost, misplaced, or misfiled. In addition to numbering the documents, which is generally considered the best method, other methods available are:

a. Document indices using reference items, such as date, author, and addressee (discussed in Section 9.0122, Indices)

b. Use of surrogate documents, such as the Document Review Form (discussed in Section 9.0132, Reviewing the Material)

c. Individual and Entity Database Form (discussed in Section 9.032, Individual and Entity Database)

d. Other indices which include the identification numbers for each document.

9.00111 Privileged Documents.   It is important to identify and segregate documents early in the review and control process which may carry any "privilege," such as that of attorney-client, attorney work product, third-party, proprietary information, or trade secrets. The documents may have to be

EXHIBIT 9-1   Documents Tracking Inventory

PRIVILEGE LOG: XYZ Construction vs Developments, Inc., et al

Date Received	Source	Date Produced	Produced To	Document I.D.	NOTES	Coded/ Imaged	Box No.
06/11/02	Company A	06/15/2004	Company B	IP000001-IP010003	Copies of Contract and Addendum	Yes/Yes	WS 14-17
06/12/04	Company A	06/17/2004	Company B	IP000001-IP014869	Correspondence Regarding Contractual Arrangements	Yes/Yes	WS 18-19
06/18/04	Company B	07/16/2004	Company A	XIP014870-XIP014877; XIP015056-	Deed of Confirmatory Assignment (Ownership Document)	Yes/Yes	WS 39

tracked in a Privilege Log, which may be required to be produced to adverse counsel. The paralegal often assists in this important assignment and should be briefed by the attorney concerning what specifically should be looked for, along with the criteria to be used, in evaluating the existence or absence of privilege. There may be significant negative ramifications of producing a privileged document including waiver of the claimed privilege on that particular document or possibly all documents claimed as privileged. It is the attorney's ultimate responsibility to provide this guidance at the beginning of the case and to provide adequate supervision throughout the process.

9.00112 Issue Recognition.   When the client is the plaintiff, it may be necessary early in the discovery operation to code into the database the documents according to the issues of the case. A substantial amount of early thought and analysis by the attorneys to identify the case issues along with some familiarity with the types of documents involved in the case is needed to accomplish this task. One of the important elements to successful issue coding is to establish a reference list of the issues that incorporates an understandable "plain language" definition. Bear in mind that as the case progresses and motions are filed and ruled on by the court, the issues may change and the issue coding will need to be updated as necessary.

When the client is the defendant in a case, issue recognition is often accomplished at a later stage when there has been more opportunity to define all the issues important to the defense. Instead, sortings may be performed according to each numbered request by the opposing party, with the issues imputed to some degree from an analysis of the nature of the documents requested. These "sortings" may be accomplished either by physical segregation of copies of documents or noted in the database which can then be queried by specific sort requirement. The latter method is preferred.

9.00113 Personnel Choices.   Deciding what personnel resources to use in gathering and indexing, coding, or imaging the relevant documents must be done early in the process. Depending on the number of documents, using the client's personnel may be a cost-effective alternative to relying solely on paralegals or hiring temporary workers. When nonlegal trained staff is utilized, it is very important for the attorney and the paralegal to closely supervise the work effort to ensure that the results are reliable and thorough, with all the records produced and properly indexed or coded. For purposes of confidentiality, especially when dealing with documents that may fall under a Protective Order, using the client's personnel versus hiring temporary workers should be evaluated.

9.00114 Paralegal Conceptual Contributions.   The attorneys in the case will rely on input regarding choosing a discovery plan. The paralegal is often tasked with performing an initial review of the files and participating in discussions on the possible paths the litigation may take. When a tentative choice of the document discovery plan is made, the paralegal may often be tasked with generating a step-by-step procedure for implementing the plan, including estimates of time, personnel, space, equipment, and cost for consideration by the attorney in making the final decision. The paralegal should be knowledgeable concerning the mechanical processes and should be a forceful advocate when necessary for the system of choice, but in the end, it is the attorney's decision.

9.00115 Attorney Reviews and Audits.   The attorney must be satisfied that the directions given the paralegal for performing document searches are clear and that the work is being properly accomplished. The paralegal should welcome, encourage, and initiate regular spot checks or audits of the work being done especially early in the process; it minimizes wasted work and reveals any weaknesses in communications.

9.00116 Documenting the Plan.   Once selected, the plan should be outlined in detail (in writing) with the control devices and procedures well explained. The terms to be used, acronyms, logos, codes, and abbreviations as well as flags, slipsheets, labels, and so on must all be analyzed, and the initial selections memorialized. The plan document will serve as a guide for use and modification as the case progresses. This plan document or "protocol" should accompany the instructional video, if made.

9.01   CLIENT DOCUMENTS

Whether plaintiff or defendant, document discovery plans always involve a minimum of five basic activities to be considered, whether the ultimate effort is small and simple or huge and complex. These essential elements, or common principles, are locating the documents, establishing document control, identifying and reviewing the documents, retrieving and producing the documents, and, ultimately, returning the documents.

9.011   Locate

If the client receives a request for production of documents, the paralegal may be involved in determining what material, if any, is responsive to the various requests and where it is located. In some types of cases, especially actions involving business entities and manufacturing processes, it will take a good part of the thirty-day response time to accomplish those tasks because of the potential volume of documents and facilities to be searched.

The paralegal is involved in locating and gathering together all the client's documents, which relate to the lawsuit prior to formal filing of the summons and complaint. This is especially critical when lawsuits are to be filed in federal court, since Rule 26 of the *Federal Rules of Civil Procedure* requires the plaintiff to make initial disclosures concerning witnesses and documents at the time the lawsuit is filed.

9.0111 Attorney and Paralegal Review and Analysis.   The first step in responding to a production request is to carefully review and analyze the formal request. Note any individual requests as to which an objection might be asserted, and discuss them with the supervising attorney.

Whether responding to a production request or gathering documents during the pretrial investigation phase, the attorney and the paralegal should carefully discuss the case to ensure both have the same understanding of the issues (actual or probable) of the case along with the parameters for locating the client's files and the reviewing and selection process that will follow. In some cases, particularly in complex litigation, it may be necessary for the attorney to assist in the early review of documents to obtain a perspective on the types of documents involved in the case in order to make the subsequent decisions. Specific parameters may need to be set up to streamline the review and should be fully documented in the protocol. The types of documents, as well as the volume, often determine the control system used in the case.

9.0112 Locating Document Sources.

The next step in responding to a production request is to send a copy of the request to the client and then follow up with the client to determine the likely location of all responsive material. If the client is a business entity, the paralegal will need to know all departments or individuals that have played a part in the contracting or manufacturing or other procedure which is involved in the subject of the litigation. If possible, it is best for the paralegal or the attorney to talk with key employees. Ask them to provide a "walk-through" of the contracting or manufacturing process, identifying all other players or departments. Be on the alert for names, as well as types of documentation, which pass between or among employees. The use of an organizational chart is helpful. Typically, several copies of interoffice memoranda and correspondence are circulated to department heads or managers. If that is the case, the paralegal should prepare a "cast of characters" list which will help in the collection of documents from all possible recipients throughout the company. In a case with a small number of issues, only one, two, or three departments may be involved, which makes it easier to gather the documents. In large document cases, it is essential to prepare a full listing of all sources of records to be reviewed for discussion with the supervising attorney since this initial step may determine the completeness of the response to the opposing party's document request. Creating a datamap of possible sites for electronic files is also helpful.

After the types of potentially responsive records and the approximate volume have been tentatively identified, a strategy session may need to be held so that the attorney and client can decide whether responsive documents will be produced as they are kept in the normal course of business or whether they will be organized and labeled to correspond with the categories in the request. Document production strategies vary widely depending on the attorney's strategic, discovery, and trial style.

9.0113 Gathering the Documents and Taking Custody.

In small document cases, this process may be as simple as receiving a few file folders or a banker's box of documents from the client. In larger document cases, the process may involve arranging for all the documents to be collected in one place for transport to the law firm or some other work area within the client's organization where they will be processed and segregated. In very large cases, this process can also involve arranging transport to a "joint document depository" which has been established by agreement among all the parties to a lawsuit or by court order. Electronic documents are discussed more fully in Section 9.05.

As each collection of documents, whether in file folders, boxes, file cabinets, or electronically stored files is identified as having a possible connection to the lawsuit, it is added to an inventory list that characterizes the location from which it was taken and the custodian (individual) who provided it, along with a general description of the contents. For instance, if the file has a number and a title, that identification should be used for clarity; if a box contains accounting records, that description along with the time period covered may be used for identification. The affixing of temporary number labels may facilitate the paralegal's tracking of the boxes. When taking possession of a large number of documents or files, an estimate of the space involved should be made as well, such as a "one-half-inch linear

EXHIBIT 9-2   Sample Inventory List

Initial Cient Document Inventory					Page No. ___ of ___	
Case: _____ Date: _____						
Source / Location	**General Description**	**Container / Size**	**Id / End**	**Produced**	**Date**	
		☐ Box ☐ Folder ☐ Loose ☐ _____ Size: _____				
		☐ Box ☐ Folder ☐ Loose ☐ _____ Size: _____				
		☐ Box ☐ Folder ☐ Loose ☐ _____ Size: _____				
		☐ Box ☐ Folder ☐ Loose ☐ _____ Size: _____				

measure" or "one full banker's box" or "one gigabyte of data." This is important because at some later date if a decision to number is made, a reference to the inclusive numbers contained within the individual files or document collections should be added to the inventory list. (*See* Exhibit 9-2.) Receipts for the documents are prepared by the paralegal team and left with the client or individual who provided them. The paralegal team then takes the documents in whatever form provided into custody for transport to a work area.

PRACTICE TIPS

■ When gathering files from a business client for your review, it is important to ascertain whether those particular records are active files. If so, every effort should be made to give those records priority for review purposes so that they can be returned to the department using them. If any active file contains material which is responsive to the request, you must devise a system to note the location of the active file and the custodian of that file so you can retrieve it for the inspection.

■ The material which was contained in the active file when you reviewed it should be marked, listed, or clipped in some manner so that employees will not disturb the portions you have already reviewed and it will be obvious if anything has been added to the file after your review; then you only have to review any new material before you produce that file for inspection. During the inspection, it is acceptable procedure to request that opposing counsel review active files first so that business interruption can be kept at a minimum. Review of electronic documents is discussed more fully in Section 9.05.

9.0114 The Evidence Room Work Area.   If the actual production for inspection will be held at the client's facility, a conference room or other working space should be selected. In most instances, that place will serve as your office for purposes of reviewing files and other records. Generally, inactive files, which contain material responsive to the request, should be segregated and kept in a designated area awaiting the production after you have reviewed them. The work area for the paralegal team should be removed from normal activity of the departments and of the functional personalities in a case. The room should be considered an "evidence room" with restricted entry and a firm control over the entry and removal of documents within it. Accurate tracking and control of the room and all its contents at all times is essential.

9.012   Control

Once the documents have been located and gathered together, some method of control for ensuring the integrity of the document collection while it is in custody must be established. The surest method is to number the selected documents as soon as the "responsive" identity is confirmed. Once each document is numbered with a unique identifying number, alphabetic character, or alphanumeric combination, the ability to maintain the documents in the same order and condition produced is certain. Additionally, unique identification numbers allow accurate records to be maintained of exactly what documents are produced to an opposing party, ensure that the source of the particular document will be easily identified in the future, allow for the creation of easily searchable information databases, allow for cross-referencing use as exhibits, and simplify accurate reference to the document during depositions.

PRACTICE TIPS

- There are several methods available to number the documents. An automatic numbering machine or "Bates Stamp" may be used. Electronic or powered numbering machines are available to stamp the documents. Computer label programs are also widely available which print a series of numbers on "peel-and-stick" labels which are then affixed to the document pages. Many copiers have the capability of numbering photocopies of documents. Some computer programs, such as Adobe, have Bates numbering features. Finally, there are vendor services which will produce printed labels similar to those which may be done in-house as well as those who will also perform the actual task of document numbering. All of these methods allow for the use of a prefix or suffix with the number, which is useful for additional source identification.

- Whichever method of numbering is used, the placement of the identifying number on the document should be consistent and regular. The number should not cover or obscure any writing or data on the original document. Nothing is more frustrating than having to hunt for the document number on a page or not being able to read a word or phrase because it has been defaced by the number. It is suggested that whenever possible, the number be placed in the vicinity of the lower right-hand corner of a page because most of us are already accustomed to looking in that area for a page number.

Although in small document cases it is not uncommon for a method other than numbering to be used, it is still the best control method. In large document cases, numbering is the only practical and reliable method, and any attempt to do otherwise is not recommended. The relationship of a document to the file from which it was taken cannot be lost, and preserving the documents in the same condition in which they were discovered is extremely important. For that reason, if the documents need to be returned to their original source and you do not have permission to number the original documents (which is often the case), make an exact copy of the original documents including labels from folders, tabs, or binder spines. Copying of original documents can also facilitate the immediate return of critical work files to the client. Bear in mind that the paralegal cannot change the character of the documents by assembling or disassembling stapled or bound material without the concurrence and direction of the attorney.

From this point forward, it is essential that whatever system of control is adopted that the paralegal ensures its integrity. By doing so, the paralegal ensures that the attorney will be able to establish that the method of production complies fully with discovery requirements and is not arbitrary, whimsical, or unreliable. The attorney may also be required to assure the opposing party and/or the court that he or she "conducted a diligent search and reasonable inquiry" into the location of relevant documents.

PRACTICE TIPS—THE DECISION TO NUMBER

- Numbering documents produced to the opposing party has great advantages for the paralegal team and, by extension, for the attorneys for whom they work. It improves control and simplifies referral, retrieval, and sorting. When the original documents are numbered, it makes it easy to provide a copy back to the client in the situation where the document is actually used by the client in its normal and continuing course of business. Numbered documents provide an easy reference between the client, the lawyer, witnesses, and other users from that point forward. When the decision to number any document or set of documents is postponed to some future time, photocopies of the responsive documents should limit possible duplicates and actual duplicates to a minimum that later will have to be located, purged, or substituted with the numbered copies.

- A numbering system is sometimes perceived as imposing additional difficulties. Irrelevant or privileged documents may be numbered that later would not be produced to the opposing party but might have to be explained. Gaps may occur where there are numbering errors, where irrelevant documents were initially included and later removed, and where privileged documents have been removed. The opposing party will want to know why these gaps exist. However, under the Federal Rules of Civil Procedure (and state rules which are similar), the opposing party is entitled to a listing of all documents withheld from production. The use of a numbering system under these provisions enhances the ability of the producing party to comply with those rules. It should be remembered that determinations of relevancy, responsiveness, and privilege may all be challenged by an opposing party and ultimately ruled upon by a judge; therefore numbering the documents is a tool which ultimately aids in this process.

- A numbering system is often more cost-effective and efficient than a "no numbering" system. In order to maintain control and to minimize problems which arise from opposing party challenges to the completeness of the production, such as claims of never receiving a document, or establishing the source of a document reviewed

continued

> by expert witnesses, consultants, and others, some offices have each document photocopied for production marked with a legend on the side, at the top, or at the bottom of the page in a distinctive location that reads essentially "Copy of an original from the file of X produced on [date]." For extra security, an exact duplicate of the material produced to the opposing party should be maintained, with any redactions noted. A numbering system allows the creation of an index of the documents produced and eliminates the need for many duplicate copies.

9.0121 Purposes.   The purpose of the document control program is to ensure the following critical points:

1. That every document made available to the opposing parties has been reviewed by the paralegals and by the attorneys.

2. That privileged documents are not inadvertently produced to the opposing party in the course of the proceeding.

3. That every document responsive to the case is produced as required but that the attorneys before its surrender exercise every appropriate defense to production of any document.

4. That every highly significant document, whether helpful or harmful to the client, (sometimes referred to as a "hot" or "critical" document) is brought to the attention of the supervising attorneys for evaluation before production to the opposing party. These documents will most likely be used as key deposition or trial exhibits.

5. That every document obtained from the opposing party is correctly handled and cross-referenced in relation to the issues and to the "friendly" documents in the case.

6. That documents are maintained in an order facilitating retrieval of any document as needed by the attorneys in a timely fashion.

9.0122 Indices.   Indexing is an essential document control task in all document cases. Good indices are cost-effective because they make the process of analyzing, sorting, and retrieving documents less labor-intensive and time-consuming. Indices are really mini databases. By creating a master index on the computer in either "table" format or in "merge data file" format the master index can be sorted in various ways to create additional indices, such as by ID number, date, author, issue, or any other combination. When the volume of documents to be indexed exceeds 1,000, it is much more efficient to use a database program (such as Access, Paradox, or dBASE) to create the master index. The essential elements of the master index include the identification number, original source, date, document type, author, addressee, any "cc" recipients, and subject or title of the document. Normally, the information for the index is collected on forms by the paralegal or document production team as the documents are reviewed and numbered for entry into the computer at a later time. Sometimes, the information is entered directly into the computer while it is being gathered. If gathering the data manually, the form used to gather the information should be in the same format and order as the electronic version will be.

Indexing may be done at the same time the documents are reviewed and identified or may be done separately. The factors that affect that decision are usually the volume of the documents, staff available to accomplish the task, and relevant time constraints. During the control phase, the only file that exists is the original document file collection. To maintain the exact integrity of the original document file collection, it is suggested that a copy or "working set" of the documents is made and that the original documents are secured as discussed later. (*See* Exhibit 9-3, Sample Master Index.)

EXHIBIT 9-3   Sample Master Index

Master Document Index

Case: _____   Date: _____

ID No.	Source	Date	Type	Author	Addressee	Other "cc"	Subj/Title/"re"
AB 10001	ABC Accounting Dept	05-01-11	Letter	John Doe	James Joyce	Annie Long	Payment of Invoice No. 77923
AB 10002							
AB 10003	ABC Accounting Dept	05-01-12	Memo	Jane Roe	John Doe		Adjustment to Joyce Bill
AB 10003							

9.0123 Document Room Control.   Control of physical documents in the document room or work area is critical for maintaining the integrity of the document collection. An original document should never leave the document room for any reason. To assure the integrity of the original documents, once the copy set is made to number and designate (if necessary), the original documents should be put in a location that is under the control of the paralegal so that one can refer back to the original set and confirm that it is exactly as collected or received. Use care when sending originals and get approval from the attorney. If the original document is requested for review, a log detailing the date sent, name of the requester, name of the person who physically removed the document, where the document is being sent, and name of who will be responsible for the document (if different from the person who requested) should be prepared. Placing an "out card" or other surrogate document in the file in place of the document is also recommended. (*See* Exhibit 9-4, Sample Check Out Form and Document Review "Out Card.") This procedure provides an essential check to ensure that the document is not lost or mislaid, and, depending on the reason the original was taken, establishes a record which be useful in certain circumstances, such as when an opposing party complains that the document was never provided or never seen or to establish what an expert has or has not reviewed. The paralegal will also be able to follow up and retrieve documents after a reasonable amount of time. It is suggested that whenever possible, a copy of the document(s) is made for review by an attorney. This procedure should be followed if the original is being sent outside the office along with a transmittal letter forwarding the documents.

9.013   Identify and Review

The third phase of the document program is concerned with reviewing and identifying the document collection. No matter the volume of the documents involved, there is no shortcut for examining each document page-by-page. The identification process is not complete until all potentially relevant or responsive documents are distinguished and separated from documents that may be privileged and from those which are irrelevant or nonresponsive documents. Remember that during this initial review, a document may be designated as nonresponsive to a request, but issues throughout the discovery process may change, affecting this designation. For this reason, the segregation of these documents with a limited description on your document review index may be helpful.

EXHIBIT 9-4   Sample Check Out Form and Document Review "Out Card"

Document Check Out Sheet

CASE: Alpha Beta Corp vs Luke Skywalker   LOCATION: File Room "A"—Sixth Floor

Doc. ID Nos.	Date Taken / Name	Purpose	Destination	Date Return / Name	Notes
AB 115000 AB 125005	2/6/06 J. Greene	Issue Coding of Docs	J. Greene's Office	2/10/06 J. Greene	
AB2 007000 ABAS 008500	2/9/06 Annie Long	Review for Damages Info	Jack Esquire's Office		

Sample Document "Out Card"

DOCUMENT(S) PULLED FOR REVIEW/PROCESSING (SEE CHECK OUT SHEET)	
ID No. Start	**ID No. End**
~~AB 116000~~	~~AB126006~~
AB2 007000	AB2 008500

For plaintiffs, the process of initial review and examining each document page-by-page often occurs during the prelitigation phase of the case and is conducted to identify all documents which may be potentially relevant to the anticipated lawsuit, as well as those supporting of and troublesome to the client's position. When done effectively, this process will also provide the necessary information needed to respond to production requests after the lawsuit has been filed as well as to provide to the adverse parties and the court during initial disclosure.

For defendants, the initial review and document examination is usually conducted to identify specific documents that fit the requirements of the production request, whether in hand or anticipated, as well as to identify documents which support or contradict the defenses asserted in the answer to the complaint.

9.0131 Paralegal Preparation and Training.

It is extremely important for the attorney and the paralegal to discuss the scope of the document review. This should be based on the issues of the legal pleadings and the discovery received or anticipated. The scope, issues, and other items deemed important to note during the review should be documented in a memo, which is then available as a

EXHIBIT 9-5 Sample Document Review Form

CASE: XYZ Construction vs Developments, Inc., et al Screened by: Jack Palance Date: 1/1/06	

Doc_ID Start: *C 100001*	Doc_ID End: *C100010*	Date: *10/2/03*	Source: *XYZ JOB FILE*

Type: ☐ Letter ☐ Memo ☐ Report ☐ Financial Notes ☐ Contract ☐ Invoice ☐ Medical ☐ Receipt ☑ Proposal ☐ Time Card ☐ Daily Job Report ☐ Meeting Minutes ☐ Other _____

From: *XYZ CONSTRUCTION*	To: *OWNER*	"cc": *ARCHITECT*

Duplicate of Doc_ID:	☑ Attached to Doc_ID: *C 099999*

☐ Subj: ☐ Re: ☑ Title: *Change Order Proposal 14*	☐ Marginalia

Privilege: ☐ AC ☐ WP ☐ Other	Protection: ☐ Trade Secret ☐ Research ☐ Development ☐ Commercial

☑ Relevant ☐ Not Relevant ☐ Helpful ☐ Problem ☑ Damaged Info ☐ Liability ☐ KEY

Issues: ☐ Fraud ☐ NMegligence ☑ Breach of Contract ☐ Bad Faith ☐ Notice ☐ Intent ☐ Reliance

Key Words: ☐ Bituthene ☑ Change Order ☑ Delay ☐ Acceleration ☐ Weather ☐ Generator ☐ Piles

Names Mentioned:

Doc. Mentioned: *Contract dated 8/1/03*

Notes/Summary: *Subcontractor's itemized proposal to add waterproof membrane sub-roofing. Total cost $150,679. Attached to Cover Letter dated 10/3/03.*

ready reference as the task is being performed. Additional items to include in the memo are standard designations for document types, issues, privilege designations, references to individuals and entities, and document sources. This ensures that references will be consistent, which is very important later when searches are accomplished and indices or databases are created. A document review form should be created which helps those performing the task to maintain consistency. (*See* Exhibit 9-5, Sample Document Review Form.) If coding is to be done after the review phase, this task will not be necessary since all relevant and critical information will be captured during this process.

When there will be a team of personnel performing the review and selection tasks, one paralegal should be designated as being the "lead." This paralegal, with the assistance of the attorneys and any professional people recruited as consultants in the case, conducts training programs to ensure that the paralegals or other personnel performing the review operation have a working knowledge of the language and functions expressed in the documents to be read and are familiar with the review memo or protocol and the review form. The training or orientation session may be a day or more, depending on the volume of the documents, complexity of technical terms, number of legal issues, and experience of the discovery team. You may want to videotape this training session(s) for consistency and for use as orientation by future review team members. This exercise will also be invaluable if there is a stay granted or a delay in the review process takes place.

9.0132 Reviewing the Material.   The paralegal or discovery team is now prepared to review all of the documents within each folder according to the criteria established in the document review memo or protocol and/or orientation session. Every page must be read and analyzed. The paralegal or discovery team reads and screens for "potential relevance" or "potential responsiveness" in this initial sorting process, sometimes referred to as a "first cut" review. If there is any question in the mind of the reviewer, the document should be included as relevant or responsive with a notation that it is questionable. The use of flags can alert the supervising attorney of the need for a relevance decision. In this first cut review, it is better to include a questionable document than not to. The final decision on whether the document is included in the final production is made by an attorney. The documents should not be changed from their original condition during this initial review process. No stapled or otherwise bound document should be taken apart to characterize some portion of it as responsive and another portion as irrelevant or nonresponsive. Where files must be transported from the review location to another place for advice or the consideration of another party, an "out card" or "slip sheet" fully identifying the document, dated, signed by the reviewer, and reflecting the person to whom the document was directed must be inserted in place of the document. (*See* Exhibit 9-4, Sample Check Out Form and Document Review "Out Card.") Return the documents as soon as possible. It cannot be stressed enough that the paralegal must maintain the integrity of the individual files at all times.

PRACTICE TIPS

- In document cases where a decision has been made to produce the file material responsive to each discovery request, rather than producing all material "as kept in the ordinary course of business," initial physical sorting of material which is potentially responsive to a production request can often be made during the screening process.

- All documents are organized in boxes for the paralegal or the discovery team to review and screen. Place marker cards are used to ensure the paralegal or discovery team is reviewing the documents progressively in order and covering all of the documents in a file. This card should be identified with the name of the reviewer, sufficiently tall so it can project vertically above a file, and distinctive in color to allow instant recognition as a "reviewing place card." The selection of responsive documents is initially indicated in the raw files by standing them vertically on their edges in the boxes. This makes it easy to pull the documents for production copying.

9.0133 Identifying and Segregating Privileged Material.   Identifying potentially privileged material is one of the critical purposes of reviewing and screening the document collection. Privileged documents should be removed from the files as they are identified. A colored or special form sheet can be made for insertion in the file, indicating that a document has been removed due to claimed privilege. This "production document" (*see* Section 9.0143, Using Production Documents) should contain the document identification number, number of pages, date, author, addressee, any other recipients of the document, document title or subject line (if any), and type of privilege claimed. This is the same information which will be taken from the document review form (*See* Exhibit 9-5, Sample Document Review Form) to create the "privilege document index" that will be used to create the "privilege log." The *Federal Rules of Civil Procedure* and many state discovery rules require that the producing party compile and produce to the opposing party a "log" of material which is being withheld on the claim of privilege. Because the privilege log is given to the opposing party, additional care is taken in the wording used to describe the type, subject matter or title of privileged document, and persons involved so that the confidential or privileged information and content is not inadvertently disclosed. (*See* Exhibit 9-6,

EXHIBIT 9-6   Sample Privilege Log

PRIVILEGE LOG: *XYZ Construction vs Developments, Inc., et al*

Priv.	Doc. No.	No. Pages	Date	From	To	cc	Nature of Communcation
AC	XYZ 1010012	2	08/26/04	Joe Client	H. Lawyer	none	Litigation Status
WP	XYZ 1079999	5	08/05/04	H. Lawyer	Joe Client	non	Analysis of Damages

Sample Privilege Log.) If the documents are coded, certain available databases and litigation support computer programs allow for this information to be queried and a report generated which can then be utilized to prepare the privilege log.

Again, paralegals should include all documents, which are "potentially" privileged. The final decision on whether a document is privileged or not is made by an attorney. What initially appeared to be a privileged document may not be. When this occurs, its "privileged" designation is removed from the index, log, and review form, and the document is returned to its original place in the responsive file with the "privileged document" production form pulled and destroyed. The paralegal must check to ensure that any copies of the document are properly redistributed. Any other indices on which the document was listed as "privileged" must be corrected, and indices listing material produced or to be produced must be changed as well.

9.0134 Types of Files Created.   The two files that are created during the initial screening and review process consist of:

   a. Original Document File. It is best to maintain this file in the same manner and condition as the documents were first found. These documents are either client originals that have been numbered and designated as confidential (if necessary as noted in a protective order) or a copy of the client documents with original numbering labels. The only exception is that privileged documents are removed with "production documents" substituted in their place. Ideally, the original documents will have been numbered, allowing the file to be maintained in numerical order. A master index of the documents is created from the information contained on the document review forms. If the documents are coded, this index can be computer-generated. This index forms the basis for preparing working files and additional indices later during the retrieval and production phase of the discovery process. An alternate manner of handling privileged documents is to have the privileged documents copied onto red paper. The color red is used because this color cannot be reproduced on a copy machine cleanly; therefore no copies of this document can be inadvertently copied and produced. It is also quickly identifiable when you are looking in a box or redwell of documents. When it is decided that this privileged document should be produced, the original white privileged document can be copied from the segregated privileged documents collected and stored, and a clean white copy can replace the red one. Be sure to update the privilege log.

   b. Privileged Document File. This file consists of all the original documents which have been determined to be potentially privileged. This file must be separated physically from the original file and stored in a secure manner to prevent inadvertent disclosure to third parties. Depending on the volume of the privileged material, this can be accomplished by placing the documents in a sealed envelope or box and/or a locked file cabinet. These documents can also be collected, placed in sealed boxes appropriately labeled, and sent to off-site storage. A copy of the privilege index and/or the privilege log should be attached to the outside or placed inside of the envelope, box, or file cabinet. Cross-reference privileged document(s) production forms (*see* Section 9.0143, Using Production Documents) or red copies of the privileged documents are inserted in the original and working sets in place of the privileged documents. Care is taken to ensure that any photocopies made of the privileged documents for review by the attorneys are destroyed. If red color copies were made of the privileged documents, it will be easy to tell which copies to destroy.

9.014   Retrieve and Produce

Documents are discovered during the course of a case to determine those that contribute to establishing facts or the reasoning that led to events, practices, procedures, or representations at issue in the case. The assembly of documents without the ability to use them effectively later in supporting the client's case or refuting the opposing party's case is virtually worthless.

The ability to retrieve any given document or set of documents reliably and timely from the assembled mass of produced material or reference material included within a document discovery file is vital. Additionally, where documents become exhibits in a case, the authors, addressees, and persons who have seen or acted upon the content of the document are potential witnesses and may need to see and examine those documents to refresh their memories. The ability to retrieve documents can be the difference between supporting or destroying a witness or winning or losing a case, so the care and maintenance of these documents is critical.

PRACTICE TIPS

Screening Documents for Privilege and Protection

Attorney/Client Privilege
Privilege May Be Asserted
1. The document is written to the attorney from the client or from the client to the attorney.
2. Third parties (other than the attorney's staff, partners, or associates) not listed as copy recipients.
3. The subject matter concerns this litigation or another litigation matter.

Privilege May Be Waived
1. Voluntary disclosure to anyone else acts as waiver either during discovery or elsewhere.

Other Considerations
1. If the document or a portion of the document is to be used at trial, it must be produced during discovery.
2. Parts of documents that are not subject to assertion of the privilege must be disclosed.

Work Product/Trial Preparation Materials
Privilege May Be Asserted
1. Document is prepared by or on behalf of an attorney.
2. Document prepared in anticipation of litigation.
3. Document prepared by a party or agent of the party.
4. Statement within a document contains mental impressions and legal evaluations of the attorney, investigator, or claims agent.

Privilege May Be Waived
1. Disclosure to another party is basis for waiver.

Confidential Information, Not Absolutely Privileged
1. Trade secrets
2. Confidential research, development, or commercial information

---

Original client documents often are assembled in a fashion that is solely a convenience for the department file clerk or an individual who has created his or her own personal reference file. The assembly of a large number of these accumulations can result in a hodgepodge of nonchronological material in no particular order. Since the document discovery file generally must serve the purpose of relating one document to another and documents seldom are generated simultaneously, a chronological sorting of copies of all of the responsive documents is always necessary. The peripheral benefits of chronological sorting will be the identification of duplicate or near-duplicate documents resulting from the juxtaposition of all duplicate or near-duplicate documents. It allows comparison of drafts, marginal annotations ("marginalia"), or distribution comments that individually may mean little but together reflect policy, decision, responsibility, and so on. It cannot be stressed enough that you must never interfere with the integrity of the original documents as received or collected from the client. For that reason, a "working set" of documents should always be made, and the "originals" should be kept separately and only used to replenish the working set should some documents become misplaced or damaged. If a chronological set of documents is desired, you can duplicate the working set and place those in chronological order. If the documents are coded and imaged, a physical chronological set of documents will not be necessary since you can sort the documents on the database chronologically and view them or print them out in that order.

Retrieving and producing documents involves working with the original document file to either prepare working copies of specific documents or categories of documents or to produce copies of documents responsive to an opposing party's discovery request. Once this is done, the originals are placed safely and securely away. In large document production management, the boxes of documents can be tracked by being given alphanumeric numbers with appropriate identifying labels outside the box for easy identification and retrieval.

9.0141 Working File and Index Categories.
The working file and index categories described following contribute significantly to the conduct of the case. Sorting and identifying the document collection to obtain these files is done very efficiently by using the master index created from the document review form during the identify and review phase of the discovery process to create indices. Using the reports from database queries makes the process of selecting the documents for inclusion much easier and less labor-intensive, which results in cost savings to the client and the attorney in terms of both time and money. Manual indices can be produced from the master index created from the document review form.

9.01411 Chronological File and Index.   A chronological index and file is always necessary on document cases. The chronological index is created by using the computer database to sort the documents index by date (the master index can be sorted by computer if you are not utilizing a database). The file is then created by printing out or photocopying the original documents, if the documents are not coded and imaged, in the same order as the chronological index. This file should exclude privileged documents, irrelevant documents, and duplicate documents. "Production document" forms that include a detailed summary may be substituted on occasion for very large or bulky documents, depending on the preference of the case attorney. (*See* Section 9.0143, Using Production Documents.)

9.01412 Issue File and Index.   This index and file is organized by each case issue identified by the attorneys. This sorting is accomplished by using the master index mentioned previously or the database created by coding of the documents to sort by both issue topic and date. When the document review form has been used to identify issues during the review and screening phase *and* that information has been included in the database or master index, this task is reasonably fast and simple because it can be done using the computer. If the issue identification is done separately from the initial review and screening, manually going back through the chronological document file to identify all issue relationships can be time-and labor-intensive. The original documents are then printed from the database or photocopied in the same order as they appear on the index and placed in notebooks for review by the attorneys and technical personnel as needed. It is not unusual that subsequent reviews will reveal that a document pertains to additional issues and should be included in other issue files or that a document no longer has relevance to an issue. When this occurs, the database or master index is corrected to include the additional information, so that the corrected issue index can be generated.

9.0143 Witness Document File and Index.   In preparation for the deposition of a witness, copies are made of each document which refers or relates to that witness in any manner. Every document which mentions the witness as author, addressee, or other recipient or mentions the witness in the text is located and compiled in a notebook along with any documents which were connected to the witness through the testimony of another individual. This is generally a multistep process which includes sorting the master index or querying the database to produce a listing of documents which contain the name of the witness and reviewing deposition testimony, declarations, or statements of other witnesses for references to documents mentioned in connection with the witness. The master index or database is updated to include any additional links to documents for that witness, and a new witness index is generated. Usually, the documents are set up in chronological order, but sometimes they are also further segregated by issue. This is generally the attorney's call based on either protocol set up for the litigation or personal comfort. These files are used either to prepare the friendly witness for deposition or to prepare for questioning an opposing party witness at deposition.

9.01414 Exhibit Files and Index.   Every document introduced for the client or by the opposing party as an exhibit, either to pleadings, at deposition, or at trial, must be identified and indexed. The index should include a historical background on the document and cross-references to other related documents or to witnesses. This can be prepared using the master index, which is first amended to include a reference to the use of the document as an exhibit, and then sorted to produce the exhibit index. If the documents have been coded, then notation in the exhibit field can be updated and a query and/ or report can be run. It is recommended that the marked exhibits be maintained with the pleading or deposition in which they were used.

9.01415 Documents Produced.   This index or file tracks what documents have been produced to the opposing party and includes information such as the date produced, receiving party, and what discovery request the production is responsive to. When a small number of documents is involved, it is usually cost-effective to maintain an exact duplicate of the documents produced along with a copy of the formal discovery response which makes them available to the opposing party. When the volume of documents is large, it is more cost-effective to prepare an index which lists the documents produced in numerical order or lists them in order of the request they are responsive to. In either case, the master index is amended to note that the documents were produced to the opposing party party. Once again, if the documents were coded, the database is updated to reflect this production and a query and/or report can save time and energy in ascertaining which documents were produced, when, and to whom. There is a general thread running here that, if at all possible, coding of documents (and imaging) is the preferable way to control documents.

9.01416 Individual and Entity Database.   In its simplest form, this is a listing of every name that appears in the case, whether discovered in documents or testimony. In its most complex form, it includes addresses, personal information and history, and a listing of each document which has been connected to that individual or entity. It is created by compiling information from a review of the master index, the opposing party documents, and depositions or by running a query and/or report from the database of coded documents. (*See* Section 9.032, Individual and Entity Database.)

9.0142 Responding to Document Requests.
Most requests generate a mixture of formal written responses which include, but are not limited to, the following: (1) a statement that the material sought will be produced at a time and place to be agreed upon by counsel; (2) a statement that the documents sought will be produced on an agreed date to the extent that any responsive documents or records exist; (3) a statement that the responding party has no documents or records responsive to the request; and/or (4) an objection to the request.

If your client has records or documents which will be produced, it is not necessary that you identify the material with any specificity in the written response. It is sufficient to state that the party does have responsive documents, which will be produced. The attorney and client can determine between the date of the written response and the date on which the material will be produced for inspection whether it will be produced as kept in the normal course of business or whether it will be organized and labeled to correspond with the categories in the request; that is a choice afforded to the producing party. That decision rests with the supervising attorney.

In some cases, where responsive documents are small in number, the required written response and the document production can be taken care of simultaneously by attaching copies of responsive documents to the written response. When this occurs, it is a good idea to assign a number or letter to each document or group of documents being produced in response to each request, if not already numbered; in this case, track this document by its original number (another good reason to number all documents). When the actual production is done in this manner, it must be remembered that if any documents or records are being withheld under a claim of privilege, a "privilege log" is also required to be provided.

When the decision is made to allow the adverse party to inspect the documents and mark those for which copies are desired, the paralegal will need to determine ahead of time how, when, and where the copies will be made of the documents the opposing counsel designates for copying. This can range from using copy facilities at the paralegal's office, the client's offices, or the use of a commercial copying service. It is important to discuss this with the client and to make sure that the client feels comfortable with the copy method selected.

The first thing to be done when the production commences is to inform the opposing party's representatives as to the preferred procedure for marking records they want copied. If this procedure includes tabbing papers with "post-it notes" or "flags," do not presume that they will bring their own. Have some handy where the inspection will take place. Be sure to tell the representatives what the copy cost will be. If you anticipate using a commercial copy center, discuss the possibility of direct billing to opposing counsel by the copy service.

Most attorneys and clients do not want the client's records produced without having a representative of the law firm present. This task is usually delegated to the paralegal. If there is a large quantity of material being produced, the paralegal may be kept busy rotating files in and out of the room where the inspection is taking place. Otherwise, it is a good practice to bring other work assignments along to help pass the time. Generally speaking, a copy machine should not be readily available to the reviewing party.

After the inspection is concluded, follow through with the arrangements made for having the documents copied. Prior to having the documents copied, annotate the master index or document database for each document being copied as well as each document that was available during the inspection. As previously mentioned in this chapter, it may be advisable to maintain one complete set of the documents copied so that there is no question about what was copied by opposing counsel; this is particularly critical when the client's documents have not been numbered and is another reason to number. If the client's documents have not been previously numbered, it is recommended that the documents to be copied be numbered at that time so that if they are utilized for any purpose in the future, there will be no question as to where they came from. There are some attorneys that feel that whatever numbering system is selected, care should be taken that the numbers are consecutive with no gaps and that the duplicate set retained has the same numbers. Other attorneys believe that for strategic reasons, gaps are preferable since there is no obligation to explain the gaps. If for some reason, the documents were originally stamped for identification and you want a consecutively numbered set to be produced, some copy services have photocopy machines which "stamp" a consecutive number on copies made from an original. In many cases, using a service such as this proves more cost-effective in terms of both time and money than numbering and producing the copies manually "in-house." You can then track the previous number on the master index or database in the "other number" field.

9.0143 Using Production Documents.

"Production documents" are divider sheets or inserts that function to preserve the original groupings or placement of materials within a document collection. When documents are obtained from clients, whether individuals or entities, they may be in folders, three-ring binders, stapled, bound, or in various forms of semipermanent binding. When these original documents or materials are selected to be photocopied, scanned, or otherwise reproduced, it becomes necessary to provide "production document" inserts which serve as placeholders for documents too large to be copied or processed and which preserve the placement and grouping characteristics of the original document collection. Because they are placeholders, they should not receive a unique document identification number but may contain the identification of the document in whose place they are substituted. Examples of production document forms commonly used are as follows:

"Begin Bound Document." This is a sheet placed ahead of photocopies made of a bound document, such as a hardbound book, government pamphlet, or any other document that normally is an assembly of permanently bound pages. This sheet is followed by a sheet "End of Bound Document." (*See* Exhibit 9-7.)

"Begin Stapled Document." This is placed ahead of a series of pages stapled together before the copying process. As the staple is pulled, the integrity of the stapled document might be lost without this particular sheet. The one that follows the last page of this document would be the "End Stapled Document." These documents look essentially the same as those depicted in Exhibit 9-7.

EXHIBIT 9-7   "Production Document" for Bound Documents

Case _____ Document ID No.: _____ **BEGIN BOUND DOCUMENT**	Case _____ Document ID No.: _____ **END BOUND DOCUMENT**

These sheets should be on standard letter-size paper and may be color-coded.

"Begin Loose-leaf Notebook." This is placed ahead of a document found contained in a three-ring binder or other loose-leaf notebook and may be supplemented, if there are divider tabs within the binder, by production sheets saying "Divider Tab" and carrying the title of the divider tab. The whole assembly at the end of the binder would be followed by "End Loose-leaf Notebook." These documents look essentially the same as those depicted in Exhibit 9-7.

"Reduced-Scale Document." This sheet would be inserted just ahead of a large document that has been photocopied in reduced size and scale to a more manageable document. It is only used where the document can be reduced to one page (either legal or book size). This will alert everyone that a document in the original file is larger than the copy produced. For handling large computer printouts, economic tabulation sheets, engineering drawings, and so on, this type of sheet is convenient and important. (*See* Exhibit 9-8.)

"Document Too Large to Copy." In some cases, a drawing or other document is too large to be copied, even with reduction, on a single sheet of paper. When this happens, the paralegal must paste several copies of portions of the document together to achieve one larger one. It is important for persons using the file to know that what they are seeing is not an accurate representation of the original document. (*See* Exhibit 9-8.)

"Begin Stapled Series of Stapled Documents." Many times, stapled documents are assembled by purpose or by chance either in central files or in personal information files of individuals under circumstances incomprehensible to the paralegal reviewing the document. It is inappropriate for the paralegal to disassemble these documents. Thus, the condition of this assembly of documents is shown by the introduction of this sheet. It would immediately be followed by

EXHIBIT 9-8   "Production Document" for Reduced-Scale and "Too Large to Copy" Documents

Case _____
Document ID No.: _____

**REDUCED-SCALE
DOCUMENT**

Original size: _____
Brief Description: _____
_____
_____

Case _____
Document ID No.: _____

**DOCUMENT
TOO LARGE TO COPY**

Original size: _____
Description: _____
_____
_____

Where located: _____

These sheets should be on standard letter-size paper and may be color-coded.

"Begin Stapled Document" and then "End Stapled Document," "Begin Stapled Document," and so on, through the total assembly of the stapled series. The last production document would be "End Stapled Series of Stapled Documents." These documents look essentially the same as those depicted previously in Exhibit 9-7.

Archiving. In large document cases, and increasingly in smaller ones, the document collection may be archived for ease of use and reference. In this instance, there may be a need for a production document entitled "Document not Processed." This would be used for bound documents, documents too large to be copied, roll charts, or other materials which may be unable to be processed. These documents look essentially the same as those depicted previously for "Document Too Large to Copy" in Exhibit 9-8. In the past, large volume files were microfilmed to create an archive. There is still a need for archiving in large document cases, although microfilming is no longer being used. Instead, archives are now being created in CD-ROM format and are processed by scanning equipment or digital photography.

Privilege. Privileged documents have been discussed in Section 9.0133, Identifying and Segregating Privileged Material. This production document is inserted in place of the "privileged" document it represents in the original file and in any file copies subsequently produced. (*See* Exhibit 9-9.) The information contained on this sheet is identical to that listed on the privilege log that is produced to any opposing party.

Other. Other production document forms may be generated as needed.

EXHIBIT 9-9   Privileged Document "Production Document"

Case: _____

PRIVILEGE DOCUMENT

Doc. ID No.:	No. Pages:	Date:
Author:		
Addresses:		
Other Recipients:		
Privilege Asserted:		
Description:		
Attachments (ID No.):		

This sheet may be color-coded.

9.015   Return and Destroy

When a lawsuit is ended or settled, original documents considered unnecessary for retention in the firm's permanent litigation file are returned to the client or source custodians from whom they were taken. Since lawsuits require extended periods of time and in the course of such lawsuits any given document may become the "best evidence," it is prudent to retain custody of the original documents until the last moment of the case. It is important to bear in mind that appeals may be filed so the "last moment of the case" may be after the time to file an appeal has elapsed.

9.0151 Use of the Review Log.   If the inventory and master index were used at the beginning of the case, returning each document and file to the original source will be much simpler. Documents should be returned in the same fashion (stapled, bound, in binders, and so on) as they were surrendered.

At the time of return, any original documents which have been entered as evidence in the court file can be so noted on a copy of the document substituted in the client's or custodian's file. Each return should be logged and receipted.

9.0152 Retention of Indices.

Every document index, whether manually prepared or reports from the database, and receipt created in the case should be preserved and stored in the case file to serve as a guide for future cases or to answer questions regarding documents the client might have at a later time.

9.0153 Destruction of Photocopies.

Once the case is concluded and all originals have been returned to the custodians, the photocopied document files should be destroyed, but only after expiration of the date for filing of an appeal. Many firms are required to keep documents much longer due to requirements by their malpractice or errors and omissions insurance carriers. The paralegal must be aware of these requirements and follow the required procedure. Destruction is exactly that: torn up, shredded, or burned, not simply placed in the trash for casual disposal. There are vendors who provide on-site document shredding, and a receipt of destruction can be obtained. Any documents or their copies covered by protective orders should be obtained from the opposing party and from the court file, the originals returned to the client or custodian, and the photocopies destroyed. Often, stipulations are entered into between the parties to concurrently destroy each other's documents covered by the protective order. This simplifies things. Once again, no destruction should take place until all efforts at appeal are exhausted and the documents will not be needed.

9.02 OPPOSING PARTY AND OTHER DOCUMENTS

Opposing party documents and documents from other parties are received as a result of discovery requests or subpoenas. They are generally numbered by the producing party, and they are handled in much the same manner as client documents. The paralegal must develop a plan to control and organize the documents as they are received; the documents must be reviewed and analyzed; a system must be established to work with the documents; and a plan developed to return or destroy the documents at the end of the case or as addressed in the protective order. Many of the same general principles discussed in handling client documents apply and will not be repeated.

9.021 Control and Organization

When discovery documents are received, the paralegal's task is easier when the opposing party has already numbered the documents. When the documents have not been numbered, decisions must be made on whether to do so or whether to implement some other control method. If not numbered, it is wise to use an alphanumeric system that readily identifies the source of the document (i.e., 3rd party Wilson = WIL00001). It is always prudent to maintain a copy of the documents exactly as they were produced. Additionally, it is important to immediately prepare an index of the documents received and add them to the document tracking inventory. *See* Practice Tips regarding Document Tracking Inventory or using a form similar to the one used to index client documents. You can also have the documents imaged and/or coded. This makes the later tasks of analyzing the produced documents in terms of responsiveness to the production request or subpoena and creating various working files, database reports, and indices much easier to accomplish.

9.022   Review and Analyzing

In general, the paralegal and the attorney should meet and review the purpose of the discovery request or subpoena to identify the items and issues which are considered important to the case. In many cases, these will be the same topics previously identified in preparation for review of the client's documents. With discovery documents there are two variables: (1) whether the documents to be reviewed are attached to the discovery request or subpoena response and (2) whether the documents and items will be inspected in another location with the paralegal or discovery team making decisions on what items should be copied and whether the items produced for inspection were responsive to the discovery request.

9.0221 Documents Received with Discovery Responses.

The documents should first be coded or indexed, added to the document tracking inventory (DTI), and then reviewed to determine if they are responsive to the discovery requests. If the correspondence accompanying the documents lists the documents produced, check to ascertain that the entire range of documents produced was indeed produced. If the discovery response to which the documents are attached indicates that documents are being withheld because of a privilege, it should be noted whether or not a privilege log has been produced as well. Privilege logs are generally kept together in a binder for easy access. The Federal Rules for Civil Procedure and many state rules have a time limitation during which the requesting party must move to compel further production from the responding party. If the appropriate motion is not filed within that time frame, the ability to require the other side to comply with the original request may be lost.

9.0222 Documents Produced for Inspection and Copying.

Preparation for the actual document inspection should include becoming familiar with the request as well as the other party's written responses. As previously discussed, it is very important to know what to look for and understand the issues and theories which are being asserted on behalf of the client. It is helpful to prepare a summary of the material sought, noting the response. The first step in the actual inspection should be to make a preliminary assessment of the material which is being produced for inspection. Compare the written responses with the categories or types of records produced. If any categories or types of promised documents appear to be missing, make inquiry as to their location or ask when they will be produced. Be sure to dictate or write a list of any material that is not produced. Also, ask if the records are being produced as they are kept in the normal course of business or whether they have been organized and labeled to correspond with the categories in your request.

PRACTICE TIPS

- Certain basic supplies are recommended for performing an on-site document inspection, including gummed notepads (post-it notes), paper clips, legal pads, and inventory or screening forms. Portable dictating machines are also very useful. If the facts in your case include important dates and key players, lists of those things will prove helpful in locating key documents and records.

- It is important to determine in advance what the page price will be for designated copies of records or photographs. Failure to do so can obligate the law firm and the client to pay exorbitant charges, incurring additional attorney's fees and expenses to object to such charges. It is much easier to negotiate a fair price and/or explore alternative arrangements for having the material copied before the inspection begins than after the fact.

Begin by taking an inventory of the files and records produced for your inspection. This may be done by using a Document Inventory Form similar to that used to inventory client documents, or it may be dictated. It is always good practice to either note on your inventory the files and/or documents designated for copying or dictate such a list. You may also find that bringing along a laptop computer and making notes of missing documents and so forth to be helpful. Make sure to always ask whether any documents have been withheld on the basis of claimed privilege. If so, ask for the required list or privilege log or ascertain when it will be given to you.

Take time to read or skim all material that is produced. This is important because another opportunity to inspect the requested records may not be offered. For this reason, a more inclusive collection may be necessary. You should also note which documents were *not* marked for copying and where those documents can be found (box number, etc.) in case the issues change during discovery and those documents previously thought not to be relevant are now at issue. You owe it to your client to be thorough. When finished with the review, be sure that the method used to mark documents for copying is clear and that a copy clerk can understand it. Generally, a good method for designating such material is by tagging it with "post-it notes" or "flags." Paper clips can be used to identify a group of documents so that time need not be wasted "tagging" every individual page. Another way to mark large groups of documents is by using colored "Start" and "Stop" sheets. By the same token, if an entire labeled folder contains documents to be copied, the folder may be tagged or "Start" and "Stop" sheets used at the front of the folder and at the end of the folder. In that way, it is clear that you want the labeled front of the folder copied as well. Whatever the method chosen, it should be uniform if more than one person is conducting the inspection for the client. A review team meeting with use of a written protocol is a way to ensure that there is continuity in the review, especially if it is to take place over a long period of time. The review team meeting can be videotaped for future use by future reviewers. It is also a good practice to add to the protocol a list of instructions for copying, particularly if you have any special requests (such as "Copy file tabs," "Insert blank page between files," etc.). Leave a business card when the inspection is complete so that the people responsible for making the copies can call if they have any questions.

When copies of the designated documents are received, the first task is to check the inventory made during the inspection against the records delivered. The next task is to determine what control method will be used. As previously mentioned, it is recommended that a master "original" set of all documents received be maintained from which a "working set" can be made for attorney and other use. The original set is then secured.

9.0223 Analyzing the Documents.

Once the documents have been indexed, imaged and/or coded, and reviewed for responsiveness to the discovery request, the next task is to analyze the documents in terms of their relationship to the legal issues in the case, how they fit in with chronologies and issue indices developed from the client documents, whether new information is contained in any document, whether additional documents should be added to witness preparation files, whether documents which appear to be duplicates contain any additional notations or other writings, whether the documents contain any additional information on known individuals and entities, and whether the documents expose the identities of previously unknown individuals and entities. A document review form similar to the one used to review client documents may be used to make the process more efficient. (*See* Exhibit 9-5, Sample Document Review Form.)

9.023   Working with the Document Indices

Just as with client documents, all the work of reviewing and analysis will be fruitless if the paralegal is unable to develop a system for retrieving and working with the documents and the information they contain. Data from the discovery documents should be used to supplement the information gathered to

EXHIBIT 9-10   Sample Production Discrepancy Form

Production Discrepancy List:	XYZ Corporation vs. Developments, Inc., et al		
Document Mentioned	**Source Document**	**Responsive to Discovery Request**	**Notes**
Memo dated 7/15/04 from J. Astor	D1 200757 Letter to Alf Landon from Jay Lender	Pltf Set 1, REP #7 dated 1/15/06	Source Document Produced 2/16/06 Cited Doc not listed on Privilege Log

create the Issues Files and Index, Witness Documents Files and Index, Chronological Files and Index, and Individual and Entity Files and Index. In addition, review of these discovery documents will provide information to create another useful file and index system to track additional potential discovery items that are mentioned in received documents, but whose existence has not otherwise been disclosed or produced by the opposing party.

9.0231 Documents Cited but Not Produced.

There will be cases where the opposing party has produced documents that refer to other documents which were not produced or show attachments which were not attached; a special indexing and file of these documents may be appropriate at some time, together with the cross-reference information needed to support a motion to compel or other motion to produce. Because of the nature of how coding is done (names referenced, mentions, and/or attachments), that information can be more readily compiled. In some cases, very significant documents within the files will refer to documents requested from the opposing party which have not been provided. These should also be identified and included in that type of file and index. The manually prepared indices or those prepared by the information from the reports from the database should be very specific as to the dates of the request, dates of the response, and the supporting but conflicting references. This may go so far as to use colored highlighting on the documents for quick and easy reference by the attorneys. During screening or review, this information may be noted on the document review form previously discussed or on a special form "production discrepancy." (*See* Exhibit 9-10, Sample Production Discrepancy Form.)

9.024   Return and Destroy

When the litigation is concluded, whether through trial or settlement, the discovery documents received from other parties should be returned if they consist of originals or material which was provided subject to a protection or confidentiality order or agreement. Other discovery documents and copies may be destroyed in the same manner described in Section 9.0153, Destruction of Photocopies, once again bearing in mind that you should wait until the time for appeal has elapsed.

9.03   CUSTOMIZING DATABASE FORMS

A database is a collection of information specifically arranged for efficient retrieval, usually pertaining to computerized information. Paralegals have been managing this task with and without computer aid for decades through the use of forms. The ability to adapt traditional paper forms to computer systems in the law office has been a welcome tool to help with document control, sorting, indexing, and analysis.

9.031   Document Databases

Document databases consist of forms which contain specific information extracted from documents obtained during the course of litigation. The forms can be "filled out" directly on a computer, or they may be sheets of paper or index cards which are filled out by hand. An example of a "paper database" would be a set of 5-by-8-inch cards. Each card represents a single document and contains specific information from the document that allows sorting of cards in chronological order, determining all documents authored by a given party, or identifying all of the letters that went from the client company to someone else on a particular topic. The same information contained on those cards can be sorted much faster, more efficiently, and in even more ways when entering it into a true computer database that digitizes the information. The master index form and the document review form are examples of database information which may be captured first on paper and later input for sorting and indexing by a computer. (*See* Exhibit 9-5.) The most important element in creating or customizing a database is to think and plan in advance the kinds of information that are necessary to track, along with the kinds of sortings, indexes, and reports which may be needed. The organization of the record form should flow from the order of importance of the data and how the data is organized within the document. An example of a sample document database form is shown in Exhibit 9-11. A listing of some common database fields or elements (in addition to those previously discussed) is shown in Exhibit 9-12.

Thought and consideration must be given as to which documents should be included in a database. Current case law trends view index listings and inventory listings which include every document in a collection as items which may be discoverable by opposing counsel if they demonstrate to the court's satisfaction a substantial need, along with inability to obtain the substantial equivalent without undue hardship by other means. Some courts have held that indexes and inventories which list only objective data, such as document number, date, author, addressee, and copy recipient, cannot by their nature contain any mental impressions, conclusions, opinions, or legal theories of the party who created them, or in other words protected "work product." The analogy is that these indexes and inventories represent the same kinds of information which are discoverable in the initial disclosures required under Rule 26(a) of the *Federal Rules of Civil Procedure* or the similar "standard" interrogatories allowed by many state rules. A few courts have required the disclosure of more extensive databases which contain summary information on the content of the documents. One of the rationales for allowing these disclosures is that the party had included every document in the collection, making it indiscreet. On the other hand, counsel who have been able to argue that their databases or discrete indexes contained only selected documents have been able to successfully demonstrate to the courts that revealing the identity of the documents selected would disclose to the opposing attorney their thought process, mental impressions, conclusions, and opinions and have successfully prevented the disclosure of such databases. These kinds of discovery skirmishes usually take place in large document cases but may occur in smaller cases as well. These discovery battles have resulted in recommendations that only selected "key" documents be input into substantive databases. To the extent that surrogate documents, such as the document review forms, contain mental impressions, opinions, and conclusions (such as whether a document relates to a certain issue, whether it may be privileged, etc.), they will remain protected work product. To the extent that inventory lists or master indexes do not contain opinion information, they are open to discovery attacks.

9.032   Individual and Entity Database

Since documents are the products of people, the creation of an identify record for each of the relevant people in a case is essential. At the time the document review form or document database form is being created, an identity record for every different name appearing on the document should also be created. The compilation of these records is sometimes referred to as a witness notebook.

EXHIBIT 9-11   Sample Document Database Form

Document Database Form	

Case: _____   Coded by: _____   Date: _____

Doc_ID Start:	**Doc_ID End:**	**Date:**	**Source:**

Type: ☐ Letter ☐ Memo ☐ Report ☐ Financial Notes ☐ Contract ☐ Invoice ☐ Medical ☐ Receipt ☐ Proposal ☐ Time Card ☐ Daily Job Report ☐ Meeting Minutes ☐ Graphic ☐ Photo ☐ Clipping ☐ Other _____

Author:	**Addressee:**	**"cc":**

☐ **Duplicate of Doc_ID:**   ☐ **Attached to Doc_ID:**

Doc. Quality: ☐ Original ☐ Photocopy ☐ Carbon Copy ☐ Torn ☐ Thermal Fax ☐ Faded ☐ Illegible

☐ **Subj:** ☐ **Re:** ☐ **Title:**	☐ **Marginalia** ☐ **Other Markings**
Privilege: ☐ AC ☐ WP ☐ Other	**Protection:** ☐ Trade Secret ☐ Research ☐ Development ☐ Commercial

Sensitivity: ☐ Relevant ☐ Not Relevant ☐ Helpful ☐ Problem ☐ Damages ☐ Liability ☐ KEY

Issues: ☐ Fraud ☐ Negligence ☐ Breach of Contract ☐ Bad Faith ☐ Notice ☐ Intent ☐ Reliance

Key Words: ☐ Bituthene ☐ Change Order ☐ Delay ☐ Acceleration ☐ Weather ☐ Generator ☐ Piles

Individuals & Entities:

Doc. Mentioned: (Not Attached):

Notes/Summary:

☐ **Deposition Exhibit**	Witness:	Ex. No.:	Date:
☐ **Pleading Exhibit** ☐ **Motion Exhibit**	Title:	Ex. No.:	Date:
☐ **Produced to Adverse**	Party:	Req. No.:	Date:
☐ **Trial Exhibit**	Witness:	Ex. No.:	Date:

Each identity record should include the last name, first initial, first/middle name, middle initial, and all aliases. All of this information is included because a party may be referred to by initials on one document and by name on another, and it may take three or four documents before anyone is certain of the exact or preferred name of a given person. The business position of the individuals and their company affiliations, addresses, and telephone numbers should all be accumulated as encountered and posted to show the month and year of the information. The form should also indicate each document where the name of the individual appears as author, addressee, copy recipient, or is mentioned. (*See* Exhibit 9-13.)

EXHIBIT 9-12   Some Common Elements to Include in a Document Database

- **The Date.** All documents must be identified by date. Where the date is shown on the document, an estimate may be used based on the document's location in the original file or other logical basis. When the date is estimated, a notation to that effect must be made. Dates should be written using six places in a year-month-day format for ease of sorting (i.e., 06-09-05).
- **Total Pages.** A space should be provided on the database form to show the total number of pages in the document.
- **Document Type.** It is very important that the legal assistant define the types of documents and provide a reference glossary for any individual who will be entering data in this field to ensure consistent information. This is done by analyzing the kinds of documents likely to be encountered and assigning certain arbitrary identification to them; for instance, correspondence between the client firm and outside parties might be called "letters," while all correspondence within the client firm or between employees are designated "memoranda." Among those to be considered are: letters, memoranda, studies, reports, contracts, graphics (such as drawings, sketches, plans, and surveys), clippings (newspapers and magazines), photos, minutes of meetings, and notes.
- **Document Quality.** This will assist in pointing out torn documents, partially illegible documents, or faded documents that are the best copy.
- **Document Sensitivity.** In some cases, content in document test or added notations are so significant in the context of the case that a document may be classified as harmful, "significant," and/or "privileged." These are simple gradiations to make, and subtle shading should not be attempted in this area. Frequently, the legal assistants are limited to "privileged" entries under "document sensitivity."
- **Individuals and Entities.** This category is to include information concerning any person or entity mentioned within the document not included within the objective fields of author, addressee, or other recipient. Reference should include the context such as mentioned, attended, or conversation with. These references may be shown by a standardized abbreviation, such as: Mnt for mentioned; Attnd for attended, and phcon for phone conversation; or con for conversation. It is also very useful to develop a standardized method of abbreviating name references for companies and other entities, such as DOJ for Department of Justice; GM for General Motors; AMEX for American Express. These kinds of standardizations should be collected in a reference list to ensure accuracy and consistency—very important when the time comes to search for this information.
- **Related Documents.** It is important to note whether a document is attached to other documents or refers to other documents. This information may become important or relevant as the case develops, or it may point to additional documents to request. This is done by noting the document ID number of an attached document (i.e., Doc# ABC-199999 attch), or the literal reference when a document is referred to but not attached (i.e., Ref: "Yesterday's Memo from Harry").
- **Issues.** If coding for issues or sorting the documents by issue, include a provision on the card to indicate issues by number or by topic. Similarly, if sorting the documents by document discovery order, a provision to indicate that appropriate paragraph on the surrogate document is very helpful.
- **Use of the Document.** An important function is to track the use of a document during the course of the case; whether it was produced to adversaries; whether it was copied by adversaries; whether it was used as an exhibit; whether it was produced to you or by you. All of these can, with proper planning, be reflected on the form.

   Note: The above elements are in addition to those listed for the document screening form. (*See* Exhibit 9-4.)

9.04 COMPUTER DOCUMENT MANAGEMENT

The paralegal's knowledge of the attorney's manner and style of conducting litigation, the information commonly needed during the course of a particular type of case, an understanding of database concepts, and familiarity with computers and various computer programs will enable the paralegal to design a document database or develop other technical solutions to common organizational or

EXHIBIT 9-13   Sample Individual and Entity Database Form

Case: _____ Date: _____ Updated: _____

☐ Individual ☐ Entity	☐ Last Name ☐ Entity Name		
First Name:		Middle Name:	
Initials:		Alias:	
Employment:		Title:	
Bus. Street Address:	City:	State / Zip:	
P.O. Address:	City:	State / Zip:	
Phone 1:	Phone 2:	Phone 3:	
Fax:	Mobil Phone:	Other:	
Related Entities:		☐ Parent ☐ Subsidiary ☐ Affiliatee	
		☐ Parent ☐ Subsidiary ☐ Affiliatee	
		☐ Parent ☐ Subsidiary ☐ Affiliatee	
		☐ Parent ☐ Subsidiary ☐ Affiliatee	
Related Individuals:		Relationship:	
Notes/Comments:			

Doc. No.	Context	Doc. No.	Context	Doc. No.	Context

information accessibility related problems. More than ever before, computer skills will make the paralegal an extremely valuable member of the litigation team.

9.041   Introduction

Electronic document management strategies are no longer only used in cases with hundreds of thousands of pages to track. The advantages of an electronically controlled document management system can help the smallest case, and with the costs of software and services decreasing, even small firms are commonly turning to electronic solutions. Some of the considerations when the decision is made to manage documents extensively using computer technology will be addressed.

Advances in technology have been tremendous in the last decade and will continue to develop for the foreseeable future. In fact, new and innovative uses for existing technology are often taking place at the paralegal's desk. Specialized service companies for projects such as electronic document numbering, document scanning, and data indexing have become widely available and are often cost-effective alternatives to traditionally popular manual methods. In order to realize the advantages these services and products offer, it helps to understand the processes involved in creating electronic images and databases. Most important is your willingness to try something new. Be diligent in your research, but be confident in your experimentation. The upside is often too great to ignore.

Some basic things to be aware of include:

a. The cost of document management generally increases early in the case and may decline during later stages of the case.

b. Attorneys and paralegals must focus earlier on the scope and issues of the case, nature of the discovery documents, and standardized terms which will be captured in the database system.

c. Attorneys must devote time to understanding and approving the computer system, database design, and service costs.

d. Staff must be taught how to operate the chosen system, unless it has been used in the past.

e. The greatest practical benefits are the ability to retrieve specific documents instantaneously and the ability to transport entire document populations to remote locations for use in depositions, hearings, and trials.

9.042   Initial Work Effort Considerations

In a document production effort (as described earlier in this chapter), every relevant document must be found, identified, controlled, evaluated, and preserved for retrieval. Computerization does not change that but adds other layers of special effort to it, which include the requirement for stringent quality control, early data entry, and additional planning considerations (such as creating a database design that is easy to understand for both the person(s) entering the information into the database and the person(s) retrieving the needed documents).

9.043   File Handling Costs

Previously, the major source of increased costs resulting from the use of electronic document control systems was the need to purchase and maintain new hardware, such as workstations, servers, and storage platforms, which also meant hiring additional information technology (IT) personnel. This may still be true in some cases, but most law firms today already have the IT infrastructure needed to implement electronic solutions. This is more accurate when one considers the wide availability of technological service providers, some of whom even host images and databases online. In this scenario, the law firm only needs basic computer hardware and a reliable Internet connection to begin realizing the practical and financial advantages of electronic document management.

Implementing an electronic document management solution presents certain budgeting challenges for the case team. The client must be convinced that the initial investment in scanning documents and indexing documents will result in overall savings. For instance, if a case will end up using a database with attached images, the documents should be imaged as early in the case as possible. In this way, the client will spend less on document numbering and labeling because electronically applied numbers and labels are 80 percent less expensive than manually applied labels. Further, the creation of production and working sets of documents costs less when those sets are generated by printing rather than by copying.

The database itself is the hardest thing to sell your client because it is very likely the largest single investment your client will make in the case, although it is the database that most significantly reduces overall case costs. Paralegal time is greatly reduced because people no longer need to physically review boxes of paper to find specific information, and paralegals no longer need to physically retrieve and replace documents for attorney review. Everything from major productions to deposition preparation can be handled by sending computer-generated reports to vendors who then print the required documents in the order you want (numerical, chronological, date, etc.). Storage costs are greatly reduced because electronic storage, disk drives and CDs cost considerably less than physical storage, whether on-site or in warehouses.

9.044   Increased Attorney Involvement

Once the decision is made to use a document database, the responsible attorney must devote time to identify case issues, objectives, topics, and discovery document types rather than having the luxury of spreading that effort over a longer period of time. Additionally, the attorneys involved must contribute to the design of the database and assist in selecting the vendor to perform the work if it will not be done in-house. The process of selecting the vendor and designing the database will involve the attorneys, the paralegals, the firm's IT professionals, the coding manager from the service provider, and often a technical consultant from the service provider. It is important that the database be designed at the beginning of the case with enough flexibility to alter the template as the case develops, if necessary. The initial design of the template is often dependent on the type of case, although often templates can be interchangeable. If the template can be used in future cases, it will save time and money in the long run.

9.045   Additional Staff Time

A manual file system is often a combination of styles and physical devices. A mix of hand printing, cursive writing, and printed material on everything from folders to redwells to boxes can be found in manual document filing systems. That changes with computerization. Everyone involved must learn and adhere to standardized formats. Everyone must understand and use the same terms, abbreviations, words, and phrases consistently, or the ability to generate accurate searches and reports from the program will be seriously compromised. The data being created, whether by an external vendor or an in-house department, should be regularly reviewed to ensure that the correct information is in the computer database in the correct format.

The extraordinary need for consistency among all persons involved in capturing electronic data from physical documents and searching the data creates a continuing need for internal training.

9.046   Benefits

The benefits of computerization are sometimes difficult to appreciate until they have been experienced. For one, the financial advantages, as were discussed previously, develop over the life of the case. Still, these are quantifiable and can be reasonably anticipated. More difficult to foresee are the numerous intangible benefits. Paralegals have more time to devote to substantial issues when less of their time is spent locating documents. Attorneys work more efficiently when a significant amount of the information they need is available from their own desktops. Both of these things mean case teams can be more aggressive in their discovery tactics when powerful information management tools are at their disposal. Perhaps the most important, though also the most subtle, advantage is that people's lives improve. Searching for missing documents, especially under time pressures, is tremendously unsettling for paralegals, attorneys, and clients. With a properly designed electronic document management system, the stress of lost information is avoidable. Thanks to a more efficient office, employees have more time to spend away from the office pursuing their own endeavors.

9.047   Evaluation Factors in Implementing Computer Document Management

There are several main factors, which should be considered prior to implementing an advanced document management system.

9.0471 Data Input Methods.

In order to search for information in a database, case information must have been input. There are two main ways of generating information for the database: creating full text through OCR or direct electronic document conversion and document coding.

9.04711 Full Text.

Full text "coding" uses one of two methods to create a text file that links to a record in a database. Often, the database record associated with a full text file only contains the beginning and ending bates numbers of the document at issue.

Most commonly, the text file is created using OCR (Optical Character Recognition) software. A scanner creates an image of the document. The OCR program "reads" the image and creates a text file that contains all of the words in the original document. The user can then search for those words using the database to locate particular documents. OCR is less expensive than manual coding because it is an automated process, but it is not 100 percent reliable. The accuracy of the OCR output depends on the OCR program used and the type and quality of documents being processed. For an additional charge, most OCR service vendors will "clean" the OCR output by manually comparing the text file to the image and then editing the text file to match the original. This can quickly become very expensive.

If documents are received in electronic format, for instance Microsoft Word documents, Excel documents, PowerPoint documents, Outlook e-mails, and so forth, the text of the documents can be extracted automatically. Usually electronic documents arrive on CD. Specialized programs, which can be bought by the firm or are already owned by service vendors are capable of converting the documents to images that can be attached to database records, numbering those images, and simultaneously creating the searchable text file. Full text files created this way are more reliable than those created by OCR, but they are also more expensive. However, it is cheaper to process electronic documents this way than it is to print the documents, scan the documents, number the documents, and scan the documents in separate steps. Many conversion programs can also extract "fielded" data from the electronic document. This data, such as creation dates, file names, and author names, can be imported into the database records, enabling the user to run searches not just on the full text file but also on specific database fields.

9.04712 Document Coding.   Document coding is a predominantly manual process in which humans physically review the documents, mentally extract pertinent information, and enter that information into the proper database fields in the proper format. Often, in order to give the attorneys and senior paralegals the responsibility for determining the most complicated and important information, such as identifying which legal issues certain documents relate to, coding forms are used. Coding forms are similar to the document review forms discussed earlier in the chapter. The document review team reviews the documents and completes the coding forms. Trained employees or service vendor personnel then enter the information from those forms into the database. The most sophisticated firms and companies use forms that look like bubble sheets from SAT tests. This is because scanners are able to read the bubble sheets and automatically populate database fields with the associated information. Data created this way should be far less expensive than data created by hand.

If the case team chooses to code documents rather than OCR for full text, it is often worthwhile to code for names in text or named referenced. In this process, the coder reviews the documents and identifies relevant people's names, company names, product names, and so forth and manually enters them into a dedicated field. This process is very time-consuming and therefore expensive, so care should be taken to minimize the number of documents that receive this treatment. However, a knowledgeable coder capturing names in text will often create a database that is far more reliable than an OCR base. Most service vendors are not qualified to determine which names are important. Of course, no one will know which names are important if that information is not gathered before coding by the attorneys and senior paralegals. Many databases use a combination of full text OCR and detailed manual coding.

9.0472 Database Design Considerations.

As mentioned earlier, all cases can benefit from some level of electronic document management. The key is to determine what the critical pieces of information are and to develop a method of capturing that data that will yield acceptable results within the client's budget. In some cases, certain groups of documents can be coded into a single record, while other types of documents receive more detailed treatment. At a minimum, the electronic database can be used as a more effective document tracking inventory than a Word or Excel program. Couple a basic inventory level database with a set of images and the time and aggravation saved by not having to repetitively hunt out each individual document or file will represent an immediate return on your investment. Not every database needs to be a complex, entirely searchable work of art. The database just needs to work for your current application. Often, less is more in this regard.

There are situations in which a highly detailed database is necessary. Usually, these databases are meant to store many thousands of document records. These projects are more taxing, but done correctly the end result can be very satisfying to the responsible paralegal. Take your time to do it right. First, develop an organized plan of attack. Find out how many documents need to be catalogued. Find out what types of documents exist. Learn the issues of the case and find out what types of information, from what time frames, involving which people or companies, are going to be the most important. This information can be used to focus your resources, allowing you to spend more time and money on the truly critical information while developing basic inventories of the surrounding information. You can always add more specific information down the line for a set of documents that was not initially thought to be critical, as long as your basic inventory is good enough to allow you to locate that information when the need arises, but you cannot "unspend" money that has gone out the door. In this respect, a layered approach can be very effective. Once the most basic coding or OCR has been done, run searches that allow you to identify target areas or documents that deserve further treatment. This approach does take more time, so it is always a good idea to start your electronic document management work as early as possible.

9.0473 Evaluating Time and Costs Estimates.   When sending a project to an external vendor, whether it is a full database project or purely an imaging project, always obtain multiple bids. Scrutinize the bids carefully and request clarification as often as needed. Many times, bids from competing vendors will come in different forms. One bid will be based on dollars per page while the other bid will be structured according to dollars per document. In this situation, it is important to determine how the number of documents will be calculated. Sometimes it is a true count of the documents coded; other times it is an approximation based on an assumed average of 3.5 pages per document. Knowing how this will be billed and what types exist in your population will allow you to find the best deal for your client. Do not confuse expense with quality. The cheapest vendor may not perform quality work. Sometimes the most expensive is not the best. Do your research and contact references. Ensure that the choice you make represents the best combination of value and service for your given project. Establish turnaround time in advance and communicate with your vendor during the project to make sure the project is running on time. Make yourself available to your vendor during the project. You will be the most qualified person to make decisions regarding the necessity of certain information or the format in which it should be presented.

9.0474 Personnel Considerations.   If your firm chooses to set up an in-house coding facility staffed with nonparalegals, recruitment can be handled in-house or through temporary help agencies. In either event, a "work sample" test is helpful in selecting people. The work sample should be a group of 20 documents of varying types. The same documents must be used for each applicant. A set of instructions should be provided that might, for example, direct that:

a. All names be circled.

b. All dates be underlined.

c. All references to money, dollar costs, expenditures, budgets, and so on be indicated on the left margin with an asterisk.

d. The number of different names shown in the document be written in the top right corner of the top page of the document.

Regardless, each applicant must be given the identical instructions and be given the same time, in the same conditions, to complete the test.

The work sample must be carefully checked before being presented to the applicant and a master file carrying all the correct entries for each page must be created. This is compared against the applicant's results to measure error rates and the time taken by the applicant to complete the test. The test will weed out inaccurate or inordinately slow applicants. Standards must be high and must be maintained. It is better at the outset to quickly identify those who can follow instructions reliably and productively from those who cannot. Inconsistency, error, and exceeding slowness are detrimental to the document coding effort. Training of selected applicants must be a well-planned endeavor. The team members must feel like a team. An orientation on the factual history of the case is desirable. Training usually is staged by succeeding degree of complexity. It includes training on all the machinery to be used, the team's filing and handling systems, the software programs, and the coding process. Refresher sessions will be needed to update procedures and to correct detected errors. Every team must have a quality control auditor assigned to monitor, spot-check, and even "work behind" each team member to ensure consistency and work quality. The audit is a check to assist each team member, not simply to criticize. It helps detect weaknesses in the training presentation and in the job-specific instructions given to each team member. It identifies ambiguities that creep into the system through nonstandard treatment of documents that may fit more than one category. The audit will reveal the quality of each person and can serve as a foundation for dismissal of the careless or unqualified worker, an unpleasant but sometimes necessary task.

9.0475 Security.   Using computers and electronic storage devices to house your mission-critical data creates a unique need for security against environmental disaster, negligent damage, or criminal compromise of the computer file. Protecting your organization from these losses requires a financial and time investment. Environmental disasters include fire, flood, and power supply aberrations that can damage or destroy the computer and essential hardware and software components. Computer data should be archived, "backed up," on tapes or other storage media, such as optical disks and CD-ROM, and stored in a separate location as a security against such happenings. The negative effect of power fluctuations can be tempered using surge protection devices. Similarly, downtime resulting from power outages can be minimized using generators or other backup power supplies. Controlling access to both the production and user databases can minimize negligent compromise of a computerized system. Every computer system can be programmed to grant access only through the use of passwords, special access codes, and "log in" identities. Thorough training of employees on not only what to do in the programs, but also what specifically not to do will further mitigate the risk. Little can be done to prevent intentional theft, espionage, or sabotage of the computerized file beyond the normal security steps. A determined thief can and will penetrate the usual protections of a client's business, vendors' facilities, or law firm's offices, including electronic infrastructure. If a security breach does occur, it is critical that you be aware that it has occurred. Lock all the doors, filing cabinets, vaults, and desks that contain essential data and/or evidentiary documents. Install security devices and passwords on computers and electronic servers to thwart and identify hacking attempts. Being burglarized is bad, but being burglarized without realizing it can be fatal to the case and to the organization itself.

9.05   E-DISCOVERY—DISCOVERY OF ELECTRONICALLY STORED INFORMATION (ESI)

While businesses modernize and technology proliferates, litigation discovery has remained relatively stagnant. Lawyers continue to pour over boxes of paper—the more sophisticated among them making sure to demand that e-mail is printed out and produced in those boxes as well. Some lawyers may scan the papers that they receive into searchable image files and load them into a litigation management program. For trial, counsel may call the court before trial to inquire whether an ELMO (a fancy overhead projector that allows one to project documents onto a screen by placing them on the ELMO) is available. More tech-savvy lawyers may prepare a PowerPoint or other computer-generated presentation for the jury. Far more can and must be done.

Recent studies indicate that more than 90 percent of business records are now produced electronically, and nearly 50 percent of those records are never reproduced in paper form.

Reasonable litigation competence therefore demands a minimum understanding of how documents are electronically created, stored, and maintained and how one ensures that all such information from an opposing party is produced or at least preserved. A working understanding of metadata, slack space, ambient data, and so forth—previously the domain of computer geeks—is now essential when engaging in electronic discovery.

This section will discuss some of the basis principles and do's and don'ts with respect to electronic discovery.

In December 2006, the *Federal Rules of Civil Procedure* were amended requiring counsel to address the issue of electronically stored information early in each case and to consider its implications throughout the discovery process. Specifically, Rules 16, 26, 33, 34, 37, and 45 were amended.

The Electronic Discovery Reference Model (EDRM - www.edrm.net) develops guidelines and standards for e-discovery consumers and providers. According to EDRM there are 9 steps in E-Discovery:

1. Records management
2. Identification

3. Preservation
4. Collection of the Data
5. Processing
6. Review
7. Analysis
8. Production
9. Presentation.

9.051   Know Your Terminology

Under the new federal rules, the courts expect parties to have done everything in their power to prepare themselves prior to the Rule 26(f) Meet and Confer. This means you have to make sure you know your terminology. The following are some basic terms with which you should be familiar:

Native file—a native file is the electronic format of the application in which an electronic file or document is normally created, viewed, and/or modified. In other words, a document created in Excel, if produced in its native format, should be produced in Excel.

Static image—a static image is a file converted from its native format into a standard image format such as Tagged Image File Format (TIF) or Portable Document Format (PDF).

TIF—Tagged Image File Format

PDF—Portable Document Format

Metadata—metadata is information embedded in a native file that is not ordinarily viewable or printable from the application that generated, edited, or modified such native file. Metadata is a subset of ESI.

9.052   Metadata Further Discussed

In order to fully understand how to produce documents during the discovery stage of your case, you must understand the different levels of metadata.

Embedded metadata—data that reflects the substantive changes made to the document by the user (i.e., when you are in litigation involving an employment contract and you are producing that contract in its native format, the opposing party will fairly easily be able to view any changes you made prior to production of the documents).

System metadata—information generated automatically such as date and time of creation of a document and date and time edits were made (i.e., if you edited a document after you received information crucial to the litigation now at hand).

9.053   Plan Early and Plan Well!

The early stages of your case are important for the planning and strategy. At the onset of the case, it is important to put together a solid team of people to staff the case:

Partner—relationship manager

Associate—drafting and research

Paralegal—document collection and processing
   Consider using an outside vendor in the collection and processing phase.

Counsel for all parties should familiarize themselves with discovery requests with which they are served while considering the details of the discovery requests that they will serve.

No matter which side you are on, become intricately familiar with your client's operation.

1. Have a planning meeting with your litigation team.
2. Discuss the issues in case to determine if ESI is relevant; specify types of ESI.
3. Have the client designate one or more employees as in-house contacts (IT coordinator and/or key executive).
4. List all hardware and software; prepare a datamap.
5. Prepare organizational chart.
6. Issue a litigation hold.
7. Indentify key persons (witnesses) and time period.

At each step of this process you should be creating or updating checklists.

No matter how organized or how seasoned a paralegal is, it is impossible to remember everything. For each case, create a binder or electronic document which contains the following checklist (which will be discussed in depth further in this chapter):

1. Contact list—should contain everyone's name, contact information, responsibilities, and deadlines.
2. Organizational chart—plaintiff can use to plan strategy of the case, and defendant can use to plan data collection.
3. Client interview—put together a form that has all the questions to ask of each witness. Reproduce the form as many times as necessary and record the answers. This is an excellent strategy. As you complete the interviews, you can share them with the rest of your team, and the attorneys can build their case based on the information contained in them.
4. Software/hardware chart—make a list of all the client's IT systems, including servers, desktop computers, laptops, PDAs, flash drives, backup tapes, off-site storage systems, and fixed storage areas.

9.054 Rule 26(f) Meet and Confer and Rule 16 Scheduling Conference

These conferences have become the battleground where the case is shaped. Be well prepared to address the essential elements of an electronic discovery plan.

The side which has a thorough understanding of the case and knowledge of the relevant IT systems will be able to frame the discovery plan in a way that helps his or her case and potentially hamper that of the other side. The team (attorney *and* paralegal) who appear without an understanding of the ESI issues may be corralled into a discovery plan that results in substantial (and otherwise avoidable) costs for their client or which allows the other side to destroy or avoid producing critical ESI.

The meet and confer is also the place where attorneys can begin to prepare the ground for arguments that the court order substantial cost shifting to the other side. Such an order, in certain cases, can translate into hundreds of thousands of dollars and, in such circumstances, may force the other side to consider settlement simply to avoid the expense.

Under the federal rules, the meet and confer must take place within approximately 99 days (70 or 30 business days) after the complaint is filed. This leaves precious little time for all that the attorneys must do to adequately prepare. This is all the more reason for you as the paralegal team member to be on top of your game. If you have prepared your organizational chart and witness interview checklist and your relevant software/hardware charts, your attorney can begin to determine his or her strategy as to what information should be agreed to preserve and produce in discovery and what should be considered burdensome and unnecessary under the circumstances.

For example, if you establish that the plaintiff in a sexual harassment case worked in an isolated department consisting of only several employees, which had little contact with other operations of a large defendant corporation, your attorney can effectively counter requests that the corporation image the hard drives of management personnel in other departments who never dealt with the plaintiff or that it discontinue use of backup tapes in departments utilizing servers unconnected to the department at issue. Likewise, if the attorney can demonstrate that all hard drives are backed up on a nightly basis to a server, requests to preserve hard drives may be challenged as unnecessary and unduly burdensome.

From the perspective of a party seeking information, an attorney who understands the other side's information system and the manner in which key players related to one another will be able to offer concrete grounds for his or her preservation requests.

Given the staggering volume of ESI available in each case, no prudent attorney would want to be buried in ESI that would be produced in response to overly broad requests. Precision and clarity are therefore the instruments with which you must work. Ask only for the ESI that you need.

It is unlikely that the meet and confer will be a onetime meeting, but rather a work in progress that will be resolved in a Rule 16 conference with the court. Prudent attorneys and their paralegals should therefore be meticulous in documenting the points of agreement and disagreement reached between the parties and the grounds that support his or her own position. To resolve disputes, courts may hear testimony on the burdens and expenses that would be incurred to comply with unreasonable preservation and production demands. Courts are more likely to support those demands that are clear, properly focused, and supported with good reason.

9.055   The Report

Within 10 days of the meet and confer, the parties are to file a joint written report with the court setting forth proposed discovery procedures.

Some specific issues to address include:

Clawback—a procedure to allow a party to obtain back from the other side any privileged documents inadvertently produced.

Quick peek—an agreement to allow the other site to review a certain set of documents before they have been thoroughly reviewed for privilege without waiving the right to later assert privileges.

Testing/sampling—a procedure to sample the other side's ESI with agreed upon keyword searches.

(*See* §9.05, Electronic Discovery for more details.)

9.056   Collection

Collection of ESI is much different than paper documents. Improper collection can permanently alter relevant data and can lead to charges of spoliation. It is expressly important that you know exactly what type of ESI you are dealing with and that only trained professionals collect ESI.

Specific types of ESI include:

E-mail and attachments

Word processing documents

Spreadsheets

Graphic and presentation documents

Images (TIFF, JPEG, and PDF)

Text files

Hard drives

Servers

Voice mail

Text messages

Audio and video files

Transaction logs

What happens if your client maintains an exact duplicate of electronic files in paper format? Do you have to retain and produce both?

The court expects parties to consider the nature of the claim, amount in controversy, agreements between the parties, relative ability of the parties to conduct discovery of ESI, and such other factors as may be relevant under the circumstances.

In addition, you must determine where all this ESI is located and how it is maintained.

- Format, location, structure, accessibility of active and archived data
- Computer systems (including legacy systems)
- Remote and third-party locations
- Network, intranet or extranet
- Tapes, disk drives, external hard drives, and other storage media

9.0561 Collection Logs.   During the collection stage of the discovery process, it is extremely important that you document everything. Now is a good time to get out another checklist!

The exact format of each checklist is different in each case. This manual will provide some instructions for creating checklists. At a minimum your processing log should contain the following columns:

Custodian

Data collected

Documents numbered (beginning Bates number and ending Bates number)

Number checking

Review of responsive/privileged documents

Format of documents collected

Produced

Final privilege review

Samples of processing logs are discussed earlier in this chapter.

You should always Bates number your documents immediately after you have collected them. If your collection was entirely electronic, have your documents branded by your local ESI vendor, and while they are branding them, have them scanned using OCR. This will give you the ability to search the text of your documents.

PRACTICE TIP

- Put checklists and document logs in Excel or Word and add a footnote with the auto date and time feature so that you can always verify the latest version of a log.

9.057   Review

During the review phase, the volume of documents that need to be reviewed for relevance and privilege will be discovered. The documents will go through several layers of review even though nothing has been printed. After the review has been completed, the next steps are to create the privilege log and produce the documents.

It is now time to determine the manner of production. In cases such as the Enron matter and other large document intensive cases, the volume of data is so unique that the courts have dictated production in electronic format to data storage vendors only. The paralegal should check with the attorney before doing anything to downgrade or eliminate the data otherwise available in the ESI. A pristine set of the ESI must always be preserved.

The manner of production largely depends on the size of the case and the sophistication of the court. Regardless of the manner of production, be very careful to record everything.

If documents are produced in electronic format, make sure to discuss whether to produce in native format, with or without OCR, and whether to scrub your documents or to initially produce static images only.

9.058   Rules Changes Discussed

9.0581 Federal Rules of Civil Procedure 26(b)(2)(B).
The Civil Rules Advisory Committee has characterized the amendments to Federal Rule of Civil Procedure 26(b)(2)(B) as establishing a "two-tier" system. The rule seeks to strike a balance between a requesting party's desire to obtain all relevant information and the staggering volume, cost, and arguably negligible benefit of investigating every piece of ESI. It limits the initial production burden to reasonable accessible sources. Rule 26(b)(2)(B) was designed to respond to "distinctive problems encountered in discovery of ESI that have no close analog in the more familiar discovery of paper documents."

For instance, some types of computer storage can only be searched with considerable effort. The client may be able to identify difficult-to-access responsive information but may not be able to retrieve the information without incurring substantial burden or cost (i.e., backup tapes, legacy data, and fragmented data that was "deleted" but remains in computer stack space). You must provide this information identified by category or type in sufficient detail.

The party from whom discovery is sought may have to allow sampling of data to test its assertion that relevant data is not reasonably accessible. (*See* amended Fed. R. Civ. P. 34(2)(1).)

The requesting party has the burden of demonstrating that its need for the discovery outweighs the burden and cost of locating, retrieving, and producing.

9.0582 Rules 33 and 34.
The change to Rule 33 to add electronically stored information recognizes that there are significant types of digital information that are difficult to characterize simply as "documents."

These new rules do not automatically grant testing and sampling rights. The amended rule recognizes that different forms of production may be appropriate for different types of ESI.

Native format

PDF

TIFF

Sometimes it is appropriate to request that data be exported into a compatible application with which the requesting party is familiar. Beware if making such a request will impede your ability to search or manipulate the data.

A party receiving a request for production in a particular format may make a timely objection; failure to do so may give the requesting party an argument at a later date that the production was not usable. Production has to be made in usable form. In most circumstances, it can not be downgraded.

9.0583 Quick Peeks, Clawbacks, and Preservation of Privilege.

The volume of electronically stored information is staggering. A single gigabyte of data may hold as many as 75,000 pages of Word documents or over 100,000 e-mail messages. In the parlance of discovery, that is about 40 "banker's boxes."

A flash drive that fits on your key chain may hold several gigabytes, two PDAs several more, and a computer hard drive likely holds 40 to 80 gigabytes. In addition, one must consider servers of several hundred gigabytes.

Given these circumstances, courts and practitioners have observed that workable solutions must be found for how to properly conduct Rule 34 discovery within a reasonable pretrial schedule while making sure appropriate discovery is produced without wholesale privilege waivers resulting from insufficient time to carefully review all responsible ESI for privilege.

A September 2005 report of the Judicial Conference Committee on Practice and Procedure specifically noted that "the volume of the information and the forms in which it is stored may make privilege determinations more difficult and privilege review correspondingly more expensive and time-consuming, yet less likely to detect all privileged information."

Inadvertent production is increasingly likely to occur. The failure to screen out even one privileged item may result in an argument that there has been a waiver as to all other privileged materials related to the same subject matter.

Quick peek agreements become increasingly attractive. Under such arrangements, the responding party agrees to provide the requesting party with an opportunity to review all, or a substantial part, of the responding party's ESI, with a stipulation that this initial examination will not constitute a waiver of any privilege or protection. The requesting party may then designate the documents that it wishes to have produced. The responding party then reviews for privilege only the documents actually requested. If a privileged document is inadvertently produced, the receiving party must promptly return, sequester, and destroy the specified information.

Another arrangement devised to address this issue is the "clawback" or "nonwaiver" agreement. Under those arrangements, the parties agree that privileged material that is inadvertently produced will be returned without the disclosure constituting a waiver. Amended Rule 26(f) encourages parties to reach such agreements and to ask the court to include them in a pretrial order. Amended Rule 26(b)(5)(B) is designed to address the procedural aspect of this issue; it establishes a process through which a party may assert privilege and work product protection claims after production. A party who has produced privileged information may notify the receiving party of the claim and the basis for it. The receiving party must promptly return, sequester, and destroy the specified information. These agreements do not change the substantive law on privilege, a law that varies from jurisdiction to jurisdiction. Parties dealing with privileged and work product protected materials must do so with great prudence and recognition of the potential loss of privilege.

9.0584 Rule 37(f).

A distinct feature of electronic information systems is that the normal operation of the system will cause "the routine modification, overwriting, and deletion of information." This rule was enacted to provide "limited protection against sanctions for a party's inability to provide electronically stored information in discovery when that information has been lost as a result of the routine operation of an electronic information system, as long as that operation is in good faith." Sanctions should not be imposed for the loss of ESI that stems from the routine, good faith operation of an electronic information system. This safe harbor applies *only* to information that is lost due to the routine operation of an electronic information system, *and* the operation of that system must have taken place "in good faith."

This rule also covers overbroad demands for ESI. A party possessing discoverable ESI must act vigilantly in response to preservation demands that are too broad. If you receive an overly broad request from opposing counsel, you must take issue with the demands—preferably in writing—and aim to reach an understanding about what will and will not be preserved. Once the scope of responsible preservation is determined, you must immediately communicate this obligation to all essential personnel at your client's place of business.

9.059 Summary

Some jurisdictions have put together teams of attorneys and judges to construct a protocol to use that makes some sense out of the uncharted waters of ESI and discovery. An example of such a protocol can be found at http://www.mdd.uscourts.gov/news/news/esiprotocol.pdf. This protocol is not a local rule nor a guideline adopted by any court; rather, it is a "working model" that was established to provide guidance to attorneys and paralegals seeking to adjust to the new lay of the land created by the amendments to the federal rules governing discovery of ESI.

Discussion about electronic discovery often focus upon the staggering volume of ESI maintained by large corporations and the difficulties of managing, preserving, reviewing, and producing such large amounts of data. Yet, though often overlooked, ESI can be the evidence that tips the scale in the most basic of cases. At times, it may even be the smoking gun that quickly forces a favorable settlement or cements a victory at trial. Most written communications these days take place by e-mail. An increasing number of people purchase and send gifts, make travel arrangements, and conclude other transactions over the Internet. Many others maintain banking records, stock portfolios, and other financial records online and/or on hard drives. Indeed, the scope of data that individuals peruse on their computer is virtually unlimited. Carefully consider and thoroughly review all of the potentially discoverable ESI that the client maintains and seek from opposing party "all ESI that may be relevant in the litigation."

Some ways in which ESI can affect a case may be understood by considering scenarios from a general family law practice. A claim for child custody, for example, will be fully undermined by evidence that a prospective custodian has visited child pornography Web sites or engaged in inappropriate chat room conversations or other electronic communications. When charges of adultery are likely to be made in a divorce action, ESI can provide another treasure trove of information. E-mails, instant messages, and chat room conversations are obvious sources. If you believe that an opposing party may have incriminating ESI that can be used against that party in the litigation, you should immediately—even well before initiating proceedings in court—send out a preservation letter demanding that all ESI be preserved. An effective preservation letter should detail with clarity and precision the particular sources and types of ESI that should be maintained.

In addition to collecting and processing ESI, you must give serious consideration to the steps necessary to ensure that you will be able to admit this ESI into evidence. For instance, you must be able to demonstrate the relevance of the ESI as well as have the ability to authenticate the ESI. *Federal Rules of Evidence* 901(b), while not focused specifically on ESI, presents various examples of how evidence may generally be authenticated. *See Lorraine v. Markel American Ins. Co.,* 2007 WL 2028409 (D. Md.).

Case law in this area is changing rapidly. Some landmark cases and some recent cases involving electronic discovery may be found following this section. Please note cases are current as of the date of this printing.

9.0591 Landmark and Recent Cases

LANDMARK CASES
Cases That Changed Legal Standard

Zubulake v. UBS Warburg, LLC, 217 F.R.D. 309 (S.D.N.Y. May 13, 2003)

Zubulake v. UBS Warburg, LLC, 230 F.R.D. 290 (S.D.N.Y. May 13, 2003)

Zubulake v. UBS Warburg, LLC, 216 F.R.D. 280 (S.D.N.Y. July 24, 2003)

Zubulake v. UBS Warburg, LLC, 220 F.R.D. 212 (S.D.N.Y. October 22, 2003)

Zubulake v. UBS Warburg, LLC, 229 F.R.D. 422 (S.D.N.Y. July 20, 2004)

Zubulake v. UBS Warburg, LLC, 231 F.R.D. 159 (S.D.N.Y. Feb. 03, 2005)

Zubulake v. UBS Warburg, LLC, 382 F. Supp. 2d 536 (S.D.N.Y. Mar. 16, 2005)

Recent E-Discovery Cases

Bergersen v. Shelter Mut. Ins. Co., 2006 WL 334675 (D. Kan. Feb. 14, 2006)

Creative Sci. Sys., Inc. v. Forex Capital Mkts., LLC, 2006 WL 870973 (N.D. Cal. Apr. 4, 2006)

Kelly v. Montgomery Lynch & Assoc., 2007 WL 4412572 (N.D. Ohio Dec. 13, 2007)

Kellogg v. Nike, Inc., 2007 WL 4570871 (D. Neb. Dec. 26, 2007)

Miller v. International Bus. Mach., 2006 WL 99160 (N. Cal. Apr. 14, 2006)

Powerhouse Marks, L.L.C. v. Chi Hsin Impex, Inc., 2006 WL 83477 (E.D. Mich. Jan. 12, 2006)

Treppel v. Biovail Corp., 233 F.R.D. 363 (S.D.N.Y. 2006)

Qualcomm Inc. v. Broadcom Corp., 2008 WL 66932 (S.D. Cal. Jan 7, 2008)

Victor Stanley, Inc. v. Creative Pipe, Inc., et al., MJG-06-2662, U.S.D.C. for the District of Maryland (unreported as of printing)

BIBLIOGRAPHY

Federal Civil Judicial Procedure and Rules. St. Paul, MN: West Group, 2008.

Federal Practice and Procedure. St. Paul, MN: West Publishing Company, 2008.

Federal Rules of Civil Procedure. St. Paul, MN: West Publishing Company, 2008.

Federal Rules of Evidence. St. Paul, MN: West Publishing Company, 2008.

National Association of Legal Assistants, *Discovery—Advanced Paralegal Certification Course,* 2008, On-line Self Study Program, www.nala-apc.org

10

Assisting at Trial

10.00 INTRODUCTION

Trials are as varied as people and have just as diverse a selection of personalities. One trial may simply contest the damages involved with the liability issue already admitted. Other cases may be solely a trial of the legal issues or only of the factual issues, the damages or remedy having been established beyond dispute or by stipulation. Criminal trials may involve only one defendant and one violation of code or statute or may be complicated by multiple issues and defendants. Business litigation, product liability, and antitrust cases may involve complex and interdependent issues of law and fact, extensive discovery that generates hundreds or thousands of pages of potential exhibits, scores of witnesses, multiple defendants and, perhaps, hundreds of plaintiffs, cross-defendants, and cross-plaintiffs. There may even be interested parties who seek standing as a friend of the court *(amicus curiae)* and file legal briefs for the court's consideration. (*See,* e.g., the briefs in the appendix 1, Amicus Brief of the National Association of Legal Assistants.)

The duties delegated to a paralegal in preparing a case for trial depend first and foremost on the unique nature of the individual case. Two additional determining factors are always: (1) how much help the lawyer feels is necessary and (2) whether the paralegal is the proper person to supply the needed assistance.

10.01 TRIAL PREPARATION

Knowing who is on the prospective juror list, having the trial materials ready, getting all the witnesses lined up and set to go, and organizing all the exhibits—these are the elements that must be combined at the right time, in the correct order, and in the courtroom for trial preparation to be successful.

Prior to trial, the paralegal should contact the clerk's office to check on the availability of the jury list and courtroom access and obtain permission to set up video equipment, if needed. The paralegal should also check on the court's procedure for marking exhibits, equipment availability (easels, monitors, etc.), if copy machines and fax machines are available, and the court's daily schedule. After determining what equipment is already available at the courthouse, the paralegal should then arrange to rent or buy any additional equipment needed.

10.011   Investigation of the Jury Panel

A listing of jury panels is available from the jury commissioner or clerk of court prior to the scheduling of a trial date for any particular case. Many firms now obtain these jury lists and supplement them by adding limited background information on each prospective juror. More detailed juror reports can often be purchased from firms who specialize in this service. If a firm handles a high volume of trials in one city, the use of such services may be advisable. In any event, obtaining jury listings and background information is often a task that is delegated to the paralegal. Investigating jury lists is not particularly difficult, but it can be expensive and time-consuming.

Obvious sources are voter registration records, tax records, credit bureaus, and, depending on access, credit records maintained by the client. Be sure to check whether any person listed as a potential juror is known by the client (and in the case of a corporation, the client's employees) and, if so, whether that information is negative or adverse. Another area of investigation is whether the prospective juror has been a plaintiff or defendant in any civil or criminal matter within the past several years. This can be checked by reviewing the records of the state trial courts, both civil and criminal. City directories give names and occupations for other household members, which can also be important in the areas of prejudice or bias. Voter registration records generally provide information on age, residence, occupation, and political affiliation. Tax records provide information on ownership of real and personal property, such as homes, cars, and boats. Depending on the case, any or all of these facts could be important. Knowing that a particular juror is or is not a homeowner, is or is not a good paying customer, has initiated litigation, or has been a defendant in a criminal matter aids the attorney during *voir dire* in the process of determining whether a juror is being truthful as well as whether the juror has any prejudices. Juror notebooks can be set up with an individual page for each potential juror.

Another way to check on potential jurors is to circulate the list through your office. This works well in smaller communities where many people are known to each other.

10.02 TRIAL NOTEBOOKS

Trial notebooks are a particularly personal and individual creation of each attorney and paralegal. A paralegal should start the preparation of a trial notebook as soon as possible since it is a very useful tool throughout the case. It can be used at depositions, witness interviews, pretrial conferences, and for

EXHIBIT 10-1   Possible Trial Notebook Sections

1.	Court Information	13.	Outlines of Proof
2.	Trial Preparation Agenda	14.	Outlines of Damages
3.	Things to Do	15.	Medical Summary
4.	Trial Briefs	16.	Deposition Index and Summaries
5.	Pretrial Motions	17.	Witness Index
6.	Law and Evidence Briefs	18.	Direct Examination
7.	Case Law and Summaries	19.	Cross Examination
8.	Pleadings	20.	Expert Witnesses
9.	Discovery Index	21.	Trial Notes
10.	*Voir Dire* and Juror Questionnaires	22.	Closing Arguments
11.	Opening Statement	23.	Jury Instructions
12.	Exhibit Index	24.	Verdict Form

trial planning and preparation. Whatever the form, the trial notebook contains the attorney's trial plan and functions as a reference manual for all matters of law and fact related to the trial. Depending on the size and complexity of the case, a trial notebook may involve one or more volumes. Many law firms also utilize electronic versions that are contained on laptop computers brought into the courtroom. Regardless of the physical form, a trial lawyer's notebook will usually include the following sections: (1) Trial Plan/To Do List; (2) Trial Notes; (3) Key Pleadings; (4) Pretrial Motions; (5) Relevant Law; (6) *Voir Dire*; (7) Opening Statement; (8) Witnesses; (9) Exhibits; (10) Closing Argument; (11) Jury Instructions, and (12) Proposed Verdict Form. Preprinted index divider tabs can be purchased covering almost every imaginable notebook section or labels can be printed for use on blank divider tabs. Exhibit 10-1 is an example of a detailed trial notebook index that might be found in a complex case. A more detailed explanation of certain notebook sections is provided in the following sections.

10.021   Trial Plan/To Do List

Each attorney expects to prove certain facts or introduce certain evidence at specific times or through specific witnesses. To do this, a trial plan must be devised to organize the questioning of each witness and the introduction of evidence in a coherent, persuasive manner, easy for the judge or jury to both understand and relate to the case issues.

Many attorneys begin the trial plan process by first preparing a brief of the case by cause of action to identify the essential elements of alleged conduct and the legal foundation for each cause of action. Then the defenses raised in the answer and affirmative defenses are briefed. Both sides' admissions (obtained from the answer to the complaint and from any responses to requests for admission or answers to interrogatories from the parties) are analyzed, and the remaining disputed elements are isolated.

A trial plan is then created which incorporates the information from the trial brief and, in addition, outlines not only the attorney's own perception of the posture of the case but countermeasures for the discerned positions of the opposing party. Once established, the trial plan falls easily into order by collating the available sources of testimony against the factual and legal demands of the trial brief. The plan then reflects the order of presentation along with the points to be covered, which are in turn cross-indexed to witnesses, exhibits, or other sources of information.

10.022   Key Pleadings

This generally contains an index with appropriate tabbed dividers for such legal documents as trial briefs, memoranda of points and authorities, case law, citations, and authorities on anticipated points of dispute, the most recent complaint and responsive pleadings, and key pretrial orders. These represent the pleadings and documents the attorney will probably need most often during the course of the trial.

10.023   Witnesses

If you are dealing with a number of witnesses, it may be more efficient to prepare a separate witness notebook. This notebook should be indexed and tabbed with a separate section for each witness, including experts, listed by the parties to be called at trial. The first sheet in each section will usually be the attorney's outline of direct or cross-examination for that witness, followed by a fact sheet which lists the identifying personal data for the witness, the dates of each statement and/or deposition, answers to interrogatories attributed to the witness, a "conflicts" index if any conflicting points or story have been detected, and identification of each exhibit that the witness may be used to introduce. A summary of each statement and/or deposition is also included in chronological order, perhaps highlighted with tabs or color markings of significant passages and cross-indexed to the separate file of statement and deposition transcripts. Expert witness sections will also include a copy of the expert's curriculum vitae, written opinions regarding the case at hand, as well as an index of prior testimony that either supports or contradicts the expert's opinion, and applicable treatises, studies, protocol, or authority relied upon by the expert in forming his or her opinions. It should also include copies of answers to interrogatories regarding that expert, a copy of any Rule 26 disclosures, and a deposition summary, if one was taken. Having a comprehensive witness notebook greatly assists the attorney at trial and in the pretrial planning stage.

10.024   Exhibits

This section contains a list of the exhibits for both sides. All federal courts and state courts whose rules follow the form of the *Federal Rules of Civil Procedure* require each side to disclose and identify trial documents or other exhibits it intends to use prior to the trial. A copy of each party's exhibit disclosure pleading should be maintained in this section, in addition to any other listing formats that may be used. (*See* Exhibit 10-2.) Many jurisdictions also require that each side mark intended exhibits with identification numbers prior to trial. Even if not required, this is a good organizational practice, which will make the presentation of the case go more smoothly.

Because proposed exhibits may not actually be utilized, a common practice is to maintain an exhibit listing in the form of a log or chart. Exhibit 10-3 is an example of an Exhibit Log for use at trial. At a minimum, the log contains the identification for each exhibit (sequentially in order of introduction as well as the opposing party's assigned number for the exhibit if it appears on their exhibits list and preassigned numbers have not been given prior to trial); a description of the exhibit; the expected introduction witness; and columns to record the exhibit's offer, its acceptance or rejection by the court as evidence. Some attorneys like to include the needed foundation for admissibility as evidence (possibly the evidence citation); whether the attorney intends to object to an opposing party's exhibit (cross-indexed to the foundation for objection, the evidence rule, and so on); or whether the attorney expects an objection from an opposing party (cross-indexed to the foundation, case law, or evidence rule which supports admission).

EXHIBIT 10-2   Sample Exhibit Disclosure Pleading

In the United States Disctrict Court
District of _____
Civil Action No.: _____

Plaintiff)	
)	
vs.)	**PLAINTIFF'S TRIAL**
)	**EXHIBIT LIST**
Defendant)	
_____)	

Plaintiff, by and through its attorneys, hereby submits its listing of exhibits to be offered at trial in accord with Local Rule 83.V.2 DSC as follows:

1. May 7, 2006 letter from John Doe to Jane Roe (Exhibit 1 to Deposition of Roe).
2. May 25, 2006 Contract of Sale for residence at 999 Governor's Road (Exhibit 5 to Deposition of Doe).
3. June 25, 2006 HUD Settlement Statement for sale of residence at 999 Governor's Road (Exhibit 7 to Deposition of Doe).

Respectfully submitted,

EXHIBIT 10-3   Sample Exhibit Log

Pltf Ex. No.	Deft Ex. No.	Obj.	Grounds	Witness	Description	Identified	Marked	Offered	Entered

10.025 Jury Panel

The jury commissioner or clerk of court usually publishes a roster of potential jury members with sufficient identification to allow some background inquiry as described earlier in Section 10.011, Investigation of the Jury Panel. The paralegal takes the information obtained on each juror and combines that data with information obtained during *voir dire* to prepare a twelve-block chart which identifies each empanelled juror.

The twelve-block chart is organized just as the chairs in the jury box and, upon completion of the jury selection process, contains the name, age, address, occupation of each juror, and the attorney's notes regarding each. Alternate jurors, if used, are identified in separate blocks and annotated in the same fashion. (*See* Exhibit 10-4, Sample Jury Roster.) Some attorneys prefer to have a new roster prepared each day, which also contains a description of how the juror is dressed. In some jurisdictions,

EXHIBIT 10-4   Sample Jury Roster

Jury Panel — Case:				Date		Alternates	
7	8	9	10	11	12	3	4
1	2	3	4	5	6	1	2

depending on how jury selection is accomplished, this form may also be used during the actual selection process to aid in determining which potential jurors are, or should be, stricken for cause.

This section also includes a compilation of questions that the attorney plans to ask the prospective jurors during *voir dire*. The questions should be designed so that the juror's responses will disclose any biases or preconceived conclusions about the case, the clients, or the litigation process in general. During *voir dire* it is one of the responsibilities of the paralegal to make notations of the juror's responses to the questions, as well as observations of body language and facial expressions. A forensic psychologist, jury consultant, or other expert profiler is sometimes used to assist in the selection process.

10.026   The Paralegal and the Trial Notebook

The trial notebook varies from lawyer to lawyer, partly as a function of the manner in which they learned their trial practice and partly through their own ideas of emphasizing their trial effectiveness. The paralegal's contribution to the trial notebook includes preparation of various indices, entry and cross-referencing of factual material, and organization for instant retrieval backup material for the various notebook sections, such as:

a. Testimony transcripts, tape recordings, signed statements, declarations, and affidavits listed in the Witness section.

b. The operative complaint and answers, requests for admissions, interrogatories, production requests, pretrial motions and supporting briefs, and pretrial orders for the Key Pleadings section.

c. The exhibits, organized, maintained, and easily available, including cross-references to summaries of depositions, requests for production, and one-line summaries of interrogatories.

d. The case books, statutes, law review articles, the benchbook, regulations, or textbooks on which the attorney relies, available either as the entire volume or copied portions for the law section. Key sections may be downloaded to the attorney's laptop or PDA.

Additionally, some matters in the law section may be drafted by the paralegal, such as jury instructions—particularly in jurisdictions where a detailed book of approved jury instructions is available and citation of the exact language from approved instructions is persuasive. Similarly, the cross-citing of the attorney's anticipated authorities to the judge's preferred reference book may be drafted for the attorney's consideration.

Where such matters are delegated, they should be completed in a timely fashion to allow time to review, edit, and verify those entries on which the case relies. If you work in a specific area of law, for example, personal injury, it is very helpful to have copies of case law, statutes, and rules dealing with issues relating to the particular area of law. For example, if an issue should be brought to the court's attention in the judge's chambers prior to trial, the attorney would have the pertinent case law or statute at hand to argue for the client. The issues may include *voir dire*, peremptory challenges, opening statements, closing statements, jury instructions, or motions in limine, which may still be pending prior to trial.

10.0261 Identities.   Another important contribution by the paralegal is the compiling of a section that contains information on all individuals and entities associated with the case. This will be several sheets on which the name of every individual or entity in the case is recorded together with addresses, telephone numbers, and the exact relationship to the case. Always include the names of the parties and their counsel, investigators and/or paralegal s if known, identified or probable witness, with an indication of the witness type, such as plaintiff, defendant, neutral, or expert witness. Include contact information for the witness and office personnel to contact in case additional information is needed, in addition to local contact information for witnesses brought into town for the trial. Also include in this section information for persons, firms, or agencies that may be called upon to provide services to the trial team, such as a company for audio-video equipment, copy services, subpoena service, or convenient hotels where accommodation arrangements can be made for experts and witnesses, as well as the trial team and clients when the trial setting takes place out of town.

10.03 THE PARALEGAL AT THE TRIAL

If the trial is expected to be of some duration, consider requesting daily transcripts. If this is done, and it usually is advisable and economical in multiparty cases, a paralegal could see that an alphabetical index to witnesses is prepared on a daily basis. The index would include names of the witnesses, the date they appeared on the stand, names of interrogating attorneys, volume and page numbers of testimony of all witnesses, whether on direct examination and by whom, whether on redirect examination and by whom, and whether on cross or recross examination and by whom. (*See* Exhibit 10-5.)

EXHIBIT 10-5   Sample Index of Trial Witnesses from a Daily Transcript

Witneses	For	Date	Direct	Cross	Redirect	Recross
Doe, Jane L. (A), (1)	Defense	7/26	Vol. III., pp3102-3300; JONES			
		7/27	Vol. IV., pp3304-3400; JONES	Vol. IV., pp34301-3475; DOW	Vol. IV., pp3475-3500; JONES	NONE
Roe, John D.	Defense	7/27	Vol. IV., pp3502-3700; ABLE	Vol. IV., pp3701-3927; DOW	NONE	NONE
Buck, James X. (d) (I) (A)	Defense	7/28	Vol. V., pp4003-4150; DOW	Vol. V., pp4153-4200; CAIN	Vol. V., pp4200-4225; DOW	Vol. V., pp4225-4229; CAIN

(A) Abstract in File   (I) Topical Index in File   (d) Testimony Presented by Deposition

EXHIBIT 10-6   Sample Index to Trial Transcript

Volume I — July 23, 2007 — Pages 1–975

Description	Page
Opening Statement by James S. DOW (Plaintiff)	175
Opening Statement by Ivan M. ABLE (Defendant Roe)	350
Opening Statement by Richard K. Jones (Defendant Doe)	500
Jason D. Shooter, sworn — DIRECT by DOW	800
Plaintiff's Exhibit 1: Letter from Roe to Shooter dated 1/15/05	803
Plaintiff's Exhibit 2: Contract between Roe and Shooter dated 2/1/05	815
Proceedings outside presence of jury — Objections to Plaintiff's Exhibit 3	845
Plaintiff's Exhibit 3: Letter from Roe to Doe dated 1/18/05	875

Volume II — July 24, 2007 — Pages 976–1500

Description	Page
Proceedings outside presence of jury—Objection to Plaintiff's Exhibit 4	976
Jason D. Shooter — Continued DIRECT by DOW	1050
Plaintiff's Exhibit 4: 1/28/05 tape recorded conversation between Shooter, Doe, and Roe	1060
CROSS of Shooter by ABLE	1149
Defendant's Exhibit 1: Letter from Shooter to Adams dated 1/26/05	1155
Defendant's Exhibit 2: Draft of 2/1/05 Contract between Roe and Shooter	1165
Proceedings outside presence of jury — Objection to Defendant's Exhibit 3	1199
Defendant's Exhibit 3: 2/12/05 Video tape of Shooter's delivery vehicle	1295
CROSS of Shooter by JONES	1400

In addition to the index of trial witnesses, an index of the entire trial transcript may also be beneficial. (*See* Exhibit 10-6.)

Many court reporters can provide daily transcripts of the proceedings that include an index. These may be obtained on diskette for use on a computer and can form the basis for the index described previously. Many court reporters can provide a service known as "real-time" reporting. This allows testimony to either be downloaded immediately to diskette for viewing on a computer or allows a connection by which testimony can be viewed at the same time it is being taken on a computer at counsel table. Not only does the availability of these "real-time" transcripts enhance the trial team's ability to prepare for the next day's courtroom activity, but they are also a good tool for use in cross-examining a witness still on the stand. If real time is not available, the paralegal should take detailed notes for the attorney to review prior to cross-examination or recross examination. The paralegal should also keep track of when exhibits are offered and received, any objections made by either party and the judge's ruling on each objection.

In some instances, testimony at trial may be presented via depositions. This should be noted in the index, along with whether the file contains a transcript, abstract, or topical index of the deposition of certain witnesses.

10.031 Witnesses, Control, and Liaison

It is normal for witnesses to be nervous and apprehensive before a trial. They have had to disrupt their daily lives to attend. Such disruption is particularly difficult when trials are delayed by the court. The paralegal should make periodic contact with each witness, informing them of the progress of the case on the trial docket, but not on substantive matters. This allows the witness the utmost personal freedom possible without discussing the case itself. Some witnesses might have to travel to the place of trial, and the paralegal often coordinates transportation, lodging, and/or meals for them. Having the witness available at the right time is critical.

The paralegal may also be called upon to help prepare the witness to testify. The degree of witness preparation depends on the type and complexity of the case. Many attorneys prepare detailed outlines of their witness examinations, which are in part based on previously prepared summaries of statements or depositions. These are often reviewed with the witness prior to trial. In such instances, the paralegal follows the planned testimony of each witness against the topical summaries previously prepared from statements or depositions to check off anticipated testimony story changes or conflicts. Another area of preparing witnesses often delegated to the paralegal involves educating them about the purpose and procedures associated with court testimony. Many law firms maintain a brief set of instructions, which are provided to the witness for review ahead of time. (*See* Exhibit 10-7.) Often a trip to the courthouse to familiarize the witness or client with the courtroom will ease anxieties about testifying. Videos available for the potential witness to view that show a person actually giving testimony and what they should and should not do while testifying.

EXHIBIT 10-7   Sample Witness Instructions

- Above all else, always tell the truth.
- Be sure you understand the question before you answer.
  - Your attorney is not allowed to ask leading questions that suggest an answer. You will need to tell all the details you remember with as little prompting from your attorney as possible.
  - If you do not understand what is being asked, say so—politely ask the attorney to rephrase the question so that it is clear.
- Answer only the question asked as briefly as possible.
  - If possible, answer the questions of the opposing attorney with a yes or no response; if it makes you uncomfortable, then ask to explain or clarify your yes or no answer. Stop and wait for the next question.
  - Do not volunteer any additional information unless asked to do so.

- Do not expand on the question.
- Do not be evasive or give "smart" or sarcastic answers.
- Admit lack of knowledge. Do not guess or speculate. "I don't know" or "I don't remember" can be a perfectly acceptable answer.
- Avoid exaggeration.
- Make an effort to speak clearly and slowly.
  - Address your answer to the jury; they are the people who must decide whether to believe what you are saying.
- Dress conventionally and act with restraint.
- Maintain a respectful and pleasant demeanor.
- Avoid nervous gestures.
- Do not qualify favorable facts.

Source: "The Whole Truth on How to Prepare a Witness," Michael K. Gaige, CLA, XXIII *Facts & Findings 2* (August 1996).

10.032   Fees, Costs, and Expenses

The paralegal frequently monitors all the fees, costs, and expenses associated with the trial. These may include witness fees; transportation and lodging expenses; meal expenses for the trial team, witnesses, and the client; parking fees; subpoena service fees; photocopying charges; audio/video equipment costs; court reporter fees; and any hotel/motel charges. Usually, the method of handling such matters is determined by established office policy and procedure. The attorney or the office manager should be consulted to determine the manner of handling any unusual situations or expenses on each case.

10.033   Exhibit/Evidence Log

The paralegal should maintain an independent log of the exhibits introduced at trial and record their marking for identification, foundation and offering as evidence, any objections, and the court's ruling. (*See* Exhibit 10-8.) During courtroom breaks and recesses, the paralegal should confer with the attorney to ensure that desired exhibits have not only been identified and marked, but have also been formally offered and entered. It is normal for the trial team to meet after court has been adjourned for the day to review the day's events. During the course of the daily meeting, discussed in more detail following, the attorney and the paralegal reconcile their logs to ensure they are consistent.

The paralegal is usually in charge of the exhibits and must be ready to provide the requested exhibit when the attorney is ready to introduce it. This is particularly important where special arrangements are needed, such as the provision of videotape machines, televisions, computers, scale models, large sketches, drawings, or photographs. If possible, the attorney and paralegal should meet prior to trial when the outlines are being prepared to determine which exhibits will be offered with specific witnesses.

In instances where there are a large number of exhibits to be offered at trial, arrangements should be made prior to trial with the trial judge and/or the clerk of court to review all exhibits presented during that day's proceeding to determine the accuracy of your records and, when necessary, to obtain on a daily basis copies of the exhibits entered. The paralegal can then supervise reproducing, tabbing, and indexing the exhibits, furnishing copies to the attorney, and returning any original exhibits obtained from the clerk to the court prior to trial the next day.

An index of these trial exhibits should contain the dates, volumes, and page numbers in the trial transcript on which the particular exhibit was identified, marked, received into evidence, and mentioned; the interrogating attorney and witness on the stand at the time; a brief description of the exhibit; the plaintiff or defendant exhibit number as actually entered in court; and the paralegal's tabbed

EXHIBIT 10-8   Sample Trial Exhibit Log

Exhibit List—Case:

P/D No.	Date	Witness	Description	Status
P 13	7/16	ROE	6/15/05 Invoice for Roof Repairs	OBJ; RR
P 14	7/16	ROE	6/15/05 $150.00 Canceled Check	O; A
P 13	7/17	BUCK	6/15/05 Invoice for Roof Repairs	OBJ; OR; A
P 15	7/17	BUCK	6/15/05 Invoice for Asphalt Shingles	O; A

O = Offered   OBJ = Objection   RR = Ruling Reserved   OR = Overruled   S = Sustained   A = Admitted

EXHIBIT 10-9   Sample Index of Exhibits Introduced at Trial

Court Ex. No.	Party Id No.	Date	Vol./Page	Examination	Description	Identified	Marked	Offered	Entered	Mentioned
(P) 12	(P) 15	7/15	IV/1753	ROE by ABLE	6/15/05 Visa Charge Slip Totaling $150.00	4	4			
		7/15	IV/1754					4	4	
		7/15	IV/1755		Explanation					4
		7/15	IV/1890	ROE by CAIN	Cross					4
(P) 13	(P) 16	7/16	IV/1987	ROE by ABLE	6/15/05 Report of Investigating Officer	4	4			
		7/16	IV/1988		Direct					4
		7/17	V/2350	ROE by CAIN	Cross					4
		7/18	VI/3675	Bull by ABLE	Direct			4	4	
		7/18	VI/3690							4
		7/18	VI/3895	Bull by CAIN	Cross					4

(P) - Plaintiff   (D1) - Joe's Bar & Grill   (D2) = Roe

document number. (*See* Exhibit 10-9.) Not all exhibits are entered in sequence of plaintiff and defendant numbers in court; therefore, an independent chronological numbering system is preferred which also allows cross-referencing to the exhibit number entered by the court. (*See* previous discussion in Section 10.024, Exhibits.) As mentioned earlier, the use of real-time or daily transcripts from the court reporter will assist in this task. Make sure you ask the court reporter to provide you with an index to each day's proceedings.

This kind of trial support may require round-the-clock assistance with the paralegal supervising a crew that might be required to work in shifts. Not all trials require this kind of massive assistance, indexing, and cross-referencing. The signs pointing to such a need are evident early in the case from the number of parties and witnesses, the complexity of issues, the factual material to be presented to the judge or jury for decision, and where it becomes obvious that, whatever the outcome, the matter will be appealed by one of the parties. Detailed transcripts and indices are invaluable to the attorney in pinpointing the points of contention to be appealed and the testimony, factual data, and exhibits supporting those contentions.

10.034 Daily Trial Review and Planning Meeting

Every day following adjournment of the court and after the witnesses have been released, the paralegal participates in the daily trial review and planning meeting. Testimony and courtroom observations are discussed. Trial notes and exhibit logs are compared, and final arrangements and plans for the next day's activity are outlined, including decisions on any changes to the order of appearance of witnesses and identification of exhibits expected to be used with each witness. It is not unusual for these meetings to result in the need to set up morning or evening meetings with witnesses, clients, or other attorneys, creation of additional exhibit enlargements, or new demonstrative exhibits. As a result of these meetings, it may also be necessary to assist with additional research and supervise the preparation of briefs on issues the trial team has decided to bring up in court. The next day's witnesses must be notified or subpoenaed when appropriate, and arrangements for transportation and other logistics must be completed. Finally, the various indices, logs, and summaries discussed earlier in Section 10.033, Exhibit/Evidence Log are revised and updated.

10.035   Trial Notes

One of the most helpful and important jobs performed by the paralegal at trial is that of taking detailed notes of the proceedings. Of particular importance are notes and observations of testimony, particularly during cross-examination of opposing party's witnesses. Cross-examination is one period where the lawyer cannot make detailed notes of the witness's response. Even when daily or real-time transcripts are available, careful and detailed notes which include courtroom observations of the testimony will aid the lawyer during breaks and recesses, as well as at the daily trial review and planning meeting. Notes may be taken in a variety of methods including the utilization of computers in the courtroom, as well as the more traditional pen and paper.

One effective method is to use a lined legal pad, notebook paper, or spiral-bound 8- x 11-inch pad, 50 to 80 pages thick (or more than one, if for a complex case). If time permits, the top margin of each page should be marked in advance with the case name and a place to fill in the date, time, and consecutive page number. This information will be entered as the case progresses, creating a chronology of the case presentation. A vertical line one-quarter or one-third of the way from the right edge of every page will create a margin for noting exhibit introduction, important admissions, important conflicts, and other courtroom observations. When trial begins, the paralegal fills in the date and time, along with the court and the judge. It is also useful to note the names of the court clerk, court reporter, bailiff/courtroom deputy, opposing party attorneys, experts, and the presence or absence of parties. For example:

Case: Smith v. Jones
Date: 6/14/09   Time: 9:30 A.M.   Lincoln Co. Sup. Crt., Courtroom 3. Judge I. M. Wright

Notetaking begins in earnest as the opening statements are made by each attorney. When the first witness is called, the entry may look like "9:35 A.M.—Thompson sworn. Darrow Direct." The testimony is then noted as given, with additional notations in the margin concerning exhibits, objections, rulings by the judge, and jury observations. As exhibits are offered, that information is also recorded on the exhibit/evidence log for identification. Although objections and rulings are recorded in the trial notes, they are not noted on the exhibit/evidence log. When an exhibit is admitted, a notation to that effect is made in both places. The current time should also be entered on the top of each new page. That chronology, along with the times recorded for breaks and recesses (logged both at the time granted and the time trial resumes), is useful in estimating when to notify witnesses to come to the courthouse, when looking back through notes during the daily trial review and planning meetings, and when requesting certain portions of the daily trial transcripts. When the trial is over, the notebook, together with the copies of the trial exhibits and the lawyer's trial book, is stored for use in appellate procedures.

10.036   Polling the Jury

When a verdict is rendered that surprises the lawyer, interviewing the jurors to identify the reasoning behind the verdict is important. What fact, exhibit, or testimony caused the result? Which witnesses did they believe, and which did they find not credible? Why did they not believe the client or the client's witness? Asking the members of the jury these kinds of questions after a verdict has been rendered and the jurors excused is often informally referred to as polling the jury. The formal use of that term refers to a demand by a party that the jury be polled to verify that the verdict is unanimous prior to the verdict being entered and the jury discharged.

Usually, there is a reasonable and understandable basis for the decision. Sometimes it is simply common sense or a spirit of equity. For instance, in a condemnation case, the landowner wanted $2,000,000, and the public agency offered only $2,000. Both sides had experts supporting their respective but opposing valuation theories. The jury awarded the landowner $200,000 in a decision which recognized the difference in the two valuations, one so unreasonably high and the other so unreasonably low, and honored the spirit of compromise, if not the facts submitted by the two sides.

In other cases, the severity and continuing nature of an injury to an individual may arouse the sympathies of the jury, leading them to decide in favor of the injured party on a compassionate basis even though there is only the slightest thread of causal connection to the defendant's conduct.

On occasion, decisions are rendered against a party because of tactics or actions that upset, anger, or offend the jury. The offending tactic or trial strategy used by the attorney may be perfectly ethical, correct, and even necessary or required, such as a tough impeachment cross-examination. The action that angered might have been an obvious lie by a critical witness or a pattern of behavior by the party that the jury acknowledged as legal but unworthy of being rewarded by it in the verdict.

Jury polling is best done immediately after the jury is discharged but can be pursued later. Each juror is interviewed, and the notes are all collated for what value such a postmortem may provide. Some jurisdictions have placed constraints on this kind of postverdict investigation, and a paralegal should never initiate this kind of action without the attorney's express authorization and without being familiar with any such restrictions.

◄◄COMMENT►►

There is nothing quite like the experience of seeing a case through to a jury verdict. The preparation in the weeks and days preceding a trial can be demanding, exhausting, and stressful. Every jury trial is a miniature stage drama, with characters, props, and carefully choreographed moves. The paralegal often functions as stage master, copywriter, propmaster, and set designer, as well as bookkeeper, concierge, limo service manager, and drama critic. This chapter is but a brief look at the way in which the paralegal aids in trial preparation and provides assistance as an integral part of the trial team during presentation of the case to a jury. (*See* Exhibit 10-10.) Trial lawyers with a great deal of experience always say that a case should be prepared from the very beginning as if there is no chance of settlement and going to trial is definite. It pays to be prepared. If you are, the attorneys cannot afford to try a case without you.

◄◄ ►►

EXHIBIT 10-10   The Legal Assistant at Trial

Courtroom Check

1. Arrange and set counsel table.
   a. Have adequate chairs for attorney(s), legal assistant, and parties.
   b. Arrange files and documents (know where everything is).
2. Check on any requested easel, video player, etc.

Jury Selection

1. Assist attorney in gathering data on jury panel.
2. Use forms for jury selection.
3. Instruct parties to take notes during *voir dire* and to communicate thoughts regarding potential jurors to you or to the attorney.
4. Take complete notes during jury selection.
5. Be prepared to give opinion regarding potential jurors to the attorney and make sure he or she sees any notes from the parties.
6. After selection, make list of sworn jurors and fill out Jury Selection Roster form.

Witnesses

1. Coordinate attendance using information provided on a witness control sheet (keep in contact prior to the time needed; make any hotel arrangements if necessary)
2. Know your witness and client.
   a. Make sure witnesses can find the courthouse, nearby parking facilities, and the assigned court-room.
   b. Make sure witness is ready to testify.
   c. Check what the witness plans to carry on to the witness stand.
   d. Help calm down or psych up the witness.
   e. Have props, magic markers, etc. ready; tell witness where they are or how he or she will get them.
   f. Have Kleenex, aspirin, mints, cough drops, and water handy.
   g. Caution witness not to talk about testimony or the case in halls or restroom.
   h. After witness is excused, check with attorney to see if he or she will be needed again. Remind witness of no obligation to discuss case or testimony with anyone. Beware of press.
3. Track outline, unanswered questions, leads, inconsistencies not caught, etc.

Handling Documents

1. Anticipate need; have ready for witness and extra copies for court and opposing counsel.

2. Stay alert and pull pleading/documents referred to by other attorneys or witnesses; hand to attorney.
3. Keep documents organized at all times.
4. Remind attorney to offer exhibit into evidence as each witness testifies.
5. Keep careful records of exhibits offered and received (by all parties) on an Exhibit Control Sheet and compare your records with those of the court clerk at the close of each day's session.

Notetaking

1. One of the most important duties you can have.
2. Use computer for notetaking, if allowed.
3. Take as extensive notes as possible. Good notes by you can alleviate the need and expense for daily transcripts. One good method is to listen to the question and the answer and try to summarize the two into a statement.
4. Make notes as to objections and court rulings.
5. Print out and make notes available to attorney at the end of each day. Make sure the attorney has a complete set of notes of all testimony for use in preparing closing argument.

Telephone Contact with Office

1. Arrange procedure with court clerk's office for incoming messages.
2. Call office at prearranged times. (Check with attorney for instructions prior to placing calls.)
3. Keep attorney contact with office to a minimum (you act as the go-between).

Overnight Recesses

1. Go over office crisis list with attorney—get instructions or answers to telephone back to the office.
2. Ask attorney what you can do to help prepare for next day.
3. Review trial notes—make list of inconsistencies of points that need elaboration or clarification.
4. Assist with preparation of jury instructions, if requested.
5. Do not make any personal plans—be available.

Closing Arguments

1. Assist attorney in preparing for closing argument.
   a. Outline pertinent testimony from trial notes.
   b. Check with clerk to make sure exhibits are in proper numerical order.
2. Monitor outline as argument is being presented.
3. Monitor time of argument for attorney.
4. Take notes of opposing counsel's closing argument.

Source: "Trial Conduct for the Legal Assistant," Karen B. Judd, CLA, XXI *Facts & Findings* 3 (November 1994).

BIBLIOGRAPHY

Federal Practice and Procedure, St. Paul, MN: West Publishing Company, 2008.

National Association of Legal Assistants, Advanced Paralegal Certification (APC) Course – Trial Practice, (Introduced January 2007), http://nala.org/apcweb/index.html

(*Copyrighted source material: All definitions followed by one asterisk have been taken from* Oran's Dictionary of the Law *[Fourth edition, Delmar Cengage Learning]. All definitions followed by two asterisks have been taken from* Legal Thesaurus/Dictionary: A Resource for the Writer and the Computer Researcher *[Third edition, Delmar Cengage Learning].*)

Introduction

Glossary of Terms

INTRODUCTION

This chapter is not a dictionary of all legal terms but rather a selection of frequently used terms. This glossary is arranged to give paralegals definitions that serve as memory aids or refreshers.

The definitions provided are accurate but do not constitute every possible definition or contextual meaning. They are the basic, generally accepted meanings; there is insufficient detail to provide the paralegal with a means of outlining the elements of proof for a cause of action. For instance, *assault* is defined as "an unlawful offer or attempt with force to do corporeal hurt to another." The elements for a civil action require a showing that there was no consent by the plaintiff. The paralegal must consult the codes, annotated cases, texts, and other references when outlining the elements of cases and their defenses.

Those seeking in-depth meanings must consult more authoritative and detailed definitions than this book can accommodate. *Oran's Dictionary of the Law* and *Legal Thesaurus/Dictionary* are recommended.

GLOSSARY OF TERMS

a fortiori With stronger reason; by force of logic. For example, if it is true that a 21-year-old person is an adult, then, *a fortiori,* a 25-year-old person is an adult.*

a posteriori From the effect to the cause. A method of reasoning that starts with experiments or observations and attempts to discover general principles from them.*

a priori From the cause to the effect. A method of reasoning that starts with general principles and attempts to discover what specific facts or real-life observations will follow from them.*

a vinculo matrimonii "From the marriage bonds." (1) A complete divorce. (2) An annulment.*

ab actis A court clerk or a registrar.*

ab initio From the very beginning; entirely and completely since the start.*

abatement A reduction, decrease, or diminution; the suspension or cessation, in whole or in part, of a continuing charge, such as rent. The suspension or cessation of a continuing charge, for example, rent.

abrogation The destruction, repealing, or annulling of a former law.*

abstract of record A complete history in short, abbreviated form of the case as found in the record, complete enough to show that the questions presented for review have been properly reserved.

abstract of title A condensed history or summary of public records relating to the title to a particular parcel of land.

acceleration clause (in a mortgage) Specifies conditions under which the lender may advance the time when the entire debt that is secured by the mortgage becomes due.

acceptance Agreeing to an offer, thereby creating a contract.

access A right vested in the owner of land to enter and leave a tract of land from a road or other highway without obstruction; the right to enter and leave over lands of another.

accident report (auto) A report filed with the designated authorities by the operators of motor vehicles involved in an accident that sets forth the names of the parties and the circumstances surrounding the accident.

accommodation An arrangement or engagement made as a favor to another not upon a consideration received.

ACP Abbreviation for Advanced Certified Paralegal; a certification earned through and awarded by the NALA to certified legal assistants who successfully complete NALA's curriculum based Advanced Paralegal Certification program.

accretion A gradual and imperceptible accumulation of land by natural causes, as out of the sea or a river.

acknowledgment An admittance, affirmation, declaration, testimony, avowal, confession, or owning as genuine.

acre A tract of land containing 43,560 square feet of land, that is, 208.71 feet square.

ad damnum clause "To the damages." An *ad damnum* clause is that part of a plaintiff's original court papers that sets out the amount of money the plaintiff is seeking.*

ad hoc "For this"; for this special purpose; for this one time. For example, an *ad hoc* committee is a temporary one set up to do a specific job.*

ad infinitum Forever; limitless.*

ad litem "For the suit"; for the purposes of this lawsuit. For example, a guardian *ad litem* is a person who is appointed to represent a child (or other person lacking legal capacity) in a lawsuit.*

ad valorem According to value. For example, an *ad valorem* tax is a tax on the value of an item, rather than a fixed tax on the type of item. An *ad valorem* tax might tax a 10-dollar hat 50 cents and a 20-dollar hat 1 dollar, while a specific hat tax might tax all hats 75 cents regardless of price or value.*

adhesion contract Standardized contract form in which one party, normally the weaker, has little or no bargaining power or choice as to its terms.

adieu interj., n. Farewell. Good-by, bon voyage, adios, sayonara, leave, departure.**

administrative law A body of law in the form of rules and regulations promulgated by an administrative body created by state legislature or Congress to carry out a specific statute.

adverse possession Physical possession of land inconsistent with the right of the owner. In most states, a party in adverse possession, after satisfying fully the requirements of the relevant statutes, thereby acquires the title to the land. Usually requires: actual possession, adverse, under claim of right, notorious, open, exclusive, hostile, continuous, and uninterrupted.

affiant One who swears to or affirms the statement in an affidavit.

affidavit A voluntary statement in writing sworn or affirmed to before an official, usually a notary public, who has the authority to administer an oath or affirmation.

affirmative defense A new matter constituting a defense to the complaint, which is not merely a denial of facts asserted by the plaintiff. The defendant generally has the burden of proving any affirmative defenses.

agent A person authorized (requested or permitted) by another person to act for him or her; a person entrusted with another's business. Some of the many types of agents include bargaining agent; independent agent (an independent contractor); and managing agent (a company employee who runs a part of the company's business and acts with independent judgment much of the time). A person need not be called an agent to be one for legal purposes.*

air rights The right to use all or a portion of the space above a designated tract of land.

alias (1) Short for *alias dictus* or "otherwise called"; a fictitious name used in place of a person's real name. (2) An alias writ or summons is a second (or third, etc.) one put out through the court if the first one did not work.*

alibi "Elsewhere"; the claim that at the time a crime was committed a person was somewhere else.*

alienation of affection Taking away the love, companionship, or help of another person's husband or wife. This is the basis for a lawsuit in a few states.*

aliquot A part; a fractional or proportional part.*

allegation A statement in a pleading that sets out a fact that the side filing the pleading expects to prove.*

allocution In criminal proceeding, the process during which the court allows the defendant to say a few words before sentencing.

ALTA American Land Title Association, a national association of title insurance companies and title abstract organizations. This term is used most frequently as part of the identification of standard policy forms adopted by that association.

alter ego Second self. If persons use a corporation as a mere front for doing their own private business, a court may disallow some of the protections that the law gives to the corporation's owners. Under the "alter ego rule" the court may hold the persons individually liable for their actions taken through the corporation.*

amicus curiae "Friend of the court." A person allowed to give argument or appear in a lawsuit (usually to file a brief, but sometimes to take an active part) who is not a party to the lawsuit.*

amnesty A sovereign act of oblivion for past acts; often conditioned on acceptance within a trial period. Amnesty is the abolition and forgetfulness of the offense; a pardon is forgiveness.

amortize To reduce debt by means of regular periodic payments, including amounts applicable both to principal and interest.

animus Mind or intention.*

answer A pleading setting forth matters or facts as defense(s) to allegations made in a complaint.

ante Before.*

anticipatory breach Before the legally required performance of a contract duty, an announcement by one party to another party to the contract that he or she will not or cannot perform his or her contract duty.

antitrust acts Federal and state laws protecting commerce and trade from unlawful restraints, price discriminations, price fixing, and monopolies.

antitrust laws Federal and state laws designed to protect trade and commerce and to prevent restraint of trade, price-fixing, price discrimination, monopoly, and unfair practices in interstate commerce; for example, Sherman Act, Clayton Act, Federal Trade Commission Act.

appeal (1) Ask a higher court to review the actions of a lower court in order to correct mistakes or injustice. (2) The process in no. 1 is called "an appeal." An appeal may also be taken from a lower level of an administrative agency to a higher level or from an agency to a court.*

appellant A party who petitions a higher court for review of a decision made by a lower court.

appellee The party against whom the appeal is taken.

appraisal A valuation of something (property appraisal). Estimate, evaluation, setting a price on, assessment, survey, calculation, measurement, computation, judgment, rating, assay, opinion, appraisement.**

appurtenances Things deemed to be incidental to the land when they are by right used with the land for its benefit.

arbitrary (1) Describes action taken according to a person's own desires; without supervision, general principles, or rules to decide by. (2) Describes action taken capriciously, in bad faith, or without good reason.*

arbitration The referring of a dispute to an impartial third person chosen by the parties to the dispute to adjudicate the dispute. An alternative method of dispute resolution as opposed to litigation.

arguendo Hypothetically and for the purpose of discussion. For example, assume something is true (whether true or false) for the sake of argument.*

articles of incorporation The document used to set up a corporation. Articles of incorporation contain the most basic rules of the corporation and control other corporate rules such as the bylaws.*

assault A willing unlawful threat or attempt to do corporeal hurt to another by force so that the intended victim has reason to fear or expect immediate harm.

assessed valuation The valuation placed upon land for purposes of taxation; however, valuation does not necessarily represent the market value of the property.

assessment A special tax levied upon property for the purpose of paying for improvements (sewer lines, sidewalks, street paving, and so on) benefiting the land.

assessor A public official who evaluates property for the purpose of taxation.

assets All the items of value owned by an individual, association, estate, business, or corporation.

assign (1) To appoint or select for a particular purpose or duty. (2) To formally transfer, for example, to deed over land to another person. (3) To point out, set forth, or specify. For example, to "assign errors" is to specify them in a legal document, and an "assignable error" is an error that can be used as the basis for an appeal. (4) See Assignment.*

assignee One to whom an assignment or transfer of interest is made, for example, the assignee of a mortgage or contract.

assignment The transfer of property, rights in property, or money to another person. For example, an assignment of wages involves an employer paying part of an employee's salary directly to someone to whom the employee owes money. Most states limit this. An assignment of income involves an attempt to have income taxed to someone else by turning over either the income or the income-producing property to that person. Tax laws make this hard to do.*

assignor One who makes an assignment, for example, the assignor of a mortgage or contract.

assumed business name The name under which an individual, partnership, or corporation conducts business.

assumpsit "He promised"; an old word meaning a promise to do or pay something. Certain types of lawsuits had this name. For example, *indebitatis assumpsit* was "he promised to pay the debt," but it was based not on an actual promise but on the fact that money was owed, whether or not there was an actual promise to pay.*

assumption of mortgage An obligation undertaken by the purchaser of land to be personally liable for payment of an existing note secured by a mortgage. As between the lender and the original borrower, the original borrower remains liable on the mortgage note.

attachment Legal seizure of property to force payment of a debt.

attestation The act of witnessing the signing or execution of a document by signature.

attorney-client privilege *See* Privilege.

attorney in fact One who holds a power of attorney from another allowing him or her to act in the other's place and stead and to execute legal documents such as deeds and mortgages. One who is appointed by another to act for him or her in specific actions described in a power of attorney or letter of attorney.

attorney work product privilege *See* Privilege.

bail To procure the release of a person from legal custody, by undertaking that he or she shall appear at the time and place designated and submit himself or herself to the jurisdiction and judgment of the court.

bailment A delivery of goods or personal property by one person to another for some particular purpose, upon a contract, express or implied, that the property will be returned to the person delivering it after the accomplishment of the purpose for which it was delivered.

bankruptcy The legal means to erase or modify debt owed. A voluntary bankruptcy begins with the filing of a petition in bankruptcy court by the debtor pursuant to the Federal Bankruptcy Code. An involuntary bankruptcy is commenced by the creditors against the debtor.

base title or **basic title** Title to an area or tract out of which parts are subsequently conveyed or from which a subdivision or development is made. Thus, the title to farm acreage that has been subdivided would be the base title to the entire subdivision.

battery An unlawful application of force to another's person, or other wrongful physical violence or constraint, inflicted on a human being without his or her consent.

beneficiary (of a trust) A person designated to receive some benefit from the trust estate.

bifurcation Separation of issues at trial.

binder or commitment An enforceable agreement that, upon satisfaction of the requirements stated in the binder, the insurer will issue the specified title insurance policy subject only to the requirements being met prior to closing and exceptions stated in the binder. A binder sets forth status of title as of a particular date.

blue sky laws A popular name for statutes providing for the regulation and supervision of investment companies and securities, offerings, and sales.

bona fide Good faith; honest; real. For example, a *bona fide* purchaser in commercial law is a person who buys something honestly, pays good value, and knows of no other person's claim to the thing bought.*

bond (1) An insurance agreement under which one party becomes surety to pay, within stated limits, financial loss caused to another by specified acts or defaults of a third party. (2) An interest-bearing security evidencing a long-term debt, issued by a government or corporation, and sometimes secured by a lien on property; (3) A written obligation; a certificate or evidence of a debt.

breach of contract Failure, without legal excuse, to live up to a significant promise made in a contract. Breach also includes refusing to perform your part of the bargain or making it hard for the other person to perform his or her part of the bargain.*

building (restriction) line or **setback** A line fixed at a certain distance from the front and/or sides of a lot or at a certain distance from a road or street that marks the boundary of the area within which no part of any building may project. This line may be established by a filed plat of subdivision, by restrictive covenants in deeds or leases, by building codes, or by zoning ordinances.

burden of proof The necessity or duty of affirmatively proving a fact or facts in dispute on an issue raised between the parties in a cause. The degree of proof necessary for a judge or jury to render a verdict in a criminal prosecution or civil lawsuit. In criminal matters, the burden of proof standard is "beyond a reasonable doubt." In civil cases, the standard is usually "a preponderance of the evidence," although in some cases the civil standard may be raised to a higher level of proof, which is "to a reasonable degree of certainty." Both civil standards are less stringent than that required for a criminal conviction.

bureau of land management A branch of the United States Department of the Interior charged with the surveying and management of natural resource lands and their resources.

bylaws Regulations, ordinances, rules, or laws adopted by a corporation or association for the regulation of its own actions and the rights and duties of its members among themselves.

calendar year The period from January 1 to December 31, inclusive.**

capacity Legal qualification (such as legal age), competency, power, or fitness.

capital The principal invested in a business.

capitalization The total amount of various securities issued by a corporation.

causa Cause, reason, or motive.*

causa mortis "Because of impending death." A gift *causa mortis* is a gift made by a person who thinks he or she is dying. If the person recovers, the gift becomes void. Occasionally, a gift *causa mortis* is found to be an attempt to avoid a tax on property given by will if the gift comes too close to death.*

cause of action The grounds, or legal theory, on which a lawsuit may be brought.

caveat "Beware"; warning. *Caveat emptor* means "let the buyer beware." While this is still an important warning, laws and court decisions provide many safeguards to the buyer.*

caveat actor Let the doer or actor beware.**

caveat emptor "Let the buyer beware." A buyer must examine and judge the product on his or her own. No warranties given, at your own risk, without guarantee.**

censure An official reprimand or condemnation.

certified shorthand reporter A shorthand reporter tested and approved as to speed and accuracy by the court and empowered to administer oaths and record sworn testimony.

certiorari "To make sure." A request for *certiorari* (or "cert." for short) is like an appeal, but one which the higher court is not required to take for decision. It is literally a writ from the higher court asking the lower court for the record of the case.*

chain and links Units of length in the measurement of land. A chain is a land measurement being 66 feet in length; a link is a land measurement being 1/100th of a chain or 66/100th of a foot. *Caveat:* Modern surveyors use a steel tape 100 feet long in manual measurement, and it commonly is called a chain.

chain of title A term applied to the past series of transactions and documents affecting the title to a particular parcel of land.

circumstantial evidence Facts that indirectly prove a main fact in question. For example, testimony that a person was seen walking in the rain is direct evidence that the person walked in the rain, but testimony that the person was seen indoors with wet clothing is circumstantial evidence that the person walked in the rain.*

civil action Action brought to enforce, redress, or protect private rights.

civil law Laws adopted by local, state, and federal governments and known as codes or statutes and that concern civil or private rights and remedies, as contrasted with criminal laws.

CLA Abbreviation for certified legal assistant; a certification earned through and awarded by the NALA to legal assistants who successfully complete an extensive written test of their general skills and specific knowledge of four areas of substantive law practice and procedure. CP is also acceptable. Both CLA and CP are registered certification marks of NALA.

CLAS See ACP.

class action A lawsuit brought for yourself and other persons in the same situation. To bring a class action you must convince the court that there are too many persons in the class (group) to make them all individually a part of the lawsuit and that your interests are the same as theirs, so that you can adequately represent their needs.*

Clayton Antitrust Act An act to supplement the Sherman Antitrust Act against unlawful monopolies and restraints.

clear title One which is not encumbered or burdened with defects.

closing (1) A process by which all the parties to a real estate transaction conclude the details of a sale or mortgage. The process includes the signing and transfer of documents and the distribution of funds. (2) A condition in the description of real property by courses and distances at the boundary lines where the lines meet to include all the tract of land.

closing costs Miscellaneous expenses involved in closing a real estate transaction, over and above the price of the land, for example, pro rate of taxes, insurance, or recording fees.

cloud on title An outstanding claim or encumbrance that adversely affects the marketability of title.

code civil The code embodying the civil law of France, framed by a commission of jurists, passed by the tribunate and legislature, and promulgated in 1804 as the Code Civil des Francais. When Napoleon became emperor, the code was changed to Code Napoleon for many years. The law of the state of Louisiana is based historically on the Napoleonic Code.

codes A systematic collection, compendium, or revision of laws, rules, or regulations enacted by legislation; statutes. *See also* Ordinance.

collateral Marketable real or personal property that a borrower pledges as security for a loan. In mortgage transactions, specific land is the collateral.

common law All statutory and case law background of England and the American colonies; laws of legal rules that are developed as a result of decisions by judges based upon accepted customs and traditions and that do not rest upon any express and positive declaration of the will of the legislative body.

community property Property owned in common (both persons owning it all) by a husband and wife. "Community property states" are those states that call most property acquired during the marriage the property of both partners no matter whose name it is in.*

competent Properly qualified, adequate, having the right natural or legal qualifications. For example, a person may be competent to make a will if he or she understands what making a will is, knows that he or she is making a will, and knows generally how making the will affects persons named in the will and affects relatives.*

complaint (1) The first main paper filed in a civil lawsuit. It includes, among other things, a statement of the wrong or harm done to the plaintiff by the defendant, a request for specific help from the court, and an explanation why the court has the power to do what the plaintiff wants. (2) Any official "complaint" in the ordinary sense, for example, a complaint to the police about a noisy party. (3) A criminal complaint is a formal document that charges a person with a crime.*

conciliation The formality of bringing the parties of a case before a judge who attempts to reconcile the parties. Common in domestic relations matters.

condemnation The process by which property of a private owner is taken for public use through the power of eminent domain.

consideration The price, motive, cause, impelling influence, or matter of inducement of a contract, which must be lawful in itself.

consortium (1) The right of a husband or wife to the other's love and services. Damages are sometimes given to one spouse to compensate for the loss of consortium that occurs when the other spouse is wrongly killed or injured. (2) A group of companies that band together for a large project.*

contempt (of court) Any act that is calculated to embarrass, hinder, or obstruct the court in its administration of justice or that is calculated to lessen its authority or its dignity.

contingent fee An arrangement between attorney and client whereby the attorney agrees to represent the client with compensation to be a percentage of the recovered amount.

contra (1) Against; on the other hand; opposing. For example, *contra bonos mores* means "against good morals" or "offending the public conscience," and *contra pacem* means "against the peace" or "offending public order." (2) In accounting, *contra* accounts are set up to show subtractions from other accounts, and *contra* balances are account balances that are the opposite (positive or negative) of what usually appears.*

contract An agreement between competent parties upon a legal consideration to do or to abstain from doing some lawful act.

conviction (1) The result of a criminal trial in which a person is found guilty. (2) Firm belief.*

cooperative An organization for the primary purpose of providing economic services for its members for their benefit or gain rather than that of the organization.

copyright The right to control the copying, distributing, performing, displaying, and adapting of works (including paintings, music, books, and movies). The right belongs to the creator, or to persons employing the creator, or to persons who buy the right from the creator. The right is created, regulated, and limited by the federal Copyright Act of 1976 and by the Constitution. The symbol for copyright is ©. The legal life (duration) of a copyright is the author's life plus 50 years, or 75 years from publication date, or 100 years from creation, depending on the circumstances.*

coram Before; in the presence of. For example, *coram nobis* (before us) is the name for a request that a court change its judgment due to the excusable failure of a defendant to raise facts that would have won the case. *Coram vobis* is a request for a higher court to order a lower one to correct the same sort of problem as raised by a *coram nobis*. These requests are no longer used in most places. *Coram non judice* means "before a nonjudge." It describes a finding or judgment by a court with no jurisdiction, which means that the judgment is void.*

corporation An organization that is formed under state or federal law and exists, for legal purposes, as a separate being or an "artificial person." It may be public (set up by the government) or private (set up by individuals), and it may be set up to carry on a business or to perform almost any function. Large business corporations owned by stockholders are governed by publicly filed articles of incorporation and more detailed private bylaws and managed by a board of directors who delegate authority to officers. The stockholders have no liability for corporate debts beyond the value of their stock. Abbreviated "Corp."*

corpus "Body"; main body of a thing as opposed to attachments. For example, *corpus juris* means "a body of law" or a major collection of laws, and a trust *corpus* is the money or property put into the trust, as opposed to interest or profits.*

corpus delicti "The body of the crime." (1) The material substance upon which a crime has been committed; for example, a dead body (in the crime of murder) or a house burned down (in the crime of arson). (2) The fact that proves that a crime has been committed. (3) The *corpus delicti* rule is the principle that the prosecutor must produce evidence that a crime has been committed even if the defendant has confessed to the crime before the trial.*

corpus Juris A legal encyclopedia that is cross-referenced with the American Digest System. *Corpus Juris Secundum* is its most recent update.*

corpus juris civilis "The body of the civil law"; the main writings of Roman law.*

cost Expenses awarded by a court to the prevailing party.

court reporter *See* Certified shorthand reporter.

counterclaim The defendant's claim against the plaintiff usually set forth in the defendant's answer to the complaint.

CP Abbreviation for certified legal assistant; a certification earned through and awarded by the NALA to legal assistants who successfully complete an extensive written test of their general skills and specific knowledge of four areas of substantive law practice and procedure.

creditor A person to whom a debt is owed.*

crime Any violation of the government's penal laws. An illegal act.*

criminal law That law that for purposes of preventing harm to society declares what conduct is criminal and prescribes the punishment to be imposed for such conduct.

cross-claim The claim by a party to a lawsuit against a co-party that arises out of the transaction that is the subject of the lawsuit or of a counterclaim to the original action (such as one defendant's claim against another).

cross-examination The questioning of an opposing witness during a trial or hearing.*

cum testamento annexo "With the will attached." Describes an administrator who is appointed by a court to supervise handing out the property of a dead person whose will does not name executors (persons to hand out property) or whose named executors cannot or will not serve.*

curia Old European word for court.*

CUSIP Committee on Uniform Securities Identification Procedures.

damages (1) Money that a court orders paid to a person who has suffered damage (a loss or harm) by the person who caused the injury (the violation of the person's rights). (2) A plaintiff's claim in a legal pleading for the money defined in definition no. 1. Damages may be actual and compensatory (directly related to the amount of the loss), or they may be, in addition, exemplary and punitive (extra money given to punish the defendant and to help keep a particularly bad act from happening again). Also, merely nominal damages may be given (a tiny sum when the loss suffered is either very small or of unproved amount).* The most common damages requested are: (a) general, which are to compensate the injured party for the injury sustained; (b) punitive or exemplary, which are to "punish" the liable party by awarding to the injured party additional sums, over and above the general damage amount, where the wrongful tort was aggravated by circumstances of violence, malice, fraud, and so forth; and (c) special, such as wage loss and medical expenses.

damnum A loss, harm, or damage.*

damnum absque injuria A loss that does not give rise to an action for damages against the person causing it.**

data Organized information often collected for a specific purpose, for example, to make a decision; (insufficient data). Facts, evidence, materials, conditions, statistics.**

de bonis non "Of the goods not (already taken care of)." Refers to an administrator appointed to hand out the property of a dead person whose executor (person chosen to hand it out) has died.*

de facto In fact; actual; a situation that exists in fact whether or not it is lawful. For example, a de facto corporation is a company that has failed to follow some of the technical legal requirements to become a legal corporation, but carries on business as one in good faith, and a de facto government is one that has at least temporarily overthrown the rightful, legal one.*

de jure Of right; legitimate; lawful, whether or not true in actual fact. For example, a president may still be the *de jure* head of a government even if the army takes actual power by force. *De jure* segregation is a separation of races that is the result of government action while de facto segregation is caused by social, geographic, or economic conditions only.*

de minimis Small, unimportant. Also, short for *de minimis non curat lex* (the law does not bother with trifles).*

de novo New. For example, a trial *de novo* is a new trial ordered by a judge when a previous trial is so flawed that it will be made void. In some states, some types of trial *de novo* are a matter of right.*

debenture A promissory note or bond issued by a corporation as evidence of an obligation to pay money.

debtor One who owes an obligation.

declaratory judgment One that simply declares the rights of the parties or expresses the opinion of the court on a question of law, without ordering anything to be done.

decree (1) A judgment of a court that announces the legal consequences of the facts found in a case and orders that the court's decision be carried out. Specialized types of decrees include consent decree, divorce decree, and decree *nisi* (one that takes effect only after a certain time and only if no person shows the court a good reason why it should not take effect). (2) A proclamation or order put out by a person or group with absolute authority to give orders.*

defamation Holding up of a person to ridicule, scorn, or contempt in a respectable and considerable part of the community; may be criminal as well as civil; includes both libel and slander.

default judgment A judgment for the plaintiff where the defendant has failed to appear or file an answer in a timely manner.

deposition A written record of the oral testimony of a witness under oath, in the form of questions and answers made before a public officer for use in a lawsuit.

depreciation An allowance for the exhaustion or wear and tear of tangible property and certain intangible assets that have a limited useful life.

dicta Views of a judge that are not a central part of the judge's decision, even if the judge argues them strongly and even if they look like conclusions. One way to decide whether a particular part of a judge's opinion is *dicta* is to examine whether it was necessary to reach the result. If it could be removed without changing the legal result, it is probably *dicta*. If it is *dicta*, it is not binding precedent on later court decisions, but it is probably still worth quoting if it helps your case.*

dictum (1) Singular of *dicta*. (2) Short for *obiter dictum* (a remark by the way, as in "by the way, did I tell you...."); a digression; a discussion of side points or unrelated points.*

director An individual appointed or elected to manage and direct the affairs of a corporation.

directed verdict Procedure whereby a judge directs that a jury reach a certain determination in cases in which the evidence is such that a reasonable person could not disagree.

discharge To release; liberate; annul; unburden; disencumber; dismiss.

discovery The ascertainment of that which was previously unknown; the disclosure or coming to light of what was previously hidden. The phase in a lawsuit when parties may use formal methods provided by court rule or statute to obtain information from other parties to a lawsuit or from nonparties.

dismiss without prejudice Dismissal of a case allowing a party to refile the same cause of action.

dissolution The termination of a corporation as a body politic. Dissolution may occur voluntarily or involuntarily.

dividend A share of profits or property; usually a payment per share of a corporation's stock.*

domestic A corporation created by or organized under the laws of the state in which it does business.

domicile A person's permanent home, legal home, or main residence. The words "abode," "citizenship," "habitancy," and "residence" sometimes mean the same as domicile and sometimes not. A corporate domicile is the corporation's legal home (usually where its headquarters is located); an elected domicile is the place the persons who make a contract specify as their legal homes in the contract.*

donatio A gift.*

duces tecum "Bring with you." A subpoena *duces tecum* commands a person to come to court with documents or other pieces of evidence.*

due process The fundamental procedural rights that must be followed by court, agency, or other entity prior to depriving an individual of life, liberty, or property. It is a protection granted by the 5th and 14th Amendments to the United States Constitution.

duress Unlawful constraint exercised upon a person whereby he or she is forced to do some act that he or she otherwise would not have done.

e.g. Abbreviation for the Latin *exempli gratia* ("for the sake of example"). It is used in most law books to take the place of "for example."*

EIR Environmental impact report.

enlargement Applies to the extension of time in legal proceedings.

equity (1) Fairness in a particular situation. (2) The name for a system of courts that originated in England to take care of legal problems when the existing laws did not cover some situations in which a person's rights were violated by another person. (3) A court's power to "do justice" where specific laws do not cover the situation. (4) The value of property after all charges against it are paid. This is also called net worth or net value. (5) Stock. Sometimes common stock only.*

ergo Therefore.*

erratum Mistake in printed or written material.*

estoppel A bar or impediment at law that prevents one from alleging or denying a fact.

et al. Abbreviation for *et alii* ("and others"). For example, "Smith et al." means "Smith plus certain other persons."*

et cetera And others, and soon, and the rest, and so forth, etc.**

et seq. Abbreviation for *et sequentes* ("and the following"). For example, "page 27 et seq." means "page 27 and the following pages."*

et ux. Abbreviation for *et uxor* ("and wife") seen in old legal documents. For example, "This deed made by John Smith *et ux.*"*

evidence Relevant information presented in accord with applicable evidence rules for the purpose of aiding the "trier of fact" in making a determination of the truth of facts at issue. Includes testimony of witnesses, documents, objects, and admissions of parties.

ex contractu "From a contract." A lawsuit based on a contract, rather than on a tort.*

ex delicto "From wrongdoing." A lawsuit based on a tort (or on a crime) rather than on a contract.*

ex necessitate legis "From legal necessity"; implied by law.*

ex officio (1) By the power of the office (official position) alone. (2) Acting as a private citizen, not as an official. (This is a popular, not legal, meaning.)*

ex parte With only one side present. For example, an *ex parte* order is one made on the request of one side in a lawsuit when (or because) the other side does not show up in court (because the other side failed to show up, because the other side did not need to be present for the order to issue, or because there is no other side).*

ex post facto After the fact. An *ex post facto* law is one that retroactively attempts to make an action a crime that was not a crime at the time it was done, or a law that attempts to reduce a person's rights based on a past act that was not subject to the law when it was done. *Ex post facto* laws are prohibited by the United States Constitution (Article 1, Section 9).*

ex rel. Short for the Latin *ex relatione,* "on relation," or "from the information given by." When a case is titled "State ex rel. *Doe v. Roe,*" it means that the state is bringing a lawsuit for Doe against Roe.*

excise tax A tax imposed by legislature on the performance of an act, the engaging of an occupation, or the enjoying of a privilege.

exemption (1) Freedom from a general duty or service (exemption from jury duty). Immunity, release, allowance, liberty, freedom, special treatment, privilege, absolution, excuse, dispensation, impunity, license. See also exception 2. (2) A privilege allowed by law to a judgment debtor by which he or she may hold designated property free from all liability to levy and sale on execution or attachment; property exempt in bankruptcy proceedings. (3) An amount to be subtracted from gross income to determine taxable income (tax exemption for a dependent.)**

exhibit (1) Any object or document offered and marked as evidence (in a trial, hearing, deposition, audit, etc.). (2) Any document attached to a pleading, affidavit, or other formal paper.*

FELA, Federal Employers Liability Act Protects employees engaged in interstate and foreign commerce. Payments are made for death or disability sustained in the performance of the duties of employment.

felony (1) A serious crime. (2) A crime with a sentence of one year or more.*

feme couvert (French) A married woman. Married women in the past had legal disabilities, such as an inability to make contracts. *Feme couvert* was used in comparison to *feme sole* (a woman alone; an unmarried woman).*

fiat "Let it be done"; a command, especially an authoritative yet arbitrary command.*

filiation Judicial determination of paternity. The relation of the child to the father.

filiation proceeding Same as paternity suit.*

filius nullius The son or child of nobody; an illegitimate child.**

fiscal year The year between one annual time of settlement or balancing of accounts and another. A period of 12 consecutive months (not necessarily concurrent with the calendar year) with references to which appropriations are made and expenditures authorized and at the end of which accounts are made up and books balanced.

flagrante delicto (1) In the act of committing the crime. (2) Popularly used to mean lovers caught together in bed.*

foreign A corporation created by or under the laws of another state, government, or country.

forum A court. For example, *forum domicilii* is a court in the place where a person lives, and *forum rei* is a court where either the thing involved with the suit is or where the defendant lives.*

franchise (1) A business arrangement in which a person buys the right to sell, rent, etc., the products or services of a company and use the company's name to do business. The person who buys the rights is a franchisee, and the person who sells the rights is a franchisor. (2) A special right given by the government, such as the right to vote or to form a corporation. (3) A sports team granted a particular territory by the league.*

fraud Any kind of trickery used to cheat another of money or property.*

garnishment A legal process, taken by a creditor who has received a money judgment against a debtor, to get the debtor's money. This is done by attachment of a bank account or by taking a percentage of the debtor's regular income. State laws set a limit on the percentage (often 25 percent) of a person's wages that may be garnished through a person's employer. The garnishment of federal wages is limited by the Federal Wage Garnishment Act, which, in addition, gives some protection from dismissal due to garnishment.*

goodwill The favor that the management wins from the public. The fixed and favorable consideration of customers arising from established and well-conducted business.

grand jury Considers whether the evidence presented by the state against a person accused of a crime warrants his or her indictment.

guardian A person who has the legal right and duty to take care of another person or that person's property because that other person (for example, a child) cannot. The arrangement is called "guardianship."*

guardian ad litem A guardian, usually a lawyer, who is appointed by a court to take care of the interests of a person who cannot legally take care of himself or herself in a lawsuit involving that person.*

habeas corpus "You have the body." A judicial order to someone holding a person to bring that person to court. It is most often used to get a person out of unlawful imprisonment by forcing the captor and the person being held to come to court for a decision on the legality of the imprisonment or other holding (such as keeping a child when someone else claims custody).*

hearsay A statement about what someone else said (or wrote or otherwise communicated). Hearsay evidence is evidence, concerning what someone said outside of a court proceeding, that is offered in the proceeding to prove the truth of what was said. The hearsay rule bars the admission of hearsay as evidence to prove the hearsay's truth unless allowed by a hearsay exception.* Second-hand evidence, as distinguished from original evidence.

hypothetical question Posing a hypothetical question involves setting up a series of facts, assuming that they are true, and asking for an answer to a question based on those facts. In a trial, hypothetical questions may be asked of expert witnesses only. For example, a gun expert might be asked: "If this gun had a silencer, could a shot be heard from a hundred feet away?"*

ibid. The same; in, from, or found in the same place (same book, page, case, etc.). Short for *ibidem.**

ignorantia legis neminem excusat "Ignorance of the law is no excuse."*

illicit Prohibited; unlawful.*

impeachment (1) Showing that a witness is untruthful, either by evidence of past conduct or by showing directly that the witness is not telling the truth. When you do this, you impeach the witness. (2) The first step in the removal from public office of a high public official such as a governor, judge, or president. In the case of the president of the United States, the House of Representatives makes an accusation by drawing up "articles of impeachment," voting on them, and presenting them to the Senate. This is impeachment. But impeachment is popularly thought to include the process that may take place after impeachment: the trial of the president in the Senate and conviction by two-thirds of the senators.*

impleader A procedure by which a new party is brought into an action on the ground that the new party is or may be liable to the party who brings him or her in for all or part of the subject matter of the claim.

in camera "In chambers"; in a judge's private office; also describes a hearing in court with all spectators excluded.*

in esse In being; now existing.*

in extremis In the last illness before dying.*

in forma pauperis "As a pauper." Describes a court filing that is permitted without payment of the customary fees or court costs if the person filing proves that he or she is too poor to pay.*

in futuro In the future; at some future time.*

in hoc In this; concerning this.*

in loco parentis In the place of a parent; acting as a parent with respect to the care and supervision of a child; acting with the power to discipline a child as a parent can.*

in pari delicto In equal fault; equally culpable or criminal.**

in personam Describes a lawsuit brought to enforce rights against another person, as opposed to one brought to enforce rights in a thing against the whole world (*in rem*). For example, a suit for automobile accident injuries is in personam because it is against the driver or owner only. A suit to establish title to land is *in rem* because, even if there is a person fighting the claim on the other side, a victory is binding against the whole world and a "thing" is primarily involved.*

in praesenti Right now.*

in re "In the matter of." This is a prefix to the name of a case "concerned with something," rather than a lawsuit directly between two persons. For example, "*In re* Brown's Estate" might be the name of a proceeding in probate court to dispose of the property of a dead person. The words are also sometimes used when a child is involved. For example, "*In re* Mary Smith" might be the name of a child neglect proceeding even though it is really against the parents. "*In re*" should not be used in an ordinary sentence as a substitute for "concerning."*

in rem Describes a lawsuit brought to enforce rights in a thing against the whole world as opposed to one brought to enforce rights against another person. Also, there is a type of lawsuit "in between" *in rem* and *in personam* called *quasi in rem* or "sort of concerning a thing." *Quasi in rem* actions are really directed against a person, but are formally directed only against property (or vice versa); for example, a mortgage foreclosure.

in specie (1) In the same or similar form or way; in kind. But see no. 2. (2) In specific; specific. For example, "performance in specie" usually is given the same meaning as "specific performance."*

in toto In whole; completely.*

incorporators Individuals who join together for the purpose of forming a corporation.

indictment A sworn written accusation of a crime, made against a person by a prosecutor to a grand jury. If the grand jury approves it as a true bill, the indictment becomes the document used against the person as a defendant in pretrial and trial proceedings.*

indorsement (1) Signing a document "on the back" or merely signing it anywhere. (2) Signing a negotiable instrument, such as a check, in a way that causes the piece of paper, and the rights it stands for, to transfer to another person. A qualified indorsement limits rights (for example, signing "without recourse") and a restrictive indorsement limits its purpose or the person who may use it (for example, signing "for deposit"). (3) The signatures themselves in definitions no. 1 and no. 2.*

inference A fact (or proposition) that is probably true because a true fact (or proposition) leads you to believe that the inferred fact (or proposition) is also true. For example, if the first four books in a set of five have green covers, it is a reasonable inference that the fifth book has a green cover.*

information (1) A formal accusation of a crime made by a proper public official such as a prosecuting attorney. (2) A sworn, written accusation of a crime that leads to an indictment. (3) Personal knowledge of something. (But "information and belief" may mean no more than a person's good faith opinion.)*

infra (1) Below or under. (2) Within. (3) Later in this book. For example, "*infra* p. 236" means "look at page 236, which is further on."*

injunction A prohibitive writ issued by a court of equity forbidding the defendant to do some act or to permit his or her servants or agents to do some act that he or she is threatening or attempting to commit.

innuendo "Meaning." The clause in some complaints for defamation that states the defamatory meaning given by the plaintiff to the words that were written or spoken by the defendant.*

insolvency Inability to pay debts as they become due in the usual course of business.

intent Generally the same as *mens rea*. The state of mind of an individual at the time of the alleged offense.

inter Among or between.*

inter vivos "Between the living." An *inter vivos* gift is an ordinary gift, as opposed to a gift made shortly before dying. An *inter vivos* trust is an ordinary trust as opposed to one created under a will upon death.*

interim Temporary; meanwhile. For example, interim financing may be a short-term construction loan, with final financing provided later by a mortgage.*

interpleader A procedure by which persons having claims against another person may be joined as parties to a suit and required to set up claims, if their claims are such that the person initiating such procedure is or may be exposed to multiple liability.

interrogatories A set or series of written questions used in the judicial examination of a party or a witness.

interstate commerce Traffic, intercourse, commercial trading, or the transportation of persons or property between or among the states of the United States.**

interstate commerce act A federal law that regulates the surface transportation of goods and persons between states; regulates rates for railroads, pipelines, etc., formerly through the Interstate Commerce Commission, now through the Surface Transportation Board of the Department of Transportation.*

interstate commerce commission Federal regulatory agency; no longer in existence, discontinued by Congress in 1996.

intervention A proceeding by which a person is allowed to become a party to a lawsuit by joining the plaintiff, joining the defendant, or making separate claims.*

intra "Within." For example, intrastate commerce is business carried out entirely within one state, as opposed to interstate commerce.

inventory A detailed list of articles of property; an itemized list or schedule of property with appraised or actual values.

ipse dixit "He himself said it." Describes a statement that depends for its persuasiveness on the authority of the person who said it. Something asserted, but not proved.*

ipso facto "By the fact itself"; "by the mere fact that."*

ita est "So it is." A formal statement put on a copy of a document by a notary public when the original document was notarized by an earlier notary.*

joinder Uniting with another person or party in some legal step or procedure.

judgment (1) The official decision of a court about the rights and claims of each side in a lawsuit. "Judgment" usually refers to a final decision that is based on the facts of the case and made at the end of a trial. It is called a judgment on the merits. (2) There are other types of judgments. For example, a consent judgment is the putting of a court's approval on an agreement between the sides about what the judgment in the case should be; a default judgment is one given to one side because the other side does not show in court or fails to take proper procedural steps; and an interlocutory judgment is one given on either a preliminary issue or a side issue during the course of a lawsuit.*

jura Rights or laws.*

juris publici Of common right; of common or public use (e.g., highways).**

jurisdiction The authority or power of a court to decide or deal with the subject matter of an issue.

jury A certain number of citizens selected according to law and sworn to inquire of certain matters of fact and declare the truth upon evidence to be presented before them.

jury panel The assembly of citizens called to court where a group will be selected for a given jury. More than one jury can be filled from one panel.

jus (1) Right or justice. (2) Law, or the whole body of law. For example: *jus belli* (the law of war, wartime rights); *jus civile* (civil law, Roman law, or the law of one country); *jus commune* (common law); *jus gentium* (the law of nations or international law); *jus naturae* (the law of nature); *jus naturale* (natural law); *jus privatum* (the law of private rights); *jus publicum* (public or governmental law); and *jus soli* (the law of a person's birthplace; also, citizenship in a country because you are born there). (3) A particular right. For example: *jus disponendi* (the right to do what you want with your own property or the right of a seller to let title pass or keep it until all payments are made); *jus dividendi* (the right to give property by will); *jus habendi* (the right to possess something); *jus sanguinis* ("law of the blood"; citizenship in a country because your parents are citizens); and *jus tertii* (the right of someone not involved in a lawsuit to property that is involved in the suit).*

keogh Plans An enactment by Congress that allows self-employed persons to establish and participate in tax-favored retirement plans similar to qualified pension and profit-sharing plans.

laches An omission to assert a right for an unreasonable and unexplained length of time under circumstances prejudicial to the adverse party.

leading question One that instructs a witness how to answer or puts into his or her mouth words to be echoed back. Questions are leading that suggest to the witness the answer desired.

legal assistant A distinguishable group of persons who assist attorneys in delivering legal services. Within this occupational category, some individuals are known as paralegals. Through formal education, training, and experience, legal assistants have knowledge and expertise regarding the legal system and substantive and procedural law that qualify them to do work of a legal nature under the supervision of an attorney.

legal ethics (1) The moral and professional duties owed by lawyers to their clients, to other lawyers, to the courts, and to the public. (2) The study of legal ethics. (3) The written rules of ethics such as the Rules of Professional Conduct.*

libel Almost any written language, picture, or sign that upon its face has a natural tendency to injure a person's reputation, either generally or with respect to his or her occupation, and is published to a third party and is not privileged or permitted and is not true.

lien A claim against specific property that can be enforced in court to secure payment of a judgment, duty, or debt. Sometimes *lien* is defined to exclude claims due to contracts or mortgages. A *lienee* is an owner of property with a lien against it and a *lienor* (or lienholder) is a person who owns a lien against property. A *mechanic's lien* is the right of a worker to hold property worked on until paid for the services. A *tax lien* is the government's placing on a piece of property a financial obligation that must be paid because taxes have not been paid. Other types of liens include landlord's, maritime, etc.*

liquidation (1) Winding up a company's affairs in order to end its existence. (2) Payment, satisfaction, or collection; realization on assets and discharge of liabilities.*

lis pendens (1) A pending lawsuit. (2) A warning notice that title to property is in litigation and that anyone who buys the property gets it with legal "strings attached."*

litigation A lawsuit or series of lawsuits.*

locus (1) Place. For example, *locus contractus* (the place where the contract was made); *locus criminis* or *delicti* (the place where the crime was committed); *locus regit actum* (the place where the act is done); etc. See *lex loci* for more examples. (2) *Locus sigilii* is "the place of the seal." (3) *Locus poenitentiae* is the "place of repentance," a final chance to change your mind before making a deal or committing a crime.*

long-arm statute A state law extending personal jurisdiction over out-of-state persons or entities who own real property in the forum state, conduct business in the forum state, or commit certain actions in the forum state, such as entering into a contract or committing an alleged tort or crime.

majority The number greater than half of any total.

mala fides Bad faith.*

mala in se Wrongs in themselves; morally wrong acts; offenses against conscience.**

mala praxis Malpractice.*

malice (1) Ill will. (2) Intentionally harming someone; having no moral or legal justification for harming someone. (3) In defamation law, with knowledge of falsity or with reckless disregard for whether or not something is false.*

malo animo "With evil mind"; malice.*

malpractice Professional misconduct or unreasonable lack of skill. This word usually applies to bad, incomplete, or unfaithful work done by a doctor or lawyer.*

malum (or mala) in se "Wrong in and of itself"; morally wrong; describes common law crimes.*

mandamus "We command." A writ of *mandamus* is a court order that directs a public official or government department to do something. It may be sent to the executive branch, the legislative branch, or a lower court.*

mediation An informal, nonbinding process wherein an impartial third party assists the parties to a dispute in a direct negotiation to resolve the dispute. An alternative form of dispute resolution as opposed to litigation in the court system.

mens rea Guilty mind; wrongful purpose; criminal intent. *Mens rea* is a state of mind that (when combined with an *actus reus,* or "criminal act") produces a crime. This state of mind is usually to intentionally or knowingly do something prohibited, but is occasionally to recklessly or grossly negligently do it.*

merger (1) The union of two or more things, usually with the smaller or less important thing "ceasing to exist" once it is a part of the other. Companies, rights, contracts, etc., can merge. The following definitions divide these mergers by type: (2) When corporations merge, it is a *horizontal merger* if business competitors selling the same product in the same area join, a *vertical merger* if a company joins with its customers or suppliers, and a *conglomerate merger* if unrelated companies join. Conglomerate mergers are of three types: it is a *pure merger* when two totally unrelated companies join; a *geographical extension merger* when companies selling similar products in different markets join; and a *product extension merger* when two companies selling related, but different products join. Finally, many states allow a quick, cheap short-form merger when a subsidiary merges with its parent company. (3) In contract law, if the persons who make a contract intend it, one contract may end and become a part of another through merger. Also, all prior oral agreements may be ended by establishing a written contract as the entire agreement by including a merger clause. (4) Two rights, or estates can merge. For example, if a tenant buys the house, the right of tenancy merges and is ended with the start of the right of ownership. Merging of rights occurs in many other areas of the law, such as divorce law, judgment law, etc. (5) Merger also occurs in criminal law when a person is charged with two crimes (based on the exact same acts), one of which is a lesser included offense of the other. The lesser crime merges because, under the prohibition against double jeopardy, the person may be tried for only one of them.*

misdemeanor A criminal offense less than a felony that is usually punishable by a fine or less than a year in jail.*

mistrial A trial that the judge ends and declares will have no legal effect because of a major defect in procedure or because of the death of a juror, a deadlocked jury, or other major problem.*

mitigate To render less painful or severe (mitigate the effect of the defeat).**

mitigation *See* mitigate.**

mitigation of damages Duty of parties to minimize damages after an injury has been inflicted or a breach has occurred.

modus Method, means, manner, or way. For example, *modus operandi* is a method of operation (that usually refers to a distinct pattern of criminal behavior).*

monopoly Control by one or a few companies of the manufacture, sale, distribution, or price of something. A monopoly may be prohibited if, for example, a company deliberately drives out competition.*

motion An application for a rule or order made to a court or a judge for the purpose of obtaining some act to be done in favor of the applicant or moving party.

motive The reason why a person does something. Not intent (*see* intent for the difference).*

Napoleonic Code *See* Code Civil.

National Labor Relations Act (Taft-Hartley Act of 1947) A federal law regulating the relationship between employers and employees or their union representatives.

negligence (1) The failure to exercise a reasonable amount of care in a situation that causes harm to someone or something. It can involve doing something carelessly or failing to do something that should have been done. Negligence can vary in seriousness from *gross* (recklessness or willfulness), through *ordinary* (failing to act as a reasonably careful person would), to *slight* (not much). (2) Criminal negligence is the careless state of mind that can make an action a crime, for example, the extreme carelessness in driving a car that might change a noncriminal homicide into manslaughter.*

nil Nothing.*

nisi "Unless." A judge's rule, order, or decree that will take effect unless the person against whom it is issued comes to court to "show cause" why it should not take effect.*

nisi prius "Unless before." In American law, describes a trial court as opposed to an appellate court.*

nolle prosequi The ending of a criminal case because the prosecutor decides or agrees to stop prosecuting. When this happens, the case is "nolled," "nollied," or "nol. prossed." (This is not *nolo contendere* or *non prosequitur*, although it is sometimes used as a synonym for *non prosequitur*.)*

nolo contendere "I will not contest it." A defendant's plea of "no contest" in a criminal case. It means that he or she does not directly admit guilt, but submits to sentencing or other punishment. A defendant may plead *nolo contendere* only with the judge's permission because, unlike a "guilty" plea, this cannot be used against the defendant in a later civil lawsuit.*

non compos mentis "Not of sound mind." This includes idiocy, insanity, severe drunkenness, etc.*

non obstante veredicto "Notwithstanding the verdict." A judgment *non obstante veredicto* (J.N.O.V.) is a judge's giving judgment (victory) to one side in a lawsuit even though the jury gave a verdict (victory) to the other side.*

nonprofit corporation A corporation or organization of which no part of its income is distributable to its members, directors, or officers.

Notary Public An official authorized by law to administer oaths and to attest to and certify by his or her hand and official seal the identity of persons executing documents.

novation The substitution by agreement of a new contract for an old one, with all the rights under the old one ended. The new contract is often the same as the old one, except that one or more of the parties is different.*

nudum pactum "Nude pact" or bare agreement. A promise or action without any consideration (payment or promise of something of value).*

nunc pro tunc "Now for then." Describes something done "now" that has the same effect as if done "then," so that it has retroactive effect. For example, a judge may issue a *nunc pro tunc* order to correct a trial made earlier, with the effect that the record is considered correct as of the date it was first made, in effect backdating the order.*

oath A formal swearing that you will tell the truth (an assertory oath) or will do something (a promissory oath). Oaths of truthfulness are required of witnesses, and oaths of allegiance and faithful performance of duty are required of many public office-holders, soldiers, etc.*

offer A promise; a commitment to do or refrain from doing some specific thing in the future.

offeree The person to whom an offer is made.

offeror The party who makes the offer.

officer A person holding office of trust, command, or authority in a corporation with the power and duty of exercising certain functions. An officer of a corporation carries out the directives of the board of directors.

omnibus Containing two or more separate and independent things. For example, an "omnibus bill" is a legislative bill containing proposed laws concerning two or more entirely different subjects.*

opinion (1) A judge's statement of the decision he or she has reached in a case. (2) A judge's statement about the conclusions of that judge and other judges who agree with the judge in a case. A majority opinion is written when over half the judges in a case agree about both the result and the reasoning used to reach that result. A plurality opinion is written when a majority of the judges agree with the result, but not with the reasoning. A concurring opinion agrees with the result, but not the reasoning. A dissenting or minority opinion disagrees with the result. (Concurring, dissenting, and minority opinions are all separate opinions.) A *per curiam* opinion is unanimous and anonymous. A *memorandum* opinion is unanimous and briefly states only the result. (3) A document prepared by a lawyer for a client that gives the lawyer's conclusions about how the law applies to a set of facts in which the client is interested.*

order (1) A written command or direction given by a judge. For example, a restraining order is a judicial command to a person to temporarily stop a certain action or course of conduct. (2) A command given by a public official. (3) "To the order of" is a direction to pay something. These words (or "pay to the bearer") are necessary to make a document a negotiable instrument (see that word). A document with these words on it is called order paper. (4) For "order *nisi,*" *see nisi.* (5) "Order of the coif" is an award, often for law school achievement. (6) Instructions to buy or sell something. In stock sales, for example, a "day order" is an instruction from a customer to a broker to buy or sell a stock on one particular day only; a "limit order" is an instruction to buy only under a certain price or sell only over it; a "market order" is an instruction to buy or sell right away at the current market price; a "scale order" is an instruction to buy or sell a certain amount of stock at each of several price levels; and a "split order" is an instruction to buy or sell some stock when it reaches one price and some when it reaches another.*

ordinance A law, statute, or regulation passed by a local governmental body below the state level. *See* Codes.

organizational meeting A meeting of the original board of directors named in the articles of incorporation at which the adoption of bylaws, election of officers, and transaction of any other necessary business usually takes place.

OSHA, Office of Safety and Health Administration A federal agency.

pactum A bargain or agreement.*

paralegal A distinguishable group of persons who assist attorneys in delivering legal services. Within this occupational category, some individuals are known as legal assistants. Through formal education, training, and experience, paralegals have knowledge and expertise regarding the legal system and substantive and procedural law that qualify them to do work of a legal nature under the supervision of an attorney.

pari delicto Equal fault or equal guilt. (1) The "doctrine of *pari delicto*" in contract law is the principle that a court should not help enforce an illegal or invalid contract except in some cases where one party is much less at fault than the other or has been manipulated by the other. (2) There are several "doctrines of *pari delicto*" in tort law. One is that in cases of approximately equal mutual fault, the defendant wins. Another is that joint tortfeasors may not get indemnity from each other (but may get contribution). A third is the requirement of clean hands in bringing a lawsuit requesting equitable relief.*

parol Oral; not in writing. For example, parol evidence is oral evidence (the evidence a witness gives). It usually refers to evidence about an agreement's meaning that is not clear from the written contract. Not parole.*

parole A conditional release; the condition being that, if the prisoner observes the conditions provided in the parole order, he or she will receive an absolute discharge from the balance of sentence, but if he or she does not, he or she will be returned to serve the unexpired term.

particeps criminis An accomplice.*

partner A member of a partnership or a firm; one who has united with others to form a partnership in business.

partnership (general) An association of two or more persons by voluntary contract, to carry on, as co-owners, a business for profit.

partnership (limited) A partnership formed by two or more persons that includes, along with one or more general partners, one or more limited partners, who, as such, are not bound by the obligations of the partnership.

patent (1) Open, evident, plainly visible. (2) A grant of a right (given by the federal government to a person) to exclusively control, for a limited number of years (usually 17), the manufacture and sale of something that person has discovered or invented. (3) A grant of land by the government to an individual.*

paternity The state or condition of being a father (a determination of the paternity of the child). Fatherhood, male parentage; ancestry, lineage, bloodline, stock, origin, extraction, breed, descent, derivation.**

paternity suit A court action to prove that a person is the father of an "illegitimate child" and to get support for the child from the father.*

pecuniary Monetary; related to money. A pecuniary interest is a right that has monetary value. A judge should not decide a case that could affect the judge's pecuniary interests.*

pendente lite "Pending the suit"; while a lawsuit is in progress. For example, support *pendente lite* is temporary support while a divorce case is in progress.*

pension plan A plan that requires the employer to make a certain rate of contribution into a retirement fund each year per employee.

per annum Yearly (9 percent per annum).**

per capita "By heads." By the number of individual persons, each equally.*

per curiam "By the court." Describes an opinion backed by all the judges in a particular court and usually with no one judge's name on it.*

per se In and of itself; taken alone; inherently. For example, some types of business arrangements are "per se violations" of antitrust acts because, even without specific proof that monopoly power has hurt competition, the arrangements are in and of themselves considered bad.*

per stirpes "By roots"; by right of representation. Describes a method of dividing a dead person's estate by giving out shares equally "by representation" or by family groups. For example, if John leaves 3,000 dollars to Mary and Sue, and Mary dies, leaving two children (Steve and Jeff), a *per stirpes* division would give 1,500 dollars to Sue and 750 dollars each to Steve and Jeff. A "per capita" division would give one thousand dollars each to Sue, Steve, and Jeff.*

peremptory challenge The right to challenge and remove a juror without giving any reasons.**

perjury Lying while under oath, especially in a court proceeding. It is a crime.*

personal injury A hurt or wrong to the physical body or reputation of a person or both.

personal property (personalty) Rights or interests a person has in things movable, for example, an automobile or furniture.

petit jury The ordinary jury for the trial of a civil or criminal action. So called to distinguish it from the grand jury.

plea (1) The defendant's formal answer to a criminal charge. The defendant says: "guilty," "not guilty," or "*nolo contendere*" (no contest). (2) For the use of the word in most modern civil lawsuits, *see* Pleading. (3) An older word for several types of civil motions, such as a plea in abatement, that have been largely replaced by a "motion to dismiss." Other types of old pleas include pleas in bar, pleas in discharge, and pleas of release.*

pleading (1) The process of making formal, written statements of each side of a civil case. First the plaintiff submits a paper with "facts" and claims; then the defendant submits a paper with "facts" (and sometimes counterclaims); then the plaintiff responds, etc., until all issues and questions are clearly posed for a trial. (2) A pleading is any one of the papers mentioned in no. 1. The first one is a complaint, the response is an answer, etc. The pleadings is the sum of all these papers. Sometimes, written motions and other court papers are called pleadings, but this is not strictly correct. (3) The old forms of common law pleadings (which were so rigid that one small technical mistake could lose the suit) included a declaration, defendant's plea, replication, rejoinder, surrejoinder, rebutter, surrebutter, etc. (4) In modern legal practice under the Federal Rules of Civil Procedure, pleading is no longer inflexible, and pleadings may be amended freely to fit facts as they develop. Modern pleadings include complaints, answers (which may include counterclaims or cross-claims), replies (or answers) to these claims, and third-party complaints and answers.*

postmortem "After death." A postmortem examination (postmortem, for short) is an autopsy.*

power of attorney An instrument authorizing another to act as one's agent or attorney. Power may be made general or specific.

praecipe A formal request that the court clerk take some action. Any motion that can be granted by the signature of a court clerk without a judge's approval. A lawyer can "enter an appearance" in a case by praecipe.*

preponderance of evidence Greater weight of evidence or evidence that is more credible and convincing to the mind. That which best accords with reason and probability.

presumption An assumption that the law expressly directs to be made from particular facts.

pretrial conference or **hearing** A meeting of the judge and counsel for the parties preliminary to the trial of a lawsuit.

prima facie At first sight; on the face of it; presumably. Describes something that will be considered to be true unless disproved by contrary evidence. For example, a *prima facie* case is a case that will win unless the other side comes forward with evidence to disprove it.*

prima facie case A case as presented that will prevail until contradicted and overcome by contrary evidence; a case consisting of evidence that is sufficient to overcome a motion for a directed verdict and to get the case to the jury.**

prima facie evidence Evidence that is good and sufficient on its face; evidence that is sufficient to establish a given fact or group of facts and will remain sufficient unless rebutted or contradicted.**

privilege An immunity which exists under law and which may constitute a defense to a tort (such as self-defense as a counter to a charge of battery); protected relationships existing under law or statute, such as attorney-client, husband-wife, or doctor-patient. The assertion of a privilege under the work product rule to protect or prevent disclosure of confidential information, such as notes, working papers, memoranda, or similar materials, prepared by an attorney (or a paralegal acting under the direction of an attorney) in anticipation of litigation or for trial. The work product rule has been interpreted to include private memoranda, written statements of witnesses, and mental impressions of personal recollections prepared or formed by an attorney in anticipation of litigation or for trial.

privileged communications Statements made by persons within protected relationships (e.g., husband-wife, attorney-client, doctor-patient, priest-penitent), which the law protects from forced disclosure at the option of the person enjoying the privilege (e.g., spouse, client, patient, penitent).**

pro bono For the good; work or services performed free of charge.**

pro bono publico "For the public good." Describes free legal work done by a lawyer to help society. Abbreviated "pro bono."*

pro confesso As if confessed. A decree *pro confesso* is like a judgment given to a plaintiff by default because the defendant did not appear in court or did not answer the complaint, so the complaint is accepted "as if confessed."*

pro forma (1) As a matter of form; a mere formality. (2) Projected. A pro forma financial statement is one that is projected on the basis of certain assumptions.*

pro rata Proportionately; by percentage; by a fixed rate; by share. For example, if Tom, Dick, and Harry are owed two, four, and six dollars respectively by John, but John has only six dollars to give out, a *pro rata* sharing would be one, two, and three dollars, respectively. A pro rata clause in an insurance policy says that the company will not pay a higher percentage of a loss than the percentage that company covers of the total insurance coverage from all companies. A *pro rata* distribution clause in an insurance policy says that the amount of insurance on each piece of property is in proportion to the value of that property compared to the total value of all property covered.*

pro se For himself or herself; in his or her own behalf. For example, *pro se* representation means that a person will handle his or her own case in court without a lawyer.*

pro tanto For that much; to the extent of; describes a partial payment.*

pro tempore (*pro tem*) For the time being (president *pro tem*). Temporarily, provisionally, for now, for a time, for the moment, fill-in, transitory, transitional, standby.**

probable cause A reasonable ground for belief in the existence of facts warranting the proceedings complained of.

probation (1) Allowing a person convicted of a criminal offense to avoid serving a jail sentence imposed on the person, so long as he or she abides by certain conditions (usually including supervision by a probation officer). Compare with parole. (2) A trial period. A period during which a person's continued employment is conditioned on "making good" in the job and during which the person has fewer job rights than permanent employees. The period is often called the probationary period, and the person is often called the probationary employee during the period.*

profit sharing plan A plan that provides the employer make contributions into a retirement fund based solely on the profits of the corporation.

promissory estoppel Legal theory that prevents one party to a contract from denying that consideration was given in that contract.

proprietorship (sole) Business completely and directly owned by a single person.

proxy (1) A person who acts for another person (usually to vote in place of the other person in a meeting the other cannot attend). (2) A document giving the right mentioned in no. 1. (3) A proxy marriage is a marriage ceremony in which someone "stands in" for either the bride or groom (or both). (4) A proxy statement is the document sent or given to stockholders when their voting proxies are requested for a corporate decision. The Securities Exchange Commission has rules for when the statements must be given out and what must be in them.*

quantum meruit "As much as he deserved." An old form of pleading used in a lawsuit for compensation for work done. The theory of *quantum meruit* (fair payment for work done) is still used in modern contract law.*

quantum valebant "As much as they were worth." An old form of pleading used in a lawsuit for payment for goods sold and delivered. The theory of *quantum valebant* (fair payment for goods delivered) is still used in modern contract law.*

quare "Wherefore." For example, *quare clausum fregit* means "wherefore he broke the close," which describes an old form of pleading in a lawsuit that requests damages from someone who committed a trespass ("broke the close") on your land. Not *quaere.*

quasi "Sort of"; "as if."*

quid pro quo Something for something; this for that. The giving of one valuable thing for another. A quid pro quo can be the consideration required for a valid contract.

quo animo "With what intention or motive."*

quo warranto "With what authority." Describes a proceeding in which a court questions the right of a person (usually a public official) to take a certain action or to hold a certain office.*

quorum The number necessary to be present in order to conduct business.

ratio decidendi "Reason for decision." The rationale for a judge's holding; the basic ideas a judge uses to come to a decision in a case.*

recapitalization Readjusting the types, amounts, values, and priorities of a corporation's stocks and bonds.*

recidivist A habitual criminal.

record (1) A formal, written account of a case, containing the complete formal history of all actions taken, papers filed, rulings made, opinions written, etc. The record also can include all the actual evidence (testimony, physical objects, etc.) as well as the evidence that was refused admission by the judge. Courts of record include all courts for which permanent records of proceedings are kept. (2) A public record is a document filed with, or put out by, a government agency and open to the public for inspection. For example, a title of record to land is an ownership interest that has been properly filed in the public land records. The official who keeps these records is usually called the recorder of deeds, and the filing process is called recordation. (3) A corporation's records include its charter, bylaws, and minutes of meetings. The record date for payment of a company's stock dividends or for voting is the date on which stockholders must be registered on the company's books to vote or to receive dividends.*

redemption Repurchase or turn in for cash. A redemption period is the time during which a mortgage or similar debt that has gone into default can be paid off without losing the property. Some states have mandatory redemption periods for home mortgages.*

registered agent of a corporation An individual resident (or corporation authorized to do business in the state), located at the listed registered office, upon which service or notice can be made on the particular corporation.

relevancy The tendency of the evidence to establish a proposition that the evidence is offered to prove.

remittitur (1) The power of a trial judge to decrease the amount of money awarded by a jury to a plaintiff. (2) The power of an appeals court to deny a new trial to the defendant if the plaintiff agrees to take a certain amount of money less than that given in the trial. Compare with *additur*. (3) *Remittitur* of record is the return

of a case from appeals court to trial court for the trial court to carry out the higher court's decision.*

reorganization The act or process of organizing again or anew. As to corporations, the carrying out, by proper agreements and legal proceedings, of a business plan for winding up the affairs of or foreclosing a mortgage or mortgages upon the property of insolvent corporations.

replevin Redelivery to the owner of the pledge or thing taken in distress. A local action to be brought where property is taken or where property is detained, unless statute regulates the matter.

res (1) A thing; an object; things; a status. (2) The subject matter or contents of a will or trust.*

res gestae "Things done"; an entire occurrence. Everything said and done that is part of a single occurrence. An assault's *res gestae* might include, for example: excited utterances, threats that are part of the assault, present sense impressions, and other words that are an integral part of the occurrence. Words spoken by others can usually be testified about even if hearsay if the words are part of the *res gestae*. Compare with verbal acts.*

res ipsa loquitur "The thing speaks for itself." A rebuttable presumption (a conclusion that can be changed if contrary evidence is introduced) that a person is negligent if the thing causing an accident was in his or her control only, and if that type of accident does not usually happen without negligence. It is often abbreviated "*res ipsa*" or "R.I.L."*

res judicata "A thing decided"; "a matter decided by judgment." If a court decides a case, the subject of that case is firmly and finally decided between the persons involved in the suit, so no new lawsuit on the same subject may be brought by the persons involved.*

rescission (1) The annulment of a contract. (2) The president's request to Congress that certain money already appropriated not be spent.*

rescission of contract Annulling or abrogation or unmaking of a contract and the placing of the parties to it in status quo.

resolution A formal expression of a decision made by an organized group (such as a club, professional organization, legislature, public assembly, etc.). Congressional resolutions may be by one house only, concurrent, or joint. A concurrent resolution is passed by one house, agreed to by the other, and expresses the "sense of Congress" on a subject though it does not become a law. A joint resolution is passed by both houses of Congress and, in general, is the same as a bill that has been passed by both houses.*

respondeat superior "Let the master answer." Describes the principle that an employer is responsible for most harm caused by an employee acting within the scope of employment. In such a case, the employer is said to have vicarious liability.*

restitution The measure of damages according to the defendant's gains rather than the plaintiff's losses.

revocation Taking back some power, authority, or thing granted; to make void a contract.

royalty A payment made to the creator of a work or the owner of a natural material for the use of that work or material. For example, a publisher might pay an author a royalty of 10 percent of the retail price of each book sold, a manufacturer might pay an inventor a royalty of $10 per invention sold, and a mining company might pay a landowner 10¢ per pound of a mineral extracted.*

rules of court Rules established by a court for the regulating of conduct of business of the court, for example, rules of civil procedure, criminal procedure, and appellate procedure.

scienter Knowingly; with guilty knowledge.*

scilicet "That is to say." An unnecessary word, often used after a general statement to introduce a list of specific examples.*

scintilla A very little bit. The word is often used in the phrase "a mere scintilla of evidence" ("is enough to let the jury decide the case"; "is not enough to let the jury decide the case").*

securities Evidences of obligations to pay money or of rights to participate in earnings and distribution of corporate, trust, and other property.

securities and exchange Acts to provide for the regulation of securities, exchanges, and over-the-counter markets operating in interstate and foreign commerce and through the mails and to prevent unfair practices covering same. The Securities Exchange Commission (SEC) is the federal agency that administers these acts.

sequester To separate or isolate, for example, to sequester a jury by requiring it to stay apart from society until a trial is concluded and a verdict returned.

seriatim One at a time; in proper or logical order.*

settle (1) To come to an agreement about a price, a debt, payment of a debt, or disposition of a lawsuit. (2) Finish up; take care of completely. (3) Transfer property in a way that specifies a succession of owners. (4) Set up a trust.*

settlement (1) *See* Settle. A settlement workup (or brochure) is a summary of facts designed to get the other side to settle a case. (2) The meeting in which the ownership of real property actually transfers from seller to buyer. All payments and debts are usually adjusted and taken care of at this time or immediately thereafter. These financial matters are written on a settlement sheet, which is also known as a closing statement.*

shareholder See Stockholder.

sherman Act or **Sherman Antitrust Act** An act to protect trade and commerce against unlawful restraints or monopolies.

sine Without.*

sine die Without day; without assigning a day for a future meeting or hearing.**

sine qua non A thing or condition that is indispensable.*

situs Site or fixed location; place. Usually the place where a thing has legal ties.*

slander Oral defamation. The speaking of false words that injure another person's reputation, business, or property rights.*

special administrator A temporary representative appointed in an emergency situation to avoid loss, injury, or deterioration of decedent's property or to provide for disposition of decedent's remains.

specific devise A devise of a specific thing or specified part of the estate of a testator that is so described as to be capable of identification; a gift of a part of the estate identified and differentiated from all other parts.

specific performance The carrying out or performance of a contract according to its exact terms. Matters of specific performance are enforced by a court of equity.

stare decisis "Let the decision stand." The rule that when a court has decided a case by applying a legal principle to a set of facts, the court should stick by the principle and apply it to all later cases with clearly similar facts unless there is a strong reason not to, and that courts below must apply the principle in similar cases. This rule helps promote fairness and reliability in judicial decision-making.*

status quo The existing state of things at any given time. The present state of affairs, the existing condition, things as they were before the change.**

statute A law passed by a legislature.* See Codes.

statute of limitations No suit, action, or criminal prosecution shall be maintained unless brought within a specified period of time.**

stipulation (1) An agreement between lawyers on opposite sides of a lawsuit. It is often in writing and usually concerns either court procedure (e.g., an agreement to extend the time in which a pleading is due) or agreed-upon facts that require no proof. (2) A demand. (3) One point in a written agreement.*

stock (1) The goods held for sale by a merchant. (2) Shares of ownership in a corporation. Stock is often divided into preferred (getting a fixed rate of income before any other stock) and common (the bulk of the stock). (3) There are various types of corporate stock. Some of these are: *assessable* (the owner may have to pay more than the stock's cost to meet the company's needs); *blue-chip* (has excellent investment ratings); *callable* or redeemable (can be bought back by the company at a prestated price); *control* (describes that amount of stock, often much less than a majority, that can control the company); *cumulative* (gets unpaid dividends before any common stock is paid); *donated* (given back to the company for resale); *floating* (on the open market for sale); *growth* (bought for an increase in value, not dividends); *guaranteed* (dividends guaranteed by another company); *letter* (a letter is required stating that the buyer will not resell before a certain time); *listed* (traded on an exchange); *participation* (gets a share of profits); *penny* (sells for less than one dollar and is often speculative); and *registered* (registered with the Securities Exchange Commission).*

stockholder A person who owns shares of stock in a corporation or joint-stock company. Shareholder, stockowner, investor.**

sub Under, below, secondary, a smaller part.*

sub nomine Under the name of; in the name of; under the title of.**

sub silentio "Under silence"; in silence; without taking any notice or giving explicit consideration; having an unstated effect. To overrule *sub silentio* is to give a result that invalidates a prior case without mentioning that case.*

subpoena A command to appear at a certain time and place to give testimony upon a certain matter.

subpoena *duces tecum* In addition to being a subpoena to appear, it requires a person to produce books, papers, documents, and other materials.

subrogation The substitution of one person for another in claiming a lawful right or debt. For example, when an insurance company pays its policyholder for damage to his or her car, the insurance company becomes subrogated to (gets the right to sue on or collect) any claim for the same damage that the policyholder has against the person who hit the car.*

substantive law That part of the law that creates, defines, and regulates rights and duties. Substantive law is the opposite of adjective or procedural law, which provides for the method of administering and protecting the rights, duties, and obligations created by substantive law. All states of a general nature are substantive law; those regulating administrative and court proceedings are adjective law.

sui generis One of a kind.*

sui juris "Of his or her own right." Possessing full civil and political rights and able to manage his or her own affairs.*

summons (1) A writ (a notice delivered by a sheriff or other authorized person) informing a person of a lawsuit against him or her. It tells the person to show up in court at a certain time or risk losing the suit without being present. (2) Any formal notice to show up in court (as a witness, juror, etc.).*

supersedeas Describes a judge's order that temporarily holds up another court's proceedings or, more often, temporarily stays a lower court's judgment. For example, a *supersedeas* bond may be put up by a person who appeals a judgment. The bond delays the person's obligation to pay the judgment until the appeal is lost.*

supra Above; earlier (in the page, in the book, etc.).*

surety A person or corporation executing the bond of a personal representative, thereby agreeing to make good any loss suffered by one interested in a decedent's estate by reason of the failure of the personal representative to carry out his or her duty.

tangible property Property that has physical characteristics. It includes movable items such as jewelry, animals, furniture, and cash.

taxable year The calendar year or the fiscal year upon which net taxable income is computed; the annual accounting period of the taxpayer.**

terminus A limit, either of space or time.**

testamentary disposition The act of disposing of property by will.

testamentary trust A trust created by a will.

testate Leaving a valid will at death.

testator A person who makes a will.*

testatrix A female testator.**

tort A civil (as opposed to a criminal) wrong, other than a breach of contract. For an act to be a tort, there must be: a legal duty owed by one person to another, a breach (breaking) of that duty, and harm done as a direct result of the action.*

trademark A distinctive mark, brand name, motto, or symbol used by a company to identify or advertise the products it makes or sells. Trademarks (and service marks) can be federally registered and protected against use by other companies if the marks meet certain criteria. A federally registered mark bears the symbol®.*

transcript of record Official record of the court; the printed record as made up in each case for appeal to a superior court.

trust A right of property, real or personal, held by one party for the benefit of another.

trustee (1) A person who holds money or property for the benefit of another person. (2) A person who has a fiduciary duty to another person, for example, a lawyer or an agent who must act for another in a position of trust. (3) A trustee in bankruptcy is a person appointed by a court to manage a bankrupt person's property and to decide who gets it, and a trustee *de son tort* (French) is a person who is held responsible for his or her wrongful or negligent acts that are performed while improperly claiming the right to take on, or while taking on, the duties of a trustee.*

trustor *See* Settlor.**

truth in Lending Act A federal act that ensures that every person needing consumer credit is provided full disclosure of finance charges, including disclosure in the advertisement of credit transactions; amended in 1970 to regulate issuance, holder's liability, and the fraudulent use of credit cards.

ultra Beyond; outside of; in excess of. For example, *ultra vires* actions are things a corporation does that are outside the scope of powers or activities permitted by its charter or articles of incorporation.*

undue influence Improper influence to control the disposition of another's property; Illegal threats or pressure that take away the other party's free will.

uniform laws Laws in various subject areas, proposed by the Commission on Uniform State Laws and the American Law Institute, adopted in whole or in part by many states.* Some of the more important uniform laws are the Uniform Negotiable Instruments Act, the Uniform Partnership Act, the Uniform Stock Transfer Act, and the Uniform Warehouse Receipt Act.

usury Charging an illegally high rate of interest.*

ultra vires Beyond the scope of the powers of a corporation, as defined by its charter or state law.**

venue The neighborhood, place, or county in which a particular lawsuit should be tried.

verification A sworn statement confirming that the allegations in the pleadings are authentic, correct, or true.

versus Against.*

vi et armis "Force and arms."*

via A right of way or road.*

vice (1) Illegal (and considered immoral) activities such as prostitution. (2) An imperfection or defect. (3) Describes a second in command or substitute.*

vice versa In reverse order. Conversely, on the other hand, in inverted order, the other way around, contrariwise.**

void; voidable That which is void is of no legal force or effect; that which is voidable may be avoided or declared void.

voir dire (French) "To see, to say"; "to state the truth." The preliminary in-court questioning of a prospective witness (or juror) to determine competency to testify (or suitability to decide a case).*

will A document that directs the disposition of the testator's property, executed in accordance with statutory requirements. The term includes codicils and a document that merely appoints a personal representative or merely revokes or revives a will.

will contest A proceeding in probate court questioning the validity of a will or codicil.

witness fees Fees for mileage and appearance in court or at a deposition that are paid to a witness and often prescribed by law.

work product privilege *See* Privilege.

workers' compensation The name commonly used to designate the method and means created by statutes for giving greater protection and security to workers and their dependents against injury and death occurring in the course of employment.

Appendix 1

APPELLATE BRIEF OF THE NATIONAL ASSOCIATION OF LEGAL ASSISTANTS
SUBMITTED TO THE UNITED STATES SUPREME COURT, 1988

Note: The issue of recovery of paralegal time in attorney fee awards is critical to the growth and acceptance of the paralegal career field. NALA filed the following *amicus* brief in the U.S. Supreme Court in *Missouri v. Jenkins,* 491 U. S. 274, 109 S. Ct. 2463 (1989), a case in which the court considered this issue. The *amicus* brief and the Court's opinion follow.

Statement

The National Association of Legal Assistants, Inc. submits this brief *amicus curiae,* pursuant to Rule 36 of the Rules of the Supreme Court of the United States, in support of respondents.[1] This brief is submitted upon the written consent of petitioners and respondents.[2]

Interest of the Amicus Curiae

Legal assistants[3] are a distinguishable group of persons who assist attorneys in the delivery of legal services. Through formal education, training and experience, legal assistants have knowledge and expertise regarding the legal system and substantive and procedural law which qualify them to do work of a legal nature under the supervision of an attorney.

National Association of Legal Assistants, Inc., Model Standards and Guidelines of Utilization of Legal Assistants (1984).

The National Association of Legal Assistants, Inc. (NALA) was incorporated in 1975 as a non-profit organization, in recognition of and in response to the burgeoning use of legal assistants in the delivery of legal services throughout the United States. Representing some 8,000 legal assistants through individual membership or affiliated associations, NALA seeks to promote professional development and continuing education for legal assistants, and to provide a strong national voice to represent this growing and significant profession.[4]

Consistent with these goals, NALA, in 1975, adopted a Code of Ethics and Professional Responsibility for legal assistants to serve as a guideline for the proper conduct by legal assistants in the performance of their duties (reprinted in full in the Appendix to this brief). In 1976, NALA administered the first national legal assistant certification examination, testing skills basic to the profession as well as substantive knowledge of law and procedure. Currently, the voluntary two-day examination program is administered three times yearly. As of July, 1988, 2,327 participants have earned the title CLA (Certified Legal Assistant).

In 1984, NALA adopted its Model Standards and Guidelines for Utilization of Legal Assistants to serve as a guide for legal assistants and supervising attorneys, by describing the role of a legal assistant in the delivery of legal services. Finally, NALA works hand-in-hand with local, state, and national bar associations to set standards for legal assistants, and provides continuing education for legal assistants through seminars, workshops, publications and videotapes.

The legal assistant is a recognized and desirable addition to the modern law office. The delegation of work, which would otherwise be performed by an attorney, to a skilled legal assistant reduces the cost of legal services to the client and increases attorney efficiency and productivity. The benefits of this cost-reducing, cost-effective delivery of legal services to the public through the attorney-supervised use of legal assistants will be promoted and encouraged if the work of legal assistants is recognized and compensated at the market rate as part of court-awarded attorney's fees.

Were the Court to reverse the ruling below by holding that the time spent by legal assistants in the successful prosecution of a civil rights case should not be compensated at the market rate, under 42 U.S.C. § 1988, the detrimental effect upon those seeking legal representation to redress civil rights violations, as well as in other types of cases in which Congress has provided for the recovery of attorney's fees, would be substantial. Such a result would either discourage attorneys from representing victims of civil rights violations, because they could not receive full compensation for their effort, or force attorneys to perform all tasks of a legal nature, thereby decreasing the utilization of legal assistants and increasing the cost of litigation.

Summary of Argument

The widespread use of legal assistants by attorneys to perform work of a legal nature which would otherwise have to be performed by an attorney at a much higher rate has significantly reduced the cost of legal services to the public and enhanced the quality of legal representation by promoting efficient utilization of attorney time. Compensation for the attorney-supervised work of legal assistants at an hourly rate less than that charged by attorneys, but high enough to cover the cost of overhead associated with the work of a legal assistant, is customarily included in attorney's fees charged private fee-paying clients.

A reasonable attorney's fee awarded pursuant to the Civil Rights Attorney's Fee Awards Act of 1976, 42 U.S.C. § 1988, should include market rate compensation for productive work of a legal nature performed by a skilled legal assistant, under the supervision of an attorney, in order to effectuate the purpose of Section 1988. Section 1988 was adopted by Congress to make available legal representation to victims of civil rights violations by fully compensating counsel for prevailing parties at a rate competitive with that charged in the private marketplace. An attorney's fee award which includes market rate compensation for the work of legal assistants is competitive with fees charged to traditional fee-paying clients, makes civil rights representation financially feasible for competent attorneys, promotes the cost-effective practice of utilizing legal assistants in the delivery of legal services, and is in accord with the goal of making available efficient and reasonably priced legal services, not only to victims of civil rights violations but also to the public at large.

Argument: The Work of Legal Assistants is Compensable at the Market Rate as Part of a Reasonable Attorney's Fee Award Pursuant to 42 U.S.C. § 1988

a. Compensating prevailing parties for the work performed by legal assistants on an hourly basis at the market rate comports with accepted practice in the private marketplace and is thus consistent with the purpose of 42 U.S.C. § 1988.

The Civil Rights Attorney's Fee Awards Act of 1976, 42 U.S.C. § 1988, provides that in federal civil rights actions, "the court, in its discretion, may allow the prevailing party, other than the United States, a reasonable attorney's fee as part of the costs." On several occasions, the Court has visited the legislative history of Section 1988, finding that the purpose of the Fees Act was to provide a remedy necessary to obtain compliance with civil rights laws, and to promote respect for civil rights through effective citizen enforcement thereof. *Pennsylvania v. Delaware Valley Citizen's Counsel for Clean Air,* 478 U.S. 546, 561, 106 S. Ct. 3088, 3096 (1986) ("*Pennsylvania I*"); *Evans v. Jeff D.,* 475 U.S. 717, 731, 106 S. Ct. 1531, 1539

(1986). Unless the attorney's fee reimbursement pursuant to Section 1988 is "'*full and complete*', the statutory rights [created by civil rights legislation] would be meaningless because they would remain largely unenforced." *Pennsylvania v. Delaware Valley Citizens' Counsel for Clean Air*, 483 U.S. 711, 737, 107 S. Ct. 3078, 3093 (1987) (Blackmun, J., dissenting) (emphasis added), ("*Pennsylvania II*").

Because most victims of civil rights violations are unable to afford legal representation, Congress found that the market itself would not provide adequate and effective access to the judicial process for vindication of rights violated. *Pennsylvania II*, 483 U.S. at 736–37, 107 S. Ct. at 3092 (Blackmun, J., dissenting); *City of Riverside v. Rivera*, 477 U.S. 561, 576, 106 S. Ct. 2686, 2695 (1986). Thus, to ensure that experienced competent attorneys would be willing to represent persons with legitimate civil rights grievances, Congress determined that it would be necessary to compensate lawyers for all time reasonably expended on a case, at a rate mirroring the prevailing market rate in the relevant community. *Pennsylvania II*, 483 U.S. at 742–44, 107 S. Ct. at 3095–96; *City of Riverside*, 477 U.S. at 578, 106 S. Ct. at 2696; *Evans*, 475 U.S. at 731, 106 S. Ct. at 1539; *Blum v. Stenson*, 465 U.S. 886, 895 (1984). Reasonable Section 1988 attorney's fees must be competitive with the private market for lawyers' services, *Pennsylvania II*, 483 U.S. at 736, 107 S. Ct. at 3092, 3093, 3095 (Blackmun J., dissenting), and "similar to what 'is traditional with attorneys compensated by a fee-paying client.'" *Id.* at 3093 (citation omitted). *See also City of Riverside*, 477 U.S. at 575, 106 S. Ct. at 2695.

Attorneys in the private marketplace traditionally charge fee-paying clients for supervised work of a legal nature performed by legal assistants at a lesser hourly rate than that charged by attorneys. Separate billing for the services of such nonlegal personnel as legal assistants and law students is an "increasingly widespread custom." *Ramos v. Lamm*, 713 F.2d 546, 558 (10th Cir. 1983).

In the not so distant past the court would have frowned upon the practice of billing paraprofessional time separate from attorney time just as it might if a firm separately recorded and billed the hours spent by a secretary on a specific client…, but the standing of paraprofessionals has improved significantly as special training has enabled them to undertake a wide variety of more sophisticated tasks previously assigned exclusively to higher priced lawyers. The advent and widespread use of the paraprofessional has meant that the cost of effective legal counsel has been reduced and its availability enhanced without impairing the quality or delivery of legal services.

In re Chicken Antitrust Litigation, 560 F. Supp. 963, 977–78 (N.D. Ga. 1980) (citation omitted). *See also Parise v. Riccelli Haulers, Inc.*, 672 F. Supp. 72 (N.D.N.Y. 1987). That attorney's fees include compensation for time spent by legal assistants reflects "the realities of the marketplace and of modern, progressive law office management." *United Nuclear Corp. v. Cannon*, 564 F. Supp. 581, 589 (D.R.I. 1983).

This court implicitly recognized and encouraged the traditional marketplace use of nonlawyer personnel in the delivery of legal services by approving an award of attorney's fees, pursuant to Section 1988, which included compensation for time spent by a law clerk. *City of Riverside*, 477 U.S. at 566, 106 S. Ct. at 2690. Every federal circuit has likewise acknowledged the validity of delegating work of a legal nature to nonlawyer personnel under the supervision of an attorney by compensating for the work of legal assistants or law clerks pursuant to Section 1988,[5] or to an analogous fee-shifting statute or rule.[6]

  b. Compensating for the work of legal assistant time on an hourly basis at the market rate promotes the cost-effective delivery of legal services and enhances the quality of legal services.

Compensating for the work of legal assistant time as attorney's fees under Section 1988 "encourages cost-effective delivery of legal services and, by reducing the spiraling cost of civil rights litigation, furthers the policies underlying civil rights statutes." *Cameo Convalescent Center, Inc. v. Senn*, 738 F.2d 836, 846 (7th Cir. 1984), *cert. denied*, 469 U.S. 1106 (1985). Skilled legal assistants are capable of performing some work of a legal nature which would otherwise have to be done by an attorney. To the extent that such work is done by supervised legal assistants at substantially less cost per hour than would have been the case had the work been done by attorneys, the overall cost of legal services to the public is reduced. A rule prohibiting recovery for legal assistant time at the market rate would discourage the cost-effective delivery of legal services.[7]

In addition to reducing the cost of litigation, the use of legal assistants enhances the quality of legal representation. Legal assistants enable the attorney to spend his or her more costly time for greater productivity in more important areas where judgment and decision-making are required. The availability of legal assistants also promotes more thorough trial preparation by permitting a more efficient and economical utilization of staff time. *Chapman v. Pacific Tel. & Tel. Co.,* 456 F. Supp. 77, 83 (N.D. Cal. 1978). *See also Todd Shipyards Corp. v. Director, Office of Workers' Compensation Programs,* 545 F.2d 117 (1976); *Beamon v. City of Ridgeland, Miss.,* 666 F. Supp. 937, 946 (S.D. Miss. 1987).

Lawfirms in the private marketplace routinely include an hourly rate charge for legal assistants as part of the attorney's fee charged fee-paying clients. Indeed, seventy-seven percent of 1,800 legal assistants responding to a recent survey indicated that their law firm received compensation for their work from clients on an hourly billing rate basis. National Association of Legal Assistants, Inc., 1988 National Utilization and Compensation Survey Report (1989). "Lawfirms, like other businesses that sell time, must set their hourly rates at an amount greater than that needed to pay their attorneys' or paralegals' salaries; they must figure into those rates all their costs of doing business." *In re Burlington Northern Inc. Employment Practices Litig.,* 810 F.2d 601, 609 (7th Cir. 1986), *cert. denied,* 108 S. Ct. 82 (1987). The hourly rate of legal assistants must reflect not only base salary, but also fringe benefits and a proportionate share of firm overhead.[8] Additionally, the routine practice of law firms seeking reimbursement for the work of legal assistants at a rate sufficient to cover both the "actual cost" and overhead costs associated with that legally related work is a fairer billing procedure.

> Unlike the work of secretaries and other supporting personnel, . . . the work of paralegals and law clerks is ordinarily charged directly to particular litigation and is therefore a clearly identifiable cost. Were it to be treated as an overhead expense, payable out of the general receipts of the attorney, the across-the-board cost of services to the attorney's clients generally would be burdened by paralegal costs incurred in connection with particular matters of no interest or benefit to other clients.

Chapman, 456 F. Supp. at 82.

Consistent with the private billing procedure, a majority of federal trial and appellate courts approve compensation for legal assistant work hours, as well as the legally related work of other non-attorneys such as law clerks, based upon a reasonable hourly rate set lower than the hourly rate of attorneys but higher than the "actual cost" and sufficient to defray the cost of overhead. *See Jacobs v. Mancuso,* 825 F.2d 559, 563 n.6 (1st Cir. 1987) (legal assistant expenses are most frequently reimbursed based on an hourly fee).[9] This Court, in *City of Riverside, supra,* approved an attorney's fee award which included compensation for time spent by a student law clerk, at the rate of twenty-five dollars an hour, clearly more than the actual wages paid to the individual, and obviously high enough to cover the overhead costs associated with the nonlawyer employee. *See* 477 U.S. at 566, 106 S. Ct. at 2690 & n.2.[10]

    c. The inclusion of compensation for legal assistants in an attorney's fee award does not offend ethical and legal tenets prohibiting the unauthorized practice of law.

Any objection to including compensation for the supervised legally-related work of legal assistants in a reasonable attorney's fee award because legal assistants are not attorneys is but a "technical" one. The work performed by legal assistants is work of the type necessary to the prosecution of the litigation which would otherwise be performed by attorneys. Indeed, this Court has recognized the validity of nonlawyer personnel performing services of a legal nature. In *Procunier v. Martinez,* 416 U.S. 396 (1974), the Court affirmed the striking of a prison administrative rule banning attorney-client interviews conducted by law students or legal paraprofessionals as constituting an unjustified restriction on the right of access to the courts. The Court agreed with the trial court's finding that prohibiting the use of law students or other paraprofessionals from conducting attorney-client interviews with prisoners would inhibit adequate professional representation of indigent inmates, or alternately, increase the cost of legal representation for prisoners. *Id.* at 419–20. Likewise, in *Johnson v. Avery*, 393 U.S. 483 (1969), the Court struck down a prison regulation prohibiting any inmate from advising or assisting another in the preparation of legal documents. The Court noted that "the type of activity involved here—preparation of petitions for post-conviction relief—though historically and traditionally one which may benefit from the services of a trained and dedicated lawyer, is a function often, perhaps generally, performed by a layman." *Id.* at 490 n. 11. *See also City of Riverside*, 477 U.S. at 566, 106 S. Ct. at 2690 (affirming attorney's fee award which included compensation for work performed by a law clerk).

Compensation for lawyer-supervised legally-related work performed by legal assistants conforms with the ethical canons and disciplinary codes governing lawyers and legal assistants. Lawyers are obligated to keep fees in check and take steps to provide efficient, cost-effective legal services. *See* ABA Model Code of Professional Responsibility EC 2-18 and DR 2-106(A)(B) (1976); ABA Model Rules of Professional Conduct, Rule 1.5(a) (1984). The delegation of tasks to lay persons is proper "if the lawyer maintains a direct relationship with his client, supervises the delegated work, and has complete professional responsibility for the work product. This delegation enables a lawyer to render legal services more economically and efficiently." Model Code EC 3-6. *See also* Model Rules, Rule 5.3.[11] Because the lawyer, or lawfirm, is the recipient of an attorney's fee for legal services and not the salaried legal assistant, the inclusion of compensation for the supervised work of a legal assistant as part of a reasonable attorney's fee does not offend ethical rules prohibiting attorneys from sharing legal fees with laymen. *See* Model Code EC 3-8 and DR 3-102.

Legal assistants recognize the ethical ramifications of their performance of legally-related work, and emphasize, in self-policing ethics codes and guidelines, that legal assistants shall not undertake tasks which are required to be performed by an attorney, such as setting fees, giving legal advice, or appearing in any way to a court, the client, or the public to be practicing law.[12] Additionally, the rules stress that all work of a legal nature performed by a legal assistant must be delegated and supervised by an attorney, who retains ultimate responsibility to the client and assumes full professional responsibility for the work product. National Association of Legal Assistants, Inc., Code of Ethics and Professional Responsibility (1975, as amended through 1988); National Association of Legal Assistants Model Standards and Guidelines for Utilization of Legal Assistants (1984) (both reprinted in full in the Appendix to this brief). It is the close supervision by an attorney which keeps the legally-related work of a legal assistant from treading upon the prohibited and unacceptable unauthorized practice of law, and makes the work of a legal assistant no more than an extension of the work of an attorney at a less costly rate.[13]

    d. Courts scrutinize attorney's fee applications to assure the hourly rates of legal assistants and the time spent and nature of the work performed by legal assistants are all reasonable.

Courts compensating for the work performed by a legal assistant in connection with the award of a reasonable attorney's fee scrutinize the reported hours, the suggested rate, and the nature of the work performed in the same manner they scrutinize lawyer time and rates. *See Pennsylvania I*, 478 U.S. at 565, 106 S. Ct. at 3098; *Hensley v. Eckerhart*, 461 U.S. 424, 434 (1983); *Ramos*, 713 F.2d at 559. Trial courts determine what portion of the work is of a clerical nature and is thus absorbed as part of the office overhead reflected in the attorney's billing rate and what portion of the work performed by the legal assistant constitutes legal services traditionally done by an attorney and which be performed by an attorney at a costlier rate. *Ramos,* 713 F.2d at 558; *Richardson v. Byrd,* 709 F.2d 1016, 1023 (5th Cir.), *cert. denied,* 464 U.S. 1009 (1983). "Such expenses are separately recoverable only as part of a prevailing party's award for attorney's fees and expenses, and even then only to the extent that the paralegal performs work traditionally done by an attorney. Otherwise, paralegal expenses are separately unrecoverable overhead expenses." *Allen v. United States Steel Corp.,* 665 F.2d 689, 697 (5th Cir. Unit B 1982). Indeed, when considering a reasonable attorney's fee award, courts have chastised attorneys for doing work which more properly could have been delegated to a legal assistant under the attorney's supervision, and have penalized the attorney by lowering the hourly rate charged.

It is appropriate to distinguish between legal work, in the strict sense, and investigation, clerical work, compilation of facts and statistics, and other work which can often be accomplished by nonlawyers but which a lawyer may do because he has no other help available. Such nonlegal work may command a lesser rate. Its dollar value is not enhanced just because a lawyer does it.

Johnson v. Georgia Highway Express, Inc., 488 F.2d 714, 717 (5th Cir. 1974). Wasteful utilization of expensive legal talent for work that may be delegated to nonlawyers is not condoned. "Routine tasks, if performed by senior partners in large firms, should not be billed at their usual rates. A Michelangelo should not charge Sistine Chapel rates for painting a farmer's barn." *Ursic v. Bethlehem Mines,* 719 F.2d 670, 677 (3d Cir. 1983). Accordingly, courts regularly reduce an attorney's hourly rate to that traditionally charged for a legal assistant, to reflect the nature of the legal work performed.[14]

e. Permitting recovery for work of legal assistants promotes the availability of legal representation to victims of civil rights violations.

If the lawyer attempts to absorb the cost of the legal assistant into his or her regular hourly rate as an overhead expense, as is done for clerical work and office supplies, or to absorb the overhead costs associated with the work of a legal assistant, then all persons employing that attorney, including victims of civil rights violations, would suffer a higher hourly rate, regardless of whether their case necessitated the assistance of a legal assistant. More likely, the work currently performed by legal assistants would be done by attorney associates and billed at the higher attorney associate rate, clearly decreasing the utilization of legal assistants and increasing the cost of litigation. The attorney performing legal tasks which could be delegated to a legal assistant, however, faces the risk that his or her fee will be reduced by a court as being unreasonably high for the quality of work performed. The only remaining alternative would be for the attorney to perform the work at a reduced rate, below and not competitive with the market rate. Such a result would make the representation of victims of civil rights violations cost prohibitive and unattractive, and discourage competent, experienced attorneys from undertaking such representation because they could not receive full compensation for their efforts.

The widespread practice of assigning less technical yet legal work to legal assistants to be performed under the supervision of an attorney promotes economy and efficiency in the administration of justice. Permitting reasonable compensation for such services at the market rate as part of a reasonable attorney's fee encourages this desirable practice, and makes legal representation more readily available to victims of civil rights violations, in accord with Congress' intent when adopting the Civil Rights Attorney's Fee Awards Act of 1976, 43 U.S.C. § 1988.

Conclusion

For the reasons set forth above, the National Association of Legal Assistants, Inc., as *amicus curiae,* respectfully urges the Court to affirm the decision of the Court of Appeals for the Eighth Circuit and permit recovery legal assistants at the market rate as part of a reasonable attorney's fee award made pursuant to 42 U.S.C. § 1988.

Respectfully submitted,
JOHN A. DEVAULT, III
  Counsel of Record

JANE A. LESTER
  Counsel

BEDELL, DITTMAR, DEVAULT & PILLANS, P.A.
The Bedell Building
101 East Adams Street
Jacksonville, FL 32202
(904) 353-0211

For *Amicus Curiae*
National Association of Legal Assistants, Inc.

Endnotes

1. The National Association of Legal Assistants, Inc., submitted this brief, in substantially the same form, as *amicus curiae* in support of petitioner, in the case *Blanchard v. Bergeron,* 831 F.2d 563 (5th Cir. 1987), *cert. granted,* 108 S. Ct. 2869 (June 27, 1988) (No. 87-1485), currently pending before the Court.

2. The original of petitioners' written consent by Bruce Farmer, Esquire, counsel for petitioners, and the original of respondents' written consent by Jay Topkis, Esquire, counsel for respondents, are being filed with the Clerk of the Court under separate cover.

3. The term "legal assistant" is preferred, as it represents those persons doing work of a legal nature under the direct supervision of an attorney, as opposed to a broader category of persons termed "paralegal," who perform work of a similar nature but not necessarily under the supervision of an attorney.

4. Projections by the U.S. Department of Labor indicate an increase in the number of legal assistants from an estimated 53,000 in 1984 to 104,000 in 1995. U.S. Department of Labor, Bureau of Labor Statistics, *Occupational Outlook Quarterly* (Spring 1986).

5. First Circuit: *Jacobs v. Mancuso,* 825 F.2d 599, 563 (1st Cir. 1987); *Eurtado v. Bishop,* 635 F.2d 915, 920 (1st Cir. 1980); Third Circuit: *Daggett v. Kimmelman,* 811 F.2d 793, 799 (3d Cir. 1987) (fee reductions would be approved for work which should have been performed by paralegals); Fourth Circuit: *Vaughns v. Board of Educ. of Prince George's County,* 770 F.2d 1244, 1245–46 (4th Cir. 1985); Fifth Circuit: *Heath v. Brown,* 807 F.2d 1229, 1232 (5th Cir. 1987); Sixth Circuit: *Stewart v. Rhodes,* 656 F.2d 1216, 1217 (6th Cir. 1981), *cert. denied,* 455 U.S. 991 (1982); *Northcross v. Board of Educ. of Memphis City Schools,* 611 F.2d 624, 639 (6th Cir. 1979), *cert. denied,* 447 U.S. 911 (1980); Seventh Circuit: *Usirak v. Fairman,* 851 F.2d 983 (7th Cir. 1988); *Camco Convalescent Center, Inc. v. Senn,* 738 F.2d 836, 846 (7th Cir. 1984), *cert. denied,* 469 U.S. 1106 (1985); Eighth Circuit: *Jenkins v. Missouri,* 838 F.2d 260, 266 (8th Cir.), *cert. granted in part,* 109 S. Ct. 218 (Oct. 11, 1988) (No. 88-64), and *cert. denied,* 109 S. Ct. 218 (1988); Ninth Circuit: *Keith v. Volpe,* 833 F.2d 850, 859 (9th Cir. 1987); *Toussaint v. McCarthy,* 826 F.2d 901, 904 (9th Cir. 1987); Tenth Circuit: *Lucero v. City of Trinidad,* 815 F.2d 1384, 1385 (10th Cir. 1987); *Ramos v. Lamm,* 713 F.2d 546, 558 (10th Cir. 1983); Eleventh Circuit: *Walters v. City of Atlanta,* 803 F.2d 1135, 1151 (11th Cir. 1986).

6. Second Circuit: *In re "Agent Orange" Prod. Liab. Litig.,* 818 F.2d 226, 238 (2d Cir.), *cert. denied,* 108 S. Ct. 289 (1987) (class action); *City of Detroit v. Grinnell Corp.,* 495 F.2d 448, 473 (2d Cir. 1974) (antitrust class action); Third Circuit: *Brinker v. Guiffrida,* 798 F.2d 661, 668 (3d Cir. 1986) (recovery for law clerk under Equal Access to Justice Act); *Citizen's Council of Del. County v. Brinegar,* 741 F.2d 584, 596 (3d Cir. 1984) (Equal Access to Justice Act); Fourth Circuit: *Yobay v. City of Alexandria Employees Credit Union,* 827 F.2d 967, 974 (4th Cir. 1987) (law clerk under Fair Credit Reporting Act, 15 U.S.C. § 1681); *Lily v. Harris-Teeter Supermarket,* 720 F.2d 326, 339–40 n.28 (4th Cir. 1983), *cert. denied,* 466 U.S. 951 (1984) (employment discrimination);

Fifth Circuit: *Concorde Limousines, Inc. v. Moloney Coachbuilders, Inc.,* 835 F.2d 541, 546 (5th Cir. 1987); *Alter Fin. Corp. v. Citizens & Southern Int'l Bank of New Orleans,* 817 F.2d 349, 350 (5th Cir. 1987) (sanctions, 28 U.S.C. § 1927); *Richardson v. Byrd,* 709 F.2d 1016, 1023 (5th Cir.), *cert. denied,* 464 U.S. 1009 (1983) (Title VII sex discrimination class action); Sixth Circuit: *Chandler v. Secretary of Dept. of Health & Human Services,* 792 F.2d 70, 73 (6th Cir. 1986) (Social Security Act, 42 U.S.C. § 406); Seventh Circuit: *In re Burlington Northern, Inc. Employment Practices Litig.,* 810 F.2d 601, 609 (7th Cir. 1986), *cert. denied,* 108 S. Ct. 82 (1987) (employment discrimination action, 42 U.S.C. § 2000e); *Spray-Rite Serv. Corp. v. Monsanto Co.,* 684 F.2d 1226, 1249–50 (7th Cir. 1982), *aff'd,* 465 U.S. 752 (1984) (antitrust, 15 U.S.C. § 1 *et seq.*); Eighth Circuit: *Hawkins v. Anheuser-Busch, Inc.,* 697 F.2d 810, 817 (8th Cir. 1983) (employment discrimination, 42 U.S.C. § 2000e); Ninth Circuit: *Thornberry v. Delta Air Lines, Inc.,* 676 F.2d 1240, 1244 (9th Cir. 1982) (employment discrimination, 42 U.S.C. § 2000e); *Todd Shipyards Corp. v. Director, Office of Workers' Compensation,* 545 F.2d 1176, 1182 (9th Cir. 1976) (Longshoremen's and Harbor Workers' Compensation Act, 33 U.S.C. § 928); *Pacific Coast Agricultural Export Ass'n v. Sunkist Growers, Inc.,* 526 F.2d 1196, 1210 n. 19 (9th Cir. 1975), *cert. denied,* 425 U.S. 959 (1976) (antitrust, 15 U.S.C. § 1 *et seq.*); Tenth Circuit: *Kopunec v. Nelson,* 801 F.2d 1226, 1229 (10th Cir. 1986) (Equal Access to Justice Act); Eleventh Circuit: *Allen v. United States Steel Corp.,* 665 F.2d 689, 697 (5th Cir. Unit B 1982) (employment discrimination, 42 U.S.C. § 2000e); D.C. Circuit: *Wilkett v. Interstate Commerce Comm'n,* 844 F.2d 867, 877 (D.C. Cir. 1988) (law clerk; Equal Access to Justice Act); *Save Our Cumberland Mountains, Inc. v. Hodel,* 826 F.2d 43, 54 n.7 (D.C. Cir. 1987) *(en banc)* (Surface Mining Control and Reclamation Act of 1977, 30 U.S.C. § 1201).

7. *See, e.g., Jacobs,* 825 F.2d at 563 *Spray-Rite Serv. Corp.,* 684 F.2d at 1250; *Todd Shipyards Corp.,* 545 F.2d at 1182; *Shorter v. Valley Bank & Trust Co.,* 678 F. Supp. 714, 724 (N.D.Ill. 1988); *Royal Crown Cola Co. v. Coca-Cola Co.,* 678 F. Supp. 875, 880 (M.D. Ga. 1987); *Chapman v. Pacific Tel. & Tel. Co.,* 456 F. Supp. 77, 83 (N.D. Cal. 1978).

8. *See Schwartz v. Novo Industri A/S,* 119 F.R.D. 359, 365 (S.D.N.Y. 1988) (citation omitted). *See also Williams v. Rowen,* 684 F. Supp. 1305, 1308 (E.D. Pa. 1988); *Garmong v. Montgomery County,* 668 F. Supp. 1000, 1011 (S.D. Tex. 1987); *Brewer v. Southern Union Co.,* 607 F. Supp. 1511, 1528 (D. Colo. 1984).

9. *See also, e.g., Ustrak,* 851 F.2d 983; *Wilkett,* 844 F.2d at 877; *Save Our Cumberland Mountains, Inc.,* 826 F.2d at 54 n.7; *Tousaint,* 826 F.2d at 904; *Jacobs,* 825 F.2d at 563 & n.6; *In re "Agent Orange" Prod. Liab. Litig.,* 818 F.2d 230, 238; *Lucero,* 815 F.2d at 1386; *In re Burlington Northern, Inc. Employment Practices Litig.,* 810 F.2d at 609; *Heath,* 807 F.2d at 1232; *Kopunec,* 801 F.2d at 1229; *Citizen's Council of Del. County,* 741 F.2d at 596; *Richardson,* 709 F.2d at 1023; *Louisville Black Police Officers Org., Inc. v. City of Louisville,* 700 F.2d 268, 273 (6th Cir. 1983); *Strama v. Peterson,* 689 F.2d 661, 663 (7th Cir. 1982); *Stewart v. Rhodes,* 656 F.2d at 1216–17; *Todd Shipyards Corp.,* 545 F.2d at 1182.

10. To highlight the need for this Court's guidance, several courts have allowed the recovery of compensation for the work of legal assistants or law clerks based on an hourly-rate at the same time calling it compensation for "expenses," rather than attorney's fees. *See In re "Agent Orange" Product Liab. Litig.,* 818 F.2d at 238; *Yaris v. Special School Dist. of St. Louis County,* 661 F. Supp. 996, 1002, 1003 n.9 (E.D. Mo. 1987); *PPG Industries, Inc. v. Celanese Polymer Specialties Co.,* 658 F. Supp. 555, 560, 565 (W.D. Ky. 1987), *rev'd on other grounds,* 840 F.2d 1565 (Fed. Cir. 1988). Some courts have held that law firms may only recover their paralegal "out of pocket" expenses, *see Thornberry,* 676 F.2d at 1244 (citing *Northcross,* 611 F.2d at 639), while others have permitted reimbursement for salary actually paid to a legal assistant, with no additional compensation for fringe benefits or overhead. *See, e.g., City of Detroit,* 495 F.2d at 473; *Illinois Migrant Council v. Pilliod,* 672 F. Supp. 1072, 1084 (N.D. Ill. 1987); *Campaign for a Progressive Bronx v. Black,* 631 F. Supp. 975, 983 (S.D.N.Y. 1986). Still others refuse to provide separate compensation for the work of legal assistants, taking the position that legal assistants represent overhead, such as clerical and office expenses, all covered by the attorney's hourly rate. *See Abrams v. Baylor College of Medicine,* 805 F.2d 528, 535 (5th Cir. 1986); *Roe v. City of Chicago,* 586 F. Supp. 513, 516 & n.6 (N.D. Ill. 1984).

11. The American Bar Association emphasizes that the work of a legal assistant "involves the performance, under the ultimate direction and supervision of an attorney, of specifically delegated substantial legal work, which work, for the most part, requires a sufficient knowledge of legal concepts that, absent such assistance, the attorney would perform the task," ABA Standing Committee on Legal Assistants, Position Paper on the Question of Licensure or Certification (1986).

12. Though the American Bar Association has shied away from defining what constitutes the practice of law, ABA Code of Professional Responsibility, it notes that "[f]unctionally, the practice of law relates to the rendition of services for others that call for the professional judgment of a lawyer." ABA Model Code of Professional Responsibility ED 3-5 (1976). Courts faced with the question have attempted to craft a definition. For example, the Florida Supreme Court has stated that the giving of advice and the performance of services which affect important rights of a person under the law, and require legal skill and knowledge of the law greater than that possessed by the average citizen, constitutes the practice of law. *The Florida Bar v. Brumbaugh,* 355 So.2d 1186, 1191 (Fla. 1978).

13. Courts awarding attorney's fees for the supervised work of legal assistants have delineated examples of legal services which would otherwise be performed by an attorney, and thus which are compensable if performed by a legal assistant. They include: investigation of the facts relating to the action, *In re Gas Meters Antitrust Litig.,* 500 F. Supp. 956, 969 (E.D.Pa.1980); assisting with discovery, including such tasks as statistical analysis, inspection and production of documents, review of answers to interrogatories, and the compilation of statistical and financial data, *Bagel Inn, Inc. v. All Star Dairies,* 539 F. Supp. 107, 111 (D.N.J.1982); *In re Gas Meters Antitrust Litig.,* 500 F. Supp. at 967; *see also, e.g., Richardson,* 709 F.2d at 1023; *Spray-Rite Service Corp.,* 684 F.2d at 1250; doing legal research, *Morgan v. Nevada Board of State Prison Comm'rs,* 615 F. Supp. 882, 885 (D.Nev.1985); locating and interviewing witnesses, *Richardson,* 709 F.2d at 1023; *Garmong,* 668 F. Supp. at 1011; organizing and communicating with class members, *Richardson, supra; Edmonds v. United States,* 658 F. Supp. 1126, 1136 (D.S.C.1987); *In re Gas Meters Antitrust Litig.,* 500 F. Supp. at 970; assisting with preparation for depositions and trial, and organizing exhibits, *Easter House v. State of Illinois, Dept. of Children and Family Services,* 663 F. Supp. 456, 460 (N.D. Ill. 1987); *In re Gas Meters Antitrust Litig.,* 500 F. Supp. at 972; assisting with preparation of settlement and settlement administration, *In re Chicken Antitrust Litig.,* 560 F. Supp. 963, 978 (N.D.Ga.1980); *In re Gas Meters Antitrust Litig.,* 500 F. Supp. at 967, 972; compiling statistical and financial data, *Bagel Inn, Inc.,* 539 F. Supp. at 111; drafting pleadings, *Parise v. Riccilli Haulers, Inc.,* 672 F. Supp. 72, 75 (N.D.N.Y.1987); *In re Gas Meters Antitrust Litig.,* 500 F. Supp. at 969; and checking legal citations, *Beamon v. City of Ridgeland, Miss.,* 66 F. Supp. 937, 943 (S.D.Miss.1987).

14. *See, e.g., Pennsylvania v. Delaware Valley Citizen's Council for Clean Air,* 478 U.S. 546, 553, 567, 106 S. Ct. 3088, 3092 (1986) ("*Pennsylvania I*") (approving a lodestar which set different hourly rates for legal work requiring varying degrees of legal ability); *Dagget v. Kimmelman,* 811 F.2d at 799 (attorney hours devoted to tasks which should have been performed by associates or paralegals would warrant an hourly fee reduction); *Northcross,* 611 F.2d at 637, (necessary services performed by attorneys which could have reasonably been performed by less expensive personnel may be compensated at a lower rate than attorney's normal billing rate); *Drez v. E.R. Squibb & Sons, Inc.,* 674 F. Supp. 1432 (D.Kan.1987) (dropping attorney billing rate to law clerk rate where three attorneys sat through trial); *Beamon,* 666 F. Supp. at 941–42 (attorney fees for purely clerical work which is easily delegable granted at reduced hourly rate); *Skelton v. General Motors Corp.,* 661 F. Supp. 1368, 1385 (N.D.Ill. 1987) (court reduces time of attorney spent on administrative tasks); *Metro Data Systems, Inc. v. Durango Systems, Inc.,* 597 F. Supp. 244, 246 (D.Ariz.1984) (gathering information and drafting answers to interrogatories not recoverable by attorney as work which could have been performed by paralegal).

THE COURT'S OPINION: *MISSOURI V. JENKINS*, 491 U. S. 274, 109 S. CT. 2463 (1989)

MISSOURI v. JENKINS
Cite as 491 U. S. 274, 109 S. Ct. 2463 (1989)

MISSOURI, et al., Petitioners

v.

Kalima JENKINS, by her friend,
Kamau AGYEI, et al.

No. 88-64.

Argued Feb. 21, 1989.
Decided June 19, 1989.

Prevailing plaintiffs in school desegregation case sought recovery of attorney fees. The United States District Court for the Western District of Missouri, Russell G. Clark, J., awarded attorney fees, and appeal was taken. The Court of Appeals for the Eight Circuit, 888 F.2d 260, affirmed. On grant of certiorari, the Supreme Court, Justice Brennan, held that: (1) Eleventh Amendment did not prohibit enhancement of fee award under Civil Rights Attorney's Fees Awards Act against state to compensate for delay in payment, and (2) separate compensation award under Civil Rights Attorney's Fees Awards Act for paralegals, law clerks, and recent law school graduates at prevailing rates was fully in accord with Act.

Affirmed.

Justice O'Connor concurred in part and dissented in part and filed opinion in which Justice Scalia joined and Chief Justice Rehnquist joined in part.

Justice Rehnquist filed dissenting opinion.

Justice Marshall did not participate.

1. **Federal Courts** ⊙➙ 265

Award of attorney fees ancillary to prospective relief in civil rights action is not subject to strictures of Eleventh Amendment. U.S.C.A. Const. Amend. 11; 42 U.S.C.A. § 1988.

2. **Federal Courts** ⊙➙ 265

Not only is award of attorney fees in civil rights action beyond reach of Eleventh Amendment, so also is question of how reasonable attorney fee is to be calculated. U.S.C.A. Const. Amend. 11; 42 U.S.C.A. § 1988.

3. **Federal Courts** ⊙➙ 265

Eleventh Amendment does not prohibit enhancement of fee award under Civil Rights Attorney's Fees Awards Act against state to compensate for delay in payment. 42 U.S.C.A. § 1988; U.S.C.A. Const. Amend. 11.

4. **Civil Rights** ⊙➙ 13.17(20)

Attorney fees under Civil Rights Attorney's Fees Awards Act are to be based on market rates for services rendered. 42 U.S.C.A. § 1988.

5. **Civil Rights** ⊙➙ 13.17(19)

Appropriate adjustment for delay in payment—whether by application of current rather than historic hourly rates or otherwise—is within contemplation of Civil Rights Attorney's Fees Awards Act. 42 U.S.C.A. § 1988.

6. **Civil Rights** ⊙➙ 13.17(19)

Federal Courts ⊙➙ 265

Eleventh Amendment has no application to award of attorney fees, ancillary to grant of prospective relief, against state; thus, it follows that same is true for calculation of amount of fee, and adjustment for delay in payment is appropriate factor in determination of what is reasonable attorney fee under Civil Rights Attorney's Fees Awards Act. 42 U.S.C.A. § 1988; U.S.C.A. Const. Amend. 11.

7. Civil Rights ☞ 13.17(18)

Phrase "reasonable attorney's fee" in civil rights attorney fees statute does not refer only to work performed personally by members of bar; rather, term refers to reasonable fee for work product of attorney, and thus, to work of paralegals as well as that of attorneys. 42 U.S.C.A. § 1988.

See publication Words and Phrases for other judicial constructions and definitions.

8. Civil Rights ☞ 13.17(20)

Reasonable attorney fee under Civil Rights Attorney's Fees Awards Act is one calculated on basis of rates and practices prevailing in relevant market, and one that grants successful civil rights plaintiff fully compensatory fee, comparable to what is traditional with attorneys compensated by fee-paying client. 42 U.S.C.A. § 1988.

9. Civil Rights ☞ 13.17(20)

Separate compensation award under Civil Rights Attorney's Fees Awards Act for paralegals, law clerks, and recent law school graduates at prevailing rates was fully in accord with Act, where prevailing practice in area was to bill paralegal work at market rates. 42 U.S.C.A. § 1988.

*Syllabus**

In this major school desegregation litigation in Kansas City, Missouri, in which various desegregation remedies were granted against the State of Missouri and other defendants, the plaintiff class was represented by a Kansas City lawyer (Benson) and by the NAACP Legal Defense and Educational Fund, Inc. (LDF). Benson and the LDF requested attorney's fees under the Civil Rights Attorney's Fees Awards Act of 1976 (42 U.S.C. § 1988), which provides with respect to such litigation that the court, in its discretion, may allow the prevailing party, other than the United States, "a reasonable attorney's fee as part of the costs." In calculating the hourly rates for Benson's, his associates', and the LDF attorneys' fees, the District Court took account of delay in payment by using current market rates rather than those applicable at the time the services were rendered. Both Benson and the LDF employed numerous paralegals, law clerks, and recent law graduates, and the court awarded fees for their work based on market rates, again using current rather than historic rates in order to compensate for the delay in payment.

Held:

1. The Eleventh Amendment does not prohibit enhancement of a fee award under § 1988 against a State to compensate for delay in payment. That Amendment has no application to an award of attorney's fees, ancillary to a grant of prospective relief, against a State, *Hutto v. Finney,* 437 U.S. 678, 98 S. Ct. 2565, 57 L. Ed. 2d 522, and it follows that the same is true for the calculation of the *amount* of the fee. An adjustment for delay in payment is an appropriate factor in determining what constitutes a reasonable attorney's fee under § 1988. Pp. 2466–2469.

2. The District Court correctly compensated the work of paralegals, law clerks, and recent law graduates at the market rates for their services, rather than at their cost to the attorneys. Clearly, "a reasonable attorney's fee" as used in § 1988 cannot have been meant to compensate only work performed personally by members of the Bar. Rather, that term must refer to a reasonable fee for an attorney's work product, and thus must take into account the work not only of attorneys, but also the work of paralegals and the like. A reasonable attorney's fee under § 1988 is one calculated on the basis of rates and practices prevailing in the relevant market and one that grants the successful civil rights plaintiff a "fully compensatory fee," comparable to what "is traditional with attorneys compensated by a fee-paying client." In this case, where the practice in the relevant market is to bill the work of paralegals separately, the District Court's decision to award separate compensation for paralegals, law clerks, and recent law graduates at prevailing market rates was fully in accord with § 1988. Pp. 2469–2472.

---

* The syllabus constitutes no part of the opinion of the Court but has been prepared by the Reporter of Decisions for the convenience of the reader. See United States v. Detroit Lumber Co., 200 U.S. 321, 337, 26 S. Ct. 282, 237, 50 L. Ed. 499.

Cite as 491 U. S. 274, 109 S. Ct. 2463 (1989)

838 F.2d 260 (CA8 1988), affirmed.

BRENNAN, J., delivered the opinion of the Court, in which WHITE, BLACKMUN, STEVENS, and KENNEDY, JJ., joined, and in Parts I and III of which O'CONNOR and SCALIA, JJ., joined.

O'CONNOR, J., filed an opinion concurring in part and dissenting in part, in which SCALIA, J., joined and REHNQUIST, C.J., joined in part. REHNQUIST, C.J., filed a dissenting opinion. MARSHALL, J., took no part in the consideration or decision of the case.

Bruce Farmer, Jefferson City, Mo., for petitioners.

Jay Topkis, New York City, Russel E. Lovell, II, Des Moines, Iowa, for respondents.

Justice BRENNAN delivered the opinion of the Court.

This is the attorney's fee aftermath of major school desegregation litigation in Kansas City, Missouri. We granted certiorari, 488 U.S. ___, 109 S. Ct. 218, 102 L. Ed. 2d 209 (1988), to resolve two questions relating to fees litigation under 42 U.S.C. § 1988. First, does the Eleventh Amendment prohibit enhancement of a fee award against a State to compensate for delay in payment? Second, should the fee award compensate the work of paralegals and law clerks by applying the market rate for their work?

I

This litigation began in 1977 as a suit by the Kansas City Missouri School District (KCMSD), the School Board, and the children of two School Board members, against the State of Missouri and other defendants. The plaintiffs alleged that the State, surrounding school districts, and various federal agencies had caused and perpetuated a system of racial segregation in the schools of the Kansas City metropolitan area. They sought various desegregation remedies. KCMSD was subsequently realigned as a nominal defendant, and a class of present and future KCMSD students was certified as plaintiffs. After lengthy proceedings, including a trial that lasted 7 1/2 months during 1983 and 1984, the District Court found the State of Missouri and KCMSD liable, while dismissing the suburban school districts and the federal defendants. It ordered various intradistrict remedies, to be paid for by the State and KCMSD, including $260 million in capital improvements and a magnet-school plan costing over $200 million. See *Jenkins v. Missouri,* 807 F.2d 657 (CA8 1986) (en banc), cert. denied, 484 U.S. 816 (1987); *Jenkins v. Missouri,* 855 F.2d 1295 (CA8 1988), cert. granted, 490 U.S. ___, 109 S. Ct. 1930, ___ L.Ed.2d ___ (1989).

The plaintiff class has been represented, since 1979, by Kansas City lawyer Arthur Benson and, since 1982, by the NAACP Legal Defense and Educational Fund, Inc. (LDF). Benson and the LDF requested attorney's fees under the Civil Rights Attorney's Fees Awards Act of 1976, 42 U.S.C. § 1988.[1] Benson and his associates had devoted 10,875 attorney hours to the litigation, as well as 8,108 hours of paralegal and law clerk time. For the LDF the corresponding figures were 10,854 hours for attorneys and 15,517 hours for paralegals and law clerks. Their fee applications deleted from these totals 3,628 attorney hours and 7,046 paralegal hours allocable to unsuccessful claims against the suburban school districts. With additions for post-judgment monitoring and for preparation of the fee application, the District Court awarded Benson a total of approximately $1.7 million and the LDF $2.3 million. App. to Pet. for Cert. A22-A43. In calculating the hourly rate for Benson's fees the court noted that the market rate in Kansas City for attorneys of Benson's qualifications was in the range of $125 to $175 per hour, and found that "Mr. Benson's rate would fall at the higher end of this range based upon his expertise in the area of civil rights." *Id.,* at A26. It calculated his fees on the basis of an even higher hourly rate of $200, however, because of three additional factors: the preclusion of other employment, the undesirability of the case, and the delay in payment for Ben son's services. *Id.,* at A26–A27. The court also took account of the delay in payment in setting the rates for several of Benson's associates by using current market rates rather than those applicable at the time the services were rendered. *Id.,* at A28–A30. For the same reason, it calculated the fees for the LDF attorneys at current market rates. *Id.,* at A33.

Both Benson and the LDF employed numerous paralegals, law clerks (generally law students working part-time), and recent law graduates in this litigation. The court awarded fees for their work based on Kansas City market rates for those categories. As in the case of the attorneys, it used current rather than historic market rates in order to compensate for the delay in payment. It therefore awarded fees based on hourly rates of $35 for law clerks, $40 for paralegals, and $50 for recent law graduates. *Id.,* at A29–A31, A34. The Court of Appeals affirmed in all respects. 838 F.2d 260 (CA8 1988).

II

Our grant of certiorari extends to two issues raised by the State of Missouri. Missouri first contends that a State cannot, consistent with the principle of sovereign immunity this Court has found embodied in the Eleventh Amendment, be compelled to pay an attorney's fee enhanced to compensate for delay in payment. This question requires us to examine the intersection of two of our precedents, *Hutto v. Finney,* 437 U.S. 678, 98 S. Ct. 2565, 57 L. Ed. 2d 522 (1978), and *Library of Congress v. Shaw,* 478 U.S. 310, 106 S. Ct. 2957, 92 L. Ed. 2d 250 (1986).[2] In *Hutto v. Finney* the lower courts had awarded attorney's fees against the State of Arkansas, in part pursuant to § 1988, in connection with litigation over the conditions of confinement in the State's prisons. The State contended the any such award was subject to the Eleventh Amendment's constraints on actions for damages payable from a State's treasury. We relied, in rejecting that contention, on the distinction drawn in our earlier cases between "retroactive monetary relief" and "prospective injunctive relief." See *Edelmen v. Jordan,* 415 U.S. 651, 94 S. Ct. 1347, 39 L. Ed. 2d 662 (1974); *Ex parte Young,* 209 U.S. 123, 28 S. Ct. 441, 52 L. Ed. 714 (1908). Attorney's fees, we held, belonged to the latter category, because they constituted reimbursement of "expenses incurred in litigation seeking only prospective relief," rather than "retroactive liability for prelitigation conduct." *Hutto,* 437 U.S., at 695, 98 S. Ct., at 2576; see also *id.,* at 690, 98 S. Ct., at 2573. We explained: "Unlike ordinary 'retroactive' relief such as damages or restitution, an award of costs does not compensate the plaintiff for the injury that first brought him into court. Instead, the award reimburses him for a portion of the expenses he incurred in seeking prospective relief." *Id.,* at 695, n. 24, 98 S. Ct., at 2576, n. 24. Section 1988, we noted, fit easily into the longstanding practice of awarding "costs" against States, for the statute imposed the award of attorney's fees "as part of the costs." *Id.,* at 695–696, 98 S. Ct., at 2576, citing *Fairmont Creamery Co. v. Minnesota,* 275 U.S. 70, 48 S. Ct. 97, 72 L. Ed. 168 (1927).

[1, 2] After *Hutto,* therefore, it must be accepted as settled that an award of attorney's fees ancillary to prospective relief is not subject to the strictures of the Eleventh Amendment. And if the principle of making such an award is beyond the reach of the Eleventh Amendment, the same must also be true for the question of how a "reasonable attorney's fee" is to be calculated. See *Hutto, supra,* 437 U.S., at 696–697, 98 S. Ct., at 2576–2577. Missouri contends, however, that the principle enunciated in *Hutto* has been undermined by subsequent decisions of this Court that require Congress to "express its intention to abrogate the Eleventh Amendment in unmistakable language in the statute itself." *Atascadero State Hospital v. Scanlon,* 473 U.S. 234, 243, 105 S. Ct. 3142, 3148, 87 L. Ed. 2d 171 (1985); *Welch v. Texas Dept. of Highways and Public Transportation,* 483 U.S. 468, 107 S. Ct. 2941, 97 L. Ed. 2d 389 (1987). See also *Dellmuth v. Muth,* 491 U.S. ___, ___ S. Ct. ___, ___ L. Ed. 2d ___ (1989); *Pennsylvania v. Union Gas Co.,* 491 U.S. ___, ___ S. Ct. ___, ___ L.Ed.2d ___ (1989). The flaw in this argument lies in its misreading of the holding of *Hutto.* It is true that in *Hutto* we noted that Congress could, in the exercise of its enforcement power under § 5 of the Fourteenth Amendment, set aside the State's immunity from retroactive damages, 437 U.S., at 693, 98 S. Ct., at 2574–75, citing *Fitzpatrick v. Bitzer,* 427 U.S. 445, 96 S. Ct. 2666, 49 L. Ed. 2d 614 (1976), and that Congress intended to do so in enacting § 1988. 437 U.S., at 693–694, 98 S. Ct., at 2574–2575. But we also made clear that the application of § 1988 to the States did not depend on congressional abrogation of the States' immunity. We did so in rejecting precisely the "clear statement" argument that Missouri now suggests has undermined *Hutto.* Arkansas had argued that § 1988 did not plainly abrogate the States' immunity; citing *Employees v. Missouri Dept. of Public Health and Welfare,* 411 U.S. 279, 93 S. Ct. 1614, 36 L. Ed. 2d 251 (1973), and *Edelman v. Jordan, supra,* the State contended that "retroactive liability" could not be imposed on the States "in the absence of an extraordinarily explicit statutory mandate." *Hutto,* 437 U.S., at 695, 98 S. Ct., at 2576. We responded as follows: "[T]hese cases [*Employees and Edelman*] concern retroactive liability for prelitigation conduct rather than expenses incurred in litigation seeking only prospective relief. The Act imposes attorney's fees 'as part of the costs.' Costs have traditionally been awarded without regard for the States' Eleventh Amendment immunity." *Ibid.*

The holding of *Hutto,* therefore, was not just that Congress had spoken sufficiently clearly to overcome Eleventh Amendment immunity in enacting § 1988, but rather that the Eleventh Amendment did not apply to an award of attorney's fees ancillary to a grant of prospective relief. See *Maine v. Thiboutot,* 448

Cite as 491 U. S. 274, 109 S. Ct. 2463 (1989)

U.S. 1, 9, n.7, 100 S. Ct. 2502, 2507, n.7, 65 L. Ed. 2d 555 (1980). That holding is unaffected by our subsequent jurisprudence concerning the degree of clarity with which Congress must speak in order to override Eleventh Amendment immunity, and we reaffirm it today.

[3] Missouri's other line of argument is based on our decision in *Library of Congress v. Shaw, supra. Shaw* involved an application of the longstanding "no-interest rule," under which interest cannot be awarded against the United States unless it has expressly waived its sovereign immunity. We held that while Congress, in making the Federal Government a potential defendant under Title VII of the Civil Rights Act of 1964, had waived the United States' immunity from suit and from costs including reasonable attorney's fees, it had not waived the Federal Government's traditional immunity from any award of interest. We thus held impermissible a 30 percent increase in the "lodestar" fee to compensate for delay in payment. Because we refused to find in the language of § 1988 a waiver of the United States' immunity from interest, Missouri argues, we should likewise conclude that § 1988 is not sufficiently explicit to constitute an abrogation of the States' immunity under the Eleventh Amendment in regard to any award of interest.

The answer to this contention is already clear from what we have said about *Hutto v. Finney.* Since, as we held in *Hutto,* the Eleventh Amendment does not bar an award of attorney's fees ancillary to a grant of prospective relief, our holding in *Shaw* has no application, even by analogy.[3] There is no need in this case to determine whether Congress has spoken sufficiently clearly to meet a "clear statement" requirement, and it is therefore irrelevant whether the Eleventh Amendment standard should be, as Missouri contends, as stringent as the one we applied for purposes of the no-interest rule in *Shaw.* Rather, the issue here—whether the "reasonable attorney's fee" provided for in § 1988 should be calculated in such a manner as to include an enhancement, where appropriate, for delay in payment—is a straightforward matter of statutory interpretation. For this question, it is of no relevance whether the party against which fees are awarded is a State. The question is what Congress intended—not whether it manifested "the clear affirmative intent…to waive the sovereign's immunity." *Shaw,* 478 U.S., at 321, 106 S. Ct. at 2965.[4] This question is not a difficult one. We have previously explained, albeit in dicta, why an enhancement for delay in payment is, where appropriate, part of a "reasonable attorney's fee." In *Pennsylvania v. Delaware Valley Citizens' Council,* 483 U.S. 711, 107 S. Ct. 3078, 97 L. Ed. 2d 585 (1987), we rejected an argument that a prevailing party was entitled to a fee augmentation to compensate for the risk of nonpayment but we took care to distinguish that risk from the factor of delay:

> "First is the matter of delay. When plaintiffs' entitlement to attorney's fees depends on success, their lawyers are not paid until a favorable decision finally eventuates, which may be years later.…Meanwhile, their expenses of doing business continue and must be met. In setting fees for prevailing counsel, the courts have regularly recognized the delay factor, either by basing the award on current rates or by adjusting the fee based on historical rates to reflect its present value. See, *e.g., Sierra Club v. EPA,* 248 U.S. App .D.C. 107, 120–121, 769 F.2d 796, 809–810 (1985); *Louisville Black Police Officers Organization, Inc. v. Louisville,* 700 F.2d 268, 276, 281 (CA6 1983). Although delay and the risk of nonpayment are often mentioned in the same breath, adjusting for the former is a distinct issue.…We do not suggest…that adjustments for delay are inconsistent with the typical fee-shifting statute." *Id.,* at 716, 107 S. Ct., at 3082.

[4, 5] The same conclusion is appropriate under § 1988.[5] Our cases have repeatedly stressed that attorney's fees awarded under this statute are to be based on market rates for the services rendered. See, *e.g., Blanchard v. Bergeron,* 489 U.S. ___, 109 S. Ct. 939, 103 L. Ed. 2d 67 (1989); *Riverside v. Rivera,* 477 U.S. 561, 106 S. Ct. 2686, 91 L. Ed. 2d 466 (1986); *Blum v. Stenson,* 465 U.S. 886, 104 S. Ct. 1541, 79 L. Ed. 2d 891 (1984). Clearly, compensation received several years after the services were rendered—as it frequently is in complex civil rights litigation—is not equivalent to the same dollar amount received reasonably promptly as the legal services are performed, as would normally be the case with private billings.[6] We agree, therefore, that an appropriate adjustment for delay in payment—whether by the application of current rather than historic hourly rates or otherwise—is within the contemplation of the statute.

[6] To summarize: We reaffirm our holding in *Hutto v. Finney* that the Eleventh Amendment has no application to an award of attorney's fees, ancillary to a grant of prospective relief, against a State. It follows that the same is true for the calculation of the *amount* of the fee. An adjustment for delay in payment

is, we hold, an appropriate factor in the determination of what constitutes a reasonable attorney's fee under § 1988. An award against a State of a fee that includes such an enhancement for delay is not, therefore, barred by the Eleventh Amendment.

III

Missouri's second contention is that the District Court erred in compensating the work of law clerks and paralegals (hereinafter collectively "paralegals") at the market rates for their services, rather than at their cost to the attorney. While Missouri agrees that compensation for the cost of these personnel should be included in the fee award, it suggests that an hourly rate of $15—which it argued below corresponded to their salaries, benefits, and overhead—would be appropriate, rather than the market rates of $35 to $50. According to Missouri, § 1988 does not authorize billing paralegals' hours at market rates, and doing so produces a "windfall" for the attorney.[7]

[7] We begin with the statutory language, which provides simply for "a reasonable attorney's fee as part of the costs." 42 U.S.C. § 1988. Clearly, a "reasonable attorney's fee" cannot have been meant to compensate only work performed personally by members of the bar. Rather, the term must refer to a reasonable fee for the work product of an attorney. Thus, the fee must take into account the work not only of attorneys, but also of secretaries, messengers, libraries, janitors, and others whose labor contributes to the work product for which an attorney bills her client; and it must also take account of other expenses and profit. The parties have suggested no reason why the work of paralegals should not be similarly compensated, nor can we think of any. We thus take as our starting point the self-evident proposition that the "reasonable attorney's fee" provided for by statute should compensate the work of paralegals, as well as that of attorneys. The more difficult question is how the work of paralegals is to be valuated in calculating the overall attorney's fee.

[8] The statute specifies a "reasonable" fee for the attorney's work product. In determining how other elements of the attorney's fee are to be calculated, we have consistently looked to the marketplace as our guide to what is "reasonable." In *Blum v. Stenson,* 465 U.S. 886, 104 S. Ct. 1541, 79 L. Ed. 2d 891 (1984), for example, we rejected an argument that attorney's fees for nonprofit legal service organizations should be based on cost. We said: "The statute and legislative history establish that 'reasonable fees' under § 1988 are to be calculated according to the prevailing market rates in the relevant community...." *Id.,* at 895, 104 S. Ct., at 1547. See also, *e.g., Delaware Valley,* 483 U.S., at 732, 107 S. Ct., at 3090 (O'CONNOR, J., concurring) (controlling question concerning contingency enhancements is "how the market in a community compensates for contingency"); *Rivera,* 477 U.S., at 591, 106 S. Ct. at 2703 (REHNQUIST, J., dissenting) (reasonableness of fee must be determined "in light of both the traditional billing practices in the profession, and the fundamental principle that the award of a 'reasonable' attorney's fee under § 1988 means a fee that would have been deemed reasonable if billed to affluent plaintiffs by their own attorneys"). A reasonable attorney's fee under § 1988 is one calculated on the basis of rates and practices prevailing in the relevant market, *i.e.,* "in line with those [rates] prevailing in the community for similar services by lawyers of reasonably comparable skill, experience, and reputation," *Blum, supra,* 465 U.S., at 896, n. 11, 104 S. Ct., at 1547, n. 11, and one that grants the successful civil rights plaintiff a "fully compensatory fee," *Hensley v. Eckerhart,* 461 U.S. 424, 435, 103 S. Ct. 1933, 1940, 76 L. Ed. 2d 40 (1983), comparable to what "is traditional with attorneys compensated by a fee-paying client." S. Rep. No. 94-1011, p. 6 (1976), U.S. Code Cong. & Admin. News 1976, pp. 5908, 5913.

If an attorney's fee awarded under § 1988 is to yield the same level of compensation that would be available from the market, the "increasingly widespread custom of separately billing for the services of paralegals and law students who serve as clerks," *Ramos v. Lamm,* 713 F.2d 546, 558 (CA10 1988), must be taken into account. All else being equal, the hourly fee charged by an attorney whose rates include paralegal work in her hourly fee, or who bills separately for the work of paralegals at cost, will be higher than the hourly fee charged by an attorney competing in the same market who bills separately for the work of paralegals at "market rates." In other words, the prevailing "market rate" for attorney time is not independent of the manner in which paralegal time is accounted for.[8] Thus, if the prevailing practice in a given community were to bill paralegal time separately at market rates, fees awarded the attorney at market

Cite as 491 U. S. 274, 109 S. Ct. 2463 (1989)

rates for attorney time would not be fully compensatory if the court refused to compensate hours billed by paralegals or did so only at "cost." Similarly, the fee awarded would be too high if the court accepted separate billing for paralegal hours in a market where that was not the custom.

We reject the argument that compensation for paralegals at rates above "cost" would yield a "windfall" for the prevailing attorney. Neither petitioners nor anyone else, to our knowledge, have ever suggested that the hourly rate applied to the work of an associate attorney in a law firm creates a windfall for the firm's partners or is otherwise improper under § 1988, merely because it exceeds the cost of the attorney's services. If the fees are consistent with market rates and practices, the "windfall" argument has no more force with regard to paralegals than it does for associates. And it would hardly accord with Congress' intent to provide a "fully compensatory fee" if the prevailing plaintiff's attorney in a civil rights lawsuit were not permitted to bill separately for paralegals, while the defense attorney in the same litigation was able to take advantage of the prevailing practice and obtain market rates for such work. Yet that is precisely the result sought in this case by the State of Missouri, which appears to have paid its own outside counsel for the work of paralegals at the hourly rate of $35. Record 2696, 2699.[9]

[9] Nothing in § 1988 requires that the work of paralegals invariably be billed separately. If it is the practice in the relevant market not to do so, or to bill the work of paralegals only at cost, that is all that § 1988 requires. Where, however, the prevailing practice is to bill paralegal work at market rates, treating civil rights lawyers' fee requests in the same way is not only permitted by § 1988, but also makes economic sense. By encouraging the use of lower-cost paralegals rather than attorneys wherever possible, permitting market-rate billing of paralegal hours "encourages cost-effective delivery of legal services and, by reducing the spiraling cost of civil rights litigation, furthers the policies underlying civil rights statutes." *Cameo Convalescent Center, Inc. v. Senn,* 738 F.2d 836, 846 (CA7 1984), cert. denied, 469 U.S. 1106, 105 S. Ct. 780, 83 L. Ed. 2d 775 (1985).[10]

Such separate billing appears to be the practice in most communities today.[11] In the present case, Missouri concedes that "the local market typically bills separately for paralegal services," Tr. of Oral Arg. 14, and the District Court found that the requested hourly rates of $35 for law clerks, $40 for paralegals, and $50 for recent law graduates were the prevailing rates for such services in the Kansas City area. App. to Pet. for Cert. A29, A31, A34. Under these circumstances, the court's decision to award separate compensation at these rates was fully in accord with § 1988.

IV

The courts below correctly granted a fee enhancement to compensate for delay in payment and approved compensation of paralegals and law clerks at market rates. The judgment of the Court of Appeals is therefore

Affirmed.

Justice MARSHALL took no part in the consideration or decision of this case.

Justice O'CONNOR, with whom Justice SCALIA joins, and with whom the Chief Justice joins in part, concurring in part and dissenting in part.

I agree with the Court that 42 U.S.C. § 1988 allows compensation for the work of paralegals and law clerks at market rates, and therefore join Parts I and III of its opinion. I do not join Part II, however, for in my view the Eleventh Amendment does not permit enhancement of attorney's fees assessed against a State as compensation for delay in payment.

The Eleventh Amendment does not, of course, provide a State with across-the-board immunity from all monetary relief. Relief that "serves directly to bring an end to a violation of federal law is not barred by the Eleventh Amendment even though accompanied by a substantial ancillary effect" on a State's treasury. *Papasan v. Allain,* 478 U.S. 265, 278, 106 S. Ct. 2932, 2940–41, 92 L. Ed. 2d 209 (1986). Thus, in *Milliken v. Bradley,* 433 U.S. 267, 289–290, 97 S. Ct. 2749, 2761–2762, 53 L. Ed. 2d 745 (1977), the Court unanimously upheld a decision ordering a State to pay over $5 million to eliminate the effects of *de jure* segregation in certain school systems. On the other hand, "[r]elief that in essence serves to compensate a party injured in the past," such as relief "expressly denominated as damages," or "relief [that] is tantamount to an award of damages for a past violation of federal law, even though styled as something else," is prohibited by the Eleventh Amendment. *Papasan,* 478 U.S., at 278, 106 S. Ct., at 2940–41. The crucial question in this case is whether that portion of respondents' attorney's fees based on current hourly rates is properly characterized as retroactive monetary relief.

In *Library of Congress v. Shaw,* 478 U.S. 310, 106 S. Ct. 2957, 92 L. Ed. 2d 250 (1986), the Court addressed whether the attorney's fees provision of Title VII, 42 U.S.C. § 2000e-5(k), permits an award of attorney's fees against the United States to be enhanced in order to compensate for delay in payment. In relevant part, § 2000e-5(k) provides:

> "In any action or proceeding under this subchapter the court, in its discretion, may allow the prevailing party, other than the [EEOC] or the United States, a reasonable attorney's fees as part of the costs, and the [EEOC] and the United States shall be liable for costs the same as a private person."

The Court began its analysis in *Shaw* by holding that "interest is an element of damages separate from damages on the substantive claim." 478 U.S., at 314, 106 S. Ct., at 2961 (citing C. McCormick, Law of Damages § 50, p. 205 (1935)). Given the "no-interest" rule of federal sovereign immunity, under which the United States is not liable for interest absent an express statutory waiver to the contrary, the Court was unwilling to conclude that, by equating the United States' liability to that of private persons in § 2000e-5(k), Congress had waived the United States' immunity from interest. 478 U.S., at 314–319, 106 S. Ct., at 2961–2964. The fact that § 2000e-5(k) used the word "reasonable" to modify "attorney's fees" did not alter this result, for the Court explained that it had "consistently . . . refused to impute an intent to waive immunity from interest into the ambiguous use of a particular word or phrase in a statute." *Id.,* at 320, 106 S. Ct., at 2964. The description of attorney's fees as costs in § 2000e-5(k) also did not mandate a contrary conclusion because "[p]rejudgment interest . . . is considered as damages, not a component of 'costs,'" and the "term 'costs' has *never* been understood to include any interest component." *Id.,* at 321, 106 S. Ct. at 2965 (emphasis added) (citing 10 C. Wright, A. Miller, & M. Kane, Federal Practice and Procedure §§ 2664, 2666, 2670 (2d ed. 1983); 2 A. Sedgwick & G. Van Nest, Sedgwick on Damages 157–158 (7th ed. 1880)). Finally, the Court rejected the argument that the enhancement was proper because the "non-interest" rule did not prohibit compensation for delay in payment: "Interest and a delay factor share an identical function. They are designed to compensate for the belated receipt of money." 478 U.S., at 322, 106 S. Ct. at 2965. As the Court notes, *ante,* at 2468, n. 3, the "no-interest" rule of federal sovereign immunity at issue in *Shaw* provided an "added gloss of strictness," 478 U.S., at 318, 106 S. Ct., at 2963, and may have explained the *result* reached by the Court in that case, *i.e.,* that § 2000e-5(k) did not waive the United States' immunity against awards of interest. But there is not so much as a hint anywhere in *Shaw* that the Court's discussions and definitions of interest and compensation for delay were dictated by, or limited to, the federal "no-interest" rule. As the quotations above illustrate, the Court's opinion in *Shaw* is filled with broad, unqualified language. The dissenters in *Shaw* did not disagree with the Court's sweeping characterization of interest and compensation for delay as damages. Rather, they argued only that § 2000e-5(k) had waived the immunity of the United States with respect to awards of interest. See *id.,* at 323–327, 106 S. Ct., at 2966–2968 (BRENNAN, J., dissenting). I therefore emphatically disagree with the Court's statement that "*Shaw* . . . does not represent a general-purpose definition of compensation for delay that governs here." *Ante,* at 2468, n. 3.

Two general propositions that are relevant here emerge from *Shaw.* First, interest is considered damages, and not costs. Second, compensation for delay, which serves the same function as interest, is also the equivalent of damages. These two propositions make clear that enhancement for delay constitutes retroactive monetary relief barred by the Eleventh Amendment. Given my reading of *Shaw,* I do not think the Court's reliance on the cost rationale of § 1988 set forth in *Hutto v. Finney,* 437 U.S. 678, 98 S. Ct. 2565, 57 L. Ed. 2d 522 (1978), is persuasive. Because *Shaw* teaches that compensation for delay constitutes damages and cannot be considered costs, see 478 U.S., at 321–322, 106 S. Ct., at 2965–2966, *Hutto* is not controlling. See *Hutto,* 437 U.S., 697, n. 27, 98 S. Ct., at 2577, n. 27 ("we do not suggest that our analysis would be the same if Congress were to expand the concept of costs beyond the traditional category of litigation expenses"). Furthermore, *Hutto* does not mean that inclusion of attorney's fees as costs in a statute forecloses a challenge to the enhancement of fees as compensation for delay in payment. If it did, then *Shaw* would have been resolved differently, for § 2000e-5(k) lists attorney's fees as costs.

Cite as 491 U. S. 274, 109 S. Ct. 2463 (1989)

Even if I accepted the narrow interpretation of *Shaw* proffered by the Court, I would disagree with the result reached by the Court in Part II of its opinion. On its own terms, the Court's analysis fails. The Court suggests that the definitions of interest and compensation for delay set forth in *Shaw* would be triggered only by a rule of sovereign immunity barring awards of interest against the States: "Outside the context of the 'no-interest rule' of federal immunity, we see no reason why compensation for delay cannot be included within § 1988 attorney's fee awards[.]" *Ante,* at 2468, n. 3. But the Court does not inquire whether such a rule exists. In fact, there is a federal rule barring awards of interest against States. See *Virginia v. West Virginia,* 238 U.S. 202, 234, 35 S. Ct. 795, 808, 59 L. Ed. 1272 (1915) ("Nor can it be deemed in derogation of the sovereignty of the State that she should be charged with interest *if* her agreement properly construed so provides.")(emphasis added); *United States v. North Carolina,* 136 U.S. 211, 221, 10 S. Ct. 920, 924, 34 L. Ed. 336 (1890) ("general principle" is that "an obligation of the State to pay interest, whether as interest or as damages, on any debt overdue, cannot arise *except* by the consent and contract of the State, manifested by statute, or in a form authorized by statute") (emphasis added). The Court has recently held that the rule of immunity set forth in *Virginia* and *North Carolina* is inapplicable in situations where the State does not retain any immunity, see *West Virginia v. United States,* 479 U.S. 305, 310–312, 107 S. Ct. 702, 706–707, 93 L. Ed. 2d 639 (1987) (State can be held liable for interest to the United States, against whom it has no sovereign immunity), but the rule has not otherwise been limited, and there is reason why it should not be relevant in the Eleventh Amendment context presented in this case.

As *Virginia* and *North Carolina* indicate, a State can waive its immunity against awards of interest. See also *Clark v. Barnard,* 108 U.S. 436, 447, 2 S. Ct. 878, 882–83, 27 L. Ed. 780 (1883). The Missouri courts have interpreted Mo. Rev. Stat. § 408.020 (1979 and Supp.1989), providing for prejudgment interest on money that becomes due and payable, and § 408.040, providing for prejudgment interest on court judgments and orders, as making the State liable for interest. See *Denton Construction Co. v. Missouri State Highway Comm'n,* 454 S.W.2d 44, 59–60 (Mo. 1970) (§ 408.020); *Steppelman v. State Highway Comm'n of Missouri,* 650 S.W.2d 343, 345 (Mo. App.1983) (§ 408.040). There can be no argument, however, that these Missouri statutes and cases allow interest to be awarded against the State here. A "State's waiver of sovereign immunity in its own courts is not a waiver of the Eleventh Amendment immunity in the federal courts." *Pennhurst State School and Hospital v. Halderman,* 465 U.S. 89, 99, n. 9, 104 S. Ct. 900, 907, n. 9, 79 L. Ed. 2d 67 (1984). The fact that a State has immunity from awards of interest is not the end of the matter. In a case such as this one involving school desegregation, interest or compensation for delay (in the guise of current hourly rates) can theoretically be awarded against a State despite the Eleventh Amendment's bar against retroactive monetary liability. The Court has held that Congress can set aside the States' Eleventh Amendment immunity in order to enforce the provisions of the Fourteenth Amendment. See *City of Rome v. United States,* 446 U.S. 156, 179, 100 S. Ct. 1548, 1562–63, 64 L. Ed. 2d 119 (1980); *Fitzpatrick v. Bitzer,* 427 U.S. 445, 456, 96 S. Ct. 2666, 2671, 49 L. Ed. 2d 614 (1976). Congress must, however, be unequivocal in expressing its intent to abrogate that immunity. See generally *Atascadero State Hospital v. Scanlon,* 473 U.S. 234, 243, 105 S. Ct. 3142, 3148, 87 L. Ed. 2d 171 (1985) ("Congress must express its intention to abrogate the Eleventh Amendment in unmistakable language in the statute itself").

In *Hutto* the Court was able to avoid deciding whether § 1988 met the "clear statement" rule only because attorney's fees (without any enhancement) are not considered retroactive in nature. See 437 U.S., at 695–697, 98 S. Ct., at 2575–2577. The Court cannot do the same here, where the attorney's fees were enhanced to compensate for delay in payment. Cf. *Osterneck v. Ernst & Whinney,* ___ U.S. ___, ___, 109 S. Ct. 987, 991, 103 L. Ed. 2d 146 (1989) ("unlike attorney's fees, which at common law were regarded as an element of costs,... prejudgment interest traditionally has been considered part of the compensation due [the] plaintiff").

In relevant part, § 1988 provides:

> "In any action or proceeding to enforce a provision of sections 1981, 1982, 1983, 1985, and 1986 of this title, title IX of Public Law 92-318, or title VI of the Civil Rights Act of 1964, the court, in its discretion, may allow the prevailing party, other than the United States, a reasonable attorney's fees as part of the costs."

In my view, § 1988 does not meet the "clear statement" rule set forth in *Atascadero*. It does not mention damages, interest, compensation for delay, or current hourly rates. As one federal court has correctly noted,

"Congress has not yet made any statement suggesting that a § 1988 attorney's fee award should include prejudgment interest." *Rogers v. Okin,* 821 F.2d 22, 27 (Ca1 1987). A comparison of the statute at issue in *Shaw* also indicates that § 1988, as currently written, is insufficient to allow attorney's fees assessed against a State to be enhanced to compensate for delay in payment. The language of § 1988 is undoubtedly less expansive than that of § 2000e-5(k), for § 1988 does not equate the liability of States with that of private persons. Since § 2000e-5(k) does not allow enhancement of an award of attorney's fees to compensate for delay, it is logical to conclude that § 1988, a more narrowly worded statute, likewise does not allow interest (through the use of current hourly rates) to be tacked on to an award of attorney's fees against a State.

Compensation for delay in payment was *one* of the reasons the District Court used current hourly rates in calculating respondents' attorney's fees. See App. to Pet. for Cert. A26–A27; 838 F.2d 260, 263, 265 (CA8 1988). I would reverse the award of attorney's fees to respondents and remand so that the fees can be calculated without taking compensation for delay into account.

Chief Justice REHNQUIST, dissenting.

I agree with Justice O'CONNOR that the Eleventh Amendment does not permit an award of attorney's fees against a State which includes compensation for delay in payment. Unlike Justice O'CONNOR, however, I do not agree with the Court's approval of the award of law clerk and paralegal fees made here.

Section 1988 gives the district courts discretion to allow the prevailing party in an action under § 1983 "a reasonable attorney's fee as part of the costs." 42 U.S.C. § 1988. The Court reads this language as authorizing recovery of "a 'reasonable' fee for the attorney's work product," *ante,* at 2470, which, the Court concludes, may include separate compensation for the services of law clerks and paralegals. But the statute itself simply uses the very familiar term "a reasonable attorney's fee," which to those untutored in the Court's linguistic juggling means a fee charged for services rendered by an individual who has been licensed to practice law. Because law clerks and paralegals have not been licensed to practice law in Missouri, it is difficult to see how charges for their services may be separately billed as part of "attorney's fees." And since a prudent attorney customarily includes compensation for the cost of law clerk and paralegal services, like any other sort of office overhead—from secretarial staff, janitors, and librarians, to telephone service, stationery, and paper clips—in his own hourly billing rate, allowing the prevailing party to recover separate compensation for law clerk and paralegal services may result in "double recovery."

The Court finds justification for its ruling in the fact that the prevailing practice among attorneys in Kansas City is to bill clients separately for the services of law clerks and paralegals. But I do not think Congress intended the meaning of the statutory term "attorney's fee" to expand and contract with each and every vagary of local billing practice. Under the Court's logic, prevailing parties could recover at market rates for the cost of secretaries, private investigators, and other types of lay personnel who assist the attorney in preparing his case, so long as they could show that the prevailing practice in the local market was to bill separately for these services. Such a result would be a sufficiently drastic departure from the traditional concept of "attorney's fees" that I believe new statutory authorization should be required for it. That permitting separate billing of law clerk and paralegal hours at market rates might "'reduc[e] the spiraling cost of civil rights litigation'" by encouraging attorneys to delegate to these individuals tasks which they would otherwise perform themselves at higher cost, *ante,* at 2471, and n. 10, may be a persuasive reason for Congress to enact such additional legislation. It is not, however, a persuasive reason for us to rewrite the legislation which Congress has in fact enacted. See *Badaracco v. Commissioner,* 464 U.S. 386, 398, 104 S. Ct. 756, 764, 78 L .Ed. 2d 549 (1984) ("[c]ourts are not authorized to rewrite a statute because they might deem its effects susceptible of improvement"). I also disagree with the State's suggestion that law clerk and paralegal expenses incurred by a prevailing party, if not recoverable at market rates as "attorney's fees" under § 1988, are nonetheless recoverable at actual cost under that statute. The language of § 1988 expands the traditional definition of "costs" to include "a reasonable attorney's fee," but it cannot fairly be read to authorize the recovery of all other out-of-pocket expenses actually incurred by the prevailing party in the course of litigation. Absent specific statutory authorization for the recovery of such expenses, the prevailing party remains subject to the limitations on cost recovery imposed by Federal Rule of Civil

Cite as 491 U. S. 274, 109 S. Ct. 2463 (1989)

Procedure 54(d) and 28 U.S.C. § 1920, which govern the taxation of costs in federal litigation where a cost-shifting statute is not applicable. Section 1920 gives the district court discretion to tax certain types of costs against the losing party in any federal litigation. The statute specifically enumerates six categories of expenses which may be taxed as costs: fees of the court clerk and marshal; fees of the court reporter; printing fees and witness fees; copying fees; certain docket fees; and fees of court-appointed experts and interpreters. We have held that this list is exclusive. *Crawford Fitting Co. v. J. T. Gibbons, Inc.,* 482 U.S. 437, 107 S. Ct. 2494, 96 L. Ed. 2d 385 (1987). Since none of these categories can possibly be construed to include the fees of law clerks and paralegals, I would also hold that reimbursement for these expenses may not be separately awarded at actual cost.

I would therefore reverse the award of reimbursement for law clerk and paralegal expenses.

Endnotes

1. Section 1988 provides in relevant part: "In any action or proceeding to enforce a provision of sections 1981, 1982, 1983, 1985, and 1986 of this title, title IX of Public Law 92-318 [20 U.S.C. 1681 et seq.], or title VI of the Civil Rights Act of 1964 [42 U.S.C. 2000d et seq.], the court, in its discretion, may allow the prevailing party, other than the United States, a reasonable attorney's fee as part of the costs."

2. The holding of the Court of Appeals on this point, 838 F.2d, at 265–266, is in conflict with the resolution of the same question in *Rogers v. Okin,* 821 F.2d 22, 26–28 (CA1 1987), cert. denied *sub nom. Commissioner, Massachusetts Dept. of Mental Health v. Rogers,* 484 U.S. 1010, 108 S. Ct. 709, 98 L. Ed. 2d 660 (1988).

3. Our opinion in *Shaw* does, to be sure, contain some language that, if read in isolation, might suggest a different result in this case. Most significantly, we equated compensation for delay with prejudgment interest, and observed that "[p]rejudgment interest…is considered as damages, not a component of 'costs.'…Indeed, the term 'costs' has never been understood to include any interest component." *Library of Congress v. Shaw,* 478 U.S. 310, 321, 106 S. Ct. 2957, 2965, 92 L.Ed.2d 250 (1986). These observations, however, cannot be divorced from the context of the special "no-interest rule" that was at issue in *Shaw.* That rule, which is applicable to the immunity of the United States and is therefore not at issue here, provides an "added gloss of strictness," *id.,* at 318, 106 S. Ct., at 2963, only where the United States' liability for interest is at issue. Our inclusion of compensation for delay within the definition of prejudgment interest in *Shaw* must be understood in light of this broad proscription of interest awards against the United States. *Shaw* thus does not represent a general-purpose definition of compensation for delay that governs here. Outside the context of the "no-interest rule" of federal immunity, we see no reason why compensation for delay cannot be included within § 1988 attorney's fee awards, which *Hutto* held to be "costs" not subject to Eleventh Amendment strictures.

   We cannot share JUSTICE O'CONNOR's view that the two cases she cites, *post,* at 2474, demonstrate the existence of an equivalent rule relating to State immunity that embodies the same ultra-strict rule of construction for interest awards that has grown up around the federal no interest rule. Compare *Shaw, supra,* at 314–317, 106 S. Ct., at 2961–2963 (discussing historical development of the federal no-interest rule).

4. In *Shaw,* which dealt with the sovereign immunity of the Federal Government, there was of course no prospective retrospective distinction as there is when, as in *Hutto* and the present case, it is the Eleventh Amendment immunity of a State that is at issue.

5. *Delaware Valley* was decided under § 304(d) of the Clean Air Act, 42 U.S.C. § 7604(d). We looked for guidance, however, to § 1988 and our cases construing it. *Pennsylvania v. Delaware Valley Citizens' Council,* 483 U.S. 711, 713, n. 1, 107 S. Ct. 3078, 3080, n. 1, 97 L. Ed. 2d 585 (1987).

6. This delay, coupled with the fact that, as we recognized in *Delaware Valley,* the attorney's *expenses* are not deferred pending completion of the litigation, can cause considerable hardship. The present case provides an illustration. During a period of nearly three years, the demands of this case precluded attorney Benson from accepting other employment. In order to pay his staff and meet other operating expenses, he was obliged to borrow $633,000. As of January 1987, he had paid over $113,000 in interest on this debt, and was continuing to borrow to meet interest payments. Record 2336–2339; Tr. 130–131. The LDF, for its part, incurred deficits of $700,000 in 1983 and over $1 million in 1984, largely because of this case. Tr. 46. If no compensation were provided for the delay in payment, the prospect of such hardship could well deter otherwise willing attorneys from accepting complex civil rights cases that might offer great benefit to society at large; this result would work to defeat Congress' purpose in enacting § 1988 of "encourag[ing] the enforcement of federal law through lawsuits filed by private persons." *Delaware Valley, supra,* at 737, 107 S. Ct., at 3093 (BLACKMUN, J., dissenting).

We note also that we have recognized the availability of interim fee awards under § 1988 when a litigant becomes a prevailing party on one issue in the course of the litigation. *Texas State Teachers Assn. v. Garland Independent School Dist.,* 489 U.S. ___, ___, 109 S. Ct. 1486, ___, 103 L. Ed. 2d 866 (1989). In economic terms, such an interim award does not differ from an enhancement for delay in payment.

7. The Courts of Appeals have taken a variety of positions on this issue. Most permit separate billing of paralegal time. See, *e.g., Save Our Cumberland Mountains, Inc. v. Hodel,* 263 U.S. App. D.C. 409, 420, n. 7, 826 F.2d 43, 54, n. 7 (1987), vacated in part on other grounds, 273 U.S. App. D.C. 78, 857 F.2d 1516 (1988)(en banc); *Jacobs v. Mancuso,* 825 F.2d 559, 563, and n. 6 (CA1 1987) (collecting cases); *Spanish Action Committee of Chicago v. Chicago,* 811 F.2d 1129, 1138 (CA7 1987); *Ramos v. Lamm,* 713 F.2d 546, 558–559 (CA10 1983); *Richardson v. Byrd,* 709 F.2d 1016, 1023 (CA5), cert. denied *sub nom. Dallas County Commissioners Court v. Richardson,* 464 U.S. 1009, 104 S. Ct. 527, 78 L. Ed. 2d 710 (1983). See also *Riverside v. Rivera,* 477 U.S. 561, 566, n. 2, 106 S. Ct. 2686, 2690, n. 2, 91 L. Ed. 2d 466 (1986) (noting lower-court approval of hourly rate for law clerks). Some courts, on the other hand, have considered paralegal work "out-of-pocket expense," recoverable only at cost to the attorney. See *e.g., Northcross v. Board of Education of Memphis City Schools,* 611 F.2d 624, 639 (CA6 1979), cert. denied, 447 U.S. 911, 100 S. Ct. 3000, 64 L. Ed. 2d 862 (1980); *Thornberry v. Delta Air Lines, Inc.,* 676 F.2d 1240, 1244 (CA9 1982), vacated, 461 U.S. 952, 103 S. Ct. 2421, 77 L. Ed. 2d 1311 (1983). At least one Court of Appeals has refused to permit any recovery of paralegal expense apart from the attorney's hourly fee. *Abrams v. Baylor College of Medicine,* 805 F.2d 528, 535 (CA5 1986).

8. The attorney who bills separately for paralegal time is merely distributing her costs and profit margin among the hourly fees of other members of her staff, rather than concentrating them in the fee she sets for her own time.

9. A variant of Missouri's "windfall" argument is the following: "If paralegal expense is reimbursed at a rate many times the actual cost, will attorneys next try to bill separately—and at a profit—for such items as secretarial time, paper clips, electricity, and other expenses?" Reply Brief for Petitioners 15–16. The answer to this question is, of course, that attorneys seeking fees under § 1988 would have no basis for requesting separate compensation of such expenses unless this were the prevailing practice in the local community. The safeguard against the billing at a profit of secretarial services and paper clips is the discipline of the market.

10. It has frequently been recognized in the lower courts that paralegals are capable of carrying out many tasks, under the supervision of an attorney, that might otherwise be performed by a lawyer and billed at a higher rate. Such work might include, for example, factual investigation, including locating and interviewing witnesses; assistance with depositions, interrogatories, and document production; compilation of statistical and financial data; checking legal citations; and drafting correspondence. Much such work lies in a gray area of tasks that might appropriately be performed either by an attorney or a paralegal. To the extent that fee applicants under § 1988 are not permitted to bill for the work of paralegals at market rates, it would not be surprising to see a greater amount of such work performed by attorneys themselves, thus increasing the overall cost of litigation.

Of course, purely clerical or secretarial tasks should not be billed at a paralegal rate, regardless of who performs them. What the court in *Johnson v. Georgia Highway Express, Inc.,* 488 F.2d 714, 717 (CA5 1974), said in regard to the work of attorneys is applicable by analogy to paralegals: "It is appropriate to distinguish between legal work, in the strict sense, and investigation, clerical work, compilation of facts and statistics and other work which can often be accomplished by non-lawyers but which a lawyer may do because he has no other help available. Such non-legal work may command a lesser rate. Its dollar value is not enhanced just because a lawyer does it."

11. *Amicus* National Association of Legal Assistants reports that 77 percent of 1,800 legal assistants responding to a survey of the association's membership stated that their law firms charged clients for paralegal work on an hourly billing basis. Brief for National Association of Legal Assistants as *Amicus Curiae* 11.

Appendix 2

The following is the text (attachments not included) of an amicus brief filed in late 2001 in the Oklahoma Supreme Court by NALA, Oklahoma Paralegal Association, Central Oklahoma Association of Legal Assistants, and the Tulsa Association of Legal Assistants. The brief concerns the use of screening procedures in a law firm to protect against the inadvertent disclosure of confidential information when an employee changes law firms.

The Oklahoma Supreme Court decision in *Hays v. Central States Orthopedic Specialists* (2002 OK 30, 51 P.3d 562 (2002)) found that under certain circumstances, screening procedures are acceptable. On this issue, the Court stated:

> [This issue]...presents an important question of first impression, which we believe should be resolved now. The importance of the issue is demonstrated by the amici curiae brief filed on behalf of several groups who represent non-lawyers who work as legal assistants in law firms. The amici claim that the failure to address this issue imposes potential impairment to non-lawyer employees of law firms who wish to change employment. Because we recognize the potential danger that our failure to resolve this issue presents, we will address it.
>
> ...
>
> ¶27 We hold that the use of screening devices may be appropriate where non-lawyer employees are involved. We hold that a per se rule that would prohibit a court's examination of the effectiveness of a screening device for a non-lawyer is not appropriate under Oklahoma law. Thus before being disqualified for having hired a non-lawyer employee from its opponent, the hiring firm should be given the opportunity to prove that the non-lawyer has not revealed client confidences to the new employer and has been effectively counseled and screened from doing so. If such proof is made to the court's satisfaction, the court should deny the motion to disqualify the non-lawyer's new firm. We expressly decline to decide in this opinion whether the use of screening devices would be appropriate in cases involving lawyers who move to a firm that represents an opponent of the lawyers' former firm.

This issue will continue to be discussed among the states in the coming years.

AMICUS CURIAE BRIEF OF THE NATIONAL ASSOCIATION OF LEGAL ASSISTANTS, OKLAHOMA PARALEGAL ASSOCIATION, CENTRAL OKLAHOMA ASSOCIATION OF LEGAL ASSISTANTS, AND TULSA ASSOCIATION OF LEGAL ASSISTANTS

I. Amicus Curiae Legal Assistant Associations

National Association of Legal Assistants, Inc. ("NALA"), Oklahoma Paralegal Association ("OPA"), Central Oklahoma Association of Legal Assistants ("COALA"), and Tulsa Association of Legal Assistants ("TALA") have obtained written consent of all parties (attached, Tab "A") to file this amicus curiae brief pursuant to Sup. Ct. R. 1.12(a)(1).

NALA was established in 1975 and is the leading professional association for legal assistants, composed of more than 18,000 paralegals,[1] through individual members and 90 state and local affiliated associations. NALA has adopted a Code of Ethics and Professional Responsibility ("NALA Code of Ethics") for its members, and holds disciplinary authority over members who breach its ethical standards.[2] NALA's activities include involvement in cases affecting professional issues which impact its members.

OPA was established in 1985 and is Oklahoma's only statewide association for legal assistants. OPA is an affiliate of NALA, and among its goals are the promotion of professionalism among legal assistants, and educating its members through continuing legal education and publications. OPA offers its members ethical guidelines, among other things.

TALA was established in 1982 to, *inter alia,* provide a forum for legal education and professional growth for Tulsa area legal assistants. TALA has organizational purposes which parallel those of NALA (of which TALA is an affiliate), including promotion of the profession of legal assistants, and cooperation with bar associations in setting professional standards for legal assistants.

COALA was established in 1984, and serves legal assistants in the central Oklahoma legal community, particularly the Oklahoma City area. COALA's purposes include providing a network of support and assistance among legal assistants, and promoting high standards of professional responsibility and conduct for its members.

II. Introduction

In the July 12, 2001 Order appealed in this case ("Disqualification Order"), the trial court disqualified appellant's law firm, holding that an ethical screen was an impermissible device to protect from disclosure confidences gained by a nonlawyer employee while employed by appellee's law firm. The trial court held that the Oklahoma Rules of Professional Conduct, 5 O.S. Ch. 1, 1991, App. 3-A ("Oklahoma Rules") prohibit *per se* the use of ethical screens to preserve confidences held by nonlawyer employees. *Id.* at 11.

The sole interest of NALA, OPA, TALA and COALA ("Legal Assistants") in this appeal is to seek this Court's rejection of the trial court's holding that "screening" of a nonlawyer employee is not permitted by the Oklahoma Rules to protect client confidences to which the legal assistant was exposed in prior employment. Legal Assistants take no position as to whether appellant's attorneys should have been disqualified in this case—which may turn on factual issues such as waiver or adequacy of the screen in this case. Legal Assistants implore the Court not to leave unaddressed (at least by *dictum*) the crucial issue of whether nonlawyer employees may be screened in Oklahoma, in the event factual issues *are* found dispositive. Legal Assistants believe that if the status of the trial court's holding on this issue is left uncertain, it will impose a continuing impediment not only to professional employment opportunities of legal assistants and a wide range of other nonlawyer employees such as law student clerks and legal secretaries, but will also cause harm to the lawyers who are deprived of their services, and ultimately to the clients sought to be served.

The rule applied by the trial court would enormously impair, if not nearly paralyze the ability of legal assistants and other nonlawyer employees to change employment, between large law firms, or within the same rural areas where limited personnel are available. Screening is regularly utilized by both large and small firms employing experienced personnel, not only to address known conflicts, but as a prophylactic measure to *prevent future* conflicts as to prospective *new* matters which may be undertaken adverse to parties represented by the incoming employee's former firm. Further, although a law firm may go to considerable trouble in employing an attorney from another law firm to seek necessary consents to resolve conflicts, and will risk the potential need to oppose disqualification motions brought to achieve some tactical advantage, such laborious measures and costs will not easily be undertaken for the sake of employing a particular legal assistant or other nonlawyer employee.

The trial court relied principally upon a recent Kansas decision, *Zimmerman v. Mahaska Bottling Co.,* 19 P.3d 784 (Kan. 2001). *Zimmerman* stands nearly alone among the numerous courts and ethics tribunals that have addressed the propriety of screening nonlawyer employees such as legal assistants. The rationale of *Zimmerman,* adopted by the trial court, is that: (1) Rule 5.3 of the Oklahoma Rules requires a lawyer to supervise legal assistants to ensure that their conduct is compatible with the professional obligations of the *lawyer;* (2) nonlawyer employees should be held to exactly the same ethical standards governing conflicts of interest that govern lawyers; and (3) an ethical screen is impermissible to protect client confidences held by a lawyer who becomes associated with the adverse side, and so must also be impermissible to preserve confidences held by a nonlawyer employee who becomes employed by the adverse party's lawyer. *Zimmerman, supra,* 19 P.3d at 790–93; Disqualification Order at 7–10.

Only the first of these propositions is correct. Virtually all authorities recognize that lawyers and their nonlawyer employees are not subject to the same standards regarding screening, for various public policy reasons discussed herein. While it is not settled either in Oklahoma or nationally whether screening is even permitted for *lawyers,* the trial court's holding is contrary to the great weight of authority in the nation with respect to the permissibility of screening a *nonlawyer employee*—including an informal opinion of the American Bar Association's Standing Committee on Ethics and Professional Responsibility, the Restatement of Law Governing Lawyers, the leading treatises on ethics and malpractice, numerous ethics tribunals, and other states' decisional law. In fact, in its Annual Meeting of August 6–7, 2001, the American Bar Association's House of Delegates provisionally approved a revision to the explanatory comments to Rule 1.10 (governing imputation of conflicts on interest) of the Model Rules, consistent with this prevailing view.

III. Screening Lawyers

This Court has not yet addressed the use of screening for lawyers, let alone disapproved its use for nonlawyers. As the trial court recognized, there is a division of authority on whether screening is permissible for lawyers. Screening for government lawyers is expressly permitted by Rule 1.11, but a dwindling majority of jurisdictions prohibit screening of lawyers in private practice. An extremely thorough and recent judicial treatment of the subject is *Clinard v. Blackwood,* 1999 Tenn. App. LEXIS 729 (Tenn. App. 1999), *aff'd,* 43 S.W.3d 177 (Tenn. 2001). The Tennessee Court of Appeals cites authority for each jurisdiction to have addressed the issue of screening lawyers in Part IV(D) (notes 60–67), and traces in detail the changes in ABA's ethics codes and efforts to reach a consensus on standards regarding screening in Part IV(C). *See also* 1 Mallen and Smith, LEGAL MALPRACTICE § 13.19 (3rd ed. West) ("Although the Model Rules are silent on whether screening is appropriate [other than for government lawyers], the courts have ignored or expressly rejected the omission and continued to utilize the device."); Moore's Federal Practice *The Federal Law of Attorney Misconduct* (3rd ed. 2001) § 808.06[2][b][iv] at p. 808–70 ("Courts in approximately half of the circuits have allowed screening devices in appropriate cases. Some appellate courts have directly approved the practice. Other circuit courts have left the issue open, which gives district courts and the federal circuit an opportunity to allow screening."). RESTATEMENT (THIRD) OF LAW GOVERNING LAWYERS expressly approves the use of screening for lawyers, but under more restrictive circumstances than it approves screening for nonlawyers. *Compare* RESTATEMENT (THIRD) OF LAW GOVERNING LAWYERS § 124(2) (approving screening for lawyer who possesses no "significant" client confidential information) *with* § 123, *comment f* (nonlawyer should not be treated like lawyer, and both job mobility of employee and client confidences may be adequately protected by screening such employee in new firm).

IV. Screening Nonlawyer Employees

The sharp difference of opinion on screening exists only as to *lawyers*—not as to *nonlawyer employees*—as to which all leading authorities and the overwhelming majority of jurisdictions readily *endorse* screening, for a variety of reasons. Briefly, these reasons are that: (a) non-lawyer employees have a greater interest in free mobility of employment, and the use of screening is more essential to them than to lawyers who change employment less frequently and for whose sake more time, expense and risk will be taken to resolve conflicts of interest; (b) significant obstacles to the mobility of nonlawyer employees will adversely affect not only them, but also the legal profession and the clients the profession serves (who may be deprived of higher quality services); and (c) the same public policies which support screening of government lawyers support screening of nonlawyer employees—*i.e.,* neither has a choice in the clients they serve, and neither has an economic interest in the outcome of the representation.

The principal ethics authorities all agree that screening of nonlawyers is proper, and the American Bar Association is now in the process of amending the explanatory comments to the Model Rules to reflect this consensus.

A. American Bar Association Informal Opinion 88-1526

ABA Informal Opinion 88-1526 is probably the most widely recognized authority on the issue of whether nonlawyers may be screened. The American Bar Association has a Standing Committee on Ethics and Professional Responsibility to lend guidance to courts, bar associations, and practitioners in interpreting the ABA Model Rules of Professional Conduct (adopted in Oklahoma) and other ABA ethics codes. The Committee adopts both Formal and Informal opinions, the only distinction being that Formal Opinions are determined to have "widespread interest or unusual importance."[3] While the Committee's views are not binding, they are considered highly persuasive by most courts and ethics tribunals.

For more than 13 years, the ABA has interpreted the Model Rules to allow screening of legal assistants and other nonlawyer employees to protect client confidences and prevent disqualification for a conflict of interest. ABA Informal Opinion 88-1526 (June 22, 1988). The Committee endorsed the view of *Kapco Mfg. Co. v. C&O Enterprises, Inc.,* 637 F. Supp. 1231 (N.D. Ill. 1985), that an ethical screen is permitted to rebut a presumption that the moving nonlawyer employee has shared confidential information with the lawyers of the new employer. The Committee explained its reasoning as follows:

> It is important that nonlawyer employees have as much mobility in employment opportunity as possible consistent with the protection of clients' interests. To so limit employment opportunities that some nonlawyers trained to work with law firms might be required to leave the careers for which they are trained would disserve clients as well as the legal profession. Accordingly, any restrictions on the nonlawyer's employment should be held to the minimum necessary to protect confidentiality of client information.

Id. at p. 3. The Committee cited Rule 5.3 (the same rule relied upon by the trial court here, Disqualification Order at 7), stating that this rule requires *both* the *new* employer *and* the *former* employer of the nonlawyer to take measures to ensure that the nonlawyer preserves confidences of the clients of the former employer. *Id.* at pp. 3–4. The former employer is cautioned to consider the need to advise the employing firm that the paralegal must be screened to preserve confidences, and if not satisfied with the adequacy of measures taken to prevent improper disclosures, to consider filing a motion to disqualify the employing law firm. *Id.* at p. 5.

B. Restatement of the Law Governing Lawyers

The Restatement (Third) of the Law Governing Lawyers, adopted by the American Law Institute, is one of the most respected and authoritative expositions of legal principles governing lawyers, including but not limited to legal ethics.[4] Restatement (Third) of the Law Governing Lawyers, like all other leading authorities, articulates standards directly contrary to the holding of the trial court here. Section 123, *comment f* discusses the imputation of conflicts through nonlawyer employees, explaining that their duty of confidentiality is not directly imputed to prohibit representation of other clients at a subsequent employer. The RESTATEMENT approves screening for nonlawyer employees to protect client confidences, stating:

> Adequate protection can be given to clients, consistent with the interest in job mobility for nonlawyers, by prohibiting the nonlawyer from using or disclosing the confidential information (see § 124) but not extending the prohibition on representation to lawyers in the new firm or organization. If a nonlawyer employee in fact conveys confidential information learned about a client in one firm to lawyers in another, a prohibition on representation by the second firm would be warranted.

See also Reporter's Note to §123, *comment f,* at p. 296, citing supporting authorities, and stating: "The position of the Comment refers to lack of imputation other than in situations in which a nonlawyer employee is assigned at the new firm to work directly on the same matter on which the employee had worked at a prior firm."

The RESTATEMENT also recognizes the material difference in treatment between nonlawyer employees and lawyers in circumstances where the nonlawyer employee later *becomes* a lawyer: "Even if the person learned the information in circumstances that would disqualify a lawyer and the person has become a lawyer, the person should not be regarded as a lawyer for purposes of the imputation rules of this Section." *Id., §123, Comment f.*

C. Hazard & Hodes, The Law of Lawyering (3rd Ed. 2001)

Hazard & Hodes, *The Law of Lawyering* (3rd Ed. 2001), has long been recognized as the leading treatise on professional ethics, and is cited in numerous opinions. Indeed, the trial court relied upon Hazard & Hodes in its Disqualification Order in this case, citing the treatise for the proposition that Rule 1.10 creates a "conclusive" (or irrebuttable) presumption that the confidences obtained by a moving *lawyer* have been imparted to other lawyers in the new firm. Disqualification Order at 6–7.

However, as to *nonlawyers* changing firms, Hazard & Hodes observes that imputation rules do not strictly apply, and that most authorities allow screening:

> On the other hand, most authorities hold that the differences between lawyers and their nonlawyer assistants instead justifies a *relaxation* of the imputation rules, at least to the extent of allowing screening in lieu of disqualification. See, for example, Restatement of the Law Governing Lawyers § 123, Comment f. There are several reasons for this view. First, inasmuch as nonlawyer personnel do not reap the financial rewards that lawyers do and do not usually have the same job security, they ought to be permitted more job mobility. More important, without relief from the imputation rule, lawyers would have difficulty hiring experienced personnel, and this would ultimately be to the detriment of clients.

(Original emphasis) Hazard & Hodes, *The Law of Lawyering,* § 14:11.[5]

D. ABA/BNA Lawyers' Manual on Professional Conduct

The American Bar Association and Bureau of National Affairs, Inc. jointly publish the LAWYERS' MANUAL ON PROFESSIONAL CONDUCT, a multi-volume treatise which includes extensive analysis and discussion of authorities (both case law and ethics opinions) regarding ethics standards under both the Model Rules and the former Code of Professional Responsibility. As to the issue of protecting confidences gained by a nonlawyer switching firms, the treatise indicates that effective screening is usually held to be sufficient protection for client confidences:

> Usually, the answer hinges upon whether the non-lawyer assistant has been appropriately informed as to his obligations of confidentiality and whether the firm has implemented strict procedures for

protecting client information and screening the assistant.... If the screening, or "cone of silence," is inadequate to prevent disclosure of confidences, the firm may be disqualified.

LAWYERS' MANUAL ON PROFESSIONAL CONDUCT (ABA/BNA 2001) § 55:317.

E. State Ethics Tribunals and Bar Associations

State ethics opinions are nearly uniform in supporting screening for nonlawyer employees.[6] Space does not permit more than citation to the relevant opinions. Copies of the opinions cited herein, arranged alphabetically by state, are attached under Tab "B" pursuant to Sup. Ct. R. 1.11(i)(1)(2). *See* Delaware State Bar Ass'n Committee on Professional Ethics Opinion 1986-1; District of Columbia Bar Legal Ethics Committee, Opinion 227 (April 21, 1992); Chicago Bar Ass'n Committee on Professional Responsibility, Opinion 93-5 (May 1994); Kentucky Bar Ass'n, Ethics Committee, Opinion E-308 (Sept. 1985); State Bar of Michigan, Committee on Professional and Judicial Ethics, Opinion RI-284 (Nov. 18, 1996); New Jersey Advisory Committee on Professional Ethics, Opinion 665; North Carolina State Bar Ethics Opinion 176 (July 21, 1994); South Carolina Bar, Ethics Advisory Committee, Advisory Opinion 93-29; Supreme Court of Tennessee, Board of Professional Responsibility, Formal Ethics Opinion 89-F-118 (March 10, 1989); State Bar of Texas Professional Ethics Committee Opinion No. 472 (June 20, 1991); Vermont Bar Ass'n, Committee on Professional Responsibility, Opinion 97-09.

Contra: Kansas Ethics Opinion No. 90-005 (December 9, 1991) (relied upon in *Zimmerman, supra,* 19 P.3d at 791–92); Nebraska State Bar Ass'n, Advisory Opinion 94-4 (screening impermissible for both private and government lawyers, and for nonlawyers).

F. Case Law

Case law also overwhelmingly supports the use of ethical screens to protect confidences of nonlawyer employees. *In Re Complex Asbestos Litigation,* 232 Cal. App. 3d 572 (Cal. App. 1 Dist. 1991), which has been cited by sixteen law review articles and two annotations, is properly described as "[t]he most comprehensive judicial treatment of the disqualification question with respect to the hiring of nonlawyer personnel by opposing counsel...."[7] In *Asbestos Litigation,* a paralegal moved from one firm to another with client confidences gained in the first firm. After extensively reviewing relevant public policy concerns and case law, the court concluded that whatever rule might be appropriate for attorneys, any presumption that a *nonlawyer* has shared confidences should be rebuttable:

> An inflexible presumption of shared confidences would not be appropriate for nonlawyers, though, whatever its merits when applied to attorneys. There are obvious differences between lawyers and their nonlawyer employees in training, responsibilities, and acquisition and use of confidential information. These differences satisfy us that a rebuttable presumption of shared confidences provides a just balance between protecting confidentiality and the right to chosen counsel. The most likely means of rebutting the presumption is to implement a procedure before the employee is hired, which effectively screens the employee from any involvement with the litigation, a procedure one court aptly described as a " 'cone of silence.' "

Id. at 593. The court concurred with the concerns as to employment mobility for nonlawyer employees, expressed by the ABA Standing Committee on Ethics, discussed above, and added that a *per se* disqualification rule "could easily result in nonlawyer employees becoming 'Typhoid Marys,' unemployable by firms practicing in specialized areas of the law where the employees are most skilled and experienced." *Id.* at 595–96. Since screening measures had not been used and the presumption that the paralegal had disclosed the confidences to lawyers in her new firm had not otherwise been rebutted, the court upheld disqualification in the case before it. *Id.* at 596–99.

An Arizona decision adds other policy considerations to the list of reasons for treating nonlawyers differently than lawyers. Arizona does not permit screening for lawyers, but like almost all jurisdictions, recognizes that a different rule is appropriate for nonlawyers:

> [W]e are wary of allowing a literal reading of a rule appropriate for lawyers to become a means of injustice to the parties when applied to nonlawyers if there are valid reasons to draw distinctions between them.

Smart Industries Corp. v. Superior Court of State of Arizona, 876 P.2d 1176, 1184 (Ariz. App. 1994). In *Smart,* the court concluded that the reasons for allowing screening of *government* lawyers under the Model Rules also applies to nonlawyers:

> We believe that this reason for treating government lawyers differently in the context of imputed disqualification cases applies equally to nonlawyer assistants, who, unlike lawyers in private practice, generally have neither a financial interest in the outcome of a particular litigation, nor the choice of which clients they serve. Moreover, in our opinion, the public perception of what is expected of lawyers as compared to nonlawyers is different...

Id. at 1184. This rationale was quoted and relied upon in *Stewart v. Bee-Dee Neon & Signs, Inc.,* 751 So.2d 196, 206 (Fla. 1st DCA 2000), which, following the "central position which balances the concerns expressed by our sister courts and by others," *id.* at 200, concluded by adopting a burden-shifting methodology for determining a disqualification motion due to a nonlawyer's change of employment, allowing screening as one device to rebut a presumption that a nonlawyer employee has shared client confidences, *id.* at 207–208. *See also id.* at 204–205, identifying the public policy interests at stake, and finding they should be balanced in accordance with the similar standards of the majority of courts and ethics committees of other jurisdictions.[8] While Florida intermediate appellate courts are divided on this issue, a majority (three out of five) approve screening for nonlawyer employees.[9]

Numerous decisions from other jurisdictions reject any *per se* disqualification rule arising from a nonlawyer employee changing employment, often expressly approving the use of screening to preserve confidences. *See Herron v. Jones,* 637 S.W.2d 569 (Ark. 1982) (screening of legal secretary approved); *Atmel Corp. v. Information Storage Devices, Inc.,* 1998 U.S. Dist. LEXIS 4241 (N.D. Cal. 1998) (approving use of standards in *Complex Antitrust Litigation, supra,* where secretary of plaintiff's lead counsel was employed by defendant's firm before litigation was filed, finding employee did not possess significant confidences and the defendant's firm showed she had not conveyed information regarding the client or the lawsuit); *Rivera v. Chicago Pneumatic Tool Co.,* 1991 Conn. Super. LEXIS 1832, 1991 WL 151892 (screening of paralegal approved); *Temkin v. Temkin,* 1993 Conn. Super. LEXIS 2442 (similar); *Kapco Mfg. Co. v. C&O Enterprises, Inc.,* 637 F. Supp. 1231, 1239–40 (N.D. Ill. 1985) (the decision cited in ABA Informal Opinion 88-1526, also cited in numerous court and ethics opinions and commentaries, holding that current law firm employer of nonlawyer employee who changed sides could show that the employee did not disclose confidences even without institutional screening, under circumstances of case); *Riddell Sports Inc. v. Brooks,* 1994 U.S. Dist. LEXIS 2290 (S.D.N.Y. 1994) (new employer of a paralegal may rebut the presumption that the paralegal has shared confidences by presenting evidence that the confidences were not imparted to the lawyers of the new firm, even without a formal screen);[10] *Latson v. Blanchard,* 1998 Ohio App. LEXIS 4619 (Ohio 1998) (relying upon standards set forth in ABA Informal Opinion 88-1526, *supra,* but finding disqualification was required because paralegal was not screened and worked on both sides of the same matter); *Phoenix Founders, Inc. v. McClellan,* 887 S.W.2d 831 (Tex. 1994) (joining the "weight of authority in other jurisdictions" to allow screening of nonlawyer employees, approving the approach suggested in ABA Informal Opinion 88-1526, and also relying principally upon *Antitrust Litigation, supra, Smart, supra,* and *Herron, supra*);

Daines v. Alcatel, S.A., 194 F.R.D. 678 (E.D. Wash. 2000) (denying motion to disqualify because paralegal had been screened, in a jurisdiction which also allows screening for lawyers); *Makita Corp. v. U.S.,* 819 F. Supp. 1099 (Ct. Intern. Trade 1993) (expressly recognizing propriety of screening a nonlawyer, approvingly citing the approach of ABA Informal opinion 88-1526 and *Kapco, supra,* while stating that this constitutes "[a] difference" from the standards applied to lawyers, *id.* at 1105).

Kansas and Nevada have definitively rejected screening for nonlawyer employees. *Zimmerman v. Mahaska Bottling Co.,* 19 P.3d 784 (Kan. 2001) and *Ciaffone v. District Court,* 945 P.2d 950 (Nev. 1997). Both of these decisions were principally relied upon by the trial court in this case.

A Nebraska decision, which was not cited either by the trial court or by *Zimmerman,* applied a rule disallowing screening of attorneys to a disbarred attorney who, before being disbarred, obtained client confidences at the former firm, and was then employed to perform clerical tasks at the adversary's firm. *State ex rel. Creighton University v. Hickman,* 512 N.W.2d 374 (Neb. 1994).

G. ABA Commission on the Evaluation of the Rules of Professional Conduct

The American Bar Association in 1997 established a Commission on the Evaluation of the Rules of Professional Conduct (popularly known as ABA's "Ethics 2000" Commission) to recommend changes to the Model Rules. The Commission recommended that the following comment be added to Rule 1.10, stating that it "represents the overwhelming state of the current case law:"[11]

> [4] The rule in paragraph (a) also does not prohibit representation by others in the law firm where the person prohibited from involvement in a matter is a nonlawyer, such as a paralegal or legal secretary. Nor does paragraph (a) prohibit representation if the lawyer is prohibited from acting because of events before the person became a lawyer, for example, work that the person did while a law student. Such person, however, ordinarily must be screened from any personal participation in the matter to avoid communication to others in the firm of confidential information that both the nonlawyers and the firm have a legal duty to protect. See Rules 1.0(k) and 5.3.

Id., p. 98, *comment [4]* (relevant excerpts attached, Tab "C"). The ABA House of Delegates provisionally adopted this comment at its annual meeting on August 6–7, 2001,[12] while amending the proposal to eliminate other language which would have also expressly allowed screening of lawyers.[13]

H. Trial Court's Analysis

The trial court relied upon Rule 5.3 of the Oklahoma Rules to lead her to the conclusion that *if* the Oklahoma Rules prohibited a law firm from screening a lawyer, they also prohibit a law firm from screening a *legal assistant.* Disqualification Order at 7.

Rule 5.3 provides that a lawyer must take measures to reasonably ensure that a legal assistant's "conduct is compatible with the professional obligations of the lawyer." The trial court quoted the comment to Rule 5.3, which states that a lawyer should give legal assistants "appropriate instruction and supervision concerning the ethical aspects of their employment, particularly regarding the obligation not to disclose information relating to representation of the client...." Disqualification Order at 7. The trial court concluded:

> This Court interprets [Rule 5.3] to mean that legal assistants are subject to the same rules as lawyers.

Id. This led the trial court to conclude that the permissibility of screening legal assistants and other nonlawyer employees must be determined by reference to the standards governing lawyers under Rules 1.9 and 1.10 of the Oklahoma Rules. *Id.* at 9-11.

The analysis misconstrues Rule 5.3. Rule 5.3 does not state that a legal assistant is bound by the same rules governing lawyers—only that a lawyer must ensure that a legal assistant does not cause the breach of the *lawyer's* ethical duties under the Rules. The ethical duties of concern *here* are those governing the *lawyers* in both plaintiff's and defendant's firms.

Here, Rule 1.6 imposed obligations of confidentiality on plaintiff's attorneys, and Rule 5.3 required plaintiff's attorneys to ensure that their employees, including April Mendoza, preserved that confidentiality. Rule 8.4(a) forbade *defendant's* attorneys from assisting or inducing any breach of these obligations imposed upon plaintiff's attorneys. However, none of these rules, including Rule 5.3, imposed upon Ms. Mendoza, a nonlawyer employee, the standards and prohibitions of Rule 1.9, which governs the duties of a "*lawyer*" with respect to the lawyer's "*former client.*" Nor was she subject to the same strictures under Rule 1.10 for determining imputation of conflicts for private lawyers (which does not recognize screening), any more than she was subject to the standards of Rule 1.11 which applies to government lawyers (and which allows screening). A legal assistant is not a lawyer (private or government), and the client is that of the lawyer, not the legal assistant. A legal assistant may have *independent* duties of confidentiality imposed by separate ethical standards governing legal assistants, such as the NALA Code of Ethics. But Rule 5.3's imposition of a duty on attorneys to ensure that a legal assistant preserves the confidences of that attorney's client does not wholesale extend all of the conflict of interest rules and standards governing attorneys to legal assistants.

Discussing Rule 5.3, the ANNOTATED MODEL RULES OF PROFESSIONAL CONDUCT (American Bar Association 4th ed.) at p. 440 explains this distinction between ensuring that a legal assistant complies with the *lawyer's* duty, and subjecting the legal assistant to all the same ethical rules governing the lawyer:

> In recognition of the fact that not every rule is applicable to *legal assistants,* the standard of Rule 5.3 is a different formulation from that of Rule 5.1, which requires the supervising lawyer to take reasonable efforts to ensure that the subordinate *lawyer* "conforms to the rules of Professional Conduct."

(Emphasis added.) *See also Smart Industries Corp. v. Superior Court of State of Arizona,* 876 P.2d 1176, 1181 (Ariz. App. 1994) (discussing lawyer's duty of supervision over legal assistants under Rule 5.3, approvingly quoting *Hazard & Hodes* statement that " 'nonlegal assistants or associates of a lawyer cannot be held to exactly the same professional standards as are lawyers.' ").

The trial court relied upon *Zimmerman's* citation of a Missouri federal district court decision to support its conclusion that "Rule 5.3 requires non-lawyers to be treated in the same manner as lawyers when considering confidentiality issues pursuant to Rule 1.10." Disqualification Order at 9. That case is *Williams v. Trans World Airlines, Inc.,* 588 F. Supp. 1037 (W.D. Mo. 1984)—which did *not* involve a moving nonlawyer employee. Rather, in *Williams* defendant's former personnel manager (Campbell Schanck), who had prepared defendant's defense against plaintiffs' employment discrimination claim, was *herself* discharged—and became a new *client* of plaintiff's lawyers. Plaintiff's lawyers proceeded to openly threaten (in writing) the defendant with use of the defendant's confidences which Ms. Schanck had readily disclosed to them. *Id.* at 1040. The opinion made clear that the *failure* to screen, and the open misuse by plaintiffs' lawyers of the confidences which its client Ms. Schanck had disclosed, was the reason for disqualification:

> [Plaintiffs'] firm has direct access to confidential information because of its representation of Campbell Schanck. No effort has been made to prevent [plaintiffs' attorneys] from having access to Campbell Schanck and any information she may furnish.... Furthermore, plaintiffs' counsel have reminded TWA that Campbell Schanck had been in a position to learn a great deal about [plaintiffs'] cases. Plaintiffs' counsel have threatened TWA with Campbell Schanck's testimony if TWA does not capitulate

to plaintiffs' settlement demand. The message was crystal clear; Campbell Schanck's knowledge about these cases is at plaintiffs' disposal and will be used if TWA defends itself.

Id. at 1045.

In fact, *Zimmerman* string cites six cases for the conclusion that "the rules applicable to lawyers are also applicable to nonlawyers employed in a private firm" (*Zimmerman, supra,* 19 P.3d at 790)—but all the jurisdictions cited except for Nevada *support* screening of nonlawyers. *Daines v. Alcatel, S.A.,* 194 F.R.D. 678 (E.D. Wash. 2000) (denying motion to disqualify because the paralegal had been screened); *Makita Corp. v. U.S.,* 819 F. Supp. 1099 (Ct. Intern. Trade 1993) (expressly recognizing propriety of screening a nonlawyer, approvingly citing the approach of ABA Informal Opinion 88-1526 and *Kapco, supra,* while stating that this constitutes "[a] difference" from the standards applied to lawyers, *id.* at 1105); *Smart Industries Corp. v. Superior Court of State of Arizona,* 876 P.2d 1176, 1184–85 (Ariz. App. 1994) (expressly approving use of screening for nonlawyers, as discussed above); *Koulisis v. Rivers,* 730 So.2d 289 (Fla. 4th DCA 1999) (while this case disallowed screening, a majority of the five Florida courts of appeal districts allow screening, as discussed above); *Ciaffone v. District Court,* 945 P.2d 950 (Nev. 1997) (Nevada is the only jurisdiction cited by *Zimmerman* that disallows screening of a nonlawyer); *Glover Bottled Gas Corp. v. Circle M. Beverage Barn, Inc.,* 129 A.D.2d 678, 514 N.Y.S.2d 440 (1987) (finding no steps were taken to ensure that a paralegal with confidential information complied with the attorney's ethical duties).[14]

Conclusion

The Court should expressly reach the issue raised by the trial court's holding that the Oklahoma Rules of Professional Conduct prohibit *per se* the use of an ethical screen to preserve client confidences held by a nonlawyer employee who changes employment. If that holding is left unaddressed, it will stand as a constant threat to qualified nonlawyer employees such as legal assistants whenever the employee even arguably possesses confidential information, since the employing lawyer will have no sure protection from a disqualification motion by use of the ethical screen which is now in regular use in almost all jurisdictions for such occasions.

All leading professional ethics commentators and virtually all ethics tribunals and courts to have addressed the matter hold that screening should be a permissible method to protect confidences held by nonlawyer employees who change employment, for the numerous public policy reasons discussed herein (and summarized at p. 6). The American Bar Association, which is the original author of the Model Rules of Professional Conduct adopted in Oklahoma, not only supports this view, but its House of Delegates has provisionally approved an amendment of the explanatory comments to Rule 1.10 to clarify that position.

This Court should adopt the prevailing view in the overwhelming majority of other jurisdictions, and expressly endorse the use of an ethical screen to protect confidences held by a moving nonlawyer employee.

Respectfully submitted,
HARVEY D. ELLIS, JR., OBA #2694
    - *Of the Firm* -

CROWE & DUNLEVY
1800 Mid-America Tower
20 North Broadway
Oklahoma City, Oklahoma 73102
(405) 235-7700
(405) 239-6651 FAX

Attorneys for Amicus Curiae National Association of
Legal Assistants, Inc., Oklahoma Association of
Paralegals, Central Oklahoma Association of Legal
Assistants, and Tulsa Association of Legal Assistants

Certificate of Service

This is to certify that a true and correct copy of the above and foregoing was mailed, postage prepaid, this _____ day of November, 2001, to:

JOHN E. DOWDELL
Christine Diane Little
NORMAN, WOHLGEMUTH, CHANDLER & DOWDELL
2900 Mid-Continent Tower
401 South Boston Avenue
Tulsa, OK 74103-4016

GRAYDON D. LUTHEY, JR.
MICHAEL T. KEESTER
R. MARK PETRICH
HALL, ESTILL, HARDWICK, GABLE, GOLDEN & NELSON, P.C.
320 South Boston Avenue, Suite 400
Tulsa, Oklahoma 74103

Endnotes

1. "Legal assistant" and "paralegal" are used herein synonymously.
2. Canon 7 of the NALA Code of Ethics imposes upon legal assistants a professional duty to protect both confidences and privileged communications of the clients of the attorneys employing such assistants.
3. *Formal and Informal Ethics Opinions,* pp. 566–67 (ABA 1985).
4. While the RESTATEMENT OF THE LAW GOVERNING LAWYERS was being drafted, University of Oklahoma College of Law Professor Judith Maute, in her article, *Symposium Issue on the Evolving Restatement of the Law Governing Lawyers,* 46 Okla. L. Rev. 1, 7 (1993) stated that "the *Restatement* is immensely important, even while tentative in form. It represents a new maturity in the law of lawyering.... As contrasted with ethics codes, which define permissible standards of conduct, the *Restatement* attempts to combine the diverse judicial, statutory, and code formulations into one comprehensive document."
5. Additional distinctions between lawyers and nonlawyers are elaborated upon in Kalish, *The Side-Switching Staff Person in a Law Firm: Uncomplimentary Assumptions and an Ethics Curtain,* 15 Hamline L. Rev. 35 (Fall 1991), *i.e.,* that because nonlawyer employees have no independent duty of loyalty to a firm's clients, the former client should have lesser reasonable expectations with respect to the employee's job mobility as long as confidences are protected. "No former client can reasonably believe that his side-switching paralegal has improperly turned against him." *Id.* at 59–60. Further, the side-switching staff person will have a concomitantly lesser financial incentive to reveal confidential information than would the side-switching lawyer, since the staff person's "salary will neither be dependent on the outcome of a particular matter nor be directly dependent on firm profit." *Id.* at 60. Finally, "[i]n contested matters a side-switching staff person is unlikely to generate confusion in the fact-finder's mind with respect to who is representing whom." *Id.* at 60.
6. Some of the opinions indicate that only nonlawyer employees may be screened, while others indicate that both nonlawyers and lawyers may be screened.
7. *Stewart v. Bee-Dee Neon & Signs, Inc.,* 751 So.2d 196, 207–208 (Fla. 1st DCA 2000).

8. The court held that these authorities properly balanced "the public's interest in the integrity of the judicial process, the parties' interest in the integrity of the particular proceeding, the client's right to chosen counsel and the financial burden on the client of replacing disqualified counsel, the nonlawyer employee's interest in open employment opportunities, the lawyers' interests in providing efficient and effective legal representation, and the court's concern that tactical abuse may underlie the motion for disqualification." *Id.*

9 Allowing screening: *Stewart v. Bee-Dee Neon & Signs, Inc.,* 751 So.2d 196, 207–208 (Fla. 1st DCA 2000); *City of Apopka v. All Corners, Inc.,* 701 So.2d 641, 644 (Fla. 5th DCA 1997); *Esquire Care, Inc. v. Maguire,* 532 So.2d 740, 741 (Fla. 2d DCA 1988). Disallowing screening: *First Miami Securities, Inc. v. Sylvia,* 780 So.2d 250 (Fla. 3rd DCA 2001); *Koulisis v. Rivers,* 730 So.2d 289 (Fla. 4th DCA 1999).

10. Moreover, New York endorses the RESTATEMENT'S position allowing screening under some circumstances even for lawyers. *Kassis v. Teacher's Ins. and Annuity Ass'n,* 717 N.E.2d 674, 677–78 (N.Y. 1999).

11. American Bar Association Report 401, *Amendments to Model Rules of Professional Conduct to the House of Delegates* (2001 Annual Meeting), Model Rule 1.10, Reporter's Explanation of Changes, pp. 101–102 (relevant excerpts attached, Tab "C"). ABA's proposed explanatory comment to the rule which Oklahoma adopted from ABA's Model Rules is a proper subject of judicial notice. *Cf., Clark v. Virginia Board of Bar Examiners,* 880 F. Supp. 430, 440–441 (E.D. Va. 1995) (considering proposal of ABA House of Delegates in review of public policy issues relating to Americans with Disabilities Act).

12. The comment will not be finally adopted until the House of Delegates acts to adopt the revised Model Rules, and is subject to change before that time.

13. Report of Select Committee of American Bar Association House of Delegates (September 14, 2001) at p. 15 (Tab "D") (approving proposal as amended); American Bar Association House of Delegates *Daily Journal* for 2001 Annual Meeting, p. 12 (showing amendment) (Tab "E").

14. New York allows the presumption of shared confidences to be rebutted even without screening. *Riddell Sports,* discussed *supra.*

Appendix 3

Syllabus

NOTE: Where it is feasible, a syllabus (headnote) will be released, as is being done in connection with this case, at the time the opinion is issued. The syllabus constitutes no part of the opinion of the Court but has been prepared by the Reporter of Decisions for the convenience of the reader. See *United States* v. *Detroit Timber & Lumber Co.,* 200 U. S. 321, 337.

SUPREME COURT OF THE UNITED STATES

Syllabus

RICHLIN SECURITY SERVICE CO. *v.* CHERTOFF, SECRETARY OF HOMELAND SECURITY

CERTIORARI TO THE UNITED STATES COURT OF APPEALS FOR THE FEDERAL CIRCUIT

No. 06–1717.   Argued March 19, 2008—Decided June 2, 2008

After prevailing against the Government on a claim originating in the Department of Transportation's Board of Contract Appeals, petitioner (Richlin) filed an application with the Board for reimbursement of attorney's fees, expenses, and costs, pursuant to the Equal Access to Justice Act (EAJA). The Board concluded, *inter alia,* that Richlin was not entitled to recover paralegal fees at the rates at which it was billed by its law firm, holding that EAJA limited such recovery to the attorney's cost, which was lower than the billed rate. In affirming, the Federal Circuit concluded that the term "fees," for which EAJA authorizes recovery at "prevailing market rates," embraces only the fees of attorneys, experts, and agents.

Held: A prevailing party that satisfies EAJA's other requirements may recover its paralegal fees from the Government at prevailing market rates. Pp. 4–18.

   (a) EAJA permits a prevailing party to recover "fees and other expenses incurred by that party in connection with" administrative proceedings, 5 U. S. C. §504(a)(1), including "the reasonable expenses of expert witnesses, the reasonable cost of any study, analysis, engineering report, test, or project . . . , and reasonable attorney or agent fees," and bases the amount of such fees on "prevailing market rates," §504(b)(1)(A). Because Richlin "incurred" "fees" for paralegal services in connection with its action before the Board, a straightforward reading of the statute demonstrates that Richlin was entitled to recover fees for the paralegal services it purchased at the market rate for such services. The Government's contrary reading—that expenditures for paralegal services are "other expenses" recoverable only at "reasonable cost"—is unpersuasive. Section 504(b)(1)(A) does not clearly distinguish between the rates at which "fees" and "other expenses" are reimbursed. Even if the statutory text supported the Government's dichotomy, it would hardly follow that amounts billed for paralegal services should be classified as "expenses" rather than as "fees." Paralegals are surely more analogous to attorneys, experts, and agents than to studies, analyses, reports, tests, and projects. Even if the Court agreed that EAJA limited paralegal fees to "reasonable cost," it would not follow that the cost should be measured from the perspective of the party's attorney rather than the client. By providing that an agency shall award a prevailing party "fees and other expenses ... *incurred by that party*" (emphasis added), §504(a)(1) leaves no doubt that Congress intended the "reasonable cost" of §504(b)(1)(A)'s items to be calculated from the litigant's perspective. It is unlikely that Congress, without even mentioning paralegals, intended to make an exception of them by calculating their cost from their employer's perspective. It seems more plausible that Congress intended all "fees and other expenses" to be recoverable at the litigant's "reasonable cost," subject to the proviso that "reasonable cost" would be deemed to be "prevailing market rates" when such rates could be determined. Pp. 4–8.

(b) To the extent that some ambiguity subsists in the statutory text, this Court need look no further to resolve it than *Missouri* v. *Jenkins*, 491 U. S. 274, where the Court addressed a similar question with respect to the Civil Rights Attorney's Fees Awards Act of 1976— which provides that a court "may allow the prevailing party ... a reasonable attorney's fee as part of the costs," 42 U. S. C. §1988— finding it "self-evident" that "attorney's fee" embraced the fees of paralegals as well as attorneys, 491 U. S., at 285. EAJA, like §1988, entitles certain parties to recover "reasonable attorney ... fees," §504(b)(1)(A), and makes no mention of the paralegals, "secretaries, messengers, librarians, janitors, and others whose labor contributes to the work product for which an attorney bills her client," 491 U. S., at 285. Thus, EAJA, like §1988, must be interpreted as using the term "attorney ... fees" to reach fees for paralegal services as well as compensation for the attorney's personal labor, making "self-evident" that Congress intended that term to embrace paralegal fees. Since §504 generally provides for recovery of attorney's fees at "prevailing market rates," it follows that paralegal fees must also be recoverable at those rates. The Government's contention that *Jenkins* found paralegal fees recoverable as "attorney's fee[s]" because §1988 authorized no other recoverable "expenses" finds no support in *Jenkins* itself, which turned not on extratextual policy goals, but on the "self-evident" proposition that "attorney's fee[s]" had historically included paralegal fees. Indeed, this Court rejected the Government's inter-

Syllabus

pretation of *Jenkins* in *West Virginia Univ. Hospitals, Inc.* v. *Casey*, 499 U. S. 83, concluding that a petitioner seeking expert witness fees under §1988 could not rely on *Jenkins* for the proposition that §1988's "broad remedial purposes" allowed recovery of fees not expressly authorized by statute. Pp. 8–11.

   (c) Even assuming that some residual ambiguity in the statutory text justified resorting to extratextual authorities, the legislative history cited by the Government does not address the question presented and policy considerations actually counsel in favor of Richlin's interpretation. Pp. 11–18.

472 F. 3d 1370, reversed and remanded.

ALITO, J., delivered the opinion of the Court, in which ROBERTS, C. J., and STEVENS, KENNEDY, SOUTER, GINSBURG, and BREYER, JJ., joined, in which SCALIA, J., joined except as to Part III–A, and in which THOMAS, J., joined except as to Parts II–B and III.

Cite as: 553 U. S. ____ (2008)

1

Opinion of the Court

NOTICE: This opinion is subject to formal revision before publication in the preliminary print of the United States Reports. Readers are requested to notify the Reporter of Decisions, Supreme Court of the United States, Washington, D. C. 20543, of any typographical or other formal errors, in order that corrections may be made before the preliminary print goes to press.

SUPREME COURT OF THE UNITED STATES

No. 06–1717

RICHLIN SECURITY SERVICE COMPANY, PETITIONER v. MICHAEL CHERTOFF, SECRETARY OF HOMELAND SECURITY

ON WRIT OF CERTIORARI TO THE UNITED STATES COURT OF APPEALS FOR THE FEDERAL CIRCUIT

[June 2, 2008]

JUSTICE ALITO delivered the opinion of the Court.*

The question presented in this case is whether the Equal Access to Justice Act (EAJA), 5 U. S. C. §504(a)(l) (2006 ed.) and 28 U. S. C. §2412(d)(1)(A) (2000 ed.), allows a prevailing party in a case brought by or against the Government to recover fees for paralegal services at the market rate for such services or only at their cost to the party's attorney. The United States Court of Appeals for the Federal Circuit limited recovery to the attorney's cost. 472 F. 3d 1370 (2006). We reverse.

I

Petitioner Richlin Security Service Co. (Richlin) is a small California proprietorship. In the early 1990's, it was engaged by the former Immigration and Naturalization Service (INS) to provide guard services for detainees at Los Angeles International Airport. Through mutual mistake, the parties' two contracts misclassified Richlin's

---

*JUSTICE SCALIA joins this opinion except as to Part III–A, and JUSTICE THOMAS joins this opinion except as to Parts II–B and III.

Opinion of the Court

employees under the Service Contract Act of 1965, 41 U. S. C. §351 *et seq.* The Department of Labor discovered the misclassification and ordered Richlin to pay its employees back wages. Richlin responded by filing a claim against the Government with the Department of Transportation's Board of Contract Appeals (Board). The claim sought reformation of the two contracts in order to force the Government to make additional payments necessary to cover Richlin's liability under the Service Contract Act. Richlin prevailed after extensive litigation, and the Board entered an award in its favor.

Richlin then filed an application with the Board for reimbursement of its attorney's fees, expenses, and costs pursuant to EAJA. Under EAJA, "[a]n agency that conducts an adversary adjudication shall award, to a prevailing party other than the United States, fees and other expenses incurred by that party in connection with that proceeding, unless the adjudicative officer of the agency finds that the position of the agency was substantially justified or that special circumstances make an award unjust." 5 U. S. C. §504(a)(1). In addition to its other fees and expenses, Richlin sought $45,141.10 for 523.8 hours of paralegal work on its contract claim and $6,760 for 68.2 hours of paralegal work on the EAJA application itself.

The Board granted Richlin's application in part. *Richlin Security Service Co.* v. *Department of Justice*, Nos. WRO–06–90, WRO–03–91, 2005 WL 1635099 (June 30, 2005), App. to Pet. for Cert. 25a. It found that Richlin met §504(b)(1)(B)'s eligibility requirements, see *id.,* at 30a, and that the Government's position had not been "substantially justified" within the meaning of §504(a)(1), *id.,* at 32a. It concluded, however, that Richlin was not entitled to recover its paralegal fees at the rates (ranging from $50 per hour to $95 per hour) at which Richlin was billed by its law firm.[1] See *id.*, at 39a. The Board held that EAJA limited recovery of paralegal fees to "the cost to the firm rather than . . . the billed rate." *Ibid.* Richlin had not submitted any evidence regarding the cost of the paralegal services to its law firm, see *ibid.*, but the Board found that "$35 per hour is a reasonable cost to the firm[,] having taken judicial notice of paralegal salaries in the Washington D. C. area as reflected on the internet." *Id.*, at 42a–43a.

A divided panel of the Federal Circuit affirmed. 472 F. 3d 1370. The court construed the term "fees," for which EAJA authorizes recovery at "prevailing market rates," §504(b)(1)(A), as embracing only the fees of attorneys, experts, and agents.[2] See *id.*, at 1374. The court declined to follow the contrary decision of the Eleventh Circuit in *Jean* v. *Nelson*, 863 F. 2d 759 (1988), aff'd *sub nom. Commissioner* v. *Jean*, 496 U. S. 154 (1990). It also distinguished this Court's decisions in *Missouri* v. *Jenkins*, 491 U. S. 274 (1989), and *West Virginia Univ. Hospitals, Inc.* v. *Casey*, 499 U. S. 83 (1991), reasoning that those cases involved a different fee-shifting statute with different "'goals and objectives.'" 472 F. 3d, at 1375–1377, 1379 (discussing the Civil Rights Attorney's Fees Awards Act of 1976, 42 U. S. C. §1988). The court instead found support for its interpretation in EAJA's legislative history, see 472 F. 3d, at 1381 (citing S. Rep. No. 98–586 (1984) (hereinafter S. Rep.)), and in considerations of public policy, see 472 F. 3d, at 1380–1381.

---

[1] Richlin was actually billed for paralegal services at rates as high as $135 per hour, but it amended its application to cap the fees at $95 per hour. See App. to Pet. for Cert. 39a; Brief for Petitioner 9; Brief for Respondent 4, n. 2.

[2] Some agencies allow nonattorney representatives, known as "agents," to assist parties with the presentation of their cases. See n. 10, *infra.* Richlin has never claimed that a paralegal may qualify as an "agent" within the meaning of §504(b)(1)(A).

Opinion of the Court

Judge Plager dissented. He believed that the authorities distinguished by the majority (particularly this Court's decisions in *Jenkins* and *Casey*) were indistinguishable. He also identified "sound policy reasons for . . . adopting the Supreme Court's take of the case, even if we thought we had a choice." 472 F. 3d, at 1383.

Richlin petitioned for rehearing, pointing out that the approach taken by the Eleventh Circuit in *Jean* had been followed by several other Circuits. See 482 F. 3d 1358, 1359 (CAFed. 2007) (citing *Role Models Am., Inc.* v. *Brownlee*, 353 F. 3d 962, 974 (CADC 2004); *Hyatt* v. *Barnhart*, 315 F. 3d 239, 255 (CA4 2002); and *Miller* v. *Alamo*, 983 F. 2d 856, 862 (CA8 1993)). The panel denied rehearing over Judge Plager's dissent, and the full court denied rehearing en banc. See App. to Pet. for Cert. 57a.

We granted certiorari. 551 U. S. ___ (2007).

II
A

EAJA permits an eligible prevailing party to recover "fees and other expenses incurred by that party in connection with" a proceeding before an administrative agency. 5 U. S. C. §504(a)(1). EAJA defines "fees and other expenses" as follows:

> "'[F]ees and other expenses' includes the reasonable expenses of expert witnesses, the reasonable cost of any study, analysis, engineering report, test, or project which is found by the agency to be necessary for the preparation of the party's case, and reasonable attorney or agent fees (The amount of fees awarded under this section shall be based upon prevailing market rates for the kind and quality of the services furnished, except that (i) no expert witness shall be compensated at a rate in excess of the highest rate of compensation for expert witnesses paid by the agency involved, and (ii) attorney or agent fees shall not be

awarded in excess of $125 per hour unless the agency
determines by regulation that an increase in the cost
of living or a special factor, such as the limited availability of qualified attorneys or agents for the proceedings involved, justifies a higher fee.)" §504(b)(1)(A).[3]

In this case, Richlin "incurred" "fees" for paralegal services
in connection with its contract action before the Board.
Since §504(b)(1)(A) awards fees at "prevailing market
rates," a straightforward reading of the statute leads to
the conclusion that Richlin was entitled to recover fees for
the paralegal services it purchased at the market rate for
such services.

The Government resists this reading by distinguishing
"fees" from "other expenses." The Government concedes
that "fees" are reimbursable at "prevailing market rates,"
but it insists that "other expenses" (including expenses for
"any study, analysis, engineering report, test, or project")
are reimbursable only at their "reasonable cost." And in
the Government's view, outlays for paralegal services are
better characterized as "other expenses" than as "fees."
The Government observes that the second sentence of
§504(b)(1)(A), which explains how to calculate awards for
"fees," refers to attorneys, agents, and expert witnesses,
without mentioning paralegals. From this omission, the
Government infers that Congress intended to treat expenditures for paralegal services not as "fees" but as "other
expenses," recoverable at "reasonable cost."

We find the Government's fractured interpretation of

---

[3] Virtually identical fee-shifting provisions apply to actions by or
against the Government in federal court. See 28 U. S. C. §§2412(a)(1),
(d)(2)(A). The question presented addresses both §§504 and 2412, but
the Federal Circuit's decision resolved only petitioner's §504 application, and the Government avers (without challenge from Richlin) that
§2412 "is not at issue in this case." Brief for Respondent 2, n. 1. We
assume without deciding that the reasoning of our opinion would
extend equally to §§504 and 2412. We confine our discussion to §504.

the statute unpersuasive. Contrary to the Government's contention, §504(b)(1)(A) does not clearly distinguish between the rates at which "fees" and "other expenses" are reimbursed. Although the statute does refer to the "reasonable cost" of "any study, analysis, engineering report, test, or project," Congress may reasonably have believed that market rates would not exist for work product of that kind. At one point, Congress even appears to use the terms "expenses" and "fees" interchangeably: The first clause of §504(b)(1)(A) refers to the "reasonable expenses of expert witnesses," while the parenthetical characterizes expert compensation as "fees." There is no indication that Congress, in using the term "expenses" in one place and "fees" in the other, was referring to two different components of expert remuneration.

Even if the dichotomy that the Government draws between "fees" and "other expenses" were supported by the statutory text, it would hardly follow that amounts billed for paralegal services should be classified as "expenses" rather than as "fees." The Government concludes that the omission of paralegal fees from §504(b)(1)(A)'s parenthetical (which generally authorizes reimbursement at "prevailing market rates") implies that the recovery of paralegal fees is limited to cost. But one could just as easily conclude that the omission of paralegal fees from the litany of "any study, analysis, engineering report, test, or project" (all of which are recoverable at "reasonable cost") implies that paralegal fees are recoverable at market rates. Surely paralegals are more analogous to attorneys, experts, and agents than to studies, analyses, reports, tests, and projects. Even the Government's brief, which incants the term "paralegal expenses," *e.g.,* Brief for Respondent 4, 5, 6, 7, 8, 9, 10, 11, 12, slips up once and refers to them as "fees," see *id.,* at 35 ("As the court of appeals explained, treating paralegal fees as attorney fees could 'distort the normal allocation of work and result in a less

efficient performance of legal services' under the EAJA
. . .").

But even if we agreed that EAJA limited a prevailing
party's recovery for paralegal fees to "reasonable cost," it
certainly would not follow that the cost should be measured from the perspective of the party's attorney.[4] To the
contrary, it would be anomalous to measure cost from the
perspective of the attorney rather than the client. We do
not understand the Government to contend, for example,
that the "reasonable cost" of an "engineering report" or
"analysis" should be calculated from the perspective of the
firm that employs the engineer or analyst. Such an interpretation would be tough to square with the statutory
language. Section 504(a)(1) provides that an agency shall
award to a prevailing party "fees and other expenses
incurred by that party." See also §504(b)(1)(A) (emphasis
added). That language leaves no doubt that Congress
intended the "reasonable cost" of the specified items in
§504(b)(1)(A) to be calculated from the perspective of the
litigant. That being the case, we find it hard to believe
that Congress, without even mentioning paralegals, intended to make an exception of them by calculating their
cost from the perspective of their employer rather than the
litigant. It seems more plausible that Congress intended
all "fees and other expenses" to be recoverable at the

---

[4] The Government contends that the question presented does not
fairly include the question whether the cost of paralegal services should
be calculated from the perspective of the litigant rather than the
litigant's attorney. We disagree. The question presented in Richlin's
petition for certiorari was whether "a prevailing party [may] be
awarded attorney fees for paralegal services at the market rate for such
services, . . . [or at] cost only." Pet. for Cert. i. A decision limiting
reimbursement to "cost only" would simply beg the question of how that
cost should be measured. Since the question presented cannot genu-
inely be answered without addressing the subsidiary question, we have
no difficulty concluding that the latter question is "fairly included"
within the former. See this Court's Rule 14.1(a).

Opinion of the Court

litigant's "reasonable cost," subject to the proviso that "reasonable cost" would be deemed to be "prevailing market rates" when such rates could be determined.[5]

B

To the extent that some ambiguity subsists in the statutory text, we need not look far to resolve it, for we have already addressed a similar question with respect to another fee-shifting statute. In *Missouri* v. *Jenkins*, 491 U. S. 274 (1989), we considered whether litigants could recover paralegal fees under the Civil Rights Attorney's Fees Awards Act of 1976, 42 U. S. C. §1988. Section 1988 provides that "the court, in its discretion, may allow the prevailing party, other than the United States, a reasonable attorney's fee as part of the costs." We concluded that the term "attorney's fee" in §1988 "cannot have been meant to compensate only work performed personally by members of the bar." 491 U. S., at 285. Although separate billing for paralegals had become "increasingly widespread," *id.,* at 286 (internal quotation marks omitted), attorney's fees had traditionally subsumed both the attorney's personal labor and the labor of paralegals and other individuals who contributed to the attorney's work product, see *id.,* at 285. We were so confident that Congress

---

[5] It is worth recalling that the Board calculated Richlin's award based on an Internet survey of paralegal salaries in the District of Columbia. Presumably the salaries the Board identified represented the market rate for paralegal compensation. The limited award that the Government wants affirmed was thus based, ironically enough, on the "prevailing market rates" for paralegal services. The fact that paralegal salaries respond to market forces no less than the fees that clients pay suggests to us that this case has more to do with determining whose expenditures get reimbursed (the attorney's or the client's) than with determining how expenditures are calculated (at cost or at market). Since EAJA authorizes the recovery of fees and other expenses "incurred by [the] party," §504(a)(1), rather than the party's attorney, the answer to the former question is plain.

had given the term "attorney's fees" this traditional gloss that we declared it "self-evident" that the term embraced the fees of paralegals as well as attorneys. *Ibid.*

We think *Jenkins* substantially answers the question before us. EAJA, like §1988, entitles certain parties to recover "reasonable attorney ... fees." 5 U. S. C. §504(b)(1)(A). EAJA, like §1988, makes no mention of the paralegals, "secretaries, messengers, librarians, janitors, and others whose labor contributes to the work product for which an attorney bills her client." *Jenkins, supra,* at 285. And we think EAJA, like §1988, must be interpreted as using the term "attorney ... fees" to reach fees for paralegal services as well as compensation for the attorney's personal labor. The Government does not contend that the meaning of the term "attorney's fees" changed so much between §1988's enactment in 1976 and EAJA's enactment in 1980 that the term's meaning in one statute must be different from its meaning in the other. Under the reasoning of *Jenkins,* we take it as "self-evident" that when Congress instructed agencies to award "attorney ... fees" to certain parties prevailing against the Government, that term was intended to embrace paralegal fees as well. Since §504 generally provides for recovery of attorney's fees at "prevailing market rates," it follows that fees for paralegal services must be recoverable at prevailing market rates as well.

The Government contends that our decision in *Jenkins* was driven by considerations arising from the different context in which the term "attorney's fee" was used in §1988. At the time *Jenkins* was decided, §1988 provided for the recovery of attorney's fees without reference to any other recoverable "expenses." The Government insists that *Jenkins* found paralegal fees recoverable under the guise of "attorney's fee[s]" because otherwise paralegal fees would not be recoverable at all. Since EAJA expressly permits recovery (albeit at "cost") for items other than attorney, agent, and expert witness fees, the Government sees no reason to give EAJA the broad construction that *Jenkins* gave §1988.

The Government's rationale for distinguishing *Jenkins* finds no support either in our opinion there or in our subsequent decisions. Our opinion in *Jenkins* expressed no apprehension at the possibility that a contrary decision would leave the claimant emptyhanded. This omission is unsurprising, since our decision in *Jenkins* did not rest on the conviction that recovery at market rates was better than nothing. Our decision rested instead on the proposition—a proposition we took as "self-evident"—that the term "attorney's fee" had historically included fees for paralegal services.

Indeed, the Government's interpretation of *Jenkins* was rejected by this Court just two years after *Jenkins* was handed down. In *West Virginia Univ. Hospitals, Inc.* v. *Casey*, 499 U. S. 83, the petitioner sought to recover expert witness fees from the Commonwealth of Pennsylvania pursuant to §1988. The petitioner looked to *Jenkins* for the proposition that the "broad remedial purposes" of §1988 allowed the recovery of fees not expressly authorized by statute. The Court rejected that interpretation of *Jenkins:*

> "The issue [in *Jenkins*] was not, as [petitioner] contends, whether we would permit our perception of the 'policy' of the statute to overcome its 'plain language.' It was not remotely plain in *Jenkins* that the phrase 'attorney's fee' did not include charges for law clerk and paralegal services. Such services, like the services of 'secretaries, messengers, librarians, janitors, and others whose labor contributes to the work product,' had traditionally been included in calculation of the lawyers' hourly rates. Only recently had there arisen 'the increasingly widespread custom of sepa-

Opinion of the Court

rately billing for [such] services.' By contrast, there has never been, to our knowledge, a practice of including the cost of expert services within attorneys' hourly rates. There was also no record in *Jenkins*—as there is a lengthy record here—of statutory usage that recognizes a distinction between the charges at issue and attorney's fees." *Casey, supra,* at 99 (quoting 491 U. S., at 285–286) (some internal quotation marks and citations omitted).[6]

Our analysis of *Jenkins* in *Casey* refutes the Government's claim that *Jenkins* had to stretch the law to fit hard facts. As *Casey* shows, our decision in *Jenkins* turned not on extratextual policy goals but on the traditional meaning of the term "attorney's fees."

III

The Government parries this textual and doctrinal analysis with legislative history and public policy. We are not persuaded by either. The legislative history cited by the Government does not address the question presented, and policy considerations actually counsel in favor of Richlin's interpretation.

A

The Government contends first that a 1984 Senate Report accompanying the bill that reenacted EAJA[7] unequivocally expressed congressional intent that paralegal

---

[6] Following our decision in *Casey,* Congress amended §1988 to allow parties to recover "expert fees as part of the attorney's fees." Civil Rights Act of 1991, §113(a), 105 Stat. 1079 (codified at 42 U. S. C. §1988(c)).

[7] The version of EAJA first enacted in 1980 had a sunset provision effective October 1, 1984. See §§203(c), 204(c), 94 Stat. 2327, 2329. Congress revived EAJA without the sunset provision (but with certain other amendments) in 1985. See Act of Aug. 5, 1985, §§1–2, 6, 99 Stat. 183–186; see also n. 8, *infra;* see generally *Scarborough* v. *Principi,* 541 U. S. 401, 406–407 (2004) (summarizing EAJA's legislative history).

Opinion of the Court

fees should be recovered only *"'at cost.'"* Brief for Respondent 29 (quoting S. Rep., at 15; emphasis in original). It next contends that the Report tacitly endorsed the same result by approving model rules of the Administrative Conference of the United States and a pre-EAJA Sixth Circuit decision, both of which had adopted schemes of reimbursement at attorney cost. See Brief for Respondent 29. We are not persuaded. In our view, the legislative history does not even address the question presented, much less answer it in the Government's favor.[8]

The Senate Report accompanying the 1984 bill remarked that "[e]xamples of the type of expenses that should ordinarily be compensable [under EAJA] include paralegal time (billed at cost)." S. Rep., at 15. The Government concludes from this stray remark that Congress intended to limit recovery of paralegal fees to attorney cost. But as we observed earlier, the word "cost" could just as easily (and more sensibly) refer to the client's cost rather than the attorney's cost. Under the former interpretation, the Senate Report simply indicates that a prevailing party who satisfies EAJA's other requirements should generally be able to "bil[l]" the Government for any reasonable amount the party paid for paralegal services.

---

[8] Richlin makes a threshold challenge to the legitimacy of the 1984 Senate Report as legislative history, observing that the bill it accompanied was vetoed by the President before being enacted by a subsequent Congress. See Brief for Petitioner 27 ("To the extent that legislative history serves as legitimate evidence of congressional intent, it does so only because it is presumed to have been ratified by Congress and the President when the relevant legislation was enacted" (citing Siegel, The Use of Legislative History in a System of Separated Powers, 53 Vand. L. Rev. 1457, 1522 (2000); and *Sullivan* v. *Finkelstein*, 496 U. S. 617, 631–632 (1990) (SCALIA, J., concurring in part))). But see *Melkonyan* v. *Sullivan*, 501 U. S. 89, 96 (1991) (relying on the same Report to interpret EAJA's 1985 amendments). Because the legislative history is a wash in this case, we need not decide precisely how much weight it deserves in our analysis.

Since the litigant's out-of-pocket cost for paralegal services would normally be equal to the "prevailing market rat[e]" for such services, 5 U. S. C. §504(b)(1)(A), the Senate Report could easily support Richlin's interpretation.

Moreover, even if the Government's interpretation of the word "cost" is correct, that interpretation would not be inconsistent with our decision today. "Nothing in [EAJA] requires that the work of paralegals invariably be billed separately. If it is the practice in the relevant market not to do so, or to bill the work of paralegals only at cost, that is all that [EAJA] requires." *Jenkins, supra*, at 288 (construing 42 U. S. C. §1988). We thus recognize the possibility, as we did in *Jenkins*, that the attorney's cost for paralegal services will supply the relevant metric for calculating the client's recovery. Whether that metric is appropriate depends on market practice. The Senate Report, even under the Government's contestable interpretation, is not inconsistent with that conclusion. On the contrary, the Report implies that courts should look to market practice in setting EAJA awards. See S. Rep., at 15 ("The Act should not be read . . . to permit reimbursement for items *ordinarily* included in office overhead, nor for any other expenses not reasonable in amount, necessary for the conduct of the litigation, *and customarily chargeable to clients*" (emphasis added)). Beyond that vague guidance, the Report does not address the critical question in this case: whether EAJA limits recovery of paralegal fees to attorney cost *regardless of market practice*. As such, the Report does not persuade us of the soundness of the Government's interpretation of the statute.

The Government's reliance on the Sixth Circuit's decision in *Northcross* v. *Board of Ed. of the Memphis City Schools*, 611 F. 2d 624 (1979), founders for the same reason. The Government contends that *Northcross* approved of reimbursement at attorney cost under 42 U. S. C. §1988 and that the 1984 Senate Report, by endorsing *Northcross,* tacitly approved of the same result for EAJA. See Brief for Respondent 30 (citing *Northcross, supra,* at 639). The problem again is that *Northcross* did not decide whether a litigant's recovery for paralegal services would be limited to his attorney's cost even in a market where litigants were customarily billed at "prevailing market rates." Although the Sixth Circuit seems to have been aware that paralegal services could be billed to clients at market rates, some language in its opinion suggests that the court assumed that attorneys billed their clients only for the out-of-pocket cost of paralegal services.[9] Since *Northcross* does not clearly address the question presented, its endorsement in the Senate Report means little.

Finally, the model rules cited in the Senate Report may actually support Richlin's position. The implementing release for the rules describes the Administrative Conference's approach to paralegal costs as follows:

> "Commenters also took varying positions on whether paralegal costs should be chargeable as expenses. We do not believe the rules should discourage the use of paralegals, which can be an important cost-saving measure. On the other hand, lawyers' practices with respect to charging for paralegal time, as with respect to other expenses such as duplicating, telephone

---

[9] Compare *Northcross,* 611 F. 2d, at 638 ("[A] scale of fees as is used by most law firms is appropriate to use in making fee awards pursuant to Section 1988. The use of broad categories, differentiating between paralegal services, in-office services by experienced attorneys and trial service, would result in a fair and equitable fee") with *id.,* at 639 ("The authority granted in section 1988 to award a reasonable attorney's fee included the authority to award those reasonable out-of-pocket expenses incurred by the attorney which are normally charged to a fee-paying client, in the course of providing legal services. Reasonable photocopying, paralegal expenses, and travel and telephone costs are thus recoverable pursuant to the statutory authority of §1988" (internal quotation marks omitted)).

Opinion of the Court

charges and the like, vary according to locality, field of practice, and individual custom. We have decided not to designate specific items as compensable expenses. Instead, we will adopt a suggestion of the Treasury Department and revise the model rule to provide that expenses may be charged as a separate item if they are ordinarily so charged to the attorney's clients." Administrative Conference of the U. S., Equal Access to Justice Act: Agency Implementation, 46 Fed. Reg. 32905 (1981).

To the extent that this passage addresses the question presented at all, it seems to take the same approach that the Court took in *Jenkins* and that we adopt today: it allows the recovery of paralegal fees according to "the practice in the relevant market." 491 U. S., at 288. But we think the fairest interpretation of the implementing release is that it does not address how awards for paralegal fees should be calculated. Instead, it addresses the anterior question whether courts may award paralegal fees under EAJA at all. See, *e.g.,* 46 Fed. Reg. 32905 (responding to comments urging that the model rules "identify particular expenses of attorneys and witnesses that are compensable"). Like the other legislative authorities cited by the Government, the model rules fail to persuade us of the soundness of the Government's interpretation because they fail to clearly address the question presented.

B

We find the Government's policy rationale for recovery at attorney cost likewise unpersuasive. The Government argues that market-based recovery would distort litigant incentives because EAJA would cap paralegal and attorney's fees at the same rate. See 5 U. S. C. §504(b)(1)(A) ("[A]ttorney or agent fees shall not be awarded in excess of $125 per hour unless the agency determines by regulation

Opinion of the Court

that an increase in the cost of living or a special factor, such as the limited availability of qualified attorneys or agents for the proceedings involved, justifies a higher fee"). The Government observes that paralegal rates are lower than rates for attorneys operating in the same market. If EAJA reimbursed both attorney time and paralegal time at market rates, then the cap would clip more off the top of the attorney's rates than the paralegal's rates. According to the Government, a market-based scheme would encourage litigants to shift an inefficient amount of attorney work to paralegals, since paralegal fees could be recovered at a greater percentage of their full market value.

The problem with this argument, as Richlin points out, is that it proves too much. The same reasoning would imply that agent fees should not be recoverable at market rates.[10] If market-based recovery of paralegal time resulted in excessive reliance on paralegals, then market-based recovery of agent time should result in excessive reliance on agents. The same reasoning would also imply that fees for junior attorneys (who generally bill at lower rates than senior attorneys) should not be recoverable at market rates. Cf. *Jenkins, supra,* at 287 ("If the fees are consistent with market rates and practices, the 'windfall' argument has no more force with regard to paralegals than it does for associates"). Yet despite the possibility that market-based recovery of attorney and agent fees would distort litigant incentives, §504 unambiguously

---

[10]"'An "agent fee" may be awarded for the services of a non-attorney where an agency permits such agents to represent parties who come before it.'" Brief for Respondent at 11, n. 4 (quoting H. R. Rep. No. 96–1418, p. 14 (1980)); see also n. 2, *supra.* Since federal courts generally do not permit nonattorneys to practice before them, the portion of EAJA governing awards for parties to federal litigation makes no provision for agent fees. Compare 28 U. S. C. §2412(d)(2)(A) with 5 U. S. C. §504(b)(1)(A).

authorizes awards of "reasonable attorney or agent fees
. . . [at] prevailing market rates." 5 U. S. C. §504(b)(1)(A).
The Government offers no persuasive reason why Congress would have treated paralegal fees any differently.
The Government's policy rationale thus founders on the
text of the statute, which shows that Congress was un-
troubled by the very distortion the Government seeks to
prevent.

We also question the practical feasibility of the Government's interpretation of the statute. The Board in this
case relied on the Internet for data on paralegal salaries in
the District of Columbia, but the Government fails to
explain why a law firm's cost should be limited to salary.
The benefits and perks with which a firm compensates its
staff come out of the bottom line no less than salary. The
Government has offered no solution to this accounting
problem, and we do not believe that solutions are readily
to be found. Market practice provides by far the more
transparent basis for calculating a prevailing party's
recovery under EAJA. It strains credulity that Congress
would have abandoned this predictable, workable framework for the uncertain and complex accounting requirements that a cost-based rule would inflict on litigants,
their attorneys, administrative agencies, and the courts.

IV

Confronted with the flaws in its interpretation of the
statute, the Government seeks shelter in a canon of construction. According to the Government, any right to
recover paralegal fees under EAJA must be read narrowly
in light of the statutory canon requiring strict construction
of waivers of sovereign immunity. We disagree.

The sovereign immunity canon is just that—a canon of
construction. It is a tool for interpreting the law, and we
have never held that it displaces the other traditional tools
of statutory construction. Indeed, the cases on which the

Opinion of the Court

Government relies all used other tools of construction in tandem with the sovereign immunity canon. See *Ardestani* v. *INS*, 502 U. S. 129, 137 (1991) (relying on the canon as "reinforce[ment]" for the independent "conclusion that any ambiguities in the legislative history are insufficient to undercut the ordinary understanding of the statutory language"); *Ruckelshaus* v. *Sierra Club*, 463 U. S. 680, 682, 685–686 (1983) (relying on the canon in tandem with "historic principles of fee-shifting in this and other countries" to define the scope of a fee-shifting statute); *Department of Energy* v. *Ohio*, 503 U. S. 607, 626–627 (1992) (resorting to the canon only after a close reading of the statutory provision had left the Court "with an unanswered question and an unresolved tension between closely related statutory provisions"); see also *Smith* v. *United States*, 507 U. S. 197, 201–203 (1993) (invoking the sovereign immunity canon only after observing that the claimant's argument was "undermine[d]" by the "common-sense meaning" of the statutory language). In this case, traditional tools of statutory construction and considerations of stare decisis compel the conclusion that paralegal fees are recoverable as attorney's fees at their "prevailing market rates." 5 U. S. C. §504(b)(1)(A). There is no need for us to resort to the sovereign immunity canon because there is no ambiguity left for us to construe.

V

For these reasons, we hold that a prevailing party that satisfies EAJA's other requirements may recover its paralegal fees from the Government at prevailing market rates. The Board's contrary decision was error, and the Federal Circuit erred in affirming that decision. The judgment of the Federal Circuit is reversed, and this case is remanded for further proceedings consistent with this opinion.

It is so ordered.

No. 06-1717

IN THE

Supreme Court of the United States

Richlin Security Service Co.,

Petitioner,

v.

Michael Chertoff,
Secretary of Homeland Security,

Respondent.

On Writ of Certiorari
to the United States Court of Appeals
for the Federal Circuit

**BRIEF *AMICI CURIAE* OF NATIONAL ASSOCIATION
OF LEGAL ASSISTANTS, PARALYZED VETERANS
OF AMERICA, AND THE NATIONAL
ORGANIZATION OF SOCIAL SECURITY
CLAIMANTS' REPRESENTATIVES
IN SUPPORT OF PETITIONER**

Pamela S. Karlan
Jeffrey L. Fisher
STANFORD LAW SCHOOL
 SUPREME COURT
 LITIGATION CLINIC
559 Nathan Abbott Way
Stanford, CA 94305

Charles L. Martin
MARTIN & JONES LAW OFFICES
123 N. McDonough St.
Decatur, GA 30030

Amy Howe
Counsel of Record
Kevin K. Russell
HOWE & RUSSELL, P.C.
4607 Asbury Pl., NW
Washington, DC 20016
(202) 237-7543

Thomas C. Goldstein
AKIN, GUMP, STRAUSS,
HAUER & FELD LLP
1333 New Hampshire Ave., NW
Washington, DC 20036

January 11, 2008

QUESTION PRESENTED

Under the Equal Access to Justice Act (EAJA), 5 U.S.C. § 504(a)(1) and 28 U.S.C. § 2412(d)(1)(A), may a prevailing party be awarded attorney fees for paralegal services at the market rate for such services, as four circuits have held, or does EAJA limit reimbursement for paralegal services to cost only, as the Federal Circuit panel majority below held?

ii

TABLE OF CONTENTS

iii

TABLE OF AUTHORITIES

v

INTEREST OF *AMICI CURIAE*[1]

1. The **National Association of Legal Assistants (NALA)** is a professional association offering continuing education and professional development programs for paralegals throughout the nation.[2] NALA was established in 1975 as a nonprofit organization under section 501(c)(6) of the Internal Revenue Code. It is composed of 6000 individual members and over 90 state and local affiliated associations, representing about 10,000 paralegals. Detailed information about the association is available at http://www.nala.org.

NALA has served as a leader in the development of the legal profession by supporting continuing education of paralegals and providing ethical guidelines. In 1975, NALA members adopted the first Code of Ethics and Professional Responsibility for paralegals in their day-to-day activities. In 1984, NALA members adopted its Model Standards and Guidelines for Utilization of Legal Assistants to serve as a guide for paralegals and supervising attorneys by describing the role of paralegals in the delivery of legal services. The Model is based on research of state-bar-association-adopted guidelines, ethics opinions, and case law related to paralegal utilization. NALA has

---

[1] No counsel for a party authored this brief in whole or in part, and no counsel or party made a monetary contribution intended to fund the preparation or submission of this brief. No person other than *amici curiae*, their members, or their counsel made a monetary contribution to its preparation or submission.

[2] In recent years, NALA has found that the term "paralegal" is a preferred term in certain geographic areas; in some states, "legal assistant" is falling by the wayside. This brief uses the terms "legal assistant" and "paralegal" interchangeably.

2

conducted a nationwide utilization and compensation survey every two to three years since 1986, and survey findings are submitted regularly to the Department of Labor.

In 1989, NALA filed an *amicus curiae* brief in *Missouri v. Jenkins*, 491 U.S. 274 (1989). In the brief, NALA explained that paralegals are a recognized and desirable addition to the modern law office. The delegation of work to a skilled paralegal reduces the cost of legal services to the client and increases attorney efficiency and productivity. Today, the contribution and value of paralegals to cost-effective delivery of legal services is indisputable and recognized even more so than it was in 1989. The paralegal occupation was then and continues to be designated as one of the fastest-growing occupations in the United States. When NALA's brief was filed in 1989, there were an estimated 53,000 paralegals (as of 1984), which was projected to rise to 104,000 by 1994. Today, the Bureau of Labor Statistics estimates that over 200,000 paralegal jobs are held in the United States. The use of paralegals continues to be promoted and encouraged when compensated at market rate as part of court-awarded attorneys' fees. In addition, the public interest is served by encouraging attorney use of paralegals where practical.

2. The **Paralyzed Veterans of America (PVA)** is a national nonprofit organization chartered by the U.S. Congress.[3] *See* 36 U.S.C. § 170101 et seq. Membership in PVA is limited to American citizens who are veterans of the U.S. Armed Forces and have a

---

[3] Detailed information about PVA is available at www.pva.org.

spinal cord injury or disease. PVA has over 20,000 members, the vast majority of whom use a wheelchair for mobility. The congressionally mandated purposes of the organization include acquainting the public with the needs and problems of paraplegics; promoting medical research regarding injuries to and diseases of the spinal cord; and to advocate for and to foster various programs on behalf of members and other individuals with spinal cord injury or disease. PVA maintains an active practice at both the U.S. Court of Appeals for Veterans Claims and the U.S. Court of Appeals for the Federal Circuit litigating cases involving veterans' benefits on behalf of its members and other veterans. The recovery of legal fees and expenses under the Equal Access to Justice Act allows PVA to continue with this important effort on behalf of its members and other veterans. Therefore, the PVA has a vital interest in ensuring that the Equal Access to Justice Act is interpreted consistently with its primary purpose of ensuring that the expenses involved in litigation do not deter citizens subject to unreasonable governmental conduct, such as veterans and other with disabilities, from seeking vindication of their rights.

3. The **National Organization of Social Security Claimants' Representatives (NOSSCR)** is a non-profit membership corporation that provides professional education and related products and services to individuals who represent individuals who claim benefits under the Social Security Act.[4] NOSSCR has filed *amicus* briefs in several other cases before

---

[4] Detailed information about NOSSCR is available at www.NOSSCR.org.

4

this Court, presenting the perspective of its membership—approximately 4000 attorneys and non-attorneys who represent Social Security claimants—and of the claimants NOSSCR represents. NOSSCR members include both lawyers and non-lawyers, in legal services organizations and in private practice, located in all parts of the country.

NOSSCR's members represent Social Security claimants before the Social Security Administration and in the courts. Overall, over five percent of all federal district court filings in the twelve-month period ending September 30, 2006 were Social Security cases,[5] and about half of those cases likely will result in some relief entitling NOSSCR's clients to seek attorney's fees under the Equal Access to Justice Act. Many of NOSSCR's members who seek EAJA fees include paralegal services in their requests. Therefore, NOSSCR has a great interest in ensuring that its members be compensated for such an integral part of their legal practice.

SUMMARY OF THE ARGUMENT

In *Missouri v. Jenkins*, this Court held that when the prevailing practice is to bill paralegal work at market rates, paralegal time should be similarly compensated for purposes of fee requests under 42 U.S.C. § 1988. Compensation at market rates, this Court reasoned, would encourage the "cost-effective delivery of legal services." This Court's holding and

---

[5] *See* Table C-3, U.S. District Courts—Civil Cases Commenced, by Nature of Suit and District, During the 12-Month Period Ending Sept. 30, 2006, *available at* http://www.uscourts.gov/ judbusiness2006/contents.html.

5

reasoning in *Jenkins* apply fully to requests for paralegal fees under EAJA: If anything, the separate billing of paralegal time at market rates is even more universally accepted now than at the time of this Court's decision in *Jenkins*, and paralegals perform substantive legal work that would otherwise be performed by attorneys, resulting in lower fees for clients and lower requests for compensation under EAJA. The Federal Circuit's assumption that allowing EAJA compensation for paralegal time at market rates would create "perverse incentives" is misplaced, as it fails to take account of both the realities of modern law practice and a court's discretion in fixing the amount of an EAJA award. The Federal Circuit's holding that paralegal fees under EAJA should instead be compensated at the attorney's cost is similarly flawed, as it too is inconsistent with the way in which law firms operate and would impose additional administrative burdens on both attorneys and courts.

ARGUMENT

I. Compensating Paralegal Time at Prevailing Market Rates Is Consistent with Practices Throughout the Country and Will Encourage the Cost-Effective Delivery of Legal Services.

1.   In *Missouri v. Jenkins*, 491 U.S. 274, 285 (1989), this Court found it "self-evident" that "the 'reasonable attorney's fee' provided for by" 42 U.S.C. § 1988 "should compensate the work of paralegals, as well as that of attorneys." When it came to assigning a value to paralegals' work, this Court concluded that when "the prevailing practice is to bill paralegal work

6

at market rates, treating civil rights lawyers' fee requests in the same way is not only permitted by § 1988, but also makes economic sense." *Id.* at 288. Specifically, the Court explained, "[b]y encouraging the use of lower cost paralegals rather than attorneys wherever possible, permitting market-rate billing of paralegal hours 'encourages cost-effective delivery of legal services' . . . ." *Id.* (quoting *Cameo Convalescent Center, Inc. v. Senn*, 738 F.2d 836, 846 (7th Cir. 1984), *cert. denied*, 469 U.S. 1106 (1985)). Noting that the separate billing of paralegals at market rates "appear[ed] to be the practice in most communities," and in particular in the local market in Missouri, this Court upheld the lower courts' decisions ordering compensation for paralegal time at market rates. *Id.* at 289.

This Court's reasoning and holding in *Jenkins* apply fully to this case. First, like section 1988, EAJA authorizes an award of "reasonable attorney fees" to parties who prevail in litigation against the government. *See* 28 U.S.C. § 2412(d)(1)(A) ("[A] court shall award to a prevailing party other than the United States fees and other expenses . . . incurred by that party in any civil action (other than cases sounding in tort), . . . brought by or against the United States in any court having jurisdiction of that action, unless the court finds that the position of the United States was substantially justified or that special circumstances make an award unjust."); 5 U.S.C. § 504(a)(1) ("An agency that conducts an adversary adjudication shall award, to a prevailing party other than the United States, fees and other expenses incurred by that party in connection with that proceeding, unless the adjudicative officer of the

7

agency finds that the position of the agency was substantially justified or that special circumstances make an award unjust."); 28 U.S.C. § 2412(d)(2)(A) ("For the purposes of this subsection, 'fees and other expenses' includes . . . reasonable attorney fees."); 5 U.S.C. § 504(b)(1)(A) ("For the purposes of this section, 'fees and other expenses' includes . . . reasonable attorney . . . fees."). There is no reason why it should be any less "self-evident" in the context of the EAJA that "the 'reasonable attorney's fee' provided for by statute should compensate the work of paralegals."

Unlike section 1988, EAJA provides specifically that "[t]he amount of fees awarded under [the Act] shall be based upon prevailing market rates for the kind and quality of the services furnished," 28 U.S.C. § 2412(d)(2)(A); 5 U.S.C. § 504(b)(1)(A). And as federal courts have repeatedly recognized (and the government did not challenge in its brief in opposition to certiorari), the practice of billing clients separately for paralegal time at market rates has become even more entrenched throughout the country in the nearly two decades since this Court's decision in *Jenkins*.[6]

---

[6] *See, e.g., Edmond v. Oxlite Inc.*, No. Civ. A. 01-2594, 2005 WL 2458235, at *3 (W.D. La. Oct. 5, 2005) (finding separate billing to be the prevailing practice in the court's jurisdiction); *File v. Hastings Entertainment, Inc.*, No. Civ. A. 2-02CV0213J, 2003 WL 21976739, at *3 (N.D. Tex. Aug. 19, 2003) (same); *Cleveland Area Bd. of Realtors v. City of Euclid*, 965 F. Supp. 1017, 1020 n.4 (N.D. Ohio 1997) (same); *Spectrum Leasing Corp. v. GSA*, 93-1 B.C.A. (CCH) P25,317, 1992 GSBCA LEXIS 279, at *30-*31 (July 27, 1992) (same for Washington, D.C. metropolitan area); *see also* Nat'l Ass'n of Legal Assistants, *What Do Legal Assistants Do?*, *available at* http://www.nala.org/whatis.htm (visited Dec. 3, 2007) (explaining that "[p]rofessionally, a paralegal's time for substantive legal work (as opposed to clerical or administrative

8

Indeed, the American Bar Association's Standing Committee on Paralegals even instructs attorneys that a "paralegal's substantive legal work (i.e., not clerical work) may be billed directly to the client just as an attorney's work is billed, or considered in setting a flat fee just as an attorney's work would be."[7]

2.   Although paralegals may have originally performed tasks that closely resembled those of a legal secretary, *see* Lisa S. Quaranta, *The Changing Role of the Paralegal*, 10 W. Va. Law. 9 (1996), they now perform, under the supervision of an attorney, substantive legal work that would otherwise be performed by an attorney – that is, precisely the kind of legal work that Congress intended to compensate under EAJA. This work may include, for example, "attending client conferences, witnessing the execution of documents, preparing transmittal letters, and maintaining estate/guardianship trust accounts,"[8] locating and interviewing witnesses, conducting investigations and statistical research, conducting legal research, drafting legal documents and

---

work) is billed to clients much the same way as an attorney's time, but at a lower hourly rate").

[7] ABA Standing Cmte. on Paralegals, *Information for Lawyers: How Paralegals Can Improve Your Practice*, *available at* http://www.abanet.org/legalservices/paralegals/lawyers.html#13 (visited July 10, 2007).

[8] ABA Model Guideline 2 for the Utilitization of Paralegal Services cmt., *available at* http://www.abanet.org/legalservices/ paralegals/lawyers.html#5 (visited Dec. 15, 2007) (emphasis added).

9

pleadings, and summarizing depositions, interrogatories, and testimony.[9]

Because paralegals are capable of handling a variety of substantive legal work that would otherwise be performed by an attorney, allowing paralegal fees to be compensated at prevailing market rates will, just as this Court noted in *Jenkins*, encourage the cost-effective delivery of legal services, thereby resulting – as the D.C. Circuit has emphasized – not only in lower fees to the client, but also in a lower request for reimbursement.[10] *See In re Donovan*, 877 F.2d 982, 992-93 (D.C. Cir. 1989) (per curiam).

Indeed, the experience of NOSSCR members also demonstrates the economic benefits that can result from the use of paralegals to perform substantive legal tasks that would otherwise be performed by an attorney. In Social Security appeals to federal court, paralegals (under the supervision of an attorney) may perform such important but time-consuming tasks as preparing a summary of the administrative record and drafting the procedural history, statement of the case,

---

[9] Nat'l Ass'n of Legal Assistants, *What Do Legal Assistants Do?*, available at http://www.nala,org/whatis.htm (visited Dec. 15, 2007).

[10] *See also* ABA Standing Cmte. on Paralegals, *Information for Lawyers: How Paralegals Can Improve Your Practice, available at* http://www.abanet.org/legalservices/paralegals/lawyers.html#role; *see also* Arthur G. Greene & Therese A. Cannon, *Paralegals, Profitability, and the Future of Your Law Practice* fig. 2.1 (2003), *reprinted at* http://www.abanet.org/legalservices/paralegals/lawyers.html (providing examples of significant savings to client by delegating work such as legal research, reviewing documents, interviewing witnesses, and drafting pleadings to a legal assistant).

and summary of the medical evidence. *See also, e.g.,* *Sandoval v. Apfel*, 86 F. Supp. 2d 601, 609 (N.D. Tex. 2000) (in Social Security case, describing work performed by paralegal and emphasizing that work "might otherwise have been undertaken by [the attorney of record] at a higher hourly rate, while consuming substantially the same amount of time"). In addition to the lower client fees and, ultimately, requests for reimbursement created by the use of paralegals in Social Security cases, NOSSCR members who use paralegals also find that their use of paralegals has the further benefit of freeing up attorney time for the most important aspects of a matter, thereby allowing the attorney to provide legal assistance to more clients than she otherwise would – a particularly important consideration given the limited number of attorneys who are willing to take on Social Security cases at all.[11]

3. In concluding that paralegal fees should be compensated at cost, the Federal Circuit relied heavily on its assumption that allowing recovery of paralegal fees "at or near the full market rate" would "create a perverse incentive." Pet. App. 18a. Because attorney fees under EAJA are capped by statute, the panel majority reasoned, allowing paralegal fees to be compensated at market rates approaching that cap would "distort the normal allocation of work and result in a less efficient performance of legal services." *Id.*

---

[11] A contrary holding would discourage attorneys from using paralegals. By forcing attorneys themselves to take on more of the work involved in Social Security cases, such a ruling would likely create delays in some federal court cases, as attorneys would be forced to seek extensions to permit them to complete their briefs.

Know friends or family members who could benefit from fast-track career training at Virginia College or via the Internet from Virginia College Online? Complete the form below and return it to the admissions department at your campus. Or invite them to visit www.vc.edu for more information and to complete the "More info" form.

Virginia V College

Your success starts here!

Name:_____

Address:_____

Email address: _____

Telephone (day): _____ Telephone (night):_____

Year of high school graduation or GED: _____

Note: For Virginia College Online, the form may be mailed to: 500 Century Park South Suite 200 Birmingham, AL 35226

Design and order your own Virginia College logo wear and other items! Go to www.vc.edu and choose your campus location to see the link to MyGarb

ISBN-13: 978-0-536-45275-7
ISBN-10:   0-536-45275-X

9 780536 452757

90000

11

Contrary to the Federal Circuit's assumption, however, allowing EAJA compensation at market rates will not create "perverse incentives." First, although EAJA imposes a cap of $125 per hour on fees for an attorney (with additional adjustment for inflation available, *see* 28 U.S.C. § 2412(d)(2)(A)(ii)), in many areas of the country there is little evidence that billing rates for paralegals are sufficiently high to create the "perverse incentives" that the panel decries. To the contrary, although courts now routinely approve EAJA fees for attorneys (when adjusted for inflation) at rates approaching $170 per hour,[12] *see, e.g., Begolke v. Astrue*, No. 06-C-0445-C, 2007 U.S. Dist. LEXIS 79689 (W.D. Wis. Oct. 26, 2007) (EAJA award for attorney's fees at $165.00 per hour for attorney services); *Lambert v. Nicholson*, No. 04-815(E), 2006 WL 2619658 (Vet. App. Sept. 7, 2006) (EAJA award included attorney's fees reimbursed at rates of $153.38 and $154.31 per hour); *see also* Br. of Pet'r 7 ("The current inflation adjusted cap is approximately $168 per hour."), both the EAJA caselaw and a recent NALA

---

[12] Indeed, in opposing proposed legislation that would have lifted the statutory cap on EAJA attorney's fees, the government expressly emphasized that, in its experience, "courts routinely take advantage of EAJA's current discretionary authority to exceed the hourly rate cap." Statement of Ryan W. Bounds, Chief of Staff, Office of Legal Pol'y, Dep't of Justice, Before the Subcommittee on Courts, the Internet, and Intellectual Property, Committee on the Judiciary, U.S. House of Reps., Concerning H.R. 435, the Equal Access to Justice Reform Act, at 7 (May 23, 2006) (citing, *inter alia, Former Employees of Tyco Elecs. Fiber Optics Div. v. U.S. Dep't of Labor*, 350 F. Supp. 2d 1075, 1093 (C.I.T. 2004), in which court awarded attorney's fees at $158.70 for work performed in 2004), *available at* www.judiciary.house.gov/media/pdfs/bounds052306.pdf (visited Sept. 20, 2007).

12

survey indicate that the rates for paralegals are generally – and often well – below $100 per hour. *See, e.g.*, *McKay v. Barnhart*, 327 F. Supp. 2d 263, 270 (S.D.N.Y. 2004) (indicating in Social Security case that "the prevailing rate for paralegal services in the Southern District of New York is $75 per hour"); Nat'l Ass'n of Legal Assistants, 2004 National Utilization and Compensation Survey Report tbl. 3.5, *available at* www.nala.org/Survey_Table.htm (visited June 21, 2007) (in 2004 nationwide survey of legal assistants, only thirty-eight percent reported a current billing rate greater than $90 per hour, and average billing rate for paralegals with five or fewer years of experience was $79 per hour).

Second, contrary to the assumption of the court of appeals, there is no reason to believe that the increased use of legal assistants will always result in the "less efficient performance of legal services." In response to a "demand for expertise," legal assistants have increasingly "develop[ed] knowledge and skills in highly technical or specialized subject areas." Nat'l Federation of Paralegal Ass'ns, *Paralegal Roles and Responsibilities*, *available at* http://www.paralegals. org/displaycommon.cfm?an=1&subarticlenbr=699 (visited June 21, 2007). When reviewing requests for EAJA reimbursement for legal assistants who specialize in a particular area of the law, district courts have expressly acknowledged that an attorney "is not necessarily able to" accomplish the tasks performed by legal assistants "in less time than it takes an experienced paralegal to do so." *Sandoval v. Apfel*, 86 F. Supp. 2d 601, 609 & n.12 (N.D. Tex. 2000) (approving EAJA award that included market rate for

13

legal assistant with "extensive experience performing paralegal work in social security disability litigation").

Third, to the extent that in some cases legal assistants may require more hours than an attorney to accomplish a particular task, the disparity between the hourly rates for an attorney and those of a legal assistant means that the use of legal assistants will remain cost-effective, as courts considering EAJA requests have repeatedly recognized. *See Nickola v. Barnhart*, No. 03-C-622-C, 2004 WL 2713075, at *1 (W.D. Wis. Nov. 24, 2004) (granting EAJA award for 33.15 hours of attorney time at $148.75 per hour and 44.2 hours of paralegal/law clerk time at $95 per hour and noting that "[a]lthough it might have taken more time for a law clerk to draft a brief than had an attorney drafted it, overall the use of law clerks in this case appears to have been a money-saving measure because it reduced the amount of time the attorney spent on the case").

Fourth, the suggestion of the decision below that, if paralegal fees are compensable at market rates, attorneys will somehow willy-nilly delegate virtually all aspects of a case to their paralegals in the hope of maximizing their compensation under EAJA is simply misplaced in at least two respects. First and foremost, although paralegals may – under the supervision of an attorney – perform a variety of substantive legal tasks that would otherwise be performed by an attorney, the attorney ultimately remains responsible for the work performed and thus has no incentive to delegate beyond the paralegal's capabilities and the point at which delegation is efficient. Thus, even if paralegals are compensated at market rates, many of the most

14

sensitive projects in a matter will be handled by
attorneys, who after careful consideration may
conclude that supervising the performance of certain
tasks by a paralegal is ultimately less cost-effective for
the client than performing the task themselves.
Second, to the extent that attorneys may be prompted
to delegate work to a paralegal, that delegation is
more likely to be attributable to other factors – such as
a client's desire to minimize her legal bills – than to
the prospect of compensation under EAJA, which is
rarely certain because the party seeking fees must
first prevail and then be prepared to demonstrate that
the government's litigating position was not
substantially justified. Third, although paralegal fees
under EAJA have long been compensated at prevailing
market rates in some circuits, *cf. Burt v. Heckler*, 593
F. Supp. 1125, 1133 (D.N.J. 1984) (compensating for
law clerk time at market rate of $25 per hour), the
Federal Circuit did not point to any evidence that the
"perverse incentives" and inefficiencies prophesized by
the decision below have come to pass.

Finally, the decision below completely overlooks
that courts may adjust fee awards under EAJA to
avoid any "perverse incentive" problem. In
Commissioner v. Jean, 496 U.S. 154 (1990), this Court
emphasized that "a district court will always retain
substantial discretion in fixing the amount of an EAJA
award." *Id.* at 163. In practice, courts have availed
themselves of that discretion to reduce fee awards to
account for inefficiencies on the part of both attorneys
and paralegals. *See, e.g., Dudelson v. Barnhart*, No. 03
Civ. 7734 (RCC) (FM), 2007 U.S. Dist. LEXIS 19124
(S.D.N.Y. Mar. 20, 2007) (approving an EAJA award
that included legal assistant fees at a rate of $75 per

15

hour but reducing the number of hours covered by the award after finding that "much of the time billed may not have been entirely productive"); *Teixeira v. Nicholson*, 2006 U.S. App. Vet. Claims LEXIS 295 (Vet. App. Apr. 4, 2006) (reducing EAJA award in light of finding that "representation by multiple counsel resulted in duplicative work and excessive billing for time spent by counsel conferring with each other").

II. Paralegal Fees Should Be Reimbursed Under EAJA at Market Rates, Rather Than at Cost.

The Federal Circuit's holding that paralegal time should be compensated at the cost to the attorney is further flawed because it is likely to impose an additional administrative burden on both attorneys and courts – a burden that can be avoided by holding that paralegal time should instead be billed at market rates.

As described in detail above, *see supra* at 7-8, attorneys overwhelmingly bill out their paralegals' time at prevailing market rates. Under this practice, attorneys have no need to calculate the per-hour cost for each of their paralegals, the majority of whom are salaried employees. *See* Nat'l Ass'n of Legal Assistants (NALA), *2004 National Utilization and Compensation Survey Report*, tbl. 2.5. Nor would it be simple for attorneys to make such a calculation for purposes of an EAJA application, as a paralegal's actual cost to his employer would necessarily include not only his salary, but also additional employer costs such as payroll taxes, workers' compensation insurance, employee benefits such as a pension plan or

16

health insurance, and overhead costs such as rent, utilities, and administrative support. Moreover, given the many variables that contribute to a paralegal's actual cost, employers would have to conduct an individual cost calculation for each paralegal for whom EAJA compensation is sought, as two otherwise identically situated paralegals – with the same level of experience and the same billing rate – could have markedly different costs to their employer depending on, for example, their seniority in the firm, the number of dependents covered by the firm-provided health insurance, and whether the paralegal is vested in the firm's pension plan. Indeed, the additional expenses associated with calculating the indirect costs of paralegal services in EAJA cases would likely discourage the use of paralegals by NOSSCR members, many of whom practice in small firms with limited accounting resources.

And even if attorneys did calculate the hourly "cost" for paralegal services, allowing compensation at cost would also require courts reviewing EAJA applications to conduct a fact-intensive inquiry to determine the reasonableness of those costs. Such an inquiry would necessarily be far more extensive than the brief Internet search conducted by the Board of Contract Appeals in this case and might include, for example, resolving as-yet-unexplored questions such as how to determine the cost of a paralegal's overtime when the paralegal worked on both EAJA and non-EAJA cases in a single day. By contrast, allowing compensation for paralegals at market rates eliminates much of the burden for both litigants and courts: Litigants can simply submit fee applications that include their market billing rates for paralegals,

17

while courts may rely on either established fee tables[13] or other cases to ensure that the rates are reasonable. *See, e.g., McKay v. Barnhart*, 327 F. Supp. 2d 263, 270-71 (S.D.N.Y. 2004) (citing other recent cases for evidence of the prevailing market rate for paralegal services).

* * * *

Compensating paralegal time under EAJA at cost would be, as noted above, inconsistent with the realities of modern law practice. Moreover, because such a practice would likely discourage use of paralegals in many small firms, including those of many NOSSCR members, a holding that required paralegal time to be compensated only at cost would directly conflict with one of the goals of the federal fee-shifting statutes – viz., to encourage lawyers to take on cases. By contrast, allowing paralegal fees to be compensated at market rates is consistent with the near-universal practice of attorneys nationwide, encourages the cost-effective delivery of legal services, and frequently will enable attorneys such as members of NOSSCR to take on more cases in which EAJA compensation may be available. Moreover, it will significantly reduce the likelihood of ancillary litigation over the reasonableness of EAJA fee requests, thereby reducing litigation burdens on successful plaintiffs, the federal government, and the courts.

---

[13] For example, the U.S. Attorney's Office for the District of Columbia publishes the "Laffey Matrix," a list of market rates that may be cited for fee awards in fee-shifting cases. *See* "Laffey Matrix 2003-2008," http://www.usdoj.gov/usao/dc/Divisions/ Civil_Division/Laffey_Matrix_7.html (last visited Dec. 17, 2007).

18

CONCLUSION

For the foregoing reasons, the judgment of the court of appeals should be reversed.

Respectfully submitted,

Pamela S. Karlan
Jeffrey L. Fisher
STANFORD LAW SCHOOL
  SUPREME COURT
  LITIGATION CLINIC
559 Nathan Abbott Way
Stanford, CA 94305

Amy Howe
(Counsel of Record)
Kevin K. Russell
HOWE & RUSSELL, P.C.
4607 Asbury Pl., NW
Washington, DC 20016
(202) 237-7543

Charles L. Martin
MARTIN & JONES LAW OFFICES
123 N. McDonough St.
Decatur, GA 30030

Thomas C. Goldstein
AKIN, GUMP, STRAUSS
  HAUER & FELD LLP
1333 New Hampshire Ave., NW
Washington, DC 20036

January 11, 2008

SUMMARY OF DEFINITIONS OF TERMS: LEGAL ASSISTANT AND PARALEGAL

Note: The following is a short summary of definitions of the terms "paralegal" or "legal assistant" found among the states. These definitions are either adopted by statute, court rule, case law, bar association attorney guidelines, or other document adopted by a bar association. This article is updated regularly and is available on the National Association of Legal Assistants (NALA) Web site at www.nala.org/terms.htm.

> National Association of Legal Assistants, Inc.
> 1516 S. Boston, #200
> Tulsa, Oklahoma 74119
> (918) 587-6828; FAX (918) 582-6772

Introduction

NALA is a professional association composed of individual members and 92 state and local affiliated associations, representing over 18,000 paralegals. Established in 1975, NALA goals and programs were developed by 800 charter members to:

increase the professional standing of legal assistants throughout the nation;

provide uniformity in the identification of legal assistants;

establish national standards of professional competence for legal assistants; and

provide uniformity among the states in the utilization of legal assistants.

One of the services of this association is tracking legislative, court, and bar association activities related to the paralegal profession. The following is a summary of the various definitions of the terms "paralegal" and "legal assistant" as of June 2004 from 27 states, the United States Supreme Court, the American Bar Association, and the National Association of Legal Assistants.

Definition of Legal Assistant/Paralegal

National associations, bar associations, legislatures, and supreme courts have addressed the definition of legal assistant and paralegal. Through discussions within each group, similarities in the identification and duties of paralegals are emerging with routine consistency. The common threads in these definitions and discussions are:

Paralegals:

1. have received specialized training through formal education or many years of experience;
2. work under the supervision and direction of an attorney; and
3. perform nonclerical, substantive legal work in assisting an attorney.

This paper summarizes these definitions.

National Organizations

The definition of "legal assistant" adopted in 1984 by NALA is as follows:

> Legal assistants (also known as paralegals) are a distinguishable group of persons who assist attorneys in the delivery of legal services. Through formal education, training, and experience, legal assistants have knowledge and expertise regarding the legal system and substantive and procedural law which qualify them to do work of a legal nature under the supervision of an attorney.

In 1986, the American Bar Association adopted the following definition:

> A legal assistant is a person, qualified through education, training or work experience, who is employed or retained by a lawyer, law office, governmental agency, or other entity, in a capacity or function which involves the performance, under the ultimate direction and supervision of an attorney, of specifically-delegated substantive legal work, which work, for the most part, requires a sufficient knowledge of legal concepts that, absent such assistant, the attorney would perform the task.

In 1997, the American Bar Association amended this definition. The 1997 version is:

> A legal assistant or paralegal is a person qualified by education, training or work experience who is employed or retained by a lawyer, law office, corporation, governmental agency or other entity who performs specifically delegated substantive legal work for which a lawyer is responsible.

Both definitions recognize the terms "legal assistant" and "paralegal" as identical terms.

In fact, in recognition of the similarity of the definitions and the need for one clear definition, in July 2001, the NALA membership approved a resolution to adopt the ABA definition.

State Legislatures

Legislatures among the United States have also addressed this question. The State of Florida statute 57.104, effective October 1, 1987, specifically states that paralegals work under the direction and supervision of a licensed attorney.

Similar legislation was introduced in 1993 in the states of Indiana and Oklahoma. These bills called for the recoverability of paralegal time in attorney fee awards. The Indiana bills (House Bill 1583; Senate Bill 424), passed April 27, 1993, now Public Law 93-6. They define paralegals as persons (1) qualified through education, training or work experience, and (2) employed by a lawyer, law office, governmental agency, or other entity to work under the direction of an attorney in a capacity that involves the performance of substantive legal work that usually requires a sufficient knowledge of legal concepts and would be performed by the attorney in the absence of the paralegal. This definition is, essentially, the same as the definition adopted by the American Bar Association.

Oklahoma House Bill 1628 defined paralegals in the same manner, using the ABA definition as a basis. This bill passed the Oklahoma House of Representatives on February 15, 1993. It did not reach the Senate floor during the session.

The California legislature enacted a statute governing the use of the terms paralegal and legal assistant. See Chapter 5.6 Paralegals section 6450 of the Business and Professions Code. This law, effective January 1, 2001, defines "paralegal" as follows:

> 6450. (a) "Paralegal" means a person who either contracts with or is employed by an attorney, law firm, corporation, governmental agency, or other entity and who performs substantial legal work under the direction and supervision of an active member of the State Bar of California, as defined in Section 6060, or an attorney practicing law in the federal courts of this state, that has been specifically delegated by the attorney to him or her. Tasks performed by a paralegal include, but are not limited to, case planning,

development, and management; legal research; interviewing clients; fact gathering and retrieving information; drafting and analyzing legal documents; collecting, compiling, and utilizing technical information to make an independent decision and recommendation to the supervising attorney; and representing clients before a state or federal administrative agency if that representation is permitted by statute, court rule, or administrative rule or regulation.

6454. The terms "paralegal," "legal assistant," "attorney assistant," "freelance paralegal," "independent paralegal," and "contract paralegal" are synonymous for purposes of this chapter. Illinois Senate Bill 995, passed and signed by the governor on July 7, 1995, sets forth a definition of a *paralegal*. Effective January 1, 1996, the bill amended the Statute on Statutes by adding Section 1.35 as follows:

Sec. 1.35. Paralegal. "Paralegal" means a person who is qualified through education, training, or work experience and is employed by a lawyer, law office, governmental agency, or other entity to work under the direction of an attorney in a capacity that involves the performance of substantive legal work that usually requires a sufficient knowledge of legal concepts and would be performed by the attorney in the absence of the paralegal. A reference in an Act to attorney fees includes paralegal fees, recoverable at market rates.

The Pennsylvania legislature has addressed paralegals in its unauthorized practice of law statutes. Effective July 11, 1996, Section 2524(a) of Title 42 of the Pennsylvania Consolidated Statutes now reads:

(a) General rule.—Except as provided in subsection (b), any person, including, but not limited to, a paralegal or legal assistant, who within this Commonwealth shall practice law, or who shall hold himself out to the public as being entitled to practice law, or use or advertise the title of lawyer, attorney at law, attorney and counselor at law, counselor, or the equivalent in any language, in such as a manner to convey the impression that he is a practitioner of the law of any jurisdiction, without being an attorney at law or a corporation complying with 15 Pa. Cons. Stat. Ch. 29 (relating to professional corporations), commits a misdemeanor of the third degree[.] upon a first violation. A second or subsequent violation of this subsection constitutes a misdemeanor of the first degree.

This statute is in response to widespread concern that some individuals using the terms "paralegal" or "legal assistant" as their occupational title and in advertisements were doing so in a way that led potential customers to believe they were authorized to deliver legal services. This legislation prohibits use of the terms "paralegal" and "legal assistant" in this fashion. Rather than serving as a definition of what paralegals may do, the statute informs the public that paralegals and legal assistants do not deliver legal services without attorney supervision and cannot hold themselves out as individuals entitled to practice law.

The State of Maine statutorily defined the terms "legal assistant" and "paralegal" in 1999. By passage of LD 0724, the legislature has not only defined the terms, it provides that a person who claims to be a paralegal or legal assistant and does not meet the statutory definition commits a civil violation for which a forfeiture of up to $1,000 may be adjudged. The adopted definition is:

"Paralegal" and "legal assistant" mean a person, qualified by education, training or work experience, who is employed or retained by an attorney, law office, corporation, governmental agency or other entity and who performs specifically delegated substantive legal work for which an attorney is responsible.

Supreme Court Recognition

The United States Supreme Court encourages and recognizes the use of paralegals working under the supervision of an attorney.

It has frequently been recognized in the lower courts that paralegals are capable of carrying out many tasks, under the supervision of an attorney, that might otherwise be performed by a lawyer and billed at a higher rate. *Missouri v. Jenkins,* 491 U.S. 274, 109 S. Ct. 2163, 2471–72 (1989).

State supreme courts have also addressed the definition of "legal assistant" or "paralegal" in their rules and in their opinions. Many of the state supreme court findings are included in this section. Further, the definitions of legal assistants or paralegals adopted by bar associations that are regulated by supreme courts are included in this section.

Kentucky.   Among the earliest to address the utilization of paralegals in its rules is the Kentucky Supreme Court in adoption of rule 3.700 on September 4, 1979. The rule, revised through 1989, lists the following definition:

> For the purposes of this Rule, a paralegal is a person under the supervision and direction of a licensed lawyer, who may apply knowledge of law and legal procedures in rendering direct assistance to lawyers engaged in legal research; design, develop or plan modifications or new procedures, techniques, services, processes or applications; prepare or interpret legal documents and write detailed procedures for practicing in certain fields of law; select, compile and use technical information from such references as digests, encyclopedias or practice manuals; and analyze and follow procedural problems that involve independent decisions.

Michigan.   Effective January 1, 2001, the Michigan Supreme Court amended its rules to provide the following:

> Rule 2.626 Attorney Fees. An award of attorney fees may include an award for the time and labor of any legal assistant who contributed nonclerical, legal support under the supervision of an attorney, provided the legal assistant meets the criteria set forth in Article 1, Section 6 of the Bylaws of the State Bar of Michigan.

Article 1, Section 6 of the Bylaws of the State Bar of Michigan states:

> Any person currently employed or retained by a lawyer, law office, governmental agency or other entity engaged in the practice of law, in a capacity or function which involves the performance under the direction and supervision of an attorney of specifically delegated substantive legal work, which work, for the most part, requires a sufficient knowledge of legal concepts such that, absent that legal assistant, the attorney would perform the tasks and which is not primarily clerical or secretarial in nature, and;
>
> (a) who has graduated from a ABA approved program of study for legal assistants and has a baccalaureate degree; or
>
> (b) has received a baccalaureate degree in any field, plus not less than two years of in-house training as a legal assistant; or
>
> (c) who has received an associate degree in the legal assistant field, plus not less than two years of in-house training as a legal assistant; or
>
> (d) who has a minimum of four years of in-house training as a legal assistant;
>
> may upon submitting proof thereof at the time of application and annually thereafter become a Legal Assistant Affiliate Member of the State Bar of Michigan.

Rhode Island.   In Rhode Island Supreme Court Provisional Order No. 18, effective February 1, 1983 and revised through October 31, 1990, "legal assistant" is defined as follows:

> A legal assistant is one who under the supervision of a lawyer, shall apply knowledge of law and legal procedures in rendering direct assistance to lawyers, clients and courts; design, develop and modify procedures, techniques, services and processes; prepare and interpret legal documents; detail procedures

for practicing in certain fields of law; research, select, access, and compile information from the law library and other references; and analyze and handle procedural problems that involve independent decisions.

The guidelines accompanying this definition emphasize that legal assistants shall work under the direction and supervision of a lawyer who shall be ultimately responsible for their work product.

New Mexico.   The New Mexico Supreme Court Judicial Pamphlet 16, 1986, states that:

> A 'legal assistant' means a person, not admitted to the practice of law, who provides assistance to a licensed lawyer and for whose work that licensed lawyer is ultimately responsible. The assistance may include, but is not limited to, record and statistical research; investigation; analysis of records, documents and facts; problem analysis; preparation of legal memoranda; assistance in drafting legal documents, interrogatories and correspondence; completion of forms which have been prepared by or under the supervision of the supervising attorney; location of reported decisions, cite checking and shepardizing; and interviews of clients and witnesses. These and other types of assistance must be provided under the supervision and direction of a licensed attorney....

The commentary to this definition includes references to the fact that the definition of "legal assistant" is intended to cover those persons usually designated as "legal assistants," "paralegals," and "lawyers' assistants."

In 1995 the Supreme Court amended SCRA 1986, 24-101 of the Rules Governing the New Mexico Bar to establish a division of the bar for legal assistants, affirming the definition and listing qualifications for division membership.

New Hampshire.   Supreme Court Administrative Rule 35, Guidelines for the Utilization by Lawyers of the Services of Legal Assistants under the New Hampshire Rules of Professional Conduct, amended through 1987, defines a legal assistant as:

> a person not admitted to the practice of law in New Hampshire who is an employee of or an assistant to an active member of the New Hampshire Bar, a partnership comprised of active members of the New Hampshire Bar or a Professional Association within the meaning of RSA Chapter 294-A, and who, under the control and supervision of an active member of the New Hampshire Bar, renders services related to but not constituting the practice of law.

South Dakota.   In Rule 92-5, March 6, 1992, the Supreme Court of South Dakota adopted the following definition of legal assistants.

> Legal assistants (also known as paralegals) are a distinguishable group of persons who assist attorneys in the delivery of legal services. Through formal education, training, and experience, legal assistants have knowledge and expertise regarding the legal system and substantive and procedural law which qualify them to do work of a legal nature under the direct supervision of a licensed lawyer.

The rule further states, that "any person having been convicted of a felony shall not serve as a legal assistant in the State of South Dakota, unless upon application to the Supreme Court of South Dakota, establishing good moral character and restoration of full civil rights, and its approval thereof."

The South Dakota rule goes on to list seven minimum qualifications as follows:

1. Successful completion of the Certified Legal Assistant (CLA) examination of the National Association of Legal Assistant, Inc.; or
2. Graduation from an ABA approved program of study for legal assistants; or

3. Graduation from a course of study for legal assistants which is institutionally accredited but not ABA approved, and which requires not less than the equivalent of sixty semester hours of classroom study; or

4. Graduation from a course of study for legal assistants, other than those set forth in (2) and (3) above, plus not less than six months of in-house training as a legal assistant; or

5. A baccalaureate degree in any field, plus not less than six months in-house training as a legal assistant; or

6. A minimum of three years of law-related experience under the supervision of a lawyer, including at least six months of in-house training as a legal assistant; or

7. Two years of in-house training as a legal assistant.

Indiana.   The Indiana Supreme Court adopted Guidelines on the Use of Legal Assistants January 1, 1994, which are part of the Indiana Rules of Professional Conduct. The rules provide:

> A legal assistant shall perform services only under the direct supervision of lawyer authorized to practice in the State of Indiana and in the employ of the lawyer or the lawyer's employer. Independent legal assistants, to-wit, those not employed by a specific firm or by specific lawyers are prohibited. A lawyer is responsible for all of the professional actions of a legal assistant performing legal assistant services at the lawyer's direction, and should take reasonable measures to insure that the legal assistant's conduct is consistent with the lawyer's obligations under the Rules of Professional Conduct.

The guidelines provide that a lawyer may delegate to a legal assistant any task normally performed by the lawyer; however, any task prohibited by statute, court rule, administrative rule or regulation, controlling authority, or the Indiana Rules of Professional Conduct may not be assigned to a nonlawyer. They also provide that a lawyer may charge for the work performed by a legal assistant. Finally, the guidelines set forth a statement of legal assistant ethics and provide that all lawyers who employ legal assistants in the State of Indiana shall assure that such legal assistants conform their conduct to be consistent with stated ethical standards.

North Dakota.   Amendments to the North Dakota Rules of Professional Conduct adopted December 11, 1996 by the North Dakota Supreme Court, with an effective date of March 1, 1997, include rules which govern legal assistants/paralegals in North Dakota. Rules 1.5 (Fees), 5.3 Responsibilities Regarding Nonlawyer Assistants, 7.2 Firm Names and Letterheads, and the Terms section of the NDRPC include a definition of "legal assistant," suggested minimum standards, and comments related to supervision of legal assistants, the unauthorized practice of law, and billing for work performed by a legal assistant.

The rules state the following definition:

> "Legal Assistant" (or paralegal) means a person who assists lawyers in the delivery of legal services, and who through formal education, training, or experience, has knowledge and expertise regarding the legal system and substantive and procedural law which qualifies the person to do work of a legal nature under the direct supervision of a licensed lawyer.

Virginia.   On March 8, 1996, the Virginia State Bar Standing Committee on the Unauthorized Practice of Law adopted a resolution stating that a legal assistant working under direction of a member of the Virginia State Bar in conformance with the Standards and Guidelines would not be engaged in the unauthorized practice of law and that the employment or supervision by a Virginia State Bar member of legal assistants who conform to the Standards and Guidelines would be in the best interest of the public.

The resolution recommends that members of the Virginia State Bar make all reasonable efforts to encourage all legal assistants to subscribe and conform to the Standards and Guidelines. This resolution adopts the following definition of a legal assistant (paralegal):

> as one who is a specially trained individual who performs substantive legal work that requires a knowledge of legal concepts and who either works under the supervision of an attorney, who assumes professional responsibility for the final work product, or works in areas where lay individuals are explicitly authorized by statute or regulation to assume certain law-related responsibilities.

Cases

Arizona.   In *Continental Townhouses E. Unit One Ass'n v. Brockbank,* 152 Ariz. 537, 733 P.2d 1120, 73 A.L.R.4th 921 (1986), the Arizona Court of Appeals considered whether the time of a nonlawyer employee may be included in attorney fee awards. In its opinion, the Court relied upon the definition of "legal assistant" formulated by the American Bar Association. The court also used the terms "legal assistant" and "paralegal" interchangeably.

New Jersey.   In 1990, the New Jersey Committee on Unauthorized Practice of Law issued Opinion No. 24, which held that legal assistants or paralegals who contract their services to attorneys are engaged in the unauthorized practice of law. The New Jersey Committee on the Unauthorized Practice of Law is appointed by the Supreme Court, thus its findings and opinions become Supreme Court Rule. This opinion was appealed to the New Jersey Supreme Court. The Supreme Court issued its Opinion on May 14, 1992, and held:

> The evidence does not support a categorical ban on all independent paralegals practicing in New Jersey. Given the appropriate instructions and supervision, paralegals, whether as employees or independent contractors, are valuable and necessary members of an attorney's work force in the effective and efficient practice of law.

The Court further stated that charges for nonlawyer's time that properly fall within the definition of "attorney fees" are those that are clearly shown to have been made (1) for the delegated performance of substantive legal work, that (2) would otherwise have to be performed by a lawyer, (3) at a rate higher than that charged for nonlawyers' time.

Oklahoma.   In *Taylor v. Chubb,* 874 P.2d 806 (Okla. 1994), the Oklahoma Supreme Court held that charges for legal assistants could and should be included by courts in attorney fee award decisions. In its decision, the court refers to the definition of a legal assistant as promulgated by the American Bar Association and specifically enumerated a list of duties that may be properly performed by legal assistants as follows:

1. Interview clients
2. Draft pleadings and other documents
3. Carry on legal research, both conventional and computer aided
4. Research public records
5. Prepare discovery requests and responses
6. Schedule depositions
7. Summarize depositions and other discovery responses
8. Coordinate and manage document production
9. Locate and interview witnesses

10. Organize pleadings, trial exhibits and other documents

11. Prepare witness and exhibit lists

12. Prepare trial notebooks

13. Prepare for the attendance of witnesses at trial

14. Assist lawyers at trials

South Carolina.   In *The State of South Carolina v. Robinson,* Opinion No. 24391, filed March 18, 1996, the court stated the function of a paralegal was addressed *In re: Easler,* 275 S.C. 400, 272 S.E.2d 32 (1980):

> Paralegals are routinely employed by licensed attorneys to assist in the preparation of legal documents such as deeds and mortgages. The activities of a paralegal do not constitute the practice of law as long as they are limited to work of a preparatory nature, such as legal research, investigation, or the composition of legal documents, which enable the licensed attorney-employer to carry a given matter to a conclusion through his own examination, approval or additional effort. *Id.* at 400, 272 S.E.2d at 32–33.

The opinions stated that while there are no regulations dealing specifically with paralegals, requiring a paralegal to work under the supervision of a licensed attorney ensures control over his or her activities by making the supervising attorney responsible. See Rule 5.3 of the Rules of Professional Conduct, Rule 407 SCACR (supervising attorney is responsible for work of nonlawyer employees). Accordingly, to legitimately provide services as a paralegal, one must work in conjunction with a licensed attorney.

Washington.   Adopted December 3, 1994, the Washington State Bar Association Board of Governors has established guidelines for the utilization of legal assistant services. The guidelines are based on the ABA Model Guidelines for Utilization of Legal Assistants and adopt the definition of legal assistant/paralegal promulgated by the American Bar Association.

In *Absher Construction Company v. Kent School District,* 29 Wash. App. 841, (1995), the Washington Court of Appeals considered the question of the award of nonlawyer time in attorney fee awards if the nonlawyer is a legal assistant. The Court defined a legal assistant as one who is "qualified through education, training, or work experience, is employed or retained by a lawyer, law office, governmental agency or other entity in a capacity or function which involves a performance, under the ultimate direction and supervision of an attorney, of specifically delegated legal work, which work, for the most part requires a sufficient knowledge of legal concepts that, absent such assistant, the attorney would perform the task." The Court set forth the following criteria relevant in determining whether such services should be compensated:

1. The services performed by the nonlawyer personnel must be legal in nature.

2. The performance of these services must be supervised by an attorney.

3. The qualifications of the person performing the services must be specified in the request for fees in sufficient detail to demonstrate that the person is qualified by virtue of education, training, or work experience to perform substantive legal work.

4. The nature of the services performed must be specified in the request for fees in order to allow the reviewing court to determine that the services performed were legal rather than clerical.

5. As with attorney time, the amount of time expended must be set forth and must be reasonable; and

6. The amount charged must reflect reasonable community standards for charges by that category of personnel.

Bar Association Activity

Bar associations in the following states have defined legal assistants as qualified and educated individuals working under the supervision of attorneys:

Alaska	New Hampshire
Arizona	New Mexico
California	North Carolina
Colorado	North Dakota
Connecticut	Ohio
Florida	Oregon
Illinois	Rhode Island
Iowa	South Carolina
Kansas	South Dakota
Kentucky	Tennessee
Massachusetts	Texas
Michigan	Virginia
Minnesota	West Virginia
Missouri	Wisconsin

The following are examples of bar resolutions or guidelines adopted by the associations to assist attorneys in the utilization of paralegal services.

Bar Association Sections and Divisions

Michigan. The Bylaws of the State Bar of Michigan, Article 1, Sec. 6, defines "legal assistant" for the purposes of membership in the State Bar Legal Assistant Section as follows:

> Any person currently employed or retained by a lawyer, law office, governmental agency or other entity engaged in the practice of law, in a capacity or function which involves the performance under the direction and supervision of an attorney of specifically delegated substantive legal work, which work, for the most part, requires a sufficient knowledge of legal concepts such that, absent that legal assistant, the attorney would perform the tasks and which is not primarily clerical or secretarial in nature, and;
>
> (a) who has graduated from an ABA approved program of study for legal assistants and has a baccalaureate degree; or
>
> (b) has received a baccalaureate degree in any field, plus not less than two years of in-house training as a legal assistant; or
>
> (c) who has received an associate degree in the legal assistant field, plus not less than two years of in-house training as a legal assistant; or
>
> (d) who has a minimum of four years of in-house training as a legal assistant...

On April 23, 1993, the Michigan State Board of Commissioners announced approval of Michigan Guidelines for the Utilization of Legal Assistants. In recognition of the professional status of legal assistants, the guidelines cite *Missouri v. Jenkins* in allowing that a fee arrangement with a client may include a reasonable charge for work performed by legal assistants at market rates.

Nevada. As part of the creation of a Division of Legal Assistants, the State Bar of Nevada has adopted the following definition of a legal assistant (December, 1994):

A legal assistant (also known as a paralegal) is a person, qualified through education, training or work experience, who is employed or retained by a lawyer, law office, governmental agency, or other entity in a capacity or function which involves the performance, under the ultimate direction and supervision of an attorney, of specifically delegated substantive legal work, which work, for the most part, requires sufficient knowledge of legal concepts that, absent such an assistant, the attorney would perform the task.

This definition is identical to that adopted by the American Bar Association in 1986.

Texas. As early as 1981, the Board of Directors, State Bar of Texas, adopted General Guidelines for the Utilization of the Services of Legal Assistants by Attorneys. These guidelines require that a legal assistant work under the supervision of an attorney and shall not give legal advice or otherwise engage in the unauthorized practice of law. An attorney may allow a legal assistant under his or her supervision and direction to perform delegated services in the representation of that attorney's clients provided: (1) the client understands the legal assistant is not an attorney; (2) the attorney maintains a direct relationship with the client; (3) the attorney directs and supervises the legal assistant; and (4) the attorney remains professionally responsible for the client and the client's legal matters. The State Bar of Texas was the first state to establish a membership division for legal assistants within its bar association.

Bar Association Guidelines

Colorado. One of the first states to establish guidelines for paralegals in July 1986, the Colorado Bar has adopted the following definition of a paralegal:

Legal assistants (also known as paralegals) are a distinguishable group of persons who assist attorneys in the delivery of legal services. Through formal education, training and experience, legal assistants have knowledge and expertise regarding the legal system and substantive and procedural law which will qualify them to do work of a legal nature under the direct supervision of a licensed attorney.

Connecticut. From a December 11, 1985 Report of Connecticut Bar Association Special Inter-Committee Group to Study the Role of Paralegals, the committee sets forth recommendations as to what the professional obligations of lawyers should be in relation to paralegals. The report uses "paralegal" and "legal assistant" as having identical meanings and define the terms as follows:

Persons employed by law offices who are not admitted to practice law but a major part of whose work is performing tasks commonly performed by lawyers and who are under the general supervision and control of lawyers. Paralegals may be salaried employees or independent contractors such as freelance paralegals utilized on occasion by lawyers or special assignments.

The Connecticut Bar Association offers associate membership to paralegals.

Georgia. Georgia Advisory Opinion No. 21, revised May 20, 1983, sets forth the following definition of legal assistant as follows:

For the purposes of this opinion, the terms 'legal assistant,' 'paraprofessional,' and 'paralegal' are defined as any lay person not admitted to the practice of law in this state who is an employee of or an assistant to, an active member of the State Bar of Georgia or of a partnership or professional corporation comprised of active members of the Sate Bar of Georgia and who renders services relating to the law to such member, partnership or professional corporation under the direct control, supervision and compensation of a member of the State Bar of Georgia.

Idaho. In State Bar Resolution 94-7, adopted November 1994, the Idaho State Bar urged the Supreme Court to adopt the ABA Model Standards and Guidelines for Utilization of Legal Assistant Services, which includes the definition of a legal assistant/paralegal promulgated by the American Bar Association.

Kansas. The guidelines were first adopted in 1988 and amended February 2004. The guidelines set forth a definition of legal assistant/paralegal, standards, guidelines for attorneys, questions and answers, information about associate membership in the Kansas Bar Association for paralegals, and an attorney checklist for working with legal assistants/paralegals.

The term "legal assistant/paralegal," as used in these standards and guidelines, is defined by adoption of the American Bar Association (ABA) definition (http://www.abanet.org/legalservices/legalassistants), to wit:

> A legal assistant or paralegal is a person, qualified by education, training, or work experience who is employed or retained by a lawyer, law office, corporation, governmental agency or other entity and who performs specifically delegated substantive legal work for which a lawyer is responsible.

The guidelines go on to state that any attorney employing a legal assistant/paralegal shall ascertain that such person is qualified to act in the capacity either by reason of formal education, special training, and/or experience.

Maryland. In 2001, the Maryland State Bar Association began offering associate membership to legal assistants. The definition and requirement states:

> Paralegal/Legal Assistant. A paralegal/legal assistant is a person qualified through education, training or work experience to perform work that requires knowledge of legal concepts and is customarily, but not exclusively, performed by a lawyer. This person shall be retained or employed by a lawyer, law office, governmental agency or other entity or be authorized by administrative, statutory, or court authority to perform this work. A paralegal/legal assistant may apply for associate membership if sponsored by an active lawyer member of the Association.

New York. The New York State Bar Association Committee on Law Office Economics and Management Subcommittee on Legal Assistants published a pamphlet entitled "The Expanding Role of the Legal Assistant in New York State." This references guidelines for the utilization of legal assistants, published in 1976, and adopts the definition of a legal assistant as promulgated by the American Bar Association.

Oklahoma. During its meeting on August 20, 1999, the Oklahoma Bar Association Board of Governors adopted a resolution defining the terms "legal assistant" and "paralegal" to provide guidance to members of the bar. The board approved the following definition as a guide to Oklahoma attorneys, corporations, or other entities to utilize the services of legal assistants/paralegals and bill their clients separately for such services:

> A legal assistant or paralegal is a person qualified by education, training or work experience who is employed or retained by a lawyer, law office, corporation, governmental agency or other entity who performs specifically delegated substantive legal work for which a lawyer is responsible, and absent such assistant, the lawyer would perform the task.

Effective September 15, 2000, the Oklahoma Bar Association adopted minimum qualification standards to serve as a guide for Oklahoma attorneys. The guidelines include the previously quoted definition, prescribe standards for qualified legal assistants, and include a recommendation for continuing legal education.

Oregon. The Oregon State Bar Association has published a pamphlet entitled "The Lawyer and the Legal Assistant" (undated). This states the terms "legal assistant" and "paralegal" are synonymous terms, and that legal assistants must work under the direct supervision of a licensed attorney.

Utah. As published in January 1994, the Office of Attorney Discipline of the Utah State Bar has set forth standards related to the ethical use of paralegals in the practice of law. The office has reviewed the National Association of Legal Assistants Guidelines for Utilizing Paralegals as well as the ABA Model Guidelines for Utilization of Legal Assistant Services and "in an attempt to provide a safe harbor for those lawyers utilizing paralegals until the Supreme Court Advisory Committee on Discipline formally considers amending Rule 5.3 and 5.5(b) of the Rules of Professional Conduct, promulgates standards and guidelines." The guidelines require attorney supervision of legal assistants and list general duties and responsibilities of a legal assistant.

West Virginia. During its annual meeting held July 16–17, 1999, the West Virginia State Bar Board of Governors approved the following definition:

> A legal assistant is a person, qualified through education, training or work experience, who is employed or retained by a lawyer, law office, governmental agency, or other entity, in a capacity or function which involves the performance, under the ultimate direction and supervision of an attorney, of delegated substantive legal work, which work, for the most part, requires a sufficient knowledge of legal concepts that, absent such assistance, the attorney would perform the task.

The members of the State Bar Legal Assistant Committee felt the adoption of the definition of a legal assistant/paralegal by the State Bar was important to the legal profession in providing uniformity in the identification of legal assistants.

Wisconsin. The following definition of a paralegal has been approved by the Wisconsin State Bar Paralegal Task Force, November 1996:

> A 'paralegal' is an individual qualified through education and training, who is supervised by a lawyer licensed to practice law in this State, to perform substantive legal work requiring a sufficient knowledge of legal concepts that, absent the paralegal, the attorney would perform the work.

Summary

All definitions describe a professional group working under the direct supervision of an attorney, and acknowledge that the terms "paralegal" and "legal assistant" are used synonymously. They intentionally exclude persons who do not work under attorney supervision even though they may perform law-related work. This direct supervision is required whether the paralegal is utilized in the course of full-time employment or is being utilized on a contractual basis by an attorney or firm. In both instances, the work product of the paralegal becomes merged into the final product of the supervising attorney.

Bar association definitions may be found in guidelines and informational materials developed by the bar associations to assist their members in understanding more about the utilization of paralegals and how this may assist their practice. In addition, bar associations that offer associate membership to paralegals include a definition of "legal assistants" or "paralegals" within the membership requirements.

Index